THE SHADOW
Emperor

THE SHADOW

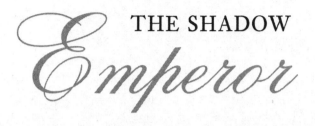

Emperor

A Biography of

NAPOLÉON III

Alan Strauss-Schom

St. Martin's Press
New York

www.stmartins.com

Library of Congress Cataloging-in-Publication Data is available upon request.

ISBN 978-1-250-05778-5 (hardcover)
ISBN 978-1-4668-6168-8 (ebook)

Our books may be purchased in bulk for promotional, educational, or business use. Please contact your local bookseller or the Macmillan Corporate and Premium Sales Department at 1-800-221-7945, extension 5442, or by email at MacmillanSpecialMarkets@macmillan.com.

First Edition: May 2018

10 9 8 7 6 5 4 3 2 1

Dedicated to Eugen Weber, 1925–2007,

Professor Emeritus, UCLA

Contents

THE SHADOW
Emperor

THE BONAPARTE FAMILY TREE

Joseph	Napoléon	Lucien	Elisa
1767–1844	1769–1821	1775–1840	(Maria Anna)
KING OF NAPLES AND	EMPEROR OF THE FRENCH	PRINCE OF CANINO,	1777–1820
OF SPAIN		FRENCH PRINCE	PRINCESS OF LUCCA
	1) m. 1796		AND PIOMBINO, GRAN
m. 1794	Joséphine de Beauharnais	1) m. 1795	DUCHESS OF TUSCAN\
Julie Clary	1763–1814,	Christine Boyer	
1777–1845	divorced 1810	1773–1800	m. 1797
|		|	Felix Bacciochi
Zénaïde	2) m. 1810	Charlotte	1762–1841
1801–1845	Marie Louise of Austria	1795–1865	|
	1791–1847		Elisa
Charlotte	|	Christine	1806–1869
1802–1839	one son	1798–1865	
	Napoléon-François-		Frédéric
m. 1826	Joseph-Charles	2) m. 1803	1813–1833
Napoléon Louis	1811–1832	Alexandrine Jouberton	
Bonaparte	KING OF ROME,	1778–1855	
1804–1831	DUKE OF REICHSTADT	|	
		Charles	
	Napoléon's stepson,	1803–1857	
	Eugène de Beauharnais		
	1781–1824	Letizia	
		1804–1871	
	m. 1806		
	Princess Auguste-Amélie	Jeanne	
	of Bavaria	1807–1829	
	1788–1851		
	|	Paul	
	seven children	1808–1827	
		Louis	
		1813–1891	
		Pierre	
		1815–1881	
		Antoine	
		1816–1877	
		Alexandrine	
		1818–1874	
		Constance	
		1823–1876	

Carlo Maria Buonaparte (1746–85) m. 1764 Letizia Ramolino (1750–1836)

Louis	Pauline	Caroline	Jérôme
1778–1846	(Paolo Maria)	(Maria Annunziata)	1784–1860
KING OF HOLLAND	1780–1825	1782–1839	KING OF WESTPHALIA
(1806–1810)	DUCHESS OF GUASTALLA	GRAND DUCHESS OF BERG	
	1) m. 1797	(1806–1808),	1) m. 1803
m. 1802 Hortense	Gen. Charles Leclerc	QUEEN OF NAPLES	Elizabeth Patterson
de Beauharnais	1772–1802	(1808–1815)	1783–1879
1783–1837			divorced 1811
	Louis Napoléon	m. 1800	(United States)
Children:	1798–1804	Joachim Murat	
Napoléon-	2) m. 1803,	1767–1815	Jerome (Bo)
Louis-Charles	Prince Borghese	KING OF NAPLES	1805–1870
1802–1807	1775–1832	1808-1815	
Napoléon Louis			2) m. 1807 (bigamous)
1804–1831	No children	Achille	Catharina of Württemberg
		1801–1841	1783–1835
Charles-Louis-			
Napoléon		Letizia	Jérôme-Napoléon
(Napoléon III)		1802–1878	1814–1847
1808–1873			
		Lucien	Mathilde
m. 1853		1803–1878	1820–1904
Eugénie de Montijo			m. 1840
1826–1920		Louis	
		1805–1889	Anatole Demidoff
Napoléon-Eugène-			1813–1870
Louis			Napoléon-Joseph-Charles-Paul
1856–1879			"PRINCE JÉRÔME"
			(Plon-Plon)
			1822–1891
			m. 1859
			Maria Clotilde of Savoy
			1843–1911
			Victor
			1862–1926
			Louis
			1864–1932
			Maria Letizia
			1866–1926

———— ◆ ————

PRINCE LOUIS NAPOLÉON

*To rule in France one must either be born in grandeur . . . or else
be capable of distinguishing oneself above all others. . . .*[1]
—NAPOLÉON I TO HIS BROTHER JOSEPH

*I believe in Fate. If my body has miraculously escaped danger,
if my soul has managed to overcome every obstacle, it is because
I have been called upon to achieve something of significance.*[2]
—PRINCE LOUIS NAPOLÉON, 1845

Fine carriages bearing famous gilded imperial coats of arms and elegant phaetons drawn by sleek, well-groomed horses were not an uncommon sight between the Rue de Mont Blanc and here before the stately mansion at 8 Rue Laffitte (then Cerutti). By four o'clock on the afternoon of Wednesday, April 20, 1808, traffic was brought to a standstill, however, and even the troops in dress uniform lining the street could do nothing about it, a queue forming as these equipages passed through the large double iron gates and into the spacious cobbled courtyard, where these very unusual guests in elegant court costume descended.[3]

Even in terms of imperial court receptions, the new arrivals were impressive, brought here on this special occasion to witness the signing of the *acte de naissance*, the certificate attesting to the birth of Holland's queen Hortense's latest son earlier this day. What was not only peculiar but unique about today's ceremony was the fact that on the document now presented, the space where the names of the newly born boy should have been printed was left blank. Nevertheless, the reason was simple enough, for Emperor Napoléon was not present, and no child of the imperial family could be named without his approval and blessing. If the emperor could be excused, the absence of King Louis, the child's father, could not, nor did his ambassador today provide a reason for his remaining in Holland. But of course the rift, the official separation of Louis and Hortense, was hardly a secret in court circles.

On the second of June, Napoléon finally announced the baby's name: Charles-Louis Napoléon, better known as Prince Louis Napoléon, the future ruler of France as Napoléon III.[4]

S ince the fall of Napoléon's Empire in 1815, existence for ex-queen Hortense, now known officially as the Duchess de Saint-Leu, had been far more complicated and painful, indeed a veritable nightmare. For as charming and delightful as the five Allied rulers found the lovely daughter of Joséphine, nevertheless she was an important "political" figure as the wife of Napoléon's brother Louis, whose two surviving sons—Princes Napoléon Louis Bonaparte and Louis Napoléon Bonaparte—stood in line to the imperial succession. The new Bourbon king, Louis XVIII, banned Hortense, and all members of the Bonaparte clan, from French soil. Traveling to Aix-les-Bains (Savoy), she and her sons had fled to Switzerland and then across the German frontier to Constance in southern Bavaria, only to be ordered out of that country. In 1816, Hortense's cousin, Stéphanie de Beauharnais, now the Grand Duchess of Baden, offered her and her sons a haven at Carlsberg, only for Hortense to find herself and her family obliged to move once more when a relentless Louis XVIII put great pressure on the Grand Duke of Baden as well. Uprooted again for at least the fifth time with young sons in tow, a by now desperate Hortense appealed to her brother, Eugène de Beauharnais, as the son-in-law of King Maximilian I of Bavaria, for help.

Overcoming the king's anxieties, Eugene's intervention proved successful, and by February 1817 Hortense was authorized by the five Allies to settle in the prosperous medieval city of Augsburg in western Bavaria.

In 1817 the Swiss Federated Government—through the council of
the northern Canton of Thurgau—also issued permission for Hortense
to settle in Switzerland. After two years of perpetual peregrinations and
anxiety, she could now purchase her own house, in fact two of them (including the nearby Swiss estate of Arenenberg). At the same time, after
long, difficult negotiations, a settlement was reached with Louis
Bonaparte. Their eldest son, Napoléon Louis Bonaparte, would remain
with his father in Italy, while his younger brother, Prince Louis Napoléon, the future emperor, would be brought up by Hortense.

The past couple of years of continuous personal upheaval and uncertainty had taken a permanent toll on both Hortense and her son
Louis Napoléon. Always at the back of her mind was the anxiety that
soldiers would once again appear on her doorstep with signed orders
from the British Foreign Office and the other four members of the
Allied coalition to expel her and her young family from yet another
country. That young Prince Louis Napoléon became as cautious and
wary as his mother of people and of the proffered friendship of new-
comers was hardly surprising. Who in the final analysis could they
really trust and rely upon? That anxiety remained with the prince the
rest of his life. And this applied within the family as well, where some of
their most determined enemies were to be found, including the otherwise mild Joseph Bonaparte.

From the day of his marriage to Joséphine, Napoléon himself had had
to contend with the open jealousy and hostility of his mother, Letizia,
uncle Fesch, brothers Joseph, Louis, Lucien, and, sporadically, Jérôme,
not to mention his sisters. This enmity was only intensified following the
imperial coronation in December 1804.

Now, more than a dozen years later, with Napoléon thousands of
miles away on St. Helena and the family dispersed to the four winds, this
Corsican animosity toward Hortense and her sons remained undimin-
ished. During the empire they had squabbled regarding the Napoleonic
succession. That Napoléon subsequently changed the order of that succession only intensified bitter familial rivalry that continued to this day,
but was now aimed at Hortense and her two Bonaparte sons, who were
high up on the list to succeed to the throne.

Napoléon I had left his imprint on France. He had created a whole new post-revolutionary society and world in his own image and with it a whole new national mystique. Millions of Frenchmen had served in his armies and his state government. Millions of families, indeed every French man, woman, and child, had been affected by this dazzling if destructive genius who had altered their lives, while at the same time rampaged across the face of Europe like a rogue boar, suppressing kingdoms, monarchs, national frontiers, and political and legal systems, filling millions of graves in the process. Hundreds of cities, towns, and villages had been destroyed, hundreds of thousands of war refugees were forced to flee their ruined homes, and many tens of thousands of women and girls were raped, all because a madman wanted to satisfy his ego and conquer the world. There had been nothing like him and his bewildering legacy in two thousand years of European history.

After the fall of Napoléon in 1815 and the dispersal of the Bonaparte clan, the question remained: How were the following generations going to deal with this ill-defined and unresolved heritage? How real and lasting was it? Would it reemerge, and if so how, in what guise? And if this imperial ghost of the past should rematerialize, who would be its heir, and what legacy would he offer? As Napoléon had rightly predicted on distant St. Helena, "It will be difficult to make me completely disappear from the public memory."

A Bonaparte heir was indeed to emerge, but it is of course quite impossible to replicate, to resurrect the past, as a France of the future under a new Napoleonic empire was to prove yet again.

For the first time in his life the nine-year-old Prince Louis Napoléon had a permanent roof over his head in 1817, his first home, in Augsburg, where he soon attended regular classes at the gymnasium, or high school, with other members of the aristocracy and haute bourgeoisie, and he was cautiously happy. Gradually, the anxiety of the volcanic events of the past three years following the fall of Napoléon I now eased with his new daily route. His classes were in German, of course, and he quickly became fluent in that language, gradually coming to the point where he spoke French at home with a German accent, which remained with him the rest of his life.

Most of the next ten years he spent at Augsburg, with occasional sojourns across Lake Constance to their estate at Arenenberg, where Hortense was supervising the reconstruction and extensions to the main house and laying out a new garden to resemble that of the Malmaison of her youth.[5] They would also spend several weeks each winter and summer in Milan, Florence, and especially in Rome, where Louis Napoléon made a few new friends, including Francesco Arese, and became fluent in Italian, a language, like the country, he loved.

Although never more than an average student, he always looked forward to the resumption of his studies in Augsburg each autumn. He was an unusually curious student and enjoyed classical history, geography and languages, mathematics, physics, and, later, chemistry. Although he had no ear for music and did not like classical concerts, he excelled in dancing and drawing. In addition, he took riding and fencing lessons, becoming adept in both. If he attended frequent hunts at the estates of the local aristocracy and of his uncle Eugène de Beauharnais, it was more for the social gatherings and the ladies in particular. Unlike the landed gentry, the Bonapartes were never renowned as sportsmen.

The center of the boy's daily existence, however, was with Hortense, especially after the removal of his brother, Napoléon Louis (1804–1831), to Florence to live with his father. The two surviving brothers remained very close, and despite the tedious necessity of having to pass all their correspondence through the police, they wrote regularly and were able to visit each other for a few weeks each year.

When Prince Louis Napoléon settled in at Augsburg, in addition to servants, he acquired several tutors, and these individuals had to be carefully vetted. Teachers, after all, introduce ideas, a dangerous commodity. The prince's education was of special interest to the Allies, and the background checks on his private tutors were rigorous. These teachers incuded Abbé Bertrand, Dr. Hase, Colonel Armandi, Messrs. Gastard and Vieillard, General Dufour, and the prince's favorite, Philippe

Lebas.[6] But in the case of Louis Napoléon, who was in line to succeed to the Bonaparte crown, that approval did not suffice so far as surveillance was concerned, and when Lebas went to visit his family in Paris each year, French police followed him to assure the Paris prefect of police (and Louis XVIII's minister of the interior) that he was not on an errand for Prince Louis Napoléon, plotting against the French government. His mail was intercepted and his private papers regularly rifled when traveling. After Hortense let one of her maids go, that woman was interrogated by the French police. Refusing to cooperate and disclose anything to the police, she instead praised her former employer "who does so much good in that country, for which she is much loved."[7] Hortense's faithful lady-in-waiting, Mlle. Cochelet, was likewise questioned when she visited Paris, and she and her son were also under constant surveillance by French agents, both in Augsburg and at Arenenberg.

This police work in Switzerland was directed through the French foreign office and by the French minister accredited to Bern, Auguste de Talleyrand.[8] All these police reports were eventually dispatched to the French foreign minister, who, in serious cases, discussed them in turn with the heads of state or foreign ministers of England, Austria, Prussia, and Russia, as signatories of the Congress of Vienna. They continued to use spies in and with contacts to Arenenberg. Bribes did work occasionally. "A tailor by the name of Joseph Gruber works for the son of Mme. Hortense," read one police report. "This tailor has few qualms when it comes to money which he is very fond of, and he turns out to be a regular gossip." Returning to Switzerland year after year, he proved a reliable source.[9] Even behind the secure doors of the chateau of Arenenberg, Louis Napoléon and the Duchess of Saint-Leu could trust no one, and the prince never came to consider it anything but a temporary abode until he could return to France permanently.

A very tight lead was kept on Hortense and her two surviving sons. When each year Prince Louis Napoléon was sent to visit his father in Florence, his brother, Napoléon Louis, went on an exchange visit to Arenenberg to stay with his mother, the two brothers passing as they traveled. But each foreign journey required weeks of prior police work to ensure that the Bonaparte clan had no secret agenda. Indeed, every member of the family was subject to rigorous control. Louis Napoléon's father personally rebuked him, however, when the Allies delayed authorization for his visit. The French police even interfered with the burial ceremony the Bonapartes had arranged for their mother, Letizia, in 1836. Napoléon's little Elban escapade in 1815 had taught them a very bitter and costly lesson indeed.[10]

From his earliest youth Prince Louis Napoléon lived in visceral fear and trepidation of his father, ex-king Louis Bonaparte, not a fear of physical abuse, but of his father's unrelenting criticism of everything the boy did. This anxiety, the constant necessity of seeking his father's approval, continued right into Louis Napoléon's late thirties and up to the time of his father's death in 1846. No one can begin to understand Napoléon III without fully comprehending the significance of that negative father-son relationship, leaving a much battered ego and sense of self-esteem helplessly suppressed and humiliated by a twisted, unstable father.

The death of their eldest son, Napoléon-Louis-Charles, at the age of five in 1807 had brought a fleeting reconciliation between a grieving Hortense and Louis. Louis Bonaparte's remaining paternal affection was then transferred to his second eldest, Napoléon Louis. As for the third son, Prince Louis Napoléon, there was to be no affection whatsoever. Thereafter there was the recurrent, if false, rumor that Louis Napoléon, living with Hortense, was illegitimate. The final proof of the ex-king's belief that he was the father came at the time of his death in 1846 when he left his entire estate to him. But from the start the relationship between father and son was most difficult, indeed painful, and to prove the greatest and most persistent source of anguish of Louis Napoléon's life.

2

A SON AND HIS FATHER

*"I fully realize that I owe a great deal to my prominent position
because my name is Bonaparte, and up to this point, nothing to my
personal achievements."*[1]
—LOUIS NAPOLÉON, JANUARY 1835

*"My dear Papa, I receive harsh words from you so often, that I ought to
be quite used to them by now."*[2]
CAPTAIN LOUIS NAPOLÉON BONAPARTE TO HIS FATHER,
—FEBRUARY 7, 1835

When Philippe Lebas, as Prince Louis Napoléon's new private tutor, arrived at the wooded hilltop estate of Arenenberg overlooking Lake Constance in the 1820s, he was no longer young, having served in the French army for several years and then as a minor civil servant. Coming from a modest family with strong Republican credentials, he had found his pupil soft, spoiled, in a very feminine ménage, and overly coached in all things Napoleonic. It took some time for Lebas to determine that this mild, charming, surprisingly unpretentious, even diffident Bonaparte prince, nearly five foot five in height with auburn hair and bluish-gray eyes, also had an unusually mature sense of will and determination dedicated to a future career as Napoléon's heir and successor. This his mother, Hortense, the former queen of Holland, had carefully nurtured over the years.

The prince's Napoleonic heritage, along with his obsessive preoccupation with his father's approval, largely governed the boy's thoughts and daily existence. There was always a distracted, distant look in his eyes. He never seemed to relax, to let his guard down. Very few could ever really get close to him. His unflappable, imperturbable attitude, even from his youth, always struck strangers. A boy who never lost his temper was a very rare creature indeed. "The prince is reserved and distant even in day-to-day affairs though always courteous and welcoming,"[3] one acquaintance noted. But as his new tutor at Arenenberg was gradually to learn, it was the arrival of those monthly letters from his father, the former king of Holland Louis Bonaparte, that had such a depressive effect on Prince Louis Napoléon and played a powerful, even disturbing role in shaping the character, outlook, life, and development of his pupil.

I give you my heartfelt blessings," his father wrote following his son's first communion in April 9, 1821. "I pray that God gives you a pure and grateful heart toward Him, He who is the author of all that is good, and that He sheds His light upon you that you may fulfill all your duties to your country [France] and your parents, and that you may understand the differences between right and wrong."[4] This was probably the most benevolent letter his father ever wrote. It was to prove as rare as the snows of the Sahara. At the same time it reveals a Louis Bonaparte generally unknown to the public, deeply devout, and even puritanical and idealistic, in such utter contrast to his elder brother Napoléon, the great scoffer of all such values.

Louis Napoléon's father took a very real if rigidly controlling interest in the boy's studies, which included a flowing stream of advice or criticism, offset by sparing praise. The results of what proved to be a rather harrowing lifelong experience had inevitable consequences. Even at the age of nineteen, Louis Napoléon's insecurity could be witnessed in every letter he wrote his father, constantly attempting to please a man who simply refused to be pleased—"the older I grow, the better I can appreciate my happiness in having such a good father instructing me by his wise counsel." And thus following Louis's advice, he continued with his studies, concentrating on mathematics up to calculus, when he stopped "following your recommendations."[5]

Clearly still very much the dutiful if intimidated son, at twenty years old, his school reports to his father sounded more like those of a quaking boy half his age. Nearly completing his formal studies in June 1828, he was always diligent and maintained the same long hours, rising at five o'clock every morning and going to bed at ten p.m. "I promise to follow the precise plan that you propose for my studies. Today for instance I duly took the works of Condillac from Maman's library. Likewise I intend to study chemistry and go hunting once a week, as you suggest."[6]

With his studies behind him, Louis Napoléon was largely preoccupied with politics and his own future. Some three months before his twenty-first birthday, Prince Louis Napoléon took the first step that would lead to the achievement of his political career. On January 19, 1829, he informed his father that he would like to enroll in the Russian army, then campaigning in the Russo-Turkish War of 1828 against the Turks in the Balkans and on the Black Sea. Through British and Prussian pressure, the Ottoman Empire's Sultan Mahmud I agreed to peace, and the Treaty of Adrianople (Edirne) was signed in September 1829, resulting in, among other things, Ottoman recognition of an independent Serbia and Greece, and the reopening to Russian and the world the maritime commerce of the Straits, the 125-mile passage from the Black Sea at the Bosphorus through the Sea of Marmora to the Dardenelles and the Mediterranean.

Reminding his father how much he loved him, he plunged in: "Mon cher papa . . . More than anything in the world I wish to join the [military] campaign against the Turks as a volunteer in the Russian Army, for which I now ask your permission. I have already spoken to Maman who feels that it would prove useful for me, and has given her full consent." Hortense had met Russia's emperor Alexander I in Paris years earlier and thought he would be amenable to the idea, and Louis Napoléon concluded that "no doubt I would be appointed to the [tsar's] general staff." Therefore he would hardly be in a dangerous position, and "Maman would select a retired army officer to accompany me. And then, at long last I could do something worthy of you, by demonstrating the courage I have received from being your son. At the same time it would draw public attention to me [for the first time]." However, in the event his father did not give his consent to this proposal, "I should die of embarrassment. . . . Adieu, mon cher Papa."[7]

Needless to say his father, a talented general officer in his own right who had won his spurs as a youth by Napoléon's side in Italy and Egypt, was not overly impressed with the idea of his son going to fight for his former enemy, the tsar. Nor was he happy with Hortense's encouragement of such a scheme. And the last thing the painfully reclusive Louis Bonaparte wanted was publicity that would inevitably affect him personally, and which would most certainly upset the Allied governments already supervising and restricting every move the members of the clan made. Surprisingly, ex-king Louis's response revealed a calm, mature assessment of the situation. It also revealed an important side of his hitherto unknown views on the role of the military in society and political philosophy.

Fighting "Muslim barbarians [the Turks]" in Greece and the Balkans was perfectly honorable, his father responded, "nevertheless you are intelligent and endowed with so many fine qualities that a little reflection on your part will calm you and will restore your sense of judgment. . . . To be sure nothing is finer than military glory. To know that everyone is talking about you," to command great armies in the field, "to be in a position to change the destinies of peoples and nations . . . all that of course is fine and attractive and cannot but excite a young gentleman's imagination. . . . Unfortunately one must also face a very real truth, one quite contrary to that noble view, and that is that *all war*—apart from that of legitimate self-defense of one's home and nation, *is in fact nothing but the act of a barbarian*, which is only distinguished from that of savages and wild beasts, by more satisfactory lies regarding its alleged necessity." Never forget, his father went on, that "one must only go to war and fight for his own country, and for no others [not for Switzerland, not for Russia]. Anyone who acts otherwise is just a mercenary, acting on contrived motives, or else is quite simply bloody minded."[8]

Undoubtedly this was one of the most important letters that Louis Bonaparte ever sent his son, in effect a complete renunciation of his brother Napoléon's entire legacy of warfare and conquest, indeed of his very raison d'être. Prince Louis Napoléon wrote that same month, abandoning his military plans for the moment: "Adieu, mon cher Papa, your devoted son. As you see I have given you true proof of my devotion by renouncing my plans [for Russia], for had I not loved you so much I should never have been able to resist my great urge to carry it out, and this I now do against my will."[9]

Just days before celebrating his twenty-first birthday on April 20, 1829, Louis Napoléon deferred to his father's wishes on this occasion. On the other hand, he was a red-blooded young man bent on adventure and excitement, and this, combined with an unquenchable idealism, was bound to resurface at the next opportunity.

3

AUGUSTE DE MORNY

"Morny . . . was certainly courageous, capable of intrigue and clever . . .
and the most impudent, the most brazen man I have ever known."[1]
—MAXIME DU CAMP

"It is rare indeed to come across such a considerate and intelligent man
like Morny, a man of solid common sense and decision."[2]
—ANTONIO PANIZZI, HEAD LIBRARIAN, BRITISH MUSEUM

In June 1830, a desperate Charles X—the last Bourbon king of France—on the advice of Prime Minister Jules de Polignac invaded Algeria. He did so not because of any real threat from, or even interest in, that nominal Ottoman province, but in order to distract from a popular revolt of the French people against the king's attempt to return to the seventeenth century and the Divine Right authoritarian rule of France of Louis XIV. Indeed Charles X had already reduced the electorate of more than five million under Napoléon I to a mere 25,000— that is, the ruling aristocracy.

On the fifth of July, 1830, the white Bourbon fleur-de-lys was hoisted over the ramparts of Algeria. By the second of August, this same Charles X had abdicated and fled to England. On the ninth of August, Louis Philippe d'Orléans was crowned "King of the French." "Most assuredly France is rich enough to afford an [Algerian] Opera Box," the Duke [Victor] de Broglie argued, "but the cost is far too dear."[3] Charles, Count de Montalembert, strongly disagreed. "So important is our occupation in Algeria that any minister who dared sign the order for its evacuation would be charged with treason!"[4] The newly crowned Louis Philippe agreed, and the French army in Algeria dug in to secure their latest colony. Little could he realize that this was just the beginning of a colonial war that France would still be waging well over a century later, costing hundreds of thousands of lives, draining the French treasury, and ultimately leading to a near national revolution in the very heart of metropolitan France.

Now completing his second tour in Algeria, a much battered Lieutenant Auguste de Morny, having narrowly survived the disastrous siege of Constantine, sailed back to France in January 1837, resigning his commission shortly thereafter. Louis Philippe had committed France to the conquest of that new colony, which was to prove the training ground for hundreds of thousands of French soldiers over the decades to follow and for a whole series of colonial governors, including Clauzel, Bugeaud, Changarnier, and MacMahon among them, who would through their actions in turn shape French politics, often directly. But Lieutenant Morny, for his part, had had enough and never wanted to see North Africa or the army again.

Charles Auguste Louis Joseph, Count de Morny was the openly acknowledged illegitimate son of one of Napoléon's favorite aides-de-camp and most courageous and highly decorated general officers, Charles Joseph, Count de Flahaut de la Billarderie. Morny was also the grandson of Bonaparte's celebrated foreign minister, Charles Maurice de Talleyrand-Périgord. And of course General de Flahaut, a staunch Bonapartist to the end, also remained a personal friend of King Louis Philippe, to whom he had earlier applied for Morny's army commission.

Second only to his father, Charles de Flahaut, women played a very real role in the formation of Morny's life. He was raised by his paternal grandmother, and surrogate mother, Adélaïde [de Flahaut] de Souza, well known as a novelist, but more importantly a close friend of Louis Philippe, with whom she had shared exile during the French Revolution. She remained close to him and his wife, the queen, Marie Amélie, during the July monarchy. Adélaïde was also one of the few to know the identity of Morny's mother, the wife of King Louis Bonaparte of Holland, Hortense de Beauharnais (the daughter of Joséphine and mother to Louis Napoléon). Separated early from her violent, unstable husband, Louis, Hortense had fallen in love with Charles de Flahaut, by whom she had one son, Auguste de Morny, and it was Adélaïde who arranged for Hortense's secret arrangements in Geneva, Switzerland, where Auguste de Morny was born on September 17, 1811, far from the prying eyes of her stepfather, Napoléon I, and his secret police.[5] In the meantime de Flahaut married the daughter of the wealthy Admiral Lord Keith in 1817 and spent most of his time in Scotland and England.

Adélaïde remained in close, if secret, communication with Hortense throughout the ensuing years, and Hortense entrusted her with a large sum for Auguste's education (largely spent by Adélaïde). In the meantime, in the 1830s, Adélaïde, as the wife of the Portuguese ambassador, Dom José de Sousa, came into contact with Fanny Le Hon, the wife of Belgium's first ambassador to France, and attended Fanny's celebrated Saturday evening soirées in the Rue Mont Blanc (today's Chaussée d'Antin).

A surprisingly close, almost mother-daughter relationship developed between Hortense and Fanny. Hortense was especially impressed by Fanny's total devotion to Morny. Their correspondence was warm, Hortense for the first time addressing a joint letter to her son, Auguste, and Fanny, closing, "A thousand thanks to you both, my dear children, you are my consolation."[6] After the death of Adélaïde de Sousa early in 1836, it was thanks to Fanny that Hortense decided to publicly recognize Auguste as her son and to adopt him legally. In addition to formal adoption, she could provide him "with complete financial independence and that is what I must do."[7] Meanwhile, aware of her own rapidly declining health (she was suffering from cancer), Hortense invited Fanny to the Schloss Arenenberg in October 1836 to draw up the final papers regarding the adoption of Auguste. It was apparently during this visit that her son Louis Napoléon learned from his mother of the existence of his half brother, Auguste, and he was deeply distraught by the news. They all dined together for the last time on the twenty-fourth of October— Louis Napoléon, Hortense, Valérie Masuyer (her lady-in-waiting),

Henri Conneau (Hortense's surgeon), and Fanny Le Hon. It was a tense affair, the main topic ostensibly Louis Napoléon's engagement to his first cousin, Mathilde, the daughter of Jérôme Bonaparte, the ex-king of Westphalia; the real issue, Hortense's recognition of Auguste, unmentioned.[8]

Of all the women in Auguste de Morny's life, it was the lovely Fanny Le Hon who was to play by far the most significant role, and by whom he was to father at least one child. The countess, born Françoise Zoë Mathilde Mosselman, was the daughter of one of the wealthiest "industrialists" of Belgium and wife of Charles, Count Le Hon, who had been instrumental in the selection of the newly created country of Belgium's first monarch, Leopold I.[9] A petite, strikingly attractive ash-blond beauty—"the lady of the iris blue eyes," the bewitched novelist Honoré Balzac described her—*une dame cultivée,* a talented linguist who spoke Greek, Latin, French, Flemish, German, and English, and an accomplished pianist, her salon dominated the Parisian diplomatic community. With her captivating, unrevealing smile, Fanny Le Hon was undoubtedly the most brilliant woman Auguste de Morny ever knew. Balzac was not alone in his rapture with the divine Fanny. *Homme de lettres,* novelist, art historian, and future director of the Théâtre Français Arsène Houssaye, with his celebrated Tolstoyan-length beard, was a friend of both Morny and Fanny, and clearly smitten with her utter sexuality, finding her "like a flower awakened by love . . . her provocative grace tantalizing . . . simply voluptuous and feline."[10] Perhaps a little more riveting than the allure of flesh was Fanny's fabled collection of Russian and Indian rubies, emeralds, and diamonds. She was reputedly the greatest heiress of the day, and her Saturday salons were always well attended by the diplomatic corps, including the Metternichs and Apponyis, the leading artists, musicians, and politicians of the day. This included the royal family: Louis Philippe, the otherwise shy Queen Marie Amélie, and her handsome sons.

Like most young aristocrats, Auguste de Morny was largely educated at home, in this case by tutors, his doting father, General de

Flahaut, and by his devoted if eccentric paternal grandmother, Adélaïde. English, Latin, Greek, history, and mathematics were the core subjects he studied prior to attending the elite Collège Bourbon of Paris. His social education was then completed during visits to Grandfather Talleyrand, who was notorious for his antipathy to children, where Auguste, the exception, was spoiled in a truly princely fashion.

Auguste, like so many brilliant students, was lazy when he could get away with it, but when it came to education, his father put his foot down and enrolled the boy at the Sorbonne at the age of fourteen, to study mathematics. When he worked, he did exceptionally well, but he soon rejected mathematics and the university altogether. His father finally completed his education by introducing him into the world of actresses.

Morny's friend and fellow member of the Jockey Club, Edmond d'Alton Shée, who had an intimate knowledge and understanding of the young man, described him in his *Memoirs*: "Having been educated throughout his youth [by his famous father] to be a dashing man of the world, Auguste managed to combine a natural nonchalance and ease with a real taste for diligence and hard work."[11] Clearly Auguste was very much his father's son, except for an atavistic distaste and respect for the military. As for his once beautiful but now ailing grandmother, Adélaïde, not only did she do nothing to discourage this type of upbringing but she assiduously fostered and rewarded it. Unfortunately, her own lifelong utter irresponsibility in money matters, a trait shared by Talleyrand, was to prove equally destructive in Morny's life as well. It was hardly surprising, then, that young Auguste turned out as he did.

Much shorter than his father, and blond and blue-eyed if prematurely bald, "while perhaps not qualifying as truly handsome, nevertheless he had fine, kindly features, and bore himself erect as a gentleman of elegance and distinction," d'Alton Shée recalled. "He was a brilliant success with the ladies of all ages,"[12] Queen Hortense's elderly companion and lady-in-waiting, Valérie Masuyer, fully concurred. "He exuded the most exquisite old world charm and manners! This boy is quite simply a born diplomat, just like his father."[13]

By the same token, his obvious intelligence and superior knowledge in most subjects inevitably led either to admiration by many or to jealousy by some. This was especially so where the ladies were concerned, including with a fellow member of the Jockey Club, Count Alexander Walewski, Napoléon's illegitimate son by his Polish mistress. The lives and politics of Walewski and Morny were to intertwine closely over the ensuing years. Nor was the Duke of Orléans, Prince Ferdinand Philippe, the eldest son and heir of Louis Philippe, any less of a competitor. In one instance the jealous young duke, as the king's son, apparently had the military records of Auguste de Morny's brief but distinguished military career destroyed, and with them any mention of citations, medals, and decorations. Much taller and more handsome than Morny, the frustrated young duke on another occasion had reputedly challenged Auguste to a duel over a woman, possibly Fanny Le Hon.

Neither Morny nor Fanny ever made the slightest attempt to conceal their very open affair, which indeed they flaunted with total disregard. The lovely wife of the Belgian ambassador appeared everywhere in public with Auguste. The jealousy and passion continued for years. The competition between Morny and Ferdinand Philippe extended to racing, common enough in a world of thoroughbred horses. Both men had fine stables and were excellent equestrians. Therefore, despite all, given Louis Philippe's powerful influence throughout society, it was fortunate indeed for Morny that the king remained on cordial terms with Morny's grandmother and father, the general, whom the king was to appoint as ambassador to Vienna. In any event, the premature death of the duke at thirty in a carriage accident removed that problem.

Morny "had an absolute faith in himself," d'Alton Shée recalled. "He was audacious and fearless whilst always remaining in complete control of events, regardless of the situation. He could act with a total aloof sang-froid at all times, combined with an exceptionally balanced mature judgment [except notably in his personal financial affairs]." A born boulevardier, he never allowed emotions to interfere with his numerous dalliances and affairs, nor did he pretend otherwise, and he was accepted by "the ladies" on those terms. No one really expected marriage as a result of a tryst. As for embarrassing emotional scenes in public or private, he avoided them like the plague. He was "a most generous chap, cheerful and positive by nature, but more capable of good fellowship than of true intimate friendship," d'Alton Shée shrewdly noted, "while remaining a loyal ally, but he more set on protecting the interests of acquaintances than of any personal devotion to them."[14]

"[Morny] greatly enjoyed social events, but never with the usual calculating eye as to how those individuals encountered might be of use or profit him. . . . His ambitions were held in another distinct category, and they were quite open and direct. And he was faithful to any personal engagement he undertook. His word in such instances was his bond," d'Alton Shée made quite clear. "He was certainly addicted to a life of ease and luxury [tempered with an unrelenting energy and restlessness]. He made absolutely no attempt to conceal from the world that he had no political principles or that he held little faith in his fellow man. Nor did he ever let anything interfere with his personal freedom [in politics, business affairs, or his private life]."[15]

And yet to those who knew him more intimately than the d'Alton Shées and *hommes des lettres* Du Camps and Mérimées, in the course of daily work at the Palais Bourbon or when sharing his unquenchable nocturnal passion for the *filles du ballet*, the theater, and the music hall, yet another Auguste de Morny emerges. "I have never known anyone so imbued with such a sincere desire to be of assistance, to help one out, and without any of the usual upper class condescension. . . . He was such a fair and fine human being!" Ludovic Halévy, his senior secretary later responsible for preparing the daily agenda and minutes of the Corps Legislatif, recalled of their daily meetings and breakfasts together at his presidential residence in the Hôtel de Lassay adjoining the Palais Bourbon. He was "such a forward looking, clear thinker! . . . And he was always so unassuming, so charming and decent! . . . He embodies in his daily life [as president of the legislative body]," Halévy found, "the same refinement that can be found in his meticulous work."[16] In addition to his official duties at the Palais Bourbon, Halévy, along with Henri Meilhac, knew Morny in his capacity as librettist for composer Jacques Offenbach, to whose work and musical world Morny gave a surprising amount of his time during the 1850s and 1860s. Offenbach, too, had only good things to say about him. "You know better than anyone all that he has done for me . . . how he went out of his way to protect us [from administrative restrictions regarding musical productions]," he later wrote Ernest Lépine, private personal secretary to Morny.[17] That Morny surrounded himself with very talented Jews—Halévy, Meilhac, and Offenbach—did not go unnoticed by a disapproving aristocracy.

On the other hand, when it came to fortune and finances, Morny again proved himself worthy of Grandfather Talleyrand. Money regularly flowed through his hands—indeed tens of millions of francs, like the endless waters of the Nile. He never played for small stakes, whether at cards, horses, or business. Because he was a supreme egotist, apart from his well-publicized personal pleasure and comfort, the drive for riches grew to be perhaps the most consistent driving force, if not obsession, in his life, not for the sake of accumulating vast wealth, however, but rather to support the easy and at times openly decadent lifestyle that wealth alone could provide. And again like Talleyrand, he lived for the moment, not the morrow, in his case perhaps as a result of having lost several young friends in battle in Algeria. As for the words "legality" and "illegality," they simply had no place in either his lexicon or his conscience. Short of murder, blackmail, or openly robbing a bank, any proposition was valid, including the evasion of importuning creditors, which drove him to England on more than one occasion. Where a highly lucrative financial proposition was involved, all scruples and professional banking loyalties were abandoned with utter disdain.

Morny's overweening confidence and sense of superiority over all men in all matters obviously intimidated and distanced all but a few. On the other hand, he could be sincere and perfectly at ease when dealing with the other classes, including peasants on his estates and the hands working in his various stud farms, and they were at ease with him. Unlike Grandfather Talleyrand, however, within his inner sanctum he lived with surprising simplicity, dining most sparingly, and in the morning no servants were present for breakfast. By nature generous to a fault, and utterly devoid of jealousy or envy, he had little patience with the mediocrity, spite, and petty attitudes of others. But in the final analysis, as Maxime Du Camp summed up, Auguste de Morny "traveled through life effortlessly, a spoiled child of fortune."[18]

4

GENTLEMANLY PURSUITS

"I have never plotted in the usual sense of the word, for the men whom I
count on are not tied to me by mere personal oaths of loyalty, but rather
by something far more enduring, by a mutual love [of France] . . ."[1]
—PRINCE LOUIS NAPOLÉON

"He absolutely believed himself to be the man of Destiny . . .
upon whom France utterly depended."[2]
—ALEXIS DE TOCQUEVILLE

Queen Hortense was without doubt the most influential person in Louis Napoléon's life, inculcating his moral and spiritual values, strengthening his ego, and enforcing his determination to achieve supreme power. He was also a prisoner of her love. "Take good care of yourself, mon enfant, if only to ensure my peace of mind, your love is the sole consolation of my existence," Hortense was to write time and again to her sheltered son even when he was in his twenties and thirties. One side of Hortense wanted to see him in a powerful political position, the other wanted only to keep him with her, devoting himself to her as the center of his existence. He had, she pointed out, "courage" and "the necessary dedication" combined with "a generous nature and noble character," she continued. "I should have admired him even if I weren't his mother." She regretted only her "inability to soften existence [financially] for him. . . . to sooth his sad and difficult destiny. . . . He deserves the truly fine things in life; he is worthy of that."[3] Fed on honeyed pap and smothered in cotton wool by an emotional, overly protective, unhealthily possessive doting mother . . . her son's future did not look hopeful. No one could even begin to understand the Napoléon III who later evolved without this knowledge of the gentle but pervasive domination and controlling role of his mother in his life. Only his surprisingly strong character and personal will to achieve something worthy of his name, the chalice of empire, to be recognized and respected by the outside world, drove him on with force enough eventually to break away from this strangling silk web.

As for Hortense, there was another side to her character, a separate world of grievances that she also shared with her son. It was a bitterly disappointed Duchess de Saint-Leu who acknowledged the profound disappointment she continued to find in people, in society. "Learn to judge men, to really know them, and in some cases when it is necessary to keep them out of your life altogether," she advised her son, "for most of them are not worthy [of your trust and respect]." Live simply, "make a comfortable private life for yourself, and avoid all politics."[4] She was full of contradictions. It was pretty grim stuff for such a young man, so full of life, ready to prepare a career of his own, and even risk his life for his country. One minute Hortense encouraged him as heir to the Napoleonic legacy to fulfill the imperial ambition, and the next to abandon people and politics. But for all this, life went on, and the young man continued to dream in a world of his own.

Hortense and Louis Napoléon had been vacationing in Italy every year since settling in Augsburg and Arenenberg, which included visits with the beautiful Antoinette, the Countess Arese (née the Marchioness Fagnini) and her son, Francesco, in Milan, before continuing down to Rome.[5]

The Areses, a very old, distinguished aristocratic Milanese family, and Hortense had gradually become close friends, meeting frequently over the years in Milan and Rome. Francesco's father Count Marc Arese had been a senior officer in the Italian corps serving in Napoléon's army, with an enduring attachment to France. With the fall of Napoléon in 1815, Austrian troops had reoccupied northern Italy, extending from

Milan in Lombardy right across to Venice and the Adriatic. Ever since, Marc Arese and his fellow ex-army officers had been plotting through secret organizations, including the Carbonari, which they, along with other influential masons, largely directed with the aim of wresting their homeland from Habsburg rule.

It was during the annual visits of their two families, the Bonapartes and Areses, including those in Rome at Hortense's Palazzo Rusconi, that their two sons became truly fast friends. And it was now that Louis Napoléon took up a new cause and became an ardent supporter of Francesco's patriotic dream to end the Austrian occupation of northern Italy, and to end the Vatican's secular administration of the medieval Papal States, covering nearly one-third of Italy. Thereafter the two boys would correspond often and almost always on one subject, plots and rebellion.

In the meantime, anti-Austrian sentiment continued to simmer dangerously in the Duchies of Parma and Modena, and of course the ever-turbulent Bologna. "My Dear Count Arese," Louis Napoléon, then visiting his older brother, Napoléon Louis, wrote from Florence on November 7, 1830. "I should very much like you to come to Rome again this winter. If that is acceptable to you I could rent a small apartment for you near the Corso [and Hortense's Palazzo Rusconi] and you could dine with us every day." Closing, he assured Francesco that he would endeavor "to render your sojourn there as pleasant as possible."[6]

Louis Philippe's seizure of France in July of 1830 had sent revolutionary shock waves reaching throughout Europe, and Italy in particular. Louis Napoléon naturally found this infectious, and given his recent disappointment in failing to join the Russian army battling the Turks, his pent-up excitement in meeting Francesco Arese (whose father was a major figure in the revolutionary Carbonari) in Rome now was hardly surprising. But the real ringleader was his recently married brother, Napoléon Louis, the only one of the three to have actually signed an oath to support the Carbonari. In addition to rendezvous with light "seductive women," as Hortense referred to them, the young men regularly visited the Palazzo Rinuccini to see Grandmother Letizia—who had finally come round to accepting Hortense. Secretly, however, Louis Napoléon was receiving Carbonari friends at the Palazzo Rusconi (when Hortense was out), which also became a communications center for the Carbonari, sending and receiving messages. Instructions to their first cousin, Napoléon's son, the Duke of Reichstadt in Vienna—whom they hoped to place on the throne of Italy—were hand delivered by members of the family only.

The time was ripe for revolution, encouraged by the overthrow of the Bourbons in France and the recent death of Pope Pius VIII, who had not yet been replaced by the College of Cardinals. Nevertheless it proved impossible for the Duke of Reichstadt—Napoléon II—to escape from Vienna, where he was under close surveillance. Moreover, in Rome, the Vatican police also had some two dozen young rebel patrician patriots under close observation. Then, to aggravate matters, a flippant Louis Napoléon took it into his head to ride madly through the streets of Rome carrying a French revolutionary tricolor from his saddle—this at a time when disturbing reports of conspiracies and demonstrations against the Austrian occupation force in Bologna and Modena were reaching the Roman authorities.

That was the last straw for an exasperated Monseigneur Capelletti, the governor of Rome, who now gave the green light to act. Early on December 11, 1830, some four dozen armed Vatican police surrounded the Palazzo Rusconi, arresting among others the exuberant equestrian Louis Napoléon. A few days later, more than twenty of these "Carbonari," including Louis Napoléon (and Uncle Jérôme and his entire family), were forcefully expelled from Rome, as Francesco Arese slipped out of the scene.[7]

No sooner had he reached Florence than he was put into contact with the conspirators in that city through one of their leaders, Colonel Pier Damiano Armandi, who just happened to have been Napoléon Louis's tutor a few years earlier. Armandi in turn introduced Louis Napoléon to the principal rebel chief there, General Ciro Menotti (of Modena), who wanted to put to immediate good use the two nephews of Emperor Napoléon.

They had gone to join these Italian patriots, Louis Napoléon now informed his disconsolate mother after the deed was done, because "the name we bear obliges us to come to the aid of the unhappy people who seek our help."[8] At the age of twenty-three he should have known better, but he was carried away with the excitement of the moment. The two Bonaparte brothers remained with the Carbonari throughout February 1831. "The enthusiasm one finds here is simply grand," Louis Napoléon wrote in continued exhilaration to his father. "This army of patriots is now marching on Rome," he continued, expecting that city to fall to them in a week's time. "For Heaven's sake don't worry about us, look to the future and you will see the peoples of Europe demanding the recovery of their lost rights."[9] Louis Napoléon was ready to fight the new pope, Gregory XVI, who had just called for Austrian reinforcements. Although knowing that "two Bonapartes" were now advancing with the Carbonari caused panic in senior circles, Louis Philippe declined to help the pope against the republican rebels.

By now, however, both Uncles Jérôme and Louis, alarmed at the spiraling violence, called on the newly promoted General Armandi—now serving as minister of war in the rebel republican army—to send Louis Napoléon and Napoléon Louis back to Florence. Although they did not stop immediately, the two firebrands finally buckled under, and by the third of March General Armandi could assure Hortense "[t]he young princes are here and perfectly fit . . . You should be prouder than ever, Madame, to have such courageous children."[10]

Fresh major forces of the Austrian army were everywhere crushing the republican rebel patriots in fierce fighting, however, including at Bologna, where the two Bonaparte brothers were last reported to have been seen. An undaunted, terribly anxious Hortense determined to extricate her uncooperative sons and, with the faithful Valérie Masuyer at her side, set out across Italy on March 12, 1831, with two English passports in hand (provided by the British Minister, Lord Seymour). Meanwhile, cut off by the advancing Austrians, Louis Napoléon and his brother reached Forlí on March 9, only to discover the city in the midst of a measles epidemic.[11]

Nothing could stop the valiant, diminutive Queen Hortense, whose carriage was literally crossing veritable battlefields under live fire, heading for Ancona. Unknown to her, however, Napoléon Louis had contracted measles on the eleventh of March and had died at Forlí on the seventeenth. With the epidemic raging and the Austrians closing in, Louis Napoléon, himself now also infected, fled with the others to Pesaro, where Hortense found him very ill in bed at a palazzo of Eugène de Beauharnais's son, the Duke de Leuchtenberg. On the twenty-third of March they all set out from Pesaro, once again in the direction of Ancona and the Adriatic coast. Reaching Austrian-occupied Ancona, they hid until the third of April, when disguised as servants they escaped, traveling rapidly westward via Siena, Lucca, Genoa, and the appalling coastal road to the last Italian city, Nice. Then, crossing the River Var, they entered France on the fourteenth of April. It was a harrowing tale worthy of Stendhal himself.[12] Meanwhile behind them the Carbonari rebels in Italy had been crushed by the Austrians, General Ciro Menotti hanged, and Francesco Arese left a fugitive in hiding in his native Milan.

On the twenty-third of April, Hortense's heavy mud-splattered Berlin traveling carriage reached Paris and finally came to a halt in the Rue de la Paix before the Hôtel de Hollande.[13] Physically and mentally exhausted after plunging through a hell usually reserved for men, the ex-queen, a still weak Louis Napoléon, and their loyal Countess Masuyer felt truly safe.

Nevertheless they were here illegally, Louis Philippe's law of 1832 having banished all the Bonapartes permanently from French soil. Undaunted, a few hours later, this determined lady dragged herself back into her coach and had herself driven over to the long, distinctive, rectangular, column-lined residence of the Orléans, the Palais Royal. The Palais was surrounded by hundreds of troops because of the violent unrest in the country and the assassination attempts on the life of the king, and Hortense scarcely recognized the place where she had once danced so gaily in her youth. But the king refused to receive her, and she returned to the Rue de la Paix.

Following the visit and an interrogation by a distinctly hostile Prime Minister Auguste Casimir-Perier about the circumstances that had brought them to Paris, Hortense Bonaparte was finally invited to a more

welcoming Palais Royal. On the evening of April 26 she was shown into
Louis Philippe's austere "little chamber," where he, his wife, the shy sympathetic Queen Marie Amélie, and his sister, Adélaïde, greeted her. As
warm as the reception was, the ever-cautious Louis Philippe promised
nothing, apart from giving Hortense and Louis Napoléon permission
to remain in Paris briefly, if incognito. The last thing the king wanted
now were spontaneous pro-Bonaparte street demonstrations. Nevertheless, the king did promise to look into her request to have her property
and valuable estates, which had been seized first by the Bourbons and
then kept by the Orléans, including 700,000 francs (more than nine
million dollars today) in back revenue, returned to her, though nothing
ever came of this. Nor was a brief letter Louis Napoléon had drafted to
the king asking for permission to return to France "as a simple citizen. . . .
as a simple soldier . . . happy to be permitted to die for my country,"[14] in
the long run ever submitted.

Alas, Louis Napoléon, ignoring their most fragile, tentative situation
in Paris and the cautious goodwill thus far demonstrated by the king,
now jeopardized everything. If he did not gallop through the streets
carrying a revolutionary banner as he had done earlier in Rome, he did
commit an even more egregious transgression now, allegedly "secretly"
visiting leaders of the political opposition. He simply could not stop med-
dling. Prime Minister Casimir-Perier immediately informed the king,
who felt deceived and humiliated by the lovely Hortense (who in fact
had known nothing of her son's activities). Prior to this, Louis Philippe
had in fact softened, offering Louis Napoléon the option of remaining
in France, if he agreed to give up the name of Bonaparte, and be known
legally as "the Duke of Saint-Leu." His reaction was not unexpected:
"I should prefer to be laid out with my brother in his coffin first!"[15] But
instead, once again he had burned his bridges, and the order by a betrayed Louis Philippe quickly followed—to leave the country forthwith.
On the sixth of May their Berlin headed toward the English Channel
and London.

They established themselves in Mayfair to bide their time. It was not
until the end of March 1831 that Louis Napoléon had received a first
communication from his father asking about his brother's death. Fear-

ful of Habsburg reprisals and being expelled from Austrian-occupied Florence, Louis's letter was devoid of all sentiment and brutally business-like, not even asking after his health. "I require information about two things: All the details possible about your fatal [Italian] escapade; 2. Idem., about the final moments of your brother's life. Did he really have measles? Are you quite sure that someone had not deliberately caused his death? . . . Did he die in your arms? Adieu, mon ami, have courage and bear up. Now is the time to demonstrate it, for yourself and your mother's sake."[16] Louis did not even ask if his son had suffered, or if Louis Napoléon was coping. "Your suspicions about someone having deliberately killed him are entirely unfounded," the prince replied. "Believe me that if such a frightful crime had been committed, I should have found the culprit personally and avenged his death then and there. . . . Oh! Mon cher Papa, how cruel life is!"[17]

Provided with fresh travel documents by French Ambassador Talleyrand, Hortense, Louis Napoléon, and Valerie Masuyer sailed from Dover on August 6, 1831, reaching the Schloss in the last week of the month.[18]

5

RETURN TO ARENENBERG

"I never had any wish to undertake anything that he was not part of."[1]
—LOUIS NAPOLÉON ON THE DEATH OF HIS BROTHER, NAPOLÉON LOUIS

"Don't you realize the revival of the Empire is at hand!"[2]
—GILBERT FIALIN

On his return to Arenenberg in August 1831, Louis Napoléon found a crate sent by his father, including his brother Napoléon Louis's gold watch, his portrait, and another of his favorite horse. There was also a letter from his father discussing the details of his brother's testamentary dispositions, a subject Louis Napoléon found most distressing. "Alas! Since it is necessary to deal with such a sad subject as my brother's estate, I can tell you quite simply that you have handled it very well," he wrote, adding that he wanted nothing for himself, apart from some personal mementos of no real value. "As for me, I have no interest whatsoever in any money that comes from such a source."[3] "I have lost the one person I loved the most in the world," he confided now to his widowed sister-in-law, Charlotte Bonaparte, the daughter of Uncle Joseph. "I never had any wish to undertake anything that he was not a part of."[4]

After returning to the schloss, a restless Prince Louis Napoléon rejoined his regiment at Thun while Hortense proceeded to visit her cousin Stéphanie, the Grand Duchess of Baden, at Mannheim, where she received a letter postmarked Milan and just forwarded from Arenenberg. In it she learned from Antoinette Arese that her son, Francesco, was, like Louis Napoléon earlier, still a fugitive from the Austrian rulers of northern

Italy, and was probably en route to Switzerland. Would Hortense be so kind as to provide him with a refuge at Arenenberg?

"I can well appreciate better than anyone a mother's distress under such circumstances," she replied, "and I shall be only too happy to allay such worries by taking care of your son and seeing to all his needs." As she pointed out, knowing only too well from personal experience that such young men of his age "are filled with all sorts of extravagant ideas, I shall do my best to calm him down." She had had some success, she felt, in the case of Louis Napoléon, "in persuading him that it is necessary to resign oneself to the fact that there is no such thing as perfection in life, and that one must settle for peace of mind in lieu of wild pipe dreams." She was instructing the staff at Arenenberg "to welcome your son." Louis Napoléon was frequently away at the Thun military school, or at his late uncle Eugène de Beauharnais's neighboring estate of Schloss Eugensberg (inherited by his daughter, Princess Eugène Hortense, after her father's premature death in 1824). "My son will be more than delighted to have a good companion with him during the [forthcoming] hunting season. And I hope that our peaceful solitude will permit him to forget some of his problems."[5]

Coming at this time with the household in full mourning over the loss of his brother, nevertheless Louis Napoléon warmly welcomed Francesco, a young man of his own age and background who had also been a friend of his late brother. Shared experiences and death brought the two young men quickly together, and Arese soon became Louis Napoléon's surrogate brother. They hunted and rode together, and later went to London on a brief journey. Hortense was as good as her word and treated him like a member of the family and was later to leave a small memento in her testament to the cheerful, outgoing Count Arese, who had become "like a son to me."[6]

But when Louis Napoléon's apparently jealous father discovered the presence of Arese at Arenenberg, he grew furious, finding him "unsuitable," and demanded his immediate departure; the prince was simply staggered. "It is truly most painful to find you like this yet again. No matter what I do you are angry. . . . Count Arese comes from one of the finest families of Milan. He is very quiet, very reliable and, what is more, he is very attached to me, and I in return like him very much. You seem to forget, Father, that I am twenty-five years old and no longer a child."[7]

As for the two young men, they had their differences, but differences they mutually respected. Unlike Arese, Louis Napoléon was both a life-long Mason and a staunch supporter of the Catholic Church. The count was to dedicate his life to fighting for only one cause: the creation of an independent kingdom of Italy, freed of the Austrians and the Vatican's control of the Papal States. Although coming from a strongly pro-French family, Francesco Arese refused to get personally involved in any aspect of French politics and later avoided any participation in or support of Louis Napoléon's plots to overthrow the July Monarchy of Louis Philippe. But Arese remained rigorously faithful to Louis Napoléon, a veritable brother, as future events were to prove. Arese was to stay at Arenenberg until 1835.

Life resumed its usual pace at Arenenberg in 1832, but there were now signs that Louis Napoléon was gaining some international attention. Juliette Récamier, first Joséphine's friend and now Hortense's, arrived one day with none other than the celebrated statesman, diplomat, and literary figure of the day, François Auguste René de Chateaubriand. After an unusually long afternoon at Arenenberg, he described his young host: "Prince Louis is a studious, educated young man. He is solemn and is governed by a sense of honor." Juliette Récamier found him "polished, distinguished looking and taciturn."[8]

A delegation of Polish aristocrats arrived at the schloss to offer the crown of their troubled country, which he gratefully declined. On the thirtieth of April 1832, Louis Napoléon was made a naturalized citizen at Thun, while beginning to champ at the bit to return "to my own country, France."

Then his life was changed in a flash with the startling news of the death in Vienna on the twenty-second of July of Napoléon I's blond, nearly six foot, twenty-one-year-old son, Napoléon II—Napoléon François Joseph Charles, the king of Rome and Duke of Reichstadt. The official alleged cause of this suspicious death was tuberculosis. A bewildered

Louis Napoléon now found himself next in the line of succession to claim the largely symbolic Napoleonic crown. (Both brothers Joseph and Louis had renounced their rights to that dignity, and of course Lucien had been excluded by Napoléon himself.) In consequence, Prince Louis Napoléon received an invitation in the autumn of that year, 1832, from Uncle Joseph Bonaparte, then in London, to visit him. He was accompanied by Francesco Arese. The meeting did not pass off well and he never met his uncle again.

"I fully realize that I owe a great deal to my present position because my name is Bonaparte," he confided to a friend, "but up to this point nothing to my own achievements. Aristocrat by birth, democrat by heart and belief, I owe everything to hereditary election." He was now bent on acting decisively in his own right so, as he put it, he might be "touched by one of the last dying rays of the sun emanating from St. Helena."[9]

And so the days passed, 1833 much like the previous year, with the exception of the publication of Louis Napoléon's first books, *Political Thoughts* and *Political and Military Considerations on Switzerland,* intended to express his personal philosophy while also praising Napoléon I's rule and his father's, King Louis's, administration of Holland. Proudly sending the first copy to his father, he looked forward to his reply, only to receive a stinging rebuke: "Ought the political policies of the head of your family, of a man such as the Emperor, be superficially judged by a mere young man of twenty-four!" He further denounced "the many falsehoods you have published on the perceived reasons behind my personal conduct of State Affairs [while king of Holland]."[10] Louis Napoléon was simply shattered.

Battered but not defeated, in the following year Louis Napoléon published his *Artillery Manual,* for which the Swiss army congratulated him with promotion from lieutenant to captain. Delighted, Louis Napoléon sent a copy of the book with the good news to his father who, as a general officer in his own right, he felt would heartily approve. "We are going to have to come to some sort of understanding, *if we are to remain good friends* [author's italics]," read another drubbing from Tuscany. "I am very happy to learn that you merit the estime and consideration of the

Swiss. . . . but for the rest . . . I must ask you to heed my words, and I cannot say this often enough," he harangued Captain Bonaparte. "Under no circumstances . . . must one serve in the army of a foreign country. To be sure the military profession is the finest and most honorable. . . . so long as one is defending one's own country; otherwise . . . it is the most contemptible of all." He knew his son no doubt was tired of these incessant criticisms; he added, "nevertheless I cannot but repeat yet again what I believe to be my duty to point out to you."[11]

So bitterly stung this time was Louis Napoléon that he ceased all correspondence for the next six months, only replying in 1835.[12] "Mon cher Papa, I receive your harsh words so very often that I should be quite used to them by now," he wrote. "Regardless, every new reproach by you does indeed wound me, and as painfully as on the very first occasion." His father had also criticized him for donating funds for the construction of a local village school, for donating a cannon to the Swiss army, and then for his poor handwriting. The growing frequency and brutality of these senseless, humiliating, wounding onslaughts was just too much for Louis Napoléon, as the ex-king attempted to continue to dominate a son who was feverishly struggling to escape his grasp. And then a stranger knocked on the door who would prove the means for hastening this escape.

In July 1835, a young man arrived at Arenenberg with a letter of introduction from Uncle Joseph Bonaparte, whom he had recently met in London. His name was Jean Gilbert Victor Fialin. Slender, dapper, with his sandy hairy falling over his brow, a neat, well-trimmed military mustache, and refined features, Fialin was presentable and spoke surprisingly well given his modest background. But it would have taken a veritable soothsayer to predict that this otherwise unprepossessing chap, the son of a provincial tax collector from Limoges, would one day become Emperor Napoléon III's public relations and party manager. Now at the age of twenty-seven, after serving as a non-commissioned officer in the army of Charles X, his transition to Louis Philippe's command had not been a success and he was cashiered for his outspoken "republicanism." Fialin had then taken up journalism, where he showed a real flair for writing in the popular press. With an inordinately strong ego and a determined drive to succeed, the ex-sergeant thus entered Arenenberg, and Louis Napoléon's life, permanently.

Fialin was a recently converted "Bonapartist," a fanatic dedicated to the resurrection of the Napoleonic legacy of the magnificent First Empire. "Don't you realize that the revival of the Empire is at hand, that it is imminent and even inevitable!"[13] Fialin argued in the press and wherever he could find an audience, with all the fervor of a reborn Christian at a fundamentalist revival. Fialin, or Persigny, as he affected to be called, had several qualities that appealed to Prince Louis Napoléon, despite Hortense's strong personal objections to the man. He was subservient and knew his place before the aristocracy—the prince appreciated that; he had compelling drive and fire when preaching the Napoleonic cause; he understood the military world and military discipline; and he was capable of undying loyalty to a superior and a cause he wanted to believe in. Furthermore, his newspaper articles established his possibilities as a most effective public relations officer . . . and finally— with no other source of revenue in sight—he was eager to start work for this holy cause forthwith.

For Louis Napoléon, alone at Arenenberg throughout 1835 and 1836, with neither his late brother nor Francesco Arese (now back in Milan) on hand, Gilbert Persigny—as he will be called hereafter—by his diligence and daily presence now filled a formal place in his new political quest and daily existence. Hereafter he was the prince's inseparable shadow every step of the way, determined to change things in France and above all to alter the prince's life beyond all his dreams.[14]

6

———— ✦ ————

ROMANCE AND RUCTIONS

"Believe me, I know my France."[1]
—LOUIS NAPOLÉON TO HIS MEN

"Certainly the prospect of this marriage pleased me, but . . ."[2]
—MATHILDE BONAPARTE REGARDING HER
ENGAGEMENT TO LOUIS NAPOLÉON

On the face of it, it hardly seemed of immediate concern to the inhabitants of Schloss Arenenberg when in the spring of 1835 newspapers announced a deadly outbreak of cholera sweeping the ancient Tuscan capital of Florence. It had happened before, many times, and the socially prominent and wealthy simply left for the countryside. Louis Bonaparte left for the seaside, while his younger, fifty-one-year-old brother, Jérôme, his ailing wife, Catharine, son "Prince Jérôme," Plon-Plon (Napoléon Joseph), and daughter Princess Mathilde, preferred the safety of Switzerland. Back in January 1831 the Jérôme Bonapartes had been obliged by the Vatican police to abruptly quit their comfortable Roman palazzo and move to Florence, thanks largely to Prince Louis Napoléon's plotting with the Carbonari to bring Napoléon's son, the Duke of Reichstadt, from Vienna to assume the crown of Italy.[3]

And now, four years later, Uncle Jérôme still resented the heavy price they had paid as a result of his wayward nephew Louis Napoléon's hell-raising, as he settled into the villa of "Mon Repos," near Lausanne, on the shore of Lake Geneva. Swiss doctors confirmed that Catherine was in an advanced stage of cancer. The once frantically gay princess rapidly succumbed, dying in the rented villa on the night of November 29–30, 1835.

The funeral of the princess was not the only thing on Jérôme Bonaparte's mind now, however, for the death of his wife also meant the immediate loss of the two main sources of the family's income, derived from two "pensions" granted her by the former tsar Alexander and her father, Friedrich I, king of Württemberg. With the family treasury suddenly depleted—thanks to Jérôme's squandering of his entire estate and his here-today-gone-tomorrow champagne mentality—and the inevitable marriage of his blossoming fifteen-year-old, dowryless daughter Mathilde to think of in the near future, for almost the first time in his erratic, sometimes violent life, libertine, gambler, and womanizer Jérôme Bonaparte had to sit down and do some serious thinking. And then once again, as it always seemed to transpire in his feckless existence, an unexpected, if still rather dim, light shone on the horizon.

Following the funeral and during his immediate sojourn to Stuttgart, nominally to visit Catherine's relatives following her burial in the family crypt, but in reality to salvage his finances, Jérôme Bonaparte received an invitation from his sister-in-law, Hortense, to come with his grieving children for a visit to Schloss Arenenberg. While Jérôme's feelings regarding his now twenty-seven-year-old nephew Louis Napoléon were not exactly warm at this stage, stripped of two-thirds of his income, this former king of Westphalia had to be realistic. The family's small convoy of calèches was soon en route to the modest château overlooking Lake Constance. Of all the Bonapartes, Jérôme was the only one who personally liked and accepted Hortense. The other clan doors had been rudely shut these past two decades, leaving few possible suitors for his daughter.

Although visitors generally found Arenenberg rather somber, heavy, and oppressive, including the ostentatious clutter of Napoleona—large family portraits and delicate miniatures, busts, swords, snuff boxes, and books—young Mathilde found the ambiance, especially the

lightened, tented chiffon ceilings in the private apartments, most inviting, and she liked her gentle, beautiful aunt Hortense, which in turn
won her over in the eyes of cousin Louis Napoléon.

Allowed to visit Hortense in the morning while she was still in bed,
Mathilde found her "pleasant and smiling, taking me into her confidence
about her daily affairs here while showing an interest in my future, even
as she attempted to better understand me personally." And Louis
Napoléon, for once relaxing in this rare intimate family gathering,
was clearly smitten with his pretty first cousin, even flirting with her.
Putting her dark mourning dress aside, one afternoon she appeared in
an embarrassingly low-cut gown, looking much older than her sixteen
years. "It was a pleasure to look at her, she was so pretty," an amused Valérie Masuyer remarked, noting that "the young prince could not take his
eyes off her."[4] Uncle Jérôme soon had to return to Stuttgart with Mathilde,
pleased that this first meeting between the young couple had gone off
so well.

Mathilde was not the only prospect in sight, however, as Hortense
and Valérie Masuyer considered the possibilities. The daughter of General Arrighi de Casanova, the Duke of Padua, was an attractive option,
with a dowry of 600,000 francs in cash, but the title was new and the
young lady a bit of a pudding so far as Louis Napoléon was concerned,
and in any event his father also rejected that candidate, just as he did
the young widowed Maria da Braganza, queen of Portugal. And although
there were rumors of German and Russian princesses, Louis Napoléon
for his part neither wished to bear the crown of, nor live in, a foreign
country. It would be France or nothing, and he was fast losing patience
with this matrimonial quest. "I do not want to run all over Europe selling myself to the highest bidder," he complained to Hortense.[5] On the
other hand there were not that many crowned heads of state wishing to
have one of those upstart "Bonapartes" as a son-in-law. Europe had
enough problems as it was, without having to add to them.

Back in Stuttgart once again, Jérôme Bonaparte and King Friedrich
had to settle Catherine's estate, Jérôme not neglecting the opportunity
of showing off the king's lovely granddaughter, Mathilde, as a potential
bride-to-be—and no doubt her worth as a dowry investment by him.

Indeed Jérôme assured the stouthearted king that he personally was a reformed man. He would put an end to his spendthrift ways of the past couple of decades. He would not only cut down on household expenses, he would sell his luxurious Florentine palazzo in exchange for the more modest villa of Quarto.

The subject of marriage between Louis Napoléon and Mathilde was now on the table. The hurdle of Bonaparte family animosity was diminished somewhat as Letizia gradually came to know and accept Hortense after her many visits to Rome, and with that matriarch's death on February 2, 1836, any possible lingering animosity was literally buried.

Money was the real problem. Jérôme was hoping for cooperation from his father-in-law, King Friedrich, who openly welcomed the idea of the marriage of that couple. Another visit to Arenenberg followed, allowing Louis Napoléon and Mathilde to spend more time together, including chaperoned moonlight boat rides on Lake Constance. The creative Jérôme Bonaparte finally proposed terms: a 150,000-franc cash dowry (which he did not possess) and the Schloss Gottlieben (near Arenenberg) that he had just acquired (entirely on credit) for the young couple. The prince's father in Florence finally condescended to the alliance (at the urging of Hortense) with the promise of another 250,000 francs. Hortense added an annual pension of 12,000 francs out of her own meager personal funds. The two poorest branches of the Bonaparte family would unite, but with a cautionary Louis adding his usual paternal advice. He was perfectly aware, he noted, that Mathilde was "charming, but that is not everything in a marriage," for the "illusions of beauty and even those of worthy feelings" frequently did not stand the test of time.[6] And that is how matters stood on the twenty-second of May, 1836, as a blooming Mathilde and a much relieved Jérôme left Switzerland on their return journey to Florence.

Little known to Hortense, however, Louis Napoléon had more pressing matters on his mind, thanks in great part to the stimulating drive of Gilbert (Fialin) Persigny. Hereafter politics superseded romance in the life of the prince.

• • •

Louis Philippe, "the king of the French," and his misrule and mass suppression of the electorate were among the principal obstacles oppressing the French people, Louis Napoléon preached to Persigny, who in turn encouraged the prince. The July Monarchy, having arrived by revolution, must in turn now be removed by it, but not by violence, not by the sword, the prince insisted. "If the government [of Louis Philippe] have committed enough mistakes to makes the people desire another revolution," he argued before Gilbert Persigny, "if the Napoleonic cause has left fond memories in the hearts of the French people, then all I should have to do is to present myself, standing quite alone, without even troops at my side, before the people and remind them of their recent grievances and past glory, and they will rally to my flag. . . . Believe me, I know my France."[7] He was completely beguiled by his own rhetoric and fervor, and convinced of the purity of his intentions. After all, "a revolution is only acceptable, only legitimate when it is made in the best interests of the majority of the people,"[8] he argued. And strongly encouraged by Persigny throughout the late summer of 1836, they sat down to work out a plan to remove King Louis Philippe and replace him with this nephew of Emperor Napoléon. Louis Napoléon decided on the seizure of the ten-thousand-man garrison of Strasbourg, followed by a march on Paris. But initial attempts to contact and win over senior army officers and officials in that city were most disappointing. The commanding general, Théophile Voirol, had not only turned him down but had notified the war office in Paris.[9] Louis Napoléon's attempt to bring in General Rémi Exelmans, a veteran of the 1812 Moscow campaign, also failed.[10] In the end, the most senior officer at Strasbourg agreeing to go along with this plot was the fifty-two-year-old Colonel Claude Nicolas Vaudrey, who had fought with Napoléon at Waterloo. Vaudrey in turn recruited Major Denis Parquin (married to Hortense's former companion, Louise Cochelet), Major de Bruce, Lieutenant (Viscount) de Querelle, and Lieutenant Armand Laity, among others. And that was how matters stood by the end of September 1836.

• • •

Fanny Le Hon had been working with Hortense as she prepared to recognize Auguste de Morny officially, by adopting him, and in the last week of October Fanny duly arrived at Arenenberg to draft the legal paperwork. It was probably about this time that Louis Napoléon received the shocking news that he had an illegitimate half brother. On the twenty-fourth of October, a somber, constrained farewell dinner was held at Arenenberg including Hortense, Louis Napoléon, Henri Conneau, Valérie Masuyer, and Fanny Le Hon. Fanny announced that she would be returning to Paris to see the lawyers regarding the adoption, and Louis Napoléon had been invited to visit cousins on a hunting party in Germany.[11] The following morning, the prince boarded his carriage and set out on his journey. Instead of heading northeast, however, hours later he crossed the Rhine into France. He would not see his mother again until the summer of the following year.

7

WHAT HATH GOD WROUGHT

"I took as my guiding principle to follow only the inspirations of my heart, my intellect and my conscience."[1]
—PRINCE LOUIS NAPOLÉON

*"The Napoleonic concept—*l'idée napoléonienne*—is not founded on the principle of war."*[2]
—PRINCE LOUIS NAPOLÉON

At six o'clock on Monday, the thirtieth of October, 1836, Swiss army Captain Louis Napoléon Bonaparte—now disguised in the uniform of a French colonel—attended by French "General" Vaudrey and ten officers (including Gilbert Persigny) marched into the Strasbourg garrison and to the barracks of the 46th Infantry Regiment, where "Colonel Bonaparte" appealed to the men to join him. Unfortunately, they completely rejected the young man and the name of "Bonaparte," much to the astonishment of the prince, and from then on it turned into a shambles. Although they managed to seize the commanding general, Théophile Voirol, in his office, he then escaped through a back door and was saved by his staff officers, joined by Voirol's hysterical mother-in-law and wife, who then pummeled the bewildered Swiss captain with a barrage of fists. By eight o'clock the coup was over, and "the invaders" were behind locked doors.[3]

In fact, even if the coup had succeeded, who was Louis Napoléon expecting to find waiting with open arms in the French capital? Unlike

Uncle Napoleon's successful coup of 18–19 Brumaire in November 1799, there was no plan after Strasbourg. The army was not behind him, and there was no newly formed shadow government of politicians in the wings ready to step in and take over the government in his name. Moreover, the prince did not even personally know a single national political leader in Paris. Indeed, he did not have a single seasoned political advisor to consult when planning the adventure.

"Ridiculous," the London *Times* summed up the fiasco. "An unbalanced young man," the *Frankfurter Zeitung* called Prince Louis Napoléon. "What on earth did he possibly expect to achieve?"[4]

Leaving behind an unprecedented early Alsatian snowstorm, his fellow conspirators now in prison, and a firmly loyal Strasbourg garrison still in place, on reaching Paris on Tuesday the first of November, Prince Louis Napoléon was handed over to the recently appointed prefect of Paris, Gabriel Delessert. The choice of this descendant of Swiss Calvinist bankers proved indeed fortunate for prisoner Bonaparte. Although he had served under Emperor Napoléon in a mere fiscal capacity, Delessert's wife, Valentine, had in her father, Count Alexander de Laborde, unusually strong Bonapartist ties. Awarded the Legion of Honor by Emperor Napoléon himself, this skilled diplomat had not only negotiated Napoléon's marriage contract with Marie Louise, but was a very close friend of the then-queen Hortense, even co-authoring her *Partant pour la Syrie* ("Marching Off to Syria"), which was to become the unofficial national anthem under the Second Empire. Now a strong supporter and friend of Louis Philippe as well, Laborde served as both a general of the Paris National Guard and as the king's ambassador to Madrid. With such unusually strong direct ties both to Emperor Napoléon and King Louis Philippe, the son of Hortense and grandson of Joséphine had a powerful "friend at court," in the guise of Prefect Gabriel Delessert.

"My dear Mother, You have no doubt been most anxious, having received no news from me," Louis Napoléon had written on the first of

November, "and now your anxiety will be all the greater when you learn what I have attempted, but failed to bring off at Strasbourg." He then broke the news: "I am in prison here . . . But you mustn't cry, for I am the victim of a worthy cause, a truly French cause. . . . Fortunately," he added, "not a drop of French blood was spilled . . . I am most proud to have raised the Imperial Eagle once again, and quite ready to die for my political convictions."[5]

And then from Paris on the tenth he broke the news: "They are sending me to America . . . but under no circumstances are you even to think of joining me there . . . in my new exile. . . . Life is of little import when the only thing that counts for me is the honor of France. But do think of the others as well, I beseech you to see that the prisoners in Strasbourg having all they need, and do take special care of Colonel Vaudrey's two sons."[6]

Rushing to Paris in the first week of November to plead with Louis Philippe, Hortense found herself stopped at the Château de Viry on the king's orders, he refusing to see her. In fact Louis Philippe had a very "hot political potato" on his hands. Holding someone by the name of Bonaparte as a state prisoner was tantamount to holding the lit fuse of a political powder keg. Ever since coming to power, unrest had threatened the Orléans regime. There had been insurrections in Lyons in 1831 and in Lyons again and Paris as recently as 1835. There had been several assassination attempts, including the bloody massacre on July 28, 1835, in the midst of the annual Bastille Day celebration of the French Revolution, when a Corsican, Giuseppe Fieschi, and his two fellow conspirators had detonated a homemade "infernal machine" at the carriage of Louis Philippe and his three sons. Eighteen people were killed outright, including four senior army officers, while another twenty-two were wounded. Although the king was slightly wounded in the head, his sons escaped unscathed, and security had been tight in Paris ever since. Seven and a half months later, Louis Napoléon Bonaparte attacked Strasbourg and attempted to overthrow Louis Philippe. By this point the king and his family were rather on edge.

In all respects the Bonapartes were in fact a very special case for Louis Philippe. During the First Empire, Napoléon had protected members of the House of Orléans, even providing financial assistance for Louis Philippe's mother and family. Moreover, Auguste de Morny's father, General Charles de Flahaut, and grandmother, Adélaïde de Souza, had been close to the king, or the Duke of Orléans, as he still was, ever since the 1790s. Further, Louis Philippe and the queen, Marie Amélie, were personally very fond of Hortense Bonaparte, whom they had known since childhood. The problem facing Louis Philippe, therefore, was great, the ramifications greater still, and the unsettling events of Strasbourg now before the public, a veritable nightmare. Moreover the Napoleonic clientele—the families of hundreds of thousands of former soldiers and administrative personnel—remained an explosive political force in itself. The king had to defuse the situation and act with quick, unwonted resolve.

A military court was ruled out and the case was instead handed over to the public prosecutor in Strasbourg for trial. On the other hand, Louis Napoléon, as an aristocrat, could have been tried separately by a court of his peers. Louis Philippe had quickly ruled that out too, as he directed Hortense to leave the country and her son to be deported. The decree of 1832 banishing the entire Bonaparte family remained in full effect. As for all the other Strasbourg co-conspirators, it was decided to have them arraigned by the public prosecutor of Strasbourg. The senior military officers clamoring for a court-martial were to be deprived of their firing squads.

Twenty-four hours after arriving in Paris, on the eleventh of November, 1836, Prince-prisoner Louis Napoléon found himself being handed into a closed carriage in the courtyard of the Conciergerie, bound under heavy escort for the channel coast where the French navy had a warship awaiting his arrival. Regardless of the situation today, like the great Napoléon in the past, nephew Louis Napoléon did not admit fallibility, did not recognize past errors of judgment. In his eyes he was a patriot, a savior of the country. As a gentleman and a Bonaparte, he had had no choice but to act as he had. Even now he would have done it all over again. "Why am I treated as such a pariah, even by my own family?" he asked his father.[7] He simply could not understand it.

• • •

Setting out from the Isle de France on the eleventh of November, the prince arrived at Lorient on the fifteenth. Before he embarked, on the personal instructions of Louis Philippe himself, Deputy Prefect Villemain handed the prisoner a purse of 15,000 francs (a little over $193,000 today).[8] That same evening the prince was taken to the small harbor where Captain Henri de Villeneuve received him aboard the modern, surprisingly spacious, and powerful fifty-two-gun frigate *Andromeda*.[9] They cast off immediately.

After being held up by contrary winds in the notoriously inhospitable Bay of Biscay for eighteen days, Captain de Villeneuve finally opened the sealed orders prepared by the Naval Ministry. At last prisoner Bonaparte learned his fate, the orders "instructing the captain to take me to Rio de Janeiro, but not to permit me to go ashore. He was also to forbid any sort of communications [with the outside world]."[10]

Finally reaching the East Coast of the United States after four and a half months at sea within the confined quarters of the *Andromeda,* Louis Napoléon, a true Bonaparte and never a good seaman, stepped ashore no longer a prisoner, but a free man under the protection of the American flag. Louis Philippe could not threaten him here.[11] Due to contrary winds, Captain de Villeneuve had diverted from his charted course to New York, and instead put in to Norfolk, Virginia, on the tenth of April 1837, thereby concluding this exhausting, frequently uncomfortable, and monotonous 8,870-nautical-mile transatlantic odyssey (more than 10,000 land miles).

During those long weeks at sea, Louis Napoléon had been entirely cut off from the world, receiving not a single letter, or a single bit of information from Switzerland, France, or Europe. When he had sailed from Lorient in November 1836, his fellow conspirators were in prison in Strasbourg awaiting trial, and Hortense had just returned to Schloss Arenenberg. This did not prevent mother and son from writing to each other, Louis Napoléon's thoughts totally preoccupied with the fate of the prisoners, and of course his mother, and public opinion of himself and his actions.

"I am leaving heartbroken in not having been able to share the same fate as my suffering companions," the prince had written Hortense from Lorient just prior to putting to sea. "My undertaking having failed . . . I wished to be the sole victim [put on trial]," he insisted, angry at having been separated from them and treated differently, as well as having been denied the opportunity to explain his aims to the press. "As a result, in the eyes of the world I am considered to be a lunatic, an opportunist and a coward."[12]

Meanwhile Hortense was sending him news that he would not receive until he had reached New York, and most of it bad. If King Louis in Florence had found his son's conspiracy quite mad, nevertheless he supported him, calling Louis Philippe's prosecution of the case "a political plot against the family." The rest of the Bonaparte clan, however, had to a man turned against Louis Napoléon, openly denouncing him, including Uncle Jérôme, who cancelled the forthcoming marriage plans to Mathilde—"I would rather give my daughter to a peasant than to him!" Jérôme then demanded that Hortense buy back from him the château he had just "purchased" (but had never paid for) as a wedding gift for the couple.[13]

"The more I dwell on the conduct of your family, the more it dismays me," Hortense wrote.[14] "I have developed such a disgust of mankind and the things of this world," she continued, "that you will well appreciate my sentiments when I say that I am only too delighted that in the end everything has turned out so badly for you." Because, as a result, "you are going to be obliged to live quietly, out of harm's way," instead of being "caught up in the world of petty political passions."[15]

Now on foreign soil, Louis Napoléon encountered his first "Americans"—he spoke fluent English, but with a German accent—as he traveled from Norfolk to Philadelphia by one of the first steam trains built in that region. There he next boarded a long, narrow steamboat, which continued up the Delaware River. Always interested in anything mechanical, the prince was fascinated by the number of uses of steam power in these still wild, relatively untamed regions.

Louis Napoléon was even more impressed, however, by "the width of this beautiful river . . . and all the steamboats which are truly magnificent!" Years later he had not forgotten these early vivid impressions, and as Emperor Napoléon III, he was to stimulate and greatly facilitate the development and expansion of both France's first rail network and international steamship lines.[16]

"I was very surprised and happy to find [Francesco] Arese here to meet me in New York [on April 20]," an unusually buoyant Louis Napoléon wrote his old family friend and tutor, Narcisse Vieillard. "It was a great consolation to have so good a friend near me at this time."[17] In fact no sooner had Arese heard the news of the Strasbourg affair than he had written Hortense for details, and then set out from Milan, to join Louis Napoléon in America. Equally unexpected, though less welcome, was the sight of three of his cousins at the pier: Joachim and Caroline Murat's two sons, Napoléon and Achille, and Uncle Lucien's hell-raising libertine son, Pierre Bonaparte. European leaders seemed determined to jettison all their black sheep in America. In any event, the Bonaparte family having always cold-shouldered Hortense in the past, the prince avoided their offspring hereafter.

On reaching his hotel, the prince found a bundle of letters from his mother and cousins. "Here I am on terra firma once again!" he responded immediately to Hortense that same day. "On landing [at New York] I learned the news of the acquittal of my friends [in Strasbourg]. You can well imagine the great joy I felt, after the long nightmare of these past months and dreading to learn of their conviction."[18]

Before leaving France, state prisoner Bonaparte had pleaded with Louis Philippe on behalf of his fellow conspirators. "They played no part in the plot," he had insisted, "the whole idea for the conspiracy was mine and mine alone."[19] In any event, Louis Napoléon had been on the high seas when the trial eventually opened in the Assize Court (Cour d'Assises) of Strasbourg on January 6, 1837.

Of the thirteen initially charged in the public prosecutor's indictment, only seven eventually appeared in court. The remaining six had "escaped," including the nimble Gilbert Persigny, now snug in London.

Obviously Louis Philippe had no wish to dramatize before the whole country the fact that a dozen of his finest young army officers (and one ex-sergeant) had betrayed him, wishing to overthrow his regime. Alas, having a highly respected national hero with a splendid military record such as the fifty-two-year-old Colonel Vaudrey testifying in an open French court of law proved unavoidable.

The court was filled with the national and international press as the jury filed in for the last time on the morning of January 18, 1837, to present their verdict. The presiding judge asked for it to be read, and it came like a bomb blast: "Not guilty." As for Prince Louis Napoléon, the publicly acknowledged ringleader, the instigator, and financier behind the attempted coup had not even been charged by Louis Philippe's government, and as a result, the jury had rightly concluded that it would have hardly been "equitable" to have imprisoned only the underlings.

"The victory bells are ringing" for the political opposition, the *Moniteur* announced on January 23. The Bourbon establishment and haute-bourgeoisie were dismayed, including Austrian chancellor Clement von Metternich, who declared the mass acquittal "a deplorable, simply detestable" decision.[20] If the authorities exonerated these culprits of their acknowledged treasonous acts, it would only encourage more brazen attempts against the government in the future.

From the moment of his arrival in New York, Louis Napoléon was swept up in a whirlwind of activity such as he had never before known. Francesco Arese took charge of his schedule, which was rapidly filled by invitations from prominent Americans. Meanwhile a fellow passenger Louis Napoléon had met while sailing from Philadelphia, the Reverend C. S. Stewart, acted as their tour guide over the next couple of weeks. The clergyman, like other Americans, found the French gentleman "shy, reserved and well mannered," while another new acquaintance, the young poet Fitz-Greene Halleck, found him a most pleasant, if "a rather dull man in the order of [George] Washington."[21] Louis Napoléon apparently found both Americans and the bustling scene around him fascinating, and despite his natural reserve he made every attempt to talk to them, even playing billiards with them at his hotel.

Encouraged by the more outgoing Arese, Bonaparte made the ideal tourist. Intelligent, most curious about everything around him, and by nature most observant, he could never see or learn enough. This was in fact a very new Louis Napoléon. He found America to be "a land of merchants" and "speculators," everyone most industrious, keen on making his way, willing to risk all and gamble their fortunes and lives in order to improve their circumstances—so utterly different from the people and mentality in France and Switzerland. This new world was invigorating. It was also in the streets of New York that he encountered slavery for the first time and found it repugnant, "a bad thing," as he put it.

Taking advantage of his fluent English, he spoke to people whenever possible, and sometimes came to rather curious conclusions. "This country possesses immense material forces, but it is entirely deficient in moral force," he summarily concluded without explanation. It was still "a colony," as he saw it, emerging from the cocoon, and far from mature. "In principle every [American] colony [state] is a real republic. It is an association of men who all, with equal rights, have agreed together to develop the products of their country. It matters little whether they have a governor or president for their chief. They require . . . only a few police regulations. . . . Here there is freedom to acquire, but not freedom to enjoy: there is the right to act, but not to think," he stated, again not developing his reasons for these rather curious assumptions. "The transition [from the colony mentality to that of a mature nation state] is going on daily . . . But I do not think the transition will be completed without its crises and convulsions."[22]

Propelled by his own driving curiosity, Louis Napoléon exhibited an almost limitless energy he had never before displayed. It was the physical, mechanical sights that really fascinated him. Keen on manufacturing, he visited numerous factories. He was also interested in schools and laboratories, where he saw an "electro-magnet" for the first time. He had only praise for the sheer physical and mental industry of the people, their astonishing will to achieve something. He was riveted by this dynamism and was never to forget it.

Nor did he fail to take an interest in some of the nation's men of letters, including his favorite American author, Washington Irving, whom he was curious to visit at his Dutch-style home overlooking the Hudson at Tarrytown. "I have read his works, and admire him both as a writer and a man," he recorded in English. He answered as many invitations as he could, introducing himself to New York society. Always known for his appreciation of a pretty face, he attended receptions, dinners, and balls given in his honor by the Bayards, Berkmans, De Pysters, Livingstones, Schuylers, Kents, the Van Nesses, the Dewitts, and the Roosevelts.[23] His days were filled from morning to night.

On his arrival at New York he had a sharp exchange of correspondence with Joseph Bonaparte over his harsh criticism of the Strasbourg affair, in the midst of which a defiant Louis Napoléon lashed out—most uncharacteristically—at his uncle: "What! I had the effrontery to undertake such a hardy business . . . that I dared throw myself into it, risking my life in the process, persuaded that my death was worthy of our cause," while receiving from him nothing but "scorn and disdain!" Yes, unfortunately, "my venture failed, but at least it announced to France that the family of the Emperor was not yet dead and buried!"[24]

Nevertheless intrigued by the widespread popularity of his uncle, and the complimentary things he had heard about him in New York society since his arrival, Louis Napoléon planned to visit his estate at Point Breeze, New Jersey, with Arese. First, despite the effort and discomfort of driving along primitive roads through the formidable virgin forests and mountains of upstate New York, a region teeming with bear, moose, deer, wolves, and mountain lions, they drove hundreds of miles to visit the fabled Niagara Falls on the U.S. Canada border. This was such a success that they next hoped to visit the newly emerging Washington, D.C., and President Andrew Jackson's recently elected replacement in the White House, Martin Van Buren.[25]

But back in New York City, barely two months after his arrival, on the sixth of June of 1837, the prince received a long-delayed letter from Henri Conneau, his mother's physician, informing him that Hortense was dying and that he must return at once before it was too late. Cancelling his forthcoming visit to Washington, D.C., he wrote to Martin Van Buren:

"Mr. President, I cannot leave the United States without expressing to your Excellency the regret I feel in not having been to Washington to make your acquaintance . . . and I [had also] hoped . . . to travel through a country which has so excited my sympathy," but due to his mother's ill health, "and [with no immediate] political consideration binding me here," he was obliged to leave. "I beg your Excellency to receive this letter as proof of my respect for the man who occupies the seat of George Washington . . . Louis Napoléon Bonaparte"[26]

Alas, his dealings with this country and another president, Abraham Lincoln, decades later were not destined to prove quite so convivial.

My dear mother," Louis Napoléon wrote from London a few weeks later, "The news I received of your health determined me to return to Europe as soon as possible. . . . You can understand how impatient I am to know how you are. I dare not believe in the happiness of seeing you again soon. . . . This all seems so unreal, everything that has happened these past few months, like some sort of dream."[27]

8

FAREWELLS AND ASYLUM

"Give up . . . what are referred to as the great affairs of the world."[1]
—LOUIS BONAPARTE TO HIS SON, 1837

"Switzerland has done her duty . . . and now I must do mine."[2]
—LOUIS NAPOLÉON, LEAVING SWITZERLAND
FOR THE LAST TIME, OCTOBER 1838

After sailing from New York (on an American passport and false name) on the twelfth of June, 1837, Louis Napoléon finally reached Switzerland and his dying mother on the fourth of August. Louis Philippe's government, fully aware of his return to Europe, turned a blind eye for the moment, out of respect for the prince's wish to be with his failing mother. In spite of the morphine administered by Henri Conneau, Hortense was by now in excruciating pain from the cancer that was killing her. Louis Napoléon spent every day at her bedside. "My mother died in my arms at five o'clock [in the morning] today," he wrote his father on the fifth of October.[3]

Three days later, the funeral service took place in the nearby church of Ermatingen before the casket was taken temporarily to Arenenberg's own small chapel. Louis Napoléon's world had collapsed around him. Nor was he permitted by Louis Philippe to accompany the casket to France for its final interment just a few miles from Malmaison in the small church of Saint Paul Saint Pierre in the village of Reuil. Among the mourners were the queen's two ladies-in-waiting, Valérie Masuyer and Madame Salvage de Faverolles; a few old soldiers, including Marshal

Nicholas Oudinot and General Rémi Exelmans; and of course members of the family, Hortense's twenty-six-year-old son, Auguste de Morny, and his father, Charles Count de Flahaut de la Billarderies, accompanied by Fanny Le Hon.[4] "My uncles Joseph and Lucien sent their condolences," the prince informed his equally absent father Louis in Florence. "Uncle Jérôme, alone, has not deigned to do so."[5] The turbulent Jérôme Bonaparte was never known for either his elementary good manners or common decency. As for the mourning twenty-nine-year-old Louis Napoléon, his was a grief that would never disappear.

G iven these circumstances, ex-king Louis's letters to his son now were mellowing, if continuing to offer gratuitous advice, in particular about his son's plans, counseling him not to go into politics "and what are referred to as the great affairs of the world." Instead, he continued, "let us enjoy some real pleasure during this brief existence of ours."[6]

Ever since their installation at Arenenberg, the French government had everyone there under police surveillance, and then following the death of Hortense in October 1837, Louis Philippe began putting enormous pressure on the Swiss to expel Louis Napoléon permanently. Out of patience with the uncooperative Swiss, on the first of August 1838, the French ambassador handed the Swiss foreign secretary an official ultimatum: if Bern did not expel Prince Louis Napoléon forthwith, the ambassador would be obliged "to ask for the return of his passport" and close the French embassy. Paris could not "allow Louis Bonaparte to remain on her territory . . . where he openly dares to resume his criminal intrigues [against the French government]." Louis Philippe "has the right and duty to demand that Switzerland cease to tolerate his presence on Swiss soil," since the prince had never renounced his French citizenship.[7] A defiant Swiss government replied that they would consider the matter in a few weeks, and the French army dispatched twenty thousand men to the Swiss frontier.

"DOES THIS MEAN WAR?" the official *Journal des Débats* responded, threatening the use of force, "if that is what is called for."[8] By exiling Louis Napoléon, "what do you achieve," *Le Siècle* countered, "in rendering a war inevitable as a result of your folly?" Moreover, thanks to all this publicity, "no one in France can ever again forget [Louis Napoléon's] name" and he will be even "more dangerous than he was before the Strasbourg affair."[9]

Although he had become a naturalized Swiss citizen in 1832, a now very anxious Louis Napoléon did not want his adopted country to suffer on his account. "Switzerland has done her duty," he informed Bern, "and now I must do mine," and on the fourteenth of October he left for England, never to return.[10] "Now what have you accomplished," *La Gazette de France* in turn asked, "by having Prince Louis in England instead of Switzerland? After all London is closer to Paris than Arenenberg."[11]

One thing remains to be seen. Are they [the French] now going to threaten Great Britain as they did the Swiss cantons?"[12] London's *Morning Chronicle* asked, tongue-in-cheek, upon the safe arrival of Louis Napoléon in London in mid-October 1838. What a public relations hash Louis Philippe's government had made of this affair, surrounding Switzerland with twenty thousands troops, making Paris the laughingstock of Europe. France had got herself into a corner. She had threatened a tiny country but could hardly menace Great Britain. She had simply moved Louis Napoléon out of one country into another.

In any event, Downing Street gave Louis Napoléon permission to come to England, and the great houses of the capital opened their doors to offer him a warm welcome once again. The foreign office followed this up by providing visas for his entire Arenenberg entourage, more than twenty in all, including Henri Conneau, who served not only as the prince's physician but more importantly as his chief of staff and principal secretary; Gilbert Persigny, the prince's general factotum; Count Giuseppi Orsi, the young Florentine banker and financier; Lieutenant Viscount Henri de Querelles; General Count Tristan de Montholon; Alfred d'Alembert, Louis Napoléon's private secretary. Charles Denis Parquin and Colonel Vaudrey, of Strasbourg fame, were also among them, as well as Louis Napoléon's chef and his two assistants, the faithful Thélin and the rest of the household.[13]

The number of army officers was extraordinary by any definition and did not escape the notice of English authorities, who undoubtedly kept the prince under loose surveillance throughout his sojourn, at a time of considerable international political tension between London and Paris. Foreign Secretary Palmerston disliked King Louis Philippe as much as Prince Louis Napoléon himself did, and he distrusted that king's hostile foreign policy from the Near East to the English Channel.

Moving the entire household was a costly logistical effort for Louis Napoléon, including their salaries and wages, not to mention room and board. Hereafter he was going to be facing one financial crisis after another. The Strasbourg Affair had cost a few hundred thousand francs in bribes, pensions, and legal costs, and as Hortense had left a total estate of only three and a half million francs, before legacies for friends and staff, and a large undisclosed sum for her illegitimate son, Auguste de Morny, that inheritance was quickly dwindling, although ex-king Louis had sent his son another 600,000 francs. In addition, the prince was preparing to support two Parisian newspapers, *Le Commerce* and *Le Capitol,* the latter alone receiving 140,000 francs directly out of Louis Napoléon's pocket, to propagate pro-Napoleonic political views and favorable public relations.[14] Publishing cost money, editors cost money. Hence the prince's decision to recruit the banker Count Orsi.

The prince settled in at the spacious and fashionable 17 Carlton House Terrace, Pall Mall, overlooking St. James's Park.[15] There were servants' quarters for half of his staff, a carriage house for his two elegant French landaus, and stabling for his nine horses. His years of modest living, of which Persigny boasted, were clearly a thing of the past, though Louis Napoléon could comfortably live in just a simple room with a table and chair, as he had done in his youth and would soon be doing again in France.

The prince's second and last principal residence was at nearby 1 Carlton Gardens, a large, handsome, white two-story corner house, now the Foreign and Commonwealth Office, then owned by the wealthy and influential Frederick John Robinson, the Earl of Ripon. Lord Ripon would open many doors to Mayfair society for Louis Napoléon, who would thereafter be seen at the Palmerstons'—this was a most important contact, especially after the creation of the Second French Empire—at Lansdowne's elegant residence in nearby Berkeley Square, at the Liverpools', at Lord Buckinghamshire's, but most frequently at Lord Malmesbury's, and Comte d'Orsay's and Lady Blessington's Gore House in Kensington, the center of arts and letters, and where Louis Napoléon first met a thirty-six-year-old member of Parliament, Benjamin Disraeli.

It was ironic that this future French head of state was to meet and know many more key English political leaders now than he himself yet knew in Paris. Palmerston was England's longest serving foreign secretary in the nineteenth century, and then, as prime minister as well throughout most of Louis Napoléon's reign as emperor, he was to be the most important political figure with whom he came into contact now. Palmerston, well traveled in both Italy and France and a fluent speaker of both languages, shared some common continental interests with the prince. For Palmerston, France was always the linchpin of his foreign policy.

As for his landlord, Lord Ripon, they did share a common interest in public education and the development of the British Museum and its new extension for printed books. As one of the most famous keepers of books at the new wing of what was to become the British Library, Antonio Panizzi, like Louis Napoléon, was a regular visitor at Ripon's, Lansdowne's (where he met Auguste de Morny), Palmerston's, and Brougham's. The prince was soon a regular visitor at the library when doing research for his political tracts, for which Panizzi gave him a private office in which to work.

L ouis Napoléon's final choice of residence at 1 Carlton Gardens turned out to be a happy one. The rooms were filled with the usual Napoleona—Isabey's portraits of Hortense, Napoléon, and Marie Louise, and another of Marie Louise and the king of Rome, Napoléon's infant son, and one of Josephine, Canova's marble bust of Napoléon, the emperor's jewels, coronation ring, and the tricolor sash he reputedly wore at the Battle of the Pyramids. There was even one of Charlemagne's relics containing a splinter of the true cross. There were books, pamphlets, and the inevitable sword.

Gilbert Persigny, in one of his initial famous public relations publications, *Letters from London,* describes the twenty-seven-year-old Louis Napoléon's typical day in the capital of the British Empire.[16] "The prince is an industrious hard-working man." He was up and at work in his study from six in the morning until noon when he stopped for a bite to eat. "Following this meal, which never takes more than ten minutes [he returns to his study where he] reads the newspapers from which he [takes] notes. . . . At two o'clock he receives visitors; at four he goes out; at five he goes riding [in the park]; at seven he dines; and then as a rule he goes back to his study to work for several hours in the evening. . . . There are no luxuries in his life. . . . He spends all his money on beneficial projects, in founding and supporting schools and centers of refuge for the poor, in studying and expanding his knowledge and on the publication of his political and military works." Persigny is generally considered the manager of Louis Napoléon's political career, whereas in reality he was more responsible for the physical fieldwork of preparing events. The manager was in fact Henri Conneau, who met with Louis Napoléon daily in long consultations, which Persigny omitted from his *Letters from London*, for personal pique.

Clearly Persigny's sketch of Louis Napoléon was an idealized public relations gesture, preparatory to the prince's anticipated return to his political fight in France. And with that in mind, Persigny's *Letters* was produced along with Louis Napoléon's *Napoleonic Ideas.* There was always much activity, not only in the prince's study, but in the offices of Persigny and Conneau, resulting in a constant flow of manuscripts to the printers.

Nor did the young man ignore the pleasures of life, receiving endless invitations to dinners and balls, including receptions in his honor. Although the French have never had clubs on as large a scale as the English, and never replicating the ambiance and purpose of English clubs, Louis Napoléon himself was a natural "club man" and a frequent visitor to the Athenaeum, Brookes's, and especially the Army and Navy

Club. Although an habitué of the theater, he had absolutely no inter-est in classical music or opera or in serious theater, preferring comedy and lighter pieces, and above all "light opera" and his scantily dressed "actresses."

Although brought up in strongly anti-British surroundings, the prince gradually came to be very fond of the British. Always a close and seri-ous observer of his surroundings, in 1839 he was greatly impressed by the English obsession with foreign travel and exotic places. It was in that year, of course, that Britain seized Hong Kong, while the East India Company occupied and claimed Aden as a future coaling station. Louis Napoléon also closely followed Britain's foreign wars, including the de-velopment of the First Anglo-Afghan War in 1839 and of course their First Opium War in China. There was nothing like this British passion for foreign places and adventures to be found in France, apart from the Algerian war, which at this early stage hardly offered attraction either to commerce or even archaeologists. He studied the reports of foreign correspondents about the Eyre expedition now setting out to explore the interior of South Australia, and the James Clark Ross expedition sail-ing to explore the Antarctic. Indian deserts and Antarctic ice: the English seemed to be hypnotized by the bleakest corners of the world. The prince was disturbed, on the nineteenth of April, to learn of the signing of the long delayed Treaty of London, announcing the official recognition of an independent Kingdom of Belgium, under Leopold I, a piece of real estate over which Louis Philippe had very much hoped to hoist the tricolor, with which Louis Napoléon commiserated.

After his own early interest in scientific studies, in 1839 the prince purchased Michael Faraday's new work, *Experimental Researches in Elec-tricity,* and Charles Darwin's *Journal of Researches into the Geology and Natural History of the Various Countries Visited During the Voyage of* HMS Beagle.

Naturally, the announcement of the launching of the first oceangoing military ironclad steamer, *Nemesis,* in November of 1839, caught the prince's attention, resulting in the creation of a file on that subject. This was just one of several that he kept for the time of his rule as emperor of France, when one of the first things he would do was to establish a new Naval Development Office to oversee the large-scale building of steam-driven ironclad ships for his new, modern French Imperial Navy.

The prince planned to go on a tour of the Midlands, beginning with Birmingham on July 4, 1839, to visit steam engine manufactures and armaments firms, but he was obliged to cancel due to the Bull Ring riots and the Chartist uprising in that city by thousands of working-class men demanding sweeping electoral reform, including the right to vote for any man at least twenty-one years of age, and a secret ballot. This, too, Louis Napoléon took note of and worried about, despite all his conflicting protestations to the contrary about Louis Philippe's suppression of French voting rights. "I wanted to establish a new government, one elected by a full popular vote [of the people]," he had told the public prosecutor after his arrest at Strasbourg on October 30, 1836. But writing in 1840, he revised his views. "The fundamental vice (which is eating away at France today) . . . is the exaggerated interpretation of the rights of the individual, of his scorn for authority."[17] This was the real Louis Napoléon speaking. The people were already too independent now. Yes, there should be popular elections, but the people must vote as they were directed. And that is precisely how he intended to run his future empire: give the masses the vote, but all voting would be dictated by *the leader* of the country, à la Bonaparte. Napoléon I had, of course, completely manipulated his national plebiscites without apologies—that system worked.[18]

But at least the Chartists could not prevent the publication of George Bradshaw's first *Bradshaw's Railway Time Tables* in 1839. England already had enough railways to warrant printing train schedules for them, while France didn't have ten miles of line in the whole of a country twice as large as Britain. That was something else Louis Napoléon took note of for the day in the future when he would be in a position of power to facilitate the rapid development of French national rail networks. France was still living in the eighteenth century, with an eighteenth-century economy and banking–financial system, and industrial development at the same level, not to mention a stagecoach transport unchanged since the days of the Ancien Régime, and all this disturbed, nay deeply humiliated, Louis Napoléon. Often lightly dismissed as a hapless, even comical individual, as indeed he appeared in some political matters, including his attempted coups d'état, in reality he was a very perspicacious, diligent, and determined gentleman who was today quietly, carefully preparing files for his day in the sun. France had been held back a whole century by blind, incompetent political leaders, and that had to be changed.

The key to Louis Napoléon's private and public life was a modest gentleman rarely mentioned by historians, but whose real role was fundamental to everything. Although Gilbert Persigny is generally considered the managing architect of the prince's career, and is certainly better known as a result of his many publications and self-promotion, it was Henri Conneau whose life and achievements would be inextricably woven with those of Louis Napoléon till the very end of the empire and who remained closest to him and his principal advisor.

Enrico François Alexandre—better known as Henri—Conneau was born in Milan in 1803, the son of a senior French-born Napoleonic receiver of taxes for that region. Conneau's early years were spent in Milan, before he undertook his medical studies in Florence, during which time he worked as a part-time private secretary to ex-king Louis Bonaparte, and where he first met Louis Napoléon, three years his junior. On achieving his doctorate in surgery, Conneau moved to Rome to practice medicine.

In any event, by 1830 both Bonaparte brothers had met Henri Conneau as fellow Carbonari members. And of course Conneau already knew Louis Napoléon's Milanese friend, Francesco Arese. In 1831 they all had to flee the Austrians and Italy, Arese eventually arriving at Arenenberg late in 1831 followed then by Conneau. But unlike Arese, Conneau gradually became a part of the Bonaparte family and remained, first in his capacity as physician to Hortense and the household, and then as a permanent member of the family. Only five years Louis Napoléon's senior—they became very close, and their mutual friendship with Arese helped form a special bond among all three. But for Louis Napoléon and Henri, it was different, because they remained together the rest of their lives.

Now in London, Conneau's position had changed. Earlier, the health of Hortense had been his principal concern, but now he had become Louis Napoléon's combined principal secretary and chief of staff. At 1 Carlton Gardens, they conferred daily as colleagues and friends and appeared together socially. It was a natural friendship of absolute trust and shared interests, French, Italian, and as fellow Carbonari. Though Arese later returned to Milan to continue in the struggle to chase the Austrians out and to create a united, independent Italy, Conneau's focus concentrated entirely on France and its political future, although the three of them continued to correspond regularly, and occasionally meet, the rest of their lives. And it was now Chief of Staff Conneau who, with Louis Napoléon, formed the decision to plot for the next coup, while Persigny, as his field man, arranged things on the ground, actually contacting and organizing the individuals to comprise this commando raid. From now on, to the very end, Henri Conneau was to remain Louis Napoléon's closest friend and confidant.[19]

9

"THIS GRAND AND GLORIOUS UNDERTAKING": BOULOGNE OR BUST

"I am the nephew of our great Emperor and I have come to occupy the throne of France."[1]
—PRINCE LOUIS NAPOLÉON

"France is like a flirting woman who sometimes enjoys seeing a prince risk his life for her."[2]
—BAPTISTE CAPEFIGUE

On a warm Monday, August 3, 1840, in the Pool of London, amid a veritable forest of towering wooden masts obliterating the view of the East India Company docks on the far shore, men were busy loading coal into the bunkers of the *City of Edinburgh,* while forward of the two great paddle wheels straddling the vessel, nine horses and a pair of elegant carriages bearing French coats of arms were lowered into the stables below. At 301 tons, the vessel had been launched near this very spot at Blackwall by Wigram and Green nearly nineteen years earlier, their very first steamer.

The following morning, Tuesday the fourth, Captain James Crow, of the General Steam Navigation Company, received the first of the passengers who had chartered this vessel for the month of July.[3] Their clothes were French, as was their speech. With the last of their trunks and crates aboard and the high tide beginning to ebb, the crew cast off as the helmsman headed the 124-foot wooden steamer downstream.

Reaching the Thames estuary at Gravesend, they stopped for the night. There they collected the local pilot; Louis Napoléon Bonaparte; General Tristan de Montholon; Colonels Voisin and Laborde; the young Florentine banker Count Giuseppi Orsi, responsible for securing the £20,000 ($2.2 million in today's value) required to finance this venture; and the retired major Denis Parquin, who boarded with a partially plucked eagle (to prevent it from flying) he had just bought in the port to serve as their Napoleonic mascot, now chained to the mast.

From Ramsgate on the fifth of August Louis Napoléon ordered Captain Crow to chart a general course for the northern coast of France. Once they were well out in the channel, the prince ordered the trunks and crates opened, and French army uniforms and arms (purchased from Birmingham) were distributed. Among those present were Dr. Henri Conneau, Gilbert Persigny, Count Orsi, the doddering Denis Parquin, his old retainer Charles Thélin, Colonel de Montauban, the recently sacked Major Séverin Le Duff de Mésonan, and General de Montholon, hired to direct the military operations (for which he would be handsomely rewarded).

With all of them decked out in their new uniforms and himself as a French major general—he had been a colonel at Strasbourg—Louis Napoléon convened all fifty-six of them in the main saloon, where he addressed them: "Friends, companions of *my destiny,* I have drawn up a plan . . . we are going to France!" [Author's italics] Wearing French uniforms and approaching the French coast, that could hardly have come as a surprise. "There we will find powerful, devoted friends awaiting us. The sole obstacle is Boulogne, but once it is removed final success is certain. And if I am supported and reinforced there, which is as certain as the sun in the sky we will be in Paris within a matter of days. Then history will say that with just a handful of such brave men as you *I* shall have achieved this grand and glorious undertaking."[4]

Of this fifty-six-man "expedition," only three—Conneau, Persigny, and Orsi—were considered a part of Louis Napoléon's inner council, privy to all. Throughout his career, the prince was to be criticized for his lack of judgment in men, of whom among this group "Major General" Tristan de Montholon, his new military commander, was by far the strangest of them all. Just about everything about him was either phony or bizarre, beginning with the title he used of "marquis"—he was only a count, and quite a new one at that. Allegedly wounded and having served with Napoléon from Hohenlinden to Waterloo, it was all lies. Indeed he not only had never served on a single battlefield, but he had refused to do so when so ordered. Not content with that, he had reneged on gambling debts and topped that off by stealing the regimental pay of his own officers. Despite all, he had somehow hoodwinked Napoléon and accompanied him to St. Helena, where he became his final confidant. Promised a major legacy from Napoléon's will, Montholon on at least two occasions administered arsenic in Napoléon's wine, greatly weakening him and leading to his death. And it was this charlatan, coward, thief, and murderer whom Louis Napoléon had now unwittingly appointed to head this campaign.[5]

The English Channel was calm, the sky clear, and the night warm and uneventful in the early hours of Tuesday, the sixth of August, 1840. Following Louis Napoléon's instructions, Captain James Crow brought the *City of Edinburgh* off the coastal village of Wimereux before two o'clock in the morning, dropping anchor a few hundred yards from the shore. They were now just four kilometers north of Boulogne, an easy march even for the older men. Although well known locally for the quality of its mussels and the village itself referred to as a port, there were no port facilities of any kind in Wimereux, neither a basin for the protection of the local fishing smacks nor breakwater. In fact, the coast was quite straight here and the extremely wide, limitless sandy beach a perfect obstacle to any ambitious politician's plans for challenging nature.[6]

The *City of Edinburgh*'s boat was lowered over the side immediately upon anchoring and succeeded in landing the initial contingent after the fourth return trip to the beach, where Lieutenants Aladenize, Bataille, and Forestier from the St. Omer garrison were waiting to guide them to Boulogne. It was still very dark, and everything had to be completed well before daybreak.[7]

Trouble started immediately when a customs officer, attracted by the commotion the men were making as they scrambled ashore, approached and challenged them. "We belong to the Fortieth Regiment and are en route from Dunkirk to Cherbourg," they said, explaining that one of the two paddle wheels of their steamer had broken. They were wearing proper French uniforms, with facings of the 40th Infantry Regiment, whereas the local regiment was in fact the 42nd. The customs officer left them to fetch his sergeant, who in turn notified his superior, Lieutenant Bally. By the time Bally arrived, the landing party was assembled in a column ready to march.

After he attempted to question the men, it soon became apparent to Bally that there was no senior officer speaking on behalf of this "expeditionary force." General Montholon should have acted forcefully and taken over, but instead remained silent, as did "General" Bonaparte. Nevertheless the customs team, a squad of them by now, agreed to act as their guides to Boulogne. Lieutenant Bally could not possibly know, of course, that more than thirty of the fifty-six smart looking troops of the 40th Infantry Regiment had never before even held a rifle in their hands. More than thirty of them were in fact members of Louis Napoléon's "staff": household servants, valets, footmen, a butler, a coachman, one messenger boy, three cooks, two gardeners, two gamekeepers (who at least could shoot), and for good measure, one tailor. And of course Orsi was a banker. Thus of the fifty-six men, several in their late forties or fifties, fewer than twenty had any military training whatsoever. It would have been better to have left the thirty civilians behind and marched with the original twenty, for it was the civilians who were going to panic and cause chaos when the shooting began. Louis Napoléon's comical "expeditionary force" had been doomed even before sailing from the Pool of London.[8]

Suddenly Colonel de Montauban shouted out impatiently, "Do you know whom you are escorting? It's Prince Napoléon himself!" He, like several of the others, had been drinking too much cognac during the crossing. Then another man cried out: "Boulogne is ours, and France will soon proclaim the prince Emperor of France!"[9]

A very suspicious Lieutenant Bally abruptly ordered the column to halt and turn back. The prince's men refused until General de Montholon, also the worse for drink, stepped forward to offer the young officer a guaranteed pension of 1,200 francs. Bewildered, Bally withdrew his men. Then Parquin, with the eagle in one hand, dropped the other to the hilt of his sword threateningly. "Forward march," he ordered. The customs men returned to Wimereux, and "General" Bonaparte's column resumed its march south to Boulogne.[10]

The merry band headed by Louis Napoléon and Montholon entered the port city of Boulogne at five o'clock that morning, now preceded by Lieutenant Aladenize, who knew the city streets. Persigny immediately ordered a couple of men to plaster the city with the proclamations that had been printed back in London: "Citizens of Boulogne, have faith in our providential mission and follow me. . . . The Bourbons d'Orléans dynasty has ceased to rule."[11]

Their first objective was to seize the barracks of the two companies of the 42nd line regiment protecting the city. They were next to occupy the castle and with it the garrison's arsenal. Or at least that was the plan. They were stopped in the Place d'Alton by a squad of five soldiers who refused to join Aladenize. The eloquent Parquin once again stepped forward with another garbled, drunken threat: "You will regret that!" No one was coming over to them, and Louis Napoléon's officers were beginning to get jumpy. Lieutenant Aladenize, angered by the soldiers' refusal to obey an officer's orders, grabbed the arm of one of them. "Come here, you! You will be sorry," he said, but still they refused, and "the expeditionary force" continued on its way, reaching the Grand Rue of the city.[12] There encountering a sub-lieutenant, Louis Napoléon addressed him, but frightened and intimidated by this unexpected mass of magnificent gold braid appearing before him, the young man ran off to inform his superior, Captain Col-Puygelier. They resumed their march, Lieutenant Aladenize bringing them before the garrison's barracks.

Inside the barracks' parade ground, Aladenize ordered: "To arms! Here is the prince!" which was repeated by a soldier on guard duty. Some of the men of the 42nd fell in and presented arms, shouting, "*Vive l'Empereur!*" When an older sergeant arrived to see what was happening, Louis Napoléon blurted out, "I shall make you a captain of the grenadiers!" Order and common sense had already been replaced by a carnival of hysterics and absurdities. Louis Napoléon then harangued the troops, offering commissions, medals, and money. Clearly Captain Bonaparte, late of the Swiss army, was no more fit to command a garrison than a squad.

Captain Col-Puygelier arrived and, drawing his sword, demanded to know what was happening and where his company was. Some of Parquin's men tried to grab him. "Captain, I am Prince Louis Napoléon. Come join us and you will be rewarded with whatever you desire." "But I don't know you," the captain replied. "You are a traitor," he called out. Then turning around to his company, he said, "Soldiers, this is a trick! *Vive le Roi!* Fall in behind me." Bonaparte's men tried to seize him again when two more officers of the 42nd arrived. Freeing himself, Col-Puygelier managed to notify the garrison commander, Colonel Sansot, and to rally some of his men. Panicking, Napoléon took out his pistol and shot an unarmed grenadier, Geouffroy, in the mouth. They were stunned, and no one more so than Louis Napoléon himself. As for the prudent Persigny, ever the survivor, he kept his head low and well behind the others.

Though Col-Puygelier's men were still unarmed—they had been issued no live ammunition—they were angered by Louis Napoléon's cowardly act, and they now chased all fifty-six heavily armed men of his "expeditionary force" from the regimental parade grounds and barracks. The drums were beating to call out the rest of the 42nd as Captain Col-Puygelier distributed ammunition and secured the barracks, while dispatching Lieutenant Maussion with a platoon of twenty men to secure the port. Col-Puygelier then set out with Lieutenant Ragon and his platoon to secure the castle and the arsenal, before this "General" Bonaparte got there.

At about this same time—it was now six o'clock and the sun was rising; the entire city was awake—the mayor of Boulogne, Monsieur Adam, aided by Deputy Prefect Launay-Leprovost, alerted the gendarmerie, the port officer, the director of customs, the commander of the national guard, and the police. With dozens of men shouting and running through the streets, the entire city was by now in an uproar.

Still clearly shaken by his own unplanned madness, Bonaparte ordered his column to continue up toward the higher ramparts and the castle. En route, while passing the offices of the sub-prefecture, the deputy prefect himself stood before the advancing column ordering them to throw down their arms and disperse. As they continued forward, someone lowered one flag standard with the large imperial eagle and rammed it into the chest of the deputy prefect, and Bonaparte resumed his march.

Pound against the solid oak double doors of the château as they might, no one surrendered, and Louis Napoléon, who had once again failed to prepare a backup plan, ordered his column up and beyond the city to the towering Column of the Grande Armée, where Napoléon's statue had once stood. There they ran up the imperial Napoleonic flag, while "General" Bonaparte just stood there silently, as if in a state of shock, for he quite simply had never even considered defeat, utter failure.

On the other hand, the garrison's able commanding officer, Colonel Sansot, knew precisely what to do and was now marching with several hundred troops plus the entire national guard directly after Bonaparte's servants, who began screaming and scattering in all directions. A hysterical Louis Napoléon took out his pistol and apparently tried to blow out his own brains but was restrained by Persigny. One soldier remained at the column, to protect the imperial flag, while several others were quickly rounded up by a handful of gendarmes as they fled across the field. Lieutenant Aladenize and Colonel de Montauban were among the first to be captured. Meanwhile the hapless Major Parquin and the equally inept Major General Tristan de Montholon were next arrested by a police inspector, Bergeret, and the national guard's commander, Captain Chauveau-Soubitez.

Most of the others, led by a remarkably swift-footed Prince Louis Napoléon, eventually reached the beach at Wimereux. There more troops were lying in wait for them, however, and most of the prince's men surrendered without a struggle. A few shouted across the water, trying to hail Captain Crow in the *City of Edinburgh,* hoping in vain for a boat to haul them to safety. At least a dozen tried to escape in the sea under a heavy hail of bullets from the national guardsmen lining the beach. Colonel Voisin, who had found a small boat, was shot twice, gravely injured, while trying to climb aboard before the boat capsized. Captain Hunin was drowned in the surf, Sergeant Faure was shot dead; two other men, servants in uniform, drowned, including a gardener, and another was badly wounded. "The national guardsmen remorselessly peppered these by now frantic unarmed men," reported the correspondent of the Parisian *National*. "One of the guardsmen called it 'a regular duck shoot!'"[13] Louis Napoléon, Persigny, Conneau, and Mésonan were among the "ducks" falling under the intensive rain of bullets as they tried to swim out despite their heavy boots, cartridge belts, and woolen military tunics. The prince was hit squarely by one bullet, which lodged in his soaked gold-braided uniform, saving his life. Like Conneau, Persigny, Mésonan, and others, he was fished out of the sea by two boats manned by the national guardsmen.

A shivering, dripping wet Prince Louis Napoléon was helped into the waiting coach of Mayor Adam and Deputy Prefect Launay-Leprovost, ready to whisk him away to Boulogne. He finally got his wish, as they passed through the now open gates of the château he had failed to seize. His only thought was to kill himself. It was the last battle that "General" Bonaparte would ever fight . . . at least for the next thirty years. Twenty-four hours earlier he had been a free man on English soil.[14] Down below in the harbor that Emperor Napoléon had built expressly for the invasion of England, French customs officers were thoroughly searching the *City of Edinburgh*, where they seized the expedition's 400,000-gold-franc war chest, which had been provided by Giuseppi Orsi. This port had never brought anything but trouble to the house of Bonaparte.

French territory has been violated by a gang of adventurers," a bulletin from the War Ministry announced to startled Parisians on Friday, August 7, 1840, who "had been thrown back into the sea from which they had just been vomited. Louis Bonaparte and all his followers have been captured, killed or drowned."[15] "Monsieur Louis Bonaparte has placed himself in such an impossible position that no one in France today can honorably feel even the slightest sympathy or pity for him," declared *La Presse*. His actions are as "odious" as they are "ridiculous," the paper continued. He was not even the head of a political party, just the "distorted caricature" of one.[16]

This attempt at Boulogne has left us with "a sense of indignation mixed with pity," the *Journal des Débats* reported. "All these eagles, all these dramatic proclamations, these absurd imperial pretensions of Monsieur Louis Bonaparte . . . this excess of madness" leaves him now looking like "the dupe of his own vanity that he is." This whole business has gone far beyond just the ridiculous, "it is crazier than even . . . the skirmish of 1836 [at Strasbourg]. It surpasses mere comedy," because this time "blood has flowed"; there were corpses.[17]

"This obsession of his as pretender [to the Bonaparte throne] really makes one wonder," the moderate *Constitutionnel* probed. "Where on earth does this incredible dementia of his come from . . . this attempt to conquer France with some superannuated sayyid-leftovers from the Empire and a troop of servants disguised as soldiers!"

Louis Napoléon's sixty-two-year-old father, Louis Bonaparte, was so outraged at the accusations and proceedings being taken against him by Louis Philippe that, resisting his lifelong detestation of the press and the outside political world, he had a letter published in an Italian newspaper in defense of his son. He was, he said, convinced that his son was "the victim of an infamous conspiracy, and seduced by flatterers, false friends and perhaps by insidious advice." His son, he declared, had fallen into "an appalling trap," otherwise "it is quite impossible that a man surely not lacking the [financial] means and common sense, should have—with his eyes wide open, willingly thrown himself over such a [political] precipice."[18] Louis Bonaparte, himself a most able general officer in his own right, was simply bewildered by this whole fiasco.

At midnight on Friday, the seventh of August, Prince Louis Napoléon was taken under heavy escort from the Château of Boulogne to Paris, and from there to the prison fortress of Ham, as Louis Philippe's government decided how to handle this most delicate situation. That king had other "Bonaparte considerations" to deal with as well, as he had ordered a frigate to sail shortly for St. Helena to collect Napoléon Bonaparte's ashes for reburial in the French capital, and that alone had required long negotiations with the British government. To have to cancel that now because of this unanticipated Boulogne incident would in itself be most embarrassing. If the reburial service did indeed take place in Paris on schedule in December, would it spark violent demonstrations and perhaps another attempt on the government of Louis Philippe? Or would the cancellation of those very ceremonies incite riots in the capitol, Lyons, Marseilles, and elsewhere throughout the country?

Twenty-five years after Waterloo, the French political scene was still very much plagued by Napoléon and his legacy.

"I make no apologies for what I have done because I have acted out of conviction," said an unrepentant Louis Napoléon. He had persisted after Strasbourg and had tried again at Boulogne. Clearly he had not heeded Uncle Napoléon's famous advice: "To know how to choose the right moment in which to act is the special quality that distinguishes great men from all the others."[19]

Louis Napoléon would have to stand trial this time, it was concluded, but by the Chamber of Peers re-forming as a Court of Peers—a decision that went against Louis Philippe's own advisors, who argued that Louis Napoléon and his men "will have for their judges today the very men who had been on the island of Elba [with Napoléon] yesterday"—they would largely be high officials appointed and promoted by Emperor Napoléon himself.[20] They were quite right, but the decision was made, with the Chamber of Peers appointing a committee to carry out a thorough investigation, beginning with the five-hour interrogation of Louis Napoléon, now back once again in the Conciérgerie, on the nineteenth of August. The newly formed Court of Peers then handed down indictments against twenty-one members of the prince's "force," charging them with "an attempt against the Security of the State." Naturally their number included the inner circle of the ringleaders, beginning with Louis Napoléon Bonaparte, Conneau, Persigny, Orsi, Montholon, Parquin, Mésonan, Montauban, Voisin, Laborde, Lombard, Aladenize, et al.[21]

The trial of Louis Napoléon Bonaparte was opened by the highly respected sixty-three-year-old president of the Chamber of Peers and chancellor, Étienne-Denis, Duc de Pasquier (Napoléon's last prefect of police for Paris), in the impressive Salle des Séances of the Luxembourg Palace on September 28, 1840.

This tale is full of history and ironies. Of the 312 peers of the realm, 160 of them were Napoléon I's senior army officers and officials who declined to appear or simply abstained, which left only 152 to sit as the jury.[22] To the right of the dais, Napoléon's old throne still stood, untouched. The public prosecutor representing the state was M. Émile Frank-Carré. Prince Louis Napoléon was represented by three of the most brilliant barristers of the day, Maîtres Pierre Antoine Berryer, Thomas Marie, and Ferdinand Barrot (the brother of Napoléon III's future statesman, Odilon Barrot).

No sooner had Chancellor Pasquier begun to introduce the proceedings than he was interrupted by Louis Napoléon. Startled, certainly, but Pasquier did not stop him. Wearing a dark frock coat with the highest order of the Legion of Honor, an elegant white waistcoat, black cravat, and of course the obligatory white gloves, a remarkably composed twenty-nine-year-old Louis Napoléon stood before this amphitheater crowded to the bursting point with more than three hundred of the highest dignitaries of the state, and calmly addressed the *salle*. "For the first time in my life I have been permitted to speak in France and to speak freely before the French people.

"In spite of the guards on either side of me, in spite of all the accusations I have just heard, I find myself here within the walls of the Senate that I had first visited as a child [with Napoléon]. In your midst, you whom I know, gentlemen, I do not believe that I have to justify myself, nor that you could be my judges.

"A solemn occasion is offered me here to explain to my fellow citizens my conduct, my intentions, my projects, what I think and what I desire. . . . The nation has never revoked the grand act of sovereignty [established by Napoléon's Imperial Constitution], and as the Emperor himself said, 'everything done without adhering to it is illegal,' and that includes this trial.

"And, too, do not think for a moment that I might have wanted to attempt any imperial restoration in France" without the backing of the people of this country through a plebiscite. "As for my undertaking at Boulogne. . . . I had no other accomplices. I alone am responsible. . . . I represent before you a principle, a cause and a defeat: one principle, the sovereignty of the people, the cause, that of our Empire; and a defeat, Waterloo. The principle [of sovereignty] you already know; the cause [the First Empire] you yourselves have already served; and the defeat you wish to avenge [were they to declare war on England again]. Therefore clearly there is no disagreement between you and me.

"As the representative of a political cause, I cannot accept a political jurisdiction to judge my wishes and acts. . . . And if you are the conqueror's men, I can expect no justice from you, and I do not ask for your generosity [charity]."[23]

Days of testimony followed, and the trial progressed, the public prosecutor Frank-Carré pointing out before him and all present that he, Louis Napoléon, was utterly incompetent, or as he put it, "The sword of Austerlitz is too heavy for your feeble hands. . . . And let me just point out to you that France has more right to claim the name of the emperor than you do!"[24]

Regardless of the surprising dignity and even unexpected eloquence of Louis Napoléon and his gifted barrister, Maître Berryer, in the final analysis, of course, there could be no denial of the fact that on the sixth of August, 1840, Louis Napoléon did, knowingly and with premeditation "invade France" and enter Boulogne at gunpoint with the intention of overthrowing the legal government of the land.

On the sixth of October, after six days of hearings, the Court of Peers rendered their judgment: Prince Louis Napoléon Bonaparte was condemned to "perpetual imprisonment in a fortress situated on the continental territory of the kingdom."[25] By noon the following day Louis

Napoléon found himself snugly locked up in the prison-fortress of Ham, where he was shortly to be joined by three others condemned that same day. And a day rich in ironies at that: Prince Louis Napoléon Bonaparte, a plucked eagle in a cage of his own making, the only member of his entire fifty-six-man ragtag "expeditionary force" to have lost his head, to have shot a French soldier.

IO

FUNERAL FOR AN EMPEROR

"Bonapartist ideas are one of the festering sores of our century. . . ."[1]
—ALEXANDRE GLAIS BIZOIN, 1840

"The ashes of Napoléon are not yet completely extinguished,
and they are already being stirred up again."[2]
—ALPHONSE DE LAMARTINE, MAY 1840

I cannot prostrate myself before the memory of [of him] . . . I am not a follower of this Napoleonic religion of his, of this cult of force . . . to deify war . . . [of] these symbols of theirs, of despotism and the sword," Lamartine declared before the Assembly.[3] But the vast majority strongly disagreed with him. Napoléon's remains should be returned to France where they belonged. "It is here that he will find his apotheosis," *Le Temps* declared, "for he has taught us to understand the existence of demi-gods," and the country concurred.

Gentlemen, the King [Louis Philippe] has commanded His Royal Highness, the Prince de Joinville [François Ferdinand d'Orléans], to take a frigate to the island of St. Helena to receive the mortal remains of the Emperor Napoléon. . . . They will be deposited in the [Hôtel des] Invalides. . . . the temple consecrated to the God of armies," Interior Minister Charles de Rémusat informed the Chamber of Deputies in the Bourbon Palace on May 12, 1840. There was "an explosion of applause across the amphitheater," the *Journal des Débats* reported.[4]

For an indecisive Louis Philippe d'Orléans, the idea of reintroducing the very name of "Napoléon Bonaparte" to the French people now, among whom he himself was in contrast never really popular, was not taken lightly. The possibility of bringing back "Emperor Napoléon's" remains from St. Helena had been reintroduced and discussed seriously for the past two years. The very idea of leaving the remains of the country's greatest hero since the times of Charlemagne on British soil, buried beneath the Union Jack, was simply anathema to the emotional nationalism of the proud French, and the Chamber of Deputies duly voted a one-million-franc budget for the return of the great man.

Jules Hardouin Mansart's elegant, dignified, and spacious French baroque Invalides Palace was selected as Napoléon's final resting place. One could easily envisage the funeral train proceeding up the long green esplanade leading up to the Invalides and the chapel, lined on either side with the statues of thirty-two kings and "illustrious captains" of France, ranging from Charlemagne to Joan of Arc, and Louis XIV to Napoléon and some of his famous marshals. If any place in the French capital was worthy of honoring the kingdom's greatest soldier of all time, then clearly it was this seventeenth-century architectural treasure, the Invalides.

Back in 1838, ex-king Louis Bonaparte had suggested that his last surviving son, Louis Napoléon, should sail down to St. Helena and fetch back his famous uncle, though of course Louis Philippe could hardly have acceded to this. But now, in May 1840, it was Louis Philippe's new prime minister–historian, Adolphe Thiers, an enthusiastic disciple of Napoléon Bonaparte,[5] who pushed the hesitating king into calling for this imperial rehabilitation of this national hero. Following the easy approval of the chambers and the authorization of the British government for this project, Louis Philippe ordered his third son, François d'Orléans, Prince de Joinville, a career naval officer, to sail to St. Helena to collect those remains.

On July 7, 1840, the handsome twenty-two-year-old Joinville, as captain of the sixty-gun frigate, *La Belle Poule,* with her freshly painted funereal black hull, attended by the corvette *La Favorite*, hauled out of the French navy's principal port of Toulon, charting the five-thousand-mile-long course for the South Atlantic that would take them to Madeira, the Canaries, Bahia, Brazil, and finally to the East India Company's little volcanic island of St. Helena.

Ninety-three days later, the two warships reached Jamestown, St. Helena, where the British laid on full honors. Napoléon's disinterred mahogany coffin was placed into a lead coffin and then into the elaborately carved ebony coffin just brought from Paris. A horse-drawn hearse took the coffin down the mountain to the port of Jamestown in a cortège led personally by the English governor, as guns from the forts fired continuous salutes until the enormous coffin was hoisted aboard *La Belle Poule*, which with *La Favorite* immediately set sail for the homeward voyage to France and the port of Cherbourg.

The remains of the great national hero and late emperor Napoléon Bonaparte were due to be honored by Louis Philippe himself in a state ceremony in Paris on December 15, while this same king was still recovering from the bewildering shock of this Prince Louis Napoléon's attempt to overthrow him and his government.

How would his situation and presence affect the current political situation? One Bonaparte in prison, another on a hero's pedestal. If Louis Philippe had judged incorrectly now, he could be swept out of office and France before Christmas Eve, a day that had narrowly proved to be Napoléon Bonaparte's own abrupt downfall forty years earlier.

• • •

On an icy eighth of December, Prince de Joinville transferred Napoléon's ebony casket from his black-hulled frigate to the steamer *La Normandie*. From Cherbourg that ship carried her historic cargo to Le Havre and the Seine. At Rouen the coffin was transferred for a final time to a much smaller iron river steamer, *La Dorade*, continuing the journey up the Seine. Many thousands of laborers and troops were everywhere still frantically making final arrangements to have all in readiness for the grand ceremonies on the fifteenth of December. The king wanted to turn this nightmarish page of French history as quickly as humanly possible.

Late on Monday, the fourteenth of December, *La Dorade* with the Prince of Joinville reached the port of Courbevoie, and the next morning the casket was carried ashore by twenty-four stout sailors preceded by the prince between lines of troops and national guardsmen, and greeted by a twenty-one-gun salute and a band playing the "Marseillaise." The casket was hoisted onto the floor of a forty-foot-long "funeral car" resting on four six-foot-high gilt wheels. The pedestal rose another seven feet and was entirely covered with gold-and-purple cloth bearing the armorial crest of the emperor. On both sides hung two velvet imperial mantles. Above this pedestal stood fourteen gilt-colored caryatides, larger-than-life statues, supporting on their heads and hands an immense gold-gilt floor in the shape of an oval shield. A mock-up sarcophagus in turn rested on it with the scepter, the hand of justice, and the imperial jewel-studded crown.

"This gold and velvet monument was drawn by sixteen black horses, yoked by fours," with each horse caparisoned with a full-length shimmering gold cloth. "The manes were adorned with gold tresses and [their heads with] white plumes, and valets, dressed in the [green] livery of the Emperor, led the horses," the correspondent of the London *Times* reported. "This whole ensemble was veiled in a long purple crêpe screen covered with golden [Napoleonic] bees." The back of the enormous car was made of "a trophy of flags, palms and laurels" and inscribed with the names of Napoléon's principal victories.

The hearse set off across the Neuilly Bridge over the Seine at eleven o'clock, passing under the shadow of an enormous temporary statue of Joséphine just erected at the foot of the bridge. "The procession commenced its march amidst the roaring of artillery," entering the long broad straight tree-lined Avenue de Neuilly filled since early morning with "400,000 or 500,000 persons," in spite of "the piercingly cold wind," including "a number of [Napoleonic] veterans of the old army, dressed in their original imperial uniforms."[6] Louis Philippe, taking no chances, had both sides of the next five miles lined with tens of thousands of regular army infantrymen, some reinforcements brought over from Algeria for this purpose, along with national guardsmen in their red-and-blue uniforms. Security above all was the byword in the event of a violent attempt on members of the royal family today.

The parade was in fact one enormous military display, including cavalry and infantry regiments and their bands of four battalions, a detachment of Polish lancers of the Imperial Guard, and the students of St. Cyr Military College and of the elite École Polytechnique, as thousands marched ten abreast, a spectacle the like of which had not been seen since the arrival of Wellington and the tsar in 1815.

All passed peacefully before the crowds, the only sound to be heard that of carriage wheels, the hooves of thousands of horses, and the tramp of boots, attended by rolling drums and solemn music. They were then unexpectedly joined by some two thousand angry university and law students marching eight abreast, carrying their own tricolored flag covered with black crêpe, and crying out *"à bas les Anglais," "à bas Palmerston," "à bas le Ministre de l'Etranger* [Soult]," *"à bas Guizot," "Guizot à la Tamise!" "Vive Thiers!"*—down with the English, down with Palmerston, down with the foreign minister, down with Ambassador Guizot, but long live Adolphe Thiers, their booming voices then chanting "La Marseillaise," followed by an occasional *"Vive le Prince de Joinville,"* or

"Vive l'Empereur [Napoléon]," though not a single cry of *"Vive le roi* [Louis Philippe]."

"Suddenly cannon thundered from three different points on the horizon," eyewitness and great admirer of Napoléon Victor Hugo recorded. "The emperor's [funeral] carriage appeared. . . . in the distance . . . moving slowly through the mist and sunlight, against the gray and red background of the trees . . . , past tall white statues . . . it emerged, a sort of golden mountain." And by the time it finally drew close enough for inspection, the thirty-eight-year-old Hugo was as delighted as a child. "It is an enormous mass, a golden glow, giving the entire ensemble an immense grandure!"[7]

The drums of the National Guard beat "Au Champs" as one regiment after another approached the 164-foot Arc de Triomphe, now draped in black and ringed by three dozen flagpoles streaming long silk tricolors bearing the names of Napoléon's famous military—the Grand Army, the Army of the Rhine, the Army of Italy, the Army of Holland, etc.—"as two batteries of twenty guns roared."

As the bier approached them "everyone fell abruptly silent," an excited reporter for *La Nation* wrote. "We saw tears everywhere and heard many a stifled sob. It seemed as if we were being transported into some other realm."[8] "It was hypnotic, we were positively riveted," Madame Delphine Gay Girardin wrote.[9]

"It would be almost impossible to calculate the number of persons assembled to witness this imposing ceremony," gathered at this point from early morning and including "numerous urchins who had climbed the trees lining the grand avenue, they affording much amusement to the spectators," despite the ice under foot. The crowd's "enthusiasm for Napoléon's memory [was gradually] cooling however as a result of the sharp northeast wind," and a temperature that had earlier plummeted to "22½ degrees [Fahrenheit] below zero." Only a Napoléon Bonaparte could have brought out hundreds of thousands of people in such weather.

Icy weather or no, passing beneath the Arc de Triomphe, the procession now entered the Champs-Élysées. Continuing into the spacious

Place de la Concorde, it turned right, with the snow-covered Tuileries gardens to the left lined with thousands of armed infantry troops, cavalry, national guards, and municipal guardsmen, which did not prevent spectators who had paid two hundred francs or more for their perches from peering from the windows and balconies of the surrounding buildings. The crowds here, diminished to only about 50,000, were well outnumbered by the estimated 84,000 troops either in the procession or lining the streets. Ironically, the only enemy to be feared at this moment were fanatical Bonapartists, possibly wanting to avenge the imprisonment of Napoléon's nephew, Prince Louis Napoléon.

The funeral procession reached the grounds of the Invalides at a quarter past one that afternoon. Meanwhile, the cannon at the nearby École Militaire continued to be fired every quarter of an hour as it had been for more than six hours now.

Turning left into the long esplanade, the funeral cortège proceeded through the principal entrance of the Invalides proper. That in turn opened into the immense rectangular courtyard, the Cour Royale, leading to the entrance of the church, the Dôme des Invalides. It was here, directly under that 351-foot high French baroque dome, that a temporary catafalque had been prepared on which to place the ebony casket from St. Helena.

Entry was by ticket that day, which in no way appeared to intimidate the crowds, including the highest nobility and civil and military officials of the kingdom.

Despite the distracting, hastily erected draped black cloth, the London *Times* correspondent was taken aback by "the splendid vista of the chapel." The great altar having been removed "from the entrance to the other extremity of the dome, the view was uninterrupted. The space under the dome, arranged as a *chapelle ardente,* was filled with a blaze of light from the thousands and tens of thousands of wax lights that hung in lustres or lined the walls, until . . . the chapel looked like one great wall of fire. In its midst was erected the *catafalque* upon which the coffin was to be placed." To each side tiers of stands "hung with black drapery" rose to accommodate the hundreds of members of the two chambers, of the government and the royal family. But "the real sight worth seeing after all . . . was the crowd itself in mourning dress that filled the chapel, first along the archways in the nave, then in the tribunes of the dome"—the government ministers in elaborate gold-braided navy-blue court uniforms, the marshals and the superior officers of the army, the high-court judges in their crimson gowns, and high-state officials. Notably absent, however, was the entire diplomatic corps, they to a man boycotting any ceremony honoring the man who had invaded, looted, and devastated their countries and economies for fifteen long years.

"The Archbishop and his magnificent train of clergy . . . [advanced] to meet the coffin and perform the rites of absolution at the entrance of the church. . . . as the funeral procession entered . . . headed by the priests." The Prince de Joinville, who had walked with the hearse all the way from Neuilly, now stopped before his father, the king, then, drawing and lowering his sword to the ground, he said: "Sire, I present to you the body of the Emperor Napoléon."

"I receive it in the name of France," Louis Philippe replied in a firm voice as General Louis Atthalin, a veteran of the Grande Armée, stepped forward with a cushion on which to lay the sword Napoléon had worn at Austerlitz in 1805. The king stepped back, turning to General Henri Bertrand, Napoléon's companion at St. Helena. "General, I charge you with placing the Emperor's glorious sword upon his coffin." But Bertrand froze, and General Gaspard Gourgaud quickly stepped forward, taking the sword from Bertrand's hands and placing it on the casket.[10]

The coffin was then slowly carried up the stone steps from the nave and placed on the catafalque directly under the center of the dome. Right on cue, outside the cannon again roared. "The mortal remains of Napoléon now reposed where he had requested . . . in the heart of his own country, in the place worthy of France's greatest general—under the dome of the Invalides.

"The crowd lingered and turned again and again to look back at the burning wax-lights, at the *chapelle ardente* and the illuminated cata-falque." So ended the funeral of an emperor, the first since Char-lemagne, and the last ever to be held on French soil. "This entire ceremeony had something strangely phantasmagoric about it," Victor Hugo ruminated as he left the Invalides, where Louis Philippe had re-mained lost in silence.[11]

"The government appears to be fearful of the very phantom it is now evoking," Hugo felt, while many miles away in a northern prison the very nephew of that phantom was already preparing the next stage . . . "it is not just his ashes," Louis Napoléon said, "it's the Emperor's plans [for France] that we must now bring back."[12]

———◆———

TO HAM, WITH LOVE, TOSH, AND TOIL

*"Of that immense empire that once covered the world, what
now remains, a grave and a prison; a grave to prove that the great
man is dead, and a prison to kill off his cause."*[1]
—LOUIS NAPOLÉON BONAPARTE, HAM

"Better to be a prisoner in France than free in a foreign land!"[2]
—LOUIS NAPOLÉON TO NARCISSE VIEILLARD, 1843

I do not want to leave my prison here in Paris without first thanking
you once more for all your noble services on my behalf," Louis
Napoléon wrote his leading defense counsel, Maître Pierre Antoine
Berryer. "I have no idea what lies in store for me now."[3]

State prisoner Bonaparte entered the Château of Ham on October 7,
1846, passing over the same drawbridge and beneath the same portcullis as King Louis XI had in 1475 after concluding the One Hundred
Years' War with England's Edward IV. Four hundred troops lined the
courtyard's ten-meter-thick stone walls and battlements, effectively
sealing this fortress off from the village of Ham and the outside world.
Prince Louis Bonaparte would not leave again for years.

"Well, here I am. I have a bed . . . a table, a commode and six chairs,"
he informed Hortense's former lady-in-waiting, Baroness Louise Salvage
de Faverolles. "As you can see, I have everything I require."[4] What he
neglected to mention was the stack of legal bills on that table from his

lawyers and the courts totaling 31,000 francs, and the more than 75,000 francs ($1,367,000, all inclusive) to repay friends, pensions, and support for the families of those now imprisoned with him.

"I have a sacred duty to fulfill," he confided to his late brother's tutor, his friend and advisor from Arenenberg and future senator of the empire, the forty-nine-year-old Narcisse Vieillard, "to support everyone who has so devotedly served me . . . and I shall do everything in my power to lessen their [financial] burden, while doing what I can to cut back here on my own personal comforts."[5] "The Boulogne enterprise," as he referred to it, had cost him the 400,000 francs in gold (or $5,160,000, today) seized at that port and at least another 100,000 francs ($1,290,000) out of pocket. The estate of his mother had all but disappeared within three years of her death, and yet he still continued to give money away to any worthy cause—including a local school and any individual with a hard-luck tale to relate. Minister of the Interior Charles de Rémusat offered a single payment of 600 francs ($7,740 today) to help defray the costs of repairing and rendering habitable the prince's "cell," in fact a fairly large two-room apartment with regular doors, and iron bars only on the small exterior windows. But nothing could be done about the damp stone walls, which were to take their long-term toll on his health.[6]

Installed with him was his faithful, good-natured thirty-seven-year-old surgeon and family companion, Henri Conneau, condemned to five years, but who was to insist on remaining with him after completing his sentence; the inimitable fifty-eight-year-old charlatan, Tristan de Montholon, sentenced to twenty years.[7] The final prisoner to join them here was the prince's loyal thirty-nine-year-old family retainer, Charles Thélin, who, although acquitted of all charges at the trial, afterward had also insisted on remaining with Louis Napoléon. Louis Napoléon always attracted this sort of blind devotion from those around him, friends and servants alike. Meanwhile Colonels Voisin and Laborde had been incarcerated for ten years in an insane asylum at Chaillot, and all the others in the ancient citadel of Doullens, north of Amiens (where Parquin—minus his eagle—was destined to die within a few years).

As for his ever resilient "campaign manager," ex-sergeant Gilbert

Persigny, sentenced to twenty years, he managed to have himself transferred to the military hospital at Versailles. Thereafter he was freed but confined within the limits of Versailles, if still cut off from all communications with Louis Napoléon. There he was to write one of the most remarkable books in French history, "proving" that all the learned French, English, and German archaeologists were wrong in declaring the pyramids to have been built as imposing mausoleums for some of the pharaohs of Ancient Egypt. No, Persigny now established that the pyramids had been constructed to prevent the Nile from silting up![8]

Ham was a medieval fortress that had undergone many changes over the centuries, and by 1840, its former château long gone, it was reduced to a traditional rectangular fortress, complete with four stout towers, including a massive "keep." The thirty-foot gates at the entrance led into the vast inner court with a single Liberty Tree dating from 1793; it was otherwise devoid of any structures, while at the end and to the right two large ugly brick barracks had been added. Louis Napoléon's "apartment" was situated at the far end of the fort.

It was soon filled with furnishings donated by friends, including rugs, curtains, paintings, a sofa, a Voltaire reading chair, and one canapé, not to mention Bonaparte family portraits, busts, books, and bric-à-brac. By the time of his visit later, Louis Blanc described the apartment as being "provided with everything that domestic comfort required." The prisoner, he claimed, was being "treated very well indeed." The government's food allowance for all three men came to a total of twenty francs a day (no provision being made for Thélin, a "voluntary guest"). Louis Napoléon made up for the shortfall, including wine and fresh game. Dinner was prepared in the prison kitchen and was served at five-thirty in the afternoon. In the evening Louis Napoléon, Henri Conneau, and the charming Montholon would play a hand or two of whist over a glass of wine, occasionally joined by Thélin or Major Demarle, the governor of the prison.[9]

Life settled into a comfortable, if monotonous, routine, thanks to the accommodating new commanding officer, though he was *très correct* and obliged by the interior minister to personally inspect their quarters four times a day. The reins were gradually loosened, however, with the governor and his wife soon inviting the convict to dinners and card games. Every morning Louis Napoléon worked in his "study" on various articles, chapters of books, or translations, including some of German playwright Friedrich Schiller's works, a favorite author of his. With the addition of shelves for chemicals, he also began carrying out simple "Volta" experiments, resulting in a paper he prepared for the Academy of Sciences on the conduction of electricity.[10]

He was given permission to buy a horse for exercise within the confines of the courtyard. More frequently he worked in a forty-square-meter garden plot on the ramparts of the fortress, always within sight of the sixty soldiers on duty at all times. "I spend a lot of time gardening," he related to Vieillard. "I plant flower seeds and shrubs. The pleasure I gain from tilling a few cubic meters of earth leads me to think that we have within us many inner resources and other unknown consolations upon which to draw."[11]

Regardless of his Germanic accent in French and English, the prince's winning Old World courtesy and mild temperament won over everyone, including the guards. Despite his notorious reputation, despite his two failed attempts to overthrow the government of France, despite his having shot an unarmed French soldier, it was simply very difficult to dislike the man.[12]

L ouis Napoléon's dramatic arrest and imprisonment had attracted much interest in France, England, and Europe, resulting in a flood of mail—all of it carefully vetted by Major Demarle, including requests for visits from the celebrated and total strangers alike. The ladies at first outnumbered the men, including the Princess Belgiojoso, Baroness de Bossi, Madame de Querelles, Éléonore Gordon (of Strasbourg fame), Hortense Cornu, and Caroline Jane O'Hara, an Irish "adventuress"— Tristan de Montholon's lastest mistress. Demarle allowed her to be installed with Montholon, while her chambermaid, Éléonore Vergeot-Camus, known as "Alexandrine," was to be become Louis Napoléon's mistress and the mother of their two illegitimate prison-born sons (in 1841 and 1845).[13]

Visitors included newspapermen and publicists, former officers, or the sons of former Napoleonic officers, as well as Lieutenant Armand Laity, the jovial Alexandre Dumas, the somber Chateaubriand, and good-natured James Harris, the third Earl of Malmesbury—the future foreign secretary, probably Louis Napoléon's closest and most reliable friend in English government circles.

Louis Blanc, a twenty-nine-year-old lawyer and celebrated socialist theoretician, was perhaps the most interesting, and the strangest of all Louis Napoléon's visitors. Launched to instant early fame in 1839 by the publication of his celebrated work, *The Organisation of Labour*, always remembered for his "National Workshops," and his formula—"Everyone according to his abilities, to each according to his needs"—Blanc had inherited his Bonapartist credentials from his father, who had served as Joseph Bonaparte's inspector general of Finances when king of Spain.

Although a Bonapartist, Blanc was against "a Napoleonic restoration," which he saw as "despotism without glory." "However my credo," the prince protested, "is the Empire. Has it not raised France to the height of her glory? . . . As for me, I am convinced that what the country wants is the return to the Empire." "When taking my leave . . . he took me quite by surprise embracing me so warmly as to leave me unable to hide the emotions I felt," Blanc confessed.[14] He later went into exile rather than face life under the Second Empire.

Discussion of leaving Ham soon cropped up among his fellow inmates. When the prince told his father that he had not even thought of seeking his freedom prior to September 1845, however, that was not true. "In the course of the year 1842 some influential gentlemen from Central America wrote to the prisoner of Ham . . . entreating him to ask for his liberty," the prince later recalled in the third person, "that he might leave for America, where he would be received," they insisted, "with enthusiasm." Although he was expected to head, or at least give his name to, one of their major commercial projects, in any event Louis Napoléon thought better of it and initially declined. Nevertheless, it started him thinking about Mexico and Central America and its many opportunities that lay before him, including escape from his prison.

Next a French naval officer about to sail for the Pacific visited the prince, explaining what a boon an interoceanic canal linking the Caribbean and the Pacific would be for the French navy and worldwide commercial shipping, lopping off thousands of miles of travel and months of sailing time. In fact the French government had just sent an engineer to Central America to study the feasibility of constructing a canal through the Isthmus of Panama. Intrigued, Louis Napoléon spent several months exploring all aspects of such a canal and in August 1845 produced a long, detailed memorandum on the subject.

Independently, Señor Dr. Francisco Castellon, the new Minister Plenipotentiary of the Republic of Guatamala (encompassing Guatamala, Nicaragua, Honduras, Costa Rica, and San Salvador), arrived in Paris to discuss the possibility of French naval protection for their coastal interests in exchange for favorable commercial concessions to the French. Louis Philippe, already bogged down in the first stages of the conquest of Algeria, while challenging an aggressive Royal Navy in the Mediterranean, dismissed the offer out of hand. Castellon had also visited Ham at the end of 1844. Although clearly interested, but going through a period of depression and indecision, Bonaparte also declined, and Castellon went on to Bruxelles, where instead he signed "a treaty" with a Belgian company supported by King Leopold.

They continued to correspond, however, and a year later, in December 1845, Castellon renewed his offer, appealing to Louis Napoléon's "magnanimity and benevolence" regarding this "great object of paramount importance to my country," noting his interest in going to that country where he could help initiate an interoceanic canal that would bring "a new era of prosperity to the inhabitants." But this occurred at a time when the prince was preoccupied with reestablishing contact with his semi-paralyzed father, and gaining a paroled release to visit him in Florence.

The foreign minister of Nicaragua then wrote informing him officially that all the powers required for organizing this enterprise had been conferred on him on January 8, 1846. The name of the projected

Canale Napoleone de Nicaragua was of course intended to flatter him. In fact, everything depended on Louis Philippe's agreeing to release him.

Louis Napoléon now wrote personally to the French king, fully explaining his situation and his ardent desire to be with his father. After residing with his dying father, he assured the king that he would then proceed to Central America for the next few years to create and launch this new canal. Subsequently, with Louis Philippe's rejection, Louis Napoléon put all travel plans to America aside permanently.[15]

His decision to attempt to take Boulogne and overthrow Louis Philippe had been timed for August 1840 because of the French government's announcement to return the remains of Napoléon I from St. Helena. Hoping to replace Louis Philippe at the Tuileries that August, Louis Napoléon had intended to be in the French capital on the fifteenth of December in his capacity as the newly acclaimed head of state to receive his uncle's remains on behalf of the French nation. It would have been a politician's dream, a public relations coup, coinciding with his own enthronement.

Instead of the Tuileries, Louis Napoléon had found himself shackled symbolically in this prison. He not only deeply resented it, but even considered it quite unfair. "The government which has recognized the legitimacy of the head of my family," the prince wrote Interior Minister Duchâtel in 1844, "is obliged therefore to recognize me as a prince [of that family] . . . The treatment I endure here is at once unjust, illegal and inhumane!" He was, he reminded the minister, the son of a king and nephew of an emperor, as well as being allied to all the sovereign heads of Europe [sic]."[16]

Since the prince no longer had secretaries to whom he could dictate and who could prepare his manuscripts, Hortense Cornu, the daughter of Hortense's Arenenberg chambermaid and his goddaughter, faithfully came to Ham regularly to collect the more important post, to prepare manuscripts for publication, to bring books to him from the Royal Library (authorized by Louis Philippe), and to carry out research elsewhere as the moment required, for example, when preparing his history of artillery. As for the actual writing, early every morning Louis Napoléon closed the door to his "study," sat down at the table, or stood at his new pulpit desk, and wrote and wrote and wrote, month after month, year after year.

Among his projects was a pamphlet, *The Sugar Question,* in support of the protected development of commerce and agriculture, including sugar production, in which his new friend and regular visitor, Count Fouqier d'Herouël, was financially involved. (The count was also influential later in raising a large sum facilitating the prince's escape.) Ironically, unknown to him, his half-brother, Auguste de Morny, was already becoming a major producer of sugar beet, near Clermont Ferrand. But the real thrust of this pamphlet focused on the urgency of the country becoming completely self-sufficent in its production of all the basic food staples and minerals.

"The first priority of a country does not consist in producing cheap manufactured goods, but rather in providing work for the people," he argued. However, while the consumer demanded lower prices for the food and goods he bought, this obliged the "bosses" to produce the maximum at the lowest possible cost, resulting in a low level of wages. "England has realized the dream of some modern economists: she surpasses all other countries by the cheapness of her manufactured products, but only by maintaining very low wages for her work force." And as for the production of food and other staples, "a nation is always guilty of leaving itself at the mercy of other countries when relying on them to supply these for them." To leave a people cut off from their source of wheat, corn, and iron "is to place their destiny in the hands of a foreign country, and that is a type of suicide." Therefore France must produce all her own wheat, corn, and sugar, coal, iron and copper.[17]

As a prisoner of the state, Louis Napoléon was convinced the best way of attracting public attention and sympathy was by writing, the mass medium of the day. In 1839, just before leaving London, he had published his little brochure, *The Napoleonic Ideas,* or values and concepts. His overall objective was "to rebuild entirely a society disrupted by fifty years of revolution," while also "reconciling 'freedom' with the necessity of 'order,' and the rights of the people with 'the principles of authority' . . . all of which based on the principles of eternal justice." This would replace the old hereditary aristocracies with a new "hierarchical system" based on merit and industry, "while ensuring social equality and guaranteeing public order. *It establishes an element of force [state authority] and stability in our democracy because it brings the discipline required to make it function* [author's italics]. . . . And thus in the end *The Napoleonic Ideas* envisages a new France whose citizens have reconciled all their differences and joined together as brothers. . . ."[18] But it was the key words "order," "discipline," and "authority" that ring with strident clarity throughout this tract and that would define the empire he anticipated.

"What then was Napoléon's supreme objective for the French people?" the prince asked, "Freedom! . . . Yes, Freedom! And the longer one studies history, the more convincing this truth becomes. . . ."[19] Louis Napoléon's views: A modern new society must be endowed with the principles of "revolutionary democracy" and voting rights for the masses, but all directed by the selected new enlightened aristocrats ruling the land. Moreover, had Napoléon had more time, his nephew insisted, he would have created a whole "new unified Europe," all joined by a "European Association [of States]" under a new "European legal code" responsible to a European "high Court of Appeals." Under this new super state, "the larger overall European interests would dominate those of individual states."[20] A European Union . . .

P erhaps the most famous work produced by Louis Napoléon while at Ham was another short pamphlet, *The Extinction of Pauperism*. It was widely praised for its apparent favorable attitude to a socialist economy, a fairer "redistribution of wealth," much as Émile Zola was to conceive a couple of decades later in his Rougon-Macquart novels. Favorable to socialism in theory, perhaps, but not in the practical day-to-day world of reality.[21]

The prince considered the solutions that socialism could offer, such as the creation of major national agricultural cooperatives as a mainstay of the economy. "The working class have nothing, and therefore we must make them property owners," he argued. "They must be given a place in society by attaching their interests to the land." To achieve this "agricultural colonies must be created, they offering bread, education, religion, and jobs for everyone out of work," he added, "and God only knows the number of the unemployed in France is high enough today!"[22]

France in the 1840s was still largely agricultural and artisanal, and Louis Napoléon wanted every *département* in France to establish one such agricultural colony, to be financed by the state. He envisaged similar pools created for industrial workers, in effect, "labor exchanges" of men to be drawn upon by captains of industry as needed. "By having all offers of employment being channeled to one center in each department, the unemployed would be far better placed to have access to this information, however poor the pay." The state would then provide 300 million francs to establish these "colonies."[23] But of course this was never enacted.

"Your preoccupations and writings prove that we shall have a splendid citizen in you," novelist George Sand wrote, congratulating Louis Napoléon in May 1844. "Now here is a prince . . . a noble example to all the powerful men in the world," she recorded in her diary.[24]

I n fact Louis Napoléon's preoccupations after September 1845 had nothing to do with fine theoretical political tracts prepared for his future Napoleonic state, nor with the country's unemployment and poverty, but with himself . . . and the old nagging problem of his relationship with his father. That shadow suspended over so much of his youth was now transforming and dissipating as alarming reports from the Florentine palazzo announcing the declining health of the perennially hypochondriacal Louis Bonaparte at last proved true, followed by news of a partial paralytic stroke.

At about the same time, Louis Napoléon's relations with his father, held in a sort of limbo since 1841, started improving dramatically thanks to a most unexpected visit in September 1845 by Silvestre Poggioli, a close friend of Louis Bonaparte, who handed the prince a letter from his father, explaining the long period of silence and about his illness. He wrote back to his father on the nineteenth of that month. "Yesterday I felt the first joy I have known in five years, on receiving your friendly letter . . . I share your opinion, father . . . that the only true happiness in this world consists in the reciprocal affection of beings created to love one other. What most touched and stirred me was the desire you express to see me again. This wish is to me a command." He now learned of the various *démarches* his father had been undertaking over the past several months, contacting influential friends and high French officials, to arrange for his release. "Thank you most heartily for the steps you have taken on my behalf."

This response to his father was the warmest and most emotional he was ever to write. "Even as late as yesterday I had decided to do nothing about leaving this prison. But to leave, to go where? To do what? To wander all alone? . . . Now a new purpose opens itself to me, to go and embrace you with my attention, to care for you . . . for nothing could ever eradicate the filial piety I feel for you." In a flash he had finally made up his mind; he would definitely leave this prison, no matter what, and go to his father.[25]

During this period, however, the British minister, Lord Malmesbury, made a most extraordinary attempt to obtain Louis Napoléon's freedom through the intervention of Prime Minister Robert Peel with Louis Philippe. But the English prime minister declined to act.[26]

Meanwhile, when the prince next asked the commandant of Ham to release him temporarily, Major Demarle referred him to Interior Minister Duchâtel. "My father, whose state of health and advanced age demand the care and attention of a son, asked the government that he be permitted to go to him," he wrote in the third person. These *démarches* proving fruitless, he finally addressed Louis Philippe himself. "I now appeal, Sire, with confidence in your Majesty's sentiments of humanity, renewing my request, and submitting it to your high and generous spirit."[27] But the king rejected the prince's request.

When Odilon Barrot suggested that the prince appeal to the king for clemency, the prisoner refused on the spot, and on the fifteenth of May Louis Napoléon met with Henri Conneau to inform him that, after more than five years' incarceration, he had had quite enough and intended to flee the prison and France. "I wished to see my father again," as he afterward related to his publisher friend, Frédéric Degeorge, "and was not prepared to put up with any more nonsense."[28]

Early on May 25, 1846, after shaving off his distinctive mustache and donning a long black wig, a workman's blue blouse and trousers, wooden sabots, with a clay pipe in his mouth, and carrying a plank over his shoulder, Louis Napoléon sauntered lazily past some of the carpenters carrying out repairs in the fort. Passing over the drawbridge and walking a further two kilometers up the road to the village cemetery, he found "my good and faithful Thélin" waiting with a cabriolet to whisk him the twenty-one kilometers northeast to St. Quentin. After a change of horses they continued north a further sixty kilometers on to the Valenciennes railway station. The four o'clock train then took them across the recently rechristened Belgian frontier. From Bruxelles another train took them to Ostende, where, with an English passport provided earlier by Malmesbury, Louis Napoléon and Thélin crossed the English Channel nearly six years after their last curious odyssey.

Louis Napoléon Bonaparte found himself once again in the capital of the British empire, safe from the French government—if on this occasion without his twenty servants—where a "Count d'Arenenberg" and his man registered at the Brunswick Hotel, on Jermyn Street in the heart of Mayfair. "The desire to see you again led me to attempt something I might otherwise have never undertaken," the prince wrote his father. "I slipped past 400 soldiers, and have now arrived in London safe and sane." "I have been very well received here," he informed Vieillard. "One really must do justice to the English; they have great independence of character."[29]

Once again the Union Jack was flying overhead and once again all was well with the world as he applied to various embassies for the visas requisite for travel to Tuscany, but the king of Belgium and the Austrian emperor personally continued to bar the way. Before he could leave London, however, he learned that Louis Bonaparte had died of a stroke on the twenty-fifth of July. There would be no more tortured letters coming from the family palazzo in Florence. The king was dead, long live the prince.

12

MARKING TIME

"For my part, I always prefer to think the best of someone, until I have proof to the contrary."[1]
—LOUIS NAPOLÉON ON COUSIN
JÉRÔME BONAPARTE, DECEMBER 10, 1846

I have been installed in my new house for the past fortnight, and for the first time in seven years I am enjoying the pleasure of living under my own roof," a freed Louis Napoléon had written Narcisse Vieillard after settling in London in February. This rather modest rented brick house in King Street reflected his new, reduced circumstances—with only a secretary, Thélin, a cook and a couple of maids, instead of the staff of twenty he had earlier had at Carlton Gardens, and a more sobered view of his situation. And he would soon be joined by his closest companion, Henri Conneau, when he was released from Ham.[2]

A terraced London house was a great difference from the freedom offered by Arenenberg and its surrounding grounds, but for Louis Napoléon it was a welcome change. There were no more immediate painful memories associated with his dying mother, while gaining a new personal security here in the capital of the British empire where Louis Philippe's police would commit no follies. So determined was he to cut himself free from Switzerland now that he ordered his agent to put Arenenberg up for sale to raise badly needed cash. This new existence for a recently liberated prisoner included seeing old friends and acquaintances, including his most loyal English friend throughout the years, James Harris, Lord Malmesbury, Foreign Secretary Lord Palmerston, Lord Shelburne (the future Lord Lansdowne), the kindly Lord Brougham, Giuseppe Panizzi, Lord Archie Montgomerie, and Count Alfred d'Orsay and his lovely Lady Blessington (Marguerite Gardiner).

Nearly six years of confinement had appreciably changed Louis Napoléon physically and emotionally, his expression continually more preoccupied and his shoulders stooped, as Malmesbury and Panizzi remarked. But he enjoyed social life all the more, free of the high stone walls that had denied him both basic physical exercise and the outside world. He was welcomed back to the aristocratic houses in and around Mayfair, while returning to his old haunts in the theater district between Piccadilly and Leicester Square. At a dinner given by the director of His Majesty's Theatre, the humorous Benjamin Lumley, the prince was introduced to the thirty-four-year-old Giuseppe Verdi, who was presenting his opera *I Masnadieri*. More to his liking was the new French acting sensation: "I have seen Rachel, and have been enchanted by her," he informed Hortense Cornu. "It is the first time I have ever seen a French tragedy played [Racine's *Phèdre*]," he confessed.[3] And if this summer he did not return to Scotland for Eglinton's jousting festival, he did regularly attend the races at Newbury, where he lost more than he won. An excellent horseman, Louis Napoléon invariably rode in Hyde Park daily, regardless of the weather. And then for good measure during the Chartist riots he briefly accepted the staff of office as a special constable, responsible for guarding dangerous Park Lane, across from Apsley House. A Bonaparte protecting the Duke of Wellington. *Alors!*

Hortense Cornu and her artist husband visited the prince in the summer at Bath, where he was taking the waters. While in the capital, Louis Napoléon had written asking Narcisse Vieillard to help build a political organization.[4] The soft-spoken Vieillard found his erratic cousin, Prince Jérôme, to be quite a prickly character. (This was the same Plon-Plon who had years earlier spent several months at Arenenberg following his mother's death. Commiserating with his old friend, Louis Napoléon conceded that his young cousin did indeed have an "unintelligible disposition." He was at times "frank, loyal and open, only to change abruptly, becoming constrained and dissimulating. Sometimes his heart seems to speak enthusiastically of the glory of a particular cause and to suffer with you for all that is great and generous. At other times he displays hardness, trickery and knavery. Who then is he really?" he asked. *"For my part, I always prefer to think the best of someone, until I have positive proof to the contrary, and while remaining ever on my guard, I continue to withhold none of my affection and friendship."*[5] [Author's italics] Louis Napoléon rarely spoke about people behind their back, and this was the only time he was ever known to have discussed his difficult cousin so freely. What many were later to take for weakness or even stupidity on his part was in fact the attitude of a mature, very decent man, one capable of understanding the foibles and limitations of those around him, while trying to continue to work with them given their limitations.

Although Louis Napoléon's name was by now as familiar in France as those of Alexandre Dumas and Victor Hugo—both of them still his admirers at this stage—unlike them, Bonaparte could not earn a living by writing, and now back in London he had to concentrate on restoring his finances. The name of Bonaparte could, nevertheless, draw financial backers, even in Italy, where Counts Orsi and Armani, in conjunction with a Mr. Rappalo, managed to borrow 250,000 francs (over $3,300,000), and the Marquis Pallavicino lent another 325,000 francs (nearly $4 million), which included a mortgage on a Bonaparte villa in Civita Nova. Fortunately, Louis Napoléon now met Joshua Bates, an American—the founder of the Boston Public Library, and senior partner of Barings Bank. From now until his death in 1864, he was to handle the prince's investments.[6] In brief, contrary to rumors, at this time he always had immediately available all the cash he needed on short call—exclusive of any funds he might receive from generous personal friends later, although he continued to live simply, apart from his gambling debts and, of course, women.[7]

Unlike his earlier stay in London, Louis Napoléon spent very little time on his public relations political tracts, though he did continue to work on the second volume of his history of artillery (the first volume having just been published).[8] After those years in Ham, naturally he took his pleasures seriously, which centered more and more around Gore House, Kensington (on the site of Albert Hall). There the lovely

Marguerite Gardiner, the Countess of Blessington, resided with her dissolute, effeminate lover and Parisian playboy, the talented painter and sculptor, Alfred, Count d'Orsay, dubbed "the Archangel of Dandyism" by Lamartine.

The self-taught daughter of a small-holdings farmer from Tipperary, Ireland, through two marriages Marguerite had gradually improved "her situation," and in 1818 had married the Irishman, Charles John Gardiner, the first Earl of Blessington, complete with his previous four children. During their extensive travels on the Continent, they had met Alfred d'Orsay, and the *ménage à trois* later settled in at Gore House, where they became renowned for their extravagant dinners and soirées attracting the artistic set, including Sir Thomas Lawrence, who painted the portrait of the ravishing brunette. Among her acquaintances she counted Lord Byron, Edward Bulwer-Lytton, Charles Dickens, and Benjamin Disraeli. Then in 1846 she introduced Louis Napoléon to her "protégée," Harriet Howard, the woman who was to become intimately associated with his name over the next several years.[9]

Harriet Howard (baptized Elizabeth Ann Haryett) was born of humble origins in Brighton in 1823. At the age of fifteen, she ran off to London with hopes of a career on the stage and changed her name to Harriet Howard. There, a wealthy married army officer, Mountjoy Martyn, provided her with a son, Martin Constantin Haryett, and a remarkably handsome fortune. She was twenty-three years old living with her son in Berkeley Street when she met the prince. Theirs was an unusual romance from the start, Louis Napoléon soon bringing his two illegitimate sons—Eugene and Louis—from Ham to live with Harriet and her son Martin, and to be brought up together with them for the next several years. Thereafter the prince spent most of his time in Berkeley Street in 1847 and the early part of 1848.

As for the situation in Paris, no one was following events there more attentively than the prince. It was just a matter of time now.

13

A PURE NEW HOLY REPUBLIC: 1848

"I grieve at the prospect of a republic in France."[1]
—FOREIGN SECRETARY LORD PALMERSTON TO AMBASSADOR
LORD NORMANBY, FEBRUARY 28, 1848

"The banks are crashing one after another."[2]
—LÉON FAUCHER, FUTURE MINISTER OF THE INTERIOR

Paris thrived on political humor, including Ludwig Börne's satirical sketch of Louis Philippe as "the emperor of the five-percenters [interest on state securities], the king of the three-percenters [bondholders], the protector of bankers, [and] the mediator of stockbrokers."[3] That financially strapped king left the realm's coffers nearly bare, with state revenue reduced to a trickle, an ossified economy unreformed, and nationwide poverty. Like Charles X in 1830, Louis Philippe, too, now seemed to understand nothing of what was happening all around him.

Nor, for that matter, even as late as New Year's Day 1848, did Baron James de Rothschild, the practical realist and usually extremely well informed head of the French House of Rothschild, who seemed to remain inexplicably oblivious to the state of the nation: "We made 19 million [francs] in 1847; if all goes well we should do 20 million this year,"[4] he noted with surprising complacency on the first of January 1848. Unlike his older brother, Nathan, in London, he thought things had never been better, there were no clouds on the horizon, at least no more than usual. He had just underwritten a 3 percent, 250-million-franc government bond issue (well over $3,200,000,000 today) at the request of Louis Philippe, and Rothschild was a very contented banker. But from the impoverished populace, "a vengeful world lurked behind society," as a more dramatic Chateaubriand recorded. In Paris a laborer earned and attempted in vain to support a family on less than two francs for a twelve-hour workday, with almost two-thirds of the city's population of one million dwelling in abject poverty. But the most ominous sign to any banker, shop owner, and member of the bourgeoisie was not only the suffering but the growing number of widespread street protests. Novelists and social artists, like the two Honorés— Daumier and Balzac—had long seen what the king and Rothschild had not, "a deadly terror" behind the hungry faces, "haggard, sallow, leathery," of desperate fathers and mothers with nothing to lose, amid an appalling mortality rate that, nevertheless, ungenerously failed to relieve the burgeoning medieval slums of the French capital.[5]

The newspapers will relate [the events surrounding the revolutionary situation here in Paris] far better than I can. Suffice it so say, I am still alive, that's all I know," Auguste de Morny wrote his half sister, Emily [de Flahaut], Countess of Shelburne, on the first of March, 1848. "If I am most fortunate in that respect, so far as the state of my finances is concerned, however, well, I am utterly ruined—everything is gone! Heaven only knows what lies in store for us."[6]

Louis Philippe abdicated without warning and under the worst possible circumstances during the early hours of February 24, 1848, leaving a trail of political mayhem and bewilderment in his wake. In fact there had been very clear signs of public unrest for many months, including a "banquet" held at Clignancourt on July 9, 1847, a forum demanding sweeping national electoral and economic reform. It had been answered by a defiant King Louis Philippe at the opening of parliament on December 28, 1847, when he had denounced "the agitation fomented by blind hotheads," a government position which Morny himself mostly supported.[7] When meeting with the conservative premier

François Guizot in February 1848 to suggest a modest compromise to ease tensions, however, Morny had been rebuffed. This call for parliamentary reform was just the beginning of their demands, Guizot had insisted. "We are not dealing here with the usual 'reformers,' these people are out-and-out revolutionaries," so there was nothing to discuss. Morny then appealed directly to the king: "Not to worry, young man," Louis Philippe reassured him, "the French government is run by loyal professional administrative officials and they know their duty very well indeed and will see us through [this crisis]."[8]

Nevertheless, widespread discontent continued, and opposition leaders insisted on government authorization for another political banquet to be held on February 19. More than six hundred paid to attend this gathering, and unlike the protests during the Revolution of 1789, this was initiated by educated men, men of property, not by angry mobs from the slums of Paris. These men today planned to meet in order to protest their denial of voting rights and parliamentary representation. As a member of the chamber of deputies, Morny was one of the two representatives designated by Guizot's government to negotiate with the leaders of this banquet. Following difficult talks, a much relieved Morny reported to his sister Emily and brother-in-law in London: "I intervened . . . and reached an agreement between the government and the opposition." The crisis seemed resolved, and the banquet was rescheduled for the twenty-second of February, 1848. But then without warning an arrogant Interior Minister Charles Duchâtel unilaterally cancelled that second banquet altogether. Appalled by this underhanded action, which had also undermined his own role, Morny, who had just been offered a portfolio in the government, recoiled. "God forbid my ever accepting such a post now in a country like ours!"[9] On that same twenty-second, thousands of businessmen and shop owners gathered to protest along the Champs-Élysées, where the banquet had been scheduled to be held. Scuffles broke out, and the situation quickly deteriorated as barricades went up, closing off one street after another. A flash flood of anger and defiance swept the city. It was all Morny's fault, and the king had betrayed them.

The explosion of events on the twenty-third, followed by the news of Louis Philippe's bewildering nocturnal flight to the coast on the twenty-fourth, caught everyone off balance, and no one more so than a shocked Auguste de Morny. The already skittish financial markets were as usual the first to panic. Rothschild's solution: "I think we should purchase some American Treasury [bonds]," he advised his nephews. "America is still the most secure country for the investment of capital."[10] Meanwhile, members of the cabinet and parliament, the war ministry, even the foreign ministry and diplomatic corps—all were left in the dark. With share prices plummeting, the Bourse immediately closed its doors, only adding to the turmoil. Long queues formed all night outside the Banque de France, the public desperate to exchange their certificates, notes, and letters of credit for gold. The National Treasury, down to a mere 192 million francs on February 22, and even that thanks in part to Rothschild's recent initial loan flotation, was hemorrhaging out of control with no tax receipts to replenish it. The government was completely closed down.

The thirty-six-year-old political insider Auguste de Morny was not the only one to be caught completely off guard by the unpredicted fall of Louis Philippe, despite his long, very close ties over the years with the ruling family through Fanny Le Hon, his late grandmother, Adélaïde de Souza, and of course his father, General Charles de Flahaut, at this very moment serving as French ambassador to Vienna.[11]

"I am simply staggered by the utter stupidity by which he [Louis Philippe] lost the day [February 23]," eyewitness Maxime Du Camp commented. The former governor general of Algeria, and now military governor of Paris, Marshal Thomas Bugeaud, could have moved in immediately with troops and nipped the uprising in the bud, Du Camp insisted, but instead "simply gave speeches." As for the king's son, the Duke de Nemours, in nominal command of the Royal French Army, "he never left the Palace and the safety of his general staff." Of the only two members of the Orléans family noted as men of action, the Prince de Joinville was with the navy and the Duke d'Aumale far away in Algeria with the army.[12] "This whole business has been so thoroughly botched [by the king]." Morny fully agreed with his friend, Du Camp. "They [the new provisional government under Lamartine] have also lacked the most elementary common sense and courage to act."[13]

Such was the situation Morny, like the rest of the people, found himself in. Powerless to act, he prepared to leave the capital. "[And now therefore] I am obliged to send all my paintings and the remaining money I am able to salvage, to you in London for safe keeping," he informed his sister.[14] With creditors literally pounding on the door and even accosting him in the streets, Morny, like so many others, sold what jewelry he could and let his servants ago, unpaid. Most of his friends had already fled the country, including the mother of his natural daughter Louise, Fanny Le Hon, her father and brother—François and Alfred Mosselman—along with nearly all the principal bankers of the capital.[15] "Tell me whether Shelburne thinks I should also send you my horses and carriages. In such volatile times as these it's quite impossible to sell them here in Paris," he wrote.[16]

Lord Shelburne, a great landowner and influential member of Parliament, who was destined to serve as undersecretary at the Foreign Office under Lord Palmerston, certainly knew the state of affairs in England. Moreover, he personally knew the nation's leaders intimately, including Peel, Aberdeen, and Prime Minister Lord John Russell. And he and Harry Palmerston had been students at Cambridge together and had even contended the same parliamentary seat there. Auguste de Morny, like his father Ambassador de Flahaut, along with Prince von Metternich and ex-king Louis Philippe, would eventually be accorded a safe haven in London. Many dozens of fellow French were not quite so fortunate, including some leading musicians, such as Jacques Offenbach, choosing other traditional refuges in times of crisis at Bruxelles, Geneva, Amsterdam, Cologne, or Hamburg.

Charles de Flahaut was not the only diplomat to be caught up in this unexpected political vortex. In Barcelona, the forty-four-year-old French consul general, Ferdinand de Lesseps, was as much at a loss about what to do as anyone else, in his case because of the absence of an official government in Paris or instructions from a silent foreign ministry. Who indeed was the minister of foreign affairs at this moment? What, Lesseps asked his family, "are they going to do with me now?" A few days later he was at last summoned to Paris where Alphonse de Lamartine personally informed him that he, Lesseps, was to replace the French ambassador at Madrid. One of his first visitors at that embassy was the Countess Eugénie de Teba (later, de Montijo), his first cousin and the future wife of Napoléon III, who implored him to intercede on behalf of some Spanish officers who were about to be executed. The long-term consequences of that unexpected meeting were to be beyond anyone's wildest dreams.[17]

All the thoughts and "theories" of a new republican-socialist order evolving after the Revolution of 1789, and in renewed form throughout the 1830s and 1840s, now converged, jumbled together, confusing, conflicting, and contradictory, all vying for political approval and ultimate domination. The shattered French economy, perhaps Napoléon I's most destructive immediate legacy, which had in turn undermined the Bourbons between 1815 and 1830, remained largely unaltered in 1848. The result: continuing nationwide impoverishment of the people, a major factor, along with the lack of electoral reform, in bringing down Louis Philippe. The deepening national depression persisted unabated, engulfing all classes, driving even the bourgeoisie to revolt and join the commercial classes in calling for the banquets of protest this February.

The names and works of the socialist and republican heroes still pervaded the atmosphere of the Isle de France this 1848: Charles Fourier, Étienne Cabet, Pierre-Joseph Proudhon—"Property is theft"—Philippe Buchez, and Louis Blanc with the National Workshops he espoused in his famous *Organization of Labour*. And then of course there was Louis Auguste Blanqui, scorning both romantic Christianity and pure unrealistic socialist theory—who, when released in 1848 after decades in prison, thought he had the answer. Instead of a call for the violent overthrow of governments, there would be a revolutionary dictatorship of his choosing calling for the end of destructive capitalism. A dangerous agent provocateur, Blanqui was immediately rearrested.

On the other hand, Saint-Simonism and its "moralistic responsibility" remained active in thought and practice, even gaining adherents for the first time from a few of the idealistic younger bankers and financiers, such as Émile and Isaac Pereire, and Michel Chevalier, and one Louis Napoléon Bonaparte. Henri, Count de Saint-Simon, had preached his own version of a "new Christianity," of brotherly love, but one combined with the practical support of commerce. Unlike Proudhon, he accepted the need for private property, but under the thoughtful administration of a government led not by politicians, but by technocrats—industrial managers, engineers, and scientists—experts capable of running a new society in the true interests of the people, and thereby avoiding the usual pitfalls of daily politics.

In defiance of the traditional closed banking establishment reserved uniquely for the wealthy and great property owners, in the 1840s and 1850s the Pereire brothers were to remain sympathetic to the Saint-Simon school. To be sure, James de Rothschild, like 99 percent of bankers and political leaders of that era, couldn't have cared less about the masses, although he did personally know Émile Pereire, a former employee, very well. On the other hand, Louis Napoléon Bonaparte continued to proclaim Saint-Simon his own personal apostle.

And then there were the new politicians sporting republicanism or Bonapartism who claimed their rightful place in these revolutionary times. Paramount among them, and at first glance the least likely, the handsome and eloquent Burgundian aristocrat, lyrical idealist, and poet, diplomat, and historian, Viscount Alphonse de Lamartine, stood out. From the first hours in February 1848, he proclaimed from the tribune of the Palais Bourbon a new democratic France, praising past republican "heroes" of the 1789 revolution in his *History of the Girodins*, including none other than the terrorist Robespierre.

This Lamartine was now to emerge as the self-appointed spokesman for the righteous in the emerging Second Republic. His highly emotional, zealous, and uncompromising espousal of the republican cause, like his mellifluous aristocratic oratory, expounded with an ethereal religious fervor—"this new, pure, holy, immortal great and peace seeking Republic, transcendent and acclaimed by the people"—clearly stirred the literate bourgeoisie, though as events turned out, not the unseen mass of hungry, unemployed workers. Meanwhile, from the Collège de France,

Professor Jules Michelet published his own purified, carefully filtered version of events in *Le Peuple*, even as he was preparing his monumental *History of the French Revolution*, in which he presented "the common man" as the hero of France. Such was the heady intellectual admixture intoxicating this immediate post–Louis Philippian era of France in 1848.[18]

Under the circumstances, the ensuing confusion in seeking a feasible solution to right the country's woes, a solution that had somehow escaped everyone since 1789, was hardly surprising. Some, such as the poet, novelist, playwright, and self-imposed social conscience of France, Victor Hugo, the son of a popular Bonaparte general, reduced it simply to insisting on the takeover of mass republican democracy, while those who feared chaos and what they saw as the aimless and rampaging destructive masses, like Auguste de Morny and his fellow aristocratic members of the Jockey Club set, instead desperately sought the security and stability of the state through a strong monarch or benevolent dictatorship. The propertied classes looked in vain to the Bourbons or Orléans, others to powerful soldiers, such as the gaunt General Louis Eugène Cavaignac, governor of Algeria, while still others reflected wistfully on the days of Napoleonic France. But for the masses who had been disenfranchised by Louis Philippe—only 250,000 qualified voters, instead of the nearly five million who had voted for Napoléon's First Empire in 1804—the old order simply had to be swept away once and for all.

As for the current situation in Paris in the early months of 1848, "I can see absolutely nothing good coming of these upheavals," a depressed Morny concluded. Prosper Mérimée agreed, "and this time we don't have a Napoléon around to save us." With no firm leadership in sight, privately Morny saw only doom and damnation. "In the final analysis no one in a position of power has behaved intelligently or courageously, least of all the royal family [Louis Philippe]," whom he dismissed as having acted "most shamefully" by abandoning their responsibilities and their people.[19]

• • •

Across the English Channel, Prime Minister John Russell's foreign secretary, Henry Temple, Viscount Palmerston, shared this suspicion and anxiety about events in France. He had always considered Louis Philippe "a tricky fellow," ever since that king's opposition to the full recognition of Ottoman suzerainty over Egypt back in 1839–1840, aiming instead for an independent Egypt with the aid of French intervention in the affairs of that province. "If we give way now," Palmerston had argued, then "France will [next] take Morocco and Tunis," as well as Algeria, and of course France eventually did just that.[20]

Political volatility in France in February 1848 did nothing to allay anxiety, and like James de Rothschild and Auguste de Morny, the British foreign secretary too wished very much indeed "to avoid these [revolutionary] upheavals."[21] "I grieve at the prospect of a republic in France," Palmerston confided to his ambassador in Paris, Constantine Henry Phipps, the Marquis of Normanby, five days after the collapse of the Orléans government. "I fear it must [eventually] lead to war in Europe," just as the creation of the First Republic in the 1790s had led to years of military conflict with France's European neighbors.[22]

Of even more immediate attention was Palmerston's growing concern over the spread of French republican egalitarianism to British shores, a contagion encouraging voting rights among Britain's still disenfranchised working class. This movement "and other mischief" the foreign secretary was determined to stanch at any price.[23] And there were already dramatic signs of similar unrest in Frankfurt, Berlin, Prague, Vienna, Rome, and Naples. Nevertheless, Palmerston in London, again like James de Rothschild in Paris, was a pragmatist. "We must deal with things as they are," he counseled the British minister to Berlin, the Earl of Westmorland, "and not as we should wish to have them."[24]

For all his misgivings, Palmerston shed no tears over the ousting of Louis Philippe—for whom he had an almost visceral loathing—and his chief minister, François Guizot, "who were more bent on reducing and crippling the power of England than any men . . . since Napoléon Bonaparte."[25]

· · ·

Meanwhile, back in Paris and facing a new reality of his own, for perhaps the first and only time in his life, the notoriously egocentric Morny, who felt himself so superior to every man and every situation, broke down on reading his sister's immediate reassurances that she and Shelburne—the future Lord Lansdowne—would guard his property and provide a roof over his head while in exile in the English capital. "Tears came to my eyes when reading your letter," an overwhelmed Morny responded, "for you do not know how dear you are to me! . . . We can never forget that we are the children of a father whom we adore and embrace with all our affection and tenderness." This was a Morny the outside world never knew. All they had in this world, he wrote, was each other and their familial love. "Apart from that, God alone knows what fate has reserved for us in the midst of this abominable chaos. As for France, my poor child, the country is lost and dishonoured."[26]

In his London exile Louis Napoléon Bonaparte maintained a vigil from a safe distance, patiently awaiting the right moment to intervene. Ironically, his old foe Louis Philippe was by now, like himself, a political refugee, also a guest of Queen Victoria, a combination of drama and farce fast at work. The Charter of 1814, the Constitution, and the government were no more, while the streets of Paris lay wide open, completely unprotected.

"It was as extraordinary as it was terrible to see," the noted jurist Alexis de Tocqueville wrote, watching spellbound in the French capital. "The whole of an immense city, filled with so much wealth, left under the sole protection of those [masses roaming the streets] who possessed nothing . . . sheer terror gripped all other classes," he later recalled.[27] Now fearing for the lives of his family, James de Rothschild rushed his wife, Bette, and their children first to the safety of their estate of Ferrières, and then to England.

"Everyone is afraid, of course," Rothschild's visiting English nephew, Nathaniel, informed his family back in London. "The town is greatly agitated . . . God alone knows what will happen."[28] From his residence in the Place des Voges an enthralled Victor Hugo, too, was gripped by these precarious events. "Something sinister seems to be brewing," he noted. "Last night more than fifteen of Paris's finest mansions were marked with a chalk cross on the door, for the crowds to pillage, among them Princess Lieven's mansion in the Rue Saint Florentin [owned by James de Rothschild]."[29] The Louvre had already been pillaged, followed by Louis Philippe's château at Neuilly.

Outside Paris another mob rampaged through Salmon de Rothschild's château at Suresnes, led by the local poultry butcher, smashing furniture and gilt mirrors while slashing paintings and stealing what they could carry, before then burning it to the ground.[30] The mob violence continued everywhere. "They no longer pay taxes of any kind, they cut down woods on private property and torch country estates and factories," a sober Prosper Mérimée observed. "But everyone is simply too terrified of them to complain." The violence spread as workers tore up tracks and burned down railway bridges at Asnières, Chatou, Croissy, and Maison-Laffitte. "Whatever happens now," Morny reflected, "there is no more *Liberté* left in this land. The only thing I wish for is that plain common sense will calm and temper the new Republic, and that we can soon return to more tranquil times once again."[31] "One never knows what to expect from a Republican government," Rothschild summed up.[32] An ad hoc triumvirate was established by Lamartine (as titular head of state) and Foreign Minister Louis-Antoine Garnier-Pagès, with the adroit lawyer-politician Adolphe Crémieux holding the justice portfolio, though most of the country's judges and police officials had also fled the capital.

Upon his return to Paris, the successful playwright Ernest Feydeau, now in his national guard's uniform, ran into the small, heavyset Rothschild, who was curious about nearby gunfire as he left his office in the Rue de la Paix and walked toward the Tuileries. " 'Monsieur le Baron,' I said, 'You could not have chosen a worse day for taking a walk.' " Seventy men had been shot before the Ministry of Foreign Affairs, then situated in the Boulevard des Capucines. "I think it would be safer if you returned home rather than expose yourself to wild gunfire." But

Rothschild replied in his heavy accent that he had to get to the Ministry of Finance. As for stray bullets, he had no time for such tomfoolery, and continued on his way.

If that banker never worried about his own personal security, he continued to be preoccupied with that of his family. And when his eldest son was called up to serve on active duty with the national guard, the reality of the national emergency struck home. "My Alphonse . . . fighting for the Republic. As a father I want to avoid these upheavals. What's more, I'm not even that much of a republican."[33]

"I feel calmer now," the banker assured his wife in London, "although the situation here is still dangerous. All we can do is to keep meeting our [banking] obligations [though the other banks had by now closed their doors]. I am even taking on new business," he exaggerated.[34] And on March 7 the Paris Bourse tentatively reopened. "Rentes" (interest yielding securities), which had been quoted at 116.10 francs back on February 22, now plunged to 89, and by the sixth of April fell to 50 francs, while dividends were more than halved, before stopping altogether. The State Treasury was now down to a mere 59 million francs. If Rothschild himself was barely scraping through, even the oldest banking establishments were not, including those of the Protestant elite, Mallet, Hottinguer, and Delessert.[35]

As for Rothschild, in addition to the collapse of the normal markets affecting his banking transactions, there remained his anxieties about the acts of sabotage by thousands of striking railway workers against the tracks, locomotives, bridges, and stations of his Paris–Lille northern line, resulting both in further falling stock values and the pressing need for currently unavailable millions to meet the cost of those repairs.

Regardless of the air of stability, the Paris office, the most junior of the five Rothschild branches—London, Frankfurt, Vienna, and Naples being the others—was indeed in jeopardy. In the ensuing weeks following the departure of Louis Philippe, the Paris branch, like those in Vienna and Naples, was obliged to suspend all credit. James even had to deny a modest loan to the wife of the English ambassador. When word of this got around, the marketplace tensed, even as Rothschild secretly implored his brother in London for a golden infusion. "Let us be courageous, let us show our greatness [at this critical moment]," the uncle wrote on March 17, attempting to buck up his nephews.[36] And at least one shrewd observer and future interior minister, Léon Faucher, knew just how grave the French national financial situation really was. "Everyone is ruined in Paris. The banks are crashing one after another. . . . Rothschild alone is still standing, albeit bled white," Faucher reported.[37]

The façade remained, but not much else. A little of "the old family magic," as Amschel Rothschild put it, was very badly needed to stave off bankruptcy. The House of Rothschild had risen since the Napoleonic era, thanks to the combined, coordinated strength of the five Rothschild brothers, and James now desperately appealed again to London, the strongest of the five family banks. But when brother Nathan in England balked, back in Germany Amschel insisted on an immediate transfer of at least six million francs (more than seventy-seven million dollars), while privately advising James to close his doors permanently and return to a less tempest-tossed Frankfurt. The proud James stubbornly refused to admit to the family that his faith in France had been misplaced and his own judgment faulty. In any event, nephew Lionel duly crossed the channel with the necessary funds and James was narrowly saved, "by a thread," as he acknowledged.

But if the Paris house had fallen, or if James had simply given up and moved to Frankfurt, the entire teetering economy of France could very well have completely collapsed, leading to a long-term economic depression. One man symbolically stood between survival and ruin. For the first and only time in his life, James de Rothschild was shaken, though he gradually pulled himself together. "If only we had stood firm and not allowed ourselves to be intimidated [by the general panic] in the first place," he belatedly understood.[38]

France was not like other countries, and the fact was that times had changed; the social and economic stability based on the assumption of a powerful stable monarch, as found in London, for instance, just did not exist in Paris and never would. Even a Napoléon Bonaparte had been overthrown eventually, leaving the nation, indeed most of Western

Europe, destitute and in utter ruin. Brother James was the first to accept the necessity of adjusting to this new daily uncertainty. "We are going to have riots, property will lose value [and income will fall], but the situation will improve and so will prices. However it will never become completely normal again," he advised the family on May 1, 1848. "It is on that assumption and reality we must work from now on."[39]

James's cautious nephew, Nathaniel, disagreed, however, with all that was being done. "I think it downright madness to plunge up to one's neck in hot water just on the odd chance of making a little money," he confided, while publicly supporting James.[40] On the other hand, James de Rothschild had many years of experience that his occasionally critical nephew Nathaniel lacked, not to mention complete faith in his own long-term good judgment and ability to analyze, and combined with the redoubtable family determination, he was resolved to carry on. And thus the House of Rothschild prevailed, and remained in Paris, and the French economy survived. But as Rothschild himself had readily admitted at one weak moment, it had all been a closely run thing, with nephew Nathaniel still advising complete family withdrawal once and for all from France and her unstable political history.

As for the 250-million-franc state loan so desperately needed by the government, and guaranteed by a 25-million-franc deposit by Rothschild, that was in turn successfully renegotiated and all parties were saved, including the Banque de France.[41] Moreover, very serious threats by the republican government to nationalize his northern railways were dropped. But James had also personally provided an imploring Louis Philippe with a last-minute four-million-franc personal loan, which would never be repaid, and that was another lesson Rothschild learned the hard way.[42] From now on, political loyalty had to be calculated more carefully; after all, crowned heads of state were not family.

The public turbulence so dramatically anticipated by James de Rothschild—"we are going to have riots"—remained the real permanent wild card in French politics (and Rothschild thinking), the quantum mechanics problem they would have to factor into all future financial equations. Nephew Nathaniel Rothschild's anxiety continued to grow concerning this 1848 French revolution, "this political cholera," as he called it, "that has infested the world,"[43] and was now spreading across the Continent, forcing even brothers Salomon in Vienna and Karl in Naples to flee for their lives.

At Whitehall, the veteran British foreign secretary, Henry Lord Palmerston, who claimed France as "the pivot of my foreign policy," and particularly wary of this latest French revolutionary contagion, was now striving to cope with the full consequences of the fall of Louis Philippe and the founding of a second republic. If anything personally sympathetic to France, a country he had known since his youth and whose language he spoke fluently, Lord Palmerston had carefully to keep himself in check. While cautiously warning that "in the uncertain state of things in France, it would be imprudent . . . to consider ourselves secure from the necessity of having to defend ourselves [from the French]."

Nevertheless, the foreign secretary remained basically optimistic about maintaining peaceful relations between Britain and France,[44] especially after long conferences with the Lansdownes—father and son— and General Charles de Flahaut and his son, Auguste de Morny. "Before the summer is over," he wrote his brother William Temple one year later, "I should not be sorry if it [the changes in the French government] ended in Louis Napoléon being made Emperor."[45]

As usual, the prescient Harry Palmerston had anticipated events, in this case four years early. On the other hand, what even he could never have possibly foreseen was just how inextricably his own destiny as England's foreign secretary and then as first minister would be linked with this very Louis Napoléon as emperor of the French and his own unique brand of "political cholera."

14

PRESIDENT OF THE REPUBLIC
BONAPARTE

"He will never be content with being merely Emperor of the Republic."[1]
—LÉON FAUCHER

*"He lacks so many of the qualities usually to be found in a man of
merit—sound judgment, knowledge [of men and the country],
the ability to express himself, and political experience."*[2]
—CHARLES DE RÉMUSAT

With the fall of Louis Philippe's July monarchy, Louis Napoléon came to Paris on a flying visit to consult Vieillard and Persigny. In May, elections were held for a new assembly and on the fourth of June Louis Napoléon was elected in his absence as deputy from three different constituencies. In a panic convening on the tenth of June an emergency meeting of the Executive Commission, now ruling the provisional government, the ministers announced that irrespective of the election results, the law of 1832 forbidding Louis Napoléon, as a Bonaparte, from living in France remained in full force, thereby forbidding his taking his rightful seat in the Palais Bourbon. The Bonapartists, well stirred up by Persigny's public relations blitz, were caught up in fighting and bloodshed, and although the commission's order was rescinded, permitting the prince to remain, on the sixteenth of June he sent a message to the assembly that, rather than be the cause "of deplorable troubles," he was resigning. "I am ready to sacrifice everything for the happiness of France," he declared and promptly returned to England.[3] The deep differences dividing the country were not merely political, but also stemmed from traditional class differences. However, poverty was a major underlining factor for the vast majority of the French, little having changed since 1789.

Then in the last week of June, between the twenty-third and twenty-sixth, the situation exploded with violent clashes between the authorities and the more than 100,000 unemployed men who were forced into the streets of Paris after having been evicted from their state-subsidized work in the National Workshops, which the government was now closing down. Once again the barricades went up and shots were fired and General Cavaignac was called in with the army and national guards to put down the unrest. Batteries of artillery soon cleared the streets but at a terrible price: more than three thousand killed, hundreds summarily executed in the streets, and thousands imprisoned or deported.[4] Even today the exact number killed remains unknown. Louis Napoléon on the other side of the channel was one of the few politicians to escape any complicity with the bloodshed of "the June Days." As for the good General Cavaignac, he was rewarded by a grateful assembly with the task of maintaining order in Paris while suppressing political clubs and hostile newspapers.

Supplementary national elections were called for, on September 17–18, when Louis Napoléon was again returned as a deputy, elected this time by five different constituencies, including Corsica and Paris, and on September 24 he returned to France permanently, taking up his new quarters in the Hôtel du Rhin in the Place Vendôme.[5] Victor Hugo could not praise Louis Napoléon enough, along with thousands of other Bonapartists. The next day the prince duly took his place in the hemicycle of the National Assembly, where he later addressed his colleagues. "After thirty-two years of proscription and exile, I finally reclaim my country and all my rights as a French citizen."[6] On the fourth of November the newly launched Second Republic's Constitution—proclaiming freedom, equality, and fraternity—was based on the principles of "Family, Work, Property and Public Order." That same day the call went out for presidential elections.[7] The results announced on the twelfth of December took everyone by surprise, as Louis Napoléon Bonaparte was declared the winner of the new republic, with 5.5 million of the nearly 7.5 million votes cast, General Cavaignac coming in a poor second place with 1.5 million, and Lamartine with less than 18,000.[8]

"This is no mere election," the astonished publisher Émile de Girardin declared in *La Presse*, "it is a veritable National Acclamation!"[9] "A puzzle . . . a caprice . . . a [national] affliction," the *Journal des Débats* had called Louis Napoléon's earlier election to the assembly, and now it reiterated its disgust, while Thiers's *Réunion de la Rue de Poitiers* saw that France had "solemnly demonstrated her great need for peace and for the return of law and order."[10] In England a shocked *Morning Advertiser* described the outcome as "the height of folly!" while *The Times* reported that shares had already shot up 8 percent, and that Paris had returned "to a state of long unaccustomed joy."[11] As for Louis Napoléon's equally bewildered arch political detractor, Charles de Rémusat, he tried to understand this electoral phenomenon as best he could. "He who in foisting his imagination up the affairs of the world and consequently succeeds in actually producing or altering these events as a result of his fantasy, possesses I don't quite know what special gift of extraordinary persistence, that immediately separates him from the masses and raises him to a place among our most famous historical figures." Louis Napoléon has, he declared "virtually altered the course of French history."[12]

P arisians awoke on Thursday, December 20, 1848, to find the Champs-Élysées lined with cavalry and infantry units, and troops on the other side of the Place de la Concorde as well, while beyond the gardens, the imposing iron gates of the Tuileries were closed. Across the Seine the Palais Bourbon, too, was well secured by the military, who were taking no chances, not this time. Unlike the angry outbursts by the thousands of members of radical political clubs and the National Workshops who had invaded this legislative palace back on May 15, 1848, just eight months earlier, and nearly succeeded in an attempt to close down the government, today security was extremely tight.

On this wintry inaugural afternoon, there were no violent crowds anywhere in sight. Like the Bourse, the Stock Exchange, the atmosphere in the Assembly itself was subdued, with little business being transacted, everyone still stunned by the outcome of the national presidential elections.

Anxious or just curious, everyone was now awaiting the principal event of the day, the swearing-in ceremony of Charles-Louis Napoléon Bonaparte as the nation's first president of this newly launched Second Republic. No one had been prepared for the results, least of all the prince. His successful nomination for the presidency and the magnitude of his electoral victory had left even the coolest calculating politicians staggered and the political pundits for once stymied and silent.

President-elect Bonaparte entered the hemicycle of the Bourbon Palace almost unnoticed. The president of the Constituent Assembly, Armand Marrast, was standing at the tribune, not far from the outgoing prime minister, Cavaignac, to be replaced today by Louis Napoléon's new premier, Odilon Barrot, and just concluding the reading of some minor reports at four thirty p.m. as Louis Napoléon made his way to his assigned seat. Dressed impeccably in white tie and black evening wear, with the rosette as deputy in his lapel, and the Grand Cross of the Legion of Honor on his breast, he bowed to those greeting him just as "the servants, attired as footmen" were turning up the gas lamps in the dim wintry light. Not far away, but unseen by the prince, his half brother, Auguste de Morny, watched most attentively.

When they finally noticed him seated among the other deputies, there was a growing murmur as they pointed to the prince, the noise becoming so great that Monsieur Marrast was obliged to strike his gavel repeatedly as he called out "Silence!" as the reporter representing *La Presse* duly jotted down notes for his article. "It's him! shhhh! He had entered incognito, without trumpets blaring and drums rolling drums," the reporter noted. He displayed no emotion, "his face was kindly and he carried himself in a dignified manner, but physically bore no resemblance whatsoever to the emperor," the journalist remarked, when Louis Napoléon was called up to the tribune to be sworn in as the first president of this Second Republic.

"All eyes were on him, and very few had a friendly expression."[13]

Bonaparte, in his first official act, walked slowly over to the tribute to address the Constituent Assembly. "A slight, slow dignified figure," he stood before Armand Marrast, who read the oath: "In the presence of God, and before the French people as represented by the National Assembly, I swear to remain faithful to the Democratic Republic, one and indivisible, and to fulfill all the duties imposed upon me by the Constitution."

And Louis Napoléon replied, "I do so swear." A profound silence followed. Now alone at the tribune facing the audience in the vast amphitheater, he bowed slightly and, taking a piece of paper from his pocket, began to read slowly in his low monotone voice, with a German accent.

"Citizen Representatives. To the electorate of the nation, to whom I have just sworn this oath, and who command my future conduct and direct my duties.

"I shall regard as enemies to the country all who may endeavor by illegal means to change the form of government," he continued in this awkwardly prepared speech.

"Like you, I desire to establish society on a true foundation. . . . This Government [his own] will be neither utopian nor reactionary," he assured the deputies. "We will make the well-being of the country our top priority and we hope that with God's blessing, even if we do not accomplish everything we set out to do, at least we shall have endeavored our best to do so." Following this brief acceptance speech the assembly rose to their feet, shouting, "Long Live the Republic!" Leaving the tribune, Louis Napoléon, who had been sitting on the dais with his prime minister designate, Odilon Barrot, went over to shake hands with a grim, reluctant Cavaignac.

Auguste de Morny, though present, apparently had not left a record of the day's events, possibly because, like most attendees, he could not even hear the speech clearly in this vast chamber filled to capacity with many hundreds of people. However, Morny had earlier heard his brother's maiden speech before the Assembly back in October. "He was shy and his voice weak, and the impression he gave, as to his competence— was most unfavorable, but as a future president of the country, he's rather promising. Barring unforeseen circumstances, then, it seems obvious to me that he will indeed be elected president of the Republic."[14]

"Prince, do not start making innovations here. Practice moderation and order," Adolphe Thiers gratuitously advised. "Accept the support of the moderate political party [i.e., Thiers's], which in turn will support your administration."[15] Little did Thiers understand this sphinx and what bombshells the fastidiously courteous, soft-spoken incumbent prince-president had in store for France. But now escorted by three questors, Louis Napoléon drove the short distance across the Seine from the National Assembly to install himself in the Élysées Palace, where he was to be responsible for directing the 400,000 state officials and employees, while not forgetting the largest standing army in Western Europe, nearly half a million strong.[16] In five days' time the bells of Notre Dame Cathedral would be ringing in Christmas across a weary history-battered French capital, and the calmest one in many a year.

15

THE ÉLYSÉE

"One finds in the human heart a depraved taste for equality,
that . . . reduces men to preferring equality in servitude
to inequality in freedom."[1]
—ALEXIS DE TOCQUEVILLE, *DEMOCRACY IN AMERICA*

"The more I see of the representatives of the people,
the more I love my dogs."[2]
—FORMER FRENCH FOREIGN MINISTER
ALPHONSE DE LAMARTINE

I do not know what to tell you about the president," Auguste de Morny wrote his sister, Emily, Lady Shelburne, in London. "Some say that he is a mediocrity, others that he is weak or stubborn, still others that he is a good, loyal chap. What do I believe? He certainly made mistakes at the beginning of his career. He could easily have been classified as a moderate. He neither knows the important people in Paris, nor is familiar with the French political scene. The legitimists [royalists] are flocking to him. What do they have in mind, I simply do not know. As for me, I have not yet met him, though he might at least have indicated an interest in having the pleasure of making my acquaintance."[3]

Moving into the Élysée Palace on the twentieth of December 1848, President of the Republic Bonaparte had everything to do. This eighteenth-century residence, formerly the home of Madame Pompadour and later bought by Napoléon I in 1808, today saw another Bonaparte moving in. Having no real organized political party in place behind him, everything was thrown together rapidly on an ad hoc basis. Literally everyone had to be appointed and everything created. Louis Napoléon began with the fifty-seven-year-old Jean François Mocquard, who was placed in complete charge of the Élysée and its administration.

Mocquard, a native of Bordeaux, was the scion of, and heir to, a highly successful colonial shipping company trading with the Caribbean. A dynamic leader and brilliant scholar, Mocquard had completed his legal studies in Paris and had then served in a diplomatic post under Napoléon I. With the fall of the First Empire, he practiced law in Paris as a barrister, and finally served as a deputy prefect under Louis Philippe until 1839. He met ex-queen Hortense back in 1817, who appointed him her financial advisor, and as a regular visitor to Arenenberg he had known Louis Napoléon as a schoolboy. In 1840 Mocquard joined the prince then in exile in London. Following the Boulogne fiasco, Mocquard published the Bonapartist newspaper *Commerce* in Paris and visited the convicted Louis Napoléon in Ham every month. Thus, now at the end of December 1848, it was a great relief for President Bonaparte to have this capable, well-tried, trusted, and loyal gentleman in charge of the Élysée Palace, and he was later to reward him with a life senatorship and the Legion of Honor.

The loyal balding Henri Conneau now finally returned to medicine after his years in Ham. Louis Napoléon would later have him organize and direct the imperial medical service. Gilbert Persigny at long last found himself in his first official post, responsible for relations between the Élysée and the nation's elected representatives at the National Assembly. In addition he was responsible for coordinating the activities of Bonapartist political clubs and public relations, including the French press. Louis Napoléon's first cousin, Felix Baciocchi, a native of Corsica and son of Elise Bonaparte Baciocchi, was charged with organizing state dinners, balls, and Louis Napoléon's discreet nightly entertainment. Colonel Claude Nicolas Vaudrey, who had been with the prince at Strasbourg and had spent years in prison for his role there, was shortly to be rewarded with a prefecture and security for the rest of his life. In brief, Louis Napoléon could count on the loyalty and devotion of his Élysée staff.

Colonel Émile Fleury was also attached to the palace staff, briefly working for Persigny. Having squandered his family's inheritance in his twenties, he had joined the army, serving under King Louis Philippe as a cavalry officer commanding Spahis, an Algerian unit, until 1848. Fleury had first met Persigny and Louis Napoléon while in exile in London when he attached himself to the Bonaparte cause. Although the newcomer here, he would command a brigade during the coup d'état on December 2, 1851, and would rise to the rank of major general. Later serving as Napoleon III's Grand Écuyer at the Tuileries, he was named Grand Officer of the Legion of Honor. This was a soldier Louis Napoléon could absolutely count on in a crisis.

If Uncle Jérôme Bonaparte had proven generally less dependable, and inevitably in debt, and despite some acts of blatant disloyalty, nevertheless Louis Napoléon was to play the respectful nephew by heaping honors and considerable wealth on him. In the final analysis, Uncle Jérôme was Emperor Napoléon's brother, and that he would never forget. Three days after being sworn in as president of the Republic, Louis Napoléon appointed Jérôme Bonaparte governor of the Invalides, with a handsome salary and splendid adjoining apartments. In spite of Jérôme's lamentable military record, in January 1850 his nephew would promote him to marshal of France, and then president of the new Senate, each position accompanied by a handsome state salary. Jérôme Bonaparte, a notorious deceiver, reprobate, and backbiter, would finally have to stop criticizing his nephew, at least in public.

On the other hand, Jérôme's only daughter, Mathilde, whose marriage plans to Louis Napoléon had been aborted in 1836, proved a surprisingly stable, loyal supporter of her older cousin and was now to serve as his official hostess at Élysée until the time of his marriage to Eugénie. At the age of twenty-nine and in her prime, the lovely brunette also held regular receptions for him at her mansion at 10 rue de Courcelles, with her lover, Alfred, Count de Nieuwerkerke. Her father, Jérôme Bonaparte, remained excluded from her home and her life.

• • •

The heady, ebullient atmosphere in the Élysée following the electoral landslide would have convinced any mortal man of his great
power and prestige in a land that had so dramatically swept him into
office. In reality, the president's position was altogether different. For
the first and perhaps only time in modern French history, a head of state
had arrived without any sort of coherent functioning party, institution,
or group behind him. "I am absolutely isolated," the prince frankly admitted to his sympathetic friend in London, Lord Malmesbury. "Those
supporting me and my views still do not know me, nor in fact do I even
know who they are, who is with me . . . I am completely alone."[4] How
could he be expected to make reliable appointments? His acceptance
of General Cavaignac's recommendation of Major General Nicolas
Changarnier as the new military governor of Paris and commander of
the national guard was not only a case in point, it was to prove the key
case in point.

Changarnier was not only a mistake, he was an affliction, according
to the author and traveler Maxime Du Camp, who had met him years
before in Algeria. In that colony he had demonstrated "tenacity" and
"decision" on the battlefield. But socially, "I have never met such a coarse
man." Short, his face pockmarked, wearing a soiled wig, he was "precious in his gestures, and pretentious in his bearing." But his language
was so utterly filthy as to upset even his own ADCs (aides-de-camp) and
fellow ordnance officers. Moreover, Du Camp found him "inconsider-
ate of others and lacking in moderation." There was only one point of
view, his. He was "disparaging of everyone including his senior officers
(behind their back)." As for Changarnier the politician, he was "a poor
specimen," lower even than Cavaignac or Lamoricière, and his speeches
were "as pompous as they were vacuous."[5] Alexis de Tocqueville, who
had also met that general when touring Algeria, found him to be
"crude" and "brutal." Even Gilbert Persigny, who at first thought he
could work with Changarnier, soon changed his mind.

Auguste de Morny, who had served under fire with Changarnier in
Algeria, was even more concerned about Changarnier's appointment as

military governor of Paris, as that general quickly revealed his true colors, speaking openly of the necessity of removing President Bonaparte, and of "locking him up in [the fortress of] Vincennes."

O f far more critical importance to the president now and to the future development of the Second Empire, however, was the one individual in Paris Louis Napoléon had long dreaded meeting. Auguste de Morny did indeed eventually receive an inevitable, if discreet, invitation to meet his half brother privately. Arriving at the Élysée unobserved through a side entrance as requested at ten o'clock on the evening of the twenty-third of January, 1849, Morny was closeted alone in the presidential apartments with Louis Napoléon, where they discussed the whole gamut of questions concerning the current situation in France. "My initial feeling was that we did not like each other," Morny recollected. "Nevertheless such a relationship could prove mutually beneficial and I felt obliged to work with him."[6] He later slipped out of the palace at two o'clock in the morning on the twenty-fourth. The two half brothers had crossed a threshold that was to change the entire course of modern French history. There may never have been any deep affection between them, but both men were realists and understood the necessity of working together.

"Were it left to me I would never have returned there [to the Élysée]," Morny later wrote. "I found him [his brother] imbued with prejudices, false conceptions of things, and smugly right in all matters," the product of "a type of sentimental liberalism." His views and opinions were hardly the stuff of measures with which to execute the very real practical business of government. As for the men with whom President Bonaparte now surrounded himself, Morny dismissed most of them as "a pack of dunderheads [Persigny in particular] . . . hardly qualified to advise the prince on the direction of his government to follow." On the other hand, he pointed out, "I had always considered myself a Bonapartist, and my conservative views were well known to all . . ." And therefore in spite of everything, in the long run "it was more natural and convenient for him and me to get on together."[7]

After hearing his brother speak in the assembly back in October, and assessing this first meeting now, Morny—in the view of the shrewd Prosper Mérimée, a surprisingly most astute politician—the temptation to be well out of it was great. Beyond just basic tactical ability, and unlike most generals, Morny was a master strategist. The country was at its most important crossroads since July of 1830. Morny found himself in a curious, certainly unique, position. Taking advantage of Louis Napoléon, as a "host" administrator, Morny could provide the input required to develop and guide the government in the right direction. Indeed in some respects Louis Napoléon was to prove the ideal "host emperor"; much as the Arab Caliphates of the Umayyads and Abbasids had proven "host civilizations," importing the culture, education, science, and art gleaned from scholars of the outside world.

"It is quite impossible for me to drop him now, especially after the position I have already taken at his side, and the confidence that I seem to have inspired in the prince," Morny confided to his father's Scottish wife a few months later. "I see him every day, more often than not twice daily. He freely discusses everything with me. In all decency can I abandon him at this critical time?"[8] Without his brother's knowledge of the men and the background to the current events, Louis Napoléon was lost, indeed was already drowning. Morny for his part needed a brother whom he could invisibly guide to return France to stability and to provide the legislation and the officials required to render a stable, prosperous state. Without this, neither France nor Louis Napoléon could survive and prosper. They would be a team of necessity.

Adolphe Thiers, as the head of the Law and Order Party's Rue de Poitiers Committee (legitimist and Orleanist), with its headquarters in the seventh arrondissement near the École Militaire and the Academy of Medicine, was Louis Napoléon's first choice as prime minister. Thiers, although having voted for him for president of the Republic, admitted that in fact Bonaparte was hardly his favorite candidate, he being "the lesser of two evils." In private he referred to the prince as "this cretan."[9]

Louis Napoléon then turned to the well-known lawyer and orator, also a leader of the Rue de Poitiers Committee, the difficult Odilon

Barrot (brother of Ferdinand Barrot, one of the lawyers who had defended him and his colleagues following the failed Boulogne coup). Although Barrot had been instrumental in bringing down Louis Philippe, this prime minister–cum–justice minister did not prove to be the best choice for Napoléon III, and their relationship would not be an easy one. As for Foreign Affairs, President Bonaparte selected Edouard Drouyn de Lhuys and the dogmatic editor of the *Courrier Français*, Léon Faucher, for the Interior portfolio.

Initially President Bonaparte and the Assembly appeared to be working in harmony, at least on Italian affairs, and the delicate question of Rome in particular. In 1830 the French government had dispatched troops to protect the pope and Rome from Austrian and republican control. In December 1848, the scene was even more complex and violent, with Giuseppe Mazzini's nationalist troops battling the Vatican's forces. On February 9, 1849, a victorious Mazzini proclaimed his new Roman Republic, forcing Pius IX to flee. To complicate matters, the Austrian rulers of northern Italy were marching troops down to oust Mazzini and his Roman Republic, while restoring papal authority. Responding to the pope's appeal, the Second French Republic under Louis Napoléon dispatched its first three brigades in April 1849, some twelve thousand men commanded by General Nicolas Oudinot. Their objective: to cleanse Rome of Mazzini's patriots and to restore Pius IX to his rightful place.[10]

Emerging from the National Assembly on December 20, 1848, as the Second Republic's first (and only) president, Louis Napoléon had found himself caught up in the midst of this Roman affair, and anything "Italian" was always of special interest to him. Unlike his uncle, Emperor Napoléon, Louis Napoléon was a lifelong practicing Catholic and supporter of the papacy, but only in its role as a temporal authority. As seen earlier, in his youth he and his brother had fought with the Carbonari against the Austrian-backed papal forces in Rome in 1830–1831. With Oudinot's troops meeting stiff resistance by the end of April 1849, Louis Napoléon ordered in reinforcements. "We must bring in the heavy artillery and put an end to this unfortunate Roman business," he confided to Narcisse Vieillard. "I deplore it, but I have no choice."[11] General

Oudinot duly crushed Mazzini's Roman Republic and restored Pius IX to the Vatican on July 13, 1849.

Louis Napoléon's first presidential act, supporting the expedition to Rome, proved popular both with the assembly and the French people, but not with his own family. The ever-unpredictable son of Jérôme Bonaparte, Prince [Napoléon] Jérôme, or "Plon-Plon," who had just taken up his post as ambassador to Madrid in April 1849, on learning of the French expedition to Rome, rushed back to Paris barely one week after arriving in Madrid. Storming into the Élysée where the president was entertaining Mathilde and Auguste de Morny, Plon-Plon accused a bewildered Louis Napoléon of having made a terrible error in authorizing the attack against Rome to save the pope. It was only thanks to his sister Mathilde's and Morny's intervention that the hysterical prince was calmed down and finally left. It was a frightening experience.[12]

The spokesman of the "red faction" in the National Assembly, Alexandre Ledru-Rollin, a forty-two-year-old hothead as violent and mentally unstable as Plon-Plon, declared on June 11 that the president of the Republic should be arraigned for having violated the Constitution. Speaking from the tribune, he threatened "red riots" in the streets of Paris and "to take up arms" against the government. Blood must flow. For once Louis Napoléon acted quickly, ordering General Changarnier to secure the streets of the city with his troops. Even as these orders were being issued, a President Bonaparte still largely unknown to the French people warned Ledru-Rollin's followers: "Your agitation causes mistrust and problems in the country. It must cease! Now it's the turn for the troublemakers to start worrying!" On Morny's advice thirty-one leftist deputies were arrested, and the dreaded riots expected on the thirteenth of June fizzled.[13] Ledru-Rollins fled the country.

From the elaborately courteous President Bonaparte there emerged a bold, resourceful commander, if one reinforced by the presence of his half brother, quite astonishing his opponents. Throughout his various writings about Emperor Napoléon and the new France, Louis Napoléon had repeatedly spoken of the necessity for "Authority" in order to maintain "a productive and free country," and now he was that executive Authority—or almost.

When his cousin, General Edgar Ney, serving with the French Expeditionary Force at Rome, also criticized his support of the pope, Louis Napoléon wrote to him, calmly pointing out the situation. "The French Republic did not send an army to Rome in order to stifle Italian liberty, but quite the contrary, to preserve it against its own excesses, and to give it a solid foundation by restoring the pontifical throne." Summing up the situation, Louis Napoléon declared, "I represent the re-establishment of the Pope's temporal power: a general amnesty, the establishment of the new administration, the Code Napoléon, and liberal government." Not only did the pope fail to thank President Bonaparte for restoring him to the Vatican, but he carried out a series of brutal reprisals against the republicans and the old Carbonari. For once outraged, Louis Napoléon publicly denounced Pius IX's "tyranny," "brutality," and "feudalistic repression."[14] This was just the beginning of a long "war" between Paris and Rome.

Louis Napoléon's fascination with Italy and her welfare was to be a veritable obsession with him over the years to come. But as a result of this Roman expedition, Count Falloux, a strong supporter of Pius IX, immediately resigned in protest as Bonaparte's minister of culture and religion. As for Pius IX, he refused to halt his retaliation against his republican opponents, while nevertheless admitting the necessity of the presence of French troops to maintain order and to prevent Austrian forces from seizing the city. With the exception of one brief period, French troops were in fact destined to occupy Rome continuously over the next two decades until the fall of Napoléon III in 1870.

Meanwhile, Louis Napoléon had not forgotten the celebrated "Miss Howard," her son, and his own two children by the laundress of Ham, all of whom he now installed in a house in the Rue du Cirque, just across from the Élysée Palace. Louis Napoléon was a daily visitor, and made no effort to conceal this situation. He was often seen in the afternoon strolling with them in the park grounds of the Élysée, or driving along the Champs-Élysées in the calèche bearing the Bonaparte arms. Harriet frequently attended his weekly Monday receptions at the presidential palace, where she would meet members of his inner circle, including cousin Mathilde, though the two ladies never got on at all well. As for the prince and Harriet Howard, they were genuinely fond of each other, and the president appeared to dote on his little family. But when it came to constant sentiment and loyalty, there was to be only one woman to whom Louis Napoléon could ever be blindly devoted, and she lay buried forever in Rueil. No woman could compete with a ghost.

16

COUNTDOWN TO EMPIRE

"I have done so little as yet for my country . . ."[1]
—PRESIDENT BONAPARTE, AMIENS, JULY 7, 1849

"There is no excuse for coups d'état."[2]
—PRESIDENT BONAPARTE, TOURS, 1849

Life in Paris tends to slow to a more languid pace after the National Assembly breaks up for its annual parliamentary recess in July, but President Bonaparte had special plans for the summer of 1849, to travel across the country to become acquainted with the land, its cities, and in particular its people. Beginning at Chartres, he celebrated the opening of the new railway linking it with the capital. The president went on to Amiens on the sixth of July to present the National Guard of the Somme with their new colors. Here where the 1803–1805 Anglo-French Truce, "the Peace of Amiens," had been concluded prior to the resumption of hostilities beginning in October 1805 with the Trafalgar campaign and the appearance of the newly created Grand Army at Austerlitz, the prince-president was warmly received.

"Although I have done so little as yet for my country," he addressed the mayor in top hat and tricolor sash, the guard in their resplendent uniforms, and the people of this city, before the Hôtel de Ville where that truce had been signed, "I am at once proud and embarrassed by this warm ovation which I attribute to my name rather than to myself. . . . Today you desire not just peace—but a glorious peace—one fertile in real benefits at home and in influence abroad." Throughout these initial early years in France, time and again Louis Napoléon was to stress that this latest Bonaparte was a man of peace, whose aim was to bring prosperity to the nation, not war.[3]

With his companion Henri Conneau at his side, the party drove southeast down to Ham where on the twenty-first of July he was warmly received at a banquet prepared by the villagers. "In this place where I suffered, I propose to you a toast in honor of the men who have resolved . . . to respect the institutions of their country." Touring the prison he and Conneau found in his former "cell" another state prisoner, the Algerian leader Bu Maza, who had been captured during the recent fighting "to pacify" the colony of Algeria. This was the first Algerian Louis Napoléon had ever met, and it would spark an awareness of that colony that would soon develop into a veritable lifelong passion. If at Chartres the prince-president had celebrated the progress of technology and the arrival of the railways, at Ham he fêted a peace-loving, magnanimous republic, and on a whim ordered the astonished governor of the prison to free the former "rebel"Algerian.[4]

This was just the beginning of a series of tours across the country over the next three years, a deliberate long-term campaign strategy to introduce himself to the people. On another occasion he traveled to Rouen, the capital of Upper Normandy, near the mouth of the Seine, where he spoke of trade, commerce, and prosperity. Then from Nantes the presidential party proceeded to Saumur and up the Loire to Angers.[5] In the heart of the Loire Valley, they made a major stopover at the Bourbon stronghold of Tours with its splendid *hôtels particuliers*, ancient university, and cathedral. "I cannot do for you all that the Emperor did," he told the receptive Tourangeaux. "I have neither his genius nor his power, but you applaud today because I represent that policy of moderation and conciliation inaugurated by the [Second] Republic." Comparing France to a mighty ship that had been battered over the years by terrible storms and had finally dropped anchor in a sheltered roadstead, he continued, "therefore it is now up to us to rebuild that ship enabling her to resume her historic journey. Trust then to the future, and forget the coups d'état and insurrections of the past. *There is no longer any excuse for coups d'état. . . .* [Author's italics] Instead put your faith in the National Assembly and your own First Magistrate [the president] . . . and above all rely on the protection of the Supreme Being who looks over France."[6]

If Louis Napoléon returned to Paris satisfied with the results of the summer's work, a surprised Auguste de Morny was even more so. "The president's journey could not have been more successful," he informed his father in Scotland, "his language and bearing were well measured and admired by everyone." Rare praise indeed coming from his oft critical half brother. Morny was especially impressed by his ability to bring up "untouchable subjects," the genuine anxieties of the people, their fears of insurrections, of 18 Brumaires, of coups d'état, associated with the name of Bonaparte, and for him to speak of them so openly, as probably no other politician could have managed so convincingly. Louis Napoléon was beginning to learn his new profession.[7]

The following year he would continue with his "whistle-stop" campaigning, literally by train when possible, though the railways were still very limited, usually short runs of ten to twenty miles. The crowds were not always warm or even reasonably civilized, and he had to get accustomed to "the hustings," to this reality. If a visit to the "Red City," Lyon, went well—not so at Besançon. Here President Bonaparte was physically jostled by crowds of angry, violent men, so that he had to be rescued by Colonels Vaudrey and Beville and the police. The Alsatian capital of Strasbourg, on the other hand, was in contrast peaceful if wary. In the end the French people were largely touched and won over by Louis Napoléon's unpretentious simplicity and sincerity, and his "ambition of being known as an honorable man."[8]

R eturning to Paris always inevitably meant bracing himself for new problems, and the autumn of 1849 was no exception. From the outset, the new military governor of the French capital, the aggressively politically ambitious General Nicolas Changarnier, was testing his strength. Taking Persigny aside, the general insisted, "Let the prince put an end to these constitutional charades and seize complete dictatorial powers of the country!" On receiving this message, Louis Napoléon responded with an adamant, "No!"[9]

That summer of 1849, while Louis Napoléon was politicking in the countryside, Auguste de Morny was in England, ostensibly to visit his sister, Emily, Lady Shelburne, and to sell another large shipment of paintings on whose profits he depended year after year. More important, he met with Emily's father-in-law, Lord Lansdowne, and then discreetly with Prime Minister Lord John Russell's foreign secretary, Henry Temple, Viscount Palmerston, at Carlton Gardens. His purpose was to sound them out as to their reaction should Louis Napoléon decide "to expand his powers."

On returning to Paris on the twenty-fifth of October, Morny proceeded directly to the Place Beavau (as he usually referred to the Élysée, that is, the small square opposite the entrance to the Élysée) to confer with his half brother. Neither 10 Downing Street nor Whitehall (the foreign office) would interfere, should Louis Napoléon carry out a coups d'état, Morny assured him. To be sure, the well-entrenched British ambassador, the fifty-four-year-old Constantine Phipps, the Marquess of Normanby—fully supported by Queen Victoria and Prime Minister Lord John Russell—as a friend of Louis Philippe, would of course still object. But professionally the ambassador was still obliged to take his instructions from the highly influential Foreign Secretary Palmerston and would follow orders, for the moment.

Lord Palmerston had in fact declared himself for Louis Napoléon even as early as 1848. "Before the summer is over. . . . I should not be sorry if it [the changes in the French government] ended in Louis Napoléon being made Emperor," he confided to his brother William Temple, "& thus [also] ridding us of both brands of the Bourbons [represented by the Comte de Chambord and the Comte de Paris]."[10] In the long run without British support of neutrality, any coup d'état would have encountered grave long-term difficulties.

More eager than his brother to follow through on the possibilities of a coup at this time, Morny, accompanied by his father, Count de Flahaut, went to see Adolphe Thiers four days after his return to France. Would Thiers, with his influential Poitiers Street Committee behind him, be willing to participate in such a coup? "The little man," as Flahaut referred to him, never known for the refinements of civilization, including elementary courtesy, arrogantly showed them to the door. Thiers would only be interested in such a coup if Thiers were made president. Everything had changed. There was no longer any place for Louis Napoléon in Thiers's France.[11]

Stymied by his inability to form a "neutral" coalition, upset with the account Morny gave him of their brusque encounter with Thiers, but emboldened by the knowledge of Palmerston's support, Louis Napoléon summoned his cabinet for an emergency meeting on the thirtieth of October. "Present circumstances leave me no choice but to place myself in a position 'to be able to dominate,' to control the country while remaining above all parties," he informed his ministers. "France is unsettled because the country lacks any sense of direction. She seeks a steady hand at the helm to direct the affairs of state," and the presidential elections of December 10, 1848, have "duly elected me as their choice to lead the country," he submitted. He then asked for their resignations.[12]

The next day, October 31, 1849, President Bonaparte addressed a special session of the National Assembly: "Time and again for nearly a year I have given proof of my self-abnegation to avoid any misunderstanding as to my motives. I have allowed men of the most opposing views to take portfolios in my cabinet, but with nothing to show for the effort. . . . I was blamed for my own weakness. . . . But there's an end to that now! Let us therefore re-establish the government's authority without reducing our fundamental rights. Let us finally calm men's fears by resolutely ridding ourselves of the [political] evil-doers. . . . Only then will we be in a position to save the country."[13]

For the first time Auguste de Morny was now in a position to help advise on the formation of a government, beginning with the selection of his trusted friend, neighbor, and fellow deputy from Auvergne, Eugène Rouher, as prime minister and minister of justice. The highly respected jurist Alexis de Tocqueville (whose works and ideas greatly impressed Bonaparte) reluctantly agreed to accept the foreign ministry while, more importantly, Achille Fould would now take the finance ministry, General Alphonse d'Hautpoul the war office, and Ferdinand Barrot would take over the critical portfolio as minister of the interior, although his brother Odilon was already beginning to abandon the Bonapartes.[14]

Finally, Alfred Pierre, Count de Falloux du Coudray, accepted the curious ministry of public instruction and religion.

T he dapper, balding, thirty-seven-year-old Alfred Pierre, Count de Falloux du Coudray, was a royalist and devout Catholic. Despite biographies he was to write of Pope Pius V and the Bishop d'Orléans, he was later to prove a strong opponent of the ultramontane Catholic extremists led by the abrasive, ever dogmatic Louis Veuillot.[15] Nominated to this ministerial post in December 1849, he was to resign ten months later over Louis Napoléon's support of the occupation of Rome, just as he was later to oppose the creation of the Second Empire. Were it not for the law he as a deputy had proposed, and which was passed on March 15, 1850, his name no doubt would have been quickly forgotten. What surprised so many, however, was the support given to this pro-Catholic education legislation by the nephew of the excommunicated Emperor Napoléon, who had sacked the Vatican, and kidnapped and imprisoned Pius VII.

"The Falloux Law," as it is still referred to, basically ended the monopoly of public, secular, state-run education—from the university level down to the village primary schools that had produced "those awful little Reds," as Falloux referred to them. This fitted in nicely with that minister's celebrated formula for running the universe: "God in education. The Pope as head of the Church. The Church as the leader of civilization."[16] Louis Napoléon supported it because it gained the Catholic vote, while reintroducing a certain order in society, and a basic set of those moral values that had been guillotined along with Louis XVI during the Revolution of 1789. And as Morny's father appreciated, "The president seems resolved on undertaking any measures required to re-establish Order [in France]."[17]

The growing opposition by Thiers to Bonaparte remaining in office, under any guise, was building in the assembly, which was now bent on ousting him as head of the French government. The introduction and swift passage of the "Electoral Law" at the end of May 1850 was a jolt not even he could ignore, reducing the eligible electorate by 2,900,000.

With the stroke of a pen President Bonaparte had lost the electoral base that had put him in office.

Once again, as in the case of the Falloux Law, Louis Napoléon astonished even his closest friends by voting for the passage of this bill. Appalled, Morny argued with him, and Hortense Cornu sharply criticized this move. "You simply don't understand a thing. One day this will encourage the Assembly to overstep themselves. . . . and when they do, I shall strike," he argued. A coup executed under those circumstances would then be welcomed by the public.[18]

Auguste de Morny later claimed that he had been right in opposing the Electoral Law, which, thanks to the newly reformed Assembly, permitted General Nicolas Changarnier to come out in the open now and, almost successfully, overthrow President Bonaparte. Before resuming his electioneering that summer, Louis Napoléon signed a special decree transferring the prefect of the Var, one Georges Haussmann, to the prefecture of the anti-Bonaparte Yonne, and then again to Bordeaux and the royalist stronghold of the Gironde, a move with far-reaching consequences.

While touring the country that summer, Bonaparte received dramatic news. His old bête noire, seventy-six-year-old King Louis Philippe, had died at Claremont, his estate in Surrey, on August 26, 1850. Although Foreign Secretary Palmerston was overjoyed by the news— this death "delivers me from my most artful and inveterate enemy"— Louis Napoléon and Morny saw it in quite a different light.[19]

As head of his family, an ailing elderly Louis Philippe had been no immediate threat and could never head a coup or personally reoccupy the French throne, but with him gone the younger generation was now free to act with vigor. Henri d'Artois, better known as the Comte de Chambord,[20] was the immediate Bourbon heir to the throne of France, in good health and only thirty-one years old, but with no male heirs to succeed him. Exiled permanently at his Austrian castle of Frohsdorf, and completely cut off from France, apart from a few die-hard royalist followers in the Assembly, Chambord had no real military or political

support. Next in the Orléans line of succession was the late Duke of Orléans's thirteen-year-old son—and grandson of Louis Philippe—
Philippe d'Orléans, the Comte de Paris. His three uncles—the Prince
de Joinville and the Dukes de Nemours and d'Aumale—were vying
with the Comte de Chambord to be head of state. Like Chambord, however, they too expected no support within France. Later they would
discuss supporting Chambord, on condition that he name them his
legal successors.

Adolphe Thiers, of course, was still actively promoting himself, preparatory to replacing Louis Napoléon as president of the Republic, either
in coordination with the Orléans, or on his own behalf. Either way
he, too, would need the army, and his co-conspirator, General Changarnier. The pot was boiling, and as the president's two-year term of office
would terminate in May 1852, the pressure to act was building up.

Both brothers, Louis Napoléon and Morny, felt this new sudden surge
of tension, as they faced the one very real threat, a combined Thiers-
Changarnier political ticket. General Bonaparte had been able to overthrow the government (the Directory) in November 1799 thanks to his
command of several thousand troops. Changarnier, as combined military governor of Paris and commander of the national guard, was now
even more powerful, with these 80,000 men under his orders. There was
only one solution, and Morny urgently sought the immediate removal
of Changarnier from both commands.

Changarnier, with his booming voice and commanding manner,
openly ridiculed and mocked the president of the Republic—that
"melancholy parrot"—behind his back. Marshal Victor de Castellane
complained before the assembly that the general was "freely letting his
new power go to his head," and finding "his bad comments about the
president all the more unfortunate for having been made in public" and
even boasted of his intention of replacing the president at the next elections. Still Louis Napoléon remained silent, but not Morny, knowing
what it meant not to face down an insulting soldier. Inaction was "the
greatest possible mistake you could make," Auguste warned. "Either

you dismiss General Changarnier, or you will be reduced to a mere figurehead." Still Louis Napoléon's only response was the dismissal of his latest cabinet, but not Changarnier.[21]

At long last, after many weeks of dithering, on January 9, 1851, President Bonaparte duly signed the decree stripping the bumptious Major General Nicolas Changarnier of all military commands. Never again would the president make the mistake of combining the commands of the military division of Paris and that of the national guards, hereafter to remain two separate posts.

Although now removed from his army post, Changarnier still retained the full support of Adolphe Thiers. The Legislative Assembly followed Thiers's lead in seeking to avenge the dismissal of their man Changarnier, and in the summer of 1851 retaliated by refusing to increase the president's civil list that funded the annual pensions for the entire Bonaparte clan. More important, they opposed Louis Napoléon's attempt to extend his term of office through a modification of the Constitution. When on July 6, 1851, Bonaparte asked his brother what the chances were of ever changing the Constitution, Auguste replied with a blunt: "In my opinion none whatsoever." And on July 19 the legislators formally rejected the president's attempted revision. The countdown to his inevitable coup had begun, almost *malgré lui*.[22]

Louis Napoléon convened a very select secret war council at St. Cloud on the twentieth of August of 1851. There Morny, Persigny, Conneau, Colonel Émile Fleury, and Paris police prefect Pierre Carlier agreed to launch Louis Napoléon's coup d'état. Meanwhile, five days earlier, the newly promoted Général de Division (Major General) Arnaud Leroy, better known as Leroy Saint-Arnaud, had arrived from Algeria—"one of those Africans," Flahaut dismissively called him. Summoned to France by Louis Napoléon on the recommendation of Fleury, it was the president's intention of appointing him the new minister of war on condition that he agree to participate in the anticipated coup.[23]

General Saint-Arnaud was certainly the most curious, if not the most bewildering, choice for this post as commander of all the armies of the land. Having been a commercial traveler, then a soldier of fortune in the Greek insurrection for independence against the Turks, followed by a stint as a greengrocer, before going on stage as a "vaudeville type" comic-singer, while spending his time in between performances at the gaming tables, where his staggering losses drove him back into the safe arms of the army of occupation in Algeria—he hardly seemed a sound, reliable candidate either for the war office or as a responsible member of a clique preparing to overthrow a government.

The next *conseil de guerre* (Louis Napoléon, Morny, Eugene Rouher—at Morny's insistence—Persigny, and Carlier) was held at the Élysée one week later, on the twenty-seventh of August. After reading the draft of a plan submitted by Police Prefect Carlier for the proposed coup, Morny turned to him and did not mince his words. "*Mon pauvre* Carlier . . . I must tell you that I find your plan positively perverse." Meanwhile General Saint-Arnaud, who had personally agreed to the intended coup, suddenly changed his mind in the first week of September, in fact holding out for an additional cash inducement.[24]

What neither Morny nor Louis Napoléon knew, however, was that Prefect Carlier was secretly meeting with the disgraced Changarnier, revealing to him both the plans and the decisions taken at these meetings. With that information in hand, the general boasted to the prefect that when the right moment came he, Changarnier, would put Louis Napoléon in a "*panier à salade*" (slang for a police wagon) and personally drive him "in chains" to the prison fortress of Vincennes.[25]

Fanny Le Hon was having breakfast at Auguste de Morny's pavilion (adjacent to her much larger sumptuous mansion) at number 15 Champs-Élysées on the twelfth of September when Gilbert Persigny arrived unannounced with a most urgent message from the Élysée. A by now desperate Louis Napoléon had decided to place the planning and execution of the coup d'état entirely in the hands of his half brother. He was to be responsible for drafting a complete set of fresh plans and then for personally directing the operations as well. Auguste de Morny, who had long been debating whether or not to commit himself irrevocably to Louis Napoléon, now had to make his fateful decision.

"Tell him that he can count on me," he informed Persigny.[26] Always ruthlessly honest about political situations, Morny knew his own worth.

"In the first place I am always in complete control of myself, never allowing emotions to interfere with my decisions. And if I take no nonsense, no abuse from others, I in turn always treat others fairly and respectfully. When on the rare occasion I do personally agree to undertake a project, I am most demanding of myself and most thorough down to the last detail in its preparations. Once I fully believe in something, I continue relentlessly until the objective has been achieved."[27] Fanny Le Hon, who had been very close to Louis Philippe and his wife, argued fiercely with Morny against throwing in his lot with Louis Napoléon. Morny was adamant, however, as he afterward confided to Countess Masuyer, Hortense's former lady-in-waiting and confidante. "I knew at once what I had to do and did not hesitate for a moment in accepting. It was a relief and made me very happy to know that I would be contributing in saving the country, and what is more I personally would be in charge of everything."[28] There would be no more Strasbourgs or Boulognes. Louis Napoléon would have no say in the matter.

The decision now made, time was of the essence. Bonaparte had called for another war council (without Carlier) at the Élysée at two o'clock that very afternoon, the twelfth of September. Louis Napoléon had finally had to acknowledge that he personally lacked the leadership and ability required, while at the same time recognizing those very qualities in his own hardly much loved half brother. As for the no-nonsense Auguste de Morny, no one had ever called him a dilettante, a dreamer, no one had ever challenged his ability to accomplish anything he had ever set his mind to do. Had he not been there to denounce the faults in Prefect Carlier's earlier plan, there would have been no Second Empire and Louis Napoléon would have found himself once again, like Louis Philippe's family, yet another political refugee in England. Instead, with Morny in charge, this was to be a meticulous military operation.

On the twenty-seventh of October, he again shuffled his cabinet, naming General Saint-Arnaud his minister of war, as promised, while placing an obscure René François de Thorigny at the ministry of the interior, and replacing Carlier with the more reliable Émile de Maupas at the prefecture of police. With the firm major general Bernard Magnan as military governor of Paris now in command of the powerful garrison there, Louis Napoléon's team was nearly complete.

November 1851 proved to be as grim as it was tense for the gentlemen at the Élysée. On the fourth of the month Louis Napoléon, in spite of the advanced preparations now under way, still wishing to avoid force and a coup, made one last attempt to abrogate the Electoral Law of May 31, 1850, that had slashed the number of the electorate. However, his new bill, which sought to revise the Constitution of 1848 by extending the presidential term of office from four to ten years, was narrowly defeated by the Assembly, 353 to 347. "A disgusting set of rogues," a dismissive Charles de Flahaut called the members of that assembly.[29] The Electoral Law of May 31 stood and with it the loss of nearly three million voters . . . and the near impossibility of the president ever being reelected.

On November 17, 1851, the desperate "intriguants" in the Bourbon Palace, now intent on ridding themselves of Louis Napoléon Bonaparte once and for all, boldly threw down the gauntlet, introducing a new bill before the Chamber of Deputies that would permit *the assembly*—no longer *the president*—to call up the army in the event of a national emergency, even against the president of the Republic himself. Once again every seat in the hemicycle was taken and the mood sober. Bonaparte's new war minister, a clearly uncomfortable Saint-Arnaud, faced intensive questioning by the opposition and hurriedly left the assembly immediately afterward. Auguste de Morny, as a deputy for the Auvergne, was also present, studying the situation closely, and like the general left early, while Deputy Eugène Rouher remained for the counting of votes, witnessing the defeat of that measure. The army narrowly remained under Louis Napoléon's command . . . but for how long?

Leaving the Palais Bourbon, Eugène Rouher then joined Morny,

Saint-Arnaud, Persigny, and the president at the Place Beauvau—the Élysée. The assembly may have lost its bid to assume control of the army, but their intention was clear as a bell, of calling for "a coup . . . against the Executive Power of the Republic," as a frustrated Lamartine put it. "There is no other word for it," he insisted, "unless it is 'suicide.' Thereafter I considered the Republic as lost."[30]

Writing from his recently acquired mansion, the Hôtel de Massa, General de Flahaut brought his Scottish wife (in London) up to date, informing her that Thiers and Changarnier, who had been counting on the easy passage of the army bill, were left in a state of shock, having to rethink their plans. Not so his son, Flahaut pointed out, the business-like Auguste de Morny, who now instructed war minister Saint-Arnaud to put the sixty-thousand-man army garrison on a standby alert. When at the insistence of Louis Napoléon Morny met with Pierre-Antoin Berryer in an eleventh-hour attempt to win him over to his side, the offer was rejected. "We can do all that is required with you, without you, or if needs be in spite of you," Morny snapped.[31]

By the last week of November 1851, there was a very visible tension in the faces at the Palais Bourbon, and panic was spreading like cholera across the capital. Another second of December was approaching—the double-anniversary of Napoléon's coronation and great victory at Austerlitz—and the Bonapartes were notoriously superstitious about such things. And yet said *Le Siècle,* "We ask ourselves how it is possible in this day and age to still find those naïve enough to believe in a Coup d'État?"[32] Reality took many forms, and everyone recognized the old familiar pall of whispers and caution in abbreviated conversations, the anxious looks and nervous bons mots.

As matters stood, the assembly, unsure of the immediate future, could no longer carry on with business as usual and was in "a state of dissolution," Flahaut reported to his wife. "The fact is, things are getting too hot not to catch fire. . . . [and] very soon indeed," and he postponed his return to England.[33]

—•—

17

THE RUBICON FILE

*"I believe I can safely say that the coup d'état would have
never taken place without me."*[1]
—AUGUSTE DE MORNY

*"It was a tremendous game we played . . . one which
necessity alone could justify."*[2]
—CHARLES DE FLAHAUT TO DAUGHTER,
EMILY, LADY SHELBURNE

I n this day and age would it be possible for one man, no matter who,
to reshape a great nation . . . transform it *overnight*, in just twenty-four
hours, and with it the destinies of 35 million [sic, 26 million] people?"
the incredulous publisher of *Le Siècle* asked in October 1851.[3] Make that
two men, and that is precisely what Louis Napoléon Bonaparte and
Auguste de Morny intended to do.

M any of the usual *habitués* of the informal Monday evening presidential receptions mingled once again at the Élysée Palace on
December 1, 1851. Louis Napoléon's half brother, Morny, was as usual at
the Opéra Comique that night for a performance of the remarkable
musketeer-violinist-composer Joseph de Saint Georges's *La Chasse*,
though, in reality of course, it was to make the rounds of some of the
most beautiful ladies of Paris. While at the Élysée his father, the handsome, still slender, sixty-six-year-old Charles, Comte de Flahaut, was on a

visit from London to take possession of his newly acquired Parisian mansion, the Hôtel de Massa, but in particular to observe the volatile political situation. He had also come to visit his granddaughter, Louise, the
daughter of Fanny Le Hon and his son Auguste. Flahaut was not the only
one speaking to Fanny tonight, this witty, highly intelligent Parisian hostess, and wife of the absent former Belgian ambassador. The men swarmed
around her, irrespective of the splendid display of her celebrated diamonds; she was reputedly the wealthiest lady in Paris. Flahaut, Morny,
and Fanny were more than very close, confidential friends, and partners
in several highly lucrative financial investments; they were "family."

During his sojourn in Paris on this occasion, because of the current
political crisis, General Flahaut had been visiting the Élysée with his son
every morning, spending hours with Louis Napoléon, and rumors were
rife that night about the situation at the Assembly and a possible coup.
In addition to the absence of Jérôme Bonaparte, another "Bonaparte,"
Napoléon I's son by his polish mistress, Alexander, Count Walewski, a
career diplomat, was across the Channel, where Louis Napoléon had
appointed him French ambassador to the Court of St. James.

The diminutive Princess Mathilde, the president's hostess tonight and
at most Élysée functions, was her usual luxuriant, laughing self, display-
ing her wares in a décolletage that caught many an eye. Since Louis
Napoléon's return to France in 1848, he and his first cousin Mathilde,
Jérôme's daughter, had resumed their old friendship. The only disagreement, unsurprisingly, concerned women, or to be more precise, Louis
Napoléon's English mistress, the beautiful twenty-eight-year-old Harriet
Howard—whose inappropriate relationship with the prince-president
Odilon Barrot had also criticized. The Élysée was already known as a
friendly "foyer" for distinguished British visitors, and tonight Harriet
appeared with her friend—and a mutual friend of the prince from his
London days—Caroline Norton (née Sheridan), poet, novelist, and
feminist leader of her day.[4]

Whenever anything important was about to happen, one of the most
colorful newspapermen in Paris was inevitably to be found there. At the
age of fifty-three, Dr. Louis Véron, a most influential pro-Bonapartist
journalist and publisher, and a close friend of Morny, was a living legend,

a figure worthy of Balzac's pen. Pockmarked, scrofulous, and of well-rounded symmetrical girth, Véron was a man of many guises. "He dressed like a lackey aping his master," critic Philarète Chasles claimed, "with the affectations and the mincing step of the salon." In brief, he was not simply "a character," but a veritable monument of surprises. An excellent violinist, Louis Véron happily exchanged his stethoscope for a pen, for journalism was his natural profession, while also directing the Paris Opéra. Like his young friend Auguste de Morny, Dr. Véron was an inveterate theater habitué. Already the publisher of *La Revue de Paris,* he also produced the Bonapartist newspaper, the *Constitutionnel,* which he was to sell to Morny in 1852.

Also present were the ubiquitous Gilbert Persigny, public prosecutor Paul de Royer, the current foreign minister, the Marquis de Turgot, Interior Minister René François de Thorigny, and the ill-at-ease prefect of police Émile de Maupas. There was also the inevitable contingent of soldiers in dress uniform, including Colonel Vieyra, chief of staff of the 2nd Battalion of the National Guard (the only officer Morny trusted in that organization), Brigadier General François Canrobert (just brought directly over by President Bonaparte from the battlefield in Algeria), Changarnier's replacement as military governor of Paris, the reliable General Bernard Magnan, and of course the new war minister, Major General Leroy Saint-Arnaud (also brought back from the front in Algeria by the president). A final guest and total stranger appearing here for the first time, Georges Haussmann, the new prefect of the Gironde, was up from Bordeaux at the special invitation of the president of the Republic, and still none the wiser as to why, any more than his puzzled boss, Interior Minister Thorigny.

By ten o'clock, the last of the guests had left, including Mathilde, as Louis Napoléon returned to his office, stopping with his chief of staff Mocquard. "Do you know what is happening out there?" he asked. "They were talking about an imminent coup d'état—that the National Assembly are preparing *against me!*"[5] he said, coming as close to laughing as he ever had. Various members of the team were already assembled there, as Persigny, his ADC, Colonel Fleury, and Jean Mocquard distributed final instructions. Meanwhile President Bonaparte then removed a file labeled "RUBICON" from his safe, containing draft copies of various decrees and proclamations announcing the coup, destined to be plastered on the walls of the city. Louis Napoléon then handed that file to Colonel de Béville, who left immediately for the Imprimérie Nationale, at the Hôtel de Soubise, which on Morny's orders was to be sealed off by a company of the Gendarmerie Mobile, preventing anyone from entering or leaving until the printing was completed.[6]

After conferring with the president, War Minister Leroy de Saint-Arnaud and Major General Bernard Magnan set out for their respective headquarters, even as two regiments were posting guards round the Élysée, the Tuileries, the Ministry of the Marine, the Interior Ministry, the Ministry of Foreign Affairs, the École Militaire, and all other important government buildings and offices.

Police Prefect Émile de Maupas, a gentleman not noted for his charm, sense of humor, or strong nerves, had perhaps the most delicate and complicated task of all, to dispatch some eight hundred gendarmes directed by nearly one hundred handpicked commissaries (carefully screened for this purpose in interviews over the previous few weeks). Once the city was quiet and the streets empty in the early hours of Tuesday morning, the second of December, the anniversary of both the Battle of Austerlitz and Napoléon's coronation, Prefect Maupas would give orders to commence Operation Rubicon, to arrest eighty-seven of the most dangerous individuals, officials, statesmen, and soldiers. Louis Napoléon had personally enjoined Maupas, however, that his men were to be "most courteous when making these political arrests, and that applies to Mr. Thiers as well." Rudeness to such powerful figures could provoke violent demonstrations by their followers in the Assembly, and Maupas was not known for his light touch. The president added an apologetic "I had hoped to avoid all these arrests, [but] M. de Morny considers them to be essential."[7]

If the police had to be careful to avoid unduly antagonizing the politicians, this was not to be confused with the orders to military commanders and their troops who, although avoiding gratuitous bloodshed by senseless fusillades or the use of cannon—were free to use lethal force when under threat.

In fact, Auguste de Morny had not been as anxious about the firmness

of the troops as he had been about Louis Napoléon's noble declara-
tions, wishy-washy indecision, and maddening dithering when it came
to giving orders and bearing full responsibility for his actions. Therefore
Morny had first had a private tête-à-tête with his half brother where
he delivered a down-to-earth sermon. Coup leaders were not forbidden
to wear white gloves on a battlefield, Morny began, "but those gloves
must not be used as an excuse for not getting a little blood on their
hands, when required." Any kind of a military operation requires firm
leaders fully committed to achieving their objective, regardless of the
price. It was the old story of having to break eggs in order to make an
omelet. Louis Napoléon wanted to seize control of a government without paying the price, without seeing anyone hurt or upset.[8]

Bonaparte then distributed the last of the cash he had in the safe,
half of which he gave to a still wavering Saint-Arnaud, to ensure his
commitment, although he was already the recipient of a previous
fifty-thousand-franc goodwill inducement. Morny did not want to find
himself with another *sauve-qui-peut* Bernadotte or Jérôme Bonaparte
abandoning him in mid-battle. In any event, there was not even a whiff
of enthusiasm in the air when the conspirators broke up and left Louis
Napoléon, not knowing whether they would find themselves successful
or dead or in shackles at this time on the morrow.

In the early hours of Tuesday the second of December at the appointed
hour, Police Prefect Maupas duly gave the order for his gendarmes
to carry out this *rafale* and sweep through Paris to make the initial arrests of the coup, beginning with the bluff General Nicolas Changarnier—
who resisted at first with a pistol in each hand—and Deputy Adolphe
Thiers, who had been preparing a coup of their own. Most of the war-
rants were served on men caught fast asleep, including Generals Cavaignac and Lamoricière. They were then brought from various points of
the city to the recently opened Mazas prison, named after the street it
faced, just opposite the present Gare de Lyon. Intended as a holding
center for political prisoners, it was unusual in two respects—it was an
immense circular structure that housed twelve hundred cells and, on

the recommendation of de Tocqueville, boasted the first individual cells in any French prison. Meanwhile Maupas was executing the next phase of his instructions, arresting the "Reds" named on a second list, whether private citizens or deputies, to be found at all their usual haunts, apartments, political clubs, cafés, and restaurants, which were to be immediately closed. By five a.m. the initial operation had ended, without incident, even as the government proclamations and decrees were going up throughout the French capital.

As for the remarkable forty-year-old Count de Morny, after leaving the ladies at the Opéra Comique, he had gone on to the Jockey Club in the Boulevard des Capucines, where he played whist with Count Paul Daru and others until nearly five in the morning of Tuesday, the second of December. Returning to his pavilion overlooking the Arc de Triomphe just long enough to wash and change his clothes, Morny, who had not slept a wink, walked next door to Fanny Le Hon's luxurious new mansion, she being the only lady in Paris to be au courant regarding the coup d'état. Morny then left moments later with her nineteen-year-old son, Léopold, in his new capacity as special secretary. Making one more stop to collect Morny's father, General Charles de Flahaut, at the Hôtel de Massa, all three got into Flahaut's cabriolet, which took them to the Place de la Concorde, already lined with hundreds of soldiers, and across the Seine to the Ministry of the Interior in the Rue de Grenelle. It was six-thirty in the morning, and Paris was still asleep. Passing through the cavalry squadron guarding the iron grill of the ministry, the carriage pulled into the large stone courtyard and drew up under the apartments of Minister Thorigny who, awakened by the soldiers and the clatter of hooves, threw open the shutters to see what the commotion was about. "Excuse me, *monsieur,* to inform you in such a brusque manner," Morny called up to him, "but I have the honor of replacing you. Would you be so kind as to get dressed and leave immediately." Morny, who had drafted the entire complicated plan for today's coup, was now personally taking charge.[9]

The interior ministry now became the general headquarters and command center directing this coup d'état. Thanks to the installation of the new American electric telegraph, messages in Morse code could be sent instantly, no longer depending on the visual problems of the semaphore system that had impaired the government's communications after the failed Strasbourg coup. Installing Achille Bouchet, the telegrapher seconded from the Bourse (where the count was a prominent figure) to run this technology, Interior Minister Morny was in a position to communicate directly with all the other ministries, including war, as well as the country's prefects. Thanks to the magic of a telegrapher's key, he could literally govern the entire country from one small room in this building. Political orders could be given, police operations launched, and units of the army deployed.

Morny, who had campaigned in Algeria, knew only too well how a large organization—military or civil—could complicate, delay, and easily foul up an operation, and he had elected to do without it, reducing his control of Paris and the country to a streamlined structure. He would give the orders; Léopold, Fanny's unusually mature and able son, and Bouchet would carry out the communications. Three men![10] The old traditional ministry civil servants were no doubt scandalized—a nineteen-year-old secretary-general of the Interior Ministry was now giving them orders![11]

The two principal elements for controlling this coup were the police and the army. As minister of the interior, Morny controlled the nation's police. The Paris prefect of police, Émile de Maupas, like every prefect of every city in the country, took his orders directly from Auguste de Morny, as did, unusually now, the well-bribed war minister, General Leroy Saint-Arnaud, commander in chief of the French army.

President Bonaparte's proclamation announcing the dissolution of the assembly had acted like a red flag as dozens and dozens of deputies rushed to the Palais Bourbon while Paris was still dark. "I assure you that when we got up at 5 o'clock [sic] and went past the Assembly, it was being occupied [by deputies], and it was anything but rassurant [reassuring]," General de Flahaut later telegraphed his anxious wife in London from the Interior Ministry. "The Chamber is surrounded with troops, who hate the Assembly," and admittedly the army was treating the deputies roughly, but the army remained "well disposed toward the President." What in fact he saw was Gilbert Persigny and Colonel Espinasse and his 42nd Line Regiment in the process of rounding up the indignant legislators. On the way to the Rue de Grenelle they had also passed General Changarnier's house. "I saw it full of *sergents de ville* [municipal police] and *Gendarmes mobiles* [mounted police units] who were arresting him," Flahaut continued in his awkward English. What is most curious is the fact that Morny had not only permitted this message—and other telegrams to follow—to be dispatched at all, but uncoded, to be delivered by a private company in London.[12]

Hardly had Morny settled in at the ministry than he received an unexpected visitor, the new prefect of the Gironde, Georges Haussmann, a complete stranger, informing him that President Bonaparte had, without explanation, invited him to call on the minister of the interior today. With orders to dispatch all over the city and the country, Morny was most impatient with this clearly perplexed gentleman. Briefly explaining the situation, he bluntly asked the prefect, "Monsieur Haussmann, are you with us?"

"I am not quite sure what is happening here, Monsieur le Comte, but I am the prince's man. You can count on me completely," Haussmann replied. Returning to Bordeaux that same day, he carried with him the minister's special decree certifying him an "Extraordinary Commissioner of the Ministry of the Interior." In another year Haussmann would be back in Paris in a very different capacity, involving very close work with Napoléon III.[13]

In the meantime, with the well over one hundred of the nation's elected representatives that had been arrested earlier in the National Assembly now en route to jail, another two hundred deputies representing the monarchist and republican parties, having escaped from the Assembly, made their way to the *mairie* (the district city hall) of the then tenth arrondissement at the junction of the Croix Rouge and Saint-Germain-des-Prés. There they were addressed by Pierre-Antoine Berryer, the celebrated barrister who had defended Louis Napoléon following the Boulogne fiasco eleven years earlier. But a very different Berryer now declared President Bonaparte "an outlaw" and demanded his removal from office and the transfer of all his powers to the assembly. General Oudinot was then instructed to raise an army under the direct control of the assembly.

When two of Prefect Maupas's special inspectors arrived and ordered the packed hall to disperse, Berryer defied them, invoking Article 68 of the Constitution, declaring Louis Napoléon's coup to be "illegal." General Magnan's troops then entered, arrested all the deputies, and packed them off to the officers' quarters of the cavalry barracks on the Quai d'Orsay. Meanwhile Count Daru, with whom Morny had been playing whist at the Jockey Club a few hours earlier, was arrested along with some friends at his home in the Rue de Lille. Odilon Barrot, who had also escaped from the Assembly, was next seized with a few ringleaders at his apartment in the Rue de la Ferme, while "Deputy [Adolphe] Crémieux and a small group of 'reds' were arrested in the Rue des Petits Augustins." Still others were found at Ledru-Rollin's flat," Léopold Le Hon continued in his running narrative.[14] "The assembly is dissolved," General de Flahaut wrote his wife, Margaret. It was an "eventful and anxious day," he confessed, "for it is not without regret that one begins by arresting respectable men whose only fault is being political enemies."[15]

In fact the city was not as quiet as Léopold Le Hon had indicated, for Colonel Fleury had encountered swelling throngs between Port Saint-Denis and Port Martin being stirred up by agitators. When a shot rang out, a bullet grazing Fleury's head, his troops opened fire and those taken with arms were seized and a small number executed. The exchange of gunfire was brief, however, and the initial barricades dismantled.

By three-thirty p.m. that same afternoon, a caravan of omnibuses was loading the deputies arrested earlier that morning, taking them to prison. "Approximately 100 deputies [including General Cavaignac] were arrested [at the Assembly]," Léopold wrote . . . "At 7 o'clock [this evening] they will be sent to Ham. . . . The reports coming in are still quite good. . . . the faubourgs [Saint-Denis, Saint-Martin, and Saint-Antoine] are quiet at present. . . . The Chief [Morny] is going to see you after the meeting at the Élysée" where he was spending the entire afternoon to keep Louis Napoléon apprised of events, and to ensure that he did not interfere. The last thing Morny needed was an impetuous order or act by his half brother, such as had taken place at Boulogne. Léopold's "Last Bulletin" of the day stated that the news from the rest of the country was "excellent—I shall stay at my desk all night, while the Chief catches up on his sleep [the first in over forty-eight hours]."[16]

While the police and army were rounding up politicians the morning of the second, President Bonaparte had decided to show the flag and to display personally that all was well and the capital tranquil. "My dear General," Louis Napoléon wrote Count de Flahaut, "I should be delighted to have your company on horseback this morning . . ."[17] The prince had invited members of his family and some senior officers and their ADCs for this occasion. Later that morning the entire equestrian party set out on horseback from the Place Beauvau and the Élysée Nationale, as that palace was still called. A heavy cavalry escort assured the security of this glittering entourage, everyone in resplendent blue-and-red military uniform. His retinue included General Charles de Flahaut, wearing a chest full of his historic campaign medals from Austerlitz to Moscow, War Minister Saint-Arnaud, Prefect of Police Magnan, Marshal Exelmans, and the newly promoted marshal, Uncle Jérôme Bonaparte, and cousin General Edgar Ney, now back from the Roman expedition—all of them attended by a bevy of aides-de-camp.[18] It could have been a Sunday promenade through the Blois.

The idea was to demonstrate to the public that the senior officials of the government were in such complete control of events that they could afford time out for a leisurely morning ride. A fidgeting Jérôme Bonaparte alone kept warning of possible trouble, advising his nephew Louis Napoléon that they were advancing too quickly into the open Place de la Concorde, where they would make clear targets for marksmen. But of course this swaggering bully was in reality a notorious coward when it came to fighting and during the First Empire had abandoned both the capital of his kingdom of Westphalia and Emperor Napoléon on the field of battle during the Wagram and Russian campaigns. Crossing the Seine, they continued up the Quai d'Orsay before returning past the now silent Bourbon Palace, still cordoned off by troops. Four brigades, some thirty-one thousand men, lined the streets, including both banks of the Seine, concentrated largely between the Louvre and the Champs-Élysées, including the presidential palace. It was an intimidating display of military might, announcing Bonaparte's intention to crush even the slightest sign of defiance or armed rebellion. This equestrian foray had been a success, attended by a presidential appeal to the people for solidarity and support.[19]

Charles de Flahaut, who had spent the day at the Élysée or with Léopold at the Interior Ministry going over the reports received from the war ministry, the prefecture of police, and from prefects across the country, returned to the Hôtel de Massa to write his wife. "Auguste has been heroic. Nothing can exceed his courage, firmness, good sense, prudence, calm, good humor, gentleness and tact during all that was going on, and at the same time [he remains] so simple, and [there is a] total absence of vanity and conceit [in him]." As for Paris, the first night passed uneventfully.[20]

Wednesday the third of December saw dozens of streets barricaded from the Faubourg Saint-Denis in the north to the Temple, the Bastille, the Faubourg Saint-Antoine a focal point, around Les Halles, congested with horses, carts, and crowds, across to the Left Bank through the narrow streets around the Sorbonne and as far as Jean-Jacques Rousseau's tomb in the Pantheon. Here in this maze of ancient, winding streets lined with crowded tenements, there were no cries of "*Vive* Napoléon." "The people in the streets do not appear to be supporting us," the police prefect reported to Morny in a masterpiece of understatement.[21]

"Most confidential," Police Prefect Maupas notified Fanny Le Hon. "I do not have enough police to secure the streets . . . The barricades are beginning to go up in the Fauburg Saint-Antoine." He advised her to remain at home,[22] even as Military Governor Magnan was advising Morny that "the barricades in the Rue Rambuteau and adjacent streets have been taken without firing a shot. . . . For God's sake, don't believe all the tales coming from the Prefecture [of Police], who exaggerate everything, even their own fear."[23] Meanwhile, War Minister Saint-

Arnaud was having warnings posted in the streets: "Any individual building or defending a barricade, or caught bearing arms, will be shot on sight."[24]

Unusual in a prefect, Maupas was very nervous and did tend "to see double," as Emperor Napoléon used to say of fainthearted officers, imagining twice as many foes and dangers as actually existed. Morny was in fact getting quite worried about Maupas's unreliability and barely disguised hostility to both him and Magnan. "The zeal of the police is now so overexcited," he advised Nadine Baroche, "that I shouldn't be at all surprised to find myself placed under arrest!"[25]

On the other hand there was no shortage of rumors circulating throughout the city fueling those fears: Louis Napoléon had been "deposed" and "outlawed," Victor Hugo claimed in one of his creative handbills. The president had just raided the Banque de France and was distributing "twenty-five million francs" among his generals and cronies. Louis Philippe's three surviving sons were about to descend upon Lille before leading an army against Paris. Another rumor placed the prince de Joinville, currently at sea, at Cherbourg at the head of troops advancing on the capital from the west. "They say that the 12th regiment of dragoons led by the Comte de Chambord is on its way from Saint-Germain!" the police prefect warned Morny at the interior ministry. "I don't believe it for a minute," Morny replied. Chambord was in fact many hundreds of miles away safely ensconced behind the high walls of his Austrian castle at Frohsdorf.[26] Other *bruits* claimed that insurgents had seized control of Lyon, Amiens, Rouen, and other cities—false, of course, as was "news" of General Lamoricière's miraculous escape from prison, and who was allegedly marching at the head of several regiments about to seize the Élysée. Lamoricière was still in prison, of course, and his regiments entirely nonexistent. "The most important thing at this stage," Louis Napoléon concluded, "is for you [Morny] to issue news bulletins assuring the people of Paris that all is quiet in the rest of the country."[27] There were no phantom armies at St.-Germain, Lille, or Cherbourg marching on the French capital.

Although new barricades were appearing on Thursday the fourth of December, as late as eight o'clock in the morning Maupas at the prefecture and Brigadier General Levasseur at the Hôtel de Ville were reporting the capital still to be relatively calm. But many hundreds of men and women were arriving from the tenements to man the barricades and "café conspirators in black broadcloth and sporting fashionable yellow gloves" were haranguing them to revolt, to act. Léopold remained optimistic, however, assuring Fanny of the president's superior forces and of the inevitability of "a complete victory, as we are now in control of the insurrection."[28]

In fact the city's garrison of sixty thousand troops supporting Morny's operations had now been deployed to deliver the coup de grâce to the network of barricades. From his temporary post near the Carrousel, Military Governor General Mangan was directing the day's events as the last of his commanders reported that all of the brigades were in their designated positions across the right bank. Unlike Saint-Arnaud, Magnan had not spent years campaigning in Algeria, instead having remained in France (and Belgium), and because of this Morny had complete confidence in him, a dedicated, honest soldier with a sense of humanity (rare in soldiers of the day) and honor. Moreover, Magnan had refused an enormous unsolicited bribe offered by Louis Napoléon prior to Boulogne in 1840, while Saint-Arnaud had just demanded—and received—a very large *pot au vin* to ensure his serving this same Louis Napoléon. Ever the gambler, the general continued to hedge his bets and ensure his "loyalty." Morny also shared his father's prejudice against and contempt for all "those African generals," several of whom he had personally served under in combat. Bypassing the war minister, Morny had in fact worked directly with Magnan in the preparation of the day's operations. In any event, every man was now in place. Astride his horse and surrounded by his staff at precisely two o'clock on this wintry afternoon, General Magnan gave the order to commence the most important, and the shortest, campaign of his career as bugles blew and ADCs dashed off to observe the field commands in action.[29]

Six full brigades began to move: Brigadier Generals Canrobert and Cotte, positioned along the Boulevard des Italiens, coordinated with General Bourgon's brigade, continuing that line between the Ports of Saint-Denis and Saint-Martin. General Dulac with his battery of six cannon held the grounds of L'Église Saint-Eustache, and just to the west along the Rue de la Paix, General Reybelle advanced with his cavalry brigade, while to the east General Courtigis's infantry had arrived from Vincennes. As for their southern flank, it was protected by the Seine. This massive envelopment-pincer movement—complicated by the meshwork of confining narrow, ancient streets—advanced simultaneously from all points, with the leaderless insurgents from the start hopelessly caught up in this bristling mass of men and guns. And that had been Morny's and Magnan's plan, fully endorsed by Flahaut, to deploy overwhelming force and crush the insurgents as quickly as possible with the least loss of life.[30]

Fighting soon erupted along most points, beginning with the boulevards of Saint-Denis and Saint-Martin, between Rue Rambeau and the Halles, across the Rue du Temple and into the heart of the Faubourg Saint-Antoine as far east as the Place de la Bastille. The insurgents, facing crack veterans from Algeria, and with few arms and no artillery or cavalry, were foredoomed. Everywhere they were surrounded and their barricades engulfed, like some human tsunami. Meanwhile, additional troops on the Left Bank were sweeping that area clean as Victor Hugo and his followers, who had escaped arrest, were forced into hiding.

There were some fierce firefights, and dozens of barricaded streets resisted the oncoming infantry; six cannons were brought up from Saint-Eustache to blast them open while General Courtigis's battery of artillery was doing the same from the east. The dead were brought to the city's morgue, and the wounded to the closest hospital, the Hôtel de Dieu, adjacent to Notre Dame Cathedral on the Isle de la Cité. Some prisoners were shot on the spot, as the war minister had warned, but most were taken to the racecourse on the grass-covered Champs de Mars to await execution, in the shadow of Napoléon's tomb in the Invalides. A bloodthirsty, spirited young Léopold Le Hon—who had never worn a uniform or seen a battlefield—gave his blessing. "Severe punishment must be meted out as an example to all those who might rise up against us!" he pronounced.[31] Morny's plan was to begin and end this operation as quickly as possible with the least casualties, based on Emperor

Napoléon's old tactics, deploying an overwhelming mass of men and guns converging on their objective.

Magnan fully justified Morny's faith in him to command today, and the operation was a complete success by Friday morning, the fifth of December, though isolated skirmishes continued, usually from apartments overlooking the streets. Count de Morny and General Magnan were acclaimed great victors by most, and as brutes and traitors by the unforgiving defeated. There had of course also been the inevitable incidents of out-of-control backstreet killings by troops.

Despite Léopold Le Hon's protestations that the provinces had remained relatively calm, reports reached Morny of "troubles" in thirty-two of the nation's departments. "Insurgents" opposing a Bonaparte takeover were found from the royalist southwest around Bordeaux to the Var in the southeast, as well as in the central part of the country and elsewhere. But it was the smaller cities and towns in relatively isolated positions that were to prove most alarming, including Digne, seized by Napoléon during his Hundred Days march after arriving from Elba.

In fact the worst hotspot only developed after Paris was secured by the fifth, in the small town of Clamecy, in the "red department" of Nièvre, where drunken mobs of the local peasantry seized and beat priests before tying them to posts and forcing them to watch the lynching of a gendarme on Saturday the sixth. This was followed by the kidnapping of thirty-eight young unmarried girls, who were stripped naked and forced to serve their "banquets," concluding with two days of gang rape in the town center by hundreds of men, ultimately leading to fifteen hundred arrests—nearly a quarter of the town's population.[32] It was an appalling barbarity worthy of the ancient Gauls or of a Zola novel, vivid echoes of 1793 all over again, of a primitive historical mentality. For Morny, the problems in the provinces meant an emergency search for at least two dozen prefect replacements. "Could you provide us with a list of candidates as prefects and deputy prefects?" A desperate Léopold curiously even asked Fanny if she could suggest a few. "Send them to me immediately."[33]

"The insurrection is suppressed in all parts of Paris," Flahaut jubilantly telegraphed 19 Grosvenor Square at 7:02 p.m. on Friday the fifth.

THE RUBICON FILE 161

"Tranquillity prevails everywhere and even enthusiasm." "It's all over," Morny, too, assured Margaret de Flahaut [in English], a half hour later. "We are victorious . . ." "Auguste is heroic. I wish all his colleagues were like him," General Flahaut wrote; he "has displayed an energy, skill and firmness that simply defies description. . . . His determination to rid Paris and France of those scoundrels who have caused all the recent revolutions holds firm. For the first time they have been shown up for what they really are, 'bandits' and 'rascals.' "[34]

Meanwhile an ever glib Prosper Mérimée, pleased with the results of the coup, dismissed any criticism of it. "There was no brutality," he claimed, and "not even much of a battle."[35] General Bernard Magnan, as a professional soldier in charge of security for the French capital, was for his part also satisfied with the results, having avoided the carnage that would inevitably have ensued had the war minister been left in command. Magnan had been given an order by the president of the Republic and had carried it out. Unlike Saint-Arnaud or Changarnier, however, he took no pleasure in killing, and had done his best to keep casualties to a minimum.

A stonishingly, despite the heated rhetoric and accusations to the contrary, the death toll was estimated at fewer than four hundred civilians and only thirty soldiers (as compared to some five thousand killed during the June Days of 1848). Morny had planned and executed a remarkably surgical textbook operation in a densely crowded city of more than one million. More than 26,000 people were allegedly arrested across the country—which seems a grossly inaccurate figure when considering the additional isolated rebellions in thirty-two departments. Jules Simon put that figure at one hundred thousand. In any event Louis Napoléon ordered the release of 11,609 prisoners within a matter of days. Nine thousand five hundred men were transported to Algeria—the French had finally found a practical use for that colony—while 250 hardliners were sent to Devil's Island in French Guiana. Another 4,500 were released from Parisian prisons and given either full pardons or commuted sentences.[36]

Of the more than three hundred deputies arrested on the second of December, eighty-four were officially "exiled" by the government "for reasons of national security," including Adolphe Thiers, François Raspail, Pierre Leroux, and Émile Ollivier. When it was reported to Morny that Thiers was quite ill, Morny personally intervened to have him taken from his prison cell to his home for medical care; he then permitted him to leave for Bruxelles. General Louis Cavaignac, a personal friend, if political foe, who had found himself imprisoned at Ham late on the second of December, the day on which he was to have been married, was released by this interior minister in order to complete that ceremony. Secretly handed a passport with the compliments of Auguste de Morny, he celebrated his honeymoon in Belgium.

There Cavaignac found himself in good company, including Changarnier, who had fled the country in disguise (as "General Bergamote"), General de Lamoricière, General Bedeau, Colonel Charras, Victor Hugo (with his mistress, Juliette Drouet), Victor Schloelcher, Émile Deschanel, François Arago, Armand Barbès, Madier de Montjau, Edgar Quinet, and even Alexandre Dumas, who had been exiled, not by Louis Napoléon, but as usual by assiduous creditors already seizing his property in Paris. Ultimately more than seven thousand French men and women were to seek refuge in Belgium.[37]

Charles de Flahaut, too, was pleased with the operation, "a tremendous game," he called it. "The events of 4 December 1851 profundly shocked me," Morny afterward reflected, "but I was Minister of the Interior . . . responsible for order and the disorder." He had done what he considered absolutely necessary to save the nation from civil war, and accepted full responsibility for his actions.[38] "Well done, my dear friend, well done! Persevere with your enlightened dictatorship and you will save France!" Count de Laubespin congratulated a thankful Morny. "Let this splendid phrase of the Prince's be your motto," he continued. " 'The time has come for the wicked to start quaking in their boots, and for decent men to be able to start breathing freely once again.' "[39]

A national plebiscite held on December 20, 1851, on whether or not to accept major changes to the Constitution, including a new ten-year period of office for President Bonaparte, passed overwhelmingly,

7,439,216 votes for, 646,737 against (exclusive of 1,500,000 abstentions). The French people were weary of these prolonged political upheavals and above all the name "Bonaparte" today meant stability, order, and peace after three years of turmoil and uncertainty. As for the prince-president, Louis Napoléon, he had at long last executed a successful coup d'état, or rather his half brother Auguste had . . . and that he could never quite forgive.

18

— • —

THE SPHINX OF THE TUILERIES

*"I only departed from the legal path in order to
return to the spirit of the law."*[1]
—LOUIS NAPOLÉON BONAPARTE

*"He [Louis Napoléon] put up with my presence very unwillingly,
and my very services were irksome to him."*[2]
—AUGUSTE DE MORNY TO CHARLES DE FLAHAUT

Every coup d'état has its victims, in this case, Thiers, Changarnier, and the Orléanists, among others, and then of course there were the unexpected. The one that shocked everyone was Henry Temple, Lord Palmerston. On December 3, 1851, the British foreign secretary wrote a personal letter to French ambassador Alexander Walewski, congratulating the prince on his successful coup, quite unaware of what a chain of events that was about to unleash. Walewski in turn passed it on to French foreign minister Turgot. Instead of forwarding it to Louis Napoléon, however, Louis de Turgot, personally resentful of the influence of Flahaut and Morny, betrayed the president by sending a copy of Palmerston's confidential letter to the British ambassador, the Marquess of Normanby, who duly passed it on to his old Cambridge chum, Prime Minister Lord John Russell. Russell was much put out that "Pam" had failed to first submit his letter to him for Queen Victoria's authorization. Summoning Palmerston on the seventeenth of December, the prime minister fired him then and there. "One of the most rash and indiscreet acts I have ever known him to commit," an incredulous Lady Palmerston in turn related to Margaret de Flahaut.[3] Nor was Louis Napoléon any happier at having lost Palmerston at Whitehall, whom he had personally known for more than a dozen years. Normanby had achieved his aim, which was to be rid of Palmerston (a known opponent of the Orléans family).

Lord Palmerston remained unrepentant in his support of Bonaparte's coup: "If the President had not struck when he did, he would himself have been knocked over," as he put it. Discussing the situation with Lord Westmorland, he pointed out that as a matter of policy, "we must deal with things as they are, and not as we should wish to have them,"[4] and Bonaparte represented the best chance for maintaining European stability, the foundation of Palmerston's foreign policy. Normanby, a poor chess player, had set off a chain reaction, bringing down his close friend Prime Minister Lord John Russell's own government a few weeks later in consequence of his dismissal of Palmerston. Ambassador Normanby went next, finding himself replaced at the Paris embassy by a much abler Henry Wellesley, Lord Cowley, while an angry Louis Napoléon in turn then sacked his disloyal foreign minister, Turgot, even as Lord Malmesbury assumed Palmerston's office at Whitehall.

On January 9, 1852, goaded by Gilbert Persigny and the Normanby betrayal, Louis Napoléon informed Auguste de Morny of his intention to seize and auction off the property of Louis Philippe and the House of Orléans in France (beginning with the Palais Royal and including the estates of the Dowager Queen Marie Amélie). As Louis Napoléon well knew, Morny and Flahaut were very close friends of the Orléans family, and therefore he was hardly surprised when Morny vehemently protested against this decree.

Louis Napoléon then instructed his brother, as minister of the interior, to sign this very government decree, literally stripping the entire Orléans family of their wealth; "a most sordid calculation," General de Flahaut called it.[5] Angered and insulted, Morny flatly refused, and on January 17, Louis Napoléon, still at the prodding of Gilbert Persigny, demanded his resignation as interior minister (a position Persigny badly wanted for himself). For once the normally phlegmatic Morny, who had just prepared an elaborate plan for the complete reorganization of his antiquated ministry, was caught completely off guard and left staggering. Morny alone had put his brother in the winner's circle, and consequently had been overly confident of his own importance, while not forgetting his unique relationship with the president. The "indispensable" Morny had not counted on the full extent of his brother's jealousy and resentment, having embarrassingly achieved what Louis Napoléon had failed to do at Strasbourg and Boulogne.

He will probably leave the Government tomorrow," a furious Fanny Le Hon informed Charles de Flahaut on Wednesday, the twenty-first of January. "His resignation has been accepted," even as Persigny promptly moved into the interior ministry. The main criticism, she pointed out, was Morny's uncompromising opposition to "the Confiscation project." But some recent articles in the London *Times* revealing his parentage also "much disturbed the President," Fanny thought. However, in the final analysis, she pointed out, "no attempt was made to keep him [Morny in the government]." In fact it was "their undisguised intention to get rid of him . . . You know . . . how much jealousy there has been and how loath a certain person [Louis Napoléon] was to accept his decisions or to act on his advice" in the execution of the coup d'état. Once the president was safely in office, his brother could now be disposed of. He was expendable. Fanny found Louis Napoléon to be just another ruthless politician. "His outward sincerity and courtesy simply serve to conceal his real, devious character," the bitter countess declared, "including his full range of evil propensities."[6]

Auguste de Morny also warned his father, Charles de Flahaut, not to be taken in by him, despite Louis Napoléon's continued invitations to dine at St. Cloud. "He put up with my presence [during the coup] very unwillingly," Morny confided, "and found my services most irksome. He has never been more unfriendly toward me than he was at that time [December 2–8, 1851, when Morny was running the show]." Summing up his brother's character, Morny described him as "mistrustful and ungrateful," liking only "those who slavishly flatter and obey him."[7] By now the situation was clear enough for a thoroughly disgusted General de Flahaut, who in turn was privately making preparations to dispose of his recently acquired mansion, the Hôtel de Massa, on the Champs-Élysées. "If I could wipe out the 2nd of December," Flahaut confided to his son, "I would willingly do so," and with that he upped stakes and returned to London.[8] So much for any lost illusions about the prince-president.

As an alternative, an apologetic Louis Napoléon first offered Auguste de Morny the powerful presidency of the newly created Corps Legislatif. When a violent Uncle Jérôme Bonaparte strongly objected to this, however, even threatening to resign as president of the Senate if Morny were so appointed, Louis Napoléon obligingly withdrew the offer.[9] "He [Louis Napoléon] is not just an ingrate, he is a perjurer [sic: liar]," a disgusted Fanny Le Hon told Flahaut. "Clearly one can never count on an adventurer like that."[10]

"I have been quite anxious for some time now," Louis Napoléon later acknowledged to Morny, "for nothing is more painful than to be torn between one's affections on the one hand and political necessity on the other, nevertheless . . ."[11] In compensation he offered the ambassadorship to the court of the tsar at St. Petersburg—*au bout du monde*, more than two thousand kilometers from Paris, far from government and the French capital and well out of harm's way. Now twice dismissed by Louis Napoléon, and twice deliberately humiliated, and despite Flahaut's recommendation to accept the embassy, Morny rejected that diplomatic option in 1852 out of hand . . . at least this time round. Trying to mitigate the brutality of his own act, Louis Napoléon offered seats in the Senate both to Morny and his father. While Morny declined this post as well, his father eventually accepted a place in the Luxembourg Palace, as a political expediency to keep a family foot in the door, if only for his son's sake. At the end of February of 1852, Persigny condescendingly offered to run Morny as an official electoral candidate for the position of deputy for the newly created legislative body. Auguste would have none of it. Defiantly standing as an independent candidate for Clermont-Ferrand, with no court backing, he won a spectacular victory over the government's candidate.[12]

Turning his back on the murky world of palace politics, Morny decided to concentrate his future activities at the center of the nation's world of commerce, trade, and finance. With Fanny's blessing he went to Bruxelles to preside over Vieille Montagne, the powerful mining corporation Fanny's late father had created, with coal, iron, and zinc mines in Belgium and nearby German states.[13] For the first time in his life real wealth was pouring in, the type of compensation Morny appreciated.

Meanwhile, Louis Napoléon, who had been patiently biding his time, was now set on implementing his long-prepared agenda for France. Following his coup, he had taken the first steps to freeing the availability of capital from the traditionally very limited source of private closed banks. Henceforth, new credit institutions would be created to provide the capital required for substantial financial and industrial investments, for mortgages and agriculture. Furthermore, his published national budget for 1852 held several surprises, including the item of 14,000,000 francs set aside for public works, improving the living conditions of the impoverished, and the expansion of roads and canals. As for the nation's first railway grid, it would be developed entirely by an expanded private sector.

After all his talk about "the empire of peace," substantial increases in the military budget caught many completely off guard, as he announced setting aside a spectacular 32,000,000 francs (the equivalent of $412,800,000 today) for the crash expansion and modernization of a vast new French navy.[14] Long impressed by Britain's military might, Louis Napoléon sought to match, or at least come close to matching, the Royal Navy, ship for ship, including the use of the latest steam propulsion technology. The design and size of warships, along with an impressive increase of gun power, were to revolutionize the French navy over the next eighteen years. He would more than match Uncle Napoleon's shipbuilding phenomenon in 1803–1805, as the initial contracts were signed for the laying down of dozens of new steam-powered ironclad warships. The fleet of wooden ships would soon be a thing of the past. There was no limit to what had to be done, and Louis Napoléon was determined to do it. Nor did he forget to offer financial inducements for academics and inventors, for example regarding the practical development of his scientific preoccupations and hopes for the country while a prisoner at Ham.[15]

On the other hand, Louis Napoléon also demanded sweeping new powers for the police and national security services. Ideas and words were as dangerous as armies, and on February 18, 1852, he confronted the nation's press head on. No new newspapers could be published without prior government authorization. Major daily French newspapers had first to deposit a 50,000-franc ($645,000) bond with the government, which could be confiscated without appeal in case of violation of strict new press regulations. All unauthorized newspapers appearing would be heavily fined and the publishers imprisoned. Nor could foreign newspapers continue to circulate without government approval—subject to large fines and imprisonment. High stamp taxes on all publishing, including books, remained in place.

All this was just the beginning of tightening state control of the press, to end "this extreme danger facing democracies of seeing crude institutions destroying the State and our rights," as Louis Napoléon put it. Certain categories of news, including the coverage of trials and the judiciary, had to be submitted for state approval prior to publication. Censorship was alive and well, and the prefects throughout the country were the local watchdogs with full control over the nation's press, which worried Auguste de Morny very much.

Equally there would be a new Parliament, the Corps Législatif, the Legislative Body, comprised of one elected assembly, "the other [the Senate] appointed by me" for life.[16] The old First Empire policy of state scrutiny was again revived, complete with the reintroduction of Uncle Napoléon's much feared Ministry of Police, directed by Émile de Maupas.

In spite of the enormous new powers Louis Napoléon wielded, following the elections of February 29 for this legislative body, he himself was now hesitant about taking the further step of replacing the revised republic with imperial rule. It was as usual an impatient Persigny who kept nudging him toward the imperial purple.

Meanwhile Louis Napoléon, through his early preemptive act of removing Auguste de Morny from the scene in January, had rejected not only his brother's sorely needed guidance, but also launched him into the significant new independent role he would play as the future broker-tsar of an entirely new French financial world. What with Morny's corporate mining interests through Vieille Montagne and his long-term agricultural commitments in the Auvergne, he was now deliberately distancing himself from Louis Napoléon and the Élysée, where his sudden sustained absence was the subject of much conjecture. Nevertheless, Morny as a deputy managed to attend most sessions of the Corps Legislatif when major issues were involved, while in the Auvergne he continued to occupy himself with his sugar beet plantations and the production of céruse (used for the hard red dye required for French army uniforms). This seemingly minor crop was to provide a profitable source of revenue for him, as he held the government monopoly for the entire army. Morny's purchase of the three-thousand-hectare (7,410-acre) estate of Nades in Basse-Auvergne, north of Vichy, was to be the center of his agricultural activities. Of illegitimate aristocratic birth, with no inherited wealth, once again he had been almost entirely dependent on his chief business partner, Fanny Le Hon, to meet the exorbitant purchase price of 450,000 francs (nearly $6 million) for this isolated property without even a proper residence. Many were misled by Morny's sometimes notorious reputation as a denizen of Parisian nightlife, whereas in reality, among his other attributes, he was a serious, most knowledgeable farmer, the owner of a new model farm here at Nades, not to mention several highly profitable stud farms. And it was here, thanks to Fanny's money, that he built the somewhat forbidding Château de Nades, situated miles from his nearest neighbor and many days' travel from Paris.

While Louis Napoléon and most of the rational world sought a good night's sleep, the indefatigable Morny worked. And even then a day did not provide enough hours, and time and again he would have to cancel appointments with Fanny and others because of his demanding business schedule. "I was overburdened with work even before I started for the Vieille Montagne Board of Directors meeting in

Belgium," he typically explained to his father. "If all this comes out well [current zinc negotiations] I shall be profitably established in business once again. I shall owe no man anything [excluding the millions borrowed from Fanny]. . . .[17] I am going to be able to repay [the banker] Coutts this very day." His annual profits from "picture sales," largely Dutch and Flemish masterpieces currently in vogue, only went to top up the pot.[18] This, too, was a side of Auguste de Morny's existence of which the prince-president remained largely ignorant. Louis Napoléon would constantly publicize and talk about his many accomplishments; Auguste de Morny just got on with it and quietly carried out his agenda in the privacy of his own world.

In March and April of 1852, the prince-president was greatly preoccupied with his sweeping new programs and expanded constitutional reach, which gave him the power to declare war and peace, not to mention increased access to vast amounts of government funds, including 25 million francs ($328 million), for his much expanded civil list—including the annual pensions for his extended family. Meanwhile he daily edged closer to empire. He had already been granted state royal hunting establishments, his name was printed atop all official documents, civil servants were obliged to swear an oath of loyalty to him, Napoléon's name was restored to the civil code, and the imperial eagles restored to the regimental standards, and Uncle Napoléon's birthday—the fifteenth of August—was made a national holiday, even as Louis Napoléon's image appeared on the coin of the realm.[19] Moreover, he had inherited one of the largest permanent standing armies in the whole of Europe, over 450,000 strong—with only those of the Russian and Ottoman Empires exceeding it.[20]

The French—like the British and Germans—loved nothing better than a display of military bravado, and Gilbert Persigny, late sergeant of King Louis Philippe's army, intended to give them that in a dazzling public relations performance in support of the country's emerging imperial status. On May 10, 1852, President Bonaparte appeared on the green expanses of the Champs de Mars (where recently rebelling French insurgents had been executed). Stirring military music played, and trumpets and drums announced the opening of the ceremony, where the prince-president stood in his uniform as a lieutenant general before a quarter of a million approving spectators, excluding the presence of some 60,000 troops, nearly the entire Paris garrison. The pretext for this convocation was the presentation of the golden Napoleonic imperial eagles, taken out of mothballs for the new regimental colors, and in turn blessed by the archbishop of Paris. The prince-president had come here to "restore these [imperial] eagles which so often led our fathers to glory," and called upon the troops now "to swear to die, if called upon, in defense of them."[21] Every day a new event, a new ceremony, each one a step closer to empire. But despite the military display and rousing music, did the nation really want a return to empire?

B eginning in July of 1852, Louis Napoléon went on a series of fresh tours of the country in order to test the prospective imperial waters. At the end of 1851, the French people had voted enthusiastically for the extension of his Constitutional powers under the Second Republic. Were they now prepared to abandon this same republic? Once again Persigny strongly urged Bonaparte to take yet another step forward, and this new tour was intended to provide the final boost required.

On September 14, Louis Napoléon and his staff left Paris for the southeast, with Lyon his first stop. Up to this point his reception had been tepid, and unknown to the president, in Lyon Persigny had to hire crowds, the inevitable claque, and pay for the construction of triumphal arches—"spontaneously built" by an enthusiastic people—and to enliven things with a few bribed "Vive l'empereurs," for the unveiling of an equestrian statue of Napoléon. At Marseille there were a few more cheers, these no longer subsidized, as he spoke of "assimilating . . . the great kingdom of Algeria" and one day of "connecting our great Western ports with the American continent by steamship lines." Louis Napoléon offered a golden future.

Bordeaux was to be the final major stopover before returning to the capital. Here the energetic prefect Georges Haussmann kept the promise he had given to Morny at the interior ministry on the second of December and loyally provided welcoming crowds. Was it genuine? Louis Napoléon apparently thought so as he addressed the people of Bordeaux on the ninth of October: "France seems to be calling for a return to the Empire. There are those out there who say that Empire means war. But I tell you that the Empire I envisage means only one thing, peace," he repeated from an earlier speech. The empire he envisaged for 1852 was not to be confused with the empire of 1815, he pointed out. This was to be no mere continuation, but instead an entirely new beginning. But on his way back to Paris via Montpellier and Orléans, he found the crowds thinner and the cheers weaker.[22]

Upon his return to the capital, it was perhaps as a result of his own nagging doubts about the wisdom of launching the empire at this time, enforced by his less than successful tour of the south, that his thoughts returned to his brother. For once completely disregarding Persigny's advice, Louis Napoléon swallowed his monumental pride and on the nineteenth of October finally reached out to Auguste de Morny for help.

"Grand times are coming soon," he wrote in a thinly disguised bonhomie. "And I hope to find you by my side in the course of achieving them."[23] It was about as close as he could bring himself to admit that his shabby dismissal of Morny back in January had been a grave error of judgment. He did need him now, and he did not think he could succeed without his support. "You know perfectly well that you can always count on me," Morny replied in his usual forthright manner, reminding him of his earlier assurances made in 1851 that he was always ready "to risk even my life for your cause." To be sure "some disagreeable incidents"—of his own doing—had led Louis Napoléon to think that Morny had withdrawn his support. "There is nothing to that," Morny added dismissively, "and I shall fully demonstrate it when the appropriate circumstances allow."[24] One could almost hear Louis Napoléon sigh with relief, and he in turn responded immediately on the twentieth of October—"*Mon cher* Morny, . . . I was really sorry not to have seen any more of you [these past several months]," and invited him to the Élysée. "Come tomorrow at three o'clock," when he would be happy "to take up where we had left off."[25] After a most unpleasant standoff for nearly ten months, the great rift had been closed. It was as close as he could bring himself to "apologizing," if that is the word, and it proved to be one of the most important acts of his career.

There was also an unexpected personal link reaffirming their relations. On the evening of October 22, 1852, the two brothers met "by chance" at the Théâtre Français, where the exotic actress Rachel was performing a reading of Arsène Houssaye's ode, *L'Empire c'est la paix*, The Empire Means Peace. Also attending this performance were his bejeweled Harriet Howard, who had contributed 200,000 francs (nearly $2.6 million) toward Louis Napoléon's coup of the second of December, while in another loge with her mother sat the lovely twenty-six-year-old redheaded beauty, the Countess de Teba, Eugénie de Montijo, whom both Morny and his brother had already known for quite some time. Morny, who personally liked the young Spanish countess, knowing of the attraction that Louis Napoléon felt to her, encouraged the couple. It was to prove the last curtain on Louis Napoléon's liaison with the unfortunate Miss Howard, whom he was shortly to remove from Paris, albeit with a 6-million-franc ($77 million) adieu, followed by a peerage as the Countess de Beauregard, complete with a handsome château by the same name, situated just a stone's throw from the Palais de Saint-Cloud. Although Miss Howard finally remarried, they would continued to meet thereafter, if most discreetly.

With Morny working behind the scenes once more, events developed quickly. On the fifth of November the prince at long last declared publicly his willingness to accept the imperial crown if offered to him. Two days later the Senate voted almost unanimously for the reestablishment of the hereditary empire. (The one negative vote was that of Louis Napoléon's former family retainer from Arnenenberg, and now senator, Thélin.) On November 21–22, a national plebiscite was held, solidly endorsing the new Second Empire, 7,824,199 votes in favor against 253,645 opposed (but with a significant two million abstentions).[26]

• • •

On Wednesday evening, December 1, 1852, an unending procession of nearly two hundred elegant carriages made its way from the Champs-Élysées in the dense wintry fog, preceded by postillions and outriders carrying torches via a dark road crossing the meadows and woodland comprising what would later become the Bois de Boulogne, forty minutes later reaching the banks of the Seine and the sprawling 918-acre park of the Château de Saint-Cloud, where Louis Napoléon was now residing.[27]

Reaching St. Cloud, the senators in their long blue velour cloaks, culottes, and black felt caps complete with sleek white feathers, led by their president, were convened amid great pomp in the 147-foot-long gold-and-white Apollo Gallery, lined with dozens of footmen in pale blue and white. It was a detailed repetition of the ceremony carried out in this very hall on May 18, 1804, when a delegation of the Senate had come to Napoléon I to proclaim the creation of the First Empire.[28] Louis Napoléon, attired in the uniform of a general officer, surrounded by his uncle, Marshal Jérôme Bonaparte, and his son, Prince Jérôme, took his place on the red velvet throne.

"This new reign which you inaugurate today," the new emperor began, "has not, like so many in history, been founded through violence, conquest or conspiracy," but rather as "the legal result of the will of the entire people. . . . Help me one and all to establish in this land, troubled by so many past revolutions, a stable Government, based upon religion, justice, probity, and care for the suffering classes." And he closed with the accession to power—"I assume from today, with the crown, the name of Napoléon III."[29] The Second Empire was born.

The following morning the procession set out on its return journey, led by Emperor Napoléon III and his three newly created marshals—Saint-Arnaud, Magnan, and Castellane—and announced by trumpets as they passed under the Arc de Triomphe and up the Champs-Élysées, on to the Place de la Concorde and the Tuileries as hundreds of cannon roared, tambours rolled, and endless church bells pealed from every arrondissement of the capital. And with that Emperor Napoléon III moved into the Tuileries, the former residence of Uncle Napoléon Bonaparte.

The staff included his new grand marshal of the palace, Marshal Vaillant, with Marshal Saint-Arnaud as grand equerry, the Duke de Bassano as the grand chamberlain, Cambacérès as grand master of the ceremonies, General Fleury as the first equerry of the palace, and of course the faithful Thélin (who had voted against the creation of this very empire) as treasurer of the privy purse. Nor had Auguste de Morny been forgotten; he was there, wearing his newly awarded Grand Croix de la Légion d'Honneur. And thus it was on yet another second of December, in 1852, that the forty-three-year-old Louis Napoléon Bonaparte, Napoléon III—"the Sphinx of the Tuileries," as the press were to dub him—spent his first night in Uncle Napoléon's bedroom. . . . his childhood dream fulfilled at last. Hortense would have been proud.

19

VIOLETS AND WEDDING BELLS

"I have preferred a woman whom I love and respect."[1]
—NAPOLÉON III, JANUARY 1853

"Tomorrow he will risk his crown rather than not share it with me."[2]
—EUGÉNIE TO PACA, JANUARY 1853, JUST BEFORE THE CIVIL MARRIAGE

In 1833 Spain was again in turmoil with the death of Ferdinand VIII and his replacement, not by his brother Carlos, but by the king's two-year-old daughter, Isabella II. Civil war followed and Don Cipriano, the Count of Montijo, and his family were caught up in the midst of it. In July 1834 Cipriano's elder brother died without issue, leaving him everything, including a veritable network of estates, accompanied by a string of ancient titles going back to the twelfth century. That same year brought cholera to the streets of Madrid. So dangerous had the situation become that Don Cipriano was unable to wait even for his brother's funeral, as he hastily dispatched his wife and young daughters from Madrid on July 18, 1834, in a mule-drawn carriage. Traveling via Barcelona, Perpignan, and Toulouse, they reached Paris around mid-August 1834.[3] There, the two girls—Eugénie now eight, and Paca nine years old, spent the next six years studying, beginning at the Sacred Heart Convent in fashionable Saint-Germain.

When Don Cipriano finally arrived in Paris the following year, it was not as a stranger, having commanded the artillery atop Montmartre in 1814 in a last effort to save Napoléon. But today in 1835, the girls' father's objective was to obtain for them a better, more modern education,

transferring them to the gymnasium (high school) run by a fellow Spaniard, Colonel Amoros.[4] Over the remaining four years in Paris, their
education was supplemented by English governesses, and in particular by Prosper Mérimée—"a small birdlike little man." Mérimée, a
brilliant scholar and linguist, was director general of Historical Monuments in France and the author of *Colomba* and *Carmen*—which was
based on the Comtesse de Montijo. He had first met Don Cipriano many
years earlier when as a student he was traveling to Granada, and had
since become a close family friend of his wife, Doña Maria Manuela,
and the children. His friend, young Henri Beyle (Stendhal), also tutored
the children in French.

It was while at school that Eugénie and her sister, Paca, met Cécile
Delessert, one year older, who was to become a very close lifelong friend
of Eugénie. Cécile was the daughter of Gabriel Delessert, a descendant
of Swiss Calvinists, and the brother of a prominent Parisian banker and
industrialist. The Delessert mansion in Passy was to prove a home and
refuge for Eugénie over the next three decades. Earlier on, Delessert
had served as a tutor to the young Auguste de Morny, another old
friend of the family. Later, as Louis Philippe's prefect of police, one of
the few civilized men to hold that post, Gabriel Delessert briefly served
as Louis Napoléon's jailer following the Strasbourg coup. It was at Delessert's that Morny and his father, General Flahaut, had probably first met
Doña Maria Manuela, and Eugénie as a schoolgirl.

Eugénie's mother's family had risen from the Spanish middle classes,
her lowland Scottish merchant father, William Kirkpatrick, having married the daughter of Belgian businessman, Baron Grivégnée, from
Malaga. On the other hand, Don Cipriano was not merely a distinguished aristocrat, but a grandee of Spain, the grand marshal of Sevilla,
and the descendant of two kings. Tall, slender, handsome if severe,
taciturn, haughty, and aloof, he had family titles more ancient and distinguished than those of the king of Prussia. In society he was known
as Cipriano de Guzmán y Palafox y Portocarrero, Count of Teba, his
wife as the Countess of Teba, as well as of Montijo (that latter title then
being transferred to Eugénie.)[5] A liberal and a Bonapartist, Don Cipriano had fought with the French under Admiral Gravina's command

against Nelson at Trafalgar in October 1805, where a musket ball had shattered his left arm. Later, as a colonel in the French army, he had supported the French invasion of Spain in 1808 and King Joséph Bonaparte at Madrid. He next lost an eye in fighting the forces of King Francisco when he was captured and imprisoned. He was saved from execution and subsequently released from prison thanks to the intervention of his wife. Meanwhile, he had inherited his late brother's vast estates and wealth, including their Madrid mansion Casa Ariza, as well as the Casa Montijo and their summer palace of Carabanchel—the three principal family residences.

If Eugénie and her sister, Paca—Maria Francisca—were close, not so Eugénie and her daunting, dynamic mother, Doña Maria Manuela, noted for an unending list of male companions in a Spain where "forthright" conversation and sexual license astonished even the French. Eugénie, on the other hand, idolized her father, and went into a prolonged depression following his death in 1839, the reason for the family returning to Spain.

Given her mother's rather promiscuous reputation and Eugénie's devotion to her father—although never a prude—her subsequent relationships with men, including her future husband, Louis Napoléon, had to be understood in consequence. Following her father's death, in her teens she became the typical rebel, challenging her mother by her independence, dressing like a man, even donning a matador's costume, on occasion smoking a cigar (though she later disliked all tobacco and smoking in her presence)—clearly associating herself with her father, as the son he never had. Unusually keen on physical fitness, she was hyperactive, highly strung, ill-tempered, and impulsive. She was a chatterbox and always spoke quickly—in Spanish, French, and English.

Like Louis Napoléon, she loved horses and rode well, if with reckless abandon. (In later years, when pregnant, she stubbornly insisted on riding powerful horses, and was thrown, losing her first child.) At the same time, only too aware of her feminine charms, she appeared at balls in exquisite gowns. A passionate aficionada of the *corrida*, she later attempted to convince her husband to have bullfights restored in Bayonne. Carrying her enthusiasm one step further, she later set up a temporary *corrida* in the grounds of the Trianon Palace. There attended by her ladies-in-waiting, she would force a wild boar and an imported Spanish cow to fight each other, prodding them on with the aid of a sharp cavalry lance. Unfortunately, the Spanish cow, which did not appreciate cold steel piercing her hindquarters, turned on Empress Eugénie, who had to make a hasty retreat. Like her father, she had a passion for blood sports and shared his love of hunting. She was to remain an enthusiastic participant of Louis Napoléon's stag hunts at Fontainebleau and Compiègne in the future, on one occasion losing her patience with him for calling off the dogs too early, who were in the midst of tearing at the stricken stag, in order to shoot it and put it out of its misery. The cries of terrified animals literally being torn apart by dogs never repelled Eugénie de Montijo. This slender, very feminine looking woman had a very real fierce, almost bloodthirsty side to her character. This clash of personalities within her was never resolved—her great compassion for human suffering and total disregard for that of animals. People were "Catholics," animals were not.[6]

In Madrid in the 1840s Doña Maria Manuela was a close friend of the very young and dissolute Queen Isabella II, who had rejected the recent proposal of marriage by the ubiquitous son of ex-king Jérôme, Plon-Plon. Doña Maria Manuela served as lady-in-waiting to the Spanish queen and was a regular visitor to the royal palace, El Prado. She was better known, however, in her own right for her sumptuous costume balls and lavish receptions offered at the Casa Ariza, as large as the royal palace and serviced by dozens of servants. Her mother thrived on the politics of the day, and all leading men, however disreputable, in and out of government, were constant guests at the Casa.

Eugénie was brought up and educated in the central political vortex of the day. She was highly strung with very strong political opinions, which inevitably led to personal confrontations with senior officials on occasion. The daughter of Doña Maria Manuela was never known for her shyness. "Even as a girl I had a taste for politics," Eugénie remarked years later, "a taste inherited from my mother, in whose house I used to hear the statesmen, diplomats, generals and publishers expounding all day long." On the other hand, Eugénie had no patience for "petty party squabbles," preferring, she insisted, loftier subjects, "the really big issues of the day, the ones where national prestige and a nation's reputation were at stake."[7] An outspoken feminist, she naturally objected when Spanish ministers spoke dismissively of female interference in politics. At one dinner party given at the Casa Ariza, a seventeen-year-old Eugénie was denouncing the violence in the streets of the Spanish capital of government troops under the dictator-general Ramón Nárvaez, these troops of this rather "fat, ugly little man with a vile expression" who just happened to be her mother's dinner guest that evening. Angered, Nárvaez turned on her, stating that it was none of her business, because it was not women doing the fighting for the government. Moreover, women would never have the courage to face a bayonet, he snapped. A furious Eugénie impulsively grabbed a knife from the dinner table and plunged it into her own arm.[8] Clearly this was the daughter of the fabled Don Cipriano, and however courageous, one very complex, tortured young lady.

Doña Maria Manuela's principal reason for returning to Spain following the death of her husband had been to find husbands for two of the most eligible daughters of the kingdom. Prospective suitors for a lovely heiress were not wanting, but the proud, arrogant Eugénie was not easy to please. There was something more to her personal hesitation to marry, for most of the men she was attracted to were physically weak, shy, and far from handsome. The Duke of Osuna proposed and was rejected.[9] She next declined the offer of her cousin, Count José de Xifre, and then Prince Albert de Broglie, the only qualified French candidate, went the way of his predecessors. Her only English suitor, the wealthy Ferdinand Huddleston, fared no better. He was turned down because at this stage of her life Eugénie was violently anti-English and would accept no Englishman, regardless of rank and fortune.

"I love and hate violently," she acknowledged.[10] Her first personal choice for a husband was a distinctly ugly distant cousin, the fifteenth Duke of Alba, whom she had known since childhood and whose ancestors were even more illustrious than her own. Her elder sister, Paca, also loved him, and the typical sisterly rivalry brought hysterics, but her mother naturally decided in Paca's favor, she being the eldest. A distraught young Countess de Montijo swallowed a concoction of home-made poison, which nearly proved fatal. "I have an awful mixture of passions, in me, all wild," she admitted, predicting she would be the ultimate victim of them, and almost was. "My life is going to end miser-ably, in a whirl of passions, virtues and follies." "Don't say I am mad," she implored the young Duke of Alba, "please, just pity me."[11] This assertion the young countess proved most dramatically when rejected by the next suitor, Pedro, Marquess de Alcañices; she again took poi-son, a lethal dose this time, and was only saved by an antidote at the very last moment. This proved too much even for the remarkably un-flappable Doña Maria Manuela, who decided it was time for a change of scenery, as mother and remaining daughter headed north for the first time in ten years, settling in post-revolutionary Paris in the early months of 1849.[12]

With the death of Don Cipriano in 1839, Doña Maria Manuela had come into personal control of one of the most fabulous family fortunes in recent Spanish history, bringing them an annual income equivalent to 500,000 francs (nearly six and a half million dollars) at a time when a crown minister might consider himself most fortunate in-deed with 30,000 francs a year. Establishing themselves in a palatial apartment overlooking the chic Place de Vendôme, Doña Maria and her twenty-three-year-old daughter—now well and truly considered by some to be "on the shelf"—Eugénie nevertheless soon became much talked about as they drove daily along the Champs-Élysées with their ostenta-tious display of diamonds and beauty, in a luxurious phaeton complete with the family coat of arms. Even her usually persistent gossipy social critic, Count Horace de Viel-Castel—who on occasion even disap-proved of the palace's weekend invitation list for Compiègne—admitted that Eugénie had "a most prepossessing manner" and a "keen sense of humor."[13] Despite her mother's phenomenal ego and confidence in every undertaking, even Maria Manuela may have had some anxieties about finding a suitable husband for such a difficult, wayward daughter. And the last thing she wanted was to see her bury herself in a convent for the rest of her life, the traditional solution for unmarriageable daughters.

Having exhausted the list of eligible bachelors in Madrid, Eugénie's mother had come to fish in the French pond, setting her sights on no one less than the president of the Republic, Louis Napoléon Bonaparte. Eugénie, with her beauty and her late father's excellent Bonapartist credentials, was received at most of the social events of the French capital. They were introduced to Countess Fanny Le Hon, Princess Mathilde, Prince Felix Bacciochi, and others, resulting in a first meeting a few years later between Eugénie and Louis Napoléon at the Élysée in 1849, followed by invitations to St. Cloud, and hunts and "house parties" at Fontainebleau, Rambouillet, and Compiègne.

The siege to Louis Napoléon's heart had been too obvious and too successful, winning the equally powerful opposition to such a marriage with "the Spanish woman," as the distinguished Spanish aristocrat was referred to contemptuously by Colonel Émile Fleury and his debauched mistress. Surprisingly, using language worthy of Henri Rochefort, Maxime Du Camp—a self-appointed enemy of Morny and the Bonapartes—in a blistering thirty-page attack in his memoirs lashed out against Eugénie's character, calling her a cheap, selfish publicity-seeker of low intelligence leading a wasteful, utterly pointless existence. In brief he declared, "I do not think she has ever had a serious thought in her life. . . . She has been a disaster." Auguste de Morny, who had warned Du Camp in advance of his arrest in December 1852, thereby permitting him to escape imprisonment, also came in for a thorough drubbing by this selfsame gentleman and fellow member of the Jockey Club. Gilbert Persigny made no pretence of concealing his feelings before or after the wedding. "From the day of my marriage I was honored with the hatred, a venomous slandering hatred," by this man, Eugénie recalled. "Sometimes he could not stop himself calling me 'the Spanish woman,' or 'the Foreigner.' "[14] And yet worse and more direct were the attacks by Mathilde and her "coarse, brutal, violent . . . jealous" brother, Plon-Plon—whose crude attempted seduction of Eugénie back in Madrid had been rebuffed as scornfully as had his earlier proposal of marriage to Queen Isabella. "You go to bed with women like Mlle. de Montijo, but you don't marry them," the bumptious Plon-Plon told Louis Napoléon, then repeated this "story" in society. Like most members of the Diplomatic Corps, the Austrian ambassador, Alexander Graf von Hübner, found Prince Jerome obnoxious, publicly describing him as "the scourge of the imperial family." Mathilde's enmity was more subtle and insidious, being feminine and dished out behind the scenes. In a vocabulary as earthy and crude as her brothers', she confided to Louis Napoléon, *"Cette Eugénie n'a pas plus de coeur que de c. . . ."*[15] Mathilde, always genuinely fond of Louis Napoléon, and perhaps regretting her father's decision to break off her earlier engagement with him, now instead advised his marrying into a ruling European family. The last person the ever jealous clan wanted to see as empress was the daughter of a distinguished grandee of Spain, an extremely attractive and wealthy foreign heiress who not only outranked them but over whom they had absolutely no influence to manipulate toward their own ends.

They then brought in reinforcements, the Bonaparte claque. Foreign Minister Drouyn de Lhuys, Ambassador Waleswki, and the onetime greengrocer, vaudevillian failure, and reprobate gambler, General Saint-Arnaud, all strongly advised Louis Napoléon against the marriage with the ninth Countess of Montijo. The outspoken former army sergeant Gilbert Persigny publicly referred to Eugénie as "that little schemer," and in private with the usual barracks vocabulary.[16] England's foreign minister, Lord John Russell, dismissed her in similar language, judging it would be "lowering of the imperial dignity with a vengeance by marrying the daughter of the 17th Marquis de Mora." "A foolish marriage," British ambassador Lord Cowley echoed; the Contessa de Montijo was just another "adventuress," he concluded, and not worthy of a Bonaparte.[17] The London *Times*, however, pointed out the absurdity of these pretensions: that unlike the parvenu Bonaparte clan—after fifty years hardly a dynasty—Eugénie came of ancient aristocratic stock going back over seven hundred years, whose titles included one duke, seven marquises, eight counts, and one viscount. Prosper Mérimée, as an old friend of the family, was so outraged by the slander and blatant character assassination of Eugénie that he had the College of Heralds in Madrid send a copy of her father's complete, most distinguished ancestry, which he then had published in Paris.[18]

Eugénie and her mother were among more than a couple of dozen guests invited by Louis Napoléon to celebrate Christmas of 1852 at the Château de Compiègne some fifty kilometers north of Paris. While out riding alone with her host on the twenty-seventh of December, he asked her outright to sleep with him. "Yes," she replied, "when I am empress." According to Maxime Du Camp, the year before, Louis Napoléon had had a secret door built into the wall of the bedroom at Fontainebleau he had assigned her to, but on entering was immediately shown out by the young lady. By now thoroughly tired of having to make herself perfectly clear to the deaf, newly proclaimed emperor of the French, the following day, the twenty-eighth of December, she and her mother departed abruptly, leaving an embarrassed Louis Napoléon behind to make his excuses to a château full of guests.[19]

At a dinner party at the Tuileries Louis Napoléon had taken his half brother, Auguste, aside, asking him for his frank opinion about marriage with Eugénie. Morny had steered him straight during his initial coup d'état in 1851, and then again during his second coup of December 2, 1852, establishing the Second Empire. Louis Napoléon put much store in his advice and assessment of the state of affairs. "She will make an excellent and most worthy spouse for an emperor," Morny assured him formally. "She will also serve as a fine symbol for the French people . . . who will appreciate . . . the choice of a girl who for a change is not a member of the traditional royal families that have been opposing your own family for the past fifty years." "Your opinion on this is more important to me than you can possibly imagine," a much relieved Louis Napoléon said.[20] He also learned from the spies of the prefect of police that Morny had, unlike the rest of his family and supporters, been praising Eugénie in public and in private as a fine choice as imperial consort for the emperor. "Mademoiselle de Montijo is lovely and carries herself with a natural dignity and grace," Morny was reported to have said. "The emperor respects the quality of a person's basic goodness, and wants to be able to love his wife without reservation."[21]

• • •

As if the past humiliations had not been bad enough, when James de Rothschild as a favor to Eugénie (her mother's friend and Paris banker) escorted her to a ball given at the Tuileries on January 12, 1853, she was about to sit down at one of the tables set aside for the ministers, when the bourgeois wife of an otherwise worthy minister of public instruction, Hippolyte Fortoul, took it upon herself to inform the elegant Countess de Montijo that she was not allowed to sit with them, with members of the government. A hush fell over the emperor's reception. A very grim Louis Napoléon immediately stepped over to the embarrassed lady, personally inviting her and Baron de Rothschild to join him and the imperial family. Holding her head high when dancing with him afterward, she told him tonight's episode was the last straw, the last insult, and that she would be leaving France permanently. The long procrastinating Louis Napoléon was in a corner.[22]

Three days later, on the fifteenth of January, Achille Fould, the emperor's much trusted minister of state, arrived at 12 Place de Vendôme to deliver a handwritten letter from Louis Napoléon to Doña Maria Manuela. "Madame la Comtesse, I fell in love with your daughter long ago. I have now come to ask you for her hand in marriage."[23] Brief and to the point. "A happy event, one destined to consolidate the government of His Imperial Majesty and ensure the future of the dynasty, is about to take place. The Emperor is to marry Mademoiselle de Montijo, Comtesse de Téba," the official newspaper, *Le Moniteur,* informed the French public at long last after months of rumors.

On Saturday, the twenty-second, the Corps Legislatif and Senate were summoned to the Tuileries to receive the official announcement. Eugénie was to become empress, he began. "French by heart, education and through the blood spilt by her father in defense of the Empire," she was endowed with all the fine qualities he sought. "A good and gracious lady she will bring to us the same virtues that Empress Joséphine brought to Napoléon. . . . [sic!] Once you get to know her I believe that you will be convinced that Providence itself played a role in discovering her." Tell France that "I have preferred a woman whom I love and respect to an unknown partner selected for me by the dictates of international politics."[24]

How true was Eugénie's love for this man after a pursuit of three years? If it was not a romantic love, it was certainly not social climbing. Perhaps she just considered it her due, given her high position in Spanish society. Her real feelings were revealed in a letter to her sister, Paca, the Duchess of Alba, just before the wedding. For all her physical posturing as a cigar-smoking matador, for all her praise of her very stoic, manly, almost unapproachable father and his exploits on the battlefield, in Louis Napoléon she found someone totally different. With him she felt completely at ease and safe. He was charming, gentle, soft-spoken, quiet, undemanding, and thoughtful. She admired his remarkable willpower, "yet without being blindly obstinate. He is capable of making the greatest of sacrifices for something in which he really believed. He will go looking for a wild flower in a wood on a wild winter's night . . . and all this just to please the whim of a woman he loves. And now tomorrow he will risk his crown rather than not share it with me. He never counts the cost once undertaking something. He is always ready to risk his whole future on a venture in which he truly believes, and that is why he always wins in the long run."[25] These very qualities she so admired in Louis Napoléon were of course the very qualities that reflected her own personal values, some found in her own thoughts and acts, others she personally lacked but so admired.

She could be very aggressive, terrifyingly obstinate, and could talk rapidly nonstop for an hour. He was a man of few words, sure of his position, which really required no public justification. He was equanimity personified, fully at ease with himself and what he stood for. Eugénie, on the other hand, was always questioning, arguing, restless, and almost hyperactive. She was rarely content with her existence and was always looking for something. She could lose her temper in a flash—as when she had stabbed herself—while, like Mathilde, she had found Louis Napoléon phlegmatic, a cold fish, extremely slow to anger. When she had a whim, she had to act on it vigorously. Louis Napoléon did not

have whims—with the unique exception of Eugénie and this marriage—
and was in any case very suspicious of "emotion" or "change" in any form.
She was more of a reader than he. She had a sense of color and decor
that he lacked. Fine art and old masters left him cold. She was tone deaf
and disliked opera, whereas he at least liked the music hall. They both
enjoyed dancing, Louis Napoléon waltzes and polkas, she only the
Spanish fandango, which she gladly performed with complete abandon
for her friends. He enjoyed a casual stroll in the gardens; she preferred
a mad ride cross-country on a powerful horse. She found in him the
peace she so desperately sought but never really found in herself.

Never in historical memory had plans for a full-scale royal wedding
been decided on and executed in less than seventeen days, including the preparations for the full pageantry of a cathedral ceremony with
thousands of invited guests—all senior officials, elected or appointed,
crown counselors, senators, deputies, judges, court officials, the entire
diplomatic corps, senior military officers, and officials of the Legion of
Honor, etc. State carriages last used by Napoléon I in 1815 had to be
found at the Trianon Palace, Versailles, cleaned, refurbished, and
brought back to Paris. Dozens of well-trained teams of horses for the
carriages had to be found and brought to the capital, including some
from as far as England. Invitations had to be printed and addressed by
hand. All the spare bedrooms and suites at the Élysée, the Tuileries-
Louvre complex, and at the Luxembourg Palace had to be cleaned and
prepared, including the acquisition of thousands of new sheets and
hundreds of additional staff. Moreover, many of the guests would be
arriving with their personal servants in tow. Feeding thousands of people
more or less simultaneously, preparing the dinner service and silver required for such state banquets, and finding enough additional well-
qualified cooks and servants, would prove a nightmarish challenge
itself. Many tons of fresh food would have to be ordered, and transported in from the countryside by cart and barge. Literally hundreds of
new gowns and a variety of costumes to be designed and sewn just for
the empress and the ladies of the court would prove a real strain and

tug-of-war, as the aristocratic ladies of the French capital all vied for the best-known couturiers. And then of course there was the demand for hairdressers skilled in current court styles.

Louis Napoléon had decided on this marriage on the twelfth of January, it being accepted by Eugénie on the fifteenth. To the utter astonishment of everyone an extremely agitated Louis Napoléon had then impetuously decided that the wedding was to take place, beginning with the civil service on the twenty-ninth of January, in fourteen days' time. Preparing the decorations for the Tuileries and the cathedral alone would take weeks, and then only with the continuous work of hundreds of men. Tons of fireworks would have to be ordered and prepared, and decorations for the capital and the ceremonial routes to and from the cathedral would require importing tens of thousands of flowers, and a few thousand flags all to be hand sewn, and an army of workers to install all this.

Napoléon III's "impulse" to set the wedding ceremonies for the twenty-ninth and thirtieth of January left the prefect of Paris little time in which to work out most complicated security arrangements for the palaces, the theaters, and the concert halls, this in a city no stranger to assassination attempts. Hundreds of known political opponents and agitators would have to be rounded up. The route to the cathedral covering the full length of the newly completed Rue de Rivoli would prove a challenge in itself, with hundreds of thousands of sightseers. In addition, at least sixty thousand troops and cavalry—not to mention thousands of national guardsmen—would have to be assigned their positions and tasks.

It was not only madness, it was impossible, all within less than a fortnight! Yet it has never been established convincingly why this mad rush had to take place now in 1853. Clearly an unusually impulsive Louis Napoléon had decided to act without planning and thinking out the consequences. It was reminiscent of his Strasbourg and Boulogne fiascos. In the present case there was no valid reason for this incomprehensible haste, when a late spring wedding would have saved enormous anguish for everyone. The famously nonchalant, phlegmatic, quiet, amiable Louis Napoléon had suddenly lost his head completely, astonishing even his closest staff and associates. Nor could anyone reason with him, nor dissuade him from launching this social tsunami. Moreover, Louis Napoléon and Eugénie decided to repeat as closely as possible everything that had been done for the marriage ceremony of Napoleon I and Marie Louise in 1810, as librarians were sent scurrying for the original plans.

Most of the crown jewels not seen since 1814 were finally located in the vaults of the ministry of finance. This included the gold, jewel-encrusted crown Marie Louise had worn, her rings and diamond-and-sapphire-studded belt. To these Napoléon III added a little surprise of his own, the celebrated Regent's Diamond, the 141-carat blue-white stone discovered in India in the seventeenth century, purchased by Governor Thomas Pitt—"the Pitt Diamond" as it was then known—eventually to be worn by Marie Antoinette, then seized during the revolution, and placed in the pommel of Napoléon I's sword. Although Marie Louise took it back with her to Vienna in 1815, her father had it returned to the newly enthroned Louis XVIII. Today Empress Eugénie wore it—at $63 million (today's value), the most expensive single gem in the whole of Europe—around her neck and would finally have it mounted in her Grecian-style crown.[26]

Meanwhile, the reception salons of the Tuileries were to be restored to their former glory, just as they had stood in Napoléon's day, including the towering Hall of Marshals, where the marriage contracts were to be signed. Not content with that enormous project, every effort was made to replicate the costumes worn under the First Empire down to Napoléon's silk knee breeches. Louis Napoléon was to wear the uniform of a lieutenant general with Napoléon I's collar of the Legion of Honor and the Order of the Golden Fleece, and Eugénie a specially designed gown of Alençon lace, complete with a twelve-foot train.[27]

On the wedding day, both sides of the Rue de Rivoli were lined with thousands of soldiers and national guardsmen restraining an estimated 600,000 onlookers, 200,000 of whom had reached Paris by the recently opened railways. The bunting, flags, flowers, and rousing military music might have been festive, but the mood of the people was almost neutral, unemotional, more curious than anything else. There were some *"Vive l'Empereur!"* and *"Vive l'Impératrice!"* but they were few and far between. A dozen carriages, each drawn by six horses and bearing high state and military officials and members of the clan, preceded Napoléon's celebrated glass 1804 coronation coach, now carrying Napoléon III and Eugénie. Drawn by eight superbly dressed horses, preceded by a squadron of guides, and followed by a full regiment of heavy cavalry, they reached Notre Dame. The hastily begun decorations in this cavernous gothic cathedral had not been completed, but in any event nothing could lighten grimy stone pillars and walls that had not been cleaned in decades.

Monseigneur the Archbishop of Paris and his clergy led Louis Napoléon and his bride up the main aisle over three hundred feet to the altar, surrounded by a vast amphitheater for all the high officials and officers of the land, although the seating assigned to foreign European royalty, as a token of their disapproval of the House of Bonaparte, remained entirely empty. The archbishop, Cardinal Sibour, performed the service as the couple exchanged vows and France was presented with its first emperor and empress since Waterloo.[28] Mass and the "Te Deum" followed, accompanied by the orchestra and choir. Eugénie was visibly nervous and "melancholy" during and after the ceremony, which passed as if in a dream, she later said, incapable of remembering any of it. The Bonaparte clan had remained openly hostile to the new empress—just as they had been to Joséphine back in 1804. Uncle Jérôme, to whom Louis Napoléon had given Louis Philippe's private property, the Palais Royal, and his son Plon-Plon, towering over Eugénie, had refused before all present to make the prescribed bow before her, the female cousins following their lead, refusing in turn to make their reverences. Eugénie had been shaken, and a visibly angered Louis Napoléon had been obliged publicly *to command* cousin Mathilde to curtsey.

Cannons roared and every church bell in Paris rang out as the procession returned along the quay to the Tuileries, where to everyone's surprise and approval the unpredictable Empress Eugénie turned and made a gracious curtsey of her own. A reception was held there for all the officials, followed by a smaller one in their private apartments. The newly married imperial couple then drove under cavalry escort to St. Cloud that same Sunday evening. There they were to spend their honeymoon, in the most secluded spot in France, completely cut off from the outside world, thanks to a strongly armed permanent garrison. Eugénie and Louis Napoléon—she always called him "Louis"—stayed in the villa of Villeneuve L'Étang near the park of St. Cloud. Louis Napoléon had made it perfectly clear that Eugénie's mother, Doña Maria Manuela, would be expected to return to Spain, as her rather promiscuous habits and staggering unpaid debts (charged to her son-in-law), her enormous wealth not withstanding, had rendered her presence an embarrassment.

M y dear Morny," Louis Napoléon wrote him a few days later, "Eugénie and I should like you to come dine with us this Saturday at six thirty [the week after the wedding] that you might witness for yourself this intimate foyer which your personal cooperation had helped bring about thanks to your devoted and enlightened friendship."[29]

Auguste de Morny, who had remained in the background at the Tuileries during the signing of the marriage contracts, and again the following day at the cathedral, lost amid the thousands, was now the couple's first visitor during their honeymoon. And thus the Second Empire began, and with it that strange relationship of two brothers who were to reshape the historical face of France. As for Louis Napoléon and Eugénie, if theirs was not to be a marriage of warmth and romance, it was to justify Morny's earlier faith in this union, which in its own certainly unique manner was to prove fruitful, reflecting a genuine mutual respect.

Eugénie was to become celebrated for her kindness and generosity, which began immediately, when the municipality of Paris offered to spend 600,000 francs on a diamond necklace for her. Gratefully declining, she asked instead that the money be used to build an orphanage for homeless girls. As a personal gift to her, Louis Napoléon had given her violets, her favorite flower, and 250,000 francs in cash, which she also dispersed for "maternal societies" and a hospice, keeping nothing for herself.

But of course she was now alone permanently in a foreign country, and Spain and family always remained in her thoughts. As she wrote to her sister, Paca, "Everyone's fate has a sad side . . . I who used to be so obsessed with my liberty am now in chains for the rest of my life . . . amid all this court etiquette, of which I am to be the principal victim." She would adapt, however, and add a whole new dimension to Napoléon III's court and empire. Here at St. Cloud she asked for only one wedding gift of her husband, that he grant pardons to the political prisoners who had been filling French prisons ever since the coup of December 1851; 4,312 men were released forthwith.[30]

20

BIRTH OF AN EMPIRE

*"It is the most charming way of making a journey. . . . We were traveling
at a terrifying speed. . . . But the jolting is hard on the stomach!"*[1]
—DELPHINE GAY DE GIRARDIN DESCRIBING HER FORTY-FIVE-KILOMETER-
PER-HOUR JOURNEY ABOARD PEREIRE'S FIRST PASSENGER TRAIN, FROM
PARIS TO SAINT-GERMAIN-EN-LAYE, IN AUGUST 1835

"There has been much talk about you and your financial dealings."[2]
—LOUIS NAPOLÉON TO AUGUSTE DE MORNY

On an August afternoon in 1849, a well-dressed fifty-year-old gentleman, dapper of stature and comfortable of girth, sat on the terrace of the spa at Baden, as he always did at this time of year. Hardly
handsome, with a wide brow, heavy face, and a remarkably serious
expression, clearly this was not a man who invited interruption. On the
table before him lay the latest newspapers from Frankfurt, Paris, and
London. "I was going through the papers," he later recalled, "and in my
lazy state read everything including the advertisements. I was struck by
one in particular, it was [Jules] Mirès's piece about his S[ocié]té Finan-
cière de la Caisse des Actions Réunies, capitalized at five million francs.
Its profits were impressive based on such a modest investment. I said to
myself if Mirès's one-man-operation could do that well, then a fully comprehensive organization with far greater financial backing could carry
out large scale operations including major industrial developments."[3]

On his return to the French capital, Finance Minister Achille Fould
approached the Pereire brothers, Émile and Isaac, who had pub-

lished articles on this subject and who, moreover, were men of known "character and intelligence."

Back in the spring of 1849, the French had been preparing for legis-lative elections set for the fourteenth of May, and Auguste de Morny was again running as deputy for the Auvergne. But even here in an elec-torally friendly area where Morny was well known and an important landowner and employer (for his Bourdon sugar refineries, near Cler-mont), elections required a liberal distribution of gold, and as usual he was for the moment broke. "If my tailor had not extended me credit, I would not have had a stitch to wear," he informed his stepmother, Margaret, the Countess de Flahaut. In fact the situation at that time was far more critical than that, for all four of the drafts he had attempted to cash in had been rejected by the bank. Desperate, he had paid a visit to the Élysée to see his brother, President Bonaparte, who then counter-signed those same four bank drafts. On resubmitting them, they were returned once again for "insufficient funds," only saved at the elev-enth hour by publisher Louis Hachette—Morny's business partner in various ventures—who obtained the money from the recently created Comptoir d'Escompte, or Discount Bank, on the guarantee of Alfred Mosselman (Fanny Le Hon's brother), who like Hachette held a major share in that private bank.[4]

With the aid of Finance Minister Achille Fould, the first thing Louis Napoléon had done in January 1852 was to concentrate on the problems afflicting the national economy. Vast amounts of money had to be injected, made available to French financial, commercial, and industrial markets, if the country was to shake itself free of the past stagnant half century and create a vibrant, modern, new France.

To begin with, the new banking–credit facilities would have to be flexible and plentiful enough to fund and support the creation of an extensive modern national transportation grid capable of facilitating new commercial and industrial enterprises. An entirely new—and as yet practically nonexistent—national rail network was the sine qua non for the development of the nation's commerce and industry. By January 1852, a few small railways had served passengers between Paris and the English Channel. The rest of the country was basically still a desert, with a total of only 3,910 kilometers of track (a quarter of what Louis Napoléon had earlier found in Great Britain, whose development in all fields remained his model to emulate). Moreover, the British had factories manufacturing everything France needed, from rails to locomotives, and upon whom the French would have largely to rely during the early days before French industry was capable of catching up.

First, financing was needed, and immediately, with which to launch these operations, and one of the last acts Morny had performed before leaving office as minister of the interior in January 1852 had been to make government funds available for this purpose. He and Louis Napoléon were of one mind in this respect. Long-term funding at low rates of interest would be required, made available through new credit institutions.

The Comptoir d'Escompte, had been founded back in 1848, but with a mere twenty million francs, it was hardly adequate for serious industrial projects. In that same year leftist politicians attempted to nationalize the early French railways but were voted down, or there would never have been the development that was to follow. Meanwhile, Louis Napoléon's finance minister, Achille Fould, upon returning from Baden back in the summer of 1849, had begun working with Émile and Isaac Pereire to create that new type of financial institution that would provide the large-scale financing required for the expansion of French railways, industry, and public works. And in November 1852, they had successfully launched the Crédit Mobilier.

On the fifteenth of November, the day on which the then prince-president signed the decree creating the Crédit Mobilier, James de Rothschild in a most unusual action broke cover and personally criticized Louis Napoléon for this act. By authorizing it, Rothschild argued, "their bank will be able to enter and control the company boards of directors managing every railway line, and every mining company in the country." In brief, Pereire's Crédit Mobilier would obtain business and profits that in the past had been the prized fiefdom and monopoly of Rothschild and the other traditional private banking houses.[5]

Initially capitalized at 60 million francs, or $774 million (that figure soon to be doubled), the Crédit Mobilier issued 40,000 shares at 500 francs per share. Benoît Fould, a conservative banker, and brother of finance minister Achille, was named president, and the ubiquitous Count de Morny (with a generous inducement of cash and free stock in his pocket) was named to its board of directors, complete with an additional salary for that service, and in turn attracted important new investors: the Duke of Mouchy (a Noaille cousin of Morny), and the equally wealthy Rafaele Ferrari (the Duke of Galliera), Ferdinand de Lesseps, several influential Jewish bankers, and hundreds of other investors from the Bourse and foreign markets. Initially the Pereires and members of their family, including Adolphe d'Eichtal, along with the Fould brothers, held controlling interest before it began its impressive expansion. James de Rothschild, however, declined to associate himself with his former protégés and their new institution—a bit of petty jealousy, perhaps, since he would emerge as a vigorous opponent of the Pereires in their future railway endeavors when they were becoming a real challenge.

The Crédit Mobilier was in fact an instant success in a market hitherto starved of large-scale investment capital, sealed with the official authorization of the state, thanks in large part to Morny and the Fould brothers; its shares soared from 500 to 2,110 francs, and the swift development of the nation's railways followed.[6]

The Crédit Mobilier, along with the banker Charles Laffitte, of the Laffitte banking house and a fellow Jockey Club friend of Morny, financed the railways into Normandy—connecting Paris with Rouen, Le Havre, Dieppe, Caen, Cherbourg, Rennes, and Brest. France now had freight and passenger service from Paris to the English Channel. Other emerging railway concessions, also refused financing by Rothschild, were completed thanks to the Crédit Mobilier, including François Bartholony's Lyon–Geneva line, the Besançon Company, and the great Paris–Strasbourg line. Crédit Mobilier funded the Compagnie des Ardennes of Mouchy, members of the Noailles family, and Baron Seillière. Naturally the Crédit Mobilier also funded the railways launched by the

Pereires in the southern and eastern regions of France, including their Compagnie du Midi, linking Bordeaux-Bayonne-Pyrénées, and on the Mediterranean side, the Perpignan–Spanish frontier line. Pereire also built the Bordeaux-Sette line. The Crédit Mobilier was excluded from the most important railway network, however, the PLM's Paris-Lyons-Mediterranean (Marseilles) lines and that of Paris-Orléans-Bordeaux—controlled by the banker François Bartholony and Paulin Talabot.[7] Pereire very badly wanted to have a long-distance rail service running out of the French capital, but when he later applied for a concession in 1856, Louis Napoléon's two new cabinet members, Eugène Rouher, minister of agriculture, commerce, and public works, and Pierre Magne, finance minister, both of them very close to Morny, turned him down.

On April 21, 1853, Count de Morny brought off what was to prove the supreme coup of his life when Louis Napoléon obliged him by issuing an imperial decree authorizing the creation of the Grand Central to establish its lucrative railway network, which would be strongly supported by the highly productive mines in the south (such as the Mines d'Aubin, and the Houillières de Carmaux). It included rail links between Limoges-Agen, and Lyon-Bordeaux via the Massif Central and Morny's and Rouher's properties, between Clermont Ferrand and Montauban, and the Rhône-Loire.

Morny's reward was indeed "imperial": he was named president of the new Grand Central, with an equally charming salary, not to mention 30,000 shares gratis worth 15 million francs, without counting their biannual dividends.[8] When news of Morny's latest coup reached the Tuileries, an alarmed Louis Napoléon took the unusual step of calling on his brother at his Champs-Élysées pavilion. "You know what brings me here today," Louis Napoléon began. "There is much talk about you and your financial dealings." "No doubt the shareholders will enrich themselves," brother Auguste replied, "but at the same time so will the country," and of course Louis Napoléon was to share in those riches, as he did in most of the other concessions he granted through decrees and legislation.[9]

In almost every major rail negotiation Morny proved to be the grand "facilitator" in return for often outrageous compensation, and frequently thanks to his brother's cooperation. As the emperor's brother, Auguste de Morny was clearly the most powerful and influential promoter in the country, attested by his very busy schedule. Then, in the midst of his complicated maneuvers involving the Crédit Mobilier and Grand Central, on June 22, 1854, a messenger brought a letter from the Tuileries.

"*Mon cher* Morny, I should like to give you another token of my friendship and esteem by naming you President of the Chambers [of the Legislative Body]. Do tell me you will accept." Morny had reaped in fortunes because of his half brother's help, and he clearly was in his debt. "*Mon cher et bon empereur*," he replied. "Let me tell you how profoundly touched I am by this offer." Nevertheless he declined a handsome salary and the luxurious Hôtel de Lassay, that went with the position. It was a job for life if he wanted it, but it would also mean losing hours daily from his own highly prosperous personal affairs. Nevertheless Louis Napoléon, renowned by now for his tenacity once he got an idea, in the last week of October that same year invited brother Auguste to dine at the Tuileries. Morny having just returned from a relaxing summer spent at his newly completed château of Nades, on his three-thousand-hectare estate located north of Vichy, Louis Napoléon was counting on finding him much more refreshed and amenable. After dinner that evening he again turned to the Corps Legislatif. "Well now, the matter of the presidency, what is it to be? You know that I have very good reasons in wanting you for this post, and not simply out of friendship." Even the brother of the emperor could not decline a second time what was in effect an imperial command, and on the twelfth of November Auguste de Morny moved into the palatial Hôtel de Lassay, contiguous to the National Assembly and addressed the Corps Legislatif as its president for the first time.[10]

In charge of the proceedings of the deputies, Morny would set the day's agenda and select the legislation they were to vote on—but they were not allowed to debate, nor were they even permitted to address their colleagues in the hemicycle from the podium (which Morny literally had removed). In brief, Auguste de Morny was working hand-in-glove with the emperor, who was de facto responsible for having the legislative proposals drawn up by the Conseil d'État and his ministers.

And because of the special relationship with the emperor, Morny had extraordinary influence in getting through some of his own pet projects, invariably motivated by enormous bribes, as in the case of the Grand Central. For instance, his help in obtaining the concession of the small Mulhouse-Besançon railway alone brought him 2.2 million francs.[11] Not only could Morny be paid for bringing parties together or for serving on a variety of company boards, he could be influential in arranging for state financing and guaranteed returns for new industrial projects. By the same token, he could draft the necessary legislation favoring his own private projects with interested parties and have these projects pushed through the chamber, all arranged agreeably enough over a champagne dinner in the Hôtel Lassay. The Senate, handpicked and appointed for life by Louis Napoléon, guaranteed swift approval.

Morny being Morny, regardless of the work at the Corps Legislatif, and his many railway, mining, and complex financial commitments, was not a man to overlook "lesser" personal opportunities, such as with his close business associate, the publisher Louis Hachette, in their Papeteries d'Essonnes (Essonnes Paper Company), which provided the paper for Hachette's burgeoning publishing empire, including books and the newly emerging magazines. The Essonnes company also held the multimillion-franc monopoly in providing the imperial government's entire paper supply, in addition to selling the paper on which the shares of the Grand Central were printed—that subtle Morny touch again. It amused him. His newspaper, *Le Constitutionnel,* was also a guaranteed customer. Through a well-rewarded Morny, Hachette gradually obtained the bookshop monopoly of the nations' railway stations beginning in 1852, while also retaining the monopoly for printing all textbooks for the nation's schools. In addition, Morny and Hachette made many cross-investments in mining and railways and remained trusted allies to the end of their lives.[12]

As a financial manipulator, Auguste de Morny was at the peak of his influence in 1855–1856, but for reasons never explained, he began stabbing old faithful friends and investors in the financial-industrial world in the back,[13] beginning with the Pereire brothers, Émile and Isaac, who had already enriched him many times over. At issue was the Grand

Central, which Morny now wanted all for himself. On April 9, 1856, he announced that he was to join the Grand Central's network with those of their archrivals, the PLM. Émile Pereire—who, like his brother, was distinguished by his integrity and fidelity in an otherwise ruthless financial world—for one had been as astounded as he was furious at this betrayal. This apparently stemmed from Morny's earlier attempt, in 1855, to gain a new railway concession independently linking the Grand Central (via Montauban and the Pyrenees) to the Franco-Spanish frontier and Madrid, bypassing Pereire and his own already existing Perpignan–Spanish frontier line. Why share any profit with loyal old friends? Not only that, but Morny had had the effrontery to ask Pereire's Crédit Mobilier for its financing, Morny apparently anticipating a 22-million-franc ($284 million) "commission" from the Spanish concessionaire, José de Salamanca.[14] Indeed, so appalled were the trusting and usually very calm Pereire brothers, and with Morny completely out of control (supported by the emperor, he too now abandoning them after refusing their Paris railway concession in July 1856), that they decided to liquidate the entire Grand Central network while at once stripping Morny of his position as CEO.

Before Émile Pereire could act, however, president of the Grand Central Auguste de Morny sabotaged the whole operation, secretly liquidating his 30,000 shares at top market value reputedly for well over 60 million francs ($774 million). What is not clear, however, is what Morny did with these fabulous sums he reaped throughout the 1850s and 1860s, though his gambling habit (inherited from Grandfather Talleyrand, no doubt) is the only probable explanation. In any event, by the time Pereire and his fellow investors heard about Morny's treachery, the price of shares had plunged. The Pereire brothers, among others, lost heavily. When the Grand Central officially closed its doors on April 11, 1857, its railways were sold to the Paris-Orléans and Paris-Lyon Lines.[15] But their principal shareholders, Bartholony and Talabot, also felt betrayed both by Morny's secret double-dealing and each other in their attempts (and bribes) to secure those lines for themselves.

By the late spring of 1856, Morny's name was irrevocably tarnished in the financial world, not to mention within the Jockey Club. For all that, however, he could not be ignored. As the emperor's brother and president of the Corps Legislatif, he remained lethally influential, capable of controlling both favorable imperial decrees and legislation affecting the Bourse and finance. Dislike and distrust Auguste de Morny as they may, the financiers and industrialists working through the Bourse would continue to be obliged to work with him unless he could somehow be removed from the scene. Murders have been committed for less.

The Congress of Paris in March 1856, bringing to a close the calamitous Crimean War, seemed the ideal time, if a most unlikely excuse, for Louis Napoléon to do something about this embarrassing half brother, whose latest escapade had left the Paris Bourse stewing in financial turmoil. Their relationship was never clearly defined, and while needing Morny, a cautious, wary Louis Napoléon well realized he had to give him a lot of leeway and tread softly by not inquiring too closely into Morny's personal affairs. As emperor, he could not afford to alienate him or ask too many questions. But now, given his highly visible role during the settlement of the Crimean War, not to mention his position before a now clamoring Corps Legislatif, as Napoléon III he had to put public distance between himself and Morny. The official coronation ceremony of Tsar Nicholas's successor, Alexander II, was to take place later in the year, and France was asked to send a delegation on a bridge-building mission after years of war and acrimony. This invitation proved providential, the most opportune moment for removing Auguste de Morny from Paris. An outspoken opponent of the Crimean War in the first place, and a lifelong Russophile, Count de Morny was hastily appointed ambassador to Russia.

It was a scramble, but on July 4, 1856, Ambassador-designate Morny— taking a leave of absence from his post as president of the Corps Legislatif—boarded a train with a special freight car filled with his baggage and the inevitable paintings and antiques he intended to hawk at the Russian imperial court, and set off with his hastily assembled diplomatic staff on his long journey via Berlin and Konigsberg to the Russian capital—leaving the wreckage and acrimony of his financial finagling far behind . . . which was no doubt a great relief to brother Louis Napoléon.[16]

At this time every phase of rail construction was in a veritable frenzy: colossal real estate transactions, iron and steel manufacture to provide the rails and the engines, the great expansion of coal and iron mining made possible by these new railways. Foreign investors, especially the English and Germans, were flocking to the Bourse to take advantage of this fantastic boom, as they were to do later in South America and the United States. Overnight France was awash with a vast new wealth that seemed to appear out of nowhere, and by 1857, the country had 14,200 kilometers of rail, into which investors had poured 2.7 billion francs—the price of a couple of wars. The economy was fueled by a series of new financial institutions. James de Rothschild, in addition to his bank, belatedly caught up with, and successfully surpassed, the Pereires by creating new large-scale investment funds for the development of industry, the railways in particular. The government created the first mortgage banks, both for private property and for farmers. The Crédit Foncier de France was established to finance real estate projects, and the Crédit Industriel et Commercial, the first great bank to accept deposits by private individuals, was used to launch large new enterprises. Louis Napoléon's government facilitated the legislation required to support this burgeoning new world, further aided by combining and centralizing the ministries of agriculture, commerce, and public works into a powerful super ministry. And then new legislation later in the 1860s would create the first *sociétés anonymes*, or corporations, resulting in the launching of the nation's great public banking institutions, including the Banque de Paris, the Crédit Agricole, the Société Generale, and the Crédit Lyonnais, all of which have continued into our own times.[17]

As for the Crédit Mobilier, it was severly hurt by Morny's actions in the Grand Central, but that financial institution's activities were not limited to railways. Real estate and construction also benefitted from its resources, along with those of the Crédit Foncier. The Pereire brothers created an exclusive new quarter of the capital, the Parc Monceau, where splendid mansions were appearing, including one Fanny Le Hon was to move into after selling her residence on the Champs-Élysées. With the city's extension of the Rue de Rivoli as far as the Hôtel de Ville by the end of 1852, and the razing of dozens of medieval tenements overlooking the Carrousel, the Louvre, and what is today the Place du Théâtre Français, the Pereire brothers built the Grand Hôtel du Louvre for the opening of the Exhibition of 1855. At the same time they were acquiring much more land around what were to become the *"grands boulevards"* of which the new Opéra would ultimately become its fashionable center. This focused on their follow-up eight-hundred-room Grand Hotel de la Paix, opposite the Place de l'Opéra, with the capital's first en suite facilities and central heating. A fabulous success, the building boom in this quarter of the city made the Pereires perhaps the greatest real estate tycoons of the day.

Real estate speculation fever was rampant throughout the Second Empire, facilitated by the development of a national railway grid across the country, for example enabling the Pereires to build an entire city resort of seaside villas for the wealthy at Arcachon, outside Bordeaux. Later Auguste de Morny was to do one better, creating the city of Deauville along the English Channel, complete with luxury mansions, restaurants, a casino, and a racecourse named after himself. Louis Napoléon and Eugénie did not share the same delight in this development, however, when the modest fishermen's huts at Biarritz gave way to another seaside resort, complete with casino, around their previously isolated Villa Eugénie.[18]

Morny's ambassadorial assignment to Russia in 1856 proved a veritable diplomatic triumph, as a result of the very close, surprisingly warm relationship established between him and the new tsar, Alexander II. This unexpected friendship astonished and perplexed many, the English in particular, who were disturbed to find these two recent belligerents, France and Russia, bitter wartime enemies in the Crimea, now almost bosom friends. The Morny–Alexander relationship was, of course, key to this diplomatic breakthrough, though in reality it was the consequence of Morny's long-term close personal relations with Russian diplomats, including Paul Kisseleff. In addition to hawking many Flemish paintings, Auguste de Morny now met and married a beautiful blond seventeen-year-old princess of the royal family, Sophie Troubetzkouï, by whom he was to have two sons and two daughters. Tsar Alexander, who attended the marriage and gave the bride away at St. Catherine's Church in Moscow on January 19, 1857, also provided her with a 500,000-franc cash dowry, equivalent to many millions today.[19]

Although Morny's diplomatic breakthrough with Russia, at a time of increasing Prussian hostility, was welcomed in Paris, news of his forthcoming marriage and the intention of returning to the French capital, was not. The fact was that Morny's name was still anathema in Parisian financial circles, and if possible, worse yet for the Tuileries. Nor was Morny himself to escape another storm, one uniquely French, which was about to burst. The heretofore stable, sophisticated fifty-three-year-old Countess Le Hon, for so long Morny's mistress, on learning of his forthcoming marriage to Sophie, went berserk, frightening everyone, including her son Léopold Le Hon, her brother Alfred Mosselman, their mutual friend, Prosper Mérimée, and Louis Napoléon in particular. "Madame Le Hon was horribly upset and even broke down in public," Edmond de Goncourt remarked. "All they are talking about now is Monsieur de Morny's marriage and Madame Le Hon's furious reaction," Mérimée reported to Madame de Montijo in mid-February 1857. Fanny responded by sending a threatening two-line note to Morny warning that if he went ahead with the wedding, "I shall publish your letters regarding the Coup d'État [of December 2, 1851] and other documents." Not content with blackmail, Fanny went to the Tuileries, causing a frightful row, demanding that Louis Napoléon refuse permission for the wedding to take place, and for Morny's right to return to France. "I made his first fortune! . . . I took him up as a mere subaltern and today leave him a minister plenipotentiary!"[20] she literally screamed over and over again, even in public. On learning of the marriage ceremony, she summoned her lawyers, now demanding the reimbursement of the seven million francs—hundreds of millions of dollars—she claimed to have lent him over the previous two decades. "Many are turning their back on

Mme. Le Hon," Horace de Viel-Castel remarked, "claiming she's taking Morny for all he is worth just out of sheer spite." In any case, he predicted, "Morny won't be coming back from Russia, because his colossal swindle of the Grand Central has left the company in ruins."[21]

On Louis Napoléon's reading of Fanny's threatening note, which Morny had rushed to him by diplomatic pouch, this potential new scandal—the publication of documents also possibly linking him personally to some of Morny's dubious financial affairs—was just too much. Across this letter Morny had written: "Must be acted upon very quickly in order to avoid a big scandal!" By return courier to Russia Louis Napoléon sent orders to brother Auguste forbidding both his marriage and his return to France. Moreover, he warned, if Auguste did marry and return to Paris, it would no longer be to the Hôtel de Lassay and his powerful post as president of the Corps Legislatif, with its million-franc perks. On the other hand, if he remained at his ambassadorial post, he would be raised in the peerage from count to be known as the "Duke de Morny." But Morny had ignored the threat and married in January, anticipating his early return to France, when his brother would, he hoped, have regained his usual composure.

Hell hath no fury like that of a jealous, superceded woman, and with Fanny's threat to make public Morny's personal correspondence, and more importantly possible lists of bribes, confidential business contracts, papers, and accounts—some directly involving the emperor—not to mention revelations about Morny's role (not Louis Napoléon's) as the real mastermind behind his coup d'état of December 1851, the emperor had to act. Shaken by this thunderbolt, a very real possible *threat to his very throne*, he immediately summoned Prefect of Police Joseph Piétri, who dispatched Inspector Griscelli to Fanny's mansion in the Champs-Élysées to seize all those potentially incriminating papers. A very uncomfortable Léopold witnessed the whole thing as a furious Fanny screamed—"I am going to tell the whole of Europe about your government's police-state tactics!"And as if the shaken emperor did not have enough on his plate, he was handed the latest grim monthly casualty figures from the battlefields in Algeria, even as ships arrived at Toulon with the French army's wounded and dead.

In the meantime, taking the spiteful Countess Le Hon at her word, Louis Napoléon took steps to ensure her silence by appointing a "neutral" commission to study the Morny-Le Hon business accounts, in order to establish a fair amount for the reimbursement claimed by her. Unfortunately, he named to head this commission his minister of agriculture, commerce, and public works, the fifty-one-year-old Eugène Rouher. This gentleman had not only been Morny's protégé and fellow deputy from Auvergne for many years, and a shareholder in some of his enterprises, including Morny's Bourdon Sugar Refinery, he also happened to be Fanny's current lover. Rouher as a lawyer, ignoring the double conflict of interests, nevertheless undertook this assignment, awarding Fanny Le Hon three million francs. Receiving only half the amount demanded, more hysterics ensued as Fanny closed her much used bedroom door to the good Eugène Rouher.

Morny, for his part, was furious on learning that his trusted friend and business associate Rouher had not only fiddled in his private affairs but had dared to render judgment against him. He had been betrayed by all of them—Rouher, Fanny, and Louis Napoléon. Outrageously claiming lack of liquidity, Morny refused to pay the three million. By now desperate to extinguish this conflagration, Louis Napoléon personally intervened decisively, paying Fanny that sum out of his own purse, while handing Auguste a contract for a short-term, interest-bearing loan for that amount. Parisians, and the many opponents and enemies of the three parties, were enjoying yet another tawdry spectacle *à la française*. After the very good year of financial profits and the most successful royal visit of Queen Victoria to Paris in 1855, the ensuing years 1856–1857 were proving to be veritable nightmares for Napoléon III.[22]

Completely oblivious to his brother's threats, orders, and current discomfort resulting from the financial scandals and the Fanny Le Hon Affair raging in Paris, Auguste de Morny chose this moment to return to France with his golden bride. Immediately on his arrival on July 2, 1857, he confronted Louis Napoléon who, with Eugénie, was taking the waters at their favorite spa in the Vosges Mountains, Plombières.

They met in the garden while Eugénie watched from a safe distance, hearing for the first and only time very loud, angry words by both brothers. The next day, an unperturbed Morny returned to Paris, installing his lovely Russian princess in the Hôtel de Lassay, and resumed business as usual. Nothing daunted Auguste de Morny. He remained president of the Corps Legislatif until the day of his premature death seven years later. The fact is that Louis Napoléon not only needed him, but could not survive without his wayward half brother.

———◆———

21

GEORGES HAUSSMANN

"I had, and continue to hold, the deepest personal conviction that the
only form of Democracy suitable to France is the Empire."[1]
—GEORGES EUGÈNE HAUSSMANN

F ollowing the treaty of Westphalia in 1864 that concluded the Thirty
Years' War with its hardened religious divisions of the Holy Roman
Empire, the Haussmanns, as Protestants, had fled Cologne. Eventually
establishing themselves outside Colmar in French Alsace in the last half
of the eighteenth century, this industrious family established a large fac-
tory manufacturing printed cotton cloth. One brother of this family,
Nicolas, the grandfather of Prefect Haussmann, was the first to become
a naturalized French citizen. Settling in Versailles during the Revolution of 1789, he became a deputy in the National Assembly and the Convention. Charged with the administration of the Department of Seine
and Oise, he also served as a commissioner—war contractor—for the
First Republic's armies of the Rhineland and the North. Retiring with a
substantial fortune, he acquired a large estate at Chaville (between
Versailles and St. Cloud), where his grandson, the future prefect, was
to spend most of his first seven years.

Twice the outsiders—as Germans and Lutherans—all the Haussmanns, including grandson Georges, consciously spent their lives proving their loyalty to the French people and the government of the day.
Like the grandfather, his son, Nicolas Valentin Haussmann, also served
with the army as a government war contractor and later as a military in-
tendant. Unemployed during the Bourbon Restoration, 1815–1830, he

resumed his work under the July Monarchy, serving under Louis Philippe in France and Algeria, retiring with the fall of his government in 1848.[2]

In 1806, Nicolas Valentin married into another German Lutheran family, the Dentzels. His bride, Eve Marie Caroline, was the daughter of a most unusual, highly decorated army officer. Born at Bad Dürkheim in 1855, Georges Frederic Dentzel had begun his career as a Lutheran pastor, moving to France, where he served first as a Protestant army chaplain under French Bourbon colors with Rochambeau in support of General Washington during the American Revolution. With the fall of Louis XVI, Dentzel continued, but in a military capacity under the French revolutionary flag. Exchanging the pulpit for a commission in the army under Emperor Napoléon, he participated as a soldier in the Prussian and Austrian campaigns, when Bonaparte appointed him military governor of Vienna. After surviving the Russian campaign of 1812, Dentzel went on to fight at Dresden and in Spain, where he was twice wounded and rewarded with a peerage as a baron and the Legion of Honor. Brigadier General Dentzel served on Napoléon's staff to the very end, then retired to Versailles. Dentzel's other son, Louis, also served with Napoléon as a lieutenant colonel until 1815. "Following the catastrophe of Waterloo, everyone in the family came home, including my uncle, Colonel Dentzel, his arm smashed by a musket ball," Georges Haussmann recalled. "But no member of the family welcomed the return of the Bourbons, and Louis Dentzel was obliged to leave the country, going to Greece, where he was killed in battle fighting the Turks."[3]

In the meantime, Nicolas Valentin and Caroline had produced a family, including the future prefect of the Seine, Georges Eugène Haussmann, born in Paris on March 27, 1809—at a time when his father was serving under Prince Eugène de Beauharnais, who acted as the boy's godfather, hence the boy's middle name. At the age of eight, Georges was sent to a new, very progressive boarding school for the aristocracy at Bagneux, some ten kilometers due south of Paris. There he was fortunate enough to be brought under the sway of the school's brilliant director and oratorian, M. Legal.

The school was dedicated to the traditional classical education based on Greek and Latin culture, along with the usual courses in geography, mathematics, languages, drawing, fencing, gymnastics, and riding. The musically talented boy sang in the choir and studied the violin and cello. In his spare evening hours, he took special courses in physics, chemistry, biology, and astronomy. He had a simply unquenchable thirst for knowledge. Despite his very real adoration of both grandfathers, Georges Haussmann was never to demonstrate any interest whatsoever in either the military or politics. Although spending only two years at this prep school, his time there certainly disciplined his mind and helped shape his future studies, interests, and attitude toward life.

At the age of eleven, the precocious Georges was enrolled in the capital's elite Collège Henri IV (formerly the Imperial Lycée, and today's Lycée Condorcet). There he resumed his passion for learning and "immediately became head of my class," where he remained. Although not gratuitously boastful, on the other hand Haussmann was never known for his modesty.[4] There he resumed a classical curriculum, in addition to music, drawing, and fencing. He also audited courses at the Sorbonne and the Collège de France, including philosophy, differential calculus, chemistry, and physics. As student Haussmann put it, "One can cram a great many things into a schedule beginning at six a.m. and lasting until midnight, and beyond."[5]

For this energetic prodigy and polymath, that did not suffice. He played the cello in the college orchestra, while concurrently taking courses at the Paris Conservatoire in harmony, counterpoint, and composition from the director of the conservatory himself, Luigi Cherubini. It was "composition" that most attracted him however. Every sonata had to have three well-balanced movements, every symphonic work the prescribed four. He did not agree with the free new romantic compositions of his friend and fellow student Hector Berlioz, preferring instead the reliable traditional works of Bach, Handel, and Haydn.[6] Well-defined and balanced composition was everything. His well-rounded studies and disciplined mind, reinforced by his Protestant work ethic, were to help shape, formulate, and dictate his approach to the great work facing him in the future when prefect of the Seine.

Meanwhile the Collège Henri IV attracted not only the best academic students, but the sons of politically prominent families as well, including Haussmann's new classmates, Auguste and Charles, the sons of Louis Philippe's prime minister, Casimir-Pierre Perier, as well as that king's eldest son, the Duke of Chartres (later Duke of Orléans), and his younger brother, the Duke of Nemours. Moreover, as one of the several industries in the hands of the wealthy Casimir-Perier family included the manufacture of printed cotton cloth, the name of Haussmann was already well known to them. All these contacts were shortly to aid Georges Haussmann's early career. In addition, other friends, including Gabriel Boucher, his closest friend (future secretary-librarian to Louis Philippe, and senator during the Third Republic), Ferdinand Le Roy (a future prefect in his own right who later under Prefect Haussmann served as his director of the Caisse des Travaux de Paris), and Ferdinand de Lesseps's brother, Jules. [7]

No sooner had I completed my studies [at the age of seventeen] with my Bachelier ès Lettres behind me, than I enrolled in the School of Law." There he concentrated on courses dealing with real estate and property contracts, mortgages, marriage contracts, inheritance, testaments, etc., all of which he would put to good use after 1853 during his prefectorial career. "With a good memory, I found my studies easy and painless." He passed his third year in law still at the top of his class before going on to the final two years' work, on his doctoral thesis.[8] Fully grown now, he was very tall and sturdy after his frequent swims, fencing, and long walks.

On completion of his thesis at the École de Droit, Georges Haussmann had to decide on a career. Rejecting an army commission and a private law practice, "with my final diploma in hand I returned to the Duke d'Orléans to declare myself ready to enter the State administration."[9]

The Duke d'Orléans tried to dissuade him, but King Louis Philippe had the new prime minister, Casimir-Pierre Perier, step in, "who then summoned me. He already knew me [through his sons] as well as my family [in Colmar as business associates]." And thus Georges Hauss-mann's career in the French civil service was launched. "I was now at-tached as Secretary General of the Prefecture of Vienne [at Poitiers]." He never regretted his choice, and his career never looked back.[10] Over the following twenty-two years he was to hold posts from the Var to the Gironde, during which he proved an exceptionally able, dedicated, and firm administrator, one not afraid to apply the authority of his office and the state to achieve his goals.

Nevertheless, the rapid promotion he had expected was checked for many years after the premature death of Premier Casimir-Perier, followed by the accidental death of Georges's classmate, the Duke of Orléans, in a freak traffic accident in 1842. Meanwhile when still a deputy pre-fect in 1838, Haussmann met and married Octavie de La Harpe, of a prosperous Swiss Protestant family that owned a large estate and vine-yards near Bordeaux. If hardly a love match, it was to prove a generally satisfying marriage, despite long periods of separation.

By 1853, a professionally disappointed Haussmann, modestly wealthy through his own family and his wife's, had been in service for more than two decades and was beginning to think about concluding his career as prefect of the Gironde in a few years' time. He was well known and well established in this region and anticipating marriages for his two daughters, when, on June 23, 1853, while dining with his deputy-prefect, a government courier arrived with a "telegram" from Interior Minister Persigny informing him that he had just been selected for the senior pre-fectureship of the country, that of the Seine. "This dispatch that I had just received not only took me aback, but more than that, caused me some anxiety. . . . Nothing had prepared me for this [new] nomination." But the arrival of a second telegram from Persigny, informing him that Louis Napoléon was personally nominating him to his post, ended any possible hesitation on Haussmann's part. In fact, he was immensely pleased, unlike his wife, who later wished to remain at Bordeaux. The prefecture of the French capital, however, was the jewel in the crown, the supreme quest.[11]

The following week, on the morning of the twenty-ninth, dressed in the state blue-and-silver-encrusted state uniform as prefect, Georges Haussmann alighted from his carriage and entered the sprawling splendor of the St. Cloud Palace. "From the vestibule I was led up the *escalier d'honneur,* the formal staircase, up to the first floor, through the great antechamber and the adjoining salons. Passing the Gobelins tapestries representing the Marriage of Henri IV and Marie de Médicis, we continued as far as the billiards room," where a ministerial meeting was drawing to a close. "[Minister of the Interior] de Persigny then came out to lead us into the Audience Chamber where Louis Napoléon was standing. On seeing me he came over to tell me how pleased he was to be able to offer me a post to which he attached such exceptional importance during the present circumstances." Persigny then assembled all the other newly nominated prefects and read out the oath: "Do you swear to uphold the Constitution and to be loyal to the Emperor?" "As the emperor took my right hand pressing it between his, I replied: 'I swear it.' I was now well and truly the Prefect of the Seine!"[12]

Later on, Haussmann was surprised by the apparent cordiality of the interior minister, his new boss: "M. de Persigny welcomed me more warmly than I had been led to expect." Little did he realize, however, what this same devious Gilbert Persigny was really thinking of him, as that interior minister's *Mémoires* reveal. "I had before me one of those most robust and vigorous types, at once wily and crafty, resourceful and audacious," a defensive Persigny began. "So self-assured about his own importance and accomplishments, this man went on to relate the full story of his career to date, and would have continued on about himself for another six hours if I had let him. . . . What a strange personality he revealed . . . underlined by a sort of brutal cynicism, so that I could not wait to see this animal of the big game variety thrown into the [political] arena against other men of equal ambition."[13] Little did Prefect Haussmann realize what hostile forces—both in Louis Napoléon's ranks, and those outside—lay before him. Fortunately for him, Persigny would soon be replaced there.

. . .

ollowing the ceremony and a reception by the ministers who had
just emerged from the cabinet meeting—Saint-Arnaud, Ducos,
Abbatucci, Magne, Drouyn de Lhys, and Fould—"the Emperor introduced me to the Empress," as they were shown into the dining room.
"Did you know that my uncle, Prince Eugène, was his [Haussmann's]
godfather?" Louis Napoléon informed Eugénie, "just as he was yours."
Haussmann added that "a general in her [his wife's] family serving with
the French army was killed while fighting in Italy, and his bust still stood
in the Hall of Marshalls." After asking the new prefect a few more questions about his family background, Louis Napoléon nodded, satisfied.
"It's quite true, you are Alsatian by origin." A true sign of approval.[14]

It was clear that the two men had taken to each other and delighted
at finding things that mutually reinforced this feeling. This was further
strengthened when Louis Napoléon learned of Haussmann's German
ancestry and that he spoke German as well, the language of Louis
Napoléon's nostalgic school days in Augsburg. For personal friendships
Napoléon III always reserved a special place for Italians and fellow
Carbonari, while for serious posts in the government he felt a special
confidence in those with German roots.

"After lunch the Emperor took me down to his [ground floor] office,"
informing him that he would be given an entirely free hand in his
work. In fact there would soon be no ministerial intermediaries; he
would be responsible directly to him and him alone. And then Louis
Napoléon came to the purpose of this visit. "The Emperor was anxious
to show me a map of Paris on which he had traced blue, red, yellow and
green lines, each color indicating the priority of the work anticipated."[15]
Only when he had explained the meaning of those lines and what they
were to encompass did Georges Haussmann begin to grasp the enormity of the project that lay in store for him. As prefect he was expected
to rebuild the entire central heart of the French capital, in the course of
which gutting and clearing hundreds of acres of medieval buildings and
ancient narrow streets, while replacing them with modern structures,
driving through spacious new boulevards, while not forgetting the

introduction of the city's entirely new sewage and freshwater systems. He was simply staggered. Although he had always been considered a brilliant student, hard worker, and efficient prefect, even for a Haussmann, this work would prove the most daunting challenge of his life. In addition, he would be responsible for the normal demanding administrative duties of running Paris, as the office of the prefect also comprised that of mayor of the capital.

Nor could he possibly foresee how this would evolve into a close daily working relationship with Napoléon III, one extending far beyond the formal official work. Indeed a relationship of trust and responsibility was to develop, resulting in Louis Napoléon depending heavily on Prefect Haussmann's judgment over the next sixteen and a half years. No other official of his senior rank in the government, apart from Achille Fould, was to hold such a position continuously throughout the Second Empire. Georges Haussmann, for his part, genuinely respected the emperor and his office, and would work faithfully to serve them both to the utmost of his very considerable ability. The final product, an entirely new Paris, would reflect their mutual dedication. There was in fact probably not another single individual in the whole of Paris with Haussmann's sweeping intelligence, splendid education, drive, integrity, indomitable spirit, determination, and sheer dedication capable of tackling this unique and most forbidding task.

22

PREFECT OF PARIS

*"Everything I have achieved I owe to the Emperor
and my own hard work."*[1]
—GEORGES HAUSSMANN

*"Yes, gentlemen, Long Live the Emperor, who wishes to make of Paris
the first city of the world, and a capital truly worthy of France."*[2]
—PREFECT HAUSSMANN'S ADDRESS TO HIS OFFICIALS, JUNE 1853

At eight o'clock on the morning following my installation [as prefect at St. Cloud on June 29, 1853], the government carriage arrived at my hotel to take me to the Hôtel de Ville [the headquarters of the prefecture of the Seine]."[3] While showing him his special map of Paris the previous evening, Louis Napoléon had outlined his general plans for completely transforming the French capital, plans for which Haussmann was to be soley responsible.

The key to everything, he explained, would be communication: straight, wide, new avenues and boulevards had to be driven through narrow, winding medieval passageways and thousands of ancient crowded tenements and shops, in order to allow all parts of the city to communicate easily and directly with one another. Thousands of properties would have to be condemned and razed to the ground. The entire process, including the seizure of private property based on the right of eminent domain, would ultimately have to be confirmed by the newly installed Legislative Body. As its new president, Auguste de Morny would soon be able to ensure the execution of Louis Napoléon's plans for the modernization of Paris.[4] Street after street, entire neighborhoods of four- and five-story tenements, teeming with hundreds of thousands of the capital's most impoverished inhabitants, were to be demolished. These buildings, thrown up over the centuries one against another and left in a state of disrepair, saw entire families of two and three generations crammed into one or two squalid rooms, while lacking running water and the most elementary forms of sanitation.

Human waste, rotting food, and debris were simply thrown into the streets reeking of urine, much of it ultimately reaching the Seine. There were horses on every street, however poor the quarter, they being the engine of all transport, leaving their uncollected manure in steaming heaps, and eventually their fly-and maggot-infested carcasses. These tenements were in turn the thriving source of debilitating illness, disease, and periodic epidemics. Cholera alone was responsible for more than 30,000 deaths between the 1830s and 1860s. More than 32,000 burials officially took place each year in the city's three principal cemeteries—Père Lachaise, Montparnasse, and Montmartre—and another untold few thousands of nameless corpses were thrown into a communal *fosse,* or pit, left to be eaten by crows, rats, and dogs.[5]

After centuries of neglect, large portions of these swelling slums were now to be cleared and replaced by new structures, with access to fresh air, running water, and underground sewers, all ensured by the prefect's plans generated around the wide new municipal highways. On the other hand, no provision was made for rehousing most of those displaced, who were destined "to disappear" into the outlying suburbs. Nor did even Napoléon III's most severe political opponents criticize him for this failure. On the other hand, however, he was personally to buy out of his own pocket some of the condemned properties near the Gare de Lyon and build a new Saint-Simon-style housing project for a few thousand people.

The funding for these vast schemes was periodically provided by the parliament, the prefecture, and the municipality of Paris. Construction companies awarded contracts by Haussmann would be obliged to complete their work within a specified period of time or risk forfeiting the very substantial bonds (*cautions*) they were required to deposit with the city, something the prefect enforced rigorously. Nevertheless, nothing could alleviate the inevitable problems resulting from these multiple construction projects, including the "temporary disruptions" to life in local neighborhoods, the unrelenting snarled traffic, and the pall of dust clouds hanging over the city, not to mention the unabated racket faced by Paris's one million inhabitants over the next two decades.[6]

The very density in numbers of these largely illiterate working-class families had also proven a very real political threat in the past whenever they had rallied en masse in violent protest against the state, troops, and police, as Louis Napoléon had personally witnessed during his December 1851 coup d'état. Time and again the Hôtel de Ville, for instance, surrounded as it was by the working-class St.-Antoine quarter, had itself been besieged. It was expected that by moving more than one hundred thousand families—up to six hundred thousand people—out of the city and into the suburbs, the possibility of such a threat in the future would be reduced immeasurably.[7]

Napoléon III therefore had many complex motives for wishing to see this sweeping transformation of the French capital, and all were genuine, including his ever present, if sometimes elusive, Saint-Simon idealism. Perhaps even to his surprise he was soon to appreciate just how very fortunate he had indeed been in naming the ideal prefect to execute this vision.

To begin with, the network required the modern new "Gates of the City," the railway stations, to link with one another as well as with the center of the city. The various government and administrative buildings were also to be connected by a good road grid, and they in turn with the very nerve centers of the empire—the Tuileries, the Élysée Palace, and the Palace of St. Cloud. As Haussmann related, "The emperor evidently believed that in a country like France where centralization of government was pushed to the extreme, that it was the duty of the Chief of State to have the reins of the capital's administration at his fingertips, at his official residence."[8] This included police and army barracks, the various ministries, as well as the National Assembly (the Legislative

Body) and the Senate in the Luxembourg Palace. As part of this plan, the Ministry of the Interior—responsible for the country's prefectures and police—would be moved immediately to a building directly across from the entrance of the Élysée Palace, where Louis Napoléon more and more frequently sought refuge from the constant bustle, pressures, intrusions, and court activities of the Tuileries.

The broad new avenues of this grid were to fan out in all directions, permitting the easy flow of all traffic, while enabling the government to dispatch police and troops to hotspots in the event of a revolt or emergency. These new thoroughfares were also intended to divide the very breeding grounds of those neighborhoods, rendering it more difficult in time of revolt for large crowds to congregate in any one place. The expansion of trade and the economy and the creation of new jobs for the large number of unemployed also remained a fundamental part of Louis Napoléon's new Paris, and these wide new corridors would greatly facilitate local commerce and industry.

Now at his new office in the Hôtel de Ville, where he and his wife and daughters would also be housed in the almost palatial apartments reserved for the prefect, he was greeted by the inner circle of his immediate personal staff, several of them brought with him from Bordeaux, and whose numbers were due to increase with the creation of some new departments, such as architecture, engineering, public transportation, park and city planning, etc. Once installed, Haussmann assembled the heads of the various departments, including those of the mayor's office. As prefect he was in effect also de jure the mayor of Paris and as such equally responsible for the administration of all traditional municipal services. Unlike his predecessor, the cautious and unimaginative Jean Jacques Berger, however, the new prefect was no courtier or charmer. Haussmann's no-nonsense Lutheran Germanic roots still governed his way of thinking, demeanor, and relentless drive. His was a once-in-a-lifetime opportunity, as he clearly grasped, and the more formidable the task, the better, for if anyone in the administration of the Second Empire liked a real challenge, it was this dynamic Baron Haussmann.

• • •

I am an old civil servant," he began, addressing the assembly, "and as
such I intend to judge each of you personally on your merits." He
wanted to know who precisely was working for him and what in consequence to expect. "Therefore do not bother having your friends dropping me a private word praising your merits. Your good work alone will
provide all the proof I need, and for which I shall personally see to it
that you are properly rewarded." And then after outlining their future
objectives, he concluded, "Now, gentlemen, that the purpose of this
meeting has been revealed, you know what I aim to achieve and what in
turn I expect of each of you." He closed, reminding them of the great
project the emperor had just entrusted to them, "to make Paris the most
beautiful city in the world."[9]

Many found him authoritarian and intimidating, others inspiring,
for his reputation as a most remarkable administrator had preceded
him. During an early reception at the Hôtel de Ville, a socially prominent lady teased him about his "bad character." " 'Madam,' I responded,
'far from being displeased about it I am delighted.' " Elaborating, he
pointed out that he was "quiet and peaceful by nature, and under
normal circumstances always courteous, but life has taught me that in
order to be left alone to be able to get on with one's work, one must
have quite a different reputation." A loud bark could be most effica-
cious in keeping fools and troublemakers at bay. If at the end of the day
he would take up his faithful cello and play Handel and Haydn, this
side of his character was the last thing he wanted the public to know.
Indeed, it was as a result of his public no-nonsense attitude, of his rigorous integrity, of his reputation as a serious man with his nose to the
grindstone and a remarkable record for getting things done, that Louis
Napoléon had appointed him to this the most demanding office, not
only in Paris, but in the entire country. The building of Paris, Haussmann later concluded, "was the greatest event of my public life."[10]

In his *Mémoires,* written many years after the demise of Napoléon
III and the Second Empire, Baron Haussmann frankly confided what

his career and his final achievement in Paris had meant to him, and surprisingly, just how tense and trying it had in fact been, even for him. "Constantly on the alert, I could never relax, indeed I was overly anxious about anything and everything, down to the last detail . . . No aspect of this immense task was neglected by me, for I found myself on slippery ground where everything, all my work [and career], could be jeopardized by the least expected mishap, by a single wrong step, and my chief concern was to prevent just this sort of slip from occurring. . . . And with the eyes of Europe and indeed the whole world upon me, I most ardently wished to succeed in my work, for the glory of my Master, and for the very honour of my Country." He was literally charged with nothing less than the greatest organized construction project in the entire two-thousand-year history of Paris.[11]

Even before getting to work in 1853, however, Haussmann was faced with a humanitarian problem, starvation, for that year the normally plentiful wheat crop of the nearby Beauce had failed, as it did again the following year. For hundreds of thousands of the poorest of Paris, bread was the one basic daily staple of existence, and the market price shot up overnight from 40 to 80 centimes per kilo. Profiteering middlemen were raking in fortunes while children starved. Fathers could not provide money they did not possess, and crime soared out of control. An outraged Haussmann took matters into his own hands, acquiring wheat from elsewhere in the country while creating a municipal "Bread Treasury." By providing subsidies as *Bons,* or script, to the city's bakers drawn on this new fund, the price of bread fell back to its old price. As for the profiteers, Haussmann prosecuted them with his usual zeal. This was the first of several unauthorized "authoritarian acts" committed by the new prefect.[12] Meanwhile, he had to get on with the plans Louis Napoléon had presented to him, the reason for his appointment.

Apart from previously funded projects prepared by Jean Jacques Berger, including the initial stage of construction of the Rue de Rivoli, and the clearing of private structures around the original, still isolated, rectangular Louvre, the Pavillion de l'Horloge, the city's large new central food markets, Les Halles, based by Louis Napoléon on London's Covent Garden, and the enlarged Rue des Écoles, all future construction projects would depend upon the availability of funding authorized by the Legislative Body, the municipal government, and the department. The first two such funding programs, finally awarded in 1855 and 1858, posed no serious problem. Thereafter, obtaining future approval for even larger amounts from an increasingly obstructive Assembly was quite another matter.

Prefect Haussmann's first task was to divide the city into four sectors by completing the Rue de Rivoli from east to west, from the Place de la Concorde eastward to the Place de la Bastille, and then beyond as the Rue du Faubourg St.-Antoine on to the Place du Trône—today's Place de la Nation.[13] On the other side of the Concorde, the Champs-Élysées would continue from where Rivoli ended, westward to the then current city limits at the Rond Point—the Arc de Triomphe—and eventually beyond to the Seine at the Pont de Neuilly. The north-south axis cut through the Rue du Rivoli at the Place du Châtelet, the new Avenue du Centre—soon to be renamed the Boulevard de Sebastopol—driving in a straight northerly line as far as the Porte de St.-Denis, from which it would then continue as the Boulevard de Strasbourg right up to the Gare de l'Est. Its southerly line, the new Boulevard St.-Michel, would extend from the Pont de St.-Michel, right through the densely cluttered Latin Quarter, as far as the present-day Denfert-Rocherau.

Several large junctions would be formed in the city, from which major avenues and boulevards would emerge, linking other parts of the city. From the Place de la Nation, today's Boulevard Voltaire would eventually drive up to the recently cleared Place de la République (Château-d'Eau), which met with the Boulevards St.-Martin and St.-Denis, and to the west ultimately joined the future Grands Boulevards—Haussmann, the Italiens, the Capucines, 4 Septembre, etc. Meanwhile, Voltaire would emerge on the north side of the Place de la République as the Boulevard de Magenta, providing access to the Gares de l'Est and du Nord, and finally reaching as far north as the Boulevard de Rochechouart.

Apart from the junction forming at the Opéra (several years into the future), the only other major junction in Paris, and by far the biggest and most impressive, was L'Étoile, personally designed by Haussmann, including the twelve thoroughfares shooting out from it in all directions like elegant spokes of a wheel. The Champs-Élysées ended here and continued westerly on the other side eventually as the Avenue de la Grande Armée. From the north side, the Avenues Carnot, MacMahon, Wagram, and Friedland. From the southern side of the Rond Point would branch out the spacious Avenues de l'Impératrice—today's Foch, and Victor Hugo, the Avenue du Roi du Rome—today's Kléber, Iéna, and Marceau. "This beautiful ensemble [L'Étoile] I certainly consider to be one of the finest achievements of my entire administration," the usually undemonstrative Haussmann declared.[14]

Each avenue was built by a separate company, the new concessionnaire whose successful bid had been accepted by Haussmann. A law passed in 1852 allowed for the large-scale application of the right of eminent domain (declaration of *l'utilité publique)*, the seizure of private property for a public project, the expropriation of houses, shops, and apartment buildings to be demolished and then cleared away. In order to ensure full compliance and the complete execution of a new avenue, each construction company was obliged to deposit a substantial bond, or *caution,* with the city as well as the amount of the indemnity to be paid each owner of expropriated property (for which a municipal subsidy would then reimburse the company).

The expropriation of thousands of parcels of privately held real estate would inevitably bring many complaints, including of inadequate compensation. The situation was soon remedied, however, when the indemnity for expropriated property was raised significantly, ironically leading to future property owners clamoring to have their land taken by the city! In order to cut through the time-consuming red tape involved in obtaining the authorization of the legislative body for release of the property subvention indemnities, in 1858 Prefect Haussmann created the Public Works Treasury of Paris. This allowed him to expedite the process by directly issuing *Bons,* or script (IOUs drawn on this fund), as a form of redeemable payment covering the city's subventions for each of these expropriations, much as he had done in the case of wheat. This, however, led to grave complications.[15]

When the original hundred-million-franc ($1.3 billion) Public Works Treasury fund was later exhausted, Haussmann, impatient with endless committees, haggling, and lost time, illegally issued an additional unauthorized seventy million francs worth of Bons beyond the Treasury's limit, in order to complete the construction under way. His growing critics immediately cried wolf, demanding his head. In any event, the Legislative Body under Morny's direction retroactively honored the payment of the bons when they were acquired by the Crédit Foncier, thanks to the cooperation of the Pereire brothers. Neither Haussmann nor the senior officials he personally appointed profited by a single centime through this transaction or any other, and the avenues were completed on time. The prefect was a rigorous taskmaster, but his actions did add fuel to the proverbial fire of those critical of his high-handed, authoritarian rule and clamoring for the removal of this wayward, incorruptible prefect of the Seine.

With the gradual completion of the new broad avenues and boulevards, there would be a greater need for public transport, and Haussmann licensed taxis, horse-drawn fiacres, and omnibus concessions for this purpose. The competition for future profits was fierce, complete with the usual attempted *pots de vin*—bribes. And once the new thoroughfares were opened, contracts were issued for the laying of underground gas pipelines, resulting by 1870 in 33,000 new gas outlets, for street lamps, public buildings, and private houses. Overnight the dark, crime-ridden medieval passageways of Eugene Sue's *Mystères de Paris* and Émile Zola's *Dram Shop* were giving way to a city of light.[16] The London Louis Napoléon had so admired years ago and attempted to imitate was in fact now being overshadowed by a modern new spacious Paris.

With the full support of the emperor, Baron Haussmann also confronted the calamitous public health problems facing the capital arising from the polluted drinking water taken directly from the Seine and older city wells, the exclusive water supply used by most of the large working-class areas of Paris. Never a man to dither, Prefect Haussmann undertook major engineering projects to bring clean sources of drinking water by the new aqueducts of Arcueil, of the Dhuys, and the Vanne, from Belleville, Prés Saint-Gervais, and elsewhere, including new artesian wells in and outside Paris. In 1860, the Compagnie Générale des Eaux was formed to take charge of the distribution of water for the capital. Simultaneously, work was done on the extensive new underground sewage canals.[17]

Haussmann also received the closest support from Louis Napoléon (and indirectly Empress Eugénie) when it came to the public welfare and medical services offered by Paris. Eugénie had always been especially interested in orphans and destitute women, for whom hospices and clinics were opened, to which she personally ultimately contributed probably more than a million francs out of her own purse. Of the city's numerous hospitals, including general hospitals, lying-in facilities for women, and others "for incurable diseases," some were modernized and extended and one or two demolished and replaced. Shelters for the homeless, too, were established. Perhaps the most famous hospital, the enormous Hôtel Dieu on the Ile de la Cité, was completely rebuilt and expanded as the few hundred older adjoining buildings were demolished, for the first time leaving a large open piazza before it and the neighboring Notre Dame Cathedral.

While serving as a deputy prefect at Ariège much earlier in his career, Haussmann had met and become friendly with an alienist, a medical doctor specializing in mental disorders. He became interested in this problem, and now as prefect of the Seine announced "a project of capital importance," as he referred to it, involving the construction of a series of asylums in Paris, crowned by the new clinic for mental disorders attached to the School of Medicine in the Latin Quarter.[18]

Since in France the state was responsible for paying the clergy and maintaining the places of worship, Prefect Haussmann also built a number of Catholic churches, to replace those demolished, at least one Protestant reformed church, in the Rue Roquépine, and two synagogues, in the Rue de la Victoire and another in the Rue des Tournelles.[19] At the same time the prefect was also responsible for the city's educational facilities, something of very special interest to Haussmann. On his instructions, many schools were modernized or enlarged, including the Sorbonne, the Faculté de Médecin, the Lycée Bonaparte (Condorcet), the Lycée Saint-Louis, the Lycée Napoléon (Henri IV), and the Lycée Charlemagne. In addition, thanks to Eugénie, the country's first École Supérieure des Filles, or high school, was built, not to mention numerous new communal schools for boys and girls.[20]

Unlike his uncle, Napoléon I, Louis Napoléon was most interested in the public buildings and monuments of the country, and at Eugénie's urging, he appointed Prosper Mérimée—who had taught her history as a child—to be the first Inspector General of Historic Monuments. Thanks to his diligence, a register of thousands of historic monuments and buildings throughout France was drawn up and hundreds of them saved and restored, including the crumbling ramparts of Carcassonne. Among the historic buildings saved and restored in Paris were Charlemagne's Sainte-Chapelle on the Ile de la Cité and the Hôtel Carnavalet in the Marais with its newly installed museum.

The prefect also had the Hôtel de Ville exhaustively refurbished, and its galleries and salons decorated by some of the most celebrated artists of the day. There the prefect and his wife were to give their stunning masked balls for six thousand *invités* every January, while not forgetting innumerable diplomatic receptions and dinners for the heads of many European states, including one for Queen Victoria and Prince Albert. The Palais de Justice, under extensive renovation and expansion ever since Louis Philippe's reign, was now finally completed. The new palatial Ministry of Foreign Affairs on the Quai d'Orsay, also initiated by Louis Philippe, then stopped mid-course during the upheavals of 1848, was officially opened by Haussmann in 1855. The Élysée Palace, Louis Napoléon's favorite hideaway in Paris, was now extensively refurbished as well. In addition to other structures, Haussmann rebuilt the Conservatoire des Arts et Métiers and of course constructed the Palais de l'Industrie for Louis Napoléon's first Exposition Universelle in 1855. In 1861, the prefect also broke ground for Charles Garnier's new Opéra.[21] It was during his tenure, of course, that all the grand railway stations of the capital were erected in their permanent form, and the first electric telegraph network was installed throughout the country.

• • •

To the French of the Second Empire, when it came to the clink of gold, everything was a *blague,* everyone had his price, every man had his vice and weakness and was susceptible to corruption. The staggering bribes received by Napoléon I's foreign minister, Prince de Talleyrand, had been the talk of every capital in Europe, and his grandson, the notorious half brother of Napoléon III, Count, and shortly to become Duke, de Morny, ably ensured the continuation of this particular family tradition. Georges Haussmann came to Paris the complete outsider, without friends or party backing, and was to leave it in the same manner. At the same time, this irritatingly honest prefect became the ideal surrogate target for Louis Napoléon's political enemies when it came to a remorseless series of well-choreographed malicious accusations and innuendo, including vicious attacks against members of his family.

Unable to attack Emperor Napoléon directly, the prefect had to bear the brunt of these afflictions. While still presiding over the Legislative Body, Auguste de Morny was in a position to ward off some of these assaults against the prefect, but after his death in 1865, that parliamentary protection ended and the abusive assaults on Haussmann's good name increased.

The fact remained, however, that as the prefect of the Seine, in charge of the herculean construction of an entirely new capital and therefore responsible for many hundreds of millions of francs annually, he was the man who made the ultimate decisions as to the selection of each new project and who was to execute it. He was inevitably the prime target for the discontented, the unscrupulous, the jealous, and the greedy. Speculators were bewildered; they simply could not fathom a man refusing a fistful of gold, bribes ranging from 400,000 to more than two million francs (nearly $26 million). How were thiefs and corrupt politicians and businessmen possibly expected to cope when confronted by a man of principle! Haussmann had to go![22]

Although Persigny had originally suggested the nomination of Haussmann for the prefecture—if hardly out of the goodness of his heart—

he and Plon-Plon, Prince Jérôme, who were very close associates and both notorious gamblers and speculators in their own right, along with General Émile Fleury, proved to be among the prefect's most dedicated and dangerous insider detractors among the Bonapartists determined to bring him down regardless of the cost. Cousin Plon-Plon and his father, Jérôme Bonaparte, were now comfortably ensconced with their "actresses" at the Duke of Orléans's confiscated Palais Royal. As for Persigny, by manipulating his own marriage contract in 1852, and blatantly coercing Églé de la Moskowa, the daughter of the late wealthy banker Jacques Laffitte, he gained a dowry of seven million francs. (Even Louis Napoléon, strongly opposed to this marriage, was unable to prevent a defiant Persigny.) Persigny's subsequent apparent direct complicity in the murder of his wife's teenage brother (whose separate seven-million-franc fortune he then gained control of) hardly qualified him as a moral judge of Haussmann or anyone else.[23] Both Plon-Plon and the devious Persigny had more than one dark secret.

One man who did work closely with Haussmann during the Second Empire, and who in fact knew him both professionally and as an old family friend, Jean Charles Alphand, a senior engineer and the former head of the Department of Bridges and Highways at Bordeaux before coming to Paris, was so offended by the continuing campaign of vilification, well after Haussmann's death, that he finally spoke out. "Even his well established single-minded dedication to his work," Alphand protested, "could not prevent the calumny of these attacks against the very honor of this distinguished high official," including crude denunciations in the press against him and his family. Moreover, Prefect Haussmann was to leave office, Alphand closed, "in the full knowledge that he had done his duty, and strictly according to the rules. Such a proud man as he could never have lowered himself, humiliated himself by entering into a dishonest transaction with such obvious culprits."[24] For Haussmann, a towering intellect, his work was everything; it was literally his pride and joy. He needed money as much as the next man and worked very hard indeed for his 50,000 francs a year and a pension of 20,000 francs—which in fact he was destined never to receive. People like Auguste de Morny may have thought Haussmann's rigid integrity to be foolish, but like Louis Napoléon, he was one of the very few individuals Morny sincerely admired and held in the highest respect.

In any event, the wild fabricated accusations of corruption against Georges Haussmann were unexpectedly checked for the moment in 1860 when it was announced that the prefect's daughter, Marie Henriette, was to wed the very wealthy Protestant Alsatian industrialist Camille Dolfuss. It was now revealed that, far from being a newly enriched public official, the baron could not even provide the full dowry expected under such circumstances. High officials of the municipality of Paris hurriedly got together and offered Haussmann a municipal award for services rendered, to help cover the dowry. Although moved by this well-meaning gesture, he rejected this generous, but clearly unacceptable, offer out of hand. Next Louis Napoléon summoned Haussmann; he, too, offered to pay all or part of the dowry. The sensitive, proud Georges Haussmann, who had reputedly fought a duel of honor in his youth, likewise declined Louis Napoléon's offer. No one could know "the shame I felt in having to be offered this financial assistance," Haussmann later wrote. His small dowry—never disclosed—had to suffice. Nevertheless, Louis Napoléon and Empress Eugénie did sign the wedding contract and attend the Protestant wedding in the Temple de L'Oratoire that June.[25]

Even before the arrival of Haussmann in Paris, Louis Napoléon had been thinking about the creation of large parks and dozens of green "squares" with which to embellish a gray, drab Paris. Haussmann brought Alphand in to deal with the complicated engineering problems. Attempts to duplicate London's Hyde Park's beautiful Serpentine had to be altered, however, resulting in two lakes at two different levels. Meanwhile the Bois de Boulogne, a tract of land transferred by the state to the city of Paris in 1852, did indeed become the showpiece in which Louis Napoléon had put so much store, the park soon completed by the further acquisition of the Plaine de Longchamp. In fact, it was thanks to the intervention and considerable persuasion of Auguste de Morny that Louis Napoléon agreed to include this additional acreage, which Morny then arranged for the Jockey Club to lease on condition of creating France's foremost racecourse, complete with extensive stabling. (The Champ de Mars, heretofore used for public races, could now revert to a thankful army for its parades and maneuvers.) Additional roads were built and extensive floral gardens and tens of thousands of trees were planted across the Bois de Boulogne's 2,090 bucolic acres, reaching from the Porte Maillot all the way down to the banks of the Seine surrounding the Palais de St. Cloud. A pleased Louis Napoléon got his longed-for park, and Morny his racetrack—both brothers were content. Longchamp, of course, remains France's premier racetrack to this day. In 1860, Haussmann next transferred the state-owned Bois de Vincennes to the municipality. In addition, much smaller parks were also created at Monceau, at the former Buttes Chaumont gravel pits, and at the Park of Montsouris along the southernmost limits of the city, today the home of the Cité Universitaire. Louis Napoléon's dream of a green Paris was indeed fulfilled.[26]

By 1867, after fourteen consecutive years, Haussmann was utterly exhausted, both physically and mentally, and requested a meeting at the Tuileries in order to tender his resignation. Louis Napoléon, who was in declining health and incapacitated much of the time, had just lost Morny two years earlier; he pleaded with Haussmann not to abandon him now. How many men could he really rely on, especially unusually talented, responsible, and *honest* men?

To Haussmann's regret, he was to stay on, while the calumnies leveled against him continued to accumulate. By January 1870, Louis Napoléon, desperate to form a new liberal government under Émile Ollivier, reluctantly agreed to the new prime minister's main condition of removing Haussmann from office. When the betrayed prefect now refused to stand down, Louis Napoléon *fired him*. Haussmann was shocked and deeply hurt and affronted. Years earlier the prefect had declined Louis Napoléon's offer to provide dowries, ultimately for both of his daughters. When, however, Haussmann now did make one personal request, to

have his grandfather's title, as baron—bestowed originally by Napoléon I, restored and transferred to him for services rendered, Louis
Napoléon declined. No reason has ever been given for this ungrateful
act—but at least Louis Napoléon had made a *duke* out of the political
hack and sergeant of dragoons, Gilbert Persigny.

By the time Haussmann stepped down in January 1870, he had overseen the demolition of 19,722 buildings, which had been replaced by
some 43,777 new structures, all with running water and sanitary facilities. He had designed and overseen the construction of ninety-five
kilometers of broad new gas-lit streets, including most of the great
thoroughfares of the capital. Despite the mud-slinging and the fabricated allegations to the contrary, he had never taken a single bribe, nor
had he speculated on or ever owned a single property destined to be
condemned and expropriated, or indeed of any kind in Paris. Altogether he had overseen the expenditure of 2,553,668,424 francs (more
than $32 billion), all of it properly accounted for to the last centime.

He had created an entirely new Paris, the envy of Europe, with a modern sewage system, fresh clean water supplies, gas lighting, handsome
buildings, vast green public gardens, and tree-lined avenues.

All this was quickly forgotten after the collapse of the Second Empire,
when Haussmann's scheduled annual pension of 20,000 francs was
suppressed, along with his senatorial stipend of 30,000 francs. Eventually he received a total of a mere 6,000 francs a year from the Third
Republic, the same pension as a provincial prefect. If after four consecutive decades of service as a public official Georges-Eugène Haussmann did not leave office a rich man, at least he had his cello, and the
knowledge of having bestowed the jewel of the Second Empire, the
City of Light, on his and all future generations.[27]

23

CROSSES, CANDLESTICKS, AND SWORDS: THE CRIMEA

"The Empire stands for peace."[1]
—NAPOLÉON III, 1852

"[We are going to Constantinople] with England to defend the Sultan."[2]
—EMPEROR NAPOLÉON III,
BEFORE THE ASSEMBLY, MARCH 2, 1854

It all started in 1535, when Ottoman sultan Suleiman the Magnificent accorded France's king François I the guardianship of the Christian Holy Places in and around Jerusalem. In 1740, those rights were confirmed, and confirmed again in 1774 for both the Latin and Eastern Orthodox Church, but now under the aegis of the tsar. This festering contest for control of the Holy Places between the Latin and Greek churches continued into the nineteenth century, with the Eastern Orthodox Church taking the initiative in 1808 by restoring the Church of the Holy Sepulcher following a disastrous fire. In 1842, the cupola of the Church of the Nativity collapsed, amid Roman Catholic and Eastern Orthodox monks quarreling over their custodial rights to take charge. By 1847 acrimony reached fever pitch with the good monks of both persuasions taking up arms—in this case heavy silver and gold crosses and candlesticks, resulting in the breaking of heads instead of bread.[3] With no apparent sensible resolution of the conflicting claims to the disputed Holy Places in sight, Louis Napoléon dispatched a fleet to show the flag in the Near East, which at once set off alarm bells in Whitehall. The last time France had done that, Napoléon had invaded Egypt! In any event, with a French fleet at hand, on May 5, 1853, Sultan Abdülmecid accepted a more conciliatory stance. Cupolas, crosses, and candlesticks were, to be sure, transparent pretexts deceiving no one as the sword was unsheathed, with Russia's recent sweeping claims to Ottoman territory very much at the heart of the matter.

Tsar Nicholas I (1796–1855) had long been pushing Russian expansion and had earlier seized the Caucasus and beyond, continuing to encroach on a rapidly disintegrating Ottoman Empire. The pending breakup of the Turkish Balkan provinces served as a catalyst to diplomatic disaster in 1827 when the Egypto-Turkish fleet, bringing Egyptian reinforcements for the Peloponnesus, was destroyed by a powerful combined Anglo-French-Russian fleet at Navarino. The Treaty of Adrianople of 1829 offered the Russians a hefty war indemnity and Greece her independence from the Turks. Meanwhile, Egypt's de facto ruler, Muhammad Ali (Mehmet Ali in Turkish), the Khedive (1805–1848), to whom the sultan had promised Greece and Crete, now instead angrily turned his Mamluk army on the Turkish province of Syria while en route to Constantinople (Istanbul). A desperate Sultan Mahmud II appealed to Europe for help against the advancing army of Muhammad Ali, and Nicholas I alone finally dispatched his Black Sea fleet, landing fourteen thousand marines on the shores of the Golden Horn in 1833. But Turkey and Russia had signed a defense pact in 1833, obliging Sultan Mahmud II to close the Dardanelles "to any foreign vessel of war . . . under any pretext whatsoever," whenever requested to do so by the tsar.[4] By now both London and Paris were alarmed by the possibility of a Russian Bosphorus eastern Mediterranean "Gibraltar" restricting the Royal Navy and the closure of profitable Anglo-Turkish trade.

Meanwhile, separately, Muhammad Ali's Egyptian army was advancing into Lebanon and Syria en route for Constantinople. The Royal Navy responded by shelling Lebanon, and Muhammad Ali agreed to withdraw his troops in exchange for the new sultan, Abdülmecid

(1839–1861), granting him hereditary rule of Egypt, while keeping it a nominal Ottoman province. In July 1841, the Straits Convention was drawn up in London, officially reopening the Dardanelles and Black Sea to French and English shipping. The Egyptian threat had ended, and Constantinople was no longer held hostage by St. Petersburg.

Meanwhile the Greek and Latin monks in and around Jerusalem continued their own little skirmishes, aided and abetted once again by Tsar Nicholas I demanding full control of the Holy Places for the Eastern Church. With the French and English fleets off Turkish waters, and two million pounds of British gold on the table—the price demanded by the sultan for his cooperation—on May 5, 1853, the Sublime Porte confirmed that both the Orthodox and Latin churches would receive concessions at the Holy Places. Sultan Abdülmecid, however, did stop at Russian demands for control over all Orthodox Christians, that is, over twelve million Greek Orthodox Christians in the Balkan provinces of the Ottoman Empire. Tsar Nicholas was not pleased, and tens of thousands of new army recruits marched through the streets of St. Petersburg.

"I fear a storm is brewing in the East," an anxious Foreign Secretary Lord Clarendon warned the forty-nine-year-old Lord Cowley, England's new ambassador in Paris. And why? Because of "all these disputes about nothing"—local squabbles, far away in a distant land. Maintaining the integrity of the Ottoman Empire "is hardly a great European necessity," Clarendon argued, and most certainly not for England.[5] At the same time he felt that his ambassador accredited to the Sublime Porte, the arrogant sixty-seven-year-old Lord Stratford de Redcliffe, a notorious loose cannon, was behind much of this, deliberately stirring up the Turks against the Russians, even going so far as to summon the British Mediterranean Fleet to the Bosphorus—without even informing London! Although briefly dismissed, Stratford was immediately reinstated, no doubt with the powerful backing of London's grateful merchants, whose growing annual exports to Ottoman markets exceeded £2,400,000 by 1850.[6]

• • •

U p until this point the Royal Navy had ruled the proverbial waves of the eastern Mediterranean unhindered ever since Admiral Nelson's destruction of the French fleet at Abukir Bay in 1798. Since then Egypt's Isthmus of Suez had become a tendentious transshipment link—combined with the East India Company's traditional sea route around the Cape, ensuring the flow of England's rich and flourishing trade with India and the East. With the Turks no longer possessing a strong navy, Russian interference theoretically could result in collateral damage to London's prosperous shipping and financial empire. The geopolitical situation was suddenly fraught with disturbing possibilities and consequences, especially if Great Britain's allies of the moment, the French, with their growing commitment to neighboring Algeria, took advantage of the situation to reassert their claims to the rest of North Africa, the eastern Mediterranean, and Egypt. And there was already talk in the Paris Bourse and the City of London of plans to build a French Suez Canal. As for Prime Minister Lord Aberdeen and Foreign Secretary Lord Clarendon, they were concentrating on the more immediate situation regarding their former Russian allies of 1827.

T he storm Clarendon had so feared finally broke in July 1853 when hawkish rhetoric gave way to war drums, as 80,000 Russian troops descended, crossing the River Pruth in an unprovoked invasion and occupation of the Turkish Danubian provinces of Moldavia and Wallachia (the future Romania). Taking advantage of a weakened and disintegrating Ottoman Empire, which had already lost Greece in 1829 and the province of Egypt to Muhammad Ali in 1841, Russian foreign minister Count Nesselrode once again leveled his sights on the Dardanelles and Constantinople, the Ottoman political capital and spiritual seat of the Sunni Islamic caliphate.

Alarmed, England's Lord Stratford notified London. The relative stalemate of the last two decades suddenly changed dramatically. If the Admiralty was ever eager to hoist Nelson's old blue pennant, ready to preserve the Royal Navy's rights now in 1853, nevertheless Whitehall and Downing Street remained just as adamantly bent on avoiding armed conflict. The Napoleonic wars had not only created a staggering national debt, they had nearly destroyed England's economy and international trade. Wars always meant more national debt.

The French too found themselves directly involved in this nominal quarrel with Russia. Scarcely ensconced on the family throne, like the English, the very last thing Louis Napoléon desired was to begin his reign with a European war. Nor could he forget the theme of his own recent referendum campaign pledge, "The Empire stands for peace," reprinted extensively in the French and English press. Above all he was most determined not to risk his assiduously fostered special relationship with the English for the sake of some cantankerous monks or a Muslim sultan upset with Russian transgressions.

Less than a month after his marriage to Eugénie, a most anxious Louis Napoléon thus appealed to London. "My most fervent desire," he assured Lord Malmesbury, "is to maintain . . . the closest and most friendly relations with your country." He was only too willing to entrust a larger share of the Holy Places to the Greek Church in order to avoid conflict. On the other hand, having inherited the Bonapartes' wariness toward this Russia that had shattered Napoléon's Grand Army in 1812, Louis Napoléon found himself in the most curiously uncomfortable position of supporting Muslim Constantinople, not Christian St. Petersburg. Political "sympathy" was one thing, war quite another. "I do want peace if it is at all possible," he instructed Ambassador Alexander Walewski in London, "but whatever I decide on, it must be fully in conjunction with England." And yet he could hardly forget Talleyrand's La Fontainian cautionary advice that "France's alliance with England is as natural as that of man and horse, just so long as one takes care not ending up the horse."[7]

The average Frenchman, however, remained anti-English. "You have no idea how the tide of public opinion is setting against us here," Ambassador Lord Cowley informed Whitehall from Paris, "and it is spreading even to the Emperor's entourage."[8] This included a peeved and very Catholic Empress Eugénie, who had shown her preference at a recent ball given by the pro-Russian princess Mathilde, by dancing with the Russian ambassador, and not with Lord Cowley. Nevertheless Louis Napoléon was adamant, and moreover, no one could override his decision.

When through the good offices of Vienna a compromise was submitted, offering France's willingness to share the custodianship of the Holy Places, nine months of intensive negotiations with England, Austria, and Prussia followed.[9] Despite Clarendon's initial resolve not to get involved "in all these disputes about nothing," the Russian invasion of Moldavia and Wallachia in July 1853 was tipping the scales, and despite Clarendon's withering strictures to the contrary, Ambassador Stratford de Redcliffe continued to egg on the Ottoman sultan.

On September 25, 1853, Sultan Abdülmecid issued an ultimatum to Tsar Nicholas to evacuate the provinces of Moldavia and Wallachia forthwith. Receiving no reply, on October 23 Turkey declared war on Russia. On the thirtieth of that month, the Russian Black Sea Fleet sailed into Sinop Bay, destroying the entire Ottoman fleet. A reluctant Ambassador Cowley finally gave in. "We should at once make a combined and vigorous attack on Sevastopol [Russia's home naval port in the Black Sea] and let the right arms of France and England be felt with a vengeance."

On January 3, 1854, a combined Anglo-French task force duly sailed into the Black Sea to confront the Russian fleet. Although Paris and London had neither signed a mutual military pact nor issued a declaration of war, the unrelenting wheels of war were rumbling forward.[10]

Bypassing Foreign Minister Drouyn de Lhuys in the newly opened offices in the Quai d'Orsay, on January 29, 1854, Louis Napoléon secretly appealed directly to Tsar Nicholas's common sense and moderation. "Do not for a moment let your Majesty imagine that there is the least animosity in my heart," he informed the tsar. In exchange for a Russian evacuation of Moldavia and Wallachia, Louis Napoléon offered the complete withdrawal of the French and English fleets from the Black Sea. "Menaces will not induce me to withdraw [from Moldavia and Wallachia]," Nicholas replied. "My confidence is in God and my rights . . . I can assure you that Russia will prove herself in 1854 every bit as formidable as she was in 1812."[11]

"The emperor of Russia is a tyrant," Prince Albert fulminated in a letter to Queen Victoria's uncle Leopold, the king of Belgium. "The poor Turk. . . . is a fine fellow . . . Down with the Emperor of Russia!" After his first meeting with Louis Napoléon, at a troop review of 100,000 men at Boulogne in September 1854, Albert reported to Belgium's king Leopold that Louis Napoléon "is ready to fight with us in the glorious cause against Russia. Napoléon [III] forever!"[12]

"We, England and France, are going there to defend the Sultan," Louis Napoléon informed the French Assembly, "we are going to defend the freedom of the seas and our own rightful place in the Mediterranean. . . . We are going to protect the rights of the Christians . . . and above all we are marching forward with everyone who cherishes the triumph of right, justice and civilization."[13] On the fourteenth of March, the Allies issued one final ultimatum for the tsar to withdraw his army, to no avail, and on the twenty-seventh of March, England and France declared war on Russia, launching the Crimean War.

The Anglo-French expeditionary force duly landed in the Crimea at Eupatoria, some forty miles from Sebastapol, in September 1854. The French under Marshal Saint-Arnaud and the English under one-armed Waterloo veteran Field Marshal Lord Raglan (leading his much smaller army of 96,000)[14] went on to fight at Alma, where the French commander came down with cholera and died days later. Immediately after this battle, one of the French emperor's divisional generals, first cousin Prince Jérôme "Plon-Plon" Bonaparte, like his father King Jérôme before him, who had deserted his men and Napoléon I en route to Russia in 1812, now in his turn abandoned his men on the field of battle, fleeing back to France and the safety of the Palais Royal, but with a new humiliating sobriquet that would haunt him the rest of his days—"Sans-Plomb," or "Gutless" Bonaparte.[15]

It was a grim beginning for what was to prove a very grim campaign under sweltering summer temperatures as dysentery, typhus, typhoid, and a most deadly cholera epidemic ravaged the ranks. On the fifteenth of October, they fought and narrowly won "the indecisive victory" of

Balaklava, where the seventh earl, the "mad" general, "Black Bottle" Lord Cardigan—Louis Napoléon's landlord during his youthful exile in London—led his historic 661-man cavalry in the "Charge of the Light Brigade," of which only 414 young men, along with some 300 horses, survived.[16] This was followed by the Allied victory at Inkerman on November 5, 1854.

And then began the unanticipated eleven-month siege against the Russian marshal Menchikov's 50,000–70,000 men and their stoutly defended port-fortress of Sebastopol. There, the French, who had failed to bring heavy artillery for this war, were obliged to strip their navy of most of their guns to form thirteen batteries of thirty- and fifty-pound cannon.[17] In May 1855, they and the British were reinforced by the first contingents of the 15,000-man Sardinian army sent by King Victor Emmanuel. In the midst of the siege, a temperamental General François Canrobert (1809–1895), another Algerian veteran, who had succeeded Saint-Arnaud, resigned in a huff following a dispute with Raglan, abandoning his army (to be replaced by the brutal General Aimable Pélissier) and returning to France. In the meantime Raglan died of illness, and was replaced by General Sir James Simpson. General Adolphe Niel, an engineer, was called in to put an end to the siege, and Patrice de Mac-Mahon with his colorful Zouaves (Algerian troops) led the bloody assaults against the Malakoff Tower and Sebastopol in September 1855.[18]

Throughout the fighting in the Crimea, the French maintained a fleet of seventeen ships under the command of Vice Admiral Ferdinand Hamelin, and the Royal Navy fifteen warships under Vice Admiral Sir Richard Saunders Dundas, chiefly involved in the bombardment of Russian coastal facilities, concentrating, of course, on Sebastopol.[19]

Meanwhile Tsar Nicholas I, who had died March 2, 1855, had been succeeded by his son, Alexander II, as Prince Alexander Menchikov continued to command the Russian army in the Crimea. And even as Queen Victoria and Prince Albert were arriving in Paris in mid-August for a royal visit to Emperor Napoléon III and Empress Eugénie, and the Exposition Universelle, or International Exhibition, the bloody siege of Sebastopol continued. One month later, the allies made their triumphal entry into the much battered city, port, and fortress of Sebastopol on

September 12, 1855, although the Russians did succeed in taking the Turkish fortress of Kars that November.

If the numerically superior French army of a quarter of a million men bore the brunt of the fighting in the Crimea, far to the north a simultaneous large-scale naval campaign was raging in the Baltic throughout 1854 and 1855. There, an Allied naval force, led by the much wounded but indomitable sixty-nine-year-old Admiral Sir Charles Napier's twenty-five ships of the Royal Navy,[20] and supported by the undermanned French fleet of twelve vessels and three newly launched steam-driven ironclad *cuirassés* under the handsome, gray-haired Vice Admiral Alexander Parseval-Deschênes, bombarded Russian ports, successfully blockading the entire coast's naval and army facilities. Kronstadt, a mighty fortress on the island of Kotlin guarding the entrance to the Gulf of Finland and just nineteen miles west of St. Petersburg, however, continued to defy even the persistent guns of the dynamic Napier. Apparently intimidated by Admiral Napier's formidable reputation and fleet, however, the Russian navy refused to leave the safety of their ports to engage the allies. Unchallenged, the Anglo-French fleet next succeeded in taking Bomarsund, and the British destroyed the arsenal of Sweaborg, near the Russian-occupied capital of Helsinki, in August 1855.

Ultimately the Anglo-French navies were responsible for suppressing most of the maritime trade throughout the eastern Baltic—Russia's only European outlet to the sea, with the Black Sea now closed—while preventing some 170,000 Russian troops in that theater from reinforcing the Crimea and Sebastopol.[21] With the allied occupation of Sebastopol now behind them, on Thursday, December 27, 1855, the neutral Austrians presented the allies' ultimatum to the new Romanov tsar Alexander in St. Petersburg, demanding his surrender.

S everal steamers and sailing transports have arrived from the Crimea within the last few days," the war correspondent of the London *Times* reported from Marseille on Saturday December 29, 1855. The British steamer *Columbian,* which had sailed from Constantinople on the eleventh, arrived with 350 sick and wounded French soldiers and 250 invalids who were lodged in the hospitals. "The American clipper *White Falcon* arrived from Kamiesh, having on board the 3rd Battalion of the French 97th Regiment of the Line, which distinguished itself during the siege of Sebastopol, and the Sardinian steamer *Victor Emmanuel* arrived yesterday with 220 invalids, some of them very badly wounded." Dozens of ships returning from the Black Sea now also crowded the harbor of Marseille; these were "chartered by the French government" from the British, Americans, and the Sardinians. In addition to these merchant vessels, a large number of warships and troop transports reached the nearby French naval harbor at Toulon, landing the survivors of the victorious siege of Sebastopol.[22]

At a quarter to twelve [in Paris on Saturday December 29, 1855] a squadron of Guides [of the Imperial Guard] with their band playing issued from the Rue de la Paix [into the Place Vendôme]," *The Times* reported, as "the Emperor [Napoléon III] made his appearance"[23] for this major homecoming ceremony.

With Napoléon III on his "splendid bay," and his bevy of general officers to either side and behind him, the first three returning veteran regiments of the 274,436 men sent to the Crimea marched into the Place Vendôme, now passing in review before the emperor in the uniform of a major general and the towering bronze column from which the statue of an imperious Emperor Napoléon I looked down. Led by General Canrobert, at the head of what remained of the battered division he had briefly commanded, each regiment was preceded by its commanding officer "raising his sword and saluting," followed by its own band, "and such of the wounded of each corps as were able to walk," "these weather-beaten warriors in their worn uniforms, the flags torn to ribands, the eagles of their standards perforated with Russian bullets." One regiment after another saluted the emperor, their faces reflecting "the dangers they had braved, the privations they had suffered, and the glory they had won"; the troops were greeted "by the most enthusiastic acclamations" as the crowds closed around them.

Watching this sobering spectacle from the balcony of the Ministry of Justice building, the imperial family, including the heavily pregnant Eugénie, Princess Mathilde, her brother, Jérôme, Auguste, Comte de Morny, and his father, the Comte de Flahaut, the other Bonaparte cousins, the Murats, the Bacciochis, and the officers attached to the Empress Eugénie's official household, observed down below as Louis Napoléon prepared to address the troops assembled before him.

> Soldiers of the [Imperial] Guard and soldiers of the Line, I bid you welcome. I am deeply moved in seeing you again, my happiness mixed only with the painful regrets for those who are no longer with us. . . . Thank God for having spared you. . . . Although the war has not yet quite ended I have recalled you [to France] now because it is only fitting that the regiments that have suffered the most be relieved by fresh troops. Everyone therefore will share in this glory. . . . But remain vigilant and . . . hold yourselves ready should I be required to call upon you in the future. . . .[24]

A thunderous spontaneous outburst of applause and cheers filled the Place Vendôme with cries of "Long live the Emperor!" and "Long live the Empress!" as friends and family swarmed around the victorious veterans of Sebastopol.[25]

If this appeared to be a joyous occasion, complete with patriotic music and celebratory fireworks, bringing this unnecessary and unwanted war to a close, Louis Napoléon did not join in the festivities at the Tuileries that evening. Because of her earlier miscarriage, Eugénie retired early to her apartments, while Louis Napoléon retreated alone to his ground-floor corner study overlooking the gardens and the dark waters of the Seine. For the brooding victorious emperor knew what a celebrating French public did not, as he reviewed the latest casualty figures telegraphed in from Toulon. This war could not have been waged without the large French army, and there was a staggering price to pay for this dearly bought "hour of glory": 95,000 French corpses (two-thirds of these the result of cholera, disease, and colossal mismanagement) buried in the trenches and mud of the Crimea. "But what does France gain by going to war with Russia?" Foreign Minister Drouyn de Lhuys had asked, unconvinced by the excuses he had received. And now Louis Napoléon was simply staggered as he read through the reports once again. Even the British, with their much smaller army, had lost 32,402 (again with a high percentage due to cholera, disease, and poor sanitation) and Sardinia lost 2,000 Italians.[26]

Meanwhile, one thousand miles away in the sprawling military hospital at Scutari, just outside Constantinople, a thirty-five-year-old Florence Nightingale, with her thirty-eight nurses and two dozen nuns remained, attending those who had not made it back to Paris for today's victory celebration. Louis Napoléon continued to brood in the dark, for in the end he well knew that he and he alone had been responsible for sending nearly three hundred thousand Frenchmen to war. He alone had had the power to do so. He alone was responsible for the deaths of 95,000 Frenchmen who might otherwise have been alive and well and with their families this night. There was something else he could not forget, and that was the high price to be paid for the support of King Victor Emmanuel's 15,000 troops serving in the Crimea, the implied price of French military aid one day soon in freeing Italy, in yet another war, with more dead young men. Above all, Louis Napoléon Bonaparte was haunted by his own earlier promise to the French people: "The Empire stands for peace."

24

A VERY SPECIAL RELATIONSHIP

"There is a great friendship sprung up between us."[1]
—QUEEN VICTORIA, FOLLOWING NAPOLÉON III'S
VISIT TO WINDSOR, APRIL 1855

"Her journey here will remain one of the greatest events of our times."[2]
—ON QUEEN VICTORIA'S VISIT TO PARIS, AUGUST 1855

They had been at war with each other and reluctant neighbors off and on for eight centuries, ever since the Norman king of France, William the Bastard, had invaded and defeated the English at the battle of Hastings in 1066. In October 1854, still living in the shadow of this cautious historical heritage, England's pretty young diminutive queen of German blood, Victoria, sent her German consort, Prince Albert, to Boulogne to meet another historical curiosity, the recently proclaimed emperor of the French, Napoléon III. England, the greatest unchallenged sea power in the world, was about to meet the most powerful country on the continent of Europe. To the surprise of the ever wary Louis Napoléon and the notoriously persnickety Albert, the two men got on very well.

On the sixteenth of April of 1855, the two nervous neighbors met for a state visit when the forty-six-year-old Louis Napoléon Bonaparte and his young empress, Eugénie, were cordially received at the Norman castle of Windsor. To the enormous relief of all parties, that visit had passed off without a hitch, both sovereign couples finding their counterparts *sympathique*. "I cannot say what indescribable emotions filled me—how much [it] all seems like a wonderful dream," Victoria confided to her diary. "He [Louis Napoléon] is so very quiet; his voice is low and soft. Nothing can be more civil or amiable, or more well-bred than the Emperor's manner—so full of tact." And she agreed fully with Albert that "it is certainly impossible not to like when you live with him, and not even to a considerable extent to admire." She found him to be "capable of kindness, affection, friendship, and gratitude."[3]

Victoria was delighted with Eugénie as well. "Her manner is the most perfect thing I have ever seen," she was so "gentle and graceful, and kind . . . so charming and modest." If Eugénie's strongly accented English was limited, it did not detract from her character, Victoria noting her to be "full of courage and spirit" accompanied by "such innocence and yet *enjouement,*" and unexpected "liveliness." And this was just the beginning of what was to become a close, lifelong friendship between the English queen and the Spanish-born empress, a friendship shared later in decades of widowhood.[4]

After having been invested with the Order of the Garter, Louis Napoléon had sworn fidelity to the English queen and to the friendship of the two great nations. "These words are valuable [coming] from a man like him, who is not profuse in phrases, and who is very steady of purpose," Victoria noted in her diary. This resolution she found fully confirmed when he addressed the Lord Mayor of London and a distinguished gathering in Guild Hall. "As for myself, I have retained on the throne those sentiments of sympathy and esteem for the English people which I professed in exile, when I enjoyed here the hospitality of the Sovereign." These sentiments, he emphasized, extended to the political relations of the two countries. "Indeed, England and France are naturally agreed on the great political and humanitarian questions which are stirring the world . . . from the Baltic to the Black Sea." The two nations "are even stronger through the ideas which they represent, than by the battalions and ships . . . at their command." As for the situation in the Crimea, "my presence among you today attests to my energetic cooperation in the prosecution of the war" and in securing "an honourable peace."[5] Queen Victoria, the Lord Mayor, Foreign Secretary Lord Clarendon, and French ambassador Walewski could not have been more pleased, and this was echoed by the strong applause of the audience. The two countries shared the same values and the same goals, their intention to see the war through to a successful conclusion together. This would put an end to any rumors of the French signing an early separate peace.

In the meantime the German-speaking Georges Haussmann, who, at Louis Napoléon's personal request, had accompanied them to England, had made arrangements with the palace and the foreign secretary for a return visit of the queen and her consort to France that August. On the twenty-second of April, Prince Albert escorted their French guests on the royal train to Dover, from where Louis Napoléon and Eugénie sailed for France. The state visit had clearly surpassed all expectations: "I am glad to have known this extraordinary man,"[6] Victoria said afterward.

But never very far from the queen's emotional feelings regarding this new alliance were her more practical down-to-earth political assessments. "He will see," she commented on her "Brother," as she now addressed Louis Napoléon in their correspondence, "that he can rely upon our friendship and honesty towards him and his country, so long as he re-mains faithful to us. Naturally frank, he will see the advantage to be de-rived from continuing so . . . if I be not very much mistaken in his character."[7] At the same time Victoria was greatly relieved that between herself and her usual bête-noire, Lord Palmerston, they, with the help of Prince Albert and Eugénie, had finally been able to dissuade a wavering Louis Napoléon from going to take personal command in the Crimea. The thought of his directing a full-scale military campaign frightened the French as much as it did the English. "Strike quickly, and Sebastopol will be ours before May 1," he had argued with Palmerston; it of course did not fall until September. After Louis Napoléon's celebrated earlier exploits at Strasbourg and Boulogne, no one took either his military as-sessments or his abilities seriously, least of all the English.[8]

On the twenty-eighth of April, six days after their return from England, Louis Napoléon was riding along the Champs-Élysées with an equerry en route to join Eugénie's carriage in the Bois de Bou-logne when an Italian "patriot" by the name of Giovanni Pianori suddenly lurched out at him and fired two shots, narrowly missing him. As usual, the unflappable Louis Napoléon shrugged it off as yet another attempt on his life. Two years earlier, on July 5, 1853, the situation had been far more harrowing when Prefect of Police Piétri had discovered a plot by fifteen terrorists lying in wait for the emperor and Eugénie at the Opéra Comique, and even more serious threats lay in the future. Nevertheless, the emperor adamantly rejected heavy security escorts for himself, except when attending the theater or an important public function with the empress, when he accepted a full military escort and even an armored carriage.

A nd now on August 18, 1855, the newly launched 2,470-ton, 360-foot royal steam yacht *Victoria and Albert*, making its maiden voyage from the Isle of Wight accompanied by a royal naval squadron of warships, was about to enter Boulogne, this harbor excavated by hand on Napoléon I's orders fifty years earlier in preparation for his invasion of England. Lord Palmerston for one had strongly encouraged these current arrangements in 1855, even as the siege of Sebastopol was continuing. Never quite trusting the French completely (any more than they did the English), the elderly and still impressive Lord Palmerston nevertheless felt this diplomatic bridge over the channel reinforcing their alliance was fundamental to lasting good relations between the two countries. He had personally known a much younger Louis Napoléon as a neighbor in London since the late 1830s. If their relationship had never been close or warm—both men were capable of considerable political reserve—it had been cautiously, modestly successful. He had taken the risk of having been the first to congratulate Louis Napoléon as head of state following his successful coup d'état, without the approval of either the prime minister or the queen, for which he had been dismissed from the foreign office. After the upheavals of 1848, he had felt that Louis Napoléon was the best solution for France and ensuring European peace and made it an integral part of his foreign policy.

Louis Napoléon, for his part, never forgot that loyal act and the price it had cost the foreign secretary. After the French imperial couple's warm reception at Windsor by Victoria and Albert, Palmerston strongly felt this new wartime alliance in the Crimea could work. As for Louis Napoléon, this very alliance avenged some of the bitter memories of a defeated post-Napoleonic France at the Congress of Vienna back in 1815. The arrival of this magnificent yacht—larger even than Admiral Lord Nelson's glorious HMS *Victory*—flying the tricolor, the Union Jack, the royal standard, and the royal ensign, dramatically symbolized the immensity of this fundamental historical sea change. England needed a strong, reliable ally on the Continent as much as France needed a friendly neighbor on the other side of the English Channel. What was most curious, if seemingly incidental, was the role of the German language, and Louis Napoléon, like Prince Albert, spoke English with a German accent.

Just before two o'clock on Saturday, August 18, 1855, a battery of guns roared out from the heights of Boulogne the traditional twenty-one-gun salute, as Captain Smithen brought the royal yacht alongside the quay, with most of her 240-man uniformed naval crew standing smartly at attention on deck. Of those present Louis Napoléon alone was aware that this was the very quay where his hired yacht had been seized along with its arms following his failed coup here back in August 1840.

"On the right jetty, along the lower stage near the water, was an unbroken line of infantry. . . . the whole port was gay with streamers, flags and garlands. . . . [Attended by] an immense multitude. . . . Her Majesty then appeared at the ship's side. . . . a stage [gangway] was thrown on board and the emperor quickly ran up the platform, and after respectfully kissing Her Majesty's hand, saluted her upon both cheeks," the *Times* reporter described. "The Emperor then cordially shook hands with Prince Albert, the Princess Royal and the Prince of Wales." As the emperor stepped across, "I met him halfway and embraced him twice," Queen Victoria recounted in her diary, "after which he led me on shore amidst acclamations, salutes, and every sound of joy and respect. The road was kept [open] by French infantry, whose drums and bugles made military music as the royal cavalcade slowly proceeded through the dense crowds to the port's railway station. . . ." Before them on a seventy-five-foot ceremonial arch decorated with flowers and flags hung a scroll bearing in large gold letters, "WELCOME TO FRANCE." "This event, fraught with so much interest to the destinies of Europe, has this day set the seal to an alliance consecrated by the blood already shed [in the Crimea]," the London newspaper appended.[9]

The queen of England was cordially welcomed by the French emperor, Lord Cowley, and the mayor and prefect of Boulogne, as Marshal Baraguay d'Hilliers's troops maintained order among a crowd of 40,000 sightseers and well-wishers, and the military band struck up "God Save the Queen." Following an embarrassingly lavish reception, the coal-fired imperial train left for Paris via Montreuil, Amiens, and Abbeville, where further receptions were laid on, complete with speeches, flowers, and bands.

"The Queen finally arrived at Paris this evening at half-past 7 o'clock," *The Times* reporter continued, as the imperial guards' band played "God Save the Queen" for the fourth time since reaching France.

The Gare du Nord being still under construction, they were rerouted to the Gare de Strasbourg (Gare de l'Est), where they were greeted by the band of the Imperial Guard playing "God Save the Queen" yet again. "The crowds along the new Boulevard de Strasbourg were greatly excited . . . myriads of foreigners from all over the world were mixing with the population of Paris, and spilling into the surrounding streets," the official *Moniteur Universel* reported.[10]

"The Emperor in full [military] uniform . . . gave his hand to the Queen as she alighted," followed by Prince Albert and their teenage children, Edward, the Prince of Wales, and Princess Victoria, the future wife of King Frederick of Prussia and later empress in her own right. Beneath a cloudless sunny sky, "General Lowenstein presented a bouquet en behalf of the 9th Battalion of the National Guard," as enthusiastic *"Vive la reine d'Angleterre!" "Vive l'Empereur!"* and *"Vive the Prince Albert!"* filled the air. The queen and Louis Napoléon, Prince Albert, and the Princess Royal entered the first carriage, drawn by four horses, followed by the Prince of Wales and Lord Clarendon, as the cortège took them to the heart of the city, avoiding the areas encumbered by the massive construction works in progress.

In fact, given the traditional animosity of the French to "Perfidious Albion" and fearful of the worst, Louis Napoléon had ordered the most extensive security operation in the history of the French capital, involving hundreds of plainclothes secret police and some 100,000 troops. Infantry and national guardsmen closely lined every foot of both sides of the entire route. "Her Majesty was greeted all along the route by the enthusiastic cheers of the population," which the Prefect Piétri put at 800,000. At eight forty-five that evening, the cortège finally arrived at St. Cloud, the event announced by salvos of artillery. "In all this blaze of light from lamps and torches, amidst the roar of cannon, and bands, and drums, and cheers, we reached the Palace," Victoria wrote.[11]

The thirty-six-year-old English queen was, as she frankly confessed, quite unprepared for the elaborate preparations made on her behalf, far surpassing anything she had laid on for Louis Napoléon during his earlier visit that April. After alighting, Victoria took Louis Napoléon's arm as they entered the palace. "The Empress [Eugénie], Princess Mathilde and the ladies, received us at the door," she noted, "and took us up a beautiful staircase, lined with the splendid Cent-Gardes, who are magnificent men, very like our Life Guards." She found her own apartments "charming . . . I felt quite bewildered [by the luxurious accommodations] but enchanted," for everything was "so beautiful."[12] At nine-thirty that first evening at St. Cloud, "their Majesties entered the Gallery of Diana for dinner"; but they retired at eleven p.m. to their spacious state apartments. Even for the indefatigable English queen, who had left Osborne on the Isle of Wight at four-thirty that morning, it had been a very long day indeed.[13]

An intimidatingly exhausting schedule of events had been arranged for this eight-day state visit. On Sunday, Louis Napoléon permitted his guests time in which to recuperate, however, beginning with religious services in the morning and a leisurely tour of the grounds in the afternoon in his phaeton. "The Emperor drove us about in the charming cool avenues of the park, of this most enjoyable, delightful palace of St. Cloud. There are a good many roe-deer running wild . . . and [he] says there is good pheasant-shooting. While we were driving I talked to the Emperor of Prince Napoleon [Plon-Plon] who had scowled when meeting us at the railway station the previous day and of my fear that he was *bien méchant* [really most unpleasant]." Louis Napoléon acknowledged that his cousin "had the unhappy talent of saying everything that was most disagreeable, and offended everyone."[14]

The next day, the official party set out for the International Exhibition's Palais des Beaux-Arts, where they were received by that same "most unpleasant" Plon-Plon, this event's president, and the more gracious Auguste de Morny, the president of the jury judging the hundreds of international works of art entered for this event, including those of artists present today, including Ingres, Delacroix, and Horace Vernet. Louis Napoléon had prepared every step of their visit with an idea to personal detail that would please his guests, and for Prince Albert he had also arranged for a special display of German paintings. It was Horace Vernet's works on Algeria that seemed to draw special attention, however, including his "Razzia," and the "Battle of Isly." And "Arab chiefs"—"Algerian visitors, in white or red bournous, were conspicuously included as guests here." As for the visiting queen, Louis Napoléon had a special surprise in mind: "A beautifully executed bust of Her Majesty stood on a pedestal in the center of the reception room."

Queen Victoria was wearing a white bonnet and gown while both the emperor and Prince Albert were dressed in "plain clothes," suits, as their open carriages, each drawn by four horses, "escorted by the Cuirassiers of the Imperial Guard," took them next to the Ile de la Cité to visit the newly restored Sainte-Chapelle, the Palais de Justice—Louis Napoléon pointing out his former cell in the austere towering Conciergerie—and Notre Dame Cathedral. At five-thirty the exhausted tourists returned to St. Cloud. After restoring themselves and dining, the royal couple was whisked off to the opera. The redoubtable Queen Victoria showed no signs of slowing down, despite the oppressive heat and unrelenting schedule.

Over the following days under a sweltering August sun, the royal parties visited the long gallery of the Exposition Universelle, including Léon Foucault's mysterious new pendulum registering the effect of the earth's rotation, and French farming equipment, both of which fascinated Prince Albert. Throughout the summer of 1855 this vast exhibition, inspired by the Crystal Palace exhibition of 1851, displaying the products of most European countries, attracted ultimately five million visitors, the wealthiest putting up at Pereire's luxurious new Grand Hotel du Louvre and sipping champagne, while the remorseless war in the Crimea and Baltic continued, forgotten by most.

A picnic in the St.-Germain Woods and a hunt followed, while Victoria stopped to sketch. Then on to Versailles to tour the State Apartments of Louis XIV, and the vast formal gardens, fountains, and pools, completing the day's tour in the gardens behind the Petit Trianon, which captivated Queen Victoria today as much as it had the unfortunate and even younger Marie Antoinette. Another day Louis Napoléon discreetly took Queen Victoria and her daughter, incognito—"in bonnets and veils" in an unmarked carriage—on a separate tour of the monuments of Paris. Baron Haussmann and his elegant wife then hosted the official state ball of this visit for the queen given in the enormous glittering palace of the Hôtel de Ville, almost outshining St. Cloud in luxury and elegance, with its several orchestras, dancing, and reception for 8,000 *invités*, followed by a fabled midnight dinner. At the same hour hundreds of kilometers to the south, at the naval base of Toulon, crews were preparing warships and troop transports to sail with reinforcements for Sebastopol.

A bove all, however, this state visit brought the two monarchs together for long talks. Louis Napoléon and Prince Albert found that they shared many common interests, which in turn pleased Victoria enormously. "He [Louis Napoléon] is so fond of Albert [and] appreciates him so thoroughly, and shows him so much confidence."[15] But it was the many talks between Louis Napoléon and Victoria, some long and leisurely, others while en route to events, that were to prove the most valuable results of this royal–imperial visit. The queen, though not finding him a handsome man, certainly not in comparison with Prince Albert, nevertheless was almost hypnotized by him, and intrigued by what she found, in spite of his habit of speaking only in brief phrases and rarely in long, complete sentences.

Albert was generally more cautious than Victoria in making friends, and "he quite admits that it is extraordinary, how very much attached one becomes to the Emperor," she noted. "I know few people, whom I have felt involuntarily more inclined to confide in and speak unreservedly to," she admitted, "I should not fear saying anything [whatsoever] to him." And then she added something she would later say of only one other national leader, Prime Minister Disraeli—"I feel—I do not know how to express it—safe with him." He most certainly has "a most extraordinary power of attaching people to him! The children [too] are very fond of him; to them also his kindness was very great."[16] Everyone noted his special fondness of children.

The surprisingly easy, affable relationship that developed quite naturally between Louis Napoléon and Prince Albert certainly was attractive to Victoria. Albert's manner, so arrogant, impatient, and conceited, so lacking in "English amiability," had in fact distanced the German prince from Victoria's English subjects, who found him the proverbial outsider. If Albert's closest friend was a German, Baron Stockmar, he had found no one equivalent in England. Therefore it was all the more to Victoria's pleasure when she found someone she not only liked and approved of, but had her choice endorsed warmly by Albert himself. And that this Louis Napoléon also genuinely liked Victoria's children, which they reciprocated, helped deepen this new relationship. The impressionable fourteen-year-old Edward, the Prince of Wales, in particular was quite captivated by the charming French emperor. Louis Napoléon, unlike the strict disciplinarian Albert, showered the prince, the future Edward VII, with attention, including long sightseeing drives alone together through Paris in Louis Napoléon's favorite two-wheeled curricle drawn by two horses. Edward, who spoke fluent French and German, immediately fell under the spell of the easygoing, unpuritanical French emperor.

Albert and Louis Napoléon enjoyed "all sorts of old German songs,"

Victoria recorded in her diary. And then "he [Louis Napoléon] is very fond of Germany . . . and there is much that is German, and very little—in fact, nothing—markedly French in his character." Although Albert was disappointed to find that his guest had no interest whatsoever in classical music, at least they both enjoyed Schiller and Goethe. Not only that, Albert shared his host's enthusiasm for artillery, with Louis Napoléon driving him across Paris to Vincennes to see some field demonstrations.[17]

Behind everything, so far as Victoria was concerned, however, remained the necessity of establishing closer, permanent relations between France and England. They had signed a military alliance before entering the war in the Crimea and were now fighting there side by side. "The Emperor is full of anxiety and regret about the campaign," she noted one day, referring to Louis Napoléon's decision to forgo leading his army in person. But she was in an extraordinarily happy mood in Paris, and was determined to divert her host from such morbid thoughts. "We talked most cheerfully together, and he was in high spirits."[18]

"Another splendid day! Most truly do the heavens favour and smile upon this happy Alliance," Victoria wrote at St. Cloud before setting out on another excursion. This was a Victoria rarely seen in England, where she spent much of her time playing the ever watchful mother of their large family.[19] More intelligent and observant than her husband, Victoria was most impressed by the elaborate preparations Louis Napoléon had made for their visit. "Everywhere everything is ready!" She was quite staggered by the vast amounts of money he was spending to entertain her. "No one can be kinder or more agreeable than the Emperor," she remarked, greatly flattered by his many tokens of esteem. She also found him to be "so quiet, which is a comfort,"[20] in comparison with the constant instructive commentaries of Albert.

At a ball given at Versailles, Eugénie had arrived later than the others because, as Albert had put it, the empress was "in expectation of an heir."[21] When Eugénie made her appearance at the ball that evening, Victoria was in admiration, finding her "looking like a fairy queen or nymph in a white dress, it trimmed in diamonds" complete with a diamond belt and "her Spanish and Portuguese orders." Taking sight of his wife, Louis Napoléon broke his habitual silence with a delighted *"Comme tu est belle!"* (How lovely you look!).[22] Victoria was equally impressed, when Louis Napoléon not only remembered Albert's birthday on the twenty-sixth of August, but arranged to celebrate it in his own inimitable manner, by summoning three hundred drummers under the prince's balcony to play "some music of his own composition," which consisted of a "splendid roll of drums!" "It was very fine, and very kind of the Emperor to think of it. He is himself particularly fond of it," she noted diplomatically. [23]

The last big event of the royal sojourn took place on Friday, August 24, when the emperor of the French was due to review the garrison, followed by a private viewing of Napoléon I's tomb. Originally planned for an earlier date, this historic event had been delayed because Louis Napoléon's pouting Uncle Jérôme Bonaparte had left town, taking the keys to the Hôtel des Invalides with him. Other keys were found, but not Uncle Jérôme, the father of the notorious Plon-Plon, who had declined the honor of bowing before her and of appearing today.[24]

This vast military review of several battalions, forty thousand strong, extended from the banks of the Seine all the way up to the Invalides.

Ignoring a heavy gray, lowery sky, at five o'clock Louis Napoléon, with Prince Albert sitting across from him in his phaeton, began the long review. "The troops rent the air with their acclamations as the Emperor took his guests along the front, battalion after battalion, squadron upon squadron." While at the south end of the immense field, Victoria and Eugénie watched the whole scene from the balcony.

Just as the review came to an end two hours later, "the rain descended in torrents, and it was in the midst of a thunderstorm that the emperor took his guests into the Hospital of the Invalides to visit the tomb of the first Napoléon," the valiant *Times* correspondent continued. "Well might nature show signs of elemental agitation while such an act of homage to the ashes of the mighty dead was in progress!" General Count d'Ornano, acting on behalf of the still absent governor, a brooding Uncle Jérôme, had torches lit as they entered the Invalides. The vault being built to serve as Napoleon's final resting place having not yet been decided on, his coffin, "covered with black velvet and gold and the emperor's orders, hat and sword . . . placed at its foot," lay on a dais in the small adjoining chapel here. The four torches flickered violently as the jarring thunder reverberated, while the chapel's organ played "God Save the Queen." Nothing seemed real as the queen of England, Prince Albert, and Princess Victoria looked on as the Prince of Wales knelt before the remains of Napoléon I.

"There I stood," Victoria recorded in her diary, "on the arm of Napoléon III, his nephew, before the coffin of England's bitterest foe; I the granddaughter of that King who hated him most . . . and this very nephew, who bears his name, being my nearest and dearest ally! . . . Strange and wonderful indeed," she thought, as the thunder crashed. With this "tribute of respect to a departed and dead foe," she felt "old enmities and rivalries were wiped out, and the seal of Heaven placed that bond of unity, which is now happily established between two great and powerful nations. May Heaven bless and prosper it!"[25]

Before leaving, the English monarch was invited back to the Hôtel dc Ville by Prefect Haussmann for one final ceremony, the inauguration of the Avenue Victoria in her honor, Louis Napoléon's way of commemorating a very special relationship. On Monday the twenty-seventh of August, Queen Victoria and Prince Albert, accompanied by Louis Napoléon, boarded the train. A festive crowd of some 45,000 greeted them at Boulogne with a deafening *"Vive la Reine!" "Vive le Prince Albert!" "Vive l'Empereur!"* Two hours later, a twenty-one-gun salvo saluted Queen Victoria as the royal yacht and the escorting Royal Squadron set sail for Dover.[26] The degree of genuine enthusiasm experienced throughout this state visit astonished even Louis Napoléon, momentarily banishing all thoughts of the war in the Crimea.

"I am deeply grateful for these eight very happy days," Victoria confided to her diary, ". . . and for the reception which we have met with in Paris, and in France generally. The union of the two nations, and of the two Sovereigns—for there is a great friendship sprung up between us—is of the greatest importance. May God bless these two countries, and He specially protect the precious life of the Emperor!"[27] And then less formally: "I shall always look back on this visit to France . . . as one of the pleasantest and most interesting periods of my life!"[28]

Nor was the notoriously phlegmatic, usually tongue-tied Louis Napoléon left unmoved by this state visit. He acknowledged his "delight" with "the remembrance of the gracious and amiable lady, of the distinguished man, and of such charming children, in whose sweet intimacy I passed days I shall never forget."[29]

Never in living memory, and well beyond, had relations between England and France been so close and confident. But although personal loyalties and friendships may resist the severe shocks of time, relationships between nations are rarely built on such firm foundations . . . as the events of the ensuing years would reveal.

25

———

A CHILD OF FRANCE

"The Map of Europe has to be redrawn. On the Continent there are only two great powers, France and Russia. Allied with England, who rules the sea, our three powers would dominate the world."[1]
—AUGUSTE DE MORNY TO COUNT KISSELEFF, SPRING 1856

"I shall see to it that he is raised with the understanding that nations must not be isolated entities, that the peace of Europe depends on our mutual prosperity."[2]
—LOUIS NAPOLÉON SPEAKING OF HIS
NEWLY BORN SON, MARCH 1856

There never was such a mess, and I see no honourable way out of it," a discouraged fifty-two-year-old Ambassador Lord Cowley, Henry Wellesley, wrote Foreign Secretary Lord Clarendon from the Hôtel de Charost, the British embassy, in the Rue du Faubourg St. Honoré in the third week of January 1856.[3] "However, in your hands it is in good keeping, and that is my only consolation." The opening days of stage negotiations to conclude the war in the Crimea were nearly as difficult as the siege of Sebastopol itself. France wanted to end the war as quickly as possible, whereas the British wished to continue in hope of achieving an even greater victory over the Russians. Count Walewski, the newly promoted French foreign minister, was informed by Persigny, who had replaced him as ambassador to the English court, that it was all the fault of the seventy-one-year-old Prime Minister Henry Temple, Lord Palmerston. "The Emperor's conviction is that Palmerston will not hear of peace," and will threaten to carry on the war, all alone if needs be. "I never felt so out of spirits as at this moment," the British ambassador confessed. "I think that a letter from the Queen to the Emperor would be of immense use," Cowley suggested to Clarendon.[4]

"Sire and Dear Brother," an equally concerned Victoria duly wrote to Louis Napoléon, "I do not doubt for a moment that this very peace that France and England have the right to expect will most certainly be obtained," despite the great pressure on the French to sign a quick accommodating peace treaty with the Russians. Be reasonable, but stand fast, "Your very affectionate Sister and Friend."[5] While to Prime Minister Palmerston the queen was more blunt, instructing him to say to Russia, " 'You have accepted the ultimatum, *pure and simple,* and have now again recognised its stipulations . . . You will, therefore . . . have to execute them.' "[6]

On the other hand jingoistic editorials of *The Times* vigorously opposed a "weak peace," indeed *any* negotiations or peace treaty now. Instead that newspaper demanded a hard-pressed final campaign that would completely destroy Russia and her influence once and for all. Great Britain will soon have one hundred warships in Russian waters, and "her army is in perfect condition." Therefore strike the final blow now and it will be "long before she again disturbs the peace of Europe."[7]

A s if Paris were not tense enough with the daily negotiations of the four allies, plus Austria meeting with Count Walewski daily at the Quai d'Orsay, compounded by the time constraints of the armistice due to expire on the thirty-first of March, and attended by the usual series of diplomatic receptions and balls, simultaneously another drama was taking place in the empress's apartments. This event was even more important to France and more crucial for the survival of the Second Empire: an heir to the throne was about to be born. Eugénie had been in labor for over twenty-two hours, and the palace was issuing periodic bulletins.

"The Emperor, the Princess of Esseling, and Madame de Montijo

[Eugénie's mother] have remained the whole of the day at the empress's apartment," *The Times* reported on Saturday, the fifteenth of March. "The dignitaries of the empire are assembled in the green drawing room, close to the Empress's chamber."[8] Outside the Tuileries, large crowds had been gathering for news of the long-awaited imperial birth. "At six o'clock [a.m.] the guns [at the Invalides] were fired one hundred and one times," announcing the birth of a male child, Horace de Viel-Castel recorded, and "the great [tenor] bell of Notre Dame has added its tolling voice to the cannon fire."[9]

At eight-thirty the emperor's brother, Auguste de Morny, as president of the Legislative Body, broke the happy news to the nation's deputies gathered in the National Assembly.[10] "Gentlemen, last night at three fifteen Her Majesty gave birth to an Imperial Prince." This announcement was greeted by clamors of "Long live the Emperor!" "Long Live the Empress!" "Long live the Prince Imperial!" The name of the new heir:[11] Napoléon Eugène Louis Jean Joseph.

"The birth of a son . . . the heir of his crown, seems to complete the measure of the marvelous prosperity which has lately marked the eventful life of the Emperor," the Paris correspondent of *The Times* summed up.[12]

"This evening I am to dine *chez* Princess Mathilde where I doubt that I will hear any praise of the Empress," Viel-Castel dutifully noted. "The princess does not like her and makes no pretense to do otherwise. It is unfortunate that division and jealousy separate the members of this family." Prince Jérôme, who had been next in the succession to the throne was now replaced by a baby boy, and he has "started to sulk and since the birth has not spoken to a soul . . . his black character now revealed in all its true ugliness," remarked Viel-Castel.[13]

"We were in some anxiety about the life of the Empress," Prince Albert wrote his old friend Baron Stockmar on the eighteenth of March, following daily palace reports that she was "weak" and suffering from "milk fever." The *accouchement* had been "a more difficult affair than the public were allowed to be told." Foreign Secretary Clarendon, who was in Paris for the peace negotiations, confided to Queen Victoria that "the Emperor's eyes filled with tears when he described the tortures of the Empress."[14]

On Tuesday, the eighteenth of March, "Napoléon received the congratulations of the diplomatic corps at 1 o'clock in the Throne Room of
the Tuileries."[15] As far as the public celebration of the birth of the new
imperial prince was concerned, apparently Count Viel-Castel did not immediately find the same level of joy among the Parisians. "Paris is illuminated, but the public's enthusiasm is not as great as at the time when
Sebastopol was captured [last year]," he pointed out.[16]

A grateful father, Louis Napoléon next thanked the Senate and the
Corps Législatif for their official congratulations. "The Senate have
shared my joy on learning that Heaven had given me a son, and you hail-
ing the happy event, the birth of a Child of France. . . . consecrated in
his cradle by the [Crimean] peace treaty we are currently preparing, with
the blessing of the Pope . . . and by the acclamations of the people—this
child, I say will be worthy of the destiny now awaiting him."[17]

For Louis Napoléon Bonaparte, hardly noted either for long speeches
or emotional displays, this was undoubtedly the most momentous and
joyful event of his life, to have a son and legal heir to carry on his name
and his dynasty. Neither Lord Clarendon nor Ambassador Cowley had
ever seen Louis Napoléon express any emotion, and they were as deeply
moved as they were almost embarrassed by this most unusual outpour-
ing. Unlike his brutal father, Louis Napoléon was to prove a doting
father, spending hours on end with his son. If the loud acclamations by
the Senate, the Corps Législatif, the Council of State, and the magistracy
of the land were largely most sincere, they also reflected their great relief in knowing that this Second Empire would continue tomorrow, and
with it not only their government posts and emoluments, but the continuation of this political stability and surging national prosperity.

Fireworks burst over the Parisian heavens, and illuminations shone
from all the public buildings, the theaters, and the Opéra as well as from
larger private properties. The emperor announced a general amnesty
for thousands of prisoners incarcerated for all crimes, short of murder. The navy and army in turn released those guilty of military of-
fenses. All public government offices and officials offered formal
congratulations. Louis Napoléon daily announced promotions to the
Legion of Honor, including the awarding of the Grand Croix to Secre-

tary of State Achille Fould and Admiral Ferdinand Hamelin. Generals Randon, Canrobert, and Bosquet were each rewarded for their services in Algeria and the Crimea with a marshal's baton. Louis Napoléon ordered the nation's theaters opened free to the public for an entire day, and Jacques Offenbach celebrated the great event by presenting his riotous new musical, *Tromb Al-Ca-Zar.*

Although Eugénie was still too weak to appear in public, Louis Napoléon gave a sumptuous banquet at the Tuileries for the negotiators of the Treaty of Paris, including Lord Clarendon and Ambassador Cowley, Austria's Counts Buol and von Hübner, Counts von Manteuffel and von Hatzfeldt representing Prussia, Russia's Count Orlov and Baron Brünnow, Sardinia's Counts Cavour and Emmanuel Pes de Villamarina. The inevitable balls for which the Second Empire was already famed were given at the Hôtel de Ville, at the Hôtel de Lassay by Morny, and by all the embassies. Celebrating the great event, Eugénie and Louis Napoléon offered many hundreds of thousands of francs to charities and foundling hospitals, and as pensions to the artists, authors, and composers of the land.

As usual, the latest numerous rumors spread by Walewski's unpopular replacement at the French embassy in London, the ubiquitous Persigny, proved to be false. This included his totally false accusation that England's new prime minister, Palmerston, was resisting every effort to resolve the peace. What Persigny did not state, however, was that Palmerston so detested the very sight of this new French ambassador that he refused even to receive him at 10 Downing Street. Persigny had been Louis Napoléon's choice for that post for which he was most ill-suited, but even emperors have to reward political favors, while the appointment also kept the perpetually interfering Persigny far away from Paris during these sensitive Crimean peace talks.

"You will not be satisfied with the peace which has been made," Cowley informed Clarendon at Whitehall later in March. "I confess that I had hoped for better things and although I endeavour to conceal it, I feel deeply the mortification of being dragged through the mud by the

French," and an obstructive pro-Russian foreign minister, Walewski in particular. "So ill do I think that both the emperor and his Ministers have behaved," Cowley admitted, "that I begged to be relieved from the intolerable burden of carrying on business." He had hoped for far harsher terms against Tsar Alexander. "However, the deed is now done and we must make the best of it."[18]

After returning to London and spending two hours with Victoria explaining the treaty, Clarendon in fact found the queen "in good humour with the Peace [settlement], and admits . . . that she is now quite reconciled to it, and does not wish that things had turned out otherwise. . . . Palmerston, wonderful man! Is not only pleased with the Peace but is extremely doubtful whether our army might not have been destroyed by disease if we had attempted another expedition to Asia Minor, and whether we might not have been beaten on our own element [the Royal Navy] at Cronstadt, so there is no discontent, and the Cabinet generally are satisfied."[19] So much for Persigny's campaign of dissimulation.

"Sire and My Dear Brother," Queen Victoria wrote to Louis Napoléon, "I highly approve of the final terms [of the treaty]." Everything realistically possible "has been concluded . . . to ensure as much has been possible the stability of European equibilibrium."[20]

On March 30, 1856, the delegates at the Congress of Paris took their places at the large round green-baize-covered table beneath the massive crystal chandelier in the Ambassadors' Room of the Quai d'Orsay to affix their signatures under the observant eyes of Winterhalter's newly painted portraits of Napoléon III and Empress Eugénie: Alexander Walewski for France, Lord Clarendon for England, Cavour for Sardinia's king Victor Emmanuel, Counts Buol and Hübner for Austria, Hatzfeldt and Manteuffel for Prussia (who crashed the party), Orlov for Russia, and the Grand Vizier Ali Pasha on behalf of the Ottoman Empire.

Following the signing of the Treaty of Paris, officially putting an end to the Crimean War, the delegates, attired in their formal uniforms complete with gold braid and a splendid array of the highest European orders and decorations, were invited into Walewski's "Elliptical Office," the large oval office with spacious bow windows overlooking the long formal gardens. It seemed only fitting to have the full-length Gobelins *tapisseries* "The Seasons of the Gods" looking down on them. Following champagne cocktails and hors d'oeuvres, the gentlemen left by carriage across the Seine to the Tuileries to be received by Napoléon III.

CONCLUSION OF PEACE," *The Times* announced on the thirty-first of March: "CONGRESS OF PARIS. Peace was signed to-day, at 1 o'clock, at the Ministry of Foreign Affairs. . . . The great question that has kept all Europe in suspense for weeks is at last resolved. . . . The moment the signatures were complete . . . the cannon from the Esplanade of the Invalides proclaimed the news [even] before the Plenipotentiaries had quitted the hall."[21]

"All Paris has gone mad—total strangers have kissed each other in the streets," Lord Cowley reported to London as the celebrations began. By evening Viel-Castel found the Place du Caroussel "simply filled with humanity, everyone shouting 'Long Live the Emperor!' "[22] "On this date 42 years ago was fought the Battle of Paris, the last act of the great drama of which Europe was the theatre," a reflective English observer remarked, and "on the following day the [triumphant] Russians entered the capital, and dictated terms of peace" to the French. "What a dramatic historical change since 1815. Today France is able to dictate, in concert with her allies, peace to Russia," finally avenging the humiliations of the Congress of Vienna. The diplomatic tables had been turned one hundred eighty degrees. "The Emperor must be proud and happy," Horace de Viel-Castel exclaimed. "France is indeed the great nation once more, the pivot round which Europe now revolves [once again]."[23]

MOST of the delegations were, to varying degrees, content after weeks of nerve-wracking negotiations and haggling. With their troops daily wasting away in the Crimean, the French and the Sardinians were certainly the happiest with the accelerated conclusion to a war that was degenerating into decline and disaster. The Turks were even more relieved to have turned out the occupying Russians. To be sure, there remained some English almost as upset as the Russians with the early conclusion of hostilities.

By now Lord Clarendon was barely talking to French Foreign Minister Walewski with his obvious pro-Russian agenda, who had vigorously opposed the war from the outset and exerted enormous pressure on England. Fortunately, in fact, the aging Prime Minister Palmerston and Queen Victoria had been eager to end this war. Unlike Prussia, Austria had been allowed to participate in presenting Allied demands to the Russians. Toward the end a muddling Walewski had pressed for close relations with Austria and a favorable outcome for Russia, not to mention a demand for Polish independence. He had his incentives, as well, handsome bribes and rewards he had received. Walewski was always in debt and a notorious gambler not only at the Bourse but at cards, and then of course there were his mistresses. Poland—the land of his birth—presented him with a handsome estate, while the Tsar Alexander, the Grand Vizier Ali Pasha, and Victor Emmanuel offered him millions of francs. Nor were Vienna and Berlin forgetful of their obligations, including the Habsburg emperor's presentation of the Grand Cordon de St. Étienne and Prussia's Frederick Wilhelm the Order of the Black Eagle.[24]

After all those deaths and months of misery in the Crimea, thanks to the insistence of Louis Napoléon, all conquered territory was to be restored to its original owners—at least in theory. That included battle-scarred Kars, a large, important commercial city in northeastern Anatolia, which the Russians reluctantly agreed to exchange for Bolgard, in western Moldavia. Unfortunately, the Treaty of Paris set a precedent, one still troubling diplomatic relations in the twenty-first century, by proclaiming the Ottoman Empire "a European power."

In a separate treaty, England, France, and Austria agreed for the first time to "respect, defend and guarantee" the independence and integrity of the Ottoman Empire. The Turkish provinces of Wallachia and Moldavia invaded and occupied by Russia were soon to gain their independence as the new state of Romania. Montenegro and Serbia would also soon follow as autonomous states. The Treaty of Paris also proclaimed the free and unrestricted use of the Danube and a neutralized and demilitarized Black Sea. Apart from small gunboats for customs and policing, all warships were banned. As for the religious sites in the Holy Land, the Ottoman emperor was now alone fully responsible for protecting them and all Christians.[25]

Theoretically peace had been restored. Nevertheless, following the signing of all treaties there are inevitably unfinished matters, of course, diplomatic loose ends. The unhappy Poles left Paris empty-handed. Kars was returned to Turkey, the Russians now in turn claiming Bolgrad (earlier promised to them by Louis Napoléon), but England for one did not want a Russian city in the future Romania. By December 1856, however, a restless Tsar Alexander II was once again threatening to take up the sword to defend his rights and Bolgrad, much as the English had feared. Fortunately, France's newly appointed special ambassador, Auguste de Morny—banished from Paris earlier in 1856 because of his notorious stock market "coup"—interceded. Employing his celebrated "Morny charm," he was able to convince Alexander to give up Bolgard—that "wretched provincial hole," as he referred to it, for which "they [the Russians] had almost set Europe on fire once again." In exchange the tsar accepted some land in Bessarabia. "This will serve as a salutary lesson, and at little cost, a cautionary lesson to all those responsible for the fate of their nations," a much relieved Morny concluded.[26]

As for "the Italian Question," Prime Minister Cavour made a dramatic appeal before the Congress of Paris for the withdrawal of all Austrian troops from his country, and that was an issue that simply would not disappear, as Mazzini's Italian assassins were soon to remind Napoléon III and the world.

Clearly Louis Napoléon had raised France to a new position of power, prestige, and international respect, and his own stature as a world leader. He had fought a successful war, with England at his side, and had capped it by bringing senior European leaders, all former enemies forty years earlier, to negotiate a peace treaty in Paris. "Triumph" was the operative world. No leader could have asked for more . . . and then Louis Napoléon blotted his copybook with "the Castiglione affair."

L ong before, Louis Napoléon had discovered that Eugénie took no pleasure in intimate marital relations—she called sex "filthy." For his part, he enjoyed the company of ladies of easy virtue, not to mention the wives of several of his senior officials, including that of Foreign Minister Walewski. The list of his conquests was not only long, it was public, including the companions and ladies-in-waiting of the empress. For all his charms and admitted interest in major social causes, including new hospitals, schools, and housing, Napoléon III was at the same time thick-skinned to the point of deeply wounding and publicly humiliating Eugénie. Harriet Howard and her children and his own prison-born bastards were long out of sight. But then there had been Augustine Brohan, Alice Ozy, Countess Parada, Countess de La Bédoyère, the Countess Walewska, Madame Rimsky-Korsakov, and now La Castiglione; and later, Marguerite Bellanger, Valtesse de la Bigne, and Countess Mercy-Argenteau, without counting "the actresses" and the ladies of the court.[27] Louis Napoléon was indeed a womanizer on an imperial scale.

Toward the end of the hostilities in the Crimea, late in 1855, Victor Emmanuel and his prime minister, Count Cavour, had come to Paris without an invitation to meet with Louis Napoléon in the hopes of enlisting his direct military support in forcing the Austrians to remove all their troops from Italy. On returning to Turin, Cavour asked his beautiful twenty-year-old-cousin Virginia Oldoini, Contessa de Castiglione, to "encourage" Louis Napoléon to take up the cause of liberating Italy. Accepting with unanticipated amiability, she hastened to Paris, without her husband, Turin's new ambassador. "A beautiful countess has enrolled in the Italian diplomatic services," Cavour confided in his friend Luigi Cibrario. "I have invited her to play the Emperor up." "You must succeed, dear cousin, by any means you wish, but succeed you must,"

Cavour instructed her. Already a friend of Count Walewski's second, Florentine-born, wife, Maria Anna de Ricci, the raven-haired, green-eyed young Contessa Castiglione was quickly absorbed into the French capital's aristocratic social circle, where she won over everyone. She is "a veritable Venus descended from Mt. Olympus!," a dazzled Pauline von Metternich exclaimed. It was at a soirée *chez* Princess Mathilde that Virginia was introduced to an immediately smitten Louis Napoléon.[28]

Then, on the twenty-fourth of June, Eugénie personally invited "Venus" to a long weekend at Villeneuve-l'Étang near St. Cloud. There Virginia joined Louis Napoléon on a boat ride. Rowing out to a wooded islet in the middle of the lake, they did not reappear until much later. Tongues wagged as the emperor's infatuation with this Florentine beauty took flame, the two openly flaunting elementary discretion at the Tuileries, St. Cloud, Compiègne, and Fontainebleau over the next several months, much to the chagrin of the new mother, Empress Eugénie.

Ambassador Cowley, for one, was as perplexed by the emperor's senseless indiscretions as he was troubled by the harm this could do his reputation in France and the international community. Moreover, following the peace talks, he found Louis Napoléon run down. He was shocked by his "apathy, irritation [and] caprice," the result of "an exhausted nervous system and diseased organs. The political consequences," the ambassador considered, "might be fearful." Discussing "the beauteous Castiglione" with Lord Clarendon, Cowley explained, this liaison "will do his nerves no good," referring to Louis Napoléon's near breakdown following the birth of his son and the conclusion of the Congress of Paris.

After his "last rendezvous" with La Castiglione, there was a hysterical row by Eugénie at Compiègne, Mérimée reported, as the maids fled for shelter, and Louis Napoléon promised "never again," once again. "All Paris is in an *émoi* at an escapade of the Emperor . . . He isn't too discreet," Cowley sighed. "The poor empress is in very low spirits. She talked to me a long time about him—with tears in her eyes the whole time."[29] "I have tried everything, even to make him jealous," Eugénie confided to the Walewskis, of all people! "It's made no difference . . . I can't take any more," and hereafter she would disappear without explanation from Paris on long sojourns to German and Swiss spas, even to England and Scotland.[30]

The implications of this first peace treaty signed at Paris during Louis Napoléon's newly established Second Empire were at once great. He had reestablished France as a major player on the European stage again, and himself as a highly respected spokesman on behalf of world peace, unlike his uncle, the perpetual war machine. Moreover, the Treaty of Paris had avenged the destruction of the Grande Armée in Russia and the humiliating collapse of the First Empire. As a result of the Crimean victory, he had also helped to break up the old coalition and balance of power aligned against France at the Congress of Vienna. Russia seemed isolated. Louis Napoléon was now no longer the nephew of a defeated tyrant, but the most prestigious head of state on the Continent of Europe. And then he made a laughingstock of himself by having to bed every silk skirt in Paris.

No sooner was one major problem resolved, however, than another emerged. The cirrus preceding the inevitable cumulonimbus was emerging over the southern Alps, the warning of a building Italian tempest. "The Italians are still complaining [about the Austrian occupation]," Horace de Viel-Castel noted. And nothing is done to stop "Mazzini who dispatches his political assassins [e.g., Pianori]," and not content "with bloodying their own country," Viel-Castel continued, now they come here "with the purpose of killing Napoléon!" This wretched Italy, he continued, "is a festering sore," and something must be done about it.[31]

No sooner had the conflict in Russia come to an end, than "the government is already preparing to send a new expedition of forty thousand men to the Kabyle region," Viel-Castel also observed, referring to the major campaign against rebellious Berber tribesmen in the mountains of northeastern Algeria that had been interrupted in 1855 in order to send General Randon and several divisions of his Zouaves to the Crimea. "Steam transports are now being assembled" near Toulon and Marseilles. There were also rumors that Louis Napoléon personally would head this new expedition, and that "he intends to form a Regency Council" to rule France during his absence, that council to be presided over by none other than Prince Jérôme, the hero of Crimea. And that idea terrified everyone, Viel-Castel included.[32] In fact, the newly promoted Marshal Randon, as the governor general of Algeria—not Louis Napoléon—would launch this campaign, ordering General MacMahon "to pacify" the Kabyle in 1857, resulting in a few thousand more French casualties, although the Algerians suffered far worse. Fortunately Louis Napoléon was dissuaded from leading his troops.[33]

For a gentleman with a reputation as a frivolous social climber, Horace de Viel-Castel certainly seemed to be very aware of the realities around him, and he was right on the mark. If not a religious man, and despite his anxieties, he continued to strongly support Napoléon III, and even offered a prayer of his own. "France is now enjoying peace and calm once again, a right she richly earned. May God will and grant us a long reign under the guidance of Louis Napoléon!"[34]

✦

26

AN ITALIAN OPERA

"Sire, do not reject the words of a patriot . . . Free Italy!"[1]
—FELICE ORSINI TO NAPOLÉON III JUST BEFORE HIS
EXECUTION ON MARCH 13, 1858

*"The French are bent on finding accomplices in this crime
everywhere and I find it hard to resist all the extreme measures
people call on me to take."*[2]
—LOUIS NAPOLÉON TO QUEEN VICTORIA FOLLOWING
THE ATTEMPT ON HIS LIFE, JANUARY 14, 1858

ATTEMPT TO ASSASSINATE THE EMPEROR NAPOLEON," read the news in *The Times* of London under the "Latest Intelligence" received from Paris on Friday, January 15, 1858:

> The emperor was fired at this evening [Thursday, January 14] at half-past 9 o'clock as he was entering the Italian Opera in the Rue le Peletier. Some persons in the street were wounded.[3]

And thus began one of the strangest episodes of the Second Empire, beginning with an assassination attempt, and nearly ending in hostilities between two staunch friends and allies, Louis Napoléon's France and Victoria's England, and in so doing unexpectedly bringing Prime Minister Palmerston's government crashing down in its wake.

• • •

The triumphant if tumultuous year of peace and birth for Napoleon III and France, after a relatively calming summer's respite at Biarritz, had drifted into a calmer 1857, the highlight of which included a visit by Louis Napoléon and Eugénie to Queen Victoria and Prince Albert at their summer retreat of Osborne, on the Isle of Wight. The results of the Crimean War, concluded back in March 1856, were discussed during that visit, along with French hopes for a revision of the peace terms of 1815 and of a Europe with new horizons. The visit also afforded the two royal families an opportunity to deepen their friendship, especially between Victoria and Eugénie. This included discussion of the preparations of the forthcoming marriage of the queen's eldest daughter, Victoria, with Crown Prince Friedrich, the son of the Prussian king of the same name and, indirectly, its effect on Franco-Prussian politics in the future. When the two ruling families separated later in August, the relations between England and France were warmer and closer than at any time in centuries. A great historical gap had been bridged; the future looked most auspicious. Then came the events of January 1858, again standing the world on its head and shaking the Anglo-French relationship to its limits, leaving this new bridge dangling over the channel.

On Thursday January 14, 1858, Louis Napoléon, Eugénie, and their party left the Tuileries in three carriages for a gala charity evening at the Italian Opera in the Rue le Peletier. Neither the emperor nor the empress liked opera or classical music of any kind, and Eugénie, who was tone deaf, found most music acutely "painful," except for Spanish folk dances. The emperor, who as a rule disdained security details, including the presence of bodyguards, did agree to a strong police presence for public occasions such as a night at the opera. In addition, the imperial carriage was escorted by twenty-four mounted lancers of the elite Imperial Guard. Tonight's program included arias and acts from a variety of pieces, including Gioachino Rossini's *Guillaume Tell,* the popular

Daniel Auber's *Gustave III,* and Gaetano Donizetti's *Maria Stuarda.* It was afterward pointed out that Rossini's work dealt with insurrection, Auber's with the assassination of a Swedish monarch, and Donizetti's with the execution of the queen of Scotland. It was almost as if the dramatic tragedy about to unfold had been choreographed by the audacious Italian nationalist Giuseppe Mazzini himself.

The imperial calèche carrying Louis Napoléon, Empress Eugénie, and aide-de-camp General Roguet turned into the narrow Rue le Peletier leading to the Italian Opera. "Last evening [the fourteenth of January], at half-past 8 o'clock just as their Majesties . . . arrived at the Opera-house, three explosions were heard which proceeded from hollow projectiles," the *Times* reported. The usual large number of sightseers had crowded around the portico of the theater lit up by "gas stands," to catch a glimpse of the beautiful empress in her diamonds and of course the popular Napoléon III in black cape and silk top hat. The police and the Paris municipal guard had considerable difficulty in keeping the crowd away from the carriage.

The first grenade was thrown under the horses as the carriage approached the theater; when "the coachman immediately tried to whip up the horses, one . . . fell to the ground," and the other one was badly wounded. A second grenade exploded, and then a third "thrown with more precision, falling beneath the carriage itself and burst with tremendous force, smashing part of it in pieces," hurtling it against the wall of the building. A piece of shrapnel hit General Roguet, who was sitting across from the emperor, in the nape of the neck, his blood splattering onto Eugénie's white crinoline gown. "The Emperor's hat was perforated by a projectile . . . [and he] received a slight cut on the side of the nose by a piece of glass from the carriage window. Another piece struck the Empress in the corner of the left eye." Police Superintendent Hébert was dashing to the coach to warn the emperor just as the third bomb ignited, shrapnel hitting him in the head and throwing him down.[4]

"All the under part of and front of the carriage had the appearance of being blown to pieces. . . . A man was seen rushing to the carriage window with a dagger and revolver," but was tackled by a *sergent*

-an-Baptiste Wicar portrait of Louis Bonaparte, for-er King of Holland, hypochondriac, and tormenter of s son, Prince Louis Napoleon. (CHATEAU DE VER-ILLES, FRANCE/BRIDGEMAN IMAGES)

Anne-Louis Girodet portrait of Hortense de Beauhar-nais, former Queen of Holland, wife of Louis Bona parte, and mother of Napoleon III. (RIJKSMUSEUM, AMSTERDAM, THE NETHERLANDS/BRIDGEMAN IMAGES)

ortrait of Napoleon III, Emperor of the French, 52–1870, by Auguste Boulard, after the lost original Franz Winterhalter. (CHATEAU DE VERSAILLES, FRANCE/ RIDGEMAN IMAGES)

Franz Winterhalter portrait of Empress Eugénie, em-press, 1853–1870, and mother of Prince Imperial Eu-gène Louis Napoléon. (MUSEUM OF FINE ARTS, HOUSTON, TEXAS/BRIDGEMAN IMAGES)

Prince Imperial Eugène Louis Jean Joseph, 1856–1879, son of Louis Napoleon and Eugénie. (PRIVATE COLLECTION © LOOK AND LEARN/ELGAR COLLECTION/BRIDGEMAN IMAGES)

Jerome Bonaparte, former King of Westphalia, fath[e]r of Prince [Napoleon] and Princess Mathilde, and di[s]loyal and most ungrateful uncle of Louis Napoleo[n]. (GRANGER)

Plon-Plon, Prince Jerome [Napoleon Charles Paul] Bonaparte, violent, unstable, army deserter, and Louis Napoleon's jealous first cousin and most constant detractor. (DE AGOSTINI PICTURE LIBRARY/BIBLIOTECA AMBROSIANA/BRIDGEMAN IMAGES)

Princess Mathilde, first cousin, former fiancée and fait[h]ful friend of Louis Napoleon, but dedicated enemy [of] Empress Eugénie. (DE AGOSTINI PICTURE LIBRARY/B[IB]LIOTECA AMBROSIANA/BRIDGEMAN IMAGES)

...uguste, Count, and later Duke, de Morny, illegitimate ...n of Queen Hortense and General Count [Charles] ...e Flahaut, and half-brother of Napoleon III. (BRIDGE-...AN IMAGES)

Fanny, Countess Le Hon, 1808–1880, longtime mistress of Auguste de Morny, mother of at least one of his children, and the benefactress and business partner who launched Morny on his profitable financial career. (ROGER-VIOLLET/THE IMAGE WORKS)

...Ienri Conneau, 1803–1877, family physician to Hort-...nse and later of the Imperial Household, and Louis ...Iapoleon's longest and most intimate friend and com-...anion. (PHOTO © TALLANDIER/BRIDGEMAN IMAGES)

Georges Haussmann, the honest, industrious Loyal Prefect and Mayor of Paris, responsible for completely rebuilding the French capital, but later betrayed and dismissed by an ailing Louis Napoleon. (MUSÉE DE LA VILLE DE PARIS, MUSÉE CARNAVALET, PARIS, FRANCE, ARCHIVES CHARMET/BRIDGEMAN IMAGES)

Edouard-Dubufe. 1856.

he Congress of Paris, painting by Edouard Louis Dubufe. The Paris Peace Conference, held at the Quai d'Orsay,
nding the Crimean War on March 30, 1856. *Left to Right:* Count Walewski, Baron Bourqueney, Count von
uolschavenstein, Baron von Hübner, Ambassador Lord Cowley, Earl of Clarendon, Baron von Manteuffel, Count
tzfeld, Count Orloff, Baron von Brunow, Conde di Cavour, Marchese di Villamarine, and Grand Vizir Ali Pasha
d Mehmet Bey of the Ottoman Empire. (CHATEAU DE VERSAILLES, FRANCE/BRIDGEMAN IMAGES)

Cellist and composer Jacques Offenbach,
the very quintessence of the spirit of the
Second Empire, befriended by Auguste
de Morny and a favorite of Napoleon III.
(© Tallandier/Bridgeman Images)

Prince Otto von Bismarck, the "Blood
and Iron" Chancellor of Prussia, who
long and secretly plotted with Field
Marshals Moltke and Roon to invade
France. (© CCI/Bridgeman Images)

Schloss Arenenberg, the home of Louis Napoleon and Hortense after the fall of the First Empire. Following the death of Hortense here on October 5, 1837, and under grave threats by Louis Philippe's government, one year later, on October 14, 1838, the thirty-year-old prince left Switzerland, never to return. (DE AGOSTINI PICTURE LIBRARY/BIBLIOTECA AMBROSIANA/BRIDGEMAN IMAGES)

A painting by Nicolas Raguenet of the Tuileries Palace, the official residence of Napoleon III and Empress Eugénie, later deliberately burned down by Parisian communards in May 1871. (MUSÉE DE LA VILLE DE PARIS, MUSÉE CARNAVALET, PARIS, FRANCE/BRIDGEMAN IMAGES)

Camden Place, Chislehurst, Kent, Louis Napoleon's final residence and where he died following surgery on January 9, 1873. (Private Collection © Look and Learn/Illustrated Papers Collection/Bridgeman Images)

de ville, who was stabbed by the assailant. "For some minutes all was confusion," and then "a squadron of mounted Paris guards from the Minime Barracks in the Place Royale came up at a gallop. Several of the Lancers of the escort who were nearest the carriage were seriously wounded and one or two . . . killed," read the initial report.[5]

Fifty-six pieces of shrapnel had struck the carriage. Louis Napoléon once again escaped with his life. The shrapnel tearing through his hat narrowly missed taking off the back of his head, while Eugénie barely escaped blindness or glass in her brain, so forceful was the blast. Nineteen of the twenty-four lancers were wounded, and one killed, and twenty of their horses were killed or wounded, kicking in all directions and crying out, adding to the noise and mayhem. "Two of the three footmen [standing behind the carriage] were [also] wounded," as were "a considerable number of people assembled before the doors of the theatre." The windows of the adjoining houses "were blown out up to the fourth story. . . . and the gas pipes running along the façade of the Opera were blown off by the explosion," as were all the street lamps. "It was dark and cold," the only light now coming from within the theater. "The canopy over the entrance was torn, and the pavement . . . covered with blood. . . . Of the six doors, five are completely broken."

Louis Napoléon and Eugénie may have been shaken and in shock, but they did not show it as they passed through the fragmented doors of the Opera. "You should have witnessed the burst of enthusiasm which greeted them on their appearance in the Imperial box—an enthusiasm that rose to the most intense pitch when the Empress advanced to salute the assembly, her dress and cheek stained with blood." The orchestra struck up the unofficial anthem of the First Empire written by Louis Napoléon's mother, Hortense, "Partant Pour la Syrie" (Departing for Syria), accompanied by rousing applause.[6]

A fterward it was discovered that "five minutes prior to the explosions, [Superintendent] Hébert . . . had recognized an Italian named [Colonel] Pieri [an escaped prisoner] who had lately returned to Paris with a false passport . . . and arrested him" just before the theater.

He was carrying "a six-barrelled revolver, a long dagger and a bomb."[7] The inspector had then rushed back to warn Louis Napoléon when the first grenade exploded. In fact Hébert had been here that evening because of a series of strong warnings received by the police prefecture over the past several weeks about some sort of assassination attempt to be made by Mazzini's men.

"It is considered very extraordinary how, with police agents so often searching [suspicious persons], that heavy projectiles of the kind could be safely carried about, and how the [well armed] assassins . . . could arrive [undetected] so very near the execution of their designs," the *Times* reporter pointed out. This was a question Louis Napoléon himself put to a flustered Prefect of Police Piétri. The men turned out to be four Italian "republicans," some wearing disguises and using false names: Pieri—a former senior army officer and personal ADC to Garibaldi—Ruddio, Gomez, and Orsini. Felice Orsini, their leader, meticulously attired in a smart frock coat and white gloves, had been the former right-hand man in Giuseppe Mazzini's violent secret revolutionary society, Young Italy. They had all arrived from London on the eighth of January and were lodging in two different hotels just up the street. In their rooms a stash of pistols and knives was discovered, along with "270 francs in gold." The bombs brought from London were "four inches in diameter . . . made of cast iron in the shape of a pear." Their contents: hundreds of nails, iron fragments, bullets, and gunpowder.[8]

Following the performance, Louis Napoléon and Eugénie returned under heavy cavalry escort to the Tuileries. They went to their young son's bed, Lord Cowley informed Lord Malmesbury, and kneeling down "at the poor child's side . . . burst into tears, the emperor crying most bitterly." Meanwhile, back in the Rue le Peletier, seven surgeons were working throughout the night in a makeshift surgery at a nearby apothecary's. "The Emperor went this morning at 8 o'clock to the Hôpital Lariboisière, accompanied by an aide-de-camp, to visit the wounded," the *Times* noted on Friday the fifteenth.[9] That afternoon Louis Napoléon and Eugénie drove along the Champs-Élysées, attended by only one officer and no military escort whatsoever. As the later police prefect Maupas put it, Louis Napoléon's "personal courage and . . . sense of fatalism rendered him quite immune to any fear for his life," as in-deed he was to prove time and again.

The captured men were brought to the recently completed Mazas prison and later to the Conciergerie. Justice Minister Napoléon Boyer ap-pointed Chaix d'Estange, the public prosecutor, to take charge, while Examining Magistrate Treilhard interrogated the four men. The trial was then set for the Assize Court in the first fortnight of February. The *Times* correspondent denounced this "infamous attempt to assassinate the Em-peror," as did *Le Journal des Débats, La Presse, L'Univers,* and every other newspaper in France, reflecting national outrage and grief. "It is believed that the investigation into the affair will be promptly terminated." The London paper reminded its readers of a similarly bloody attack by an "infernal machine" against First Consul Napoléon Bonaparte at the Opéra [then in the Place Louvois] back in December 1800. The final police report recorded eight killed outright and 156 wounded, including men, women, children, police, and lancers. "In the annals of crime, there is no deed blacker than that which was perpetrated on Thursday [Janu-ary 14] in front of the Italian Opera," the English editorial concluded.[10]

Prefect of Police Pierre Piétri's very intensive investigation was effi-cient and conclusive, and the accused, defended by Jules Favre and others, were duly tried on February 25–26, 1858, found guilty, and moved to La Roquette Prison, on the other side of the Place de la Bastille. Orsini and Pieri alone were condemned to be executed by the guillotine, the other two given life sentences.

The whole conspiracy had been concocted and directed by the hand-some, bearded, meticulously attired thirty-eight-year-old Felice Orsini, a native of the Romagna near Forli, where Louis Napoléon's elder brother had died while serving as a member of the Carbonari to free a united Italy. After reading law briefly at the University of Bologna, Orsini had participated in an insurrection against the Austrian army of occupation. Captured in the fighting and arrested by the Austrians, he was released two years later, only to join Mazzini and his forces in 1848. In early 1849, Orsini had fought in Rome against papal forces until their brief new republic was suppressed by the French. In 1855, he was again imprisoned by the Austrians, escaping in 1856 and fleeing to London to resume his terrorist activities. There in 1857 he met a former French naval surgeon, Simon Bernard, who was assisted by an English chemist (who later fled the country). Together they manufactured four heavy "contact" grenades or bombs. Orsini also recruited the other Italian "patriots" to assist him in executing his plan to assassinate Louis Napoléon. Though heavily armed, they had passed through both English and French customs un-challenged and undetected, reaching Paris on January 8, 1858.[11]

On the revelation that this was not only another Italian attack—after the Pianori attempt three years earlier—but that the assassins had just come from London, where they had been fully armed, the French public exploded with age-old hatred for England. They let this happen! For Louis Napoléon, on the other hand, it was almost an insult; the cul-prits were Italians, the very people whose cause he and his brother had loyally supported against the Austrians in his youth. In public, however, he lashed out at the English for having protected the culprits and then permitted them to travel to France to carry out their dastardly attack. "Does one offer hospitality to assassins?" Anglophobe foreign minister Walewski chided Ambassador Persigny in London. "Should English leg-islation be allowed to favour such conspiracies . . . these flagrant acts!" "We had a gloomy Cabinet meeting to-day thinking of the universally dreadful consequences [of] this crime," Clarendon explained just before handing over the Foreign Office to Malmesbury. "I can see but one feel-ing predominant here [in France]," Lord Cowley answered, "and that is hatred of England."[12] "Irritation against England is at fever pitch," Count de Viel-Castel echoed. Meanwhile in London's Hyde Park, violent counter-demonstrators were denouncing France and calling for French blood.[13]

Caught in the middle, disturbed and under great pressure from all sides, Louis Napoléon addressed an angry Senate on Tuesday the second of February, reflecting his frustration with England, while following it pri-vately with a most conciliatory letter to Queen Victoria.[14] Meanwhile, his half brother, Auguste de Morny, convening the Corps Legislatif, joined the mob demanding English blood. Louis Napoléon immediately created a Privy Council, empowered to form as a Regency Council, "should events require it." The next attempt on his life might be more successful.[15] While, unusually, Morny was demanding vengeance against England, Persigny just as unusually was pleading loudly for moderation and the necessity of avoiding insults and hostilities with London. Nor did Louis Napoléon's recent orders for dozens of powerful new armored steam-driven warships, exclusive of a crash order for seventy-five steam-powered troop transports capable of landing 40,000 men, help reduce fears of a rumored French invasion. (The transports were in fact intended for the sole purpose of transferring reinforcements for the current campaign in Algeria. It had not occurred to Louis Napoléon that Victoria or Palmerston would seriously think he was intending to land the French army on English shores.) The bridge of friendship with Queen Victoria so laboriously constructed over the channel had been smashed with the first grenade.

For once Ambassador Persigny, in the English capital, was aware, however, that there was much more to the world than France and French anxieties. What the French government and press seemed to forget at this moment in 1858 was that England was much more preoccupied with, indeed still reeling from, the continuing great Indian Mutiny that had broken out in May 1857 as the war office and navy were expediting all available military units to Bombay and Calcutta. Thousands of British troops, civilians, women, children, and even babies had been butchered or wounded by rampaging Indians, and some 100,000 mutinying Indian troops and civilians were in turn eventually killed by British troops. Most of the London press coverage throughout 1858, therefore, was understandably preoccupied with the immensity of the tragedy in India and the very real possible loss of that crown colony itself, where some 40,000 British troops were attempting to regain control of 300,000 armed sepoys. And should India fall, the repercussions in the City and entire British economy were incalculable. This was something the fulminating Walewski chose to ignore altogether. France had not been England's only concern in the early months of 1858.[16]

The French doctor providing the bomb and funds for Orsini was tried that April at the Old Bailey and completely exonerated by the criminal court. Everyone was dismayed and shocked, and no one more so than an increduous Queen Victoria, declaring that the verdict left her "with indescribable stupefaction." "This acquittal of Dr. Bernard is a very painful business . . . [and] a disgrace to our country," Lord Malmesbury, Clarendon's successor at the foreign office, agreed. But as the veteran statesman Lord Clarendon pointed out, "Let it be remembered also that a large number of desperate Italians now in this country *have been deported here [in the first place] by the French Government* [including Pieri and Orsini]," where they had been obliged to seek refuge.[17]

The tension in France grew throughout February and March when Orsini wrote personally appealing to Louis Napoléon on behalf of his cause. "Sire, do not reject the words of a patriot. . . . Free Italy and the benediction of twenty-five million people will accompany your name to posterity!"[18] "Fancy the Emperor telling me yesterday that he felt the great sympathy for Orsini," an appalled Cowley recounted to Clarendon, "and the empress [Eugénie] is even begging him to pardon him!"[19]

A furious Morny went over to the Tuileries and read the riot act, telling his brother to get a grip on himself. The public demanded vengeance, justice, and if the emperor did not act decisively now, he would lose an enormous amount of respect and prestige in the country. A most anxious Ambassador Cowley finally intervened. "I told him . . . what I believe to be the truth, that any weakness in dealing with Orsini would have the very worst effect." Undeterred, assassins would continue to come. And then on Sunday March 14, 1858, Viel-Castel recorded: "Orsini and Pieri were executed [by guillotine] yesterday." It was over and no one was more remorseful than Louis Napoléon, or as Cowley put it, he was "regularly bitten by his miscreant."[20]

But there had also been another victim of the Orsini plot. Reacting to it and the criticism that England had harbored and aided the four

Italian assassins, Prime Minister Palmerston had taken immediate action by introducing the Conspiracy to Murder Act, with the full blessing of Queen Victoria. England must not be used as a base for terrorists. This bill presented to Parliament allowed for the prosecution of any individual conspiring in England to kill someone in another country. At the last minute Lord John Russell and others unexpectedly swung against Palmerston, however, defeating the bill by just a few votes.

Back in France Louis Napoléon demanded a new General Security Act to reinforce an 1848 law to permit the expulsion of dangerous foreigners. But for all their outrage with the English, it took all Morny's arm-twisting to get this new "aliens bill" through Parliament (even General MacMahon voted against it). Although narrowly passing, it was never applied, which of course did not prevent these same French politicians from weighing into the outrageous English for doing precisely the same thing.

That very day, February 19, 1858, Viscount Palmerston paid the price for failing to pass his Conspiracy to Murder Act and was obliged to resign, returning the seals of office to Queen Victoria. For the second time in his career he had been forced out of office as a direct result of actions related to Louis Napoléon and his Second Empire. The Orsini conspiracy added a whole new dimension to this latest tumultuous ongoing Italian opera.

Whether Napoléon III would acknowledge it or not, the Orsini plot served as a powerful catalyst in pushing France into another dramatic act of foreign intervention. The various different Italian states, duchies, and principalities wanted independence, some from papal political interference and most from the Austrian occupation of the northern half of the country. As for Mazzini, he would continue to send out his assassins against Napoleon III until all foreigners, including the French troops occupying Rome and protecting the pope, were out of the country. As Ambassador Cowley had remarked with some anxiety throughout the late spring and early summer of 1858, Louis Napoléon looked physically and emotionally shattered as a result of the pressure on him from the peace talks, the constant military demands, and the unrelenting monthly arrival of casualties from Algeria and the Kabyle.

But above all, ever since the recent plots against him uncovered by Police Prefect Piétri, it was the unresolved vexing problem of Italy that most preoccupied Louis Napoléon. It was not just the constant possibility of terrorist violence, physical threats against himself and Eugénie, which he simply shrugged off with almost a sense of philosophical inevitability, but the threat against his long-awaited heir and with him the very continuation of his empire, that was tormenting him and now focusing his resolution. No one could deny his undisguised lifelong love and singular attachment to Italy and its people. He too wanted to rid that country of the Austrians. It was the Orsini attempt, or rather the slaughter and dramatic fright it had created in the heart of the French capital, and curiously enough the guillotining of Orsini himself, that had hardened his resolve and commitment to act.

In the third week of July, Louis Napoléon dispatched his closest friend and confidant, Henri Conneau, officially in charge of the entire medical service of the imperial household, on a delicate, top-secret, spur-of-the-moment mission to Turin—unknown either to Persigny or his foreign minister—to meet with King Victor Emmanuel and Prime Minister Cavour. Louis Napoléon summoned Cavour to meet with him urgently, alone, in less than a week's time. The place designated was the isolated spa of Plombières south of Épinal in the heart of the Vosges Mountains, where they were to draft their tentative plans for a new Italy. Louis Napoléon had had long talks with Cavour during earlier visits to France, and the two men had got on surprisingly well together. They held the same views about the role of the church and the pope, and shared the same overriding desire to see Italy freed of the Austrian occupation once and for all. Curiously enough, however, there appeared to be no interest in or even discussion of the possibility of creating a unified kingdom of Italy. Their sole aim was to establish "a country" composed of different states and regions, all under the loose "presidency" of the pope. Moreover, this pope would have reduced territorial claims and powers.

• • •

Camillo Benso, Count of Cavour, was the son of an old aristocratic family of Turin, his father one of the leaders of the new "Risorgimento"—resurrection or revival of Italy.[21] Unusual in that Roman Catholic country, his mother came from a Protestant family of Geneva. The short, stout, bespectacled Cavour was privately tutored, spoiled, undisciplined, and a lazy student. Preferring hunting to books and without any strong guiding interests, at the age of fourteen he was placed as a cadet with the army and later served with the engineers of the Sardinian army. Frustrated with military life, at the age of twenty-one Cavour resigned his commission. Restless, still without aim or interests, at the age of twenty-four he began traveling, spending more than two months in Paris meeting pro-Bourbon political leaders and attending parliamentary sessions, then going on to England, a country that had long fascinated him. His basic intelligence and curiosity were finally focusing and maturing as his interests narrowed to national politics and administration. Cavour met with leaders of Westminster and "the City" and made extensive visits to hospitals, prisons, the clubs of Pall Mall, the House of Commons, and manufacturing centers as far as the Midlands. All the while he had an uninterrupted series of mistresses, but was destined never to marry. Returning to France, he studied at the Sorbonne for a while and met many of the famous literary giants of the time, including Alexandre Dumas, Charles Augustin Sainte-Beuve, Prosper Mérimée, Théophile Gautier, and politicians including Adolphe Thiers, Louis-Mathieu Molé, Auguste de Morny (at the Palais Bourbon), and Morny's father, General de Flahaut. Cavour also visited Belgium, various Germanic states, and Switzerland. His family having always been officially associated with the French ever since Napoléon I, Cavour remained strongly pro-French the rest of his life. Politically, he was drawn to the activists demanding Italian independence from Austria and he joined Mazzini's secret society, Young Italy, for a while, though later broke away from it because of its violence. He preferred negotiation and political process to assassination and bombs. After 1848, Cavour began an intensive political career associated with the young king of Sardinia, Victor Emmanuel II (1820–1878).[22]

Taking office in Turin as prime minister of Sardinia (joining mainland Piedmont and Savoy with Sardinia), an office he held from 1852 to 1859, he supported the Risorgimento, and the abolition of the privileges of the clergy. He openly confronted the expansive power and privilege of the Vatican, while arresting the archbishop of Turin. Like Louis Napoléon in France, Cavour desired to bring Piedmont out of the eighteenth century, encouraging the construction of its first railways (including the Mont Cenis railway tunnel) and the introduction of a modern steam-powered navy. He also successfully negotiated commercial treaties or customs unions with Belgium, Greece, the German states, and Austria. During an official visit to London in 1852, he met with Cobden, Disraeli, and Gladstone, as well as with Lords Clarendon, Lansdowne, and Palmerston, thereby extending his political contacts at the highest levels.

Appointed foreign minister as well in January 1855, he concluded new alliances with England and France, while of course representing Sardinia at the Paris peace conference on March 30, 1856, that ended the Crimean War. And such was the situation when in July 1858 he found himself suddenly summoned to France by Louis Napoléon. His king, Victor Emmanuel, ten years his junior, was a close family friend, but also largely a dolt. Towering over Cavour with his powerful physique, of which he was inordinately vain, and boasting a long, thick, upturned mustache of royal proportions, that king of Sardinia was more interested in the latest conquest to his bed than politics, and for the most part he rubber-stamped Cavour's political aims.

Ostensibly the French emperor went to the thermal spa of Plombières in the heart of the Vosges Mountains to escape the heat of the French capital. But unknown to anyone in Paris (except Henri Conneau), there on the twenty-first of July Louis Napoléon secretly met with a very determined prime minister Cavour. The result of this intense nearly five-hour conference was an agreement for war. In brief, Louis Napoléon would commit upward of 200,000 French troops in support of the much smaller Sardinian army to oust the Austrians from the whole of northern Italy, from Milan and Lombardy to Venice and the Adriatic Sea. In return, the French would be rewarded with the miniature mountain kingdom of Savoy, just below Geneva. There was also vague allusion to Nice as well, but nothing conclusive. With the Austrians out, they would agree to make the pope some sort of figurehead president, over a loosely formed Italian confederation. There was neither interest in nor mention of a unified Italy. On the other hand, Victor Emmanuel was to do everything in his power to prevent Mazzini from exporting his terrorists to France. This Plombières accord would be sealed by the marriage of Louis Napoléon's first cousin, Prince Jérôme, to Victor Emmanuel's fifteen-year-old daughter, Clotilde, immediately after the signing of a formal defense pact between France and Sardinia. No time frame was stipulated for the eventual signing of that military pact.

In any event, in this Plombières agreement, Louis Napoléon committed his country to another war, unless Austria could be persuaded to make a peaceful withdrawal from Italy. After all, this was the only reason Victor Emmanuel had sent troops to support the French in the Crimean War, for a quid pro quo in Italy. Moreover, the ex-Carbonaro Louis Napoléon was finally coming to grips with his lifelong obsession, shared earlier with Hortense, of one day seeing "a free Italy," and his brother's tragic death would be avenged at long last. Meanwhile, the final casualties from the Crimea continued to reach Toulon. As for the stream of dead and wounded arriving at that port from the shores of Algeria, where their own war of colonial conquest was still raging, such news would be suppressed altogether in the French press. France was no democracy, and Louis Napoléon, despite his genial smile and warmhearted sentiments, remained the most powerful autocratic ruler of any European country, apart from the Russian tsar. As for the endless war in Algeria begun back in 1830, it was no more popular than that in the Crimea had been.

Despite his repeated peaceful protests in public that, unlike Uncle Napoleon, he had no interest in conquest or war, Louis Napoléon was secretly committing the uninformed French people to just that, another war, enormous new drains on the French treasury, the inevitable new war taxes, and of course more French corpses on yet another foreign battlefield. Moreover, this time he promised Cavour personally to lead a French army of 200,000 men into battle.[23]

27

RETURN OF A CARBONARO: ITALY, 1859

"Our cause is good, our army is excellent . . . and he
[Louis Napoléon] is as pleased about it as I am."[1]
—EMPRESS EUGÉNIE ON THE EVE OF THE WAR OF
ITALIAN INDEPENDENCE, MAY 1859

"I can remember no period of equal confusion and danger."[2]
—PRINCE ALBERT, 1859

Italy had not been united since the fall of the Roman Empire until its conquest and foreign occupation by Napoléon Bonaparte and the French. With the collapse of the First Empire, 1814–1815, and the blessing of the Congress of Vienna, the Habsburgs and their Austrian army had been given free reign in the conquest and occupation of northern Italy, from Milan in Lombardy to Venice and the Adriatic . . . and ever since "the Italians" had been demanding independence. As for Louis Napoléon Bonaparte, apart from regaining his place in France, he had dreamed of little else except personally liberating the unhappy Italian peninsula from the Austrian yoke. "The dearest dream of my life, the strongest desire of my heart," he declared, "is the independence of Italy."[3] An enormous political volcano long overdue to erupt, it was now merely a question of when.[4] And the French emperor was paying the price for the amount of pressure building up all around him. Ambassador Lord Cowley reported to London finding him a chain-smoker, "cast down . . . very much out of humour," physically run-down, and unusually nervous.[5] The Italian situation had to be resolved once and for all.

I can remember no period of equal confusion and danger [in the world]," a much troubled Prince Albert confessed in 1858. Modern technology, in his case, "the new electric telegraph," he pointed out, had brought news of disasters and threats of disaster "from all quarters of the globe"—China, the Middle East, Africa, and Europe. "Suspicion, hatred, pride, cunning, intrigue, covetousness, dissimulation, dictates and despatches" have been raining down upon us, he complained to Baron Stockmar, turning the world topsy-turvy, "and in this state of things we cast about to find a basis on which peace may be secured."[6] This world of suspicion, intrigue, and dissimulation was affecting and altering his own outlook, turning him, almost abruptly, against this same very new friend, Louis Napoléon (and his France), who had so delighted him back in 1855. These negative views he now shared with his Coburg cousins, including Uncle Leopold, the king of Belgium, and the Prussian royal house itself, through his new son-in-law, prince and heir to the throne, Crown Prince Friedrich.

As for Queen Victoria, she soon found herself uncomfortably in the middle, unexpectedly having to make excuses for this emerging anti-French attitude, which she personally did not share and resisted as best she could. And Louis Napoléon, himself no stranger to paranoia and suspicion, soon felt this unanticipated swelling "German animosity" as he became more actively involved in the fate of Italy. "Two Germanies [separated and unallied] I could not mind," he confided to the fifty-seven-year-old Hungarian exile Lajos Kossuth, "but one [big] Germany," for example, the various combined German states, perhaps allied with Austria—"that I find quite unacceptable."[7]

F or Louis Napoléon, the countdown to conflict and war in Italy moved with the inexorable force of historical predestination, as his European neighbors were beginning to realize. Aware of this growing anxiety, Louis Napoléon's aim was not necessarily to enroll new allies or to disturb the European peace, but rather to avoid interference in future actions by ensuring the neutrality of neighbors, beginning with England.

In a fence-mending gesture, Queen Victoria and Prince Albert sailed to Cherbourg on August 5, 1858, nominally to celebrate the opening of the new facilities of this port (left uncompleted by Napoléon I), where Louis Napoléon naïvely insisted on unveiling the first of his new steam-powered, armor-plated naval vessels. If on this occasion Victoria displayed an anxious smile, an arrogant Albert, in the best Coburg manner, did little to conceal his new distrust of the French emperor. The show of new military might at this moment of "diplomatic reconciliation" was not fortuitous. Later in December, in her annual New Year's speech for 1859, the English queen spoke of her hope for the continuation of the two governments "cherishing their cordial understanding" and ensuring European "happiness and prosperity." Louis Napoléon in turn assured her that his personal efforts would always be directed "in maintaining a sincere alliance" between France and England. Moreover, the presence of Victoria and Albert at Cherbourg, he closed, "had put an end to those absurd rumors about our strong political differences." Despite the very real sincerity on both sides, all the old cordiality, warmth, trust, and confidence of 1855 had been replaced with stiff, cautious phraseology, tinged with anxiety.[8]

"I regret that relations between our two governments are not more satisfactory," Napoléon III told Austrian ambassador Hübner at his annual New Year's Day reception January 1, 1859, for the diplomatic corps at the Tuileries, while from his throne in Turin, King Victor Emmanuel lamented that he could hardly "ignore the cry of pain" of the peoples of Italy.[9] Reflecting this unease, shares at the Paris Bourse plunged, notably those concerned with new Rothschild and Pereire railway construction projects in Italy and the Austro-Hungarian Empire. Events went ahead of course, and on January 29, 1859, a secret Franco-Sardinian military pact was duly signed, fulfilling the earlier Plombières accord. Four days later Prince Jérôme and Princess Clotilde of Sardinia were married.

And then for good measure, on February 4, 1859, the none-too-subtle

Louis Napoléon sounded the clarion, adding to the momentum toward war by publishing M. de La Guéronnière's booklet entitled *Emperor Napoléon III and Italy,* further fanning alarm across Europe. "I have always had the intention of creating a free, independent Italian nation," Louis Napoléon had declared back in 1854, which was now repeated. This publication also declared the necessity of seeing the Vatican reduce and reform its secular Papal States as part of a new, larger, federated Italian state. The Austrians too were in need of reforming the medieval administration of their empire, this tract suggested.

While there was no mention of the creation of a large, completely unified Italy, it did call for a loose Italian confederation under the presidency of the pope. And this was the form Louis Napoléon hoped it would take. Regardless of the ultimate political form adopted, it was clear that unless the Austrians renounced their claims to Italy and withdrew permanently, war seemed inevitable.[10] Given the present political tension, Louis Napoléon's forthcoming annual throne speech on the seventh of February announcing the opening of Parliament was now awaited with great anxiety by everyone, since he was expected to declare himself at long last.

The policy of his Second Empire, Louis Napoléon that day affirmed, was "to reassure European stability while returning France to her proper role as a leader in the affairs of the world." Nor did he dodge the nagging question of the hour. "For some time now the abnormal state in which Italy finds herself—and where order has been maintained only with the assistance of foreign troops, has been troubling the diplomatic world." In attempting to resolve these conflicting issues, "I regret to say that we have found ourselves on a collision course with the Government of Vienna." Whether talking about the consequences of the Crimean conflict and the Danubian provinces, or Italy, France was rightly concerned and involved, for "the interests of France are to be found wherever the cause of justice and civilization are to be upheld. . . . Therefore, it is hardly startling that France should draw closer to Piedmont [Sardinia], this country that stood by us as faithful allies earlier in the Crimea," a position strengthened by the recent marriage of "our beloved cousin, Prince Jérôme, with the daughter of the King Victor Emmanuel."

Under the circumstances, then, he felt that "the Italian situation" had to be resolved. "But my Government will neither be pushed to act or be intimidated to withdraw [from this dispute. Nevertheless] "peace, I hope, will not be disturbed,"[11] and he suggested a solution: the convening of an international congress in Paris to resolve the Italian problem. Austria immediately rejected the idea.[12] The lines were drawn.

In mid-April 1859, Victor Emmanuel started mobilizing the Sardinian army. On the twenty-third of April, Vienna issued an ultimatum, ordering Turin to disarm and disband the Sardinian army. Cavour returned a defiant public refusal. On the twenty-ninth of April, an Austrian army ultimately totaling 250,000 men under Field Marshal Stadion emerged from the Tyrol and crossed the small Ticino River below Lake Maggiore, "entering Sardinian territory." The next day the French Parliament easily voted the war credits Louis Napoléon would need for the forthcoming campaign. On the third of May, Louis Napoléon issued a proclamation denouncing Austria. "May the responsibility [for this aggression] rest upon those who were the first to arm," he declared a few days later as French troops under Generals Canrobert and Baraguey d'Hilliers entrained for Italy. But instead of the 200,000 French troops promised at Plombières, initially only 104,000 were ready at the start of the campaign, nor was logistical support any better prepared. Nothing had been learned since the disastrously managed "victory" in the Crimea, nor from the decades of fighting in Algeria. Fortunately, Sardinia, a kingdom of only five million, was able to field another 60,000. "Our cause is good," the patriotic Empress Eugénie boasted in Paris, "our army is excellent, and he [Louis Napoléon] . . . he is as happy as I am about it."[13]

The object of this war . . . is to restore Italy to the Italians," which in turn will assure France of having on her frontiers "a friendly people, owing their independence to us," Louis Napoléon proclaimed. And therefore "I am about to place myself at the head of our army. . . . Courage, then and Forward! . . . Ours is a holy cause."[14] Commander in chief Louis Napoléon and the advance divisions of his army duly debarked at Genoa on May 12, 1859, although Émile Fleury, a court insider, for one, openly voiced his reservations about the emperor's ability to command. Napoléon III was in overall strategic command of five corps, led by Sebastopol veterans Achille Baraguey d'Hilliers, Patrice de MacMahon, François Certain Canrobert, Adolphe Niel, and in theory, Prince Jérôme, "Sans-Plomb," while Auguste Regnault de Saint-Jean d'Angély directed the Imperial Guard. The Austrian army, initially under the command of Field Marshal Stadion, was directed in the field by Field Marshal Ferenc Gyulay, whose artillery outgunned the combined Franco-Sardinian force by nearly three to one.

With the names of Uncle Napoléon's celebrated victories in Italy inspiring him—Arcola, Lodi, Marengo, and Rivoli—Louis Napoléon was determined to sweep the Austrians back across the frontier. The first battle against Gyulay at Montebello, on the twentieth of May, proved sluggish and indecisive, however. On the fourth of June, the French army under General MacMahon next clashed with the Austrians at the bridge before Magenta, which was only won by the French thanks to the arrival of last-minute reinforcements. After burying General Espinasse on the field of battle, Louis Napoléon rewarded MacMahon with the marshal's baton and the title of Duke of Magenta, an act the emperor would later live to regret.

Lombardy was won, and on the eighth of June Louis Napoléon and the victorious French army made their triumphant entry into Milan. "I have been welcomed as their *liberator!*"[15] he wrote excitedly to Eugénie. Meanwhile, Baraguey d'Hilliers was successfully pushing back the Austrians over the Chiese. On the twenty-fourth of June, General Adolphe Niel launched an early-morning attack at Solferino, as Louis Napoléon awaited the results nearby at Castiglione delle Stiviere. For once the fighting was really fierce on both sides, the battle only decided in favor of the French several hours later as the bloodied Austrians withdrew to the northeast across the Mincio. Inspired by the French, the people of Tuscany, Modena, Parma, and the Papal States joined in the rebellion against the startled "elite" Austrian army. But once again cholera and dysentery took a heavy toll on both sides.

Even as Louis Napoléon was pressing on to Venice, however, word reached him from Berlin of the mobilization of an army of 200,000 Prussians that could reach France in fifteen days' time. With the threat of their advance on the Rhine, a cautious Louis Napoléon ordered an abrupt halt to his pursuit, over the objections of the Sardinian commander. With only five French divisions, perhaps fewer than 50,000 men, available around Strasbourg, King Friedrich Wilhelm IV could easily invade and occupy French Alsace. Another nagging anxiety was Prince Jérôme's personal proposal to save the world by raising a new, separate army of 300,000 troops and attacking the Prussians.[16] If the Prussians then joined forces with Emperor Franz Josef's Austrian armies . . .

Regardless of the rumors and scaremongering, there was just enough reality behind the Prussian threat to cause Louis Napoléon to stop his advance. He had to return to Paris as quickly as possible. The fear of revolution spread by Mazzini's agents, combined with growing international distrust, was beginning to unsettle the whole of Europe. Having swept most of northern Italy free of the occupation force, a wary Louis Napoléon called for a premature truce, which a much embarrassed Austrian monarch readily accepted, and on the tenth of July the two sovereign heads of state met just south of Verona at Villafranca.

One hour later, hostilities were suspended by an armistice valid until mid-August, and general terms of a peace treaty were agreed upon. Refusing to negotiate directly with Sardinia, Austria renounced its occupation of Lombardy, whose territories and cities would be handed over to Louis Napoléon, who would in turn then hand them over to Victor Emmanuel. Franz Josef, now faced with unexpected defeat in Italy and the very real threat of revolution in Hungary—in the very heart of his empire—rapidly agreed to the creation of a new Italian Confederation under the presidency of the pope. The fortresses of Mantua and Legnano along with Venice were, however, to remain in Austrian hands.

Angered and humiliated by Austria's refusal to negotiate face-to-face with him, Victor Emmanuel felt let down by Louis Napoléon, who had reluctantly acquiesced to this procedure, including Vienna's retention of Venice. Equally outraged by what he saw as a French betrayal, Cavour resigned from office in a huff. Despite rumors to the contrary, there was still no discussion or mention of a unified Italy. Moreover, as Louis Napoléon had failed to capture Venice as promised earlier, Victor Emmanuel provisionally renounced the promised rewards of Savoy and Nice.

Rushing back to St. Cloud on the nineteenth of July, a victorious Napoléon III addressed the nation: "To help achieve Italian independence I went to war in defiance of hostile European public opinion, but later when finding my own country, France herself, imperiled [by the threat of a Prussian invasion], I concluded [an early] peace with the Austrians." "My one persistent great and disinterested objective," he told Austrian ambassador Hübner, "has always been to . . . see Italy freed and returned to her own people," and that he had largely achieved.[17] His boyhood dream had been fulfilled, and on the fourteenth of August, Louis Napoléon, the conquering hero, once again reviewed a victorious French army in the Place Vendôme.

In September of 1859, following full plebiscites by their citizens, the Duchies of Modena and Parma, along with the Grand Duchy of Tuscany and most of the Papal States were annexed by the Kingdom of Sardinia. Garibaldi's subsequent successful expeditions to Sicily and Naples then added these territories as well to the Italian crown.[18] After some modifications, the final peace treaty was duly signed at Zurich on November 10, 1859, thereby bringing to a conclusion Italy's final war of independence.

Meanwhile, following further plebiscites on March 24, 1860, Piedmont duly ceded Savoy to France, followed by Nice on the fifteenth of April, against English protests and a positively bitter denunciation by Nice's most famous native son, Giuseppe Garibaldi. By September 29, 1860, the Marches of northern Italy and Umbria had also joined Victor Emmanuel's enlarged state. The fighting was not over, however, and when an uprising against Francis II, king of the Two Sicilies, forced him to flee his capital, Palermo, in April 1860, Cavour dispatched General Garibaldi and his "red shirts" to seize that city. With his arrival at Palermo that May, peace was restored, and by September that popular general had captured Naples as well. And on March 17, 1861, Parliament officially proclaimed the creation of Victor Emmanuel's new Kingdom of Italy, of which Rome was to become the capital ten years later.[19]

With the ceding of Venice by Vienna in October 1866, the unification of Italy was more or less complete. The hope for quick victory and establishment of an independent Italy had proven optimistic, however, and the complications due to an unprepared French army, and foreign pressure to end the war in 1859 prematurely before Venetia, too, could be secured for the new Italian state, had left everyone dissatisfied.

Despite their remarkable success, Victor Emmanuel remained upset with Louis Napoléon over the delay in obtaining Venice from the Austrians. No matter what he did, or how fine his motives, no one seemed to appreciate his efforts, other than the French with the addition of Nice and Savoy and nearly 700,000 new citizens.

The resultant political structure of the new Italy did surprise Louis Napoléon, of course, who had anticipated a group of independent states continuing to be ruled by their traditional dukes and princes, if under constitutional reforms. Instead he found a centrally administered nation of twenty-two million, ruled—not by the pope, but by the vain, pleasure-loving King Victor Emmanuel. At least the Austrians were out of most of Italy, however, and hereafter Italians would be ruled by Italians. And his late brother, whom he had buried in Fiorli under Austrian fire decades earlier, would be proud and at peace.

A major chapter of Louis Napoléon's life was closed at last, and it was a renewed beginning for the modern state of Italy, an Italy that could not have been created without his personal goodwill, devotion, and steady determination, supported by the military might of the French people. France had received Nice and Savoy in return, baubles required for national honor. Despite the later accusations of his political enemies and some historians, in reality Louis Napoléon would have done it all over again without any reward, simply for the deeply felt personal joy of seeing the fulfillment of this long-sought boyhood dream. It was in a sense his finest hour. But the decline in his health observed earlier by Lord Cowley was to prove more than a passing indisposition. There was, it seemed, always a price to pay for success and happiness.

28

FOUR SEASONS

"She did indeed look the part [of an empress] and really was a
most accomplished woman of the world."[1]
—PRINCESS PAULINE VON METTERNICH ON EMPRESS EUGÉNIE

"He had that wonderful simplicity about him, an absolute want of pose,
that distinguishes great gentlemen from all the others."[2]
—PAULINE VON METTERNICH ON NAPOLÉON III

His Majesty, the Emperor!' the usher announced from the doorway of the Galérie de Diane as Napoléon III entered the Throne Room followed by Eugénie who curtsied three times," Princess Pauline de Metternich, wife of the Austrian ambassador, noted in her memoirs. After greeting the ambassadors accredited to the Tuileries and their ladies, at nine-thirty "the Emperor offered his arm to the Empress, and, passing through several drawing-rooms, and followed by the entire diplomatic Corps, . . . made their way to the Salle des Maréchaux," for the evening's ball.[3]

A solemn march accompanied by the orchestra in an upper gallery announced their appearance as the imperial couple ascended the dais "from which the Empress again curtsied three times to her assembled guests. These balls then always opened with a waltz." The ladies wearing flowing, hoop-skirted, décolleté gowns and jewels were attended by "the men [who] were either in full [military or diplomatic] uniform or in court dress, including cashmere knee-breeches, silk stockings and pumps."[4] Empress Eugénie, "a miracle of grace and dignity impossible to surpass" often wore white satin and "in her hair [Queen Marie-Antoinette's] celebrated [140.5 carat] Regent Diamond surmounted by a tift of white feathers shimmering with smaller diamonds, while round her neck she wore three superb rows of pearls."[5] Louis Napoléon addressed Eugénie in the informal you, *tu,* while she invariably used the formal you, *vous.* He pronounced her name "Ugenie," and she for her part followed the ritual of always rising whenever he entered a room, even when *en famille* informally.

After eleven o'clock the court went in to a supper, which was served at the buffet in the Galérie de Diane. Their majesties would then retire, while the younger couples danced until two or three o'clock. Such was a typical ball at the Tuileries, which the young journalist-novelist Émile Zola described in his twenty-volume *Social History of the Second Empire* as a den of iniquity and a vortex of corruption and decadence.[6]

For Princess von Metternich, still in her twenties and an eyewitness and participant, unlike Zola, who never met Louis Napoléon and Eugénie, or even entered the Tuileries, the reality was slightly different. The imperial couple, while discouraging serious gambling and overzealous drinking, were invariably gracious and thoughtful. Nevertheless, a strict, remorseless protocol ruled every aspect of their lives, and at these official balls the wives of ambassadors were required to remain seated throughout, denied all dancing, although admittedly "it was an extremely fine sight." But Princess Pauline added, "for sheer unmitigated boredom they surpassed—in my opinion—anything that can be possibly imagined."[7] And this was the routine she was obliged to adhere to over the next decade. Much more to the princess's liking were Eugénie's "Mondays," unofficial balls given in the Blue Saloon, when the empress's private apartments were thrown open to the guests, and "everyone could dance to one's heart's content" in less formal circumstances.

Like all European courts, that of the Second Empire had its well-regulated "seasons," including periodic changes of residence and activity. From mid-December through the month of May, the Tuileries

Palace was the heart and nerve center of the empire. Here Louis Napoléon received petitions, met with his ministers, or conferred with
his Privy Council, received diplomats and distinguished visitors, met
several times a week with Baron Haussmann on the current stage of
construction, oversaw the very extensive programs he was preparing
for his model farms, cattle and horse breeding stations, and major agricultural reforms, and held meetings with the war minister of the day
to prepare for the annual army maneuvers at Châlons, much needed
army reforms, and to go over the latest daunting casualty reports coming from Algeria. He also saw Auguste de Morny frequently to discuss
the latest bills to be presented before the legislative body, while holding
frequent work sessions with Minister Fould, who had the disagreeable
task of reminding Louis Napoléon of excessive state expenditures and
the necessity of practical budgetary constraints.

Relief and distraction were to be provided at the end of the work-
day, however, when Louis Napoléon received one of his numerous
mistresses—his wife having forbidden all marital relations for many
years—or attended receptions, balls, and frequently visited "the opera,"
music hall attractions, in the company of brother Morny, Mouchy, and
Haussmann. The daily demands on the emperor were relentless, and by
the early 1860s they were beginning to take their toll. If he never did
drink to excess, his chain-smoking was having an effect on his lungs. In
any event, he was too conscientious to escape this unrelenting self-
imposed schedule demanding his attention and decisions. Without the
authority of the Second Empire and without himself at the helm, his
many plans for transforming the country into a modern France would
never have been fulfilled. At particularly dark moments, he confided in
the English ambassador, Lord Cowley, about abdicating, an idea that
caused considerable anxiety for Lord Clarendon and Downing Street,
who feared a return to chaos and republican government. "We are wavering back and forth between anarchy and absolute power," an anxious
Prosper Mérimée observed. Once compromise with "the republicans"
begins, "there is no going back."[8] And although still holding wide,
sweeping powers as emperor, he was already fighting "the opposition,"
at his own court and in political circles.

• • •

E very year in the middle of May, the entire court transferred to the
Palace of St. Cloud, a forty-minute drive by phaeton from the Tuileries via the Bois de Boulogne. There Louis Napoléon and Eugénie
stayed at the nearby secluded villa of Villeneuve-L'Étang, while the
official receptions and dinners were held in the palace itself. In mid-
June the court would then transfer again, this time to the southeast of
Paris, to the elegant palace of Fontainebleau, with its vast forest, a palace that Pauline von Metternich found to be "far more luxurious than
Compiègne."[9] Fontainebleau was a favorite of François I, Louis XV,
and Napoléon I before him; Louis Napoléon would now invite large
numbers of guests in the more relaxed midsummer warmth to enjoy
the endless round of picnics, shooting parties, boating, equestrian and
charabanc excursions, dancing, and love-making.

In July and August Louis Napoléon and Eugénie would abandon the
court and retreat to the fashionable Vosges Mountain spa of Plombières
once again to take the waters for his crippling rheumatism, contracted
as a prisoner at Ham, and especially to rest and recuperate after escaping the unrelenting pressure and demands in governing the country.
Then, in the early 1860s, he replaced it with a new, relatively unknown
spa on the River Allier at Vichy, which quickly filled up with courtiers
and the wealthy, accompanied by its first luxurious hotels.

September then found the imperial family, including the young prince
imperial, at the Atlantic coastal fishing village of Biarritz, just twenty-
two miles north of the Spanish frontier. Louis Napoléon built the
"Villa Eugénie," far from Paris and the court. The solitude of the
broad Basque village beach overlooking the Bay of Biscay was soon
encroached upon, however, by the inevitable casino, hotels, and villas
of the wealthy. The guests invited to the Villa Eugénie, unlike all other
imperial residences, official or unofficial, were limited to close immediate
friends and family like Prosper Mérimée and the Delesserts, Eugénie's
sister, Paca, the Duchess of Alba, and her children and family. But occasional "tourists" did drop in on them, including one Otto von Bismarck and his wife. This was Eugénie's favorite residence, where she was

seen daily strolling across the sand with her famous yellow parasol, her young son at her side.

The court season would then resume at the Tuileries in October and continue until about the eighth of November, when Louis Napoléon and Eugénie moved north to the enormous fourteenth- to fifteenth-century palace of Compiègne, entirely rebuilt in the eighteenth century by Louis XV, where they would remain for the next month.

Compiègne was a world unto itself unlike any other, and the most highly selective one so far as the great names of the empire were concerned. "About a hundred carefully selected guests were invited [for the first week]," according to Princess Metternich, "and it can be readily imagined how eagerly and jealously the invitations were sought after."[10] Officially, Louis Napoléon's cousin, the first chamberlain, Count Felix Baciocchi, was responsible for drawing up the four "series" selected, that is, for the four one-week slots. In the final analysis, of course, it was Eugénie who decided, a task she executed with painstaking consideration, finding the right balance of names and positions in society—politicians, diplomats, foreign visitors, artists, writers, scientists, all of whom were known to get on well with everyone else (to avoid spats, female rivalry, personal vendettas, and embarrassing out-of-date mistresses). One of the irritating problems was "the Duke of Persigny's pretentious wife," and others were eliminated from the list because of one scandal or another. Those surviving this scrutiny received a large gold engraved invitation:

> By order of their Imperial Majesties, XX—is, or are, invited to spend a week at the Palace of Compiègne from the ___ of November to the ____ of November. The visitors and their servants will travel by a special train, which will also bring their luggage. It will leave the Gare du Nord at three o'clock.[11]

Pauline von Metternich, as the wife of the second most important ambassador accredited to the court after the English delegation, was one of the most frequent to receive the royal summons, and she relates her experiences from the day of their arrival. "At Compiègne we were met by brakes to which some of the most beautiful horses in the Imperial stables were harnessed. Starting at a full gallop, we reached the Palace where we found Count Felix Baciocchi standing at the head of the steps to receive us." The number of baggage and portmanteaux brought for the sixty members of the initial party was phenomenal, even by aristocratic standards of the day. "One day we counted as many as 900! . . . I was the proud possessor of eighteen of these cases," just for her gowns, without counting another dozen boxes for her hats. The maids and valets "shouting at the top of their lungs" swarmed over "a veritable mountain of trunks" heaped unceremoniously before the main entrance of the château in order to sort out theirs. It turned into a veritable free-for-all, the maids even "fisticuffing and swearing at one another!"[12]

The guests gathered in a drawing room that evening included the Duchess of Alba (Paca), the second Countess de Walewska, the Countess de Pourtalès, the Countess de la Bédoyère, the Baroness de la Poëze, the Marquise de Gallifet, Baroness Alphonse de Rothschild, the Duchess of Sutherland, and the Duchess of Manchester, among others . . . "all the youth and beauty of Paris." Nor were the men forgotten, including novelist and playwright Alexandre Dumas, *fils*; prolific novelist and playwright Octave Feuillet; popular novelist, playwright, and journalist Edmond About; the shy writer Gustave Flaubert; the composer of operatic and sacred works Charles Gounod; chemist Louis Pasteur; the physicist Jouvert de Lamballe; artists Ingres and Jérôme; barristers Lachaud and Chaix d'Estange; the Duke and Duchess de Morny,[13] ministers, diplomats, local landowners, the Marquis and Marquise de l'Aigle, the commanding general of the local garrison, and the prefect of the region. And there was almost always a small, frequently last-minute British contingent including the Lansdownes, the Malmesburys, the Clarendons, and "some Scots in kilts," the Duke of Athol and Lord Danmore.

At Compiègne there were usually ninety to one hundred guests for dinner, Princess Mathilde or the wife of the senior ambassador always seated at Louis Napoléon's right. Princess de Metternich was astonished to find only silver-plated, not sterling silver, cutlery. Having found no cutlery when he moved into this palace, Louis Napoléon refused to pay five million francs for this basic item. "At least we will not have to worry about burglars," he laughed.[14]

After dinner—which never lasted more than sixty minutes—at eight-thirty the guests walked two by two to the drawing room, when Louis Napoléon would withdraw alone to his study to smoke a cigarette, and the other gentlemen went to the smoking room. On their rejoining Eugénie and the ladies, a chamberlain arrived and stood by the side of a small upright mechanical player piano and began to crank the handle. "We were obliged to dance to this hideous and monotonous music," Princess Pauline complained, as he "ground out one frightful little tune after another." Most of the guests, however, "collapsed on the hard little benches set round the room yawning." These soirées, which usually continued until about half past eleven, "were the least agreeable of all our experiences at Compiègne," the princess confessed. "They bored us to death."[15]

Most evenings were more entertaining, however, when the emperor would suggest the latest Strauss waltz, which he had introduced in Paris, or *La Boulangère*, or the *Sir Roger de Coverley*. They would often just sit chatting, and the empress "went on talking with extraordinary verve and animation, with a complete absence of pose of any sort." Louis Napoléon was himself an accomplished raconteur. He told "some good stories and thoroughly enjoyed those told by others as well," Princess Pauline remembered. Group activities were the key attractions, however, including charades, *tableaux vivants,* or short plays composed then and there. "How many delightful little plays were given in the drawing-room." A permanent stage had been built at one end and "my husband Richard [von Metternich] conducted the chamber orchestra." "We once acted out Caesar's *Commentaries.* On another occasion, at the insistence of Louis Napoléon, Auguste de Morny presented his little play, *The Bonnet Inheritance* (later put to music by Offenbach). The Marquis de Massa prepared a revue in which Pauline von Metternich played the part of a Zouave Cantinière, Madame Portalès looking "radiantly beautiful as 'France' and Madame de Galliffet as 'England.'" The prince imperial dressed as a Grenadier Guardsman—"he was a dear little boy."

Louis Napoléon always withdrew from the drawing room early, but "we were obliged to remain till it pleased her Majesty to retire. A tea-table was brought in for her, but no one touched either the tea or the cakes. The Empress alone had a cup of tea to which were added some drops of orange-flower water." And then Eugénie rose and left, followed by her guests.[16]

Prosper Mérimée relates several stories about unscheduled events taking place at Compiègne, including one about his host. One evening Louis Napoléon was spotted prowling along the corridors of a guest wing, when suddenly Edouard Delessert dashed out of a room before him "dressed like a wild woman" ["*habillé en femme sauvage*"]. Startled and bewildered by this extraordinary vision, the timorous host quickly retreated to his own quarters. On another occasion Prince Jérôme— Plon-Plon—was briefly visiting Compiègne, when one evening after charades, they all sat down to champagne cocktails, the emperor inviting his cousin to propose the empress's health, next to whom he was seated. "He [Jérôme] frowned." "I am a little afraid of your speeches," Eugénie quickly warned, "however eloquent they may be." "I am no good at public speeches," Plon-Plon mumbled. "And if Your Majesties permit, I will dispense with one now." Absolutely outraged by this un-couth behavior, his cousin, the young Prince Murat jumped to his feet, and, trembling, made the toast. "Their Majesties betrayed no emotion," Mérimée informed Countess de Montijo, but Prince Jérôme was never again invited to Compiègne.[17] One day Mérimée encountered the pre-cocious eleven-year-old imperial prince Louis lecturing his mother on her speech. "Certainly you speak French well, Maman, but you are still a foreigner and fail to understand the subtleties of our language."[18]

On other evenings complete professional plays would be performed in the little palace theater by troops of actors brought up by special train from Paris, including from the Comédie Française, the Vaudeville, or the Gymnase. The stage was surrounded by the imperial box, with smaller ones on either side. Everyone wore full dress. After the curtain dropped, the emperor and empress would bow to the audience, who re-turned their obeisances. After the performance the artists were always invited to the imperial box, where they were congratulated by their majesties. But when it came to music, Louis Napoléon, Eugénie, and the royal court were less than satisfying as far as the good Viennese Pauline von Metternich was concerned. Or as she subtly put it, "There never existed a set of people of less musical ability than those attached to the Court of Napoléon."[19] She was equally disappointed later when she persuaded Richard Wagner to come to France to present his *Tannhäuser,* only to see him all but booed off the stage.

The day's activities began "at the stroke of twelve as we all assembled in the salon for luncheon. Our dress was perfectly simple, little woolen costumes." Although the great House of Worth prepared her formal dresses, here Eugénie wore "a woollen skirt—generally black, a red cotton shirt, and a leather belt round her waist." They settled at the table, where a great many dishes were served, "and in my opinion it was superior to dinner." At one o'clock they returned to the drawing room to make their plans for the rest of the day.

At two o'clock a veritable caravan of elegant carriages arrived "when we usually went for a drive in the beautiful forest of Compiègne," or the emperor took his guests to the castle of Pierrefonds, which Violet-le-Duc was restoring. But of all the events planned during this week in midwinter, the most elaborate and dramatic was a big hunt. These shooting and stag-hunting parties were usually comprised of ten to twelve guns, and the amount of game daily bagged could come to hundreds, including a great number of hare.

"The Emperor was a superb shot. He used to walk slowly alongside Eugénie's carriage, swaying slightly as was his wont . . . he seldom missed a shot . . . Soldiers were brought in to act as beaters. . . . The men wore Imperial colors, green coats, braided gold, red facings, white leather breeches, top boots and three-cornered hats." While the ladies wore "green cloth riding-habits; the bodices braided in gold with red facings, and like the men also wore three-cornered hats. The effect was charming. . . . Everyone was well mounted, the pack [of bloodhounds] was very fit, the huntsmen and whips chosen from among the best in France." On this day the emperor shot a fine seven-year-old stag with a large set of antlers, "and he presented a foot to one of the ladies present. I still possess the one he presented to me." Later on, the emperor gave each of the beaters a cigar. After the carcass had been carved and antlers removed, and with the bugles blowing, the first whip brought out the stag's head to which the hide was still attached, and the hounds were free to eat it. "They devoured all that remained in less time than it takes to write . . . It was a very pretty sight!" the princess acknowledged.[20]

But enough was enough for the wife of the Austrian ambassador after they were invited to extend their stay for another week . . . "The fact is it was most dreadfully exhausting to go through an entire fortnight of incessant entertainments. On our return to Paris I felt such a wreck that I did not stir from the embassy for a good week."[21]

If Compiègne was renowned for its splendid hunts, it was the Second Empire's fabulous masked balls in Paris that revived Princess Pauline and Tout Paris. Not only did they attract the most beautiful women of the day, including Comtesse de Mercy-Argenteau, Mesdames de Pourtalès, de Galliffet, Le Hon, Walewska, and the Marquise de Las Marsemes, but the originality and sheer luxury of their costumes defied imagination. The new wealth of the empire created vast new personal fortunes, and the great names of the empire vied with one another with their balls, including those offered by Princess Mathilde, Mesdames de Fleury, Rouher, Delessert, and the Baroness de Rothschild.

For Pauline von Metternich, however, "the most gorgeous fancy balls of all were those given at the Quai d'Orsay by Count Walewski, at the Admiralty in the Place de la Concorde by the Marquis de Chasseloup-Laubat, and at the Présidence du Corps Legislatif [the Hôtel de Lassay] by the Duke de Morny."[22] One of the high moments of each ball was the introduction of the quadrille, with four women to a group, and its unique motif. For the princess the most dazzling was entitled "The Four Elements of the Universe": "Earth," with four society ladies "wearing nothing but emeralds and diamonds"; "Fire," with the beauties of the day "wearing only rubies and diamonds"; "Water," represented by gowns strewn with pearls and diamonds; and "Air," with the titled ladies wearing sheaths of diamonds and turquoise, "borrowed from the Princess Lise Troubetskoi."[23]

A quadrille given at an Admiralty Ball selected a more artistic approach based on the theme of "The Four Quarters of the Globe," with Madame Bartholony making her grand entrance as an "African Queen," wheeled in in a golden chariot covered with flowers. Madame de Chasseloup-Laubat, "an excessively pretty woman," outdid even her as "she was carried into the ballroom by slaves in a palanquin adorned with enormous multi-coloured peacock feathers." But for sheer beauty "the sensation of the evening was undoubtedly the entrance of the lovely Madame Ernest Feydeau, wife of the celebrated novelist." She appeared wearing a large white hat with plumes in a white satin, gold-embroidered tunic and cape "based on one in a portrait of Louis XIV as a boy, complete with a short pleated skirt that fell to her knees," in an age when it was scandalous for ladies even to show their ankles. "I have never seen any human being more fascinating and altogether delicious," a famously plain Princess von Metternich sighed. This ball was held at a time when the reforms in Algeria were still meeting imperial hopes, and thus it seemed only fitting that "Louis Napoléon appeared as a Bedouin, wearing a flowing white burnous and white woolen turban . . . with a bejeweled dagger in his belt."[24]

29

INQUISITION AT BADEN: 1860

"Nothing . . . could be further from his [Louis Napoléon's]
thoughts, than to seize any territory from Germany."[1]
—PRINCE REGENT WILHELM VON HOHENZOLLERN,

BADEN, JUNE 1860

Louis Napoléon had been simply flummoxed by the outburst of universal, even hysterical, anti-French denunciations following the War of Italian Independence in July 1859, concluding with the Treaty of Zurich that September and the pending transfer of Savoy and Nice to France.[2] In particular he was hurt and dismayed by Palmerston's leading role in this criticism. Several months later, however, the British were partially assuaged by Prime Minister Cavour's revelation of the actual terms of the Franco-Sardinian agreements officially offering France these two territories after the war in gratitude for help in liberating the country. And the subsequent plebiscites held in Savoy and Nice overwhelmingly approved their attachment to France, further softening this trenchant indignation. Clearly French bayonets were in no way involved.

Meanwhile, despite the verbal fireworks and histrionics of the English press and at Westminster throughout the autumn of 1859—"Savoy . . . poisons everything. . . . we may soon be fighting France single-handed!"— in the Far East, strong Anglo-French naval forces were working closely together as they advanced up river to Peking to oblige the Chinese government to open its ports to their commerce. British hostility over the acquisition of Nice and Savoy had somehow conveniently overlooked the coordinated military cooperation of the Royal Navy and the French

Imperial Navy in their invasion and siege of that foreign capital. Lord John Russell did finally relent halfheartedly in 1859–1860 regarding the distribution of Sardinian real estate. As usual, there was no shortage of hypocrisy in the foreign chancelleries of Europe.[3]

But what was also beginning to dawn slowly on the French emperor during the last half of 1859 was that he had gradually become isolated, not just by England—even Queen Victoria, through loyalty to, and under great pressure from, a highly mercurial Albert, distanced herself, at least in public—but by the whole of Europe. Prussia had refused to fight the tsar in the Crimea, though it took part later in the peace talks in Paris. A defeated, humiliated Austria was now an angry foe, following the French army's successful intervention in 1859, shortly to result in the new independent state of Italy. As for "German" animosity toward Louis Napoléon, it was now being more and more carefully orchestrated by Prussia's prince regent Wilhelm, who had been ruling Prussia since his brother's incapacitating stroke in 1857.

When Napoléon I had dismantled the sprawling, loosely organized Holy Roman Empire in 1806, he had suppressed well over three hundred governments, three hundred independent kingdoms, principalities, duchies, and cities, reorganizing them eventually into a few dozen larger German states to constitute his new Confederation of the Rhine. All member states were now occupied by French bayonets and administered by pro-French officials and Bonaparte Diktat, their economies, trade, and military embondaged to Paris. With the fall of Napoléon in 1814–1815, the Congress of Vienna had disbanded what remained of the original French Confederation of the Rhine, including its four kingdoms, eighteen duchies, and seventeen principalities, which became free and independent of all foreign rule whatsoever.[4]

Now Emperor Napoléon III in 1860 found himself facing thirty-nine reconstituted free independent German states and governments. Under the circumstances it was hardly surprising, then, that he felt the full weight of those glowering "new" German states so disapproving of *this French* Louis Napoléon's recent actions and foreign acquisitions.

What was next, they asked, Belgium, Luxembourg, the Rhineland provinces? Only a collective "meeting of the minds" could dispel this toxic atmosphere, and it was agreed that in the interests of clearing the air that a conference would be held by the interested parties at Louis Napoléon's late cousin Stéphanie's Grand Duchy of Baden.

On June 16, 1860, Louis Napoléon and Wilhelm von Hohenzollern, the sixty-three-year-old prince regent and heir to the Prussian throne, duly met secretly at Baden, joined by a bevy of distinguished German royal princes, to discuss and clarify German anxiety over the perceived threat of French foreign expansion once again. Given the death of his cousin Stéphanie in Nice back in January of that year, Louis Napoléon found having to return to her Baden summer residence, now for the last time, extremely disconcerting. Stéphanie, who had been so close to him and his late mother, Hortense, to whom she bore a remarkable resemblance, physically and in character, had been the last of the Beauharnais of that generation, after the earlier premature demise of Uncle Eugène. Today, Louis Napoléon was the nominal guest of the Grand Duke of Baden, the handsome, bearded thirty-four-year-old Friedrich I. In addition to Prince Wilhelm, they were joined in the grand duke's apartments by the kings of Württemberg, Bavaria, Saxony, and Hanover, along with the Grand Dukes of Hesse-Darmstadt and of Saxe-Weimar, as well as the dukes of Saxe-Nassau and of Saxe-Coburg-Gotha. It was an extraordinary congregation of German royalty, a dramatic setting worthy of the great Richard Wagner himself . . . and for the French emperor, a most intimidating gathering of peers coming here, in effect, to pass judgment on him.

Louis Napoléon agreed to appear at this extraordinary "inquisition" to explain more fully his treaty with Victor Emmanuel and its secret clauses and under what circumstances he had annexed minuscule Savoy and Nice, and why this action was not the prologue to further French expansion either along the Rhineland or anywhere else.

What Louis Napoléon did not know, however, was that at the insti-

gation of Queen Victoria's consort, Prince Albert, Wilhelm von Hohenzollern, the Prince Regent, destined to accede to the Prussian throne
in the New Year, along with the Austrian emperor Franz Josef, had privately agreed to transmit all communications they received from Louis
Napoléon to Prince Albert. Louis Napoléon's intuitive paranoia was
indeed well founded.

This conspiracy was unprecedented, and based on their fears that
Louis Napoléon sought all-out war to avenge the allied defeat of France
at Waterloo. "What had happened to Nice and Savoy," Wilhelm reported
to London, "he [Louis Napoléon] said, was quite exceptional and due to
special circumstances," an explanation that Wilhelm said he personally
had found "most satisfactory." As for the accusations now leveled at Louis
Napoléon of preparing to invade the German Rhineland, Wilhelm explained they simply astonished the French emperor. "Nothing . . . could
be further from his thoughts, than to seize any territory from Germany
and incorporate it with France," the future king of Prussia now assured
Prince Albert. "So clamorous, however, was the outcry of the German
press, that something had to be done by him to convince Germany of his
sincerity." Left in this humiliating position, Louis Napoléon then insisted before the assembled German sovereigns that "his desire [was] to
leave Germany undisturbed" and that this message should be made
known "throughout the country." The uncontrolled press throughout the
German states was largely responsible for this warmongering, he further
asserted. "The current fears about a French invasion of Belgium were
equally incomprehensible and absurd," he stated. As for his peaceful intentions, Louis Napoléon could point proudly to the new Free-Trade Commercial Treaty just signed with England in January of that year (1860).[5]

In any event, at this meeting in Baden on the sixteenth of June, it was
felt necessary to publish a "disclaimer of any aggressive intention" by the
French. Although he met no open animosity—Bismarck was still serving
as the Prussian ambassador in faraway St. Petersburg—and despite the
apparently friendly atmosphere here among so many crowned German
rulers, the tone of this day-long inquisition had hardly been sympathetic.
Louis Napoléon was "in the dock" surrounded by his "judges" demanding

justification of his actions, like a truant schoolboy before his teachers. Thanks to Napoléon I's sweeping invasions, German suspicion of Louis Napoléon's intentions was deep-seated, and prodded invisibly by Prince Albert. Nor did the French emperor yet know that this handsome Prince Wilhelm had—with generals von Roon and von Moltke—earlier, on the twelfth of January, introduced legislation to greatly enlarge and completely reorganize the Prussian army, reforms that soon, under the supreme leadership of Bismarck, were ultimately to make possible the German invasion of France ten years later.

When Wilhelm's special courier hand-delivered a long report to Prince Albert of all that had transpired at Baden, Albert in turn wrote to his daughter, Victoria—the wife of Wilhelm's son Friedrich—that he hoped the conclusions of the gathering would result in the thirty-nine German states closing ranks and "thereby contribute toward the unity of Germany."[6] Albert's destructive role in secretly encouraging the ensuing encircling and isolation of France was deliberately kept secret from Queen Victoria and the English government. The significance of this convocation at Baden has been ignored by historians, along with an appreciation of the great anxiety it caused Louis Napoléon in subsequent months and years. But if Prince Albert served as an effective agent provocateur in preparing Europe for a new period of international anti-French agitation and even rearmament, it was another man, a Prussian, who made such intentions a reality.

Louis Napoléon returned directly to Paris, having at least established a truce of sorts at Baden, while gradually realizing that he was well and truly being isolated from and hemmed in by the European powers, including all the German states, Austria, and perhaps Russia as well. Good natured at heart and well meaning, this left Louis Napoléon perplexed by such intense, deep-seated hostility. He little suspected the significant role played by "his friend" Albert. No sooner had he returned to the French capital than he found himself on the fourth of July heading the funeral cortège of the cantankerous long-ailing Uncle Jérôme to join his illustrious brother in the Invalides. Despite the large crowds of the curious, there was no cheering for Jérôme, indisputably the most unpopular of all the Bonapartes, apart from his bumptious son, Sans-Plomb. The gloom of the Baden inquisition blended in seamlessly with the stormy skies over Paris.

In six months' time, the Prince Regent, the bald if handsome Wilhelm von Hohenzollern, would assume the throne as King Wilhelm I of Prussia, and select a Prussian-styled Talleyrand of his own, a decision that was to change the history of both Germany and France and undermine the peace of Europe for decades to come.

A fter leaving Baden that June 1860, nothing would ever again quite be the same for Louis Napoléon Bonaparte, and he sensed it deeply. There were continuing rumors of a 200,000-man Prussian army driving down the Rhine to seize everything as far as south as Lake Constance, but in the end these proved to be totally unfounded. Indeed, far away at the war ministry in Berlin, General von Roon was just beginning to draft the first basic legislation that would completely modernize the Prussian army and nearly double its strength. At the same time his colleague army chief of staff von Moltke was ordering new weapons and preparing new tactics and strategy that would one day render just such an invasion possible. With Bismarck's appointment in September 1862 as minister-president of Prussia, the unique troika—Bismarck, Roon, and Moltke—would then be in place over the next eight years as they meticulously prepared for a unification of Germany cemented by the invasion of France and the destruction of the Second Empire.

I t was a brooding, deeply depressed Louis Napoléon who returned to Paris from Baden in 1860. Nor was there any letup in the bad news greeting him in Paris, including a new crisis in the Near East. Back in April and May there had been bloody clashes between the French-backed Maronite Christians of Beirut and the English-supported Druze, leading to "massacres" as far as Damascus. Both France and England had dispatched warships to the Lebanese coast to rescue thousands of fleeing refugees, although, of course, with Lebanon being a province of the Ottoman Empire, theoretically the Turkish government should have been doing the policing. Such was the situation when the latest news reached Paris on the sixteenth of July of 1860.

Louis Napoléon ordered his new foreign minister, Édouard Thouvenel, to convene the powers in Paris on the third of August. Meeting at the Quai d'Orsay, the representatives of France, England, Prussia, Austria, and Russia agreed to dispatch a 6,000-man peacekeeping expeditionary force under French general Beaufort d'Hautpoul, with a limited six-month mandate. This military force quickly restored peace, while obliging the Ottoman authorities to step in and maintain order thereafter, which they duly did. But London was fearful of the French remaining in Lebanon and Syria—they were already well established in Algeria, and now excavating the new proposed Suez Canal. "We do not wish . . . to give France another pretext for an indefinite occupation of this land as well," as Lord John Russell put it. Sultan Abdülmecid gave in to the West and provided Lebanon with a Maronite Christian governor of the province, and all the European troops and ships left the country, including the French. And thus another diplomatic clash between England and France was narrowly resolved.[7]

Louis Napoléon, however, had a veritable gift for embroiling himself in totally unnecessary controversies and difficulties, and thus continued his ill-concealed assignations with the lovely Countess Virginia Castiglione, which did nothing to improve the tranquility of the palace or the painful scenes with Eugénie.

Meanwhile, the Anglo-French military expedition in China battling its way upriver had finally entered Peking on October 13, 1860, thereby securing peace and open ports of commerce for the future, news that would not reach Louis Napoléon until November, as he was caught up once again in the daily affairs of state. These now largely centered around the introduction of the first elements of the new Saint-Simon liberal empire he had been discussing and planning ever since his days as a prisoner in Ham. Against the advice of his conservative minister,

Eugène Rouher, but with the full support of half brother Auguste de Morny presiding over the assembly, Louis Napoléon took the initial step on November 24, 1860, by issuing a decree for the first time allowing the Legislative Body and Senate the right to debate freely about the emperor's annual throne speech before the opening of the parliamentary year. This decree was warmly welcomed by the majority, if rejected by the "imperial clientele," with Hippolyte Carnot calling it "the death knell of the Empire," which would open the floodgates to further relaxation of imperial authoritarian rule.

Louis Napoléon explained that he wished to give Parliament "a more direct participation in the general policy of my Government." The Senate and Legislative Body could now reply to the emperor's speech, introduce amendments to bills and new legislation (with some exceptions), and for the first time allow the full public parliamentary debate to be published in the daily newspapers. This decree also suppressed the short-lived Ministry of Algeria, that country reverting to the Ministry of the Marine and Colonies.[8]

Back in September of 1860, Louis Napoléon and Eugénie had escaped the mournful claustrophobia of the Tuileries, taking a special train first for a brief tour of the newly acquired Savoy, continuing via the recently completed railway to Marseille and then to Nice, where they were again warmly received by thousands of new French citizens. They next sailed from Toulon in the imperial steam yacht the *Aigle* for Corsica to pay their respects to Napoléon's birthplace in Ajaccio, before continuing on the final leg of their journey, complete with a screening frigate escort to Algeria, a colony Louis Napoléon had long wished to visit.

Arriving at the port of Algiers on Monday, the seventeenth of September in 1860, Governor Prosper de Chasseloup-Laubat had an intensive schedule prepared for his imperial guests. Louis Napoléon was dramatically struck by this exotic setting. Governor de Chasseloup-Laubat, the able former minister of the marine and colonies, had prepared a vast banquet in honor of the emperor and empress, offering dozens of dishes, including a galantine of gazelle, camel, and ostrich.

This was followed by a spectacular equestrian "fantasia," as some 10,000 "Arab" tribesmen in traditional costume galloped past the grandstand, shouting and firing their guns wildly into the air. The usually phlegmatic Louis Napoléon smiled with delight, carried away by the excitement of the moment, spellbound by his first glimpse of "the Orient," and falling passionately in love with the country and its people. His ADCs and companions, even Eugénie, were as startled by this extraordinary transformation as everyone else who knew him. "Our conquest of this country obliges us to concern ourselves with the welfare of these three million Arabs [Berbers]," he later commented, "and to raise them to the level and dignity of free men!"[9]

On the second day of their tour, the festivities came to an abrupt halt, however, when Louis Napoléon was informed of the death of Eugénie's forty-five-year-old sister, and closest friend, Paca, the Duchess of Alba, on the sixteenth of September. He now had to break the news to her. The Duchess of Alba had been suffering from "an undiagnosed disease of the spine" for months, but this news shattered Eugénie. Abruptly cutting short the festivities, they sailed for France the next day.

On the fourteenth of November, an extremely distraught, grieving forty-four-year-old Eugénie left Paris abruptly without warning for London with a retinue of fourteen retainers, where she registered at Claridge's under the name of the Comtesse de Pierrefonds, before going on a bizarre shopping spree. Her unannounced arrival in the English capital took even Foreign Secretary Malmesbury by surprise. After a flying visit to Scotland to see her husband's cousin, the Duchess of Hamilton, on her return journey to France she spent two days with a bewildered Queen Victoria—"She gave me a melancholy impression." An equally bewildered Louis Napoléon met her at Boulogne that December.[10]

Meanwhile, this brief introduction to Algeria was to have a profound and lasting impact on Napoléon III and his reign. He would return again, he said, and next time he would stay not days, but weeks, in order to travel extensively and study the country and its people. France would never be the same again as Louis Napoléon focused his energies on the hitherto largely overlooked Islamic world.

30

OFFENBACHLAND

*"Che disgrazia! to think that I am the only sovereign unable to
attend this* Grand Duchess [of Gerolstein]*!"* [1]
—APOCRYPHAL COMMENT ATTRIBUTED TO POPE PIUS IX

"Piff, Paff, Pouff." [2]
—GENERAL BOUM'S SONG AND RESPONSE TO THE WORLD
IN *THE GRAND DUCHESS OF GEROLSTEIN*

Despite some savage cuts by the state censor, on the freezing evening of Saturday, December 17, 1864, dozens of elegant carriages
stopped one after another in the Rue de Montmartre before the Théâtre
des Variétés for a very special event: a new Offenbach production, *La
Belle Hélène.* Now, at the age of fifty-one, Offenbach was a household
name, synonymous with musical extravaganza, elegant French comedy,
and a new form of music, *opéra bouffe* (comic, or light opera), beginning with his witty *Ba-Ta-Clan* back in 1855. But there had been no new
major production by this small caricature of a man—"a skeleton sporting a pince-nez," an otherwise humorless Edmond de Goncourt called
him[3]—since his successful *Orpheus in the Underworld* six years earlier.
And more than one jealous fellow composer was ready to write him off,
beginning with the outspoken Hector Berlioz, not to mention writers
and politicians, including a presumptuous, musically illiterate Émile
Zola—"that wily Italian," Goncourt called him, who had never met
him but who dismissed Offenbach as "a public enemy" and "a monstrous
beast!"[4] A young professor of philology at Basel, Friedrich Nietzsche,

disagreed with these critics, however, calling Jacques Offenbach "an artistic genius," and Rossini, Debussy, Mussorgsky, and Rimski-Korsakov fully concurred, praising "this Mozart of the Boulevards."[5] But even Offenbach's close friend and principal librettist, Ludovic Halévy, had to admit he found the great man, like so many gifted and successful artists, an egotistical tyrant and "the most badly brought up man I know," when rehearsing his cast.[6] If Offenbach was no paragon of the social graces, he was a notoriously soft touch for any musician who had fallen on hard times. He also encouraged promising students and even established composers, including Vienna's Johann Strauss, recommending his return to writing full-length operettas once more. As for the premier of *La Belle Hélène* tonight, it would either ensure Jacques Offenbach's position as the grand composer of this new musical form, or mark his downfall.

The lobby was filling with bejeweled ladies of the court and bearded gentlemen in silk top hats intrigued, even excited, with anticipation about the latest work of this extraordinary Offenbach. Why had the state censors taken such chunks out of this piece when the emperor, Napoléon III, and his lovely consort Eugénie were themselves here in the Imperial Loge also anticipating the grand event? It was said that a reference to Eugénie's friend, Pauline von Metternich, wife of the Austrian ambassador, and certain political innuendos had been removed. And the same applied to the sensual attractions of Hélène, played tonight by the great lady of the theater, Hortense Schneider—the former mistress of both Offenbach and Louis Napoléon—which had to be toned down. But even the good-humored Louis Napoléon could not help smiling later during the premiere of the *La Grande Duchesse de Gerolstein,* in which Offenbach openly satirized the army.

Curiosity, a fascination for gossip and intrigue, and above all a genuine passion for and an addictive delight in Offenbach's melodious, rollicking, frequently outrageous works now brought them to the theater once again, including the tone-deaf imperial couple—Empress Eugénie and Louis Napoléon, the latter openly laughing at his own ignorance and insensibility to beautiful music, painting, and literature, his total lack of appreciation of the arts. "It's like gout, don't you see, it skips a generation," he quipped. "But perhaps my son will like them!" Back in 1855 during the first international exhibition, Auguste de Morny as president of the Jury of the Salon des Tableaux of the new painters, was acting as Louis Napoléon's guide when they stopped before a panoramic canvas of mountains centered around Mont Blanc. A serious Louis Napoléon looked at it disapprovingly. "The painter should have indicated the altitude of each of the peaks." And when on another occasion the emperor was attending a benefit for the arts, he turned to his hostess, Madame Delessert, and asked: "What can I do to support the arts?" She curtseyed and replied, "Sire, you have to appreciate them first."[7]

Offenbach was the living caricature of what the composer of this new "outlandish" music should be, wrapped in a voluminous fur coat with an enormous collar almost engulfing his diminutive body— balding prematurely, with straggling long, thin blond-gray hair hanging from the sides and back of his head, his eyes hidden by a gold pince-nez attached by a dangling silk ribbon, his mutton-chop whiskers descending down to his clean shaven chin, and a smelly Havana cigar that never seemed to leave his mouth. Like the chain-smoking Louis Napoléon, who had to have a large fire in every room rendering his wing of the Tuileries almost tropical, he also suffered from gout, and the slender, dapper Offenbach—shorter even than Louis Napoléon—was always cold, wearing his famous fur coat inside the house and theaters, even in summer, and inevitably gesticulating with his cane in one hand and a score or cigar in the other.

Now on this Saturday evening the seventeenth, every seat of the Variétés was taken, with overflowing crowds outside on the pavement. Offenbach's lovely, long suffering, much admired wife, Herminie, whom even the usually acid-tipped pen of Edmond de Goncourt found "*sympathique*" and "*spirituelle*," was in her loge. Around the imperial box were to be seen a veritable who's who of the Second Empire, while backstage the composer's two talented librettists, Henri Meilhac and Ludovic Halévy, were going through the inevitable last-minute changes.

For the sleepless, compulsive-worker Offenbach personally, much was riding on this latest three-act *opéra bouffe*, the form he had created, but he had produced only lesser works, including *Le Papillon, Barakouf,* and *Monsieur Choufleur* (with lyrics by one M. de Rémy—Morny), since *Orpheus.*[8] This extravaganza, *La Belle Hélène,* into whose production he had invested his last centime, could make or break his reputation as well as his pocketbook.

Many of the serious music critics claimed his career had already peaked, and that he was in effect burnt out. Indeed the management of his usual theater, the Bouffes-Parisiens, had had a falling out with the composer, hence the scandalous change of venue tonight. And of course his future triumphs, including *La Vie Parisienne* with its famous can-can, and the enchanting *Grande Duchesse de Gerolstein,* had yet to be written. But this dynamic little man gesticulating in a cloud of cigar smoke also needed a success tonight to pay off production costs and hobbling gambling debts here in Paris, at Ems, Baden-Baden, Nice, and Monte Carlo. Then there were the expenses of maintaining his large apartment in the Boulevard des Capucines and supporting his beautiful forty-three-year-old wife, Herminie, and five children, including four daughters who would soon require important dowries worthy of such a celebrity. Nor was the expense of maintaining his latest mistress, Zulma Bouffar, and their two illegitimate children insignificant. In addition, his imposing family seaside resort home at Etretat, the Villa Orphée, with its separate staff, also continued to drain his hemorrhaging purse. Thus a successful box office with a long run of weeks and months was critical. But none of those anxieties could be discerned by watching the imperturbable maestro with his sardonic "Mephistophelian smile" as the curtain was about to go up tonight.

Perhaps even the phenomenal Jacques Offenbach had reached too far, too high, and misjudged his own abilities. And yet today's middle-aged composer had already become a national figure, a legend, indeed almost the very personification of this soaring, energy-infusing, new Second Empire. The whole of Europe, even the English, was in awe of this remarkable creation, of Louis Napoléon's new France, as they witnessed a totally transformed Paris, in the explosive growth of the Bourse and the economy, in the blossoming new literature and arts of the nation, and in the millions of international visitors drawn to the first Universal Exhibition of 1855. And this "skeleton sporting a pince-nez," with his heavily German-accented French—like Louis Napoléon himself—was the very symbol of this entirely new world, he and Louis Napoléon, two characters stepping right out of an Offenbach production.

Paris was the musical capital of Europe. Every major musician and composer had to present his credentials here at some stage, including Meyerbeer, Chopin, Liszt, Schumann, Verdi, and Wagner. Therefore why not this musical genius? But the great difference distinguishing Offenbach from Wagner, Verdi, and Schumann was his unique ability to find something intrinsically French in his music that appealed to, and touched, the very soul of the people, not to mention his mischievous mocking of state authority, the nation's political leaders and generals. It was quite extraordinary that this Rhineland Jewish cellist could step into French society and understand it so instinctively, so intimately, as to be able to produce a very French ambiance. Similarly, a German-speaking Frenchman had arrived from the wilds of Switzerland, taken a Spanish wife, created a new empire, and then dismantled the entire heart of the French capital and rebuilt it stone-by-stone in his own image. French history was standing on its head! No wonder Jacques Offenbach seemed to be so natural a part of the Second Empire, indeed it was hard to imagine it without him.

As it turned out, the premier this Saturday, the seventeenth of December, 1864, was to prove a financial and musical success far beyond all expectations, the contagious "crazy" enthusiasm continuing the following nights and months thereafter. One ecstatic contemporary witness aptly summed up the essence of Offenbach's unique music and the contribution made by *La Belle Hélène*: "It is our world today that he presents here, it is our society, it is us, it is our beliefs, tastes and sense of joy."[9]

Jacques Offenbach would have been as utterly inconceivable during the incessant military campaigns and in the Salle des Maréchaux

[Tuileries] of Napoléon I's reign as he would have been under the grim arch-aristocratic Bourbon reign of the severe, witless Louis XVIII and Charles X. There was only one moment in history when an exotic Offenbach could have suddenly appeared out of nowhere and thrived, and it was under Louis Napoléon's Second Empire. Offenbach was "the king of comic opera," *L'Univers Illustré* declared with the successful launching of *La Belle Hélène*.[10] In this new production one found "Rossiniesque hijinks," the inherent soul of the French people, satire, a nostalgia, tenderness, wit, and vivacity, touching their deepest basic feelings while at the same time introducing the most elegant melody all culminating in a uniquely Offenbachian "rhythmic frenzy,"[11] casting its spell over the audience, leaving the theater gripped and intoxicated. Such was the magic of Offenbach, which he himself summed up as the *la vie Parisienne*, the soul of Paris, that his magical spell quickly swept over the whole of Europe from Berlin, to Prague, Budapest, Vienna, Ems, Baden-Baden, Gilbert and Sullivan's London, and eventually New York's Broadway.

Jacques—originally Jacob—Offenbach had been born in the Jewish ghetto of Cologne in 1819, in the nearly impoverished home of a musically endowed father, a part-time cantor at a local synagogue, and music teacher—guitar, piano, flute, and violin. Jacques was one of five siblings with unusual musical abilities of varying degrees who formed their own chamber group. A child prodigy by the age of seven, Jacques was an accomplished violinist who then turned to the cello, for which he would later become famous in Paris.[12]

Thanks to a dedicated father, Jacques and his brother Jules were brought to Paris in 1833 and enrolled in the prestigious Conservatoire de Musique de Paris, under the direction of the seventy-three-year-old Luigi Cherubini, a prolific composer of chamber and sacred music as well as operatic works in his own right (e.g., *Eliza* and *Médée*). Considered cantankerous and notoriously difficult to please, he recognized great talent in the brilliant, wayward, and already independent Jacques as a cellist and composer, and was decidedly disappointed when the boy resigned from the Conservatoire one and a half years later. At the age of fifteen the boy was very determined to go his own way. He wanted to earn a living, and got a series of part-time jobs as a cellist in the orchestras of theaters and the opera, and by the age of twenty-one emerged as a well-known cellist of the concert stage. He was bursting with songs and scores, music pouring out of him like a musical fountain, sometimes melodious and sensuous, sometimes puckish and mischievous, conveyed by an endless stream of highly original, entrancing rhythm and themes. Impatient for success, he composed for hours at a time, day after day, when he was not giving concerts or playing in orchestras. Almost tortured by the new, unrelenting ideas, melodies, and scores swirling in his head, he slept and ate little. At eighty-five francs a month, at least the young musician could pay his bills, and fortunately had not yet become an addicted gambler, like so many men in the arts. Thanks to his relationship with the family of Léon Halévy and later his son Ludovic, and Leon's father, the celebrated handsome composer Fromental Halévy (remembered for his opera *La Juive*), doors were opened, easing the pace of his entry into the Paris musical world as a concert cellist.

The regulations and laws controlling theaters, dramatic and musical presentations under the Second Empire were still very primitive and restrictive as to the number of performers and the type of theatrical or musical production. By his twenties a driven Offenbach was composing as fast as he could write, but unable to find outlets for his full-length productions requiring a large orchestra and a cast of singers that defined his new art of comic light opera.

It was in the 1840s that the *flâneur*, nightly habitué of the music halls, the opera, and of the *coulisses du ballet*, Auguste de Morny, encountered Jacques Offenbach, seven years his junior. Ignoring the traditional rigid French class and religious barriers separating Christians and Jews, Morny was attracted to Offenbach through the composer's captivating new music and devilish sense of humor, and thus they became friends. Above all he respected his wonderful talent and determination to succeed. As Morny became more familiar with the difficulties Offenbach was encountering due to the still severe government restrictions on theatrical productions, he intervened on occasion through Louis Napoléon—who had also met Offenbach occasionally at musical productions—and his officials to ease the way for the composer.[13] By 1855, at the age of thirty-six, a much frustrated Offenbach was determined to leave his cello and the classical concert stage behind in order to compose full-time and produce his own works, and for this he required a permanent theater of his own.

It was at this time during the Universal Exhibition of 1855 that Offenbach found a building, the Carré Marigny near the Palace of Industry. But when he applied to the state minister in charge, Achille Fould, a license was refused. The famous tragedian, Rachel, currently Fould's mistress and previously Offenbach's, was now prevailed upon to intervene on his behalf. More important, the highly influential Morny in his capacity as a member of the Opera Commission, governing the administration of the city's theaters, also stepped into the picture.[14] Although best known for his financial scandals, the emperor's brother did not ask for or take a single centime for all the work he did for Offenbach.

Thanks largely to Morny's perseverance and unique position at court, Offenbach duly opened his new Bouffes-Parisiens on December 19, 1855, with the premier of his riotous one-act Chinese musical, *Ba-Ta-Clan,* to be followed subsequently over the years by the premiers of more than four dozen new works here. Morny, himself an amateur librettist, made this great breakthrough in Offenbach's career possible, and that musician never again appeared on the concert stage with his cello.

Morny and Offenbach met frequently over the following years, and it was through him that Morny met his gifted young collaborator, Ludovic Halévy, whom he eventually hired at the National Assembly. The count (later, duke) also cleared the bureaucratic channels in arranging for the granting of the composer's naturalization as a French citizen in January 1860, followed by his induction as a member of the Legion of Honor the following year. In 1862 Morny served as godfather to Offenbach's only son, Auguste. In addition he twice arranged for Offenbach's concerts at the Hôtel de Lassay (National Assembly) in 1861 and 1864, over which he presided. They included two of Morny's own libretti (under the name of "M. de Saint-Rémy"), *Monsieur Choufleur* and *La Succession Bonnet,* written in collaboration with Offenbach. And it was through his patron that Offenbach was invited to the Tuileries and to

Compiègne. Jacques Offenbach was shattered by the news of Morny's unexpected demise less than three months after the premier of *La Belle Hélène,* at the age of fifty-three in March 1865, and broke down during his burial at Père Lachaise Cemetery.

In the 1850s and sixties nearly every composer or musician of international repute appeared in Paris; it was obligatory. Meyerbeer, Offenbach's predecessor, was still very popular here despite maintaining Berlin as his home and musical venue. If Franz Liszt performed here only briefly—as a student he had been refused admission to the Conservatoire—Frédéric Chopin had made France his home and he had always been well received, both in the influential salons of Saint-Germain and on the concert stage. Rossini was another Parisian favorite, but when Richard Wagner, with Louis Napoléon's unstinted encouragement, produced *Tannhäuser* here in 1861, he was met by dismay, boos, and total incredulity by the Mozart-loving Parisians.

Although not liking classical music any more than he did "art," Louis Napoléon, with Eugénie's help, nevertheless made every effort to support and encourage art, music, and literature, including personal and state sponsorship scholarships and financial help. Most of the major authors of the day were invited to the Tuileries and on occasion to Compiègne. This even included the more "notorious" authors currently being prosecuted in the courts for "immoral" content, ideas, and scenes, e.g., the jolly Alexandre Dumas, *fils* (for his *Dame aux Camélias*) and Gustave Flaubert (for his *Madame Bovary*). Flaubert's appearance at the Tuileries in particular caused quite a sensation, not because of his "notoriety" so much as because of his reputation as a Norman recluse of Giverny; his visits to Paris were very rare events indeed. For his part Louis Napoléon privately gave the proscribed authors his support with the authorities. In fact, almost in spite of Louis Napoléon's considerable personal deficiencies, the arts flourished as never before in nineteenth-century France. With the wholesale reconstruction of the city, several of the old theaters along the Temple were transplanted around Châtelet. The enormous new wealth produced by Louis Napoléon's economic and commercial policies made new demands on entertainment, on the theater, operas, and music halls. New publishers appeared, and the numbers of artists increased for the new illustrated magazines and books, as well as for the portraits of the nouveaux riches. The subdued classical qualities of the Barbizon school of Corot and Courbet gave way to the lighter palette and freer forms of the impressionists represented by Degas, Manet, Monet, Renoir, Pissarro, and Sisley, among others—all thanks to the unfettered ambiance of a new liberated Second Empire, an artistic revolution previously so utterly inconceivable under the Bourbon Restoration or even during Louis Philippe's July Monarchy. New colonial motifs now appeared in their works as well, Algerian and oriental scenes inspiring paintings, literary and travel works, not to mention the interior décor of upper-class Parisian homes. Even Gustave Flaubert found himself captivated, wrenching himself away from his beloved Normandy to sail to Egypt and climb the Great Pyramid of Khufu.

The last vestiges of the eighteenth century were carried away with the rubble from the demolished medieval buildings. A fresh breeze wafted across the French capital, transforming not only the avenues and architecture but the entire attitude and outlook of the people liberated from the restraining values and ideas of the past. Thanks to Louis Napoléon's emphasis on public education, the working classes were finally taught to read and write, and new book publishers, new newspapers, reviews, and magazines multiplied, bringing literary creation as well as news from across the world and the ever expanding empire.

Broad tree-lined boulevards were terraced with sidewalk cafés where novelists, poets, dramatists, and journalists met daily, expounding their ideas with little fear of an overzealous police, though there were limits. Louis Napoléon employed no Joseph Fouché. Avenue after avenue boasted handsome *hôtels particuliers,* while elsewhere new department stores, *le grands magasins,* Bon Marché, Louvre, Printemps, and Samartaine, opened their doors to the middle classes. This phenomenon, the Second Empire, had changed the face of French history, and Jacques Offenbach and his strutting General Boum were an intricate part of the soul of this new world, until one fourth of September in the future, when the spirit of this Offenbachland was destined to vanish forever. The elegant broad avenues would remain, along with Haussmann's handsome architecture, but the esprit and soul would be lost forever with the sound of the first Krupp cannon and the sight of a strutting Prussian field marshal replacing the gentler General Boum and his "Piff, Paff, Pouff."

31

FIELDS OF EMPIRE

*"England will use the full might of her Empire . . . to teach
the viceroy [Sa'id of Egypt] to see reason."*[1]
—THE LONDON *TIMES* THREATENING AN ENGLISH
INVASION OF EGYPT SHOULD SA'ID PASHA REFUSE TO SCUTTLE
WORK ON THE SUEZ CANAL, SUMMER 1859

*"How is it, M. de Lesseps, that everyone is against
your [canal] enterprise?"*[2]
—FERDINAND DE LESSEPS, QUESTIONED BY LOUIS NAPOLÉON,
ST. CLOUD, OCTOBER 23, 1859

The cry of imperiled French Catholic missionaries in the 1850s in
what came to be called Indochina had been answered by the French
Imperial Navy. With much pressure from the Catholic Church, Empress
Eugénie's wholehearted support, and growing commercial interests,
combined with the loosest of instructions, the Ministry of the Marine
and Colonies had authorized naval intervention and the landing of a
token force of marines—this the first foothold. Such were some of the
pretexts for the acquisition of a new empire that Louis Napoléon had
for the most part not even sought. It was senior naval officers, often thousands of miles from Paris, who were destined largely to take it upon
themselves as to when and where to plant the French tricolor.

It was financial gain and debt, however, that brought the French,
Spanish, and English to Mexico. Auguste de Morny had drawn Louis
Napoléon's attention to the situation in the recently created independent

Republic of Mexico, following a visit to the Hôtel de Lassay by the Swiss banker Jean Baptiste Jecker. Owed seventy-five million francs by the Mexican government, or so he claimed, Jecker had offered Morny one-third of anything that could be recovered. Although the French government was owed an additional sixty million francs in its own right, Louis Napoléon was not seriously interested in getting involved in that distant, largely unknown land, although he did order the French navy's Caribbean squadron to bombard Veracruz briefly, if without results. Mexican investors represented by Señores Almonte and Hidalgo then sailed to France and appealed directly to a sympathetic Empress Eugénie for more persuasive measures, stressing the missionary role of the Catholic Church in that country of hundreds of "heathen" Indian tribes.

In the end, a most reluctant Louis Napoléon was talked into signing the Convention de la Soledad with Spain and Portugal on February 19, 1862. They agreed to send a small joint military force to recover Mexico's defaulted debts from a defiant President Benito Juárez. Meanwhile, the United States, although hostile to any European intervention in Mexico, was otherwise preoccupied with its convulsive Civil War. The original landing force of a few thousand men proved ineffectual, leading London, Lisbon, and Madrid to withdraw. The amount owed simply did not warrant the military expense or diplomatic headaches. Now alone, but still badgered by his Spanish wife and avaricious half brother, Louis Napoléon agreed to go it alone. It was another "Algerian fly swatter incident," with the slightest pretext, a national debt, now replacing that diplomatic instrument—France was not to be insulted by a few Mexican *banditos*!

The substantial costs of a new, larger, entirely French expedition quickly surpassed the amount of the original Mexican debt, but by now the French emperor, prodded by Eugénie, was considering something far more important: a new Roman Catholic monarchy (replacing the Mexican Republic) along the frontier with the "Protestant" United States. The absurd enormity of the size required of such a military undertaking if it were to have a realistic chance of succeeding—Napoléon I had failed to conquer a much smaller Spain with 250,000, and that had not required a powerful fleet and hundreds of transports to land and maintain such a force nearly four thousand miles away from home—simply appeared to escape Louis Napoléon's historical memory and elementary common sense. Moreover, Louis Napoléon had forgotten another basic history lesson—Uncle Napoléon's spectacular fiasco in 1803–1805 when devoting the entire French annual budget to his failed attempt to launch 110,000 troops across the mere twenty-five miles of sea separating Calais and Dover. And then of course there had also been his uncle's earlier catastrophic Egyptian expedition back in 1798.[3]

In any event, Archduke Maximilian, the brother of the Austrian emperor Franz Josef, was available to assume the Mexican crown for Louis Napoléon's Mexican venture. And his beautiful if immature young wife, Princess Charlotte—the daughter of Belgium's king Leopold—was actively encouraging Eugénie during her recent lobbying visit to the Tuileries. This new unexpected relationship with the Habsburg ruler in fact also appealed to Louis Napoléon. Such a political alliance could also, hopefully, facilitate Austria's evacuation of Venice in favor of Victor Emmanuel. At the same time it would also strengthen the French hand against the increasingly aggressive Prussians.

Of course Mexico would prove a useful satellite kingdom next to Catholic Nicaragua and its proposed interoceanic canal. That project suddenly loomed large again, and was almost as much of an attraction as Mexico itself with its vast mineral wealth, including badly needed silver for the French treasury. With the Spanish, Portuguese, and British now out of the picture, however, it was the French taxpayer who would foot the Mexican bill.

They were no longer talking about a coastal landing party of six or seven thousand men, but of a full-scale military campaign, of an army marching many hundreds of miles across unknown hostile roadless mountains and deserts to seize the capital of Mexico City. Nevertheless, in defiance of history and over the strongest protests of both War Minister Randon, with his vivid recent memories of Algeria still in mind, and of the aging Finance Minister Achille Fould, not to mention of the legislative body, Louis Napoléon committed France to war. And after hardship and tactical defeat, General Achille Bazaine eventually did bring the thirty-three-year-old "Emperor" Maximilian and his bride, Charlotte, to Mexico City in June 1864, even as a grave new major revolt was raging in the colony of Algeria, requiring additional troops. Louis Napoléon's total army of 450,000 men could only go so far, because his requests for military reforms and massive new reserves had been rejected.

On the financial side, Maximilian's emissaries had duly signed the initial draft of the Miramar Convention with France in the autumn of 1863, committing Mexico to reimburse France 270 million francs, and then a minimum of twenty-five million francs annually for the next three years.[4] A despairing Fould threw up his hands and predicted disaster. In the meantime a fresh supply of French gold did nothing to reconcile the growing differences between Maximilian and his commanding general, Bazaine. Since allegedly marrying the niece of an earlier president of Mexico, that mediocre general had become more arrogant and more independent. With mixed loyalties and promises of great personal Mexican wealth and power, the fifty-four-year-old Bazaine, a hardened veteran of campaigns in Algeria and the Crimea, was "going native" and could no longer be counted upon. Maximilian and Charlotte suddenly found themselves completely isolated in the center of a hostile country with never more than 50,000 men behind them, including the French Foreign Legion (from Algeria) and one battalion of African slaves from the Egyptian Sudan.[5]

The young emperor was considered a gracious Viennese dilettante, totally incapable of governing, and as Eugène Rouher remarked, Emperor Maximilian was "simply not doing anything right."[6] With the American Civil War now behind him, in October 1865 President Andrew Johnson demanded the evacuation of all French troops, threatening to send the American army across the Mexican frontier. By now an extremely depressed Louis Napoléon, mired in the Algerian revolt and badly needing the return of his troops from Mexico for that theater, advised his Austrian protégé to abdicate.[7] In a panic, Maximilian sent Charlotte back to France and Belgium to plead for help.

Then catastrophe struck. General Benito Juárez defeated the French, captured Maximilian, and executed him by a peasant firing squad on

June 19, 1867, while his lovely raven-haired widow went insane, reputedly while visiting Pope Pius IX in the Vatican. The original French government debt of sixty million had cost the French taxpayer 336 million francs, and as for that fabled Mexican silver . . . In addition to the conservative loss of six thousand French troops, Louis Napoléon's Mexican adventure had put enormous strain on the already hard-pressed military facing revolt in Algeria.[8] As for the role of his brother Auguste de Morny in all this . . . So ended the Mexican saga, one Louis Napoléon had never wanted in the first place. Nor was Emperor Franz Josef, now in mourning for the death of his younger brother, terribly impressed with the emperor of the French. If this page of imperial history had proved to be disappointing, a very different chapter was now being written in Egypt.

Ferdinand de Lesseps came from a unique diplomatic family, ennobled by King Louis XVI, and his brother, father, uncle, cousins, and grandfather had served or were serving the French government abroad. His father, Mathieu, had already distinguished himself under Napoléon I by the time Ferdinand was born at Versailles on November 19, 1805, one of the three surviving children. Ferdinand's half-Spanish mother, Catherine de Grévigné, was the sister of the Countess de Montijo, his aunt and mother of the empress Eugénie, whose two families remained very close. Ferdinand and his elder brother, Théodore, were educated at the Collège Henri IV along with two of their friends, the sons of the future King Louis Philippe, and a younger Georges Haussmann.

Apprenticed in his father's consular office in Italy, Ferdinand also served as assistant vice consul under his uncle, Barthélemy de Lesseps, in Lisbon, and then in Tunis, where his influential father was now consul general. It was there, in 1830–1831, that his father worked closely with Marshal Bertrand Clauzel, advising him on the establishment of the first French administration of Algeria. Ferdinand was next appointed vice consul at the Egyptian Mediterranean port of Alexandria. His friendship with the sons of the newly enthroned Louis Philippe proved useful, and the young man, who was already fluent in Arabic, next served as consul in Cairo before passing his final years in Alexandria until 1837.

Back in France that December of 1837, Ferdinand married the beautiful eighteen-year-old Agathe Delamalle, who was to give him five sons, of whom only Charles and Victor survived. It was an unusually close and warm family. Ferdinand was later transferred to the consular offices in Rotterdam, then Málaga (his mother's home), and in 1842 became consul general at Barcelona. Arriving just in time for the bombardment of that city during a violent insurrection throughout Catalonia, he spent much of his time providing medical help and shelter for the victims of both sides of the fighting. Humanity always came first with the Lesseps. In the revolutionary year 1848, he was rewarded with the ministerial post in Madrid, but his work was interrupted in 1849 when he was dispatched to Rome to negotiate the return of Pope Pius IX to Rome. Disobeying the Quai d'Orsay's instructions, he attempted to reach a compromise solution to that crisis. Having prevented General Oudinot from entering Rome, that angry general had Lesseps recalled to Paris, resulting in an early retirement, but only after being awarded the prestigious Grand Cross of the Legion of Honor.[9]

Two days before the wedding of Ferdinand de Lesseps's cousin Eugénie to Louis Napoléon on the twenty-ninth of January, 1853, Lesseps's mother died. That July, his thirty-four-year-old wife, Agathe, came down with scarlet fever, brought home by her teenage son, Charles, and died on the thirteenth, which was followed by the death of their youngest son, Ferdinand, before the month was out. These deaths left Ferdinand de Lesseps stunned and shattered. Having lived abroad all his life and without any home of his own, his wealthy mother-in-law invited him and his two remaining sons, Charles and Victor, to share her large estate, La Chesnaye, in the Indre. There he remained withdrawn from the vicious world of Parisian politics. Such was the situation in 1854 when he received a telegram from the new khedive of Egypt, Sa'id Pasha, requesting his presence at an urgent meeting.[10]

On November 7, 1854, a restored Ferdinand de Lesseps reached Egypt and the port of Alexandria after a ten-day journey by sea from Marseilles. It had been seventeen years since his last sojourn here when he had served as French consul. The openly Francophile and reform-minded Sa'id Pasha had just replaced the previously strongly anti-French khedive Abbas Pasha (assassinated four months earlier). That permitted the Frenchman to deal with the object of his visit, and on the thirtieth of November, Sa'id Pasha issued the firman, or decree, assigning the Suez canal concession to Ferdinand de Lesseps personally. He was awarded "the exclusive power to found and direct a company with the purpose of building a canal through the Isthmus of Suez."[11] At the age of fifty, de Lesseps's life's work was only just about to begin. And his old dream, going back more than twenty years, could now be realized . . . or so it seemed.

There was nothing new about an interest in building a canal connecting the eastern Mediterranean or the Nile with the Red Sea and Indian Ocean. From possibly as early as 1840 BC the pharaohs of Ancient Egypt had attempted or completed canals, most of them between the Nile and the Red Sea, as did the Persian conqueror, Darius I, some five hundred years BC, and the Khalif Umar in the seventh century AD. It was hardly surprising that another invader, General Napoléon Bonaparte, in 1798, had vaguely considered the possibility of reconstructing such a canal, but surveyors estimated that because of at least a thirty-foot differential between the levels of the Mediterranean and the Red Sea that was impossible. In 1830, however, the English engineer F. R. Chesney calculated that in fact there was little difference between those sea levels, and that a canal without locks was a practical reality. The idea did not interest London, but it did the Egyptian Mamluke ruler, Muhammad Ali, and in 1846 Barthélemy Prosper Enfantin made fresh studies for a canal.[12]

Muhammad Ali's grandson, Abbas Pasha, who succeeded him as ruler of Egypt, while hostile to the French, did welcome the British, and in 1851 signed a contract with Robert Stephenson's engineering firm, which built a wide-gauge railway link connecting the Mediterranean Sea at Alexandria with Cairo and Suez. It was Abbas's successor, Sa'id Pasha, who inaugurated the opening of that railway at the Red Sea port of Suez in 1858. Anglo-Indian trade and personnel would now be able to pass between the two seas, reducing costs and weeks of travel time. Nevertheless, the rail service was still very restricted, primitive, slow, and the route twice as long as any canal and no substitute for a canal permitting heavy, large-scale commerce and a passenger service.

In 1857 everything changed, the Indian army mutinied, hundreds of thousands were killed, and the very existence of the British in that country was threatened over the following years.[13] Taken off guard and overwhelmed, London had to rush tens of thousands of troops and hundreds of thousands of tons of military equipment and supplies to India. Stephenson's small railway was overtaxed and proved to be completely inadequate, and hundreds of ships were contracted by the British government to carry the troops and the vast bulk of arms and war materiel around the cape of South Africa to India. All this in addition to the normal commercial shipping traffic. The need for a canal, saving the Royal Navy and commercial shipping 4,300 miles of travel one way, was now imperative and obvious. The needs of expanding empires alone demanded it.

Like the Saint-Simeon leader Prosper "Père" Enfantin, Ferdinand de Lesseps had foreseen the necessity for such a canal long before any mutiny, indeed possibly as early as the 1830s when he was serving as a vice consul in Alexandria. Enfantin's bid had been rejected by Muhammad Ali years earlier. Now, two decades later, following the news of Lesseps's canal concession granted by Sa'id Pasha in November 1854, a desperate Enfantin used all his influence with Lord Palmerston to prevent the construction of that canal.[14]

Enfantin's opposition was nothing, however, compared to that of the British government, which from the first day attacked Lesseps with a ferocity that bewildered that Frenchman, Viceroy Sa'id, Napoléon III, and just about everyone else. The cornerstone of the French emperor's foreign policy, however, remained unaltered and unshaken: to do absolutely nothing that would antagonize or undermine good Anglo-French relations, especially after the terrific diplomatic row over the transfer of Savoy and Nice to France.

Although Louis Napoléon had refused any endorsement of or help for Lesseps's canal, Lord Palmerston pulled out all the stops in his attacks on that project, especially after the groundbreaking ceremony on April 25, 1859, at the site of the new Port Said. A peverse Ambassador Persigny in London now supported Palmerston's opposition against a French canal.

Literally the entire might, power, influence, and prestige of the British Empire was leveled at the Ottoman ruler, with British ambassador Henry Bulwer-Lytton instructing the sultan to order a halt to all construction or face the consequences. The London *Times* threatened Sultan Abdülmecid with "the full might of the Empire," bringing in "our fleets and armies from Malta, Corfu, Aden and Bombay . . . to teach the Egyptian government to see reason!"[15] In the event of a war between England and France, it argued, the French would be in a position to close the Suez Canal to all British shipping. After all, that is precisely what the Turks had done during the Crimean War, closing the Dardanelles to the Russians. An anxious Lesseps then arranged to meet with Prime Minister Palmerston. "I was beginning to ask myself whether I would find myself before a statesman or madman!"[16] Lesseps remarked.

Meanwhile Lesseps tried to bolster a by now intimidated Sa'id Pasha, reminding him of his "sacred undertakings, publicly executed before the civilized world."[17] The Royal Navy threatened to bombard Alexandria, and Khedive Sa'id was caught in the middle. What to do? While at 10 Downing Street Palmerston was analyzing a desperate plan submitted by the French consul Sabbatier in Cairo, in which Sultan Abdülmecid would invite Egypt's Sa'id Pasha to a meeting in Beirut, Lebanon, in July 1859, where he would kidnap that khedive, while the Royal Navy sailed to Egypt's Port Sa'id to close down Lesseps's construction site. Outraged, Palmerston rejected the plan out of hand.[18]

At about the same time, in Paris, Lesseps and his Suez Company administrators came up with a compromise solution—a legal fiction—for Sa'id to submit to Constantinople. The Egyptian workforce would be withdrawn and replaced entirely by Europeans, and Viceroy Sa'id agreed to reimburse Lesseps's company for all its expenses. But the khedive had no authority to stop the French labor force, he insisted; only the international diplomatic community could do so. The French were on their own, and he could not prevent them, Sa'id informed the British.[19]

Upon his return to Paris in the summer of 1859, Lesseps met at the Quai d'Orsay with Foreign Minister Walewski, submitting a detailed memorandum listing all the difficulties he and the construction project had encountered since 1854. Total collapse of the prospective canal was now imminent if the government, that is, Louis Napoléon, did not act at once. Although Alexander Walewski personally brought the memorandum over to the Tuileries, days passed and then weeks, but no summons from the palace came.[20]

Lesseps spent his time impatiently at the imposing offices of the Compagnie Universelle du Canal Maritime de Suez at 16 Place Vendôme, where he carried out intensive correspondence with his engineers and the companies providing the supplies he needed in Egypt. Under the present adverse circumstances, funding of the construction remained the basic stumbling block. After the creation of this company back in November of the previous year (1858), a subscription had been launched offering 400,000 shares to the public, at five hundred francs a share. Despite all the problems, the entire offering was snapped up within a matter of days. A total of 107,000 shares went to the French, followed by 95,517 to the Ottoman Empire (which, ironically, still had not even authorized construction of the canal they were investing in), and the Khedive Sa'id Pasha put his name down for another 85,506 (but never payed for them); 24,000 shares were acquired in England. That was a year earlier, however, and since then the sultan continued to refuse to lift his ban on construction and Louis Napoléon to give his blessing. The Sphinx of the Tuileries remained silent and inscrutable, and anxious shareholders began reneging on payment, including minor investors like the Americans and Russians, withdrawing completely. Collapse of the Suez Canal company was imminent.[21]

At his wit's end, Ferdinand de Lesseps finally swallowed his pride and went to the Tuileries himself to ask his first cousin, the empress, to intercede. Eugénie had an immediate word with Louis Napoléon, who agreed to see Lesseps at St. Cloud on the twenty-third of October (1859). "Monsieur de Lesseps, how is it that everyone is against your enterprise?" he asked his guest. "Sire, that is because everyone believes you are not going to back the Canal." If Louis Napoléon did not appreciate the implied reprimand, he at least understood. "Very well," he responded, submitting to the inevitable, "put your mind at ease, you can count on my protection from now on."[22] Once again Eugénie had swayed her husband. After five years of open harassment and even most undiplomatic threats by the British, Louis Napoléon at last acted.

With these official assurances, Ferdinand de Lesseps once again set sail for Constantinople, this time to meet with the new Grand Vizier, Mehmet Rushdi Pasha, who on December 19, 1859, agreed to refrain from any further interference in the construction of the Suez Canal. On the twenty-ninth of December, a much relieved, if by now thoroughly exhausted, Lesseps sailed out of the Bosphorus for Egypt to bring the good news to Sa'id Pasha and his engineers. The Suez Canal would be completed.[23]

Simultaneously Louis Napoléon was also creating a completely new empire, one largely unanticipated or planned, as the French navy and marines provided new leaders, some household heroes to this day, taking the initiative in planting the French flag abroad. The western coast of Africa in Senegal was occupied by France in the eighteenth century, but it was only after 1852 that full development of that colony began, with the arrival from Algeria of Louis Faidherbe, its future commanding general, governor, and the founder of its principal port, Dakar. Later exploration along the coast and in the interior would lead to a vast, new unbroken French empire extending from the Atlantic to the Nile. On the eastern side of Africa, the French occupied the strategically important tip of the Horn of Africa at Djibouti in 1862, thereby providing an outlet for colonial trade and a coaling station for the French navy, while sharing England's Aden Protectorate on the opposite shore. Farther south, off the east coast of that still unexplored continent, France established commercial treaties with Madagascar in 1862 (ultimately a French protectorate) while expanding trade with its long-occupied

Comoros Islands. Deep in the Indian Ocean, Louis Napoléon also reinforced the island-colony of Mauritius.

Cutting the last French ties in India by 1859, Louis Napoléon adjusted his sights elsewhere, beginning with the seizure of new territory in Indochina. In 1861 Admiral Bonard landed hundreds of troops to claim and occupy much of the lower part of the country. This resulted in the June 1862 treaty signed aboard that admiral's flagship, giving France its first protectorates in the southern region of Indochina, around Saigon, though it would take another twenty years of fighting before French troops secured Tonkin in the north. In 1863, the kingdom of Cambodia became the next French protectorate, later joined by Laos. Earlier, in 1853, Louis Napoléon had sent the French navy to the Southwest Pacific, where they seized New Caledonia to serve as a penal colony for France's worst political desperados.

Between 1852 and 1870, Louis Napoléon would acquire another 700,000 square miles of territory, tripling the size of the Second Empire, along with a new population exceeding that of France itself. In contrast Louis Napoléon's lifelong hero, Emperor Napoléon I, apart from the Caribbean colonies and St. Pierre-Miquelon, had left a France reduced to her old frontiers, complete with bleak memories of former glories, and a remorseless chancellor Bismarck bent on revenge.

32

AN ARAB KINGDOM

"I am the emperor of the Arabs as well as Emperor of the French."[1]
—NAPOLÉON III

"The Emperor does not wish to trouble or upset the natives."[2]
—A SARCASTIC DUKE DE MORNY TO BARON JÉRÔME DAVID

This was not how he had planned it, a far cry from that triumphant return anticipated back in September 1860. Instead, today, on this first day of May 1865, Louis Napoléon found himself once again aboard the two-thousand-ton, 295-foot *Aigle*. Flanked by a squadron of recently launched ironclad frigates of the French Imperial Navy, her powerful Mazeline engines drove the luxurious yacht at a top speed of fifteen knots across the Mediterranean on a southerly course. Algeria, the crown of his hopes and dreams for this new empire, was on fire, and a desperate Napoléon III was coming to put it out.

Little had he realized, when news had reached him in March 1864 of a fresh insurrection by tribesmen in the mountainous Kabyle region of eastern Algeria, that one year later this rebellion would continue unchecked, requiring fresh reinforcements from France. Due to the unanticipated call for French troops overseas in Indochina, China, West Africa, and Mexico, the remaining 60,000-man army in Algeria now had to be strengthened to 85,000. Month after month, dozens of steamers and new naval transports were now ferrying military supplies and troops from Toulon and Marseille to North Africa, returning with the dead and wounded. The former governor general of Algeria, Marshal Pélissier, the hero of Malakoff, who had died in May of 1864, was finally succeeded in September by the younger and much more determined Marshal Patrice de MacMahon.

In fact nothing had gone right for Louis Napoléon since 1864, ending in December with the death of his faithful Jean-François Mocquard, who had managed his office since the Second Republic. A loyal, intimate friend and daily presence, he was greatly missed. Moreover, international affairs were becoming much more complex, a veritable game of three-dimensional chess, and in the end it was not on his foreign ministers that Louis Napoléon relied, or Persigny, and certainly not on that erratic Bonaparte cousin, Prince Jérôme, but on his half brother, Auguste de Morny. On occasion Morny would call at the Tuileries to discuss legislative problems or to solicit a favor. More frequently, however, it was Morny who received an urgent summons to the Tuileries or the Palace of St. Cloud.

At these conferences the two brothers would closet themselves, just the two of them, to solve the problems of the moment. As president of the Legislative Body for more than a decade, Morny was the one man who could be relied upon for keeping his head, never panicking, never giving in to the howls of the masses or outraged deputies—except briefly during the anti-English outcry following the annexation of Savoy and Nice. Highly intelligent, objective, and certainly one of the best informed private individuals in the country regarding foreign affairs, Morny could always be counted on for a straightforward answer to Louis Napoléon's questions and problems; his answers were not always appreciated, perhaps, but usually right and always honest. Morny had no patience for the usual political games. There was not another man like him for integrity unless it was the ailing Achille Fould.

Despite the thirty advisors and staff members he now brought with him aboard the *Aigle*, Louis Napoléon, always a very private man, remained in his cabin, lost in his thoughts as to the course of action he would take on reaching Algiers. But one thing was clear, the situation had to be stabilized and quickly. And yet he was more alone at this moment than at any other time in his life, ever since two months earlier

when on Monday the tenth of March he had received a message that his
fifty-three-year-old half brother, Auguste de Morny, had died in bed at
the Hôtel de Lassay at 7:55 that morning.[3] Eugénie, deeply attached to
Auguste, perhaps her closest confidant, who had stood by her from the
very first hour, broke down. A stunned Louis Napoléon took to his bed
and did not leave it for twenty-four hours. Despite their sometimes
great differences, and occasional considerable rows—he was the only person with whom Louis Napoléon had ever lost his temper—they shared
the same family blood, the same mother, and the same loyalty to France.

The increasing number of this fifty-seven-year-old Louis Napoléon's
own health problems was alarming. Crippling bouts of rheumatism,
stabbing attacks of gout, hemorrhoids, headaches, a hacking cough
resulting from his chain-smoking, not to mention a heart attack in 1864—
all were becoming a growing concern in court and political circles, as
Ambassador Cowley reported back to an equally concerned British
government.[4] The emperor's unrelenting debilitating trysts, especially
with the indefatigable young beauty Marguerite Bellanger, certainly
did not help matters. And then recently his surgeon, Dr. Larrey, the
son of Napoléon's army doctor, diagnosed a new persistent, sometimes
agonizing, lower abdominal pain, believing it to be a gallstone. His
recommendation: an operation to remove it before it grew any bigger.
More and more frequently it even prevented Louis Napoléon from taking his daily ride in the Bois. Another day, he said, understandably
postponing a painful and dangerous operation.

But now even Morny was gone, with Auguste's distraught elderly
father, Charles de Flahaut, left to mourn the son to whom he was so attached. Indeed they had been almost like brothers. And thus they had
all followed the enormous funeral cortège to Père Lachaise Cemetery
on March 13, 1865. There had always been something very special
about Morny, despite his execrable failure to feel shame for his philan-
dering and the pain that had caused Fanny, and later his wife, Sophie,
or any remorse for his flagrant dishonesty in financial matters, which he
openly joked about. For those who knew him and worked with him daily,
however, especially his legislative secretary at the assembly, Ludovic
Halévy (Offenbach's favorite librettist), there was quite another Morny:

charming, loyal, and humorous, and they like so many in Morny's inner circle were almost fanatically devoted to him. It did not go without comment that many were Jews or, like Offenbach, Jewish converts.

Meanwhile, now in May 1865, Louis Napoléon was leaving Eugénie behind to rule in his stead as imperial regent, under the guidance of his privy council and the mercurial Sans-Plomb, whom she positively loathed, and whom Louis Napoléon had never trusted. The faithful Mocquard was no longer there to keep an eye on the situation in his absence or to protect the interests of the empress.

The Algeria that had so fascinated Louis Napoléon during his first visit five years earlier had since become a colonial nightmare. Obviously the people of Algeria did not know how to administer their own country and their own lives, at least as the enlightened Louis Napoléon saw it. They did not share his values and French Christian views as to how a traditional Algerian Muslim tribal society should live and be governed. He was intent, therefore, on changing the entire country, although of course he had never seriously studied Algerian history or Islam, and of course did not speak Arabic or any of the Berber dialects (the indigenous languages of North Africa except for Egypt). The Turks had governed Algeria as a province of the Ottoman Empire until 1830 and had done nothing for them, according to Louis Napoléon's lights. Apart from collecting taxes, the Turks had let them run their own lives, leaving traditional tribal affairs and customs unchanged. They had not encouraged them to abandon tribal life, acquire private property, or try to produce agricultural surplus beyond their own tribal needs, for overseas sales. All this was wrong in the eyes of Louis Napoléon Bonaparte.

The Algerians needed "guidance" in entering the modern world of European civilization. Everything had to change, but it must be done patiently and respectfully. They must be given equal rights, the same rights as the French population; such an idea, of course, had never even occurred even to the most enlightened Algerian. Tribal councils, popularly elected and chosen throughout the centuries, should now be disbanded, and along with them tribal chiefs. Dismantle the tribe and its administration and become like France, he insisted. And yet Louis Napoléon specifically forbade the creation of *cantonnements*, or "reservations."[5] His knowledge of the wholesale transportation and relocation of the American Indians, he said, had cautioned him enough not to repeat that experiment. Louis Napoléon had his own elaborate plans for the 362 Algerians tribes. This long sea voyage gave him much time for contemplation.

I t was a very somber, much preoccupied Louis Napoléon who reached Algeria in the early morning hours of May 2, 1865, even as the continuing rebellion was spreading to other tribes in Titteri, Dahra, and the Flehas. He and his staff, under General Fleury's direction, had prepared an extensive agenda, including a series of meetings with French colonists and senior military officers, and Algerian leaders throughout the country. He was sure that through an extensive investigative tour of the colony he could come to a better understanding of the problems causing the revolts, and in so doing find solutions for the outstanding problems. But what indeed had gone wrong to produce this present state of affairs? In March 1864 tribal chief Si Sliman[6] had rebelled against the French presence and then massacred four dozen French troops sent to subdue them.

Since then, reinforcements were continuing to arrive to restore order, including strong measures to discourage future rebellions. Villages were torched and rendered uninhabitable in Oran Province, the south, and in the west along the ill-defined Moroccan frontier.[7] And yet heavy resistance to the French was continuing. Louis Napoléon's idea for civilian administration of the colony, including the extension of democratic rights and institutions for the Algerian people as well— most of whom could neither read nor write—seemed to have failed in a most calamitous manner. Crisis gripped the colony.

A s early as June 1858, Louis Napoléon had decided to reduce the influence and role of the French military in Algeria. He created a special ministry for that colony and appointed none other than his ineffable cousin Prince Jérôme as both its minister and civil governor. Succeeding Marshal Randon, he had arrived with his Parisian hangers-on and an impressive agenda of liberal, "democratic" reforms to improve the lot of both the Algerians and the colonists in the summer of 1858. This Plon-Plon, or Sans-Plomb ("gutless")—he was still referred to by both sobriquets—cousin Jérôme may frequently have been highly un-predictable in speech and actions, but he was a consistent political lib-eral, wishing to democratize the entire world through his "idealism." And that idée fixe was perhaps his one saving grace in the eyes of the long-suffering Louis Napoléon. Plon-Plon had an identical blueprint ready to apply to every French colony in Africa and Asia.

As Algeria's first civil governor under the newly constituted Minis-try of Algeria, Jérôme had called for much greater colonization of the country's "vast vacant spaces," as Marshal Randon referred to confiscated tribal land. His plans also called for a political merging of Algeria with metropolitan France. Civilians would replace army officers as prefects and in daily administration, and colonists would send deputies to the Legislative Body in Paris. General—as he still was in 1858—Patrice Mac-Mahon and all senior army officers had most vigorously opposed Plon-Plon and these revolutionary actions. Without the army there would be no order or security in this still largely unconquered land. Civilian officials from Paris did not possess the extensive local knowledge or the trained police required to replace seasoned soldiers, they had argued. Moreover, Jérôme also intended to reorganize the judicial system of the colony. The French military were no longer allowed to accuse, try, pun-ish, or imprison Algerian Muslims, who now had to be tried instead under Qu'ranic law or in tribal courts. A storm of indignation directed by MacMahon obliged Louis Napoléon to retreat, allowing some mili-tary participation when Muslims were involved. The government's "Arab Bureaux," comprised of army officers,[8] at least knew the land, the people, the customs and languages, unlike the French civilian judges and offi-cials freshly off the boat from France. In brief, without the French army in control, the army argued, Algeria would revert to chaos, and France might even lose the colony.

On the other hand, the brooding Plon-Plon personally knew nothing about Algeria, its history, or its people, and had no plans to learn by touring the country or, indeed, even to leaving the capital of Algiers. He was only interested in introducing his personal theoretical liberal reforms. But when for instance on February 16, 1859, he announced from France (where he had returned in December 1858) that "the natives" would be free to sell or acquire land, including tribal land, all sides were up in arms. Strictly defined lands could no longer be easily confiscated by the state.[9] The result: tribes would eventually break up, disintegrate, and disappear. As the totality of their tribes literally constituted Algeria, this meant the entire social structure protecting the members of each tribe would no longer exist, resulting in a veritable diaspora of tribesmen. It also meant that the government's "Arab Bureaux" would lose hands-on control of the tribes. An angry MacMahon and the army brass bullied, ranted, and threatened mass resignations, and yet again Louis Napoléon gave way, abrogating the law, for the moment.[10]

One of Plon-Plon's final liberal acts as governor was to reduce the severe editorial restrictions muzzling the independent French press in Algeria, which was so opposed to the untouchable, high-handed rule of the country by an arrogant military like those found in all French colonies. Unshackled highly critical editorials immediately flooded the colony, even resulting in two duels by army officers challenging publishers. In any event, safe and far away from the chaos he had left back in Algeria, in January 1859 Governor Prince Jérôme had duly married Princess Clothilde, the daughter of King Victor Emmanuel, and on March 21, 1859, resigned his dual post as governor and colonial minister of Algeria. He never again visited Algeria, or even mentioned that colony, like his abortive (one week) Spanish embassy and his abandoned troops in the Crimea.

Clearly Louis Napoléon had made more mistakes, for Algeria had not yet been ready for a civil administration, a "resident general" as governor, and in July 1864 he officially suppressed that post, that colony returning to the Ministry of the Marine in the Place de la Concorde. So much for Louis Napoléon's desire for a liberal, more progressive

Algeria. What the colony needed now was a forceful authoritarian restoration of peace and order, and in September 1864 he appointed the
old Algerian hand Marshal Patrice de MacMahon, destined to rule Algeria with an iron hand until July 1870.

P atrice de MacMahon was born in the family chateau of Sully in Bur-
gundy on June 13, 1808, the sixteenth child of a redoubtable aristocratic mother. Like his father, he intended to be a soldier. Educated at
the Collège Saint Louis in Paris, Patrice de MacMahon then began his
military studies, emerging with a commission from the École Militaire
de Saint Cyr in 1827. Serving in Algeria under Charles X and then King
Louis Philippe, he was among the first to capture the capital, Algiers,
in 1830. Continuing in that colony under Louis Philippe through 1837,
he participated in the siege of Constantine, when he probably met
Auguste de Morny for the first time. As a major, MacMahon commanded
a battalion fighting Algeria's most famous leader, Abd el-Kader, in 1841.
In 1849 he was appointed General Pélissier's chief of staff in western
Oran Province.
     A politically savvy officer, the shrewd MacMahon supported Louis
Napoléon's coup of December 1851 and was immediately promoted to
major general. In his forties he finally married the very wealthy Elisabeth
de La Croix de Castries, placing him at once in the most influential court
circles. During the Crimean War of 1855, MacMahon had gained fame
by taking Sebastopol, for which he was rewarded by Louis Napoléon
with a senatorial seat. Declining the supreme command of the French
metropolitan army, the by now very wealthy MacMahon chose to return to Algeria, where he put down a new rebellion in the ever turbulent Kabyle region. In the 1859 Italian War of Independence against
the Austrians, he was instrumental in winning the battle of Magenta,
for which he was rewarded with a marshal's baton and the title of Duke
of Magenta.
     Up to this point Louis Napoléon had greatly admired MacMahon the
soldier, a man of his own age, and unlike so many senior officers, a gentleman of the old school, at least superficially. He had full confidence in

his restoring order in Algeria, and in a civilized manner, but had long before learned to look the other way when an ugly price had to be paid to achieve a necessary goal.

A s governor general, MacMahon certainly did not flinch from vigorous and even brutal military action, including massacres of entire villages. Algeria, however, was a vast land, its nearly three million people scattered over hundreds of thousands of square miles, and not an easy land "to pacify," a favorite term of the French. On the other hand, the long-term solutions sought for this colony were political, not military. Emperor Napoléon had ruled France and Europe with the bayonet. His nephew preferred the rule of law, common sense, and an understanding of the people's needs if at all possible. On the twenty-third of April, 1863, Louis Napoléon signed a new decree stamped with the approval of the Senate that shook the establishment in Algeria, the military, and the colonists alike.

The colony was to be surveyed, for the first time in history, something even their predecessors, the Turks, had never attempted. Paris would now "protect" the property rights of the tribes. In Algeria the country—with the exception of some urban commercial real estate, Muslim waqfs (large charitable institutions), and official government property—was largely communal, as it had been for centuries. Each tribe had its unfenced, but legally recognized, boundaries. Once surveyed, all this would change. Ironically, this also meant that the military was no longer permitted to seize entire swathes of "vacant land."

T hese Hamitic tribes were efficient, time-tested democratic communities. A group of respected men, usually elders, ruled each tribe, and they in turn selected their tribal chieftain. All matters concerning the tribe as a whole were dealt with by them through the tribal council. When water was scarce, or the flocks had to be moved seasonally to the greener uplands, it was the council that made the decision for the entire tribe. If a tribe were attacked by a neighbor, the tribal council decided on a collective defense. The council made the decisions on its "foreign policy," for there was neither a ruling king nor any sense or concept of nationhood. Indeed, the average Algerian had no idea what a country called "Algeria" meant. He never called himself "Algerian," only by his tribal name. Indeed, he did not know that there was such an entity as "a country." Everything began and ended with his tribe and its immediate neighbors. At the same time no one went hungry in the tribe, for the well-being of the people was the overall responsibility of the tribe, their community. Depending on the traditions of each tribe, families were free to raise sheep, goats, and camels. Dishonesty was not tolerated, and when a crime was committed, the tribal council and its chief dealt with it. As there were no tribal prisons, all legal matters had to be decided and dispatched on the spot. A thief would lose a hand, or a crime would be resolved by "financial" compensation, e.g., by so many animals awarded to the injured party, or in extreme cases an offender could be outlawed, "deported," rendered homeless and "stateless." That was the worst penalty for an Algerian. These people were not urban dwellers, they were shepherds and farmers who transformed themselves into warriors when threatened. There were few towns or cities, or "madinas," and those were inhabited and run by Christians, Jews, or foreign merchants. Daily existence was essentially simple, and safe, and tribal life, while never luxurious or even very comfortable, met the needs and aspirations of the people. Everyone was safe, protected, and well fed, and above all everyone belonged to his tribal community. The tribe was their anchor. All was well in the world, and this, tragically, was something that Louis Napoléon simply could never begin to fathom or appreciate.

The emperor girded with Saint-Simeon ideology, Christian charity, and his superior French civilization, while finding these "Arab customs" colorful, also considered the Algerians "a race in decline," as he put it. In fact there had been no "decline," it was just a very different society, living under very different rules, values, and customs, which had remained unchanged from time immemorial. All that was wrong, however, and Louis Napoléon was determined to rescue them from their "decline," remaking them in his own image, complete with modern cities, paved streets, gas lighting, neat houses with running water, railways, and French-style "parliamentary democracy." In effect they could still keep their camels, but as pets.

"Today we must do more to convince the Arabs that we have not come to Algeria to oppress and despoil them, but rather to bring them the benefits of [French] civilization," Louis Napoléon had instructed Marshal Pélissier in 1863, after having personally invited five Algerian tribal leaders as his guests the previous year to see modern Paris for themselves, including a weekend of shooting at Compiègne. "We must endeavor to seek every possible means at our disposal to bring about a reconciliation with this proud and intelligent race of warriors and farmers . . . The natives therefore, like the colonists, have an equal right to my protection. I am after all as much the Emperor of the Arabs as I am Emperor of the French."[11]

Despite his poor state of health, aggravated by the sweltering North African heat, Louis Napoléon insisted on carrying out a long, detailed tour of Algeria in May and June. Both the colonists and the Algerian tribes received him with enthusiasm, an appreciation not shared, however, by the army. Following four most intensive weeks in the colony, on the seventh of June, 1865, Louis Napoléon was escorted by General MacMahon back to the port of Algiers. After a formal farewell ceremony, complete with the military band and an imperial gun salute from the ancient walls of the fort, the *Aigle* set sail for France that same day.[12]

Never before had any French head of state, or even any governor general, carried out such a comprehensive inspection of this colony, resulting in the hundreds of pages of notes and reports, maps and photos with which a conscientious Louis Napoléon was now returning to France. He had taken a risk in absenting himself from Paris for so long, not to mention the dangers incurred while touring areas still under live fire by defiant tribesmen. But he hoped he could bring the revolts in Algeria under control.

This was not the end of it, however, for once back in Paris Louis

Napoléon sat down with his staff to prepare a program and analysis for General MacMahon, resulting in an eighty-eight-page document. "This country is at once an Arab kingdom, a European colony as well as a French military camp," he began, and it was therefore essential to administer it equally "in the interests of the natives, the colonists and the military. . . . This intelligent people of warriors merits our understanding and support. Humanity and our interests require our participation in this endeavor. . . . And ultimately the manner in which we treat a conquered people will be regarded by the Arabs everywhere as an intervention 'ordered by Providence itself,' " we having been sent here with "a mission of resurrecting this race" from the low state into which they have fallen.[13]

Louis Napoléon then closed his instructions to the governor general that twentieth of June, 1865, by defining the new role of colonization in Algeria. For the past seventeen years such plans had been erratic, ending in failure. He now proposed limiting all European colonization to the coastal regions of the Mediterranean, reserving the remainder of the country for the Algerians, completely rejecting Pélissier's (and Mac-Mahon's) land-grabbing plans. This new overall program would then "appease the passions and satisfy the interests of all parties." And in so doing "Algeria will no longer remain a heavy burden for us, but will be transformed, becoming a whole new source of strength. Once reconciled to the French the Arabs will provide us with troops and a colony that will flourish. . . . resulting in highly successful commercial relations with Metropolitan France." Such was Louis Napoléon's Algerian Testament, his dream.[14]

A furious MacMahon and the army rejected outright Napoléon III's views and plans for Algeria. Everything Louis Napoléon now did and said throughout the 1860s resulted in hostile protests from the military and colonists alike, and frequently from the Algerians as well. Largely dismissing this criticism following his June "letter" to Mac-Mahon, on Bastille Day, July 14, 1865, a defiant Louis Napoléon issued a new decree that left the entire colonial and military community simply dazed: French citizenship was offered to the Algerians—Muslims and Jews alike! "Why, we are offering the natives rights and a French citizenship that they had never even dreamt of asking for themselves!" Pélissier had earlier protested. And although the fine print clearly stipulated that no French passports would be issued to any Algerians until they first converted to Christianity, the entire French community damned their emperor, this madman and his blasted Saint-Simeon liberalism. It was difficult to say who outraged the French military and colonists more, Muslims or Jews. In any event, by 1870, only two hundred Algerian Muslims and 151 Jews had accepted Christianity and naturalization, out of a total population of more than two million.[15] But it was a very important first step that would open the floodgates in the twentieth century to mass naturalization.

Not content with that little bombshell, on that same July day Louis Napoléon then managed to fan the flames with another ill-timed political act by welcoming the former Algerian "rebel" leader, Abd el-Kader, to the Tuileries for a special ceremony, presenting him with the Grande Croix of the Legion of Honor. French officers worked their entire careers for such an honor, and they were now sharing it with "an Arab!"[16]

Following the revolts of hundreds of thousands of Algerians, the colony was next swept by misfortunes of veritable Biblical proportions in 1867 and 1868: a calamitous, unrelieved drought, the worst in living memory, was followed by vast swarms of grasshoppers blackening the sky and destroying crops and every living plant, olive tree, and orange grove, which combined with the drought decimated millions of goats, sheep, camels, and horses. And then, just for good measure, devastating earthquakes leveled villages and destroyed many of the new buildings, bridges, roads, and irrigation canals Marshal Randon had begun, and this was followed by cholera and typhus epidemics. Louis Napoléon came to dread the next dispatch from General Headquarters in Algiers.

And then there was the human toll, some 300,000 "Arabs" alone having perished through starvation and pestilence within a four-year period. An appalled and ailing Louis Napoléon had no more suggestions, no more plans, to offer Governor General MacMahon. For the first time in his career he was beaten, while Eugénie offered prayers and lit candles for the Algerians. In addition there was the matter of another 350,000 dead, Algerians most likely killed since 1861 by the French army in battle or through ethnic cleansing, reports of which had been largely concealed from the emperor of the French.[17]

What had Louis Napoléon achieved? The additional 25,000 troops rushed to Algeria helped quell the rebellion for a while, but as a result of the subsequent grief and misery resulting from the natural disasters, angry new rebel leaders were soon stoking the fires of revolt again. What good had the French brought them? Algerians asked. Their richest agricultural land confiscated, Algerian tribal power and authority usurped, and a railway that no "Arab" ever rode, as well as drought and devastation that no French science or army could prevent or alleviate. Louis Napoléon took this very personally, depressed by the failure of his well-meant decisions and acts and the promises he could never keep. Years of dreaming and planning dashed.

Nevertheless, his survey of the country, or at least the first stage, was executed. Twenty million acres of it would be completed by 1870. All tribal land was now fixed on a map, some three and a half million acres registered as private property, and another two and a half million acres held as public domain for the state.[18] Tribes were broken up administratively, and the title of much of their best land transferred privately to the government, colonists, and powerful Paris-based financial interests. With the removal of this communal land, a new historical phenomenon occurred: suddenly penniless, homeless Algerians, completely self-sufficient before the French had arrived, began their long trek to the cities along the coast, where there was neither food, nor housing, nor work for them, a relentless human movement that has since spilled over into France. All this because the French government considered it their God-given right to break up a society, sanctioned by the arrival of Louis Napoléon, he the catalyst instrumental in hastening this humanitarian tragedy, one still exploding today—five million North Africans in the suburbs of Paris, Lyon, Orléans, Clermont, Bordeaux, Marseilles, and Nice.

Back in Algeria, some 200,000 colonists had arrived by the late 1860s, perhaps half of them French, and most of them ended up in the coastal cities. And the government finally stopped giving away free agricultural land to attract them. On the other hand, one could not help but commiserate with a most bewildered Louis Napoléon. Prior to the arrival of the French, the Algerians had controlled nearly thirty million acres; by 1870 the French had reduced tribal holdings to three and a half million acres. Their policy of tribal deracination was in full swing, a veritable crime against humanity.

Upon his return to France in 1865, Louis Napoléon was already preoccupied with fresh distractions. That October the president of the United States ordered him to withdraw all French troops from Mexico. France, he was informed, was in violation of the Monroe Doctrine. And then that same month, while vacationing at Eugénie's seaside villa in Biarritz, Louis Napoléon received a most unwelcome visitor, the minister-president of Prussia, Otto von Bismarck. With all his wealth and all the imperial palaces and châteaux at his disposal across France, the emperor of the French could no longer find peace anywhere. "Black clouds are gathering on the horizon," he now warned the French nation in a public address.[19]

33

BISMARCK: WAR WATCH

"The great questions of the day will not be settled by fine speeches and parliamentary votes . . . but by blood and iron."[1]
—BISMARCK BEFORE THE LANDTAG'S APPROPRIATIONS COMMITTEE, 1862

"Mind you take care, that man [Bismarck]; he means what he says."[2]
—DISRAELI TO COUNT VITZTHUM VON ECKSTÄDT, JULY 1862

Otto von Bismarck was haunted by the past historical legacy of Frederick the Great, and personally determined now to restore Prussia in his own image. It was only fitting, then, that he had been born in one of the most historically significant years of the nineteenth century, 1815, just before Waterloo and the fall of Napoléon Bonaparte, the man who had laid waste to Prussia, his country, in 1806, and whom he was destined to avenge fifty-five years later.

Bismarck was a Junker, a member of the ruling landed Prussian aristocracy, born with a sword in hand and a brash natural sense of superiority that was to keep every prince in a state of obedient subjugation. Otto von Bismarck was the ultimate Junker, magnifying those class attitudes, qualities, and racial idiosyncrasies a thousandfold; indeed his arrogance in ultimately defying a hapless Prussian king Wilhelm I time and again, left him in a permanent state of intimidation and trepidation. As the Hohenzollern king admitted, if there was one man in the whole of Prussia he dreaded to be left alone in a room with, it was Bismarck.

· · ·

Otto Eduard Leopold von Bismarck was born at his father's principal estate of Schönhausen, in Brandenburg, Saxony, on April 1, 1815, the son of Karl Wilhelm Ferdinand von Bismarck and Wilhelmine Louise Mencken. Otto's father was remembered as open, kindly, indolent, and unpretentious—none of which were traits his famous son inherit. "I really loved my father," Bismarck belatedly wrote long after his death, recalling "his truly boundless, unselfish, good-natured tenderness for me."[3] He was at the same time a country gentleman who preferred his hounds, fields, and forests to books, Bach, cities, and life at the royal court, values he did in fact share with his sons, including the Junker contempt of Jews, Catholics, and Poles—Bismarck was never to employ Polish labor on his extensive Pomeranian estates. As a boy, however, Otto had a very difficult relationship with his father. "I [later] felt remorse concerning my conduct toward him," for having returned paternal kindness "with coldness and bad grace."[4] But his father had also bitterly recalled the old days at the time of Napoléon's invasion of Prussia and of the destructive occupation of Schönhausen and the neighboring estates by the French army, and Prussians had a very long memory.

Bismarck described his mother, Wilhelmine Mencken—the daughter of the chief cabinet officer of the king—as "cold and unpleasant, though she was very intelligent." There was nothing cheerful about his early years, and "as a small child I hated her." Wilhelmine was both a strict Lutheran and insistent on the importance of a good education. Constantly at odds with his father, kept at a distance by his mother, young Bismarck grew up in blustering rebellion, and remained so the rest of his life. Even as a boy his temper tantrums terrified the stable hands. But he remained close to his simpler, unambitious elder brother, Bernhard, and later to his much younger sister, Malwine.[5]

He spent most of his youth at their perennially overcast, heavily forested Pomeranian estate of Kniephof before being sent away to boarding school. Both he and Bernhard attended the elite Friedrich Wilhelm and Gray Cloiser gymnasia in Berlin, before Otto matriculated to Göttingen University in 1832 to read law. Bismarck, then well over six feet

tall and ever the Junker anti-intellectual, was a member now of the du-
eling society and primarily interested in establishing a reputation for himself as a fearsome swordsman. He challenged more than twenty students,
his sword successfully prevailing in all instances.[6] At Göttingen, Otto
met an American student, a Bostonian who was to become a senior diplomat and one of his very few lifelong friends, John Lothrop Motley.
More important, during the summer break, he was invited by a classmate,
Moritz von Blanckenburg, to join him in a government topographical
surveying project directed by his uncle, Lieutenant Albrecht von Roon.
The usually prickly Bismarck got on very well with the handsome, formal army officer and his wife, Anna. As it turned out, Roon was to play
a pivotal role in the career of Otto von Bismarck the statesman.[7] Although not a Junker, Roon, the son of a Danish officer, had also suffered at the hands of Napoléon Bonaparte, who had left his father's
estate in ruins, and himself reduced to his army pay.

While serving his one-year annual army reserve service, Lieutenant
Bismarck attended agricultural classes at the Greifswald College, and
then completed his legal studies at Berlin. Foregoing a legal career for
politics, Bismarck first served as an elected member of the local Land-
rat, or Diet (Assembly), where he quickly established a reputation for a
sharp tongue, royalist views, and reactionary politics. When the rever-
berations of revolutionary France in 1848 reached and jolted Berlin, and
Friedrich Wilhelm IV refused to put down antigovernment demonstrations with military force, Bismarck carried out his first attempted coup,
trying to convince Queen Augusta to replace her husband on the throne
with their teenage son. An outraged Augusta rarely spoke to Bismarck
again over the ensuing years.

In 1851 the Prussian king appointed Bismarck envoy to the Diet of
the German Confederation, in Frankfurt. There Bismarck's reputation for a foul temper and stinging repartee in debate quickly raised
him to prominence, as did yet another inevitable duel. With the
now partially paralyzed Friedrich Wilhelm no longer capable of ruling
Prussia, he appointed his younger brother, Wilhelm, to replace him as

his regent, who in turn appointed Bismarck Prussian ambassador to St. Petersburg, a safe distance from the royal court and Berlin politics. Bismarck had to watch from the sidelines during Victor Emmanuel's (and Louis Napoléon's) Italian war for independence against Austria.

Meanwhile, Bismarck carried out a bitter correspondence with Berlin for refusing to promote him from lieutenant to major general, the usual rank for an ambassador. The theme of his struggle for military promotion was to continue for years. During Bismarck's absence in Russia, Regent Wilhelm nominated Helmuth von Moltke to head the Prussian army as its new chief of staff, charged with completely reorganizing and modernizing that military machine, its equipment, and training, while introducing a whole new school of strategy and tactics. More important to Bismarck's future was a second appointment, that of his friend, and now general, Albrecht von Roon, as minister of war.

Finally, in 1861, Bismarck received instructions from the Wilhelmstrasse to betake himself to Paris as Prussia's new senior diplomatic representative, although without his wife, a humorless provincial lady who rarely appeared in public with him. Although he had met Louis Napoléon briefly during the Universal Exhibition of 1855, it was only after presenting his credentials at the Tuileries in May 1862 that he was to get to know the French emperor a little better as an imperial guest at St. Cloud.

At the end of June 1862, Bismarck was sent to London to study the mood and policies of the British government and to meet Prime Minister Palmerston and Foreign Minister Earl Russell, as well as a Conservative MP, Benjamin Disraeli. Before leaving London on the fourth of July, Bismarck attended a Russian diplomatic reception given by Ambassador Brunnow. The impression Bismarck gave here closely resembles that of another occasion witnessed by General Stosch: "It was the first time I saw Bismarck at a social occasion, and I must confess that the impression I got . . . nearly overwhelmed me. The clarity and grandeur of his views gave me the greatest pleasure. He was assured and fresh in every respect."[8]

And that is precisely the impact he had on the former chancellor of the exchequer and future prime minister, Disraeli, during a forthright conversation at the Russian embassy, as Bismarck outlined his personal future political plans. He would be "compelled" to take over the leadership of the Prussian government, he modestly explained to an astonished Disraeli. "My first care will then be to reorganize the army," and once that has been achieved, "I shall seize the first pretext to strike at Austria, dissolve the German Diet, subdue the minor states and unify Germany under Prussian leadership." Perhaps it was the vodka, but by any estimate it was an extraordinary thing to announce before the ambassadors of Austria and Russia, not to mention an influential English statesman. While a bemused Austrian Count Friedrich Vitzthum von Eckstädt later dismissed the Prussian's remarks, a more perceptive Benjamin Disraeli warned: "Mind you take care, that man means what he says," as history would well attest.[9]

Back in Paris that September of 1862, Ambassador Bismarck received a telegram unexpectedly recalling him to Berlin. The Prussian Diet had just refused to allow the king to reorganize the army, and at the strong urging of minister for war, Albrecht von Roon, the king had most reluctantly sent for Bismarck, appointing him minister-president of Prussia. Wilhelm needed all the powerful guns he could gather to support the reforms the army needed, and with Moltke, Roon, and Bismarck, he had a perfect troika behind him. "We are in the middle of a ministerial crisis," Bismarck's banker, Gerson von Bleichröder, informed banker James de Rothschild in Paris. "Herr von Bismarck-Schönhausen as the new Minister-President is occupied with forming a new cabinet. . . . an entirely reactionary government." The highly influential Ludwig von Gerlach thought that was precisely what was needed at this critical hour. "However great my reservations are about Bismarck . . . I would not even dare to work against him, for the simple reason that I know of no other person better suited to the task."[10]

Enormous pressure was applied to Wilhelm I, obliging him to act urgently on the defense of the country. Upon his return to Berlin, Minister-President Bismarck addressed the Appropriations Committee of the Landtag on the thirtieth of September 1862, giving his celebrated "blood and iron" challenge to the kingdom and the world: "Prussia must concentrate and maintain its power for the right moment to strike [to launch its armies]. . . . for Prussia's boundaries devised by the Vienna Treaties [of 1815] are not favorable to the healthy requirements of the nation," he announced in a deceptively quiet conversational tone. "The great questions of our time are not going to be resolved by fine speeches and parliamentary votes. . . . but by *blood and iron!*"[11]

While the Junker officer corps toasted their new spokesman, this frank speech greatly worried many civilians, including the celebrated historian Heinrich von Treitschke. "When I hear so shallow a country-squire as this Bismarck chap boasting about the 'blood and iron' with which he intends to subdue the whole of Germany [the independent German states], the meanness of it seems to be exceeded only by the very absurdity of the idea."[12] However, Bismarck's previous violent speeches and tactics within the government had not gone unnoticed, and concern over this first minister's new agenda quickly spread. Nor was the first test of Bismarck's intentions long in coming.

When Denmark's king Frederick VII died in November of 1863, there was some question as to who was to rule the two provincial Danish duchies of Schleswig and Holstein. When Frederick's successor, Christian IX, naturally claimed them for Denmark, Bismarck and Austria protested, demanding the return of Schleswig to Austria. Denmark refused, and Prussia and Austria successfully invaded and occupied the two provinces. A reluctant Austria agreed to give Schleswig to Prussia, while keeping Holstein for herself. When in 1866 Austria reneged, however, violating the Gastein Convention, Bismarck launched the Prussian army against his Austrian allies. Bismarck had already secured Prussia's southern frontiers by forming a secret alliance with Italy's Victor Emmanuel, thereby forcing the Austrians to divide their armies. The combined reorganization and modernization of the Prussian army now paid off, with Moltke defeating the Austrians at Königgrätz (Sadowa), and concluding with the Peace of Prague in 1866. The German Confederation was dissolved and Prussia annexed both Schleswig and Holstein, along with Frankfurt, Hanover, Hesse-Kassel, and Nassau. As for the new Kingdom of Italy, she was of course then rewarded with Venice (much to the satisfaction of Louis Napoléon).

True to his word, with "Blood and Iron," Bismarck now forced the twenty-one smaller German states north of the River Main into joining a newly formed North German Confederation (1867), based largely on Napoléon Bonaparte's old Confederation of the Rhine. Bismarck also personally drafted the new constitution governing this tightly knit, Prussian-style confederation. It was now controlled directly by the king of Prussia, a grateful Wilhelm I appointing Count von Bismarck his first chancellor, while the Reichstag and Bundesrat in Berlin governed the new confederation. Holding the dual post as Prussian chancellor and foreign minister, Bismarck effectively ruled all the states, while sealing them off from the outside world, much as Napoléon had done with his Confederation of the Rhine. A grateful Landtag awarded him a generous grant with which he acquired the 20,000-acre estate of Varzin, Pomerania (now in Poland). The bumptious Bismarck was toasted and fêted as a national hero, appearing from now on in the uniform of a general officer.

"We drank a lot of champagne," German ambassador Kurd von Schlözer acknowledged. "There is no denying that people have always been impressed by his [Bismarck's] dash and brilliance. From now on *he is a man to be reckoned with*!" "The scale of Bismarck's triumph cannot be exaggerated," biographer Jonathan Steinberg concedes. "He alone brought about a complete transformation of the European international order." He alone had succeeded in unifying the German states, where all predecessors had failed. For the next twenty-eight years, Prussia and the German states were to be ruled by Otto von Bismarck, or as he modestly put it, "I have beaten them all, every one!"[13]

That Bismarck had arrived at this astonishing position, equipped with overwhelming power and authority exceeding that of many a minor king or prince, was extraordinary, but then he was a phenomenon, a Prussian political Napoléon Bonaparte. As Steinberg points

out, he had no army behind him, unlike Napoléon; he had no important political party behind him; and the public certainly did not like
the man throughout most of his life. He had no parliamentary majority, and senior diplomats disliked and distrusted him. Moreover even
"the Royal Family hated him" and King Wilhelm I always felt quite ill at
ease in the great man's presence. He feared his domination. Diplomats
and heads of state alike vied with one another in attempting to understand this hulk of a Junker, but it was perhaps the British ambassador,
Sir Robert Morier, who best summed up one of the abilities that so
distinguished this backwoods Pomeranian squire from his opponents
on the international stage. Bismarck, he said, was "a colossal chess
player capable of the most daring combinations . . . and who will sacrifice everything, even his *personal hatred,* to the success of his game."[14]

Bismarck even challenged Moltke frequently, two very strong-willed
giants, neither man conceding to the other. Minister for Defense Albrecht von Roon alone remained Bismarck's close friend and loyal
ally.[15] Nevertheless, it was those three men as a team who were ultimately
capable of defeating even their most formidable opponents, as they were
to prove time and again.

For all his demands of power and absolute obedience, Otto von Bismarck was the only first minister and foreign minister in Europe to live
without palatial trappings, scores of servants, soldiers, and guards, and
most certainly without the pomp and circumstance associated with formal government ministries. For a man of his formidable arrogance and
power, this startled most foreigners, but not Germans. It represented
the real Bismarck, the squire *en ville.*

Bismarck moved into the Prussian foreign ministry at 76 Wilhelmstrasse in the autumn of 1862, shortly after his appointment. Arriving
at the age of forty-seven, he would remain here until 1890, leaving at
the age of seventy-five, with a cane, a bald head, and white walrus mustache. Here he was to combine the offices of foreign minister and
chancellor, directing the affairs of state and later of empire. Rather
than an elaborate formal magisterial building, complete with Roman
statues and Gobelin tapestries, number 76 was quite simply a large
stone eighteenth-century private residence acquired by the govern-

ment and converted into offices. Here Bismarck received his visitors in "a plain sparsely furnished office."[16] Despite the threats and assassination attempts on his life—one assassin shot him, hitting him five times—no soldiers stood guard before the entrance, nor even so much as a uniformed porter. For a man who always appeared in public in the uniform of a major general, this, too, seemed baffling. The Prussian legation in Athens was far more imposing.

Bismarck was as awesome in the dining room as he was in the chancellery. Dinner at 76 Wilhelmstrasse included at least seven very generous courses, the following being a typical evening's menu: heaps of Baltic oysters, caviar, venison soup, trout, morel mushrooms, and smoked breast of goose, wild boar, a saddle of venison, apple fritters and cheese, topped off with full plates of marzipan, chocolate, and apples—and then of course there were the wines. Louis Napoléon preferred a variety of women, Bismarck a well-stocked larder, and of course there had been the usual fortifying lunch earlier that day. After such daily feats, of course he would complain. "I am sick to my stomach and have gall bladder problems . . . and have spent the entire night throwing up. My head feels like a glowing oven . . . I fear that I am about to lose my mind."[17]

It is not unreasonable to attribute the much-dreaded Bismarck "rage" in some small measure to a perpetual state of indigestion, although his childhood resentment of a glacial mother always remained an underlying factor. Then of course the unending political rows with senior government officials, including the strong-willed Field Marshal von Moltke, proved an inevitable source of aggravation and frustration for him. But if on occasion he personally made a mistake, and it was discovered, he would invariably blame his staff. Otto von Bismarck was never wrong, especially when clashing with the military, accusing them of "seriously disrupting his own political agenda." "The King fears Bismarck's rages," General von Storsch noted, "Moltke wraps his anger in aristocratic silence, and Roon becomes ill."[18]

Despite the intensity of their particular relationship, two themes bound the three men, Bismarck, Roon, and Moltke: unification of the German states (under Prussian control) and the continued development of the crack new Prussian army, for Bismarck was bent on creating an empire. And his long-term simmering antipathy to the Napoleonic legacy was always there, as it was for Roon, and to a lesser degree for Moltke. He was just waiting for the right moment to pounce.[19]

In the meantime Roon and Moltke were pressing steadily on, preparing the Prussian army and their new North German Confederate allies for a major war, honing in on "our well-trained, well-oiled [military] mechanism," Crown Prince Friedrich Karl boasted.[20] Depots were prepared, military commanders instructed in new tactics, strategy, and weapons while training the large new army reserves—new reserves the Legislative Body had opposed for France. And all was coordinated with up-to-date maps and carefully prepared mobilization and railway transport schedules. The Prussian general staff were the finest in Europe. France had done nothing equivalent, with inadequate reserves left untrained, and most of her commanders veterans of Algerian guerilla warfare, hardly competent to fight a modern, full-scale European engagement. Bismarck and Roon were just biding their time awaiting a pretext to attack.

Having largely achieved German unification, Bismarck could no longer afford to wait beyond 1870 to find his excuse for attacking France. He could not act, launch a war, without War Minister Roon at his side, but after fifty years' service in the army he was ailing, a physical wreck, crippled by severe asthma who would be obliged to retire any day now. It would have to be 1870 at the very latest or never. Without Roon, Bismarck literally could not go to war. The final ornament needed to cap Bismarck's career was the creation of the Reich, or Empire. And only the threat of war, of a besieged Fatherland, could induce the various German states to vote to accept this new empire.[21] If Bismarck could somehow entice Louis Napoléon into declaring war against Prussia and the German states, all Germans, including the Bavarians, would automatically rally around a new imperial flag.

But first Louis Napoléon had to be prodded into declaring war against them. The year 1870 would be critical for Otto von Bismarck, "the right moment to strike," as he put it. A *"Krieg-in-Sicht"* atmosphere enthralled the country, and one German paper declared, Prussia was "On a War Watch."

34

EBB TIDE

"As I look beyond our frontiers, I am pleased in seeing foreign powers intent on maintaining friendly relations with us."[1]
—LOUIS NAPOLÉON ADDRESSING THE OPENINGS
OF THE CHAMBERS, NOVEMBER 29, 1869

"Everything I have done has been inspired by a desire to promote the interests and greatness of France."[2]
—LOUIS NAPOLÉON OPENING THE CHAMBERS, JANUARY 18, 1869

During the First Empire Napoléon Bonaparte was called "the Troublemaker of Europe." Today, in the 1860s, that title was accorded to Prussia's intimidating chancellor, Otto von Bismarck. News of Austria's totally unexpected defeat by Prussia at Sadowa in July 1866, leaving the victor to scoop up the former Danish provinces of Schleswig and Holstein, resounded through the chancelleries of Vienna, London, and Paris. "There has never yet . . . been recorded in history such a collapse as that of [Habsburg] Austria," an astonished Foreign Secretary Lord Clarendon declared.[3] Just a month before that battle, on June 12, 1866, Austria had signed a secret agreement with Louis Napoléon, ensuring French neutrality in the conflict between Austria and Prussia. Should Austria win the war, Franz Josef would carve a new Rhineland state (out of German territory) for the French. In the event of defeat, nevertheless, Austria would cede Venice to Italy, via Louis Napoléon's good offices. If Louis Napoléon had been dismayed and troubled by the future implications of that remarkable Prussian victory, at least Austria kept her

word, transferring Venice to King Victor Emmanuel's Italy the following year. But as a result of the conflict in the Crimea and the break with
Russia, and now this recent Austro-Prussian war, the balance of power
in Europe recognized in 1815 was irrevocably shattered.

The dramatic transformation of Wilhelm I's formerly inconsequen-
tial provincial Prussian army into a powerful, modern, well-trained, elite
700,000-man fighting machine came as a shock to everyone. Bismarck's
sudden aggressive intrusion into international politics was equally disturbing. If the chancellor's first priority was to unify "Germany," his second objective was to divide the allies by isolating France, separating her
from England and Italy. He also intended to prevent any future alliance
between France and Russia, which he successfully did by strengthening
the close family relationship between Russia's tsar Alexander II and his
Prussian uncle, Wilhelm I.

Bismarck first dangled the prospects of a French historical reunifi-
cation with Belgium. But Louis Napoléon had his own priorities, and
as Morny had earlier emphasized time and again, France must never
jeopardize her relationship with England, and thus Leopold's Belgium
(with its family ties to Victoria's England) would remain untouchable.
As Louis Napoléon frankly explained to Ambassador Cowley, he was
not after fresh European territorial conquests for the traditional *gloire
de la France,* but rather for French national security: secure national frontiers against the undisguised menace of a rapidly expanding militaristic
Prussia and her confederation of German states.

Thanks to Bismarck, "the Prussians [had become] the most swaggering robbers who were allowed to despoil their neighbours," Lord
Clarendon declared, fully sharing Louis Napoléon's anxieties. "I have
no faith in the friendship of Prussia," Cowley concurred. And unfortunately, as Clarendon pointed out, in July 1866, and Louis Napoléon
himself so blindly failed to see, "France is no longer the first Military
Power [on the Continent]."[4] Empress Eugénie was equally despondent,
by 1866 fearing "the beginning of the end of our dynasty." Her pessi-
mism was echoed by her husband, privately acknowledging at least that
France was suffering from "a malaise and general discontent."[5]

On July 27, 1866, Louis Napoléon summoned Prussia's ambassador,

Count von der Goltz, to the Tuileries, to present him with a list of demands, real estate to be ceded to France to provide her with a security buffer, including the Grand Duchy of Luxembourg, the district of Saarbrücken, the Palatinate, the fortress of Mainz, and a "track of the Rhine" belonging to Hesse-Darmstadt. In exchange, France would accept Bismarck's incorporating the northern German states into a confederation (but *not* the southern ones or Bavaria as well).[6] Bismarck rejected this out of hand, however, and discussions continued amid an atmosphere of saber-rattling both in Paris and Berlin. By the spring of 1867, buffeted by loud calls by the French "to march on Berlin," a most reluctant Louis Napoléon, pushed by Eugénie, seriously considered invading Prussia to salve his national pride and teach the Prussians a lesson. Bismarck had insulted France!

Even as the Great International Exhibition opened in Paris in April 1867, the threat of imminent war between Prussia and France was so acute that a by now desperate Ambassador Cowley intervened, suggesting an immediate peaceful resolution of this "problem" by convening a conference at London. Quickly expedited, an accord was signed by Paris and Berlin on the twelfth of May of 1867, eliminating from discussion all the other areas—with the exception of Luxembourg—demanded by Louis Napoléon. In fact Bismarck agreed to only one concession, to evacuate the Prussian forces from that Grand Duchy and to demolish its powerful fortress, and Louis Napoléon walked away with a defused time bomb, but without obtaining one inch of German or Dutch (Luxembourg was under Dutch sovereignty) territory. The hostile Teutonic wall facing the northern French frontier remained intact. At best this was a truce, a minor Munich Pact, for in reality the fuse was still burning.[7] The northeastern French Rhineland remained heavily fortified with the French on continued alert at Metz, Strasbourg, Belfort, and Lyon, and the Franco-Prussian cold war lingered on. But at least they had narrowly avoided another "senseless—and therefore abominable war," a much relieved Clarendon sighed.[8] Meanwhile in Austria, Franz Josef continued to find himself even more isolated by a "swaggering" Prussia and an undisguised, ever ravenous Russia encroaching from the east.

Nor in fact were relations much better between the new Kingdom of Italy and France. Louis Napoléon wanted Victor Emmanuel to maintain an army along his northern frontier. In exchange the Italian king wanted all French troops out of Italy and to move the current capital from Florence to Rome (still occupied by those same French troops, protecting the Vatican and opposing the threat of Garibaldi's republican forces). Louis Napoléon, again under pressure from the old aristocracy, the Vatican, and Eugénie, dithered, and it was not until December 1866 that all French troops were eventually withdrawn from Rome, leaving Louis Napoléon criticized from all sides.

"The fact is I find myself in an invidious position. For eighteen years I have been the Pope's mainstay and now I am accused of abandoning him," he lamented. Pius IX for his part rejected Louis Napoléon's insistence on the Vatican's renunciation of its secular political control of the Papal States.[9] That the French emperor had succeeded in liberating Italy from Austrian occupation and returning Venetia to that country apparently did nothing to mollify Victor Emmanuel's hostility toward France, egged on by his new son-in-law, Plon-Plon, as well as by Bismarck. But when Garibaldi later attacked Rome and the Vatican in September 1867, Louis Napoléon would be obliged to dispatch a fresh expedition to Italy to recover the Holy See, thereby intensifying King Victor Emmanuel's resentment of the French emperor. No matter what he did, a stymied Louis Napoléon was denounced, by one side or the other.

Such was the situation as the new year introduced 1867. It began with the lingering standoff with Prussia over Luxembourg. Louis Napoléon was also preoccupied with the health of his thirteen-year-old son, Prince Louis, who had to undergo surgery for a crippling "abscess" on his thigh that March. "Today it was found necessary to repeat the operation," Cowley reported to Clarendon in April 1867. "The Emperor is in a great state of mind about it."[10] For Louis Napoléon, who was always much closer to his son than Eugénie was, it was difficult to tear himself away from the boy's bed and concentrate on the affairs of state.

As if he did not have enough on his plate with the ever threatening

Bismarck, his son's illness, his personal health problems, and the anticipated arrival of heads of state for the opening of the Paris World Exhibition on the first of April, Algeria, swept by grasshopper infestation,
cholera, drought, and famine, accompanied by renewed fighting, once
again became a growing concern, as more and more French casualties
were landed at Toulon.

At this critical hour in 1867, as head of state Louis Napoléon would
now be called upon to receive the monarchs of Europe at the Paris Exhibition with charm and a smile, while he was eating his heart out with his
anxieties of state, and his health suffered as a result. But to his detractors,
like Victor Hugo, Henri Rochefort, and a young Émile Zola, he was just
a frivolous host enjoying the endless state banquets, the elegant balls,
beautiful ladies, and glittering champagne receptions at the Tuileries.

The longest lasting and certainly the most complex conflict of the
Second Empire was the battle between Louis Napoléon Bonaparte,
the follower of Saint-Simon, and the Emperor Napoléon III, the leader of
his country, the struggle for a liberal constitution finally emerging in open
battle after the mid-1860s. He also renewed his sympathies with the working classes now by creating a type of state-guaranteed annuity that would
protect workers in old age and in case of accident, for which they would
have to contribute only a modest sum. At the same time he suppressed the
very onerous national identity "passport" that Napoléon I had created for
the working classes, that all workmen were always required to carry with
them, attesting to their character, type of work, and any military or criminal record. The bearers of these identity passports had also been required
to inform the police of their whereabouts and were restricted both in
their movement and the type of work they performed.[11] Louis Napoléon
also sent a delegation of workers, all expenses paid, to attend a trade fair
in London. This he considered to be positive practical education.

Amid increasing criticism of the authoritarian nature of his regime,
and demands for a loosening of the reins of power, combined with a
fresh independence of spirit brought about by this new prosperity,
Louis Napoléon decided to take a few initial steps. He had already

allowed the Senate and the assembly to publish their debates, and to discuss and reply to the emperor's annual throne, or "state of the empire," speech. The Legislative Body was then permitted to debate and vote on a line-item budget for the first time. Republican politicians demanded a greater transfer of power to elected officials, and following the introduction of unpopular free-trade legislation and fears of a slowing economy, national elections had revealed some two million voters supporting his opponents to the right or left.

Under the influence of Émile Ollivier, who broke with his fellow Republicans, Louis Napoléon revised a Revolutionary law to allow organized strikes, although permanent labor unions remained illegal until 1868. With the earlier appointment of Victor Duruy as minister of education, free compulsory primary education, adult education, and an attempt at equal education for girls (with Eugénie's blessing) were introduced. Duruy was also responsible for lifting the restrictions on teaching and discussing current history—current affairs, including the revolutions of 1830 and 1848—in the high schools, or lycées. Historical plays, however, remained subject to severe censorship. Although Duruy was highly unpopular with many politicians, he was a decided favorite of Louis Napoléon, who also selected him as his principal collaborator in the preparation of his biography of Julius Caesar.

In January of the critical year 1867, while still on a collision course with Prussia, Louis Napoléon remained preoccupied with internal affairs, assuring a reluctant prime minister Eugène Rouher that he now intended to introduce more liberal policies, "to develop further the institutions of the Empire and extend all public freedoms and participation in government."[12] This included the problem of state censorship, which took many forms, including control of the nation's press. Prior to this, no newspaper or magazine could be published without the prior approval of Louis Napoléon, who could also issue an official "warning." Those restrictions were now dropped, although papers still had to deposit a bond, and the courts could and did still pursue publishers, from Émile de Girardin to Henri Rochefort.

By January 18, 1869, however, Louis Napoléon was having second thoughts about the new liberties he had granted, due to a growing highly critical press, and the boisterous demands of the newly created labor unions. "The press and public meetings have created . . . an unhealthy agitation across the land," he acknowledged as strikes broke out and political criticism grew more disruptive. A few of the members of the newly unshackled press made no attempt at moderation, inciting the public against the Tuileries. Louis Napoléon was sincere about wanting a liberal empire so long as it respected "my insistence on maintaining order." With every step forward, he stopped to look back, anxious that he was going too far, too quickly.[13]

Further changes were in the wind, and at the insistence of Émile Ollivier, in July 1869, Louis Napoléon sacrificed his loyal, uncompromising premier, Eugène Rouher, demanding his resignation, to be followed by that of an equally loyal Georges Haussmann a few months later. With even more sweeping reforms under consideration, reforms handing over more power to Parliament, one impatient senator bitterly quipped: "It would appear the best way to avoid being overthrown by a coup d'état is by overthrowing one's self!" And Adolphe de Forcade La Roquette agreed. "France is not a country made for "liberté," he asserted. A wavering Louis Napoléon appealed to Parliament, "France wants its freedoms, but with Order. Gentlemen, help me establish our freedoms." More and more uncertain of himself, with Morny gone and his own health failing, it was almost a plea for help. He now cautiously espoused a constitutional monarchy, but feared its constraints. He was in fact no longer in control of his own destiny. His solution was a balance between no change at all and the sweeping away of everything now in place—an impossible compromise that would forever escape him.[14]

Ever since his successful Universal Exhibition, held along the Champs-Élysées in 1855, scientific and industrial advances had been developing at a rapid rate, thanks to the infusion of vast new wealth in the empire, Louis Napoléon's firm commitment to the improvement of education and research facilities, and his continued belief in and support of progress and a better world. He was also the first French head of state to develop a full-scale program for the improvement of the environment, including agriculture and the protection of forests.[15] Moreover, the colonial empire had been expanding, making available to the economy new products and natural resources. Inspired by the original English Crystal Palace Exhibition held in Hyde Park in 1851, Louis Napoléon now desired to display the proud achievements of *his France* in all fields, from the traditional fine arts to industry.

And the world literally came to its doorstep, to the Great Paris Exhibition, flooding the French capital from all points of the compass, from the United States and South America, the whole of Europe, and as far as China and Japan. A hundred thousand people queued up at the entrance at the Champs de Mars for the grand opening on the first of April, 1867. A veritable world's fair, there was a tangible air of excitement and curiosity as Gioachino Rossini conducted his new composition, "L'Hymne à Napoléon III et à Son Vaillant Peuple," and the emperor welcomed the visitors to some 50,000 exhibits to be found in every corner of the 119-acre Champs de Mars, from the banks of the Seine where the Eiffel Tower now stands all the way to the guns of the École Militaire. Most of the exhibits were to be found in the 1,600-foot-long ovular structure enclosing four smaller galleries, barely completed on time after two intensive years' work by some 26,000 men. Another fifty-two acres of agricultural and horticultural products were on display on the nearby island of Billancourt.[16]

Forty-two countries displayed their wares in the main ovular galleries and in the surrounding lush, freshly planted gardens, dotted with dozens of specially commissioned statues—including two of Napoléon I and one of Empress Joséphine—and kiosks, national pavilions, international restaurants and cafés, fountains, and even a lighthouse. A towering Chinese pavilion boasted the silks and wares of that kingdom, and similar full-scale Moorish and Siamese pavilions offered the products of North Africa and Asia, in addition to national exhibits by every country in Europe.[17]

A specially built railway brought visitors to the exhibits of their choice, where one could find anything from the most modern French locomotive to Prussia's latest Krupp cannon, the American Charles Otis's new elevator, complete with a safety brake, an American pressurized diving suit, a ten-foot-high French conical pendulum clock, and Professor Plazanet's argyrometric "scales" for weighing the properties of precious metals. Louis Napoléon was personally interested in the recent English Bessemer converter, permitting mass production of steel for the first time, an invention that was to revolutionize the engineering world, from shipbuilding to industrial construction. Next there was the new refined zinc processing system, which Morny had earlier encouraged, and the latest in engine designs, while not forgetting the presentation of the new lightweight metal, aluminum, that was to create a whole new industry.

The might of the new French empire was on view in the Colonial Pavilion, displaying the products and architecture of all the new French colonies, from West Africa, Algeria, Indochina, and New Caledonia, which drew some of the biggest crowds, thanks to a fascination with a world most French men and women had only read about in newspapers and novels. And it was imposing, as were the visitors it drew, including the ubiquitous Goncourt brothers, who were captivated by "this monster of an exhibition," and the "Egyptology Park" in particular, with its artifacts, model temples, and recently excavated mummies.[18] Even the reclusive expatriate Victor Hugo finally returned to France after an absence of fifteen years just for this event. Others included Ernest Renan, a youthful Émile Zola, Charles Sainte-Beuve, Hans Christian Andersen, Théophile Gautier, Alexandre Dumas, *fils*, a very young Anatole France, and Jules Verne, Hector Berlioz, Georges Bizet, Charles Gounod, Giuseppe Verdi, Richard Cobden, Pierre Berthelot, Louis Pasteur, and Lords Granville and Malmesbury. Thousands of visitors came from England via special boat trains laid on just for this event. Louis Napoléon made arrangements for many thousands of French schoolchildren to see the exhibition gratis. The Goncourt brothers braved the fresh air and sunlight for this event, finding the whole spectacle delightfully bewildering. "I am leaving the Exhibition with the impression as if I had just visited the future, one that left our present day Paris looking like some sort of curiosity preserved out of the past."[19] With the sight of

Empress Eugénie rising over the city in an immense helium-filled balloon, the future had indeed arrived.

On leaving the Champs de Mars, visitors found a flotilla of the first thirty newly constructed steam-powered bateaux-mouche, providing a relaxing excursion along the Seine and a survey of Haussmann's new Paris.[20] Back on shore, Offenbach, who had first performed his *Ba-Ta-Clan* for the 1855 fair, now directed his latest sensation, the *Grande Duchesse de Gerolstein*. Never had Paris and the Second Empire seemed more vibrant and glorious.

I t is going to be raining kings," Edmond Goncourt had predicted.[21] And international royalty of Europe did indeed cascade in, complete with their numerous retinues; Italy's sulking king Victor Emmanuel I alone declined Louis Napoléon's personal invitation. Most of them began arriving in May and June, including the Austrian emperor Franz Josef, Russia's Alexander II and his two sons, who were put up at the Élysée Palace, Prussia's Wilhelm I and his inevitable shadows, Bismarck and Field Marshal von Moltke, sword-by-sword, assigned to the Marsala wing of the Louvre, Queen Maria of Portugal, the Prince of Wales (the future Edward VII), King Ludwig II of Bavaria, the Japanese crown prince, Tokugawa Aitake, Prince Henry of Holland, Prince Oscar of Sweden, the Ottoman sultan, Abdul Aziz, Khedive Ismail of Egypt, the former Algerian rebel leader Abd el-Kader, and dozens of lesser German dukes and princes.

The month of June proved to be the high, and low, point of this summer of festivities and balls held at the Tuileries, St. Cloud, the Hôtel de Ville, and the Quai d'Orsay, with boating on the lakes of the Bois de Boulogne and the races at Morny's new Longchamp racecourse popular daily attractions. On June 6, 1867, Louis Napoléon with his eleven-year-old son Prince Louis and Tsar Alexander II looked on as 30,000 French troops representing every regiment of the army passed in review at Longchamp, followed by a cavalry charge with a loud *"Vive l'Empereur!"*

Afterward, the various heads of state returned to their carriages and started back to Paris through the Bois de Boulogne. Suddenly a young Polish student fired a pistol at the tsar. Thanks to an alert equerry, the

Marquis de Caux, charging forward, the shot hit his horse instead of Alexander, as Lord Cowley, an eyewitness, explained to Clarendon. Four years earlier this same tsar had ordered a bloody suppression of a Polish nationalist uprising, resulting in the deaths of thousands. "The scene was . . . terrible, for both the Emperor [Alexander], and particularly the Grand Dukes [his sons, who] were covered with the blood of the wounded horse, and each thought that the other had been shot." The tsar blamed the whole thing on Louis Napoléon, Cowley noted, because of "the encouragement the Emperor Napoléon had given to the Poles." As for the tsar, the English ambassador found him most unpopular and "haughty." Wilhelm I and Bismarck, on the other hand, surprisingly, were well received during these festivities. After dinner that evening, Bismarck related to Cowley that "he had expected to be treated like 'a mangy dog,' as he says, but instead has been shown the greatest respect," particularly by a fascinated Eugénie and Prosper Mérimée, who found him "most pleasing" and "very polite."[22] In any event, the tsar kept to himself, cutting short his visit and with it what little friendship remained between France and Russia.

And then the news of the execution in Mexico of Austrian emperor Franz Josef's brother, Maximilian, reached Paris on the thirtieth of June. Louis Napoléon had earlier personally conceded that his Mexican venture was a grave error, advising "Emperor Maximilian" back in August 1866 to abandon that chimera and return to Europe. This was reinforced by a warning from President Andrew Johnson, regarding the French violation of the Monroe Doctrine.[23] Louis Napoléon was fond of Maximilian and close to his brother, the Austrian emperor, and the responsibility for his military and financial support of the entire fiasco weighed heavily on him. Nevertheless, the Great Paris Exhibition had a life of its own and continued to draw capacity crowds. By the time it closed in October 1867, nearly eleven million visitors had passed through its portals.

The strain of events in 1867 and 1868, including the continuing tension with Prussia, the haunting guilt over the death of Maximilian, and Eugénie's angry jealous scenes—"Spanish blood and Spanish jealousy have often begotten imprudences," as Lord Cowley put it—were taking their toll on Louis Napoléon, not to mention aggravating problems with his health. "He says he feels very old and is terribly depressed and discouraged," Marshal Vaillant noted. "He told me straight out that if 'they' continue to harry and pester him with these unrelenting [political] problems and if there were to continue to be too many more difficulties . . . then he would abdicate."

He was simply overwhelmed and had no one with whom to share the burden of office. More and more he missed his half brother. "People may say what they please, but Morny is a great loss to the Emperor," Ambassador Cowley confided to Foreign Secretary Clarendon, and he was "much cut up [by his death]. In critical moments Morny had great calmness and firmness, and even his enemies admit that his judgment in political affairs was sound." The ambassador also felt that he had "made a very good and impartial President of the Legislative Body. . . . Peace be to his ashes!"[24] But there was never anyone to replace him. Then came the most disappointing elections to date in June 1869.

Louis Napoléon could take no more, and on August 9, 1867, he collapsed. When he failed to appear for the long-awaited celebration of the centenary of the birth of Napoléon I on the fifteenth, wild rumors spread through court circles, the Assembly, foreign embassies, and the Bourse, where stocks and shares plunged. Would the emperor survive? Was it the end of the newly developing constitutional government, or even of the Second Empire itself? Eugénie herself asked these same questions, indeed worrying more about her son than her husband. Would Prince Louis have a crown to inherit? Meanwhile the pain from his gallstone became so acute that Louis Napoléon could only move about in a wheelchair. Henri Conneau treated him with opium, and he became delirious, the Tuileries issuing daily reports on his health. By the end of the month the crisis had passed, however, and he was again able to walk without support, and just in time, for there was much agitation across the land.

The nation's new prosperity and Louis Napoléon himself had driven up everyone's expectations, including those of the workers, who rightly complained about their conditions, while also demanding a sharp increase in wages that had remained unchanged for at least a generation. Most were living in, or near, poverty. In the first week of October there were strikes and even riots across much of the country, in the Loire region, at St. Étienne, Carmeaux, Vienne, Rouen, Elbeuf, and Aubin, followed by those at Eugène Schneider's Le Creusot Works. Resentment was particularly great in mining regions, where mine managers and engineers were physically attacked and severely beaten and company property smashed and looted by angry men having to work under notoriously dangerous conditions. Clashes with the police led to hundreds of arrests and some deaths, and editor Henri Rochefort had a field day: "The Empire continues to extinguish poverty. Twenty-seven dead, forty-eight wounded."[25]

Louis Napoléon had regained his strength sufficiently by 1868 only to face a new barrage of attacks against his regime by the press, Adolphe Thiers, and especially by Jules Ferry, if indirectly aimed at Prefect Haussmann, falsely accusing him of blatant corruption. And then in August 1868 at an important ceremony at the Sorbonne, General Cavaignac's son turned his back on Napoléon III's son, Louis, refusing to accept a prestigious award from his hands. General Cavaignac had deliberately insulted the emperor. It was a serious sign of the growing opposition to Louis Napoléon's regime. Ever since the untimely death of Auguste de Morny in 1865, followed by that of Achille Fould two years later, Louis Napoléon had been virtually without guidance, wavering more and more, and he had already put considerable distance between himself and Gilbert Persigny.

By 1869 Louis Napoléon decided to call for new national elections for the Legislative Body, but the results that May proved a further shock, his government receiving only 4.4 million votes against the swelling opposition of 3.3 million, followed by more violent industrial strikes. Prince Jérôme, Persigny, Maupas, Fleury, Ollivier, and the president of the Legislative Body Conti had demanded that Louis Napoléon sacrifice Prime Minister Rouher. The political crisis continued throughout August and September, Louis Napoléon failing to appear in public due to acute pain from the crippling gallstone. A regency council was again established just in case.

Even as Louis Napoléon was again appealing to the Legislative Body,

renewing the call for "our freedoms, but with order," Empress Eugénie
was preparing to set out for the long-awaited opening ceremonies of the
Suez Canal. Crippled by his gallstone and unable to make a nearly six-
thousand-mile round-trip journey with Eugénie, and hardly in a position to leave his politically volatile capital, Louis Napoléon had no choice
but to remain in France at this critical hour.

E
ugénie and her entourage, forty strong, including her thirteen-
year-old son, the Prince Imperial, Louis, her confessor, Monsignor
Bauer, the American dentist Thomas Evans, and Eugenie's late sister Paca's two daughters, set out from St. Cloud by train for Egypt on September 30, 1869. Stopping at Venice, she was greeted by King Victor
Emmanuel, a floating orchestra, and large, enthusiastic crowds. Now
boarding the sleek 295-foot imperial yacht L'Aigle, they proceeded to the
Piraeus and Athens, where Eugénie was received by King George I and
again by very large friendly crowds. As she was now discovering, despite
strikes and troubles in France, Napoléon III's magnificent Second Empire
was greatly admired across much of the world. Next, as they anchored off
the Asiatic shore of Constantinople, Ottoman sultan Abdul Aziz himself
came out to fetch Eugénie on his lavish imperial barge.[26] As one of Turkey's few major European allies against the Russians, this state visit also
took on full diplomatic dimensions, though no one forgot the great difficulty Lesseps and Khedive Ismail of Egypt had had in obtaining the approval and authorization of Abdul Aziz to build the new canal.[27]

L'Aigle finally steamed into the ancient Egyptian port of Alexandria
on the fifth of November, shortly after the Khedive Ismail had drowned
ninety-seven shackled criminals offshore.[28] A special English train then
took the entire imperial party to a specially illuminated Cairo, which
Eugénie visited "incognito" in a jewel-encrusted Egyptian dress, visiting
a souk, a wedding, the pyramids, and later the Luxor-Karnak temple
complex, where she sailed on the Nile in a traditional lateen-rigged dhow.
Returning to Alexandria, L'Aigle took the party to the new partially completed city of Ismailia, at the mouth of the Nile.

Here the Khedive and Ferdinand de Lesseps welcomed Empress

Eugénie for the opening ceremony of the canal held on a high lavishly decorated platform under the Egyptian, Ottoman, and French flags. The khedive and Lesseps addressed a largely European audience of several thousand, including the Norwegian playwright Henrik Ibsen, German Egyptologist Richard Lepsius, and the French artist Jean Léon Gérôme. This was followed by a banquet prepared by 500 chefs for 6,000 guests in Ismail's nearly completed local palace. During the day fire-eaters, snake charmers, Egyptian singers, "whirling dervishes," Arab horsemen displaying their skills, camel rides, and the inevitable belly dancers entertained the guests. The first of several balls followed at Ismailia under a shower of fireworks to celebrate the opening of this 433-million-franc ($43 billion) engineering feat.

The thirty-nine-year-old Ismail, the grandson of Muhammad Ali, the founder of modern Egypt, was the most Western-looking ruler of Egypt. Like many of his Mamluke predecessors, Ismail was of Albanian descent, and after completing his studies in France at the École d'État-Major, he had returned to Egypt, succeeding his uncle Said as khedive six years ago. He intended to make Egypt a progressive country, with new schools, a developing economy, an impressive railway system, a vast building program including an entirely new suburb for Cairo, while not forgetting the construction of fifty palaces for his guests along the Nile for today's event. "My country is no longer in Africa," he proclaimed, "we are now part of Europe." His recent visit to the Paris Exhibition had been a great success, but this opening of the Suez Canal now greatly increased the swelling state debt. He would eventually be obliged to sell his shares in the canal to England in 1875 for £3,976,582, ($395 million today), leading to his own deposition by the Sublime Port and exile with his fourteen wives four years later.[29]

A very proud Lesseps also received Eugénie, his cousin, at his large house here, where he had been working for many years. Across from Ismail's new palace, some 1,200 luxurious multicolored tents were prepared like a scene out of the *Arabian Nights* to accommodate the visitors, most of whose transport to and from Egypt had been paid by the khedive. In addition to a theater, Ismail had built an 850-seat opera house, where Verdi's popular *Rigoletto* was produced before an audience of gentlemen in white tie and ladies in tiaras and the latest Parisian gowns. Although paid 150,000 francs (over half a million dollars today) to compose *Aïda* for tonight's performance, Verdi, who never visited Egypt, was not to complete that opera for another two years.

"The ceremonial opening of the canal took place at eight o'clock in the morning of 17 November," Eugénie recalled many years later. "Fifty vessels, all flying their flags, were waiting for me at the entrance to Lake Timsa. My yacht, *L'Aigle,* took the head of this flotilla, and the yachts of the Khedive, the Emperor Franz-Joseph, the Crown Prince of Prussia and Prince Henry of the Netherlands followed. . . . The night was one of such magnificence, proclaiming the grandeur of the French Empire so eloquently that I could scarcely contain myself—I rejoiced, triumphantly . . . For the last time I was convinced that a wonderful future lay in store for my son. And I prayed to God that He would help me with the crushing burden which I might soon have to shoulder if the emperor's health showed no improvement."[30] Never had the Second Empire seemed more powerful and influential, as crowned heads and future monarchs of Europe followed Empress Eugénie through the 103-mile-long Suez Canal to Port Suez and the Red Sea. With the result of the labor of more than one million men, Ferdinand de Lesseps had achieved his dream and Napoléon III's Second Empire the admiration of the world.

Back in Paris, Louis Napoléon concluded the year 1869 addressing the Chambers on a note of hope. "As I look beyond our frontiers today I am pleased in seeing foreign powers engaged in advancing civilization, intent in maintaining friendly relations with us."[31] Meanwhile in Berlin, at 76 Wilhelmstrasse, Chancellor von Bismarck, War Minister von Roon, and Field Marshal von Moltke were meeting to finalize their methodical plans for unleashing their armies across the French frontier and seizing Paris.

35

COUNT BISMARCK'S WAR: 1870

"What a stroke of luck it was that the French committed such a folly!"[1]
—BISMARCK REUNION WITH ROON AND MOLTKE, 1877

"At no time has peace ever been so assured."[2]
—PREMIER ÉMILE OLLIVIER BEFORE PARLIAMENT, JULY 1, 1870

Prussia had been an undisguised threat since defeating first the Danes, and then the Austrians (Sadowa, in 1866). Field Marshals Albrecht von Roon at the war office and Helmut von Moltke commanding the army had transformed the provincial Prussian troops into an imposing, well-trained, battle-blooded fighting force that now included the North German Confederation as well. Sweeping new well-coordinated war plans prepared by an efficient, modern general staff left nothing to chance, including the well-rehearsed rapid national mobilization plan using the nation's railways.

Despite the glorious victories and conquests of Napoléon and his Grand Army resulting in the occupation of Western Europe, which the French people continued to celebrate under the Second Empire, serving in the French military was in fact no more popular in the 1860s than it had been half a century earlier. Louis Napoléon's demand for better training and arms, expanded reserves, reinforced by an increased military budget, had been voted down. Even before taking office in January 1870 as the new liberal French prime minister and minister of justice, Émile Ollivier had used all his considerable influence and skills of oratory to fight the allocation of any new money for this largely old-fashioned army. By 1870, Prussia had the finest trained army in Central and Western Europe and made little attempt to conceal the possible threat it posed to France, a threat most French politicians chose to ignore. If it came to war, the patriotic French army was invincible. Unlike Premier Ollivier, however, Louis Napoléon Bonaparte had his doubts.

In fact Louis Napoléon was increasingly losing his grip on affairs throughout 1869 and 1870. The few remaining members of the old guard were now startled and troubled by his choice of the republican Émile Ollivier as prime minister in January. This was borne out later in May and June when Ollivier again successfully opposed the emperor's increased military budget and army reserves in the face of growing Prussian military might. "The Budget of the Ministry of War is always under attack by politically motivated deputies with short-term agendas and aims in order to gain public applause," Louis Napoléon argued. "They fail to take into consideration the long-term disruption they cause to our army." As for temporary short-term measures, "they never result in significant budgetary costs. . . . And now faced as we are with the reality of a Germany capable of *mobilizing one million crack troops,* these very politicians talk about reducing our army! Clearly they have learned nothing from the experiences of the past."[3] Instead Ollivier demanded the *reduction* of the army by ten thousand men. He was overwhelmingly supported by Parliament and cousin Jérôme. "At no time has peace ever seemed more assured," Prime Minister Ollivier informed Parliament and the nation. Three weeks later war was declared.

New Year's Eve celebrations at the Tuileries were the quietest since the proclaiming of the Second Empire, and this almost gloomy ambiance deepened when shocking news reached Louis Napoléon on the tenth of January, 1870. Another notoriously troublesome first cousin, Pierre Bonaparte, the son of his late uncle Lucien, had just shot and killed a young man. A French journalist by the name of Victor Noir had arrived on Pierre Bonaparte's doorstep with a colleague, representing

Paschal Grousset, another journalist with the violent anti-Bonapartist paper, *La Revanche*, demanding a retraction of an earlier abusive article by Pierre Bonaparte.[4] An irate Pierre grabbed a pistol and shot the unarmed Noir. No one denied the facts.

The newly installed prime minister–justice minister, Émile Ollivier, personally intervened, ordering the arrest of Pierre Bonaparte, who was locked up in the Conciergerie. The funeral cortège of the left-wing editor Victor Noir, forming at Neuilly on the twelfth of January, promised to be a spectacular occasion, as some 100,000 boisterous left-wing supporters would be led by Auguste Blanqui, Louis Delescluze, and the wildest of them all, the current editor of *La Marseillaise,* Henri Rochefort, who was also a parliamentary deputy. As the Revolution of February 1848 had begun with just such a very angry crowd turning into a political demonstration, this was something the authorities were most anxious to avoid. Thousands of troops were deployed along the route all the way to the Tuileries. Beyond some scuffles, all passed off reasonably well, but Deputy Henri Rochefort subsequently had his immunity withdrawn, and on the seventh of February was sentenced to six months in prison—not for the first time in his life.

Louis Napoléon had no wish to follow in the steps of the July Monarchy and lose his crown as well. On March 27, 1870, the High Court hearing the case against Pierre Bonaparte pronounced him innocent! There was vigorous national and international consternation, as demonstrators marched through all the large cities of the country. Louis Napoléon lost more political support and no doubt privately cursed his wretched relatives. Although personally wishing to see his cousin put away behind bars, unfortunately Pierre's name was Bonaparte, and apart from paying an indemnity to the victim's family, he quite literally got away with murder. But at least the emperor had the right to deport his cousin from France, which he promptly did.[5]

As it was, there was much unrest in France throughout the new year, including two bloody strikes at the Le Creusot ironworks, which were put down through civil procedure, thanks to their influential owner and president of the Corps Législatif, Eugène Schneider, who promptly fired a hundred of the ringleaders.[6] In the meantime, as part of his agreement with Prime Minister Ollivier, Louis Napoléon ordered the official reforms for the 1852 constitution to include additional liberal changes. This he was to cap by a national plebiscite on May 8, 1870, which overwhelmingly approved these reforms—and Louis Napoléon's Second Empire—by more than seven million three hundred thousand ayes, against one and a half million nays.[7] Despite some growing liberal opposition, Louis Napoléon still held overwhelming support, or so it would appear.

For some time there had been rumors from Madrid that General Juan Prim (1814–1870), Spanish prime minister from 1868 to December 1869, had offered the vacant Spanish throne (to replace Queen Isabella II, whom he had earlier deposed) to a German prince, Leopold von Hohenzollern-Sigmaringen. On the second of July, 1870, Louis Napoléon was informed that Prince Leopold had accepted the offer of the Spanish crown. When the official government organ, *Le Journal des Débats*, released this information, there were protests and angry demonstrations in the French capital. War Minister Marshal Edmond Leboeuf did not improve the situation by ranting about this "Prussian insult" before the Assembly.

In fact Bismarck, who had been patiently waiting, month after month, year after year, for the right moment to attack and destroy the French army to gain his vengeance once and for all, was now deliberately taunting France by placing a German on the Spanish throne and a German-controlled Spanish army along the French frontier.

No one could defy history, according to Curzio Malaparte and Leo Tolstoy, and the remorseless momentum toward war continued to build up, day by day, thanks in large part to Prime Minister Ollivier's feckless newly appointed fifty-one-year-old foreign minister, Antoine Alfred Agénor, the Duke de Gramont. Scion of an ancient family, the haughty Agénor de Gramont enjoyed an idle, undisciplined, luxurious childhood that gave way to a long series of youthful affairs and scandals with society women, resulting in several abrupt changes of habitation. After attending the École Polytechnique, Gramont then briefly served in the army until the age of twenty-one, when he turned to a diplomatic career, serving as minister to various German states, Victor Emmanuel's Piedmont, and the Vatican. In May 1870 he was recalled from his last embassy in Vienna to take charge of the Quai d'Orsay.

Given Gramont's wide travel throughout the German states and Europe, and his fluent German and personal familiarity with a dozen German kings and princes, including Prussia's Wilhelm I and Austria's Franz Josef, it might be expected that after twenty-five years' diplomatic experience, Louis Napoléon could rely on this man. What his personnel record did not reveal, however, was a fatuous, self-indulgent, opinionated fossil of the Ancien Régime. This was in fact a man who knew everything and listened to no one, including Prime Minister Ollivier and the Gentleman in the Tuileries. He was thus destined to play a calamitous role in the events to follow in the summer of 1870, even as a much weakened Louis Napoléon faded helplessly into the shadows of his own throne.

Meanwhile, touring the spa of Bad Ems, just south of Coblenz, with his troupe, Jacques Offenbach, appearing in his famous sky blue jacket, bright yellow trousers, and green Italian peacock hat, was invited by King Wilhelm I, also at Ems, to present the composer's one-act light opera *La Chanson de Fortuno* at a special anniversary celebration of the Prussian victory of Sadow on the third of July, to be attended by his guest Tsar Alexander. It was a success and Wilhelm roared with delight, but following that performance, a most uneasy Offenbach departed that resort posthaste.

Back in Paris, international tension continued to grow, and on July 5, 1870, Foreign Minister Gramont complained to British ambassador Lord Lyons of the German "insult," presented by Prince Leopold's candidacy for the Spanish throne . . . "a slap in the face to Louis Napoléon," Jules Hansen called it.[8] The next day he addressed a ministerial statement to the assembly, informing them that if Bismarck's Hohenzollern candidate for the Spanish throne were not withdrawn forthwith, Gramont would know how to defend "French national interests and honor." An emergency cabinet meeting was held in the Tuileries that same day, with War Minister Marshal Edmond Leboeuf personally assuring Louis Napoléon that "the French Army is ready and prepared for anything."[9] Nevertheless Gramont insisted that "the wisdom of the German people would never possibly permit a war to break out between Prussia and France."[10]

That same sixth of July, the Prussian ambassador to the Tuileries, Albrecht Werther, was summoned to Ems for consultations with Wilhelm I. Vincent, Count Benedetti, the French ambassador to Prussia, also at Bad Ems, was personally informed by the seventy-three-year-old Prussian king that he would approve of the withdrawal of the German prince, Leopold, as a candidate if that prince and his father requested it. But the following day, on the seventh of July, Gramont issued new instructions to Benedetti "to insist" on the Prussian king advising Leopold to withdraw. With drunken French mobs clamoring to march on Berlin, the ultra-patriot publisher Émile de Girardin fanned the flames, demanding that the French army drive "the Prussians across the Rhine with the butt of their rifles!" even as the tsar was privately advising "caution and abstention" on the part of the Prussian king.[11]

"If the [Prussian] king will not advise Prince von Hohenzollern to reject the Spanish throne, then it means war," a haughty Gramont pronounced. "I have Bismarck to thank for this wretched state of affairs!" Wilhelm I declared angrily on the eighth after learning that Prince Leopold was changing his mind after talking to Bismarck and would now consider accepting the crown after all. But it was not until two o'clock in the afternoon of the twelfth that Ambassador Benedetti finally received Wilhelm's final response: "The King has consented to give his entire and unreserved approbation to the withdrawal of the Prince of Hohenzollern. He will do nothing beyond that." And independently that afternoon Prince Leopold von Hohenzollern duly sent a dispatch to General Prim in Madrid, formally renouncing the Spanish crown once and for all. "We have what we want—Peace!" a jubilant Prime Minister Émile Ollivier informed the Assembly.[12]

While Paris was celebrating Leopold's renunciation of the Spanish prize, not so the gentlemen at 76 Wilhelmstrasse—the three "vons," Roon, Moltke, and Bismarck (who afterward related the events of that afternoon of the twelfth of July to his son Herbert). Moltke was angry upon learning of the news "because he had just made the journey [to Berlin] for nothing, finding the war he had long planned now slipping away from him. . . . [And] Old Roon was depressed as well. Until now," Bismarck continued in his letter, "I thought I was standing on the verge of the greatest of historical events [his war with France], and instead all I will end up with is the interruption of my spa cure [at Varzin]!" It looks as if there will be "no battlefield promotion for you after all," he informed his son Herbert.[13]

Back in Paris on this twelfth of July, everyone was rejoicing over what the normally phlegmatic François Guizot enthusiastically summed up as "the most superb diplomatic victory I have ever seen. We have got our peace!"[14] Some in Paris, however, were as disappointed as Bismarck in Berlin, including War Minister Edmond LeBoeuf and General Charles Bourbaki, and in particular the by now hysterical foreign minister Agénor de Gramont, who was at an emotional breaking point. Prince Leopold had renounced the throne, but for the overwrought Gramont that did not suffice. Still on edge and under the influence of the emotional Gramont and patriotic Eugénie, and his aggressive war minister Leboeuf calling for blood, Louis Napoléon now made the most dreadful decision of his life. At ten p.m. that evening, he authorized Gramont to instruct French ambassador Benedetti—still in Bad Ems—to submit a final humiliating ultimatum, insisting on "a guarantee" that Wilhelm I renounce the Spanish throne "for all German princes in the future." At midnight the relentless Gramont duly dispatched the fatal telegram to Benedetti at Ems.[15]

When Benedetti attempted to see the Prussian monarch in the Kurgarten at nine a.m. the next morning, the thirteenth of July, to present the Quai d'Orsay's latest demands, however, he was informed by an aide-de-camp that Wilhelm saw no reason for another meeting as he had nothing to add to what he had already said. The king then sent a dispatch to Bismarck instructing him to respond formally to Benedetti. "Let the Ambassador be told through an adjutant that he had now received from the Prince [Leopold] confirmation of which Benedetti had previously received from Paris and therefore had nothing further to say to the Ambassador." For the long-plotting Bismarck, this was "the moment," the opportunity he had been seeking, as he sat down to draft his own edited version of the official Prussian response for the Quai d'Orsay: "His Majesty the King has . . . refused to receive the French Ambassador again and let him know through an adjutant that His Majesty had nothing further to communicate to the Ambassador." France was duly insulted, and the Ems Telegram entered history.[16]

Deliberating at three emergency meetings held at the Tuileries during the course of the fourteenth, a shocked Foreign Minister Gramont, confronted with the rude consequences of his own blunder, now somehow still expected a peaceful solution. He suddenly favored an international congress to act as mediator. A clearly unhappy Louis Napoléon, facing this unanticipated crisis, lost in silent gloom, most definitely wanted to avoid war. By ten o'clock that evening, at the third and final cabinet meeting of the day, after learning of fresh insulting verbal remarks by Bismarck to British ambassador Lord Loftus, a saddened, reluctant, and beaten Napoléon III—with a strong nudging from an arrogantly superior Eugénie at his side—decided on war against Prussia. (She had been indignant at the very idea of a "German king" being foisted upon the Spanish throne.) France had been humiliated and insulted. National honor required it, because of the utterly irresponsible actions of Gramont, and a weak, vacillating Louis Napoléon's acceptance to go along with it. At this point Louis Napoléon could have stepped in from the shadows and overruled everyone and refused to go to war— he alone had the authority to do so—but he lacked the will and character required at the most critical moment of his life. Later that evening of the fourteenth of July, Bastille Day, War Minister Marshal Leboeuf announced the mobilization of the French army.

On the sixteenth, an anguished Wilhelm I, badgered in turn by Bismarck, reluctantly authorized the mobilization of the Prussian army for a war he, too, did not want, but like Louis Napoléon, he lacked the intelligence and moral courage to confront his blustering, warmongering chancellor, not to mention Moltke's army, already sharpening their swords.

Bismarck wanted war, War Minister Roon demanded it, and Moltke would accept nothing less.

On July 19, 1870, Louis Napoléon Bonaparte declared war on Prussia. Otto von Bismarck was a very happy man. "What a stroke of luck it was that the French committed such a folly." They had taken the bait.

36

TO BERLIN!

"This unfortunate man so afflicted with pain, and scarcely able even to cope with the daily affairs of State in peacetime, was now called upon to direct a full-scale war!"[1]
—MAXIME DU CAMP ON NAPOLÉON III

On the warm summer's morning of Friday, July 28, 1870, a sixty-two-year-old Louis Napoléon, with the Imperial Prince, his fourteen-year-old son Louis, both in military uniform, took leave of Empress Eugénie at the small private station at Villeneuve-l'Etang near St. Cloud and boarded the six-car train that would take them and the imperial staff to war. "It is better to die than live without honor," Eugénie afterward wrote her mother, although even Princess Mathilde[2] had implored her that the ailing Napoléon III was hardly fit to take a long journey across France, let alone command an army on a battlefield.

The severe pain caused by the advanced state of his gallstone—his doctors having urgently advised exploratory surgery earlier that month—should have been reason enough for his not assuming personal command of the army. The by now daily problem of incontinence, the total lack of urinary control caused by the pressure of the stone, would be aggravated by a long journey aboard a primitive train and later by hours in jolting carriages and on horseback with the troops. It would also prove most embarrassing for him and his staff. To Eugénie, however, the state of his health was quite irrelevant. He was *the Emperor* and must think of his position! *She* would have been humiliated had he not led his men on the battlefield. "That is the man you are sending to war!"

an appalled Mathilde had said, pointing to her shrunken cousin, who needed the assistance of his son to board the train.[3] As Louis Napoléon himself had explained to the country on the nineteenth, "There are solemn moments in the life of a people when an outraged sense of national honor becomes an irresistible force, overwhelming everyone and ends in dictating the very destinies of the country. Just such a decisive hour has now struck in France."[4]

Although War Minister Marshal Leboeuf had reassured him that the army was "ready for anything," Louis Napoléon had taken nothing for granted and had been negotiating for several months to engage the support of two allies, Austria and Italy. As late as mid-July he had dispatched cousin Prince Jérôme to Florence, the current capital of the newly unified Italy, to seal this critical pact that would provide, at the very least, an armed neutrality including a strong Italian army along her northern frontier, and an Austrian army along the Austro-German border. Moltke would be obliged to divide his forces. Louis Napoléon's foolish hesitation in withdrawing French forces from Rome, as demanded by Victor Emmanuel, had killed any hope of an early Italian signature to such a pact. Austria and Italy instead now decided to wait and observe events as those hostilities broke out before committing themselves.[5]

Louis Napoléon and his staff reached the new railway station at Metz late on the twenty-eighth, where he assumed supreme command of the Army of the Rhine. "Soldiers—I am about to place myself at your head to defend the honor and soil of the country," he told the troops on his arrival, reminding them that "nothing is impossible for the soldiers of Africa, the Crimea, Italy and Mexico." The eyes of France and the world were on them, therefore "let every man do his duty, and the God of battle will be with us." But what Louis Napoléon found upon his arrival at Metz on the twenty-eighth of July, where the main part of the army was forming, came as a shock, even as Bismarck was lambasting the French in the German press for having "deliberately and unjustly provoked this war!"[6]

Louis Napoléon's army today had neither an experienced, capable chief of staff, nor a professional general staff. Nothing had changed since the Crimea, and the foul-ups were now repeated. In a subsequent report Louis Napoléon recorded in the third person what he now found: half of most regiments lacked even basic muskets and munitions, and most of them "had not even been drilled in the use of the new arms," including the excellent Model 1866 chassepot breech-loading rifles. The same applied to the newly manufactured grapeshot machine guns, or Reffye Mitrailleuses, capable of spewing out 100 *balles* a minute.[7] In fact only a few dozen French officers were instructed in the use of the 190 machine guns currently available for the entire French army, and even these few were treated more like rifles for short-range use. As for the much vaunted French artillery, it still remained the same muzzle-loading bronze cannon that had been used at Waterloo in 1815. Moltke, on the other hand, had the faster firing, longer ranged (four miles), far more accurate and destructive new steel 6.6-pound Krupp breech-loading guns.

Although no army could be expected to win a victory over his enemy without a well-prepared war plan, to his dismay Louis Napoléon now found in 1870 that his utterly incompetent Marshal Leboeuf had in fact prepared no such plan. France was going to launch a war and had no precise objective. Louis Napoléon did not know where he was going or what to do—apart from killing Prussians. In fact every phase of French preparation for this new campaign was woefully inadequate, including the missing encampments for the anticipated 400,000 men expected here. Thousands of tents were missing, and as for field kitchens . . .

Unlike Marshal Leboeuf's "general staff," Moltke's had a special deputy staff just to prepare all the railway schedules well in advance of collecting and transporting troops, munitions, and supplies quickly to the French frontier. When Prussian troops arrived, they would find everything in readiness, including well-designated bivouacs and field kitchens. Moreover, Moltke and his senior officers had visited the anticipated battlefields over the preceding months and years, unlike most of the French marshals and senior generals from Algeria, who were totally unfamiliar with the topography of French Alsace and Lorraine, not to mention adjacent southwestern Germany. As for their equipment, Louis Napoléon discovered that everything was "still stacked, chiefly [in the warehouses] at Vernon and Satori," while the army's entire medical supplies were at the Invalides in Paris, but not here.[8] Someone had neglected to ship them. Sending an additional ten thousand troops to Metz, for instance, required enormous provisions of food stores, but nothing had been anticipated, obliging the entire army corps to "live off the land," as Napoléon had done in Russia—multiply this forty-fold, and the campaign before them was an impending disaster waiting to happen. Even staff officers at best had maps dating back to the First Empire, that is, not even indicating the rail network, improved roads, and new canals.

Thus tired, disgruntled troops, thrown together on what trains that could be found at the last minute, arrived at Metz, where nothing was ready for them. Instead of having well-fed men, enthusiastic about advancing into Germany, Marshal LeBoeuf presented a disorganized, unprepared, untrained army, where the demoralized troops' anger was vented not against the enemy, but against their own commanding officers. Men without tents, food, arms, or hope. A general staff straight from Algeria, without even a general campaign or battle plan or accurate, up-to-date maps. Confusion was rife, and hungry recruits and veterans alike turned surly, defiant, and brazenly disobedient. Such was the situation Louis Napoléon encountered at Metz on Friday, the twenty-eighth of July, a fortnight after the orders had been issued to mobilize the French Imperial Army. That day he must have known that the war was lost.

On reaching Metz Louis Napoléon had expected to see the 350,000 troops and 100,000 Gardes Mobiles as announced by War Minister Marshal Leboeuf. Instead he found a total of only 220,000 unorganized, unfed troops, "the most striking and deplorable proof of the failings in our own military organization," he admitted. But this, of course, was superseded by his own even greater personal "failing" in having declared war on Prussia without even having a "war plan" ready to put into execution.

What was the war's objective? To march on Berlin? To remove King Wilhelm I from the throne? To replace Bismarck, Moltke, and the government? To defeat and destroy the Prussian army and occupy Prussia? In fact neither Louis Napoléon, his war minister, nor army commanders had a primary objective. They were angry about Bismarck's political bravado and crude insults, and had responded by declaring war. It was utter madness, irresponsibility at the highest level. And of course then there was the little matter of a nonexistent war plan. Ultimately Louis Napoléon would be mobilizing more than half a million men without knowing what he wanted to do with them.[9]

Marshal Niel's original 1868 "war plan," a nebulous offensive against "Germany," had been set aside by Marshal Leboeuf, replaced with an ill-defined ad hoc defensive campaign, that is, for the army remaining in France to protect the nation from an invasion wherever that happened to occur. How this was to be achieved Leboeuf failed to say, only that close to 500,000 troops would be divided into two forces, the Army of the Rhine, at Metz, and the Army of Alsace, at Strasbourg, while the inexperienced reserves would be called up and ordered to assemble at Châlons-sur-Marne (in Champagne). But to where exactly, to link up with the armies at Metz and Strasbourg? The clamor by the French press—including the Le Gaulois, Le Figaro, La Presse, Le Temps, and Le Siècle[10]—and by an assembly of deputies demanding action, roused by the equally impatient boisterous crowds in the streets of Paris singing the revolutionary "Marseillaise" and "Le Chant des Girodins," and calling for a march on Berlin, had rattled an unprepared Louis Napoléon, forcing him to act, as he quite frankly acknowledged.

As the well-respected insider and homme des lettres Maxime Du Camp now witnessed, even the dovish premier, Ollivier, had overnight become "the bellicose soul incarnate of the Gaul warrior of our ancestors," demanding blood. Indeed "it is in the very nature of the Frenchman to prick up his ears at the first sound of the tambour," Du Camps added, "and to tremble with patriotic fervor when the bugles sound out calling the nation to arms."[11] And when that author, who had just returned from Prussia and seen the extensive war preparations there, expressed his doubts about an inevitable French victory, he was sharply rebuked by the super patriot Premier Ollivier himself, he who had just weeks earlier denied the army an increased budget and reserves. "You really do not love your country!" he said turning on Du Camp. "It is a crime to ever lose faith in your own country! . . . Prussia has already as good as lost the war, why we have only to reach out and take Berlin!"

On the thirty-first of July an impatient commander in chief Napoléon III ordered an unplanned attack from Metz across the German frontier at Saarbrücken. There on the second of August General Frossard's II Corps and Marshal Bazaine's III Corps easily overran the Prussian 40th Regiment (of the 16th Division). Total casualties: eighty-six French, against eighty-three Prussian. France had won its first "battle" of the war and, as it turned out, its last. "Seizing the offensive our army crossed the frontier and invaded Prussian territory," Louis Napoléon proudly telegraphed Eugénie. "Louis has just come under his baptism of fire, and has kept a musket ball as a souvenir . . . he was remarkably calm throughout the fighting."[12]

Paris was ecstatic.

Like Uncle Napoléon before him, Louis Napoléon had no permanent intelligence staff, relying instead on a few occasional advance patrols. There were no secret agents or paid informers in the Prussian camp, with the Prussian general staff, or even in the towns along their route. Thus rumors replaced serious intelligence reports. "The Prussians are coming!" was repeated, though no one had any idea exactly what force the combined Prussian North German Confederation or Bavarian armies actually had in the field or when and where they would reach the French frontier.

In fact three Prussian armies were closing in on northeastern France: Field Marshal Karl von Steinmetz's First Army of 50,000 men around Saarlouis and Saarbrücken, Prince Friedrich Karl's Second Army, 134,000 strong, around Forbach and Spicheren, and Crown Prince

Friedrich's Third Army of 120,000 descending on Wissembourg. There were also vague reports of a Bavarian force moving in from the southeast.

Meanwhile Louis Napoléon, in a great deal of pain from traveling over rough country roads, was in no state to lead anyone. Attempting to mount a horse, he nearly fainted and had to be helped into a carriage. With reports now coming in of heavy Prussian troop concentrations at Saarlouis, instead of driving ahead or digging in to prepare for the enemy while waiting for supplies, artillery, and reinforcements, it was decided to withdraw from Saarbrücken and retreat, but to where? They had no plans. After the first day's fight, the French had suddenly lost any incentive to launch an offensive. No French army would be crossing into Germany during this war. Mentally the French had already surrendered. The army had men and guns, but it did not have leadership.

Louis Napoléon wrote Prime Minister Émile Ollivier that he had already given up any idea of a quick, short campaign like that fought earlier in Italy with Victor Emmanuel. "We must be prepared for a long war, since it is quite impossible to end it with one big knockout blow," and, as he had warned his troops at the outset, "this is going to be a long and difficult war." Uncle Napoléon had had his ill-conceived, indeed catastrophic, Egyptian, Spanish, and Russian campaigns, and Louis Napoléon now had one of his own in 1870.[13]

On the fourth of August, General Douay's division at Wissembourg, part of a screening operation by Marshal MacMahon's I Corps to intercept the advancing Prussians from the northeast, was attacked and defeated by units of one Bavarian and two Prussian corps of Crown Prince Friedrich's powerful Third Army. Easily overwhelming the much smaller French force in a brief if fierce firefight in which General Abel Douay, the divisional commander, was killed, the French abandoned Wissembourg abruptly, after suffering 1,000 casualties. This was to prove to be but the first in a long series of French defeats and retreats. MacMahon's retreating corps were next defeated by the Prussians on the sixth of August between Wörth and Froeschwiller, while General Frossard was attacked and defeated with a smaller force at Spichern (near Forbach). In a matter of days the incompetent MacMahon abandoned this entire northern part of Alsace, and at the end of September came the dramatic loss of Strasbourg, where another French soldier would not be seen in the streets again until nearly half a century later during the First World War. The enormity of this tragedy in progress was just beginning to be felt in Paris.

Moltke's armies were now driving westward into Lorraine, as most of the French Army of the Rhine fell back to a very crowded and chaotic Metz, amid serious talk of a further withdrawal of the entire French army to Châlons-sur-Marne in order to protect Paris. All this less than a week after the first fighting had begun. At Metz on the seventh of August, most general officers refused to retreat any farther, however, while in Paris Eugénie as regent was convening a series of emergency privy council meetings with equally disastrous results. That same day War Minister Leboeuf offered to resign, and a dejected Louis Napoléon, feeling utterly useless, sent a telegram to Eugénie stating his intention of returning to the French capital. "Have you considered the consequences that would result from your returning to Paris with two defeats behind you!" Eugénie responded angrily. Louis Napoléon remained with the army.[14]

What he did not tell his wife, however, was just what a weak, depressed, and even suicidal state he was in. Earlier he had deliberately and repeatedly exposed himself to intensive Prussian fire, one of his aides-de-camp killed at his side and two others wounded, while he emerged without a scratch. His stone caused him such severe pain at times he nearly collapsed, as one member of his staff witnessed. "His face was ashen and he was doubled over in pain. The least jolting by his carriage would make him groan. He could only sit a horse at the cost of agonizing stabs of pain. On one occasion . . . he stopped, leaning his head against a tree, he so terribly tortured by the spasms of his bladder," and even during meals he could be seen "shivering uncontrollably by the pain." Twice a day "his surgeon tormented him with a catheter, as he could no longer urinate."[15] Louis Napoléon desperately wanted to die, but none of this was related to the empress in Paris, who simply condemned him as a coward. In the meantime he had sent his son Prince Louis to Belgium and on to the safety of an English exile.

• • •

All the while, however, Louis Napoléon continued to add to his long list of poor military judgments by now appointing the disastrous François Achille Bazaine, late of Mexico, to take command of the Army of the Rhine at Metz. He was the son of General Pierre Bazaine, one of Napoléon I's favorite officers, but unlike his father he had washed out of the École Polytechnique. Thus began Bazaine's slow career to the top, enrolling as a private and finally achieving a commission in Algeria in 1833, where he then spent many years. After briefly being seconded to Queen Christine's Spanish army for a couple of years, Bazaine returned to Algeria, where in 1851 he was given command of the French Foreign Legion, followed by an unhappy marriage to a Spanish woman the following year. Next serving in Mexico, he had undermined Maximilian's rule and lost battles. Astonishingly, Louis Napoléon awarded him a marshal's baton in 1864, after which that soldier had served in both the Crimea and the campaign for Italian independence.

Bazaine duly assumed command of the Army of the Rhine on August 13, 1870, while yet another incompetent Algerian soldier, MacMahon, attempted to link up with the Army of Châlons, of which he had just been given command. "On the morning of the 14th the retreat began," Louis Napoléon, an eyewitness to these events, explained, as they too headed west toward Verdun. But they were then "compelled to evacuate their quarters without warning," he continued, as they came under direct enemy fire on the fifteenth "with part of the army at Gravelotte." Cut off from all communication with Paris, however, it became imperative as head of state that the emperor get to Châlons as quickly as possible. Setting out at four o'clock on the morning of the sixteenth with an escort of two regiments of the Imperial Guard, Louis Napoléon reached Châlons later that evening.[16]

There the French emperor and MacMahon found Prince Jérôme, Eugène Rouher, and General Louis Trochu, as they discussed the situation in a war council. Back in Paris, betraying Napoléon III, Jules Favres and Leon Gambetta were actively fomenting a political revolution to overthrow the French government. The army had to act decisively against the Prussians if the Second Empire were to survive. Plon-Plon chaired the meeting and gave the orders, while a confused Louis Napoléon looked on. Jérôme insisted on General Trochu assuming command as military governor of Paris, and a dazed Louis Napoléon acquiesced as usual. Eugénie had convoked the Legislative Body in his absence and illegally removed Ollivier as prime minister, replacing him with Count de Palikao, General Charles Cousin-Montauban, who took over the portfolios as prime minister and minister for war.[17] Moral authority no longer lodged with the army facing the Prussians; it had returned to the capital, as Louis Napoléon acknowledged. Action was required.

Marshal MacMahon was now given command of the entire French army, and a resigned Louis Napoléon, a broken man, agreed to follow it "whatever its destination might be," as he put it. Crippled by pain, depression, and foreboding, Napoléon III was no longer in control of the government and events in Paris, or of his own army in the field. Indeed he only got through each day thanks to the attentions of Henri Conneau. At this moment, in effect, no one ruled France. As Louis Napoléon put it in the third person, he had been "shorn of the rights he held from the nation. . . . and watched as his army marched into an abyss before his very eyes!" He found himself "the powerless witness of a hopeless struggle," and felt his "life and death to be quite irrelevant now," as MacMahon directed the new Army of Châlons to link up with Bazaine's Army of the Rhine, still at Metz.[18]

Back on the sixteenth, Bazaine had ordered Marshal François Canrobert's VI Corps to reconnoiter the road between Metz and Verdun, which he found already partly occupied by the Prussians. Following a brisk skirmish at Mars-la-Tours that same day, Canrobert withdrew his veteran VI Corps to a stronger position between the forts of St. Quentin and Rozerieulles and St. Privat La Montagne (near Gravelottes), six miles from Metz. In good health at the age of fifty-nine, but looking ten years older with his massive head of thinning gray hair, the marshal took the high ground behind St. Privat, where he ordered his infantry and artillery—120,000 men—to dig in. On the eighteenth the Prussians, now at neighboring Gravelottes, moved in following Moltke's plan for a co-ordinated pincer attack by Field Marshal Karl von Steinmetz's First Army of some 50,000 and Prince Friedrich Karl's Second Army of nearly 134,000 against Canrobert at St. Privat La Montagne.

Steinmetz, whose family had also fallen victim to Napoléon's marauding Grand Army during the First Empire, had no more love of the French than did Bismarck himself, and now this gruff, impatient seventy-four-year-old soldier, disregarding Moltke's order of battle, was determined to take matters into his own hands. Revenge has no age. At noon on the eighteenth of August, Steinmetz's Krupp guns opened fire on Marshal Canrobert's VI Corps who were well dug in on the wooded heights of St. Privat. Two and a half hours later, the Prussian commander launched his 50,000 men in a full-scale attack, which Canrobert's single corps nevertheless twice successfully repulsed, forcing Marshal von Steinmetz's much bloodied First Army to withdraw from the battlefield with very heavy casualties. The long dormant spirit of the Grand Army briefly flickered after an absence of five and a half decades.

Unlike the other Algerian veterans, Canrobert was now in his element, and he dispatched an aide-de-camp the six miles to Metz for urgent reinforcements and munitions from Marshal Bazaine. Considering the battle hopeless, however, Bazaine ignored the plea of a colleague in arms for help, refusing to send a single unit of his 100,000-man army, an army that could possibly have made the difference. Meanwhile Prince Friedrich Karl's Second Army, 134,000 strong, reached St. Privat, replacing the routed Steinmetz on the battlefield. Short on food and munitions, exhausted after hours of fighting, and vastly outnumbered and outgunned, Canrobert nevertheless held his ground amid the burning buildings of that village. But as dusk settled after ten o'clock that evening, the guns of both sides gradually fell silent. Although still in place, the following morning, the nineteenth, Canrobert, now greatly outnumbered by a vastly superior force, and abandoned by a cowardly and incompetent Bazaine, had no choice but to fall back to Metz, and to a commanding officer he utterly despised. In this battle he had lost 12,175 killed and wounded, the Prussians 20,163. Completely surrounded by Moltke's armies, Bazaine, after failing to cut a deal for himself with the

Prussians, was to surrender Metz and his Army of the Rhine to them at the end of October. There would be a place in the Invalides reserved for the brave Canrobert, but only a prison cell for Bazaine.[19]

In the meantime, far to the west, Marshal MacMahon—this soldier who as governor general of Algeria had denounced Napoléon III and his recommendations for that colony in 1865—now in full command, like Canrobert earlier, found the road between Verdun and Metz still closed by the Prussians. MacMahon instead moved to the northeast via Reims, still hoping to link up with Bazaine. "I am bound to say—for justice demands it . . . that I and I alone ordered the movement [of the Army of Châlons] in the direction of Metz," the sixty-two-year-old Patrice de MacMahon later stated for the historical record. (Louis Napoléon had privately been against it.) By the thirtieth of August, they found themselves on the heights of Mouzon with the twelfth corps, where they heard the distant guns of General de Failly. Units of the French army having been defeated at Beaumont on the thirtieth of August, MacMahon was intent on getting most of his Army of Châlons—120,000 strong—across to the right bank of the River Meuse.

MacMahon had wanted a by now physically disabled Napoléon III to proceed first to the safety of Carignan where V Corps had, he hoped, secured that village and established new general headquarters. Less than an hour later, however, General Ducrot suddenly arrived from there with news that the V Corps had been routed and was falling back helter-skelter to their position here at Mouzon. MacMahon decided to seek temporary shelter at Sedan, just six miles or so south of the Belgian frontier. Leaving his horses, carriages, and strong military escort of Guides behind, Louis Napoléon took the short train journey from Carignan to Sedan.[20]

Founded in the tenth century, Sedan by 1870 had a prosperous population of 14,000, protected beneath a towering rocky outcrop on which stood Vauban's sprawling seventeenth-century fortified castle. In theory the place was well protected, with the hills to the north and east covered by an ancient, impenetrable forest of the Ardennes stretching all the way up into Belgium. To the west, the Meuse looped around Igey, forming a narrow peninsula. To the south Sedan and its citadel overlooked the River Meuse, whose swampy banks were of little use to infantry or cavalry, and moreover there was only one bridge from Donchery crossing the river directly before the entrance to Sedan. A few kilometers to the east, the only other bridge, built for the new Remilly-Aillicourt railway, crossed the Meuse at a point leading to the village of Bazeilles on the right bank. A panicked MacMahon rushed his disorganized army forward in some confusion, with two Prussian armies close on his heels. In his haste that French commander neglected the obvious, to have those two critical bridges blown up, and the Prussians would soon be streaming across them. If Sedan looked like a temporary staging or regrouping point before escaping to Mézières eighteen kilometers to the west, it was also immediately apparent that if bottled up here by the Germans, the entire army would be completely isolated, with no escape possible. The thoroughly incompetent MacMahon had failed to take that into consideration as well.

Opposing the French, Helmut von Moltke now personally took command of the III and IV Armies, some 200,000 troops and 774 pieces of artillery, as opposed to MacMahon's paper strength of 120,000 men and 564 muzzle-loading guns. Having completely separated MacMahon's Army of Châlons from Marshal Bazaine's Army of the Rhine, surrounded by the Prussians at Metz some 150 kilometers (93 miles) away, Moltke now had MacMahon precisely where he wanted him, though he was unaware of the presence of Louis Napoléon here.

At four o'clock on the morning of the first of September, Bavarian units of the III Army began pouring over the railway bridge into the village of Bazeilles. MacMahon himself was one of the first victims, wounded near Balan two hours later while observing the fighting at nearby Bazeilles. He was briefly replaced by General Ducrot, before General Emmanuel Wimpffen now arrived to take over full command and cancel any orders for a retreat to the west. The Army of Châlons would stand and fight. Meanwhile, behind the massive stone walls of the citadel French artillery was in place, along with troops behind it forming a large circular perimeter facing Illy to the immediate north, Givonne to the east, Glaire to the west, and Floing to the north and northwest. To the northwest Prussia's Wilhelm I and Field Marshal von Moltke, now joined by Bismarck from Berlin, established their general headquarters on a hill near the village of Frénois. Given this unique terrain, there was no large area either for the deployment of cavalry or large infantry formations except on the plateau before Illy. Geography dictated the parameters of battle.

The earliest and most persistent fighting continued in and around the by now much battered Bazeilles, where the Bavarians and a unit of the French marines fought back-and-forth in hand-to-hand battle to hold this village of a few hundred. By two o'clock there was also heavy fighting behind the fortress on the Plateau of Illy and at Floing, where General Jean Margueritte three times charged the Prussians with his Algerian Chasseurs, before being cut down. South of Sedan, the Prussian Third and Fourth Armies were continuing to cross the main Donchery bridge leading to the city center of Sedan. Any escape to Mézières and the west was quite impossible by now, as was flight to the north to Belgium. Thousands of MacMahon's untrained reserve troops now fled the shelling of the plateau in complete confusion, pouring into the streets of Sedan below. There, congestion brought any real movement to a halt as horses, alive and dead, hundreds of carts, guns, caissons, and troops attempted to flee Moltke's mortars and batteries of lethal Krupp artillery.

Louis Napoléon watched helplessly in Sedan, as a baffled MacMahon advanced from chaos to final disaster. Completely cut off from all sides and all directions, amid raining shells and now house-to-house fighting, and with major fires raging in various parts of Sedan, the French emperor described the situation before him. The troops, "having fought for twelve hours without rest or food," were completely discouraged and "all those who had not been able to reach the town were now massed in the trenches and against the walls. . . . The time had come, a decision had to be made," he explained. When there now remained the inevitable "death facing the remaining 80,0000 men," as their sovereign "he could not let them be massacred under his very eyes." Hemmed in on all sides, being pounded by a vastly superior artillery, their situation was hopeless. "The citadel as well as the streets [of Sedan] were gorged with soldiers who had taken refuge there," but General Wimpffen failed to answer Louis Napoléon's call for the hoisting of a white flag. Therefore, continuing his narrative in the third person, "the Emperor assumed the responsibility for raising the flag of truce." He knew full well that he would later be accused by his critics for this action, but his only concern was for saving lives. Wimpffen immediately tendered his resignation; Louis Napoléon rejected it, reminding him "not to desert his post under these critical circumstances." Louis Napoléon then sent a message to the Prussian king, Wilhelm I, "by which he placed his sword in his hands." In fact until this point the Prussians had still been quite unaware of the presence of Napoléon III at Sedan.

"On the morning of September 2 Napoléon III"—he continued in the third person—"attended by the Prince de la Moskowa," Marshal Ney's son, along with Henri Conneau, "entered a carriage drawn by two horses to drive to the Prussian lines," where General André Reille had been dispatched to notify Bismarck of his arrival. "As the portcullis of the south [Torcy] gate of Sedan was lowered [behind him], the [Algerian] zouaves saluted him with the cry of 'Vive l'Empereur!' " When just a few miles from Donchery, "the Emperor stopped at a little roadside house there to await the arrival of the Chancellor." Bismarck arrived shortly thereafter, stating that Moltke alone was empowered to answer any questions. Louis Napoléon explained he was there in his personal capacity, not as the ruler of France; he could surrender himself and the Army of Châlons, but not France. Only the regent, the ministers, and the chamber in Paris could open peace negotiations, he stated. When Field Marshal Moltke then arrived, Louis Napoléon insisted on speaking directly to Wilhelm I and no one else.

"A few minutes later the King of Prussia arrived on horseback, accompanied by the Prince Royal and a few officers." The cordiality of their last meeting three years earlier, when Wilhelm was Louis Napoléon's guest during his state visit to the Universal Exhibition in Paris, was effaced by the present circumstances. The king demanded an immediate cessation of all fighting, and "declared it was impossible to afford more favorable conditions to his army." The entire Army of Châlons now surrendered, nearly 90,000 men remaining, along with Marshal MacMahon and more than thirty general officers, including Wimpffen and Ducrot. Louis Napoléon was informed that he was to be imprisoned at the palace of Wilhelmshöhe, near Cassel. "Then the Prince Royal advanced and shook him affectionately by the hand and in a quarter of an hour the King retired," prisoner-of-war Louis Napoléon related before being placed under a strong Prussian military escort for the long journey to the northeast and Wilhelmshöhe. For Napoléon III the war was over on this second day of September 1870.[21] He would never again see France. The cost of this one-day battle at Sedan: 17,000 French killed or wounded, opposed to 8,300 for the Prussians. With the loss of this last free French army and Bazaine refusing to fight, the road to Paris was wide open.

37

"WERE YOU AT SEDAN, HENRI?"

"We weren't cowards at Sedan, were we?"[1]
—A DYING LOUIS NAPOLÉON TO HENRI CONNEAU,
JANUARY 9, 1873

*"I think France is quite ungovernable unless her
vanity and self-love are satisfied."*[2]
—EUGÉNIE TO HER MOTHER, DOÑA MARÍA MANUELA

S he was pale and looked terrible, her eyes were hard, gleaming with anger, her face distorted by emotion," is how Augustin Filon, the young Prince Louis's tutor, described Empress Eugénie and the events breaking at the Tuileries late in the afternoon of the second of September, 1870. "Do you know what they are saying?" she said, handing a telegram to Filon and her private secretary, Eugène Conti, "That the Emperor has surrendered [at Sedan], that he has capitulated! Surely you don't believe it?" Clearly in a state of shock from this news that Interior Minister Henri Chevereau had just given her moments earlier, and hardly in control of herself, she angrily burst out, "Why didn't he kill himself! . . . Didn't he realize he was disgracing himself? What a name to leave to his son!" "We remained there speechless and stunned," after this veritable "torrent of mad, incoherent words," Filon recalled.[3] This sudden outbreak of war, Louis Napoléon insisting on commanding an army when he was crippled by so many maladies, and now followed by days without any news of him whatsoever; Eugénie was beside herself, and for the first time since declaring the empire, Louis Napoléon had left no reliable official to advise her. Since mid-August quite literally no one had been governing France.

Despite loud protests and even serious threats against the empire and Louis Napoléon, Eugénie, as regent in her husband's absence, defied them all. "I am quite prepared to face any danger," she insisted. "My one personal concern is to fulfill all my duties [and] . . . not to desert my post."[4] By Sunday the fourth of September, however, the Tuileries was surrounded by a raging mob of some 200,000 men and women from the St.-Antoine slums, hurling abuse as they attempted to break through the heavy wrought-iron gates before the palace. It was no longer a matter of directing the affairs of state, or even of remaining there.

Eugénie found herself a veritable prisoner. Long a fan and admirer of Queen Marie-Antoinette, the empress feared sharing the same fate as that beautiful young queen, beneath the blade of a guillotine. Nevertheless, even at this desperate hour, Eugénie refused to permit the handful of remaining troops to fire on the threatening masses. "I would prefer the dynasty to perish rather than lose a single French life," she told General Mellinet, who was in charge of the dwindling palace security. "I wasn't frightened of dying," she later explained, but "what did frighten me was falling into the hands of those thugs," who would defile her in a crude death, and "I could already imagine them lifting up my skirts and hear their savage laughter."[5]

By now, on this sweltering September Sunday, Eugénie having been abandoned even by her devoted ladies-in-waiting, it became clear that there was no choice left but flight. Apart from Admiral Jurien de la Gravière and Henri Conneau's son, Eugène, only Austria's ambassador, Richard von Metternich, and the Italian ambassador, Constantin Nigra, remained with her. The French had abandoned her. Nigra, braving the pressing crowd, finally hailed a passing cab in the Rue de Rivoli. A young hooligan lunged out to grab Eugénie, but was held back by the two diplomats as she and Mme. Lebreton-Bourbaki, her reader, friend, and sister of General Charles Bourbaki, narrowly escaped in the hired open one-horse fiacre.[6]

Leaving with neither money nor jewels and only the black dress and veil she was wearing, Eugénie was never to see her entire life's possessions

and the Tuileries again. After driving in vain for hours seeking the protection of friends, late that afternoon the two by now utterly desperate
ladies finally reached the mansion of Louis Napoléon's American
dentist and personal friend, Thomas Evans, in Haussmann's recently
constructed Avenue de l'Impératrice (today's Avenue Foch), near the Arc
de Triomphe. Intending to avoid the obvious ports of Calais and Boulogne, setting out before dawn in Evans's closed landau the following
morning, Monday the fifth, they safely reached the late Auguste de
Morny's recently built coastal resort of Deauville the afternoon of the
sixth. Evans, attended by his nephew, approached Sir John Burgoyne, a
former officer of the Grenadier Guards, and the owner of a splendid English yacht in that small harbor, the sixty-foot *Gazelle,* to ask for his
services in secreting the empress to England. More Flashman than
Guardsman, he refused outright. In fact a powerful gale was churning
the channel into a sailor's nightmare, with most fishing smacks seeking
a lee shore. In any event, the gallant Sir John was not about to risk a
French prison or worse for a French woman, not even for an empress.
Fortunately, Burgoyne's wife was able to overrule him. Late that night
the two ladies and Evans were whisked aboard the yacht. Storm or no,
and despite a foundering ship of the Royal Navy, the *Gazelle* braved the
worst, reaching Rye at four a.m. on Thursday the eighth.[7]

By the end of the month the plump, ever resourceful American
Evans had found and rented the small Georgian mansion of Camden
Place, in Chislehurst, Kent, just a few miles southeast of London. There
mother and son were gratefully united after weeks of separation. She
was also now joined by Augustin Filon, the palace butler, the maître
d'hôtel, and the principal chef of the Tuileries. Her immediate aim was
to see her fourteen-year-old son, Louis, enrolled in the British army at
Woolwich Barracks, and to prepare Camden Place for her husband upon
his release by the Prussians.[8] It proved to be a longer wait than expected.

This period of anxiety, pending the arrival of the prisoner's first letters,
provided time for thought, and in the case of Eugénie, time for a reassess-
ment of her marriage. And it is to her credit that after her terrible, angry
Latin explosion, including a scathing condemnation of Louis Napoléon,
she now felt remorse, pity, and the need for reconciliation. Her letters

from Chislehurst were to reflect a renewed concern and sense of compassion for a man who had in his personal relations so egregiously betrayed and alienated her over the years. It was not simply the failure of the war that drew her anger, but his years of abandonment, the acute pain and humiliation he had inflicted on her through his incessant, ill-concealed series of affairs and trysts. With a surprisingly rapid change of attitude, she now looked eagerly for her wayward husband's arrival when they could spend their final years together peacefully in this English exile.

There was always in Eugénie two persons, the gracious empress and the Spaniard, the one feminine and compassionate, the other the hardened, disciplined daughter of her father, a grandee of the Spanish aristocracy, a proud, distinguished, and courageous soldier. Then when, by the third week of August, Louis Napoléon, too weak and in too much pain even to sit a horse, no longer capable of providing even the symbolic leadership the army so desperately needed, had written to Eugénie pleading to be allowed to return to Paris, the "Spanish" side of her had replied like a thunderbolt, "ordering him" to remain with the Army of Châlons. "If you return now it won't be just rocks the people will be hurling at you in the streets, but dung!" Augustin Filon, still at the Tuileries as her son's tutor, was appalled. But she had been outraged, for *an emperor* to abandon his own army in the field, to surrender in mid-battle. To Eugénie it was simply inconceivable. He might not be able to appear on horseback, or even be able to stand up, but at least he would be present on the battlefield. "Don't you realize . . . he is doomed if we don't stop him [from returning here]!" she had screamed hysterically at a bewildered Filon.[9]

On the fifth of September Louis Napoléon reached the splendid château of Wilhelmshöhe, where he would remain in gilded bondage until March 19, 1871. Here, along with an entourage of fourteen, including his oldest and dearest companion, Henri Conneau, and his other doctor, Adolphe Corvisart, his young Corsican private secretary, Franceschini Piétri, Achille Murat, and five captured generals—Castelnau, Ney, Reille, Pajol, and Waubert de Genlis—and equerries, they settled in for the duration.[10] Louis Napoléon was assigned a suite of six elegant rooms and extensive use of the enormous park, gardens, and wood. The thoughtful Prussian queen, Augusta, sent servants and her own chef from the palace in Potsdam. It was ironic that Wilhelmshöhe, near Cassel, had been chosen as Louis Napoléon's "prison," as it was the former palace (then called Napoleonshöhe) of his late uncle Jérôme Bonaparte, the father of Plon-Plon, when King of Westphalia, from which Jérôme had fled decades earlier against Napoleon's orders at the approach of allied troops.

Louis Napoléon, who had been prostrate on his arrival, gained strength slowly, while automatically falling into exactly the same routine he had followed as a prisoner at Ham in the 1840s, rising early and spending most of each day closed up in his study with his secretary, books, and papers. The defeated emperor had three primary preoccupations here: the developments of the war and tentative peace negotiations, the volatile political situation in Paris, and his son and Eugénie. The relations between himself and his wife over the past few years had deteriorated considerably, they each going their own way. The only thing bringing them together were their public obligations and an abiding love of their much cherished son, Imperial Prince Louis, or the Comte de Pierrefond, as he was now officially known in exile. Tragedy frequently heals divisions and brings families together, and it was with great trepidation that in the third week of September Louis Napoléon opened his wife's first letters from England.

Nothing remains of the imperial grandeur of the past, nothing separates us any longer," a calm, resigned Eugénie now wrote. "Instead we are reunited closer than ever by our sufferings and our hopes, all concentrated on our dear little Louis. The darker the future appears, the greater our need for mutual love and support." Enormously relieved, but never an eloquent man himself when it came to expressing deep personal emotion, Louis Napoléon gratefully thanked Eugénie for "the tender expression of these letters, which have done me *so much good*," simple emotions he had not written or expressed since the death of his mother, Hortense, more than two decades earlier. The barrier of acrimony and distrust of the past few years was broken. There would never again be a harsh word spoken between them.[11]

A much reassured Louis Napoléon buried himself in his study from morning to night with his young secretary, Franceschini Piétri, to help him with his documents and books. Above all Louis Napoléon was intent on setting down all aspects of the historical record of this war of 1870, a project he would continue later in England.[12] Once again he and Henri Conneau dined together, and those long, uneventful evenings in the salon, often with Corvisart, Piétri, and his cousin, Achille Murat, the son of Joachim and Caroline (Bonaparte). Occasionally the generals, now discarding their military uniforms, also participated. The army, once the center of Louis Napoléon's existence, no longer held the same attraction or garnered the same admiration. Following lunch he would take a short walk through the lovely gardens, the long rides and hunts of the past, just memories.

Louis Napoléon was allowed visitors, including the loyal Hortense Cornu, Lord Malmesbury from England, his faithful friend Count Francesco Arese coming all the way from Milan, and the Duchess of Hamilton, the daughter of his favorite cousin, Stéphanie de Baden. The most important visitor of all, however, was Eugénie, who arrived on the thirtieth of October for just three days. Their reunion was complete; she remained dutifully devoted to him till the day he died. But he did decline her offer to share his internment there. Bismarck for his part quite naturally rejected Louis Napoléon's request to have units of his own Imperial Guard brought there. On the other hand, rather surprisingly, he was allowed to invite several of his marshals here, Patrice de Mac-Mahon alone declining that honor. Apparently Bismarck did not fear a new plot by Napoléon III. A German journalist, Mels Cohen, interviewed the French emperor several times, who talked freely on every aspect of the war, international affairs, and his life as a prisoner of the Prussians.[13]

Louis Napoléon remained greatly preoccupied with the continuing current campaigns of the war and Bismarck's subsequent terms for a peace agreement. He followed the news of the daily events of both the war and Parisian politics through the French, Italian, German, and English newspapers placed at his disposal. General Louis Trochu, the commanding general protecting Paris, Plon-Plon's appointment assigned to protect Eugénie, had immediately abandoned her without so much as a by-your-leave to join Jules Favre and Léon Gambetta in their coup d'état on the fourth of September, when they took over the Hôtel de Ville. From Prefect Haussmann's old office they announced the demise of Napoléon's Second Empire and the creation of "a republic," to be ruled by the new Government of National Defense, with none other than this selfsame Major General Louis Jules Trochu as its president.

Paris was an armed camp with ample army supplies, and some 2,000 pieces of artillery placed atop Montmartre and Belleville. But Trochu was as devious a politician as he was incompetent a soldier. An intensive German bombardment of Paris began in January 1871, and by the eighteenth of that month Prussia's victorious King Wilhelm I, now installed at Versailles, at long last pronounced himself emperor, kaiser, of "Germany." Bismarck had achieved the unification of the German states, including Bavaria. On the twenty-eighth of January, Adolphe Thiers (who finally joined the government) and Jules Favre signed an armistice with Bismarck and nominally surrendered Paris and France. In February, Thiers became Head of the Government of National Defense (and president of the republic that August).

With the signing of the armistice, when Prussia's Wilhelm I planned to send in hundreds of cartloads of food for the people of the French capital now cut off from the rest of the country, the mercurial Bismarck exploded in an "outburst of rage." "Count Bismarck has won for himself the reputation of being the instigator of all the cruel reprisals we have, alas, been forced to carry out," a frustrated Prussian crown prince confided to a friend. "They even say that he intends to establish a reign of terror in Paris!"[14] On the first of March of 1871, Kaiser Wilhelm I, Bismarck, Moltke, and the Prussian army concluded their victory celebrations with a grand parade of 30,000 meticulously turned-out troops down the Champs-Élysées to the Arc de Triomphe. The humiliated French were literally in tears. On their return to Berlin, a similar victory parade was held at the Brandenburg Gate.

Even as the newly elected French government convened in Bordeaux on the twenty-sixth of March, the people of Paris, who had rejected any armistice or talk of peace, formed a government of their own, the Commune, fighting the French army, while the Prussians looked on in astonishment. This Commune, begun on the eighteenth of March, was suppressed on the twenty-eighth of May, 1871, but only after fierce fighting between the Communards and the French army, not to mention the path of destruction those Communards left behind, including the burnt-out Palace of St. Cloud (shelled earlier by French guns) and the deliberate arson attacks by drunken working-class men and women, who looted and burned the Tuileries, the Imperial Library of the Louvre, the Palais de Justice, part of the Palais Royal, the Palais de la Légion d'Honneur, the Hôtel de Ville, the Théâtre Lyrique, and the Théâtre Porte Saint-Martin, while seriously damaging the Odéon, Le Châtelet, the Théâtre de Cluny and the Bataclan, and dozens of businesses and other buildings, private and public, in the heart of the French capital.

And then came the shocking results of the war's battles: over 281,000 French dead and wounded, exclusive of 474,414 French prisoners of war—*138,871 French coffins.* The Germans had suffered 116,696 casualties. Perhaps another 25,000 French were civilians killed or starved during the Commune of 1871. Bismarck should have been a very happy man.[15]

M eanwhile Louis Napoléon, who was gradually recuperating but still suffering from the gallstone that was to lead to his death, watched events helplessly from Uncle Jérôme's study and the enervating peaceful isolation of Wilhelmshöhe. Back in France on February 8, 1871, French national elections took place, the people unanimously overthrowing Napoléon III and his dynasty. Only the French would hold national elections while in a state of war and surrounded by hundreds of thousands of German soldiers. Of the 650 new deputies elected to the assembly, a mere twenty represented the Bonapartists. It was all Louis Napoléon's fault, the new assembly declared. Of course no one knew then or indeed for many decades to come that Bismarck, von Roon, and von Moltke had for the past eight years been planning to take this revenge on France, regardless of the country's leader. The extent of the sweeping Prussian success across the battlefields of 1870, however, took the French completely by surprise, as Maxime Du Camp discovered upon returning to Paris.

I saw that to contest the position any longer would be futile, an act of desperation," Louis Napoléon later reflected. "The honor of the army having been saved by the bravery already demonstrated, I exercised my sovereign right and gave orders to hoist a flag of truce. I claim the entire responsibility for that act. The further destruction of another 80,000 men [of the Army of Châlons] could not have saved France. . . . My heart was broken, but my conscience was clear.[16]. . . Now that the struggle is suspended, that the capital, in spite of a heroic resistance has fallen, and with it all hope of a national victory has vanished, it is time for everyone to demand an accounting from those who have usurped power from us in September."[17]

He remained optimistic, however, and felt that the impressive endorsement by universal suffrage that had placed him on the throne would soon restore that empire and a place for his son. On the other hand, he was never under any illusions. "Power is a heavy burden," he acknowledged, "because one cannot always succeed in doing everything one hopes to achieve for the people, and because your peers rarely acknowledge or appreciate what you are attempting to accomplish on their behalf."[18]

The final months at Wilhelmshöhe did at least assure Louis Napoléon of a warm welcome in England upon his release. "You and Louis mean everything to me," Eugénie wrote. "You take the place of family and country for me." But the brilliance of their past and court life meant nothing to her, she insisted. "For us simply to be together now, that is all I wish for, my poor *cher ami*." She wanted to share the much-welcomed new peaceful refuge with him. "What matters above all else now is seeing you again," a contrite Eugénie wrote from her new home at Camden Place. "These long days are so difficult for me, too. . . . And I am quite sure God has reserved a happier future for us. . . . My love and tenderness for you continue to grow again. I would make any sacrifice to make life happier for you."[19] But he was returning a broken man haunted by Sedan and the fall of his empire and everything he had striven to achieve.

Hardly known for his moderation, Otto von Bismarck now inflicted a five-billion-gold-franc war indemnities bill on France—the equivalent of the staggering war indemnity Napoléon I had extracted at gunpoint from Prussia in 1807. For good measure, Bismarck then took large swathes of Alsace and Lorraine, forcefully seizing 1,600,000 French men, women, and children. Bismarck had achieved his ultimate goal of avenging "the mistreatment and humiliation" inflicted on the Prussians by Napoléon, avenging their "hatred of that foreigner," as he put it.[20] In the process he finally unified the whole of "Germany" including Bavaria, without which World War I could never have been fought. Furthermore, ironically, Bismarck could never have executed this unification of the German Confederation had not Napoléon I, upon invading the whole of the German states comprising the Holy Roman Empire, completely suppressed and restructured it with a new, tightly knit structure under French command. Bismarck had simply replaced it with Prussian administration and troops. In the end it was in part thanks to Uncle Napoléon I's legacy of rampant aggression that nephew Napoléon III ultimately fell.

Neither Prussia's Wilhelm I nor Bismarck had realized what a sick man they had on their hands when they decided to hold Louis Napoléon a prisoner of war. His dying while in their custody would have brought the wrath of God upon them and international condemnation, an alienation even their sweeping victory over the French could hardly efface. But with terms of peace now in the works, on the nineteenth of March Bismarck put Louis Napoléon and Drs. Corvisart and Conneau on the kaiser's special train, taking them to the Belgian frontier, where

Louis Napoléon's cousin Mathilde came to bid a tearful final *adieu*, and then on to the Channel port of Ostende. King Leopold, hardly a close friend or admirer, nevertheless placed his yacht at the disposal of the deposed emperor, even as disastrous news of a fresh revolt in Paris reached him, news of the creation of the brief but bloody "Paris Commune." Louis Napoléon's party reached Dover the following day, and by dusk on that twentieth of March he was driving up the alley of ancient elms leading up to Camden Place, his final home. Despite rumors to the contrary, he was no longer a rich man with a reputed twenty million francs stashed away in the strong rooms of Barclays alone. In reality he had a total of only 260,000 gold francs (a little over three million dollars) to his name, but at least he was a free man, exiled safely under the protection of the English once again.[21]

After the enforced immobility as a German prisoner of war at Wilhelmshöhe and despite his plague of physical preoccupations, Louis Napoléon established a surprisingly busy agenda in Chislehurst. Following Eugénie's arrival back in September 1870, members of the family, friends, and opportunists had descended on the Kentish village, some as permanent residents and members of the household, including the family of Henri Conneau, Dr. Lucien Corvisart, Count Adolphe Clary and his wife, Augustin Filon, Franceschini Piétri, Napoléon Hugues Maret (the Duke of Bassano), the Grand Chamberlain of the Tuileries, and Louis Napoléon's new secretary and former journalist, Alfred de La Chapelle. In addition, a steady stream of visitors also came from France, including former premier Eugène Rouher, the Duke and Duchess of Mouchy, related to Eugénie, Louis Lucien Bonaparte, and the late Jérôme Bonaparte's bastard son, Senator Jérôme David, to name a few of a very long list.[22]

To the disapproval of the newly anointed emperor of Germany, Wilhelm I, Otto von Bismarck, and of many French and English political figures as well, Queen Victoria was one of Eugénie's earliest and most regular visitors at Camden Place. "At the door stood the poor Empress in black, [and] the Prince Imperial," the queen noted in her sharply slanting handwriting hand on the thirtieth of November, 1871. "She is very thin and pale, but still very handsome. There was an expression of deep sadness in her eyes." Her fifteen-year-old son, Louis, she found to be "a nice boy but rather short and strumpy." Moreover, the diminutive queen, herself still in black as well—Albert had died a decade earlier—described this, the first of many, as "a sad visit . . . like a strange dream."[23] The two grim ladies continued to see each other frequently thereafter. The Prince of Wales, the future Edward VII, too, was the first to greet Louis Napoléon upon his arrival at Camden Place. "He has grown very stout and gray and the moustaches are no longer curled and waxed," Victoria noted, but there remained "the same pleasing, gentle and gracious manner." Nor could she but admire the stoic attitude of the fallen emperor, he bearing "his terrible misfortunes, [with] dignity and patience," just like Albert during his last illness.[24]

At a time when she was being attacked brutally, even crudely, in Paris and by the French press in particular, the continuing kindness the queen of England so publicly bestowed on her and Louis Napoléon—including reciprocal invitations to Windsor, Balmoral, and Cowes—meant a very great deal to a proud Eugénie. "You could never believe all the delicate attentions she lavished on us in those first bitter days of our exile. She always treated us as sovereigns," Eugénie later reminisced. "Her visits to Chislehurst really lifted our spirits."[25]

Alas the same could not be said of the ever smug Prince Jérôme of Crimean "Sans-Plomb" repute, who persisted on arriving uninvited with his gratuitous advice and presumptuous orders. Rarely did one meet a man whose repulsive physical appearance so brutally reflected his actual character. One day Eugénie's dignified Spanish blood, no longer able to tolerate his latest interference, suddenly turned on him. "Monsiegneur, for eighteen years we have had to put up with your constant criticism of the Empire. . . . But you were *never* there to help out when really needed, and especially at the most *dangerous moments!*"[26] "Gutless" Bonaparte left for Paris. A couple of years after the death of Louis Napoléon, this same thoughtful cousin Jérôme would return to Camden Place yet again, not to see what he could do to alleviate the situation facing Eugénie and her son, to offer his aid, but to bully her again. On this occasion he pointed out that her son needed a man to take charge of his education and insisted that Prince Louis return to Paris and live with him! As Louis positively loathed this bumptious individual as much as his mother did, their disappointed visitor yet again returned to Paris, alone.[27]

As for Louis Napoléon, he really did become a homebody now, apart from occasional excursions to the clubs of Pall Mall, visits with the queen, or country tours. Most of his time, when not spent in his study, he devoted to Eugénie and his son. He was especially preoccupied with Prince Louis's education and watched with satisfaction his progress as a cadet officer at the nearby Woolwich Barracks. Whenever he and Eugénie visited there, the ex-emperor was always very popular with the young men and the staff. Louis Napoléon also had him enrolled in a couple of courses at King's College, London. And when Eugénie was out of the country, in Spain on family business, or up in Scotland, Louis Napoléon would proudly take his handsome son on excursions to Torquay, Bath, London, and elsewhere. They now became very close, much to Eugénie's delight. What a difference from Louis Napoléon's most painful relationship with his own father.

In one respect Louis Napoléon had not changed, however, for like his uncle, Napoléon, he was a born conspirator. There were always rumors to be picked up in the clubs of Pall Mall about "French plots." Both the Bourbons and Louis Philippe's sons were always up to something. The Comte de Chambord wanted the crown for himself. And of course now that Louis Napoléon was once again exiled in England, his attempted coup at Boulogne was remembered. What was he up to now at Camden Place? In fact both the English and French governments had spies in Chislehurst, one visibly perched in a windmill overlooking the small estate.

It was the inimitable Plon-Plon who first broached the subject of Louis Napoléon's return to Paris, and gradually formulated a plan. Although adamantly declining to participate in any more active conspiracies, ultimately he gave a reluctant nod of the head, and by 1872 one was well in hand. Louis Napoléon's former ADC, écuyer, and confidant, the fifty-seven-year-old General Émile Fleury, was coordinating everything.

The old Napoleonic guard in France and exiles in the surrounding countries were willing to back this operation, depositing sufficient funds with the Bank of England. Newspapers were acquired or subsidized to keep Louis Napoléon's name alive and his activities reported, if often laced with enthusiastic embellishment. The emperor was alive and well and preparing for the day of his return. Moreover, General Fleury had received word from Chancellor, and now Prince, von Bismarck, through the good offices of the Russian diplomat Count Shuvaloff, that Prussia would welcome such a coup against Thiers's new republic.

It was the old Hundred-Days-Elba-scenario all over again, with one variation. Instead of approaching from the south of France like his uncle, Louis Napoléon would sail to Holland and pass through Germany to Switzerland. From Thonon on the French side of Lake Geneva, they would descend to Chambéry to be joined by the local regiment, and thence down to Lyon, where the commanding general, Charles Bourbaki, would have his entire eastern army corps ready to march on Paris, when Plon-Plon would join them.

Such were the plans Prince Jérôme reviewed with Louis Napoléon at Camden Place on December 9, 1872. They now set the date for the operation to begin: January 31, 1873, in seven weeks' time. Louis Napoléon's health was clearly a factor, but he seemed well enough at this stage. He would just have to sit in a coach and watch. Eugénie, only too happy with her new refuge—"Camden Place," she was later to comment, "for me it was heaven," compared to palace life in Paris—certainly would have put a stop to these plans for a coup, but Louis Napoléon was the master of secrecy. Jérôme probably felt that should anything happen to Louis Napoléon en route, he, Plon-Plon, could act as regent in his name, or in that of his son, Louis. Such was the situation as Plon-Plon then returned to Paris. Everything was set for D-day, the thirty-first of January.[28]

Despite Louis Napoléon's gallant attempt at a new life, and Eugénie's complete support, later in December his health deteriorated rapidly. Back on the eighteenth of November three specialists had met at Camden Place: Sir Henry Thompson, Sir James Paget, and at the urging of Queen Victoria, her personal physician, Sir William Gull. After a fresh

examination under chloroform in the first week of December, they came
to a unanimous conclusion. The greatly enlarged stone had descended,
completely blocking the flow of urine, they had to operate; there was no
choice in the matter. But still Louis Napoléon hesitated, perhaps wishing to complete his appointment with Jérôme on the ninth. Later, when
attempting to set out to visit his son at Woolwich, however, he barely
reached the gates of the estate before collapsing in pain.

The first operation, on the second of January, 1873, failed, and the
London newspapers were filled with columns written on the French emperor's health. Louis Napoléon suddenly became the focus of national
attention, and long articles appeared on his career and personal life. Suddenly the whole country wanted to know something about the fabled
"Sphinx." Daily health bulletins appeared in the *Times* and the *Morning Chronicle*, just as they had done during Prince Albert's last days—
always the sign of impending death. Edward, the Prince of Wales, now
thirty-one, who had been devoted to Louis Napoléon from the day of
their first meeting in Paris during the Universal Exhibition of 1855, wrote
almost daily on behalf of himself and Queen Victoria.

A second operation on the sixth was as painful as it was unsuccess-
ful. Louis Napoléon was put on opium and chloroform from now on,
and Eugénie wanted to send for their son at Woolwich, but her husband
would not allow it. A third operation was planned for noon on the ninth
of January. Eugénie sat by his bed night and day, refusing to leave him.
Prince Louis had been sent for. The specialists were there, including
Henri Conneau, Louis Napoléon's daily companion since Arenenberg.
By the morning of the ninth the patient was delirious much of the time,
and the end seemed near. When relatively lucid, he seemed preoccupied
with only one thing—Sedan, and those nearly 139,000 French coffins
for which he was solely responsible. "We weren't cowards there, were
we? . . . Were you at Sedan, Henri?"[29] Eugénie held Louis Napoléon's
hand as Father Goddard administered the last rites. When horses were
finally heard pulling up before the house, Eugénie rushed to the door
and took her by now tall sixteen-year-old son in her arms. "You are all
I have left now." It was 11:45 a.m. Louis Napoléon Bonaparte, Emperor
of the French, had died thirty minutes earlier.[30]

38

ELEGY FOR AN EMPEROR

*"All the pomp and ceremonies of Notre-Dame Cathedral could not have
begun to compare with the scene in the little church of St. Mary."*[1]
—LADY COWLEY TO QUEEN VICTORIA, JANUARY 1873

It was a mild day under a thin wintry sun at eleven o'clock on the morning of Wednesday, the fifteenth of January, 1873, as the coffin of Louis Napoléon Bonaparte was placed in the hearse outside the entrance to Camden Place. "There must have been 20,000 persons [including two thousand French visitors] at Chislehurst" attending the funeral, the London *Times* reported.[2] "The early morning trains from London brought down their thousands, and in addition special trains were laid on," while still others brought French mourners arriving from Dover. "The lodge gates were in a state of siege, and the entrance was imperatively refused to all but those who had received special permits."[3] Anticipating the large numbers now arriving and possible disruptions or even an assassination attempt on the late emperor's son and heir, on special orders from the Home Office, Scotland Yard's Superintendent Mott had dispatched 800 constables from London to maintain order. After the scandal of the Orsini plot traced back to England years earlier, the last thing Her Majesty's Government desired to see was an attempt on the life of another Bonaparte, this time on English soil.

Meanwhile Eugénie, who had been at Louis Napoléon's side night and day during his illness, had then prayed next to his embalmed body where he lay in state in the uniform of a lieutenant general in the *chambre ardente*, with his sword on one side, his hat at his feet, next to a bouquet of yellow immortelles, the favorite flowers of his mother, Hortense. His hands were crossed on his chest, on which were placed a crucifix, the Grand Cordon of the Legion of Honor, the Médaille Militaire, and other decorations. He wore both his own wedding ring and that of Napoléon I's on his left hand. Photographs of Eugénie and his son were placed next to him.[4] Prostrate from emotion and exhaustion the empress was unable to attend the funeral today, while the other ladies were being escorted separately to the small Catholic church of St Mary's.

Beyond Camden Place, the entire half-mile country route to the church was lined on both sides by those coming to pay their respects as the funeral cortège proceeded from the heavily guarded lodge gates across the heath. The emperor's son and heir, the sixteen-year-old Prince Imperial [Napoléon] Louis, tall, slender, outwardly in "quiet self-possession [of his emotions] . . . his face pale, his carriage, unfaltering and dignified," bareheaded in a long black mourning cloak, led the procession on foot followed by his cousins, Princes Jérôme, Charles, and Lucien Bonaparte, and Princes Joachim and Achille Murat, former prime minister Eugène Rouher, Marshals Canrobert and LeBreton—Marshal MacMahon, who had led the French army to defeat at Sedan having declined the honor—along with Queen Victoria's personal representative Viscount Sidney, and Lord Suffield, representing the Prince of Wales, Lord Cowley, Lord Buckhurst, the physicians Sir Henry Thompson and Sir William Gull, the pallbearers, and the French and English priests "chanting the offices for the dead."[5]

The French government had refused to give any state recognition to this funeral and sent no official representatives—thereby preventing the English government or Queen Victoria and the royal family from participating. This did not hinder more than two thousand French citizens, however. They were followed by a delegation of thirty-four French workers, clad in their smocks and trooping the tricolor, and some six hundred official mourners six abreast. Separately the Lord Mayor and the high sheriff of London, former high French imperial officials—including General Fleury, the Princes de la Moskowa and Poniatowski, the Dukes de Bassano, Cambacérès, Gramont, and de Tarente, seven admirals, fifteen generals, eight ambassadors [but not of France], twenty-seven former ministers, forty prefects led by Baron Haussmann, and 190 former or present senators, deputies, and high officials—all in official uniforms or black mourning attire, were followed by a delegation of four senior Italian army officers in blue, silver, green, and gold, representing King Victor Emmanuel.[6] Ignoring Paris, the Austrians also sent their ambassador. Among those notably absent today were Prosper Mérimée, who had died in September 1870, and Victor Fialin de Persigny, who died in January 1872.

The glass-enclosed hearse drawn by eight black, richly caparisoned horses "led by mutes carrying rings of yellow immortelles on their arms" drew up the end of the procession. The hearse, its sides swept by a purple velvet pall emblazoned with the golden imperial arms, and its roof covered with wreaths of violets and white roses, slowly wound its way through the heath and the straggling village of Chislehurst.

The long black procession reached the small Catholic church of St. Mary's at half past eleven, when "the coffin, preceded by the [Rev. Dr. Daniels] Bishop of Southwark, Monseigneur Bauer, Abbé Goddard and other ecclesiastics, was borne into the Chapel," and placed on pedestals, with tall candles at either end. The ladies, including Madame Le Breton, the Vicomtesse d'Aguado, Princess Mathilde, Princess Clothilde, the Duchesse de Malakoff, the Duchess de Montmorency, the Comtesse Clary, the Comtesse Walewski, Comtesse Fleury, Madame de Saint-Arnaud, the Marquise de La Valette, Madame de Canrobert, and the Duchess de Mouchy, among others, had arrived earlier, and were already seated on the left side of the church. The men then filed into the right side, 184 in all, as the small organ played the *De Profundis.* "While the bishop was robing the *Miserere* was sung [by the Southwark boys' choir], of which the *Missa de Profundis* by a plain chant. The whole Mass, followed by the Libera and the Benedictus [accompanied by the organ], was rendered with great solemnity,"

After absolution was pronounced, the wreaths of flowers on the coffin were replaced by the purple velvet pall embroidered with a gold cross, a crown, and the initial "N." Prince Louis knelt before his father's coffin, followed in turn by Prince Jérôme and the other princes, sprinkling holy water and making the sign of the cross. "The congregation then silently awaited the departure of the Prince Imperial before attempting to leave the chapel," an Irish correspondent noted. "All bowed low as he passed down the double line of sympathisers with himself and friends of the Imperial dynasty." And then as he "emerged from the edifice, the French spectators, to the number of five or six hundred in the churchyard, raised a loud and unanimous shout of "Vive l'Empereur! Vive Napoléon IV!"[7]

The interment was the most touching scene I have ever witnessed," Lady Cowley acknowledged to Queen Victoria. "In the Church everyone was sobbing . . . even the dignitaries carrying the coffin . . . All the pomp and ceremonies of Notre-Dame Cathedral could not have begun to compare with the scene in the little church of St Mary." The Royal Standard at Windsor was lowered to half-mast as Queen Victoria and the Royal Court went into mourning for fifteen days, as did the Italian and Austrian royal families. "I should think France would now feel some remorse," Princess Alexandra wrote Lady Cowley from Sandringham.[8] But of course there was no official remorse, as immense heaps of rubble continued to smolder where the Tuileries Palace once stood. The French government did not mourn Louis Napoléon's death; no flags were lowered at half-mast before the National Assembly, the Luxembourg Palace, the Invalides, or at the Élysée. The new French Republic would literally remove Napoléon III and the Second Empire from the nation's history books, and Marshal Patrice MacMahon, in return for surrendering the entire French army to Bismarck in 1870, would be elected president of the Republic.[9]

Later the remains of Louis Napoléon were placed in a handsome sarcophagus donated by Queen Victoria, and the Royal Banner from Windsor Castle was suspended over his tomb. Six years later the twenty-three-year-old Prince Louis, Napoléon IV, a serving officer in the English army in South Africa, was killed in a Zulu ambush. His coffin was brought back to Chislehurst and placed next to his father's.[10]

AFTERWORD

As a student of the UC Berkeley school of historiography, I am interested in hard historical facts and getting at their sources. I am not interested in myth, the suppression or distortion of historical truth in order to support "national glory," or the reputations of alleged heroes currently in vogue. And as my late friend and colleague Eugen Weber also took great pains to point out, "nothing is more real and concrete than history, and nothing less interested in theories and abstractions." He had no patience for myths and falsifications, as his distinguished published works attest.

Nor has Berkeley been the only influence on my approach to writing history. Edward Gibbon's *The Decline and Fall of the Roman Empire* was much concerned with the cause and effect of historical events and the individuals who created them. In the eighteenth century when he introduced this vigorous analytical history, the world was shocked, and many dismayed. Gibbon strove for the truth in order to better understand events, regardless of the cost. Barbaric invasions swept away corrupt imperial government and organizations, he acknowledged with a strategic view to history. The early church, which he so much admired, was replaced by a new church introducing superstition, polytheism, paganism, venality, and simony. He was immediately denounced by Christians from Canterbury to the Vatican. Gibbon was interested in fact, not superstition, or in gaining the approval of powerful elite organizations. How can one possibly understand history, our past, existence itself, when closing one's eyes to disagreeable truths? he asked.

When I wrote my history of the initial stages of the U.S. naval operations in the South Pacific during World War II, *Eagle and the Rising Sun*, two retired flag officers contacted me to inform me of their disapproval of my rejection of their particular heroes and version of events as taught at Annapolis. I must alter my professional findings, they insisted, removing the names of some of the real leaders, e.g., Admirals Mitscher and Turner, of whom they did not approve, while reinstating Admiral Husban Kimmel. I reminded these gentlemen that my statements and conclusions were based entirely on documentary evidence submitted by noted military historians and the U.S. government during various subsequent official investigations. (And I was pleased that a neutral party, the late Admiral of the Fleet and First Sea Lord, Sir Henry Leach, RN, for one, fully concurred in all respects with my evaluations and conclusions.)

When I wrote my biography of Napoléon I, I was denounced by what my late friend and fellow historian David Chandler (Sandhurst) referred to as the "Napoleonic clientele." In France, too, there are those, including well-known historians, willing to dismiss and suppress well-documented historical facts, in order to appeal to mass public opinion, however hysterical or ill-founded. In my biography *Napoleon Bonaparte,* I pointed out that as his career attested, that celebrated soldier lived for war, and could not justify his existence without one military campaign after another, right down to the blood-drenched fields of Waterloo. I further pointed out, over the objections of the current school of French historians—though they could hardly deny it—that Napoléon's serial invasions terrorized the whole of Europe, which included the destruction of hundreds of towns and villages, resulting in the creation of hundreds of thousands of war refugees left homeless and displaced, three million men dead, and tens of thousands of women and girls raped and forgotten during Napoléon's glorious rule of France. Thomas Jefferson, author of the Declaration of Independence and the third president of the United States, dismissed Bonaparte as "destructive" and "a tyrant."

• • •

*T*he *Shadow Emperor* is, I believe, the first major biography of Louis Napoléon to be written in the United States. Largely dismissed by French historians for more than a century after the death of Napoléon I, it has been only in the past few decades that serious research in this field has begun in earnest. The French government is also finally showing interest in having the remains of Louis Napoléon Bonaparte transferred from England to France. Important biographies of key participants of the Second Empire are beginning to appear as well, including those of Napoléon III, Auguste de Morny, and Georges Haussmann. It is to be hoped that many more badly needed serious studies will follow, such as of Eugénie, Achille Fould, Eugène Rouher, Eugène Schneider, Gabriel Delessert, Charles de Flahaut, Léopold Le Hon, Prince [Napoléon] Jérôme Bonaparte, his sister Mathilde, and most important, Louis Napoléon's closest friend and daily companion, Henri Conneau; the list is long.

As a biographer-historian, I am interested in the personalities and their interrelationships, those individuals who create or are involved with, if only indirectly, the events that shape "the outcome of history." My biography of Napoléon I was a composite of just such biographical sketches and the resultant interplay of those individuals.

In the case of Napoléon III, Louis Napoléon Bonaparte, the historian is dealing with a totally different personality from that of Napoléon I. Although carefully groomed in the long shadow of his uncle, indeed he worshipped the great man's name and achievements, Louis Napoléon had his own youthful hopes of emerging one day as a new, very different Bonaparte, a leader worthy in his own right. Ironically, what Louis Napoléon never admitted to himself, however, was his rejection of almost everything his uncle stood for, beginning with the military. Napoléon I was a war-lover, a brilliant military officer who felt adrift, lost, in peacetime. While praising the military, his nephew Louis Napoléon was himself an incompetent military officer, rather thriving instead on peace, in rebuilding, modernizing France, its economy, commerce, and industry, its education, science, urban redevelopment, and agriculture. Over and over again he proclaimed, "The Empire stands for Peace." There would be no "Napoleonic Wars" during his watch. Nevertheless wars and international blunders followed. He committed a militarily unprepared France to the unnecessary Crimean War, which in the end accomplished very little, and the even more senseless invasion of Mexico (against his own better judgment). At the same time, his successful military support of Victor Emmanuel's forces against the Austrians did have the positive result of freeing the country of the Austrian occupation and in creating the modern independent state of Italy. In the final analysis, if Napoléon I wished to be remembered for his great victories on the battlefield, Louis Napoléon wanted to be appreciated and remembered for the sweeping peacetime transformation and projects he planned and achieved for the country.

Napoléon I cut down the nation's forests to build forts and warships, Louis Napoléon reforested the country in order to build homes and commerce. Napoléon I regimented all schools in a rigid, military-run state system to meet *his* manpower needs for the military and the nation's administration. Louis Napoléon removed this regimentation and greatly expanded the curricula to meet the needs of the modern new world he was creating, stressing the study of recent history and modern science. Napoléon I virtually drove France into bankruptcy, emptying the treasury and all but destroying the nation's banks and commerce in order to fund *his* military campaigns (even selling the "Louisiana Purchase" to finance his failed invasion of England). Louis Napoléon instead encouraged the vast expansion of commerce and industry, aided and abetted by the opening of public and private coffers, and new banking systems and credit facilities made available to the wider public. Napoléon I had little interest in agriculture, apart from introducing the sugar beet to replace the regular source cut off from the West Indies by his self-inflicted wars against England. Older breeds of cattle, sheep, and horses were dying out, a process dramatically reversed thanks to intensive programs drafted by Napoléon III. Louis Napoléon introduced recent agricultural methods, creating numerous model farms, and supported Louis Pasteur and other scientists in their research. He also supported the creation of public and private sector banking credit facilities for the advancement and expansion of agriculture. Millions of acres of wasteland and swamp were reclaimed on his orders and turned into agricultural production, this at a time when there was neither public environmental interest in, nor demand for, such government programs. As a result of his determination, corn and wheat production soared, as did the nation's wine output. The living and working conditions of the working class—totally ignored by Napoléon I— became a lifelong preoccupation with Napoléon III. Crowded medieval tenements, contaminated drinking water, and the lack of sanitary facilities and sewage disposal resulted in tens of thousands of deaths in Paris alone every year. Louis Napoléon razed perhaps one-third of Paris, encouraging modern, airy new buildings with clean drinking water and sanitary facilities, although little was done in the way of replacing housing for the working-class families displaced by this transformation of Paris. At the same time, the vast rebuilding of the capital put many tens of thousands of the unemployed to work. Louis Napoléon also introduced farsighted job-creation and old-age pension schemes for the working class, not to mention mandatory education at the primary school level. The physical and chemical sciences were also greatly encouraged with fresh funding and prizes, and new specialist hospitals were built throughout the country.

Louis Napoléon launched an impressive shipbuilding program, introducing the country's first steam-powered ironclad navy, second only to the Royal Navy in strength, while surpassing the British in modern gunnery. He introduced the first nationwide electric telegraph communications. Simultaneously, he enthusiastically supported and encouraged the rapid development of the nation's first comprehensive rail network, linking Paris with the capitals of the rest of Europe not to mention the country's Channel and Mediterranean ports. This in turn supported the launching of the first international French steamship lines providing regular service to America, North Africa, the Middle East, and the burgeoning French colonies in Asia, including Indochina and New Caledonia, at once hastening and expanding the French colonial developments so praised in the nineteenth century. Napoléon I's wars had obliterated most international commerce; Napoléon III instead now gave it his full support, including free-trade pacts with England and his continental neighbors. Although Algeria became the focus of his colonial "dreams," it was to prove a long-term disaster for the Algerians and France, draining its wealth and youth, as a despondent Louis Napoléon followed the continuing monthly casualty reports to the very end. Little did he realize that his standing army of 60,000 men in Algeria would one day be increased to more than half a million, and eventually lead to the complete withdrawal of the French from the whole of North Africa.

Louis Napoléon's misjudgment of international affairs unwittingly brought him into confrontation with England on several occasions, and deliberately with Prussia, whose growing power he feared, and which would ultimately bring down his own empire. And here one encounters another final irony, for the summer of 1870 was the last time when Bismarck was in a position to launch his long-anticipated invasion of France, which depended on the close cooperation of three men— Bismarck, Moltke, and Roon. Without all three such a war could not have taken place, but as Bismarck pointed out in a letter to his son, Herbert, Field Marshal Roon was very weak and ill even now, barely able to get to Berlin to attend their last war council in July 1870 when the decision was made to attack France. These circumstances coincided with a complacent Kaiser Wilhelm playing a passive, hapless role, surrendering to Bismarck's incessant bullying, while also accepting his editorial finagling of the "Ems Telegram," and of course the kaiser alone had the authority to declare war on France. This then was the last time when all the basic elements were in place enabling Bismarck to act. If the Prussian army had to stand down and demobilize now, there would not be another "propitious moment" for at least another year, by which time "old Roon" would have been too weak and feeble to play his critical role as war minister. Bismarck for his part could not have hoped for history conveniently repeating itself, providing another precisely similar set of circumstances, another opportunity, with the kaiser in a continuing compliant mood, and Napoléon III badgered by Foreign Minister Gramont, and foolish and weak enough to play into Bismarck's hands. One year later the situation would inevitably have been quite different and "a justified war" and the invasion of France would most likely have been quite impossible. For a most desperate Otto von Bismarck, July 1870 was the last time to strike. It was now or never, and without this war he could never have united all the German states in creating the Prussian Empire. Without this Germany could never have declared war and invaded France in 1914. Individual actions count and History is relentless.

A very dynamic and demanding Napoléon I had dominated the empire he created, while a far less vigorous and egotistical Louis Napoléon happily remained in the shadows of the very empire he in turn created. And yet despite some errors of judgment, obvious lack of organizational skills, and sometimes maddening indecision, beneath that quiet, good-humored exterior, Louis Napoléon achieved vastly much more in the long run for France than did the brilliant, swaggering soldier Napoléon I. His Second Empire now left France one of the most prosperous, modern, and progressive states in Europe. Rarely in the history of any country does it fall to one head of state to so completely alter the face and future of his civilization, to bring one's country and its infrastructure out of an older traditional century into a thriving modern age. This most unlikely Louis Napoléon Bonaparte was just such a man.

Acknowledgments

I am greatly indebted to the recent scholars who have prepared the groundwork for this study, unearthing the millions of facts that transform into the structure of this long ignored period of French history, including Eric Anceau, Michel Carmona, Pierre Milza, and especially the extensive works of Roger Price, e.g., *The French Second Empire: An Anatomy of Political Power.* As usual I am equally indebted to numerous librarians and archivists, including Helen McGinley at the Trinity College Dublin library, the Rothschild Archives, London, the Southampton University Archives, the Library of the University of California, Berkeley, in France at the Archives Nationales, St.-Denis and the Bibliothèque Nationale, Musée Carnavalet, Musée d'Histoire Contemporaine, Musée de l'Armée at the Invalides, the Vincennes Archives of the Service Historique de la Défense, the Musée de la Marine, the Biblioteca Nazionale Centrale di Firenze, the Library of the Scuola Normale Superiore di Pisa, and of course the Bodleian Library, Oxford—Mr. Alan Brown in particular. Friends and colleagues have helped with their comments and advice at various stages, including the late Eugen Weber at UCLA, who had first encouraged this project years ago, my late colleague and dear friend at UCSB, Alex Deconde, a perceptive Colonel John Greenwood, RA, Commander Phil Ingham, RN, Général de Division, Bruno Chaix,

Professor Emeritus David Ellis, University of Kent, Steve Kenis, Françoise Comenisle, Rob and Madette de Warren Sanner—the best of France— my late father-in-law and distinguished Oxford historian, Richard Leslie Hill, the late Bruce McCully, FRCS, for his amazing faith in my work over the years, my late aunt, Rose Ellison, Thornton Wilder, who decades ago instilled his own unique understanding of history when I was writing my study of Émile Zola, and last but not least my most able editor at SMP, Daniela Rapp.

Notes

1. Prince Louis Napoléon

1. Napoléon to Joseph Bonaparte, December 1805, Frédérick Masson, *Napoléon et sa Famille* (Paris: Ollendorff, 1919), v. 2, pp. 450–451; and Alan Schom, *Napoléon Bonaparte* (New York: HarperCollins, 1997), p. 339.
2. Louis Napoléon to M. Peauger, 3 février 1845, *La Nouvelle Revue,* v. 1, p. vi, n. 1, and Hippolyte Thirria, *Napoléon Avant l'Empire* (Paris: Plon, Nourrit, 1895).
3. Thirria, op. cit., v. I, pp. 1–2.
4. Thirria, Ibid., v. I, p. 2, and *Le Moniteur Universel,* 3 juin 1808. Prior to 1848 Prince Louis Napoléon was known as Prince Louis, and later as Napoléon. To avoid confusion, I shall refer to ex-king Jérôme Bonaparte's son, Napoléon—who was also known as Prince Jérôme, or Plon-Plon, but never as Prince Napoléon.
5. Fernand Giraudeau, *Napoléon III Intime* (Paris: Ollendorff, 1895), p. 18.
6. Thirria, op. cit., p. 5, and Giraudeau, op. cit., p. 16.
7. Giraudeau, Ibid., p. 16.
8. Giraudeau, Ibid., p. 15.
9. Giraudeau, Ibid., p. 18.
10. Giraudeau, Ibid., pp. 18, 8–9.

2. A Son and His Father

1. Louis Napoléon to M . . . January 1835, Thirria, op. cit., v. I, p. 10.
2. Captain Louis Napoléon Bonaparte to his father, February 7, 1835, Giraudeau, op. cit., p. 36. Giraudeau collected several dozen Bonaparte letters, parts of which I quote in this chapter and elsewhere in this work.

3. Thirria, op. cit., v. III, p. iii; and an article on this subject in *Le Constitutionnel,* Sept. 23, 1850.

4. Louis Bonaparte to son Louis Napoléon, April 9, 1821, Giraudeau, op. cit., p. 20. This was one of several letters published in *Le Figaro,* Dec. 8, 12, and 13, 1894.

5. Louis Napoléon to his father, Nov. 17, 1827, in Giraudeau, op. cit., p. 21, and in Thirria, op. cit., v. I, p. 3.

6. Louis Napoléon to his father, June 23, 1828, Giraudeau, op. cit., p. 21.

7. Louis Napoléon to his father, Jan. 19, 1829, Giraudeau, Ibid., pp. 23–24.

8. Louis Napoléon to his son, February, 1829, Giraudeau, Ibid., p. 24.

9. Louis Napoléon to his father, March 3, 1829, Giraudeau, Ibid., pp. 24–25.

3. Auguste de Morny

1. Maxime Du Camp, *Souvenirs d'un Demi-Siècle, 1830–1870* (Paris: Hachette, 1949), v. I, p. 228.

2. Michel Carmona, *Morny, Le Vice-Empereur* (Paris: Fayard, 2005), p. 499—Antonio Panizzi.

3. Louis Blanc, *Histoire de Dix Ans, 1830–1840* (Paris: Pagnerre, 1849), v. IV, p. 305.

4. Pierre de La Gorce, *Louis-Philippe* (Paris: Plon, 1931), p. 51.

5. Hortense, *Mémoires de la Reine Hortense* (Paris: Plon, 1928), pp. 272 ff; Carmona, op. cit., p. 42. On Hortense see: Constance Wright, *Daughter to Napoleon, A Biography of Hortense, Queen of Holland* (New York: Holt, Reinhardt & Winston, 1961); Duc de Castries, *La Reine Hortense* (Paris: Tallandier, 1984). See also: Françoise de Bernardy, *Son of Talleyrand, Charles Joseph de Flahaut* (London: Collins, 1956).

6. Carlo Bronne, *La Comtesse Le Hon et la Première Ambassade de Belgique à Paris* (Bruxelles: La Renaissance du Livre, 1952), pp. 120–123; Charles Fresne, *Morny, l'Homme du Second Empire* (Paris: Perrin, 1983), p. 85.

7. Bronne, op. cit., p. 118; Hortense to Fanny Le Hon, August, 1836. Hortense had developed code words for their communications. Bronne, Ibid., p. 117, discusses adoption. Cf. also Jules Bertaut, *Le Roi Jérôme* (Paris: Flammarion, 1954), p. 228, ending of the engagement.

8. Bronne, Ibid., p. 117. Cf. also Jules Bertrant, *Le Roi Jérôme* (Paris: Flammarion, 1954), p. 228.

9. Bronne, op. cit., p. 46.

10. Bronne, Ibid., pp. 85–86.

11. Edmond de Lignières d'Alton Shée, *Mes Mémoires (1826–1848)* (Paris: Librairie Internationale, 1868), vol. II, p. 9.

12. D'Alton Shée, Ibid., pp. 9, 66.

13. Cf. Françoise de Bernardy's *Walewski, 1810–1868, Le Fiul polonais de Napoléon* (Paris: Perrin, 1976); Carmona, op. cit., p. 84.

14. D'Alton Shée, op. cit., p. 9.

15. D'Alton Shée, Ibid., p. 9.

16. Ludovic Halévy, *Carnets* (Paris: Calmann-Levy, 1935), v. I, pp. 55–56. See also Jean-Claude Yon, *Jacques Offenbach* (Paris: Gallimard, 2000), p. 314; and Carmona, op. cit., p. 450, also discussing his traits.

17. Carmona, op. cit., p. 451; Jacques Offenbach to Ernest Lépine, March 13, 1865; Yon, op. cit., p. 314.

18. Maxime Du Camp, op. cit., v. I, pp. 228, 229.

4. Gentlemanly Pursuits

1. Armand François Rupert Laity, *Relation Historique des Événements du 30 Octobre 1836* (Paris: private printing, 1838), pp. 28–29; Thirria, v. I, p. 57.

2. Alexis de Tocqueville quote from Louis Girard, *Napoléon III* (Paris: Fayard, 1895), p. 103.

3. Giraudeau, op. cit., p. 40.

4. Giraudeau, Ibid., p. 41. Letter to a friend, Feb. 2, 1833.

5. Giuseppe Grabinski, *Un ami de Napoléon III: Le Comte Arese et la Politique italienne sous le Second Empire* (Paris: L. Bahl, 1897), p. 27. The Grabinskis served as military commanders of the Carbonari against the Austrians.

6. Grabinski, Ibid., p. 19. Letter of Nov. 7, 1830, first published by Romualdo Bonafidini, *Via di Francesco Arese* (Torino: Roux, 1894), pp. 20–21.

7. Prof. Milza, in his excellent work, gives the best general coverage of the turbulent political situation in Italy at this time: Milza, op. cit., e.g., pp. 60–61.

8. Louis Napoléon to Hortense, Jan.–Feb. 1836, Hortense, *Mémoires,* v. III, pp. 215–217.

9. Prince Louis Napoléon to his father, Louis Bonaparte, Feb. 25, 1836, AN 400 AP 40.

10. General Pier Damiano Armandi to Queen Hortense, March 3, 1836, quoted by Hortense, *Mémoires*, v. III, pp. 224–225.

11. Milza, op. cit., p. 67.

12. Valérie Masuyer, *Mémoires de Valérie Masuyer, Dame d'Honneur de la Reine Hortense* (Paris: Ladvocat, 1836–1838), pp. 156–172.

13. Milza, op. cit., p. 74.

14. Letter, April 1831, Louis Napoléon to Louis Philippe, in *Mémoires de la Reine Hortense*, vol. III, p. 278.

15. Milza, op. cit., p. 81.

16. Louis to his son, March 24, 1831, Giraudeau, op. cit., p. 26.

17. Louis Napoléon to his father, n. d. [1831], Giraudeau, Ibid., pp. 46–47.

18. Milza, Ibid., p. 81.

5. Return to Arenenberg

1. Louis Napoléon to his sister-in-law, Charlotte Bonaparte, n.d. 1831, Giraudeau, op. cit., pp. 27–28.

2. Pascal Clément, *Persigny: L'Homme qui a inventé Napoléon III* (Paris: Perrin, 2006), p. 13.
3. Louis Napoléon to his father, Aug. 31, 1831, Giraudeau, op. cit., p. 27.
4. Louis Napoléon to his father, April 9, 1831, Giraudeau, Ibid., p. 20. This was one of several letters published in *Le Figaro*, Dec. 8, 12, and 13, 1894.
5. Hortense to Antoinette Arese, letter, n.d. [August 1831?], Romauldo Bonfadini, *Vita di Francesco Arese* (Torino: Roux, 1894), p. 34; Grabinski, op. cit., pp. 44–45.
6. Grabinski, Ibid., p. 45.
7. Louis Napoléon to his father, May 10, 1832 [or 1833], Giraudeau, op. cit., p. 29.
8. François Auguste René Chateaubriand, *Mémoires d'Outre-Tomb* (Paris: Penau, 1850), vol. 12, p. 5; Giraudeau, op. cit., p. 47; and Thirria, op. cit., v. I, p. 8.
9. Louis Napoléon to Dr. Coremans, June 1834, Thirria, op. cit., v. I, p. 10.
10. Louis Bonaparte to his son, Sept. 12, 1834, Giraudeau, Ibid., pp. 30–31.
11. Louis Bonaparte to his son, Sept. 16, 1834, Giraudeau, Ibid., p. 33, n. 1.
12. Louis Napoléon to his father, Feb. 7, 1835, Giraudeau, Ibid., p. 36.
13. Clément, op. cit., p. 13.
14. See Jean Gilbert Victor Fialin, Duc de Persigny, *Mémoires du Duc de Persigny* (Paris: Plon, 1896), throughout.

6. Romance and Ructions

1. "Croyez moi, je connais la France," quoted by Arman François Rupert Laity, *Relation Historique des Événements du 30 Octobre 1830* (Paris: Plon, Nourrit, 1895), pp. 19–31.
2. Mathilde Bonaparte regarding her engagement to Louis Napoléon, Jules Bertaut, *Le Roi Jérôme* (Paris: Flammarion, 1954), pp. 227–228.
3. Bertaut, Ibid., pp. 211–212.
4. Bertaut, Ibid., pp. 223–224.
5. Milza, op. cit., pp. 93–94.
6. Jean Des Cars, *La Princesse Mathilde* (Paris: Perrin, 1996), p. 61, Milza, op. cit., p. 95; Bertaut, op. cit., p. 226.
7. Laity, op. cit., pp. 29–30; Thirria, op. cit., vol. I, p. 57.
8. Laity, op. cit., pp. 19–32, 28–29; Thirria, op. cit., vol. I, p. 56.
9. Louis Napoléon to Gen. Voirol, 14 août 1836, Thirria, op. cit., vol. I, pp. 60–61.
10. Thirria, Ibid., vol. I, pp. 63–64, Exelmans to Major de Bruc, août 1836.
11. Bronne, pp. 117–121.
12. See Bronne for this generally unknown background regarding Hortense and Fanny Le Hon. They had been corresponding for months regarding the necessity of recognizing Auguste de Morny as Hortense's son, and of his inclusion in her Last Will and Testament. But these papers had not yet been drawn up and signed by the time of Hortense's death.

7. What Hath God Wrought

1. Louis Napoléon to his former tutor, Narcisse Vieillard, 28 fevrier 1834, AN. 400 AP41.

2. Louis Napoléon, *Des Idées Napoléoniennes* (Paris: Plon, 1860), p. 156.

3. Thirria, op. cit., vol. I, pp. 60–74.

4. The London *Times,* and the *Frankfurter Zeitung,* both of Nov. 2, 1836.

5. Louis Napoléon to Hortense, November 1836. Thirria, op. cit., vol. I, pp. 80–84; Giraudeau, op. cit., pp. 60–62, and Laity, op. cit., pp. 25–30. Louis Napoléon to Hortense, 19 novembre 1836, Giraudeau, op. cit., p. 61, and Napoléon III, *Oeuvres de Napoléon III* (Paris: Plon-Amyot, 1854–1869), vol. II.

6. Louis Napoléon to Hortense, 10 nov. 1836, Giraudeau, op. cit., pp. 60–61.

7. Louis Napoléon to Louis Bonaparte, 12 juillet 1836, Giraudeau, Ibid., p. 70.

8. One pound sterling equaled 35 French francs in 1836. Thirria, op. cit., vol. I, p. 87, n. 3; François Guizot, *Mémoires pour servir à l'Histoire de Mon Temps* (Paris: Plon, 1858), vol. IV, p. 298.

9. Thirria, op. cit., vol. I, p. 87, n. 2.

10. Blanchard Jerrold is the best source for the American phase, *The Life of Napoleon III* (London: Longmans, Green, 1882), vol. I.

11. Giraudeau, op. cit., p. 6.

12. Louis Napoléon to Hortense, Nov. 14–15, 1836, Thirria, op. cit., vol. I, p. 87.

13. Bertaut, op. cit., pp. 226–229. Five years later Mathilde married the extremely wealthy and sadistic Anatole Demidoff, resulting in a permanent separation. Mathilde received a handsome annual settlement, of which her father, Jérôme, helped himself to 20 percent. Jérôme also "borrowed" her dowry from the bridegroom, and never repaid it. Humiliated, Mathilde never invited her father to her home and rarely ever spoke to him again.

14. Hortense to her son, 26 décembre 1836, Giraudeau, op. cit., pp. 64–66; Hortense to her son, 17 février 1837, Giraudeau, Ibid.

15. Hortense to Louis Napoléon 16 déc. 1836; Hortense to Louis Napoléon, 3 janvier 1837; Giraudeau, Ibid., p. 65.

16. Jerrold, op. cit., Philadelphia to New York.

17. Jerrold, Ibid. Arese was there to greet him.

18. Louis Napoléon to Hortense, 21 avril 1837, Giraudeau, op. cit., p. 67.

19. Thirria, op. cit., vol. I, p. 84.

20. Thirria, Ibid., vol. I, pp. 90–92, and Clement von Metterich, *Mémoires et Ecrits Divers laissés par le Prince de Metternich, Chancelier de Cour et d'État* (Paris: Plon, 1883), vol. VI, p. 190.

21. Jerrold, op. cit.

22. Jerrold, Ibid.

23. Jerrold, Ibid.

24. Louis Napoléon to Joseph Bonaparte, 21 avril 1837, Giraudeau, op. cit., p. 67.

25. Francesco Arese elected to remain in America until the following year. He wrote extensively on his travels. See Gravinski, op. cit., pp. 58–63. *Septentrionale* was published in the appendix of Bonfadini's work on Arese.

26. Louis Napoléon to President Martin Van Buren, June 1837, Giraudeau, op. cit., pp. 69–70.

27. Louis Napoléon to Hortense, London, June 1837, Giraudeau, Ibid., pp. 69–70.

8. Farewells and Asylum

1. Giraudeau, op. cit., pp. 75–76, Louis Bonaparte to Louis Napoléon, ca. 1837.

2. Thirria, op. cit., vol. I, pp. 136–139. Louis Napoléon advising the Swiss of his permanent departure from the country.

3. October 8, 1837, Giraudeau, op. cit., p. 74.

4. Louis Philippe quickly acceded to Louis Napoléon's request to have Hortense buried next to her mother, Joséphine, in France. Giraudeau, Ibid., pp. 74–76. Milza, op. cit., pp. 108 ff.

5. Carmona, op. cit., pp. 83–84.

6. Giraudeau, op. cit., p. 75.

7. Thirria, op. cit., vol. I, p. 115.

8. *Journal des Débâts,* 8 septembre 1838; and Thirria, vol. I, pp. 133–134.

9. *Le Siècle,* of this date, and Thirria, op. cit., v. I, pp. 131–136.

10. Thirria, Ibid., v. I, pp. 136–137.

11. *Le Siècle,* October 1838.

12. The *Morning Chronicle,* Oct. 15, 1840.

13. Thirria, op. cit., vol. I, pp. 166–169. They later formed the nucleus of the Boulogne landing party.

14. Thirria, Ibid., vol. I, p. 155.

15. Thirria, Ibid., vol. I, pp. 141 ff.

16. Thirria, Ibid., vol. I, pp. 141 et seq. for his London sojourn.

17. A statement made by Louis Napoléon after his arrest in Strasbourg, October 30, 1836, Giraudeau, op. cit., p. 59. Quote from his latest (1840) publication, *De L'Avenir des Idées Impériales.*

18. E.g., Napoléon's December 1804 plebiscite approving the creation of his new Empire. Cf. Schom, op. cit., p. 333, for the Empire. See also the rigged plebiscite of 1800 ending the Directory and creating the Consulate, p. 235.

19. Conneau later married a Corsican, Juliette Pasqualini, by whom he had two children; she was the great niece of Marshal Sébastiani. Conneau headed the Imperial medical service under Louis Napoléon and remained his personal physician. He was elected to the Chamber of Deputies, then named senator and Grand Officier de la Légion d'Honneur.

9. "This Grand and Glorious Undertaking": Boulogne or Bust

1. Giraudeau, op. cit., p. 83.
2. Baptiste Capefigue, *L'Europe depuis l'avénement du Roi Louis-Philippe Histoire des années 1830 à 1847* (Paris: Editions Chapitre, 1847), vol. II, p. 288.
3. Thirria, op. cit., vol. I, p. 171.
4. From the subsequent court deposition, Thirria, Ibid., vol. I, p. 173.
5. For details on Montholon's remarkable career, see Alan Schom, op. cit., pp. 775–779, 783–787.
6. Alan Schom, *Trafalgar, Countdown to Battle, 1803–1805* (New York: Oxford University Press, 1991), pp. 100–107.
7. Thirria, op. cit., vol. I, pp. 110 ff., here gives the best coverage of these events.
8. Thirria, Ibid., vol. I, pp. 166–169, where he lists the members of the expedition.
9. Captain Crow later testified to the heavy drinking of most of the men during the crossing. Adrian Dansette thought that Montholon had been serving as an informer for Minister of the Interior Charles de Rémusat. Hardly implausible.
10. Cf. depositions made by Lieutenant Bally and the local prefect, Thirria, Ibid., vol. I, p. 175. Hippolyte François Athale Sébastien Bouffet de Montauban, age forty-six, "Colonel of Volunteers." All conversations given here come from depositions taken following the arrest of Louis Napoléon and his men. See also Thirria, Ibid., vol. I, pp. 174 ff.
11. Thirria, Ibid., vol. I, pp. 162–164.
12. Thirria, Ibid., vol. I, pp. 162, 164, 176, and for the events taking place hereafter, pp. 176–180.
13. *Le National,* 7 août 1840.
14. Thirria, vol. I, pp. 180–183.
15. Signed by War Minister General Amadée de Cubières, Thirria, vol. I, p. 182: *Circulaire du Ministère de la Guerre,* 7 août 1840.
16. *La Presse,* 8 août 1840.
17. *Journal des Débats,* 7 août 1840.
18. Quoted in Thirria, op. cit., vol. I, pp. 188–189.
19. Giraudeau, op. cit., p. 71. The quote, "to know how to choose the right moment," by Napoléon, in Schom, *Napoléon Bonaparte,* p. 453.
20. *La Gazette de France,* and Thirria, op. cit., vol. I, p. 187.
21. Thirria, Ibid., vol. I, pp. 189 et seq. Commission d'Instruction.
22. Thirria, Ibid., vol. I, p. 203.
23. Thirria, Ibid., vol. I, pp. 190–193. The quotes that follow are from Leopold's speech.
24. Thirria, Ibid., v. I, pp, 193–194.
25. Thirria, Ibid., for testimony of the proceedings, pp. 200–201, and Milza, op. cit., p. 133. Of those declining to vote against Napoléon III: cf. Thirria, Ibid., vol. I,

pp. 105–196. Among those voting for conviction (Thirria, Ibid., vol. I, pp. 203–205)—Count Portalis; the Duke de Broglie; Count Molé; Count de Ségur, the son of General Exelmans; the Marquis de Rochembeau, Count Siméon. (Morny's father, Charles de Flahaut, voted against the conviction.)

10. Funeral for an Emperor

1. Alexandre Glais Bizoin regarding the return of Napoléon's remains: *Journal des Débats,* May 1840.
2. Lamartine quote by Guy Antonetti, *Louis-Philippe* (Paris: Fayard, 2002), p. 817.
3. Alphonse de Lamartine, 25–26 May 1840—before the Chambres des Députés, *Journal des Débats,* May 27, 1840.
4. *Journal des Débats,* May 13, 1840.
5. Thiers unstintingly and uncritically praised Napoléon's reign in his twenty-volume *Histoire du Consulat et de l'Empire.* This work, like his earlier history of the French Revolution (of 1789), was strong on dogma, anti-royalist rule, anti-Socialist, and anti-pure republicanism, while generally weak on facts and historical accuracy, substance, and judgment. Karl Marks described his works as "historically unfair."
6. For an eyewitness account see the articles by the correspondent of the London *Times,* December 15–17, 1840, as well as those of *The Morning Chronicle,* the *Moniteur Universel,* and the *Journal des Débâts*—for the period 8–17 December 1840.
7. Hugo quotations are from the notes taken that day: "15 décembre 1840, Funérailles de l'Empereur. Notes prises sur place." *Choses vues*—in *Oeuvres completes, Histoire* (Paris: Robert Laffont, 1987), pp. 808–809, 815.
8. *Le National,* 16 déc. 1840.
9. Delphine Gay Girardin seconded in her husband's paper, *La Presse,* 16 déc. 1840.
10. Louis Philippe quote receiving the coffin. Quoted from the official newspaper, *Le Moniteur Universel,* mercredi, 16 déc. 1840.
11. Victor Hugo's poem, "Le Retour de l'empereur." Quote, Note, Dec. 15. 1840 in Hugo's "Funérailles" article, quoted above, op. cit., *Oeuvres Complètes,* p. 815.
12. Louis Napoléon, from his *Idées Napoléoniennes* and cited by Giraudeau, op. cit., vol. I, p. 80.

11. To Ham, with Love, Tosh, and Toil

1. Louis Napoléon's diary at Ham, Giraudeau, op. cit., p. 99.
2. Louis Napoléon to Narcisse Vieillard, 1843, Giraudeau, Ibid., p. 101.
3. Louis Napoléon to Maître Berryer, 7 août 1840, Thirria, vol. I, pp. 201–202.
4. Louis Napoléon to Mme. Salvage de Faverolles, 16 oct. 1840, Giraudeau, Ibid., vol. I, p. 90.
5. Louis Napoléon to Narcisse Vieillard, 10 avril 1842, Giraudeau, Ibid., vol. I, pp. 105–106.

6. Giraudeau, Ibid., vol. I, pp. 86–87. Narcisse Vieillard, 1791–1857, a cultured gentleman, a graduate of the École Polytechnique, had served as a young officer under Napoléon.

7. Prof. Adrien Dansette thought that Montholon was serving as an informer for Charles de Rémusat, Louis Philippe's minister of the interior. Jerrold, op. cit., vol. II, pp. 345–346, 385–386. Louis Napoléon later had to pay him off, to keep him out of Paris.

8. Thirria, op. cit., vol. I, p. 201. Persigny's *De la destination et de l'utilité des Pyramides,* published privately in Paris in 1845.

9. Thirria, Ibid., vol. I, p. 208, n. 5; Louis Blanc, *Révélations Historiques* (Bruxelles: Méline, 1859), vol. II, p. 220.

10. He submitted a paper entitled "Production des Courants Électriques" on metal conductors, to François Arago at the Académie des Sciences.

11. Thirria, op. cit., vol. I, pp. 209–210. Louis Napoléon to N. Vieillard, 20 février 1841.

12. Thirria, Ibid., vol. I, pp. 209–210, and on 210 n. 3. See *Moniteur Universelle,* 19 février 1849, article under "Variétés."

13. Louis Napoléon's two illegitimate sons: Alexandre Luis Eugène (Comte d'Orx) born in Dec. 1842, and Louis Ernst Alexandre (Comte de Labenne) born in March 1845. Both sons were raised first by Harriet Howard along with her son, Martin, until about 1853, and then by Hortense Cornu.

14. Thirria, op. cit., vol. I, p. 209, n. 2. Quotes are from Louis Blanc's *Révélations Historiques,* vol. II, p. 221.

15. *Le Canal de Nicaragua ou Projet de Jonction des Océans Atlantique et Pacifique au moyens d'un Canal.* Blanchard Jerrod, *The Life of Napoleon the Third* (London: Longmans, Green, 1875), regarding this canal project, vol. II, pp. 312–331. Louis Napoléon to his father, 19 Sept. 1845.

16. Louis Napoléon to Int. Min. Duchâtel, May 28, 1844, Thirria, op. cit., vol. I, pp. 216–217.

17. *Analyse de la Question des Sucres,* published in 1842; Thirria, Ibid., vol. I, pp. 245–249.

18. Thirria, Ibid., vol. I, p. 236; Jerrold, Ibid., vol. II, 98.

19. Thirria, Ibid., vol. I, p. 238.

20. Thirria, Ibid., vol. I, p. 240.

21. See Alan Schom, *Emile Zola, A Bourgeois Rebel* (New York: Henry Holt, 1988), and as an ebook, 2015, Endeavour Press, Amazon.

22. Thirria, op. cit., vol. I, pp. 259–264.

23. Thirria, Ibid., vol. I, pp. 259–264.

24. May 1884, Georges Sand to Louis Napoléon, Thirria, Ibid., vol. I, p. 259, n. 2

25. Fort de Ham, 19 Septembre 1845, quoted by Jerrold, op. cit., vol. II, footnote on pp. 309–310. He informed Hortense November 12, Jerrold, vol. II, pp. 311–312.

26. Jerrold, Ibid., vol. II, p. 306. Jerrold mentions Malmesbury's role in April 1845.

27. Thirria, Ibid., vol. I, p. 218. Louis Napoléon to the Inter. Min., Dec. 25, 1845.

28. Louis Napoléon to Louis Philippe, 14 janvier 1846, Jerrold, op. cit., vol. II, p. 335. See also Thirria, vol. I, p. 246.

29. Thirria, Ibid., vol. I, pp. 222–227; Giraudeau, op. cit., p. 108; Jerrold, op. cit., vol. II, p. 354, Louis Napoléon to his father, Londres, le 27 mai 1846; Jerrold, Ibid., vol. II, p. 357, n. 1. Louis Napoléon to Vieillard, June 1, 1846.

12. Marking Time

1. Louis Napoléon to Narcisse Vieillard, Dec. 10, 1846, on problems with Plon-Plon, Jerrold, op. cit., v. II, p. 381. Jerrold gives the best coverage of London now.

2. Louis Napoléon to Vieillard, Feb. 25, 1847, Jerrold, Ibid., vol. III, p. 382.

3. Louis Napoléon to Hortense Cornu, July 26, 1846, Jerrold, Ibid., vol. II, p. 460.

4. Louis Napoléon to Narcisse Vieillard, August 3, 1846, Jerrold, Ibid., vol. II, p. 460, and by him to her on August 17, 1846, Ibid., and again to her on Sept. 3, 1846, Jerrold, vol. II, p. 461.

5. Louis Napoléon to Narcisse Vieillard, 10 Dec. 1846, Jerrold, Ibid., II, 381.

6. The Boston Public Library published *Memorial of Joshua Bates* in 1865.

7. Jerrold, vol. II, pp. 384–385.

8. His *Etudes sur le Passé et l'Avenir de l'Artillerie,* this volume printed privately by Bonaparte in Paris in 1847.

9. Margaret Blessington, *The Literary Life and Correspondence of the Countess of Blessington* (London: Longmans, 1855), 3 vols.; and Nick Foulkes, *The Last of the Dandies, The Scandalous Life and Escapades of Count d'Orsay* (Boston: Little, Brown, 2003).

13. A Pure New Holy Republic: 1848

1. Viscount Palmerston to Marquis of Normanby, Feb. 28, 1848, Evelyn Ashley, *The Life of Henry John Temple, Viscount Palmerston* (London: Richard Bentley, 1867), vol. 1, pp. 178–182.

2. Léon Faucher's article in the newspaper, *La Revolution Démocratique et Sociale,* December 17, 1848, were reprinted in Faucher's *Correspondance* (Paris: Hachette, 1967), v. I, p. 234; Thirria, op. cit., vol. II, p. 475.

3. Anna Muhlstein, *Baron James, The Rise of the French Rothschilds* (New York: Vintage Books, 1984), p. 177.

4. Lord Rothschild, *The Shadow of the Great Man* (London: Stellar Press, 1982), p. 49.

5. Michel Carmona, *Haussmann* (Paris: Fayard, 2000), pp. 177, 179. Carmona cites the 1846 figure for Paris: population 945,000, of which 650,00 lived below the poverty level. National literacy rate between 14 and 43 percent.

6. Michel Carmona, *Morny, Le Vice-Empereur* (Paris: Fayard, 2005), p. 112.

7. Morny's article in *La Revue des Deux Mondes,* Jan. 1, 1848, Carmona, Ibid., p. 108.

8. Carmona, *Morny,* pp. 109–110.

9. Carmona, Ibid., pp. 110–111. Authorization for the 22nd finally came through, but too late. Louis Désiré Véron, *Mémoires d'un Journaliste* (Paris: E. Dentu, 1873),

vol. IV, p. 233, vol. VI, p. 127; Jean Hippolyte Villemessant, *Mémoires d'un Bourgeois de Paris* (Paris: Librairie Nouvelle, 1856), vol. 5, pp. 239 ff.

10. James de Rothschild to nephews, Feb. 22, 1848, RAL [Rothschild Archives, London] 109/65.

11. Carmona, *Morny,* p. 115. Morny's grandmother, Adélaïde, had been a close friend of the king and his late sister, an intimacy later shared by Flahaut, Morny, and Fanny Le Hon. Emily-Jane was the daughter of Morny's father, Gen. Charles Joseph de Flahaut, and his Scottish wife, Margaret Mercer Elphinstone, 2nd Baroness Keith (the daughter of Admiral Lord Keith).

12. Maxime Du Camp, *Souvenirs d'un Demi-Siècle, Au Temps de Louis-Philippe et de Napoléon III* (Paris: Hachette, 1949), p. 90.

13. Carmona, Ibid., pp. 110, 112.

14. Carmona, Ibid., p. 112.

15. Carmona, Ibid., p. 9.

16. Morny to Emily, Carmona, Ibid., p. 112.

17. Ghislain de Diesbach, *Ferdinand de Lesseps* (Paris: Perrin, 1998), pp. 77–78, 81. Ferdinand de Lesseps to Mme. Delamalle, 5 mars 1848.

18. Lamartine quote: "La République nouvelle, pure, sainte, immortelle, populaire et transcendante, pacifique et grande est fondée."

19. Prosper Mérimée to Countess de Montijo, Carmona, *Morny,* p. 115. Morny quote, his letter to Emily, March 1, 1848, Ibid., p. 112; Véron, op. cit., vol. IV, p. 233; Henri d'Alméras, *La Vie Parisienne sous Louis-Philippe* (Paris: albin Michel, 1920), pp. 213 ff; Eugène Pierron, *Virginie Dejazet* (Paris: Ollendorff, 1856), pp. 188 ff.; Louis Girard, *Napoléon III* (Paris: Fayard, 1997); Frédéric Loliée, *Frère d'Empereur, Le Duc de Morny et la Société du Second Empire* (Paris: Emile-Paul, 1909).

20. Jasper Ridley, *Lord Palmerston* (London: Constable, 1970), pp. 583, 584, 589. For the Trelawny quotes, *The Parliamentary Diaries of Sir John Trelawney, 1858–1865,* ed. T. A. Jenkins (London: Royal Historical Society), Camden fourth series, vol. 40, 990, p. 221, entry dated Aug. 7, 1862. David Brown, *Palmerston, A Biography* (New Haven: Yale University Press, 1012), p. 232.

21. Brown, op. cit., 2003.

22. Palmerston to Normanby, Feb. 26, 1848, Ashley, op. cit., vol. I, pp. 76–78.

23. Brown, op. cit., p. 307; Ashley, op. cit., vol. I, pp. 78–82.

24. John Fane, Earl of Westmorland, K. Bourne, *The Foreign Policy of Victorian England, 1830–1902* (Oxford: Clarendon Press, 1970), p. 191.

25. Palmerston to Colonel Secretary Henry George Gray, 3rd Earl Gray, March 28, 1848, PP GC/Gr/2408 (Palmerston Papers, Southampton University Library Archives); and Brown, op. cit., p. 307.

26. Morny to Emily, Carmona, *Morny*, pp. 112–113.

27. Alexis de Tocqueville, *Souvenirs* (Paris: Gallimard, 1942), p. 93.

28. Nathaniel Rothschild to his brothers, Feb. 23, 1848, RAL 109/65.

NOTES

29. Victor Hugo, op. cit., *Choses Vues*, vol. II, p. 172.
30. Muhlstein, op. cit., pp. 175–176.
31. Carmona, *Morny,* pp. 116–117; and also Carmona's *Haussmann,* pp. 66–68.
32. Muhlstein, op. cit., p. 181.
33. James de Rothschild to nephews, June 4, 1848, RAL 109/66.
34. Rothschild to wife Bette, March 4, 1848, RAL 109/65.
35. Carmona, *Morny,* p. 115.
36. James de Rothschild, to nephews, March 17, 1848, RAL 109/65. All the figures for the House of Rothschild are not available, but those for 1828 give the Frankfurt branch (Amschel), that of Vienna (Salomon), Naples (Karl), and Paris (James), a total capital of £19,693,750 each, while Nathan's London bank reached £28,200,000. Muhlstein, op. cit., p. 221.
37. Léon Faucher, op. cit., vol. I, p. 234.
38. Muhlstein, op. cit., p. 182.
39. James de Rothschild to nephews, May 1, 1848, RAL 109/66.
40. Nathaniel Rothschild to brothers, June 9, 1848, RAL 109/66.
41. Muhlstein, op. cit., pp. 183–184.
42. Muhlstein, Ibid., p. 168, regarding that loan.
43. Nathaniel to brothers, June 4, 1848, RAL 109/66.
44. Palmerston to brother William Temple, Sept. 1, 1850, PPGC/TE/335; Brown, op. cit., p. 314. The Palmerston Papers, Southampton University Archives.
45. Ibid.

14. President of the Republic Bonaparte

1. Léon Faucher's article in the newspaper, *La Révolution Démocratique et Sociale,* Dec. 17, 1848; and Thirria, op. cit., vol. II, p. 475.
2. Rémusat, *Mémoires,* quoted by Giraudeau, op. cit., p. 104.
3. Carmona, *Morny,* op. cit., p. 127; Anceau, op. cit., pp. 122–125.
4. Paul Gagnon, *France Since 1789* (NY: Harper & Row, 1972), p. 155, estimates up to 3,000 killed.
5. Anceau, op. cit., p. 129
6. *Moniteur Universel,* 17 oct. 1848.
7. Anceau, op. cit., p. 103.
8. Anceau, Ibid., p. 143.
9. Thirria, op. cit., vol. II, p. 471; *La Presse.*
10. Thirria, Ibid., vol. II, p. 346.
11. The *Times,* Dec. 15, 1848.
12. Quoted by Giraudeau, op. cit., p. 104.
13. Jerrold, op. cit., vol. II, p. 15; Thirria, op. cit., vol. II, pp. 348–349; and Giraudeau, op. cit., p. 128. Giraudeau quotes, p. 128: Louis Napoléon to Malmesbury. Original French quote, "En presence de Dieu."

14. Carmona, *Morny*, op. cit., p. 132.

15. Adolphe Thiers to Louis Napoléon. Carmona, op. cit., pp. 143–145.

16. Giraudeau, op. cit., p. 104.

15. The Élysée

1. Alexis de Tocquville, *De la Démocratie en Amérique* (Paris: Michel Levy Frères, 1864), vol. I, Première partie, Ch. III.

2. Former foreign minister Alphonse de Lamartine, Jerrold, op. cit., vol. III, p. 37.

3. Auguste de Morny to his sister, Emily, Lady Shelburne, ca. late December 1848. Louis Napoléon invited Morny to the Élysée, 10 p.m., Jan. 23–24, 1849—their first meeting. See also, Milza, op. cit., p. 199, and Carmona, *Morny,* pp. 138–140.

4. Louis Napoléon to Lord Malmesbury, M. Du Camp, op. cit., vol. I, p. 107, n. 1.

5. Du Camp, Ibid., vol. I, p. 105.

6. Carmona, op. cit., pp. 140–141.

7. Morny's reflections following his first official meeting with his brother, Jan. 23–24, 1849—in his unpublished notes, *Souvenirs et Correspondance;* and Carmona, op. cit., p. 119.

8. Morny to Margaret, Comtesse de Flahaut, May, 1849, Carmona, op cit, p. 119; Fleury's *Souvenirs* (Paris: Plon, 2899–2908), vol. I, 1837–1859, p. 114; and Carmona, op. cit., p. 119.

9. Dec. 3, 1848, Adolphe Thiers to Frédéric Boutet of the *Echo Rochelais;* and Jerrold, op. cit., vol. III, pp. 12–13. "Le Parti de l'Ordre."

10. "Notre honeur militaire est engagé."

11. Louis Napoléon to Vieillard, June 4, 1849, Jerrold, op. cit., vol. III, 25.

12. Carmona, op. cit., p. 152.

13. Giraudeau, op. cit., p. 130.

14. Louis Napoléon, in the *Moniteur Universel,* 7 sept. 1849; and Carmona, op. cit., p. 155; 13 juin 1849, Jerrold, op. cit., vol. III, p. 25.

16. Countdown to Empire

1. Pres. of the Republic Bonaparte, Amiens, July 7, 1849, Jerrold, op. cit., vol. III, p. 29.

2. Pres. Bonaparte to audience, Tours, 1849, Jerrold, Ibid., vol. III, p. 30.

3. Jerrold, Ibid., vol. III, p. 29.

4. Speech delivered at Ham, July 29, 1849, Milza, op. cit., p. 213; Jerrold, op. cit., vol. III, p. 29.

5. Giraudeau, op. cit., pp. 312–332.

6. Carmona, *Morny,* p. 156; Giraudeau, op. cit.; Jerrold, op. cit., vol. III, p. 30. A citizen of Tours or of Touraine is called "Tourangeau" and "Tourangelle."

7. Louis Napoléon to General Count de Flahaut, September 17, 1850. Carmona, op. cit., p. 163.

8. Jerrold, op. cit., vol. III, pp. 29–30.

9. Milza, op. cit., p. 217; Carmona, op. cit., p. 156.

10. Henry Temple to brother William Temple, July 7, 1849, Southampton University Archives, PP. GC/TE/327; David Brown, op. cit., p. 314.

11. Carmona, op. cit., pp. 156–157. "Le petit homme."

12. Carmona, Ibid., pp. 156–157.

13. Jerrold, op. cit., vol. III, p. 35.

14. Jerrold, Ibid., vol. III, pp. 33–35.

15. Falloux was the author of *Histoire de Saint Pie V,* and of *L'Évêque d'Orléans,* followed by his *Mémoires d'un Royaliste.*

16. From Falloux's *Mémoires:* "ces affreux petits rouges." "Dieu dans l'education. Le pape à la tête de l'Eglise. L'Eglise à la tête de la civilization."

17. Carmona, op. cit., p. 158, Flahaut to Morny, Oct. 1849.

18. Carmona, Ibid., pp. 159–160.

19. Brown, op. cit., p. 324, Henry Temple to William Temple, Sept. 1, 1850, PP GC/TE/335.

20. Count de Chambord, 1820–1883, grandson of Charles X and legal next in line to the throne, he was considered by Bourbon followers to be Henri V, King of France and Navarre.

21. Louis Girard, op. cit., p. 128; Carmona, op. cit., p. 164.

22. Carmona, Ibid., p. 170.

23. Carmona, Ibid., p. 171.

24. Carmona, Ibid., p. 173; Jerrold, op. cit., v. III, p. 62.

25. Jerrold, op. cit., vol. III, p. 62.

26. Carmona, op. cit., p. 173.

27. Claude Defresne, *Morny, L'Homme du Second Empire* (Paris: Perrin, 1983), p. 131.

28. Carmona, op. cit., pp. 173–174. Morny to Valérie Masuyer, Sept. 12, 1851.

29. Flahaut to his wife, Margaret, Nov. 24, 1851—all his letters to her were in English. Philip Guedalla, *The Secret of the [Dec. 1851] Coup* (London: Constable, 1924), p. 115.

30. Giraudeau, op. cit., p. 138; Carmona, op. cit., p. 175.

31. Jerrold, op. cit., vol. III, p. 63. No original French available.

32. *Le Siècle,* 15 oct. 1851. Adolphe Granier de Cassagnac, *Histoire de la Chute du Roi Louis Phillipe, de la République de 1848 et du Rétablissement de l'Empire, 1847–1855* (Paris: Plon, 1857), 2 vols. An insider's history of these events.

33. Flahaut describes his work to his wife as "violent," letter to wife, Nov. 24, 1851. Guedalla, op. cit., pp. 115–116.

17. The Rubicon File

1. Dufresne, *Morny,* op. cit., p. 131.

2. Charles de Flahaut to his daughter, Emily, Lady Shelburne, Paris, Saturday, Dec. 6, 1851, Guedalla, op. cit., p. 126. (Original letter in English.)

3. *Le Siècle,* 15 oct. 1851.

4. Caroline Elizabeth Norton's major lifelong work lay in social legislation: The Custody of Infants Act, the Matrimonial Causes Act, and the Married Women's Property Act.

5. Jerrold, op. cit., vol. III, p. 68, quoting Maxime Du Camp in English.

6. Dufresne, op. cit., pp. 139–140; Carmona, op. cit., pp. 181 ff.; Guedallla, op. cit., pp. 117 ff.; and Jerrold, op. cit., vol. III, pp. 64 ff.

7. Carmona, op. cit., p. 184.

8. Frédéric Loliée, *Frère d'Empereur, le Duc de Morny, et Société* (Paris: Emile-Paul, 1909), p. 155.

9. Carmona, op. cit., pp. 185–186.

10. That Auguste de Morny, a notorious taskmaster, placed this nineteen-year-old Léopold Le Hon, and not the boy's elder brother, in charge of this office at the Ministry of the Interior throughout the coup d'état, speaks for itself as to the extremely high regard in which he held Léopold, whom he had known since birth. He was half brother to Louise Le Hon, the natural daughter of Auguste and Fanny. There is a strong possibility that Morny was also Léopold's father.

11. See Alan Schom, *Napoleon Bonaparte, A Biography* (New York: HarperCollins, 1997), Ch. 34.

12. Flahaut writing in English to Countess de Flahaut at their London town house, 19 Grosvenor Square, Telegramme, 7:02 a.m., Dec. 2, 1851, Min. of the Interior. South Eastern Electric Telegraph, 11:10 a.m. in Guedalla, op. cit., p. 119. In fact the electric telegraph between England and France had been inaugurated by South Eastern Railways just three weeks earlier. Sent in clear, Flahaut obviously intended them to reach Palmerston at the Foreign Office. See also, Carmona, op. cit., p. 187.

13. Georges Haussmann, *Mémoires* (Paris: Victor-Havard, 1890), vol. I, pp. 476–477.

14. Carmona, op. cit., p. 193; Bronne, op. cit., p. 148. Léopold, handwritten note to Fanny, Dec. 2, 1851.

15. Flahaut to wife, Tuesday, Dec. 2, 1851, and again Wednesday morning, nine o'clock, Dec. 3, 1851, in Guedalla, op. cit., p. 120.

16. Bronne, op. cit., pp. 148–149. Cavaignac was to have been married on the second, but was released on Morny's personal orders, on condition that he leave France (with his fiancée) immediately.

17. Louis Napoléon to General de Flahaut, Élysée Nationale, Dec. 2, 1851, Guedalla, op. cit., p. 118.

18. Carmona, op. cit., pp. 190–191.

19. Jerrold, op. cit., v. III, p. 71.

20. Flahaut to wife, Dec. 3, 1851, Guedalla, op. cit., p. 121.

21. Carmona, op. cit., p. 191.

22. Jerrold, op. cit., vol. III, p. 82; Bronne, op. cit., pp. 150–153.

23. General Magnan to Int. Min. Morny, in Bronne, op. cit., pp. 152–153; Jerrold, op. cit., vol. III, p. 82. There was a great deal of sharp rivalry between the prefect and

the military governor. Prefect Maupas, although directly under Morny's orders, did his best to undermine him now and in the future, as Léopold noted.

24. Milza, op. cit., p. 260.

25. Morny to Nadine Baroche, Dufresne, op. cit., p. 158.

26. Carmona, op. cit., p. 193.

27. Jerrold, op. cit., vol. III, p. 83; Bronne, op. cit., p. 154.

28. Jerrold, op. cit., vol. III, p. 83; Bronne, p. 151.

29. Jerrold, op. cit., vol. III, p. 83.

30. Jerrold, Ibid.

31. Léopold to Fanny Le Hon, Dec. [?], 1851.

32. Carmona refers to uprisings and riots in thirty-two departments. Horace de Viel-Castel, *Mémoires sur le regne de Napoléon III, 1851–1864* (Paris: Guy Le Prat, [1942]), t. vol. I, p. 232.

33. Bronne, op. cit., p. 154, Léopold to his mother, Dec. [?], 1851.

34. Guedalla, op. cit., p. 125. Flahaut to wife, Dec. 5, 1851; Morny to Mme. Flahaut, Dec. 5, 1851; Flahaut to wife, Dec. 17, 1851—in Dufresne, op. cit., p. 158.

35. Jerrold, op. cit., vol. III, p. 86.

36. Prof. Louis Girard provides these figures, op. cit., p. 155; and Milza, op. cit., p. 267, as well as Carmona, op. cit., p. 186.

37. André Maurois, *Les Trois Dumas* (Paris: Hachette, 1957), p. 261; Bronne, op. cit., pp. 160–162.

38. Carmona, op. cit., p. 196.

39. Guedalla, op. cit., p. 130, Count de Laubespring to Morny, lundi, 9 dec. 1851.

18. The Sphinx of the Tuileries

1. Louis Napoléon Bonaparte, Jerrold, op. cit., vol. III, p. 96.

2. Auguste de Morny to his father, Jan. 26, 1852, in Guedalla, op. cit., p. 157.

3. Emily, Lady Palmerston to Margaret de Flahaut, Jan. 3, 1852, Broadlands, Guedalla, op. cit., pp. 171–172.

4. Palmerston to Laurence Sullivan, Dec. 16, 1851, Brown, op. cit., p. 327; see also, Palmerston to his brother William Temple, Dec. [?] 1851. p. 307.

5. On the value of the Orléans estate, see Jerrold, op. cit., vol. III, pp. 105–106, 108; Flahaut to Morny, Jan. 19, 1853, Guedalla, op. cit., p. 194.

6. Fanny Le Hon to Flahaut, Wednesday, Jan. 16, 1852, Guedalla, op. cit., pp. 197–198.

7. Morny to his father, Friday, Jan. 23, and Monday, Jan. 26, 1852, Guedalla, op. cit., pp. 199–200, and 201–202.

8. Fanny to Charles de Flahaut, Wednesday, Jan. 21, 1852, and Flahaut to Morny, Jan. 27, 1852, Guedalla, op. cit., pp. 203–205; on the sale of the Hôtel de Massa, e.g., see Morny to Margaret de Flahaut, Dec. 17, 1852, Guedalla, Ibid., pp. 242–243.

9. Louis Napoléon to Morny, March 2, 1852, Guedalla, Ibid., pp. 225–226, 227; Carmona points out Jérôme's insensate hatred of Morny, in his biography, op. cit., p. 217.

10. Fanny to Flahaut, Jan. 1852, Dufresne, op. cit., pp. 176–177.

11. Louis Napoléon to Morny, March 2, 1852, Guedalla, op. cit., pp. 225–226. Cf. Dufresne, op. cit., pp. 176–177, citing a good quote, although I have not used it (Louis Napoléon to Morny).

12. Carmona, op. cit., p. 216. Morny, 24,374, the government candidate, 797. Contrary to orders the prefect of Clermont had supported Morny over his government-sponsored rival. Morny was continuously elected a deputy from his twenties until the time of his death.

13. Bronne, op. cit., pp. 179–180.

14. Jerrold, op. cit., vol. III, pp. 108–109.

15. Jerrold, Ibid., vol. III, p. 109.

16. Jerrold, Ibid., vol. III, p. 110.

17. Bronne, op. cit., p. 180. Ironically, Morny's fabled citadel of Nades burned down in 1879. Everything he had built in his ephemeral world seemed to vanish the moment he died, apart from his children, Deauville and Longchamps, of which more anon later in this book.

18. Morny to Flahaut, Sunday, April 15, 1852, in Guedalla, op. cit., pp. 232–234.

19. Jerrold, op. cit., vol. III, p. 115.

20. Jerrold, Ibid., vol. III, p. 116. Between January 1 and December 31, 1852, Louis Napoléon had reduced the army from 446,000 to 400,000 men.

21. Jerrold, Ibid., vol. III, p. 115.

22. Carmona, op. cit., p. 221. While many historians including Jerrold claim this tour to have been quite successful (Jerrold, vol. III, pp. 115–116).

23. Carmona, Ibid., p. 221.

24. Carmona, Ibid., p. 222.

25. Paul Gagnon, *France Since 1789* (New York: Harper & Row, 1972), p. 165. Jerrold, op. cit., vol. III, p. 118; Girard, op. cit., p 183; Carmona, op. cit., p 223.

26. Jerrold, op. cit., vol. III, p. 119.

27. The Senate announced this at St. Cloud on May 18, 1804. The procedure was different then, however, for the national plebiscite confirming this only took place on the sixth of November, although the voting was dramatically rigged in Napoléon's favor. The coronation in Notre Dame Cathedral took place on December 2, 1805. Schom, *Napoléon Bonaparte*, pp. 333–334. In the November 1804 plebiscite on the acceptance of the empire 3,572,328 had voted for it, only 2,569 against. Napoléon again broke world records, with 99.999 percent of the French electorate voting for him. There is no evidence that Louis Napoléon or his staff had tampered with the tabulation of votes on Nov. 21–22, 1852; the two million abstentions alone attest to this, they obviously refused to support his empire.

28. Jerrold, op. cit., vol. III, pp. 118–119.

29. Jerrold, Ibid., vol. III, p. 220.

19. Violets and Wedding Bells

1. Jerrold, op. cit., vol. III, p. 122.
2. Impératrice Eugénie (Duke of Alba and Gabriel Hanotaux, eds.), *Lettres familières de l'Impératrice Eugénie* (Paris: Plon, 1871–1872), vol. I, p. 53; Desmond Seward, *Eugénie, the Empress and Her Empire* (Gloucestershire: Sutton Publishing, 2004), p. 40.
3. Seward, op. cit., pp. 4–5.
4. Seward, Ibid., p. 6.
5. Seward, Ibid., p. 1.
6. The Trianon *corrida* fight, in Seward, Ibid., p. 68. She described sexual relations as "*sale*," dirty, and was greatly embarrassed by her mother's endless affairs.
7. Seward, Ibid., pp. 15, 19.
8. Lord Malmesbury's description of Gen. Nárvaez, Seward, Ibid., p. 12, the stabbing, pp. 15 and 19.
9. Seward, Ibid., p. 18.
10. Seward, Ibid., p. 14.
11. Seward, Ibid., p. 14.
12. Seward, Ibid., pp. 20–22.
13. Seward quotes Viel-Castel, p. 31.
14. For Maxime Du Camp's tirade against Eugénie, see his *Souvenirs,* op. cit., pp. 146–176; Seward, op. cit., p. 45.
15. Prince Jérôme—Plon-Plon—met Eugénie in Madrid in 1843, "unbalanced," "crude"—Seward, op. cit., p. 13. Anna Bicknell's description of Jérôme—"coarse," "brutal," "violent," etc. Anna Bicknell, *Life in the Tuileries: Under the Second Empire* (London: Longmans, 1895), pp. 64–65. Von Hübner, who very much admired Eugénie, left a very rich anecdotal coverage of his diplomatic tour in Paris, in his *Neuf ans de souvenirs d'un ambassadeur d'Autriche à Paris sous le Second Empire* (Paris: Plon, 1905), see vol. I, p. 310; Seward, op. cit., p. 75.
16. Carmona, *Morny,* op. cit., p. 224. Eugénie and Louis Napoléon suffered from the crudest pornographic vilification. The good Goncourt described Louis Napoléon as a "reptile" and "lizard."
17. Seward, op. cit., p. 39.
18. Full list of of her father's titles.
19. There are several versions as to how, when, and where this event took place.
20. Dufresne, op. cit., p. 207.
21. Dufresne, Ibid., p. 208.
22. Once again there is more than one version of this event. It was not the wife of the foreign minister, but of the minister of public instruction. Seward, op. cit., pp. 36–37; Jerrold, op. cit., vol. III, pp. 427–428.
23. Seward, op. cit., p. 37. The original letter is in the Alba Archives, Liliria Palace, Madrid.

NOTES 451

24. Jerrold, Ibid., vol. III, p. 429. *Moniteur Universel,* 17 janvier 1853. Napoléon III, *Oeuvres de Napoléon III* (Paris: Plon, 1869), vol. 3, pp. 357–359; Milza, op. cit., p. 294.
25. Seward, op. cit., p. 40; original in Eugénie, *Lettres Familières,* p. 53.
26. Today the Regent Diamond is on display in the Louvre, valued at £48 million ($71 million).
27. Jerrold describes some of the clothing, op. cit., vol. III, pp. 432–433; see also Schom, *Napoleon Bonaparte,* pp. 337 ff.
28. Jerrold, Ibid., vol. III, Appendix VII, pp. 433, 475–478, and in greater detail in the *Moniteur Universel* and *The Times,* etc.
29. Carmona, op. cit., p. 226.
30. The dispensing of charity from her *corbeille de marriage* fund, Jerrold, op. cit., vol. III, pp. 431–432: 100,000 francs to "maternal societies," the remaining 150,000 francs for a new wing of the Hospice des Incurables in Paris. Seward, op. cit., p. 39, her letter to sister Paca. Louis Girard, op. cit., mentions 3,000 pardons, while Jerrold, op. cit., vol. III, p. 435, gives the more accurate figure of 4,312.

20. Birth of an Empire

1. Delphine Gay de Girard, *Lettres Parisiennes,* quoted by Guy Fargettes, *Emile et Isaac Pereires, L'Esprit d'Entreprises au XIXeme Siècle* (Paris: L'Harattan, 2001), p. 55. She was describing her first rail journey in August 1835 aboard Pereire's new railway to St.-Germain.
2. Michel Carmona, *Morny, Le Vice-Empereur* (Paris: Fayard, 2005), p. 145.
3. Jean Autin, *Les Frères Pereires, Le Bonheur d'Entreprendre* (Paris: Perrin, 1984), p. 110.
4. Carmona, op. cit., p. 146.
5. President Louis Napoléon signed the decree creating it, Nov. 15, 1851. Also Carmona, op. cit., pp. 231 ff.
6. Autin, op. cit., pp. 121, 139–141. See also Gille Bertrand for banking background: *La Banque en France au XIXe Siècle* (Paris: Droz, 1970).
7. Carmona, op. cit., 138–139; Autin, op. cit., 139–141.
8. Carmona, op. cit., pp. 234, 236–238.
9. Carmona, Ibid., p. 234; Claude Dufresne, *Morny, L'Homme du Second Empire* (Paris: Perrin, 1983), p. 200.
10. Carmona, op. cit., 260.
11. Carmona, Ibid., 235. One side gave him 1 million francs, the opposition slipping him another 1.2 million.
12. Carmona, Ibid., 246–247, 294; Jean-Yves Mollier, *Louis Hachette* (Paris: Fayard, 1999), pp. 123 ff., regarding educational books, government, pp. 262–263, 294, 299 ff., regarding railway concessions (inspired by W. H. Smith). Morny was also president of the Essonnes Paper Co.
13. Overconfident individuals often blot their own copybook at the peak of their careers. Morny's case may also have been caused in part by extreme abdominal

pain he was suffering more and more every year, as a result of a medicine called "perles" (pearls) taken for sexual enhancement. It had an arsenic base.

14. Carmona, op. cit., p. 238; Autin, op. cit., pp. 122, 133, 304, 316.
15. Carmona, Ibid., pp. 236–239.
16. Carmona, Ibid., pp. 176–277.
17. Autin, op. cit., pp. 140–141.
18. On Pereires' property investments, see Autin, Ibid., p. 178 ff.; re the properties around the Louvre, etc., Carmona, *Haussmann* (Paris: Fayard, 2000), pp. 292, 459–460 (Hôtel de la Paix).
19. Carmona, *Morny*, p. 316.
20. Carmona, Ibid., pp. 312–313. After "l'affaire Le Hon" and the Grand Central scandal, Fould thought Morny was finished.
21. Carmona, Ibid., pp. 312–313, Goncourt Journals for February 1857; Prosper Mérimée, *Correspondance Générale* (Toulouse: Privat, 1941–1964), vol. VIII, p. 239. Mérimée to Mme. de Montijo, Feb. 1857. Fanny may have been a countess, but she was no lady. Between 1832 and 1856 she gave Morny seven million francs, of which he repaid two million. But this did not include the one million francs he provided as the dowry for their daughter Louise, who married Prince Poniatowski on June 12. 1856, and money he gave Léopold Le Hon—AN Fonds Morny 116 AP2 dossier 9. Jacques Griscelli de Vezzani, *Mémoires de Griscelli, dit Le Baron de Rimini, Agent Secret de Napoléon III (1850–1858)* (Bruxelles: private printing, 1867), pp. 49–54. Viel-Castel, *Mémoires,* op. cit., vol. IV, p. 96—dimanche, 5 juillet 1857.
22. Carmona, op. cit., p. 314. For the continuing Morny–Fanny saga see AN Fonds Morny 116 AP dossier 9. Details of the Griscelli involvement, including Fanny's note to Morny when in Russia are revealed in Griscelli's *Mémoires,* op. cit., pp. 45–46, 52, 53. He claims that Morny paid him 6,000 francs—a year's salary—for his discretion and silence. In the end Griscelli permitted Léopold Le Hon to carry the box with the documents, personally handing them over to Louis Napoléon, who subsequently ordered the suppression of Griscelli's book, one copy of which, however, I found in the Bodleian Library, Oxford.

21. Georges Haussmann

1. Georges Haussmann, *Mémoires du Baron Haussmann* (Paris: Victor Havard, 1890). vol. I, p. vii.
2. On family background see Haussann, Ibid., vol. I, pp. 5–14 and 21. Allegations reported by Pierre Milza of dishonest actions of both Georges Haussmann's father, Nicolas Valentin, and Georges Haussmann himself, have been unsubstantiated by bona fide documentary evidence. Then as now successful men inevitably attract the "criticism" of jealous peers.
3. Haussman, Ibid., vol. I, p. 21.
4. Ibid., vol. I, p. 26.

5. Ibid., vol. I, pp. 30–31, 35.
6. Ibid., vol. I, p. 34, "la construction symétrique d'une symphonie."
7. Ibid., vol. I, pp. 27–29.
8. Ibid., vol. I, pp. 30, 37.
9. Ibid., vol. I, p. 46.
10. Ibid., vol. I, pp. 47, 48.
11. Ibid., vol. II, pp. 1–3.
12. Ibid., vol. II, p. 45.
13. Jean Gilbert Victor Fialin de Persigny, *Mémoires du duc de Persigny* (Paris: Plon, Nourrit, 1896), pp. 253–255.
14. Haussmann, op. cit., vol. II, p. 51.
15. Haussmann, Ibid., vol. II, pp. 51–53.

22. Prefect of Paris

1. Georges Haussmann, *Mémoires du Baron Haussmann* (Paris: Victor Havard, 1890), vol. II, Préfecture de la Seine.
2. June 1853, Haussmann, Ibid., vol. II, p. 87.
3. Ibid., vol. II, p. 93.
4. Decree of March 26, 1852, re expropriations.
5. Parisian cemeteries were fast running out of space, a problem Haussmann was prevented from solving while in office. By 1869 he reckoned on up to 42,000 burials a year.
6. By 1870 the population of Paris would reach about two million. In 1853 the population had been about 1.2 million, before the city limits were extended to include suburbs, adding several hundred thousand. Haussman, op. cit., vol. II, pp. 452–458.
7. Haussmann, Ibid., vol. II, p. 458. Official figures 117,500 families having been left homeless, or perhaps as many as 600,000. Most of them moved into the outlying suburbs, before they in turn were incorporated in an extended Paris.
8. Ibid., vol. II, pp. 59–60; Michel Carmona, *Haussmann* (Paris: Fayard, 2000), p. 16.
9. Haussmann, op. cit., vol. II, pp. 85–86, 89.
10. Ibid., vol. II, pp. 89–90, 91–92.
11. Ibid., vol. II, pp. 89–90; Paris was allegedly founded by the Celtic Parisii in the third century BC.
12. Carmona, op. cit., pp. 355–357. This special *Caisse de la Boulangerie* functioned between September 1, 1853, and September 1, 1856, and again in 1867.
13. For the history of the streets of Paris, see Jacques Hillaret's excellent *Dictionnaire historique des rues de Paris* (Paris: Editions de Minuit, 1963), 2 vols.
14. Haussmann, op. cit., vol. II, p. 76; Carmona, op. cit., p. 312.
15. Haussmann, Ibid., vol. II, p. 367. Expropriations were dealt with by the Imperial Decree of March 16, 1852—cf. Ch. XVI. The Law of 27 May 1858 created the Caisse des Travaux de Paris—the Public Works Treasury, intended to provide these sub-

ventions on which the municipal Bons, IOU vouchers, were drawn. (Somewhat similar to the system used earlier for the Caisse des Boulangeries.) By drawing directly on this Caisse, Haussmann could pay for work directly without having first to seek approval of the Legislative Body. Haussmann, Ibid., vol. II, pp. 357–404, 556–557 cite Haussmann's explanation for the extraordinary use of "Bons" in this situation. For gas lighting, see Haussmann, Ibid., vol. II, p. 214.

16. Haussmann, Ibid., vol. II, p. 214.
17. Ibid., vol. II, pp. 514–516.
18. Ibid., vol. II, pp. 489–491. New asylums included the Asile de Sainte-Anne, that of the Ville Évrard, Vaucluse, Bicêtre, and La Salpétrie.
19. Ibid., vol. II, p. 524.
20. Ibid., vol. II, pp. 527–528. He also built La Santé prison in the Enclos de la Santé, and the new police barracks at St.-Denis and at Sceau. Ibid., vol. II, pp. 489–490.
21. Ibid., vol. II, pp. 507–508. Charles Garnier's Opéra—known as the Théâtre Impérial de l'Opéra under the Second Empire—was not inaugurated until Jan. 5, 1875, built at a cost of 35 million francs ($4.5 billion today).
22. Jacques Offenbach's popular *Tales of Hoffmann* was currently being performed at the Opéra Comique. On various attempts to bribe Haussmann, see Carmona, *Haussmann*, p. 458, as well as Haussmann's *Mémoires*, vol. II, p. 543 ff.
23. Jacques François Griscelli, a police agent working for Prefect of Police Pierre Piétri. Previously he had been involved in obtaining Fanny Le Hon's papers. He provides information re the unsavory background to Persigny's (forced?) marriage and the 14 million francs that Persigny eventually "obtained" from that marriage. Griscelli strongly implied Persigny's involvement in the most curious death of his bride's seventeen-year-old brother, from which he was to profit by some seven million francs. See *Mémoires de Griscelli, Agent Secret de Napoléon II (1850–1858), de Cavour (1859–1861)* (Bruxelles: privately printed, 1867), pp. 54–58. As minister of the interior, Persigny had placed a police spy in Laffitte's home, presumably for personal reasons. Persigny and Police Prefect Piétri were very close friends. See also "Persigny" in Jean Tulard's *Dictionnaire du Second Empire* (Paris: Fayard, 1995), pp. 995–997. Ironically, he left a far greater estate on his death than did Emperor Napoléon III.
24. Carmona, *Haussmann,* p. 461.
25. Haussmann, op. cit., vol. II, pp. 108–109. Here he discusses his embarrassment regarding Louis Napoléon's offer to help with that prefect's daughter's dowry. See also, Carmona, *Haussmann*, op. cit., pp. 430–431.
26. See also Haussmann, vol. II, p. 514 ff.
27. Ibid., vol. II, pp. 337–340. His annual 30,000-franc honorarium as senator also ceased with the fall of the Second Empire. Although his wife, Octavie, had inherited her parents' 1,000-hectare estate-winery, phylloxera decimated the vines, a financial catastrophe. Haussmann received no income from the family cotton

mills in Alsace, and was now obliged to sell his own vacation home, an old mill outside Nice. Attempting various business ventures to restore his fortunes, Haussmann returned to Bordeaux even poorer. His detractors would have rejoiced.

23. Crosses, Candlesticks, and Swords: The Crimea

1. *"L'Empire, c'est la paix."* Repeated by Louis Napoléon throughout 1852–1855.
2. *Moniteur Universel,* 2 mars 1854; see also, Anceau, op. cit., p. 279.
3. Sydney N. Fisher and William Ochsenwald, *The Middle East, A History* (New York: McGraw-Hill, 1990), p. 294.
4. Fisher and Ochsenwald, Ibid., pp. 269–270. Mehmet Ali (Muhammad Ali, in Arabic form) was the self-declared khedive of Egypt, 1805–1848, while remaining under the nominal authority of the Ottoman sultan. See also in Fisher and Ochsenwald, pp. 167, 178, 194–297. For summaries of the Treaties of Adrianople and Hunkiar Iskelesi, see these same authors, pp. 168–270. See also *The New Cambridge Modern History, Vol. 10: The Zenith of Power, 1830–1870,* the 1960 edition. Ch. XVIII, "The Crimean War."
5. Clarendon to Cowley, April (?), 1853, Henry R. C. Wellesley, Earl Cowley, *The Paris Embassy of Lord Cowley* (London: Butterworth, 1928), p. 26—this is a most instructive work. Lord Stratford de Redcliffe, Stratford Canning, British ambassador to the Subime Porte, 1841–1858. See also David Wetzel, *The Crimean War, A Diplomatic History* (New York: Columbia University Press, 1985), Ch. 3, "The Eastern Crisis, 1853." Nicholas I ruled from 1825 to 1855. The 4th Earl of Clarendon, George Villiers, served as foreign secretary, Feb. 1853–Feb. 1858; Nov. 1865–July 1866, and again Dec. 1868–June 1870; the first Earl Cowley, Henry Wellesley, 1804–1884, nephew of the Duke of Wellington, served as British ambassador most ably during the critical period, 1852–1867. He had a special relationship with both Louis Napoléon and Eugénie—who trusted him implicitly.
6. Fisher and Ochsenwald, op. cit., p. 291. By 1850 Brit. exports worth £2.4 million. England also imported a substantial amount of wheat from Russia and Turkey.
7. Anceau, op. cit. 278. Louis Napoléon to Lord Malmesbury, Feb 1853. Louis Napoléon to Ambassador Walewski in London, May 25, 1853, in Milza, op. cit., p. 385. Talleyrand quote, Giraudeau, op. cit., p. 346.
8. Cowley, op. cit., Lord Cowley to Foreign Secretary Clarendon, Jan, 28, 1854, p. 39, and Eugene, p. 37.
9. See Françoise de Bernardy, *Walewski* (Paris: Perrin, 1976), pp. 127 ff.
10. Cowley, op. cit., p. 39, Cowley to Clarendoon, Jan. 2, 1854; Milza, op. cit., p. 383, 386; Anceau, op. cit., pp. 279–280; Nap. III, *Oeuvres de Napoléon II* (Paris: Aymot, 1869), vol. III, p. 162; and AN 400 AO47 on the exchange of notes, between Louis Napoléon and Nicholas I, January 1854.
11. Jerrold, op. cit., vol. IV, pp. 10–11. Correspondence between Napoléon III and Nicholas I, Jan. 17 and 29, 1854, Tsar Nicholas demanded complete control of all

Holy Places, the Danubian provinces, etc., and the rejection of the Five-Power Treaty of July 1841. To avoid war Louis Napoléon was willing to share custodianship of Jerusalem, etc. Bernardy, op. cit., pp. 134–138. See also *The New Modern Cambridge History,* vol. 10, op. cit.; and Pierre Renouvin's classic, *La Politique Extérieure du Second Empire* (Paris: Centre de Documentation Univérsitaire, 1940).

12. Jerrold, op. cit., vol. IV, pp. 11 and 23 for the Boulogne meeting.

13. Jerrold, Ibid., vol. IV, pp. 40–41. Anceau, op. cit., p. 278. *Moniteur Universel,* 2 mars 1854, Supplément Extraordinaire, p. 245. See also Anceau, op. cit., p. 178.

14. Marshal Armand Jacques Leroy de Saint-Arnaud, 1798–1854, a veteran of the long war in Algeria, died of cholera, Sept. 1854, *Dictionnaire du Second Empire, or DSE,* op. cit., pp. 1153–1154. First Baron Raglan, Fitzroy James Henry Somerset, 1788–1855, *ODNB (The Oxford Dictionary of National Biography)* (Oxford Univ. Press, 2004), vol. 51, pp. 582–586, Raglan was succeeded by the less than successful Sir James Simpson, 1792–1868, *ODNB,* vol. 50, pp. 693–694.

15. The other two divisional commanders were Canrobert and Bosquet, both promoted to the rank of marshal. "François Canrobert, 1809–1895," *DSE,* pp. 229–230. Plon-Plon's desertion is suppressed by editor Jean Tulard in, *DSE,* article, "La Guerre de la Crimée," by Jean Ganiage, pp. 378–379, Jérôme later abandoned his post in Algeria as well—Bertaut, *Jérôme,* op. cit., pp. 154–155; and Louis Madelin's *La Catastrophe de Russie* (Paris: Plon, 1949), p. 139.

16. James Thomas Brudenell, 7th Earl of Cardigan, 1797–1868, *ODNB,* vol. 8, pp. 344–347. It was because of the scandal re the appalling living and medical conditions, and the lack of clothes and supplies in the Crimea that Lord Aberdeen's government fell in January 1855.

17. *DSE,* op. cit., "Crimée," p. 382.

18. Gen. Aimable Pélissier, 1794–1869, becoming commander in chief of the French army, May 16, 1855–1856. He, supported by Gen. MacMahon, directed the taking of Malakoff Tower, *DSE,* p. 991. Gen. Adolphe Niel, 1802–1869, *DSE,* pp. 910–911. An incompetent Sir James Simpson, 1792–1868, was next replaced in Nov. 1855 by Sir William Codrington, see "James Simpson," *ODNB,* vol. 50, pp. 693–694.

19. *DSE,* "Crimée, Aspects de la Campagne Naval," by Etienne Taillemite, p. 381. Hamelin was relieved of his command by Adm. Bruat at the end of 1854, while Richard Dundas was replaced by Admiral Lyons. Dundas was then transferred to the Baltic to replace "Black Charley" Napier in Feb. 1855. Dundas, 1802–1861, was the highly influential second son of Viscount Melville, *ODNB,* vol. 17, p. 288. Admiral Bruat, 1796–1855, died of cholera, Nov. 1855, *DSE,* "Armand Joseph Bruat," pp. 214–215. Admiral Ferdinand Alphonse Hamelin, 1796–1864, *DSE,* p. 613.

20. *Dictionnaire du Second Empire,* op. cit., p. 382; Vice Adm. Sir Charles Napier, 1786–1860, see the *NODNB,* vol. 40, pp. 151–156. Adm. Alexandre Parseval-Deschênes, 1790–1860, *DSE,* p. 971.

21. Étienne Taillemite gives these figures, *DSE,* p. 382.

22. *The Times*, Monday, Dec. 31, 1855, p. 7; *Moniteur Universel, Journal Officiel de L'Empire Français,* dimanche, 30 déc., 1855, p. 1442.

23. *The Times,* Ibid., Dec. 31, 1855.

24. The full address, in the *Moniteur Universel,* dimanche, 30 déc. 1855, p. 1442.

25. *The Times,* Dec. 31, 1855, p. 7.

26. Anceau, op. cit., p. 285. 95,000 French troops killed in battle, or died of wounds or disease, chiefly cholera. His figure of 22,000 British dead is incorrect. See the *New Cambridge Modern History,* vol. 10, p. 485, for British casualties: 2,755 killed in action, 11,848 died of wounds, and 17,799 of sickness, for a total of 32,402. See also *DSE,* op. cit., p. 382; and Orlando Figes, *Crimea* (London: Penguin, 2011), p. 252. According to Austrian Ambassador Alexandre, Count von Hübner, in August 1855 the Russians had 66,000 infantry, 2,000 cavalry, and 20 batteries of artillery in the Crimea. Hübner, *Neuf ans de Souvenirs d'un Ambassadeur d'Autriche à Paris, 1851–1859* (Paris: Plon, 1905), p. 339, and yet Nicholas II claimed 500,000 casualties. If he also had another 170,000 troops around the Baltic, there would appear to be a discrepancy somewhere.

24. A Very Special Relationshp

1. Queen Victoria, April 1855, quoted in Jerrold, op. cit., vol. IV, p. 88.

2. *Le Moniteur Universel,* lundi, 29 août 1855, p . 1.

3. Jerrold, op. cit., vol. IV, pp. 66–67.

4. Jerrold, Ibid., vol. IV, p. 67.

5. Jerrold, Ibid., vol. IV, pp. 71–73.

6. Jerrold, Ibid., vol. IV, p. 74.

7. Jerrold, Ibid., vol. IV, pp. 76–77.

8. Jerrold, Ibid., vol. IV, p. 62.

9. *The Times,* Monday, Aug. 20, 1855, p. 7, with the report from Boulogne of Saturday, Aug. 18. For the complete coverage of her arrival see The *Times,* Aug. 20–29, 1855; *Moniteur Universel,* Aug. 19–20; and Jerrold, op. cit., vol. IV, p. 79.

10. *Moniteur Universel,* Aug. 19, 1855, p. 1. For details of this visit see Queen Victoria, *Leaves from a Journal, 1855* (London: Andre Deutsch, 1961), comprised of the Queen's diary entries covering both the April and August visits, e.g., beginning with p. 73. See also Queen Victoria, eds. Arthur Christopher Benson and Viscount Escher, *The Letters of Queen Victoria, A Selection, 1837–1861* (London: John Murray, 1908), vol. III—1854–1861.

11. *Moniteur Universel,* dimanche, 19 août 1855, p. 1. Queen Victoria, *Leaves,* entry of Saturday, August 18 [1855].

12. Jerrold, vol. IV, p. 80.

13. *The Times,* Monday, Aug. 20, 1855, pp. 6 and 7. "The Visit of the Queen to Paris." By Submarine and British Telegraph.

14. Victoria, *Leaves,* Sunday, Aug. 26, p. 129.

15. Jerrold, op. cit., vol. IV, p. 90.
16. Jerrold, Ibid., vol. IV, p. 89.
17. Jerrold, Ibid., vol. IV, p. 82.
18. Jerrold, Ibid., vol. IV, pp. 82–83.
19. Jerrold, Ibid., vol. IV, p. 82.
20. Jerrold, Ibid., vol. IV, p. 81.
21. Jerrold, Ibid., vol. IV, p. 80.
22. Jerrold, Ibid., vol. IV, p. 85.
23. Jerrold, Ibid., vol. IV, p. 86; Victoria, *Leaves,* p. 129.
24. Jerrold, Ibid., vol. IV, p. 84. For full coverage of this event see *The Times,* Aug. 27, 1855, pp. 7–8, citing article of Saturday, Aug. 15; see also *Moniteur Universel,* samedi, 27 août, p. 7, citing article dated vendredi, 24 août. The following descriptions have been taken from these two newspapers.
25. Victoria, *Leaves,* pp. 116–117.
26. For the "Avenue Victoria" ceremony, Carmona, *Haussmann,* p. 332; *The Times,* Tuesday, Aug, 28, 1855, p. 12; *Moniteur Universel,* of the same day.
27. Jerrold, op. cit., vol. IV, pp. 88–89.
28. Jerrold, Ibid., vol. IV, p. 90.
29. Jerrold, Ibid., vol. IV, p. 90.

25. A Child of France

1. Anceau, op. cit., p. 287.
2. Milza, op. cit., p. 397.
3. Cowley, op. cit., p. 90. The British embassy was bought from Pauline Bonaparte Bacciochi by the Duke of Wellington following the fall of Napoléon.
4. Lord Cowley suggests this to Clarendon, Cowley, op. cit., p. 91.
5. Victoria to Louis Napoléon, Feb. 15, 1856, in Victoria, *The Letters of,* op. cit., pp. 172–173. All of her correspondence to him was in French.
6. Victoria to Palmerston, Feb. 27, 1856, Victoria, *Letters,* op. cit., pp. 172–173.
7. Leader of *The Times,* Wed., March 19, 1856, p. 6. Also a very long article on the serious decay of the administration and government of Turkey.
8. "Foreign Intelligence": "Accouchement of the Imperial Empress," dated Sunday, March 16, reported in *The Times,* Tuesday, March 18, 1856, p. 8.
9. Horace de Viel-Castel, *Mémoires du Comte Horace de Viel Castel sur le Règne de Napoléon III (1851–1864)* (Paris: Chez Tous les Libraries, 1884), vol. III, pp. 213–214.
10. For Morny's speech, *Moniteur Universel,* lundi, 17 mars 1856, p. 1.
11. *The Times,* Tuesday, March 18, 1856, p. 8.
12. *The Times,* Ibid.
13. Viel-Castel, op. cit.
14. Jerrold, op. cit., vol. IV, p. 111. The hourly palace "Bulletins de Santé" referred to *"fièvre de lait"* though of course a wet nurse was in fact breast-feeding the baby.

15. *The Times,* Thursday, March 20, 1856, p. 9.
16. Viel-Castel, op. cit., vol. III, p. 221, mardi, 1 avril 1856.
17. On Saturday the twenty-ninth of March. Jerrold, vol. IV, p. 112; and *Moniteur Universel,* 18 mars 1856.
18. Cowley to Clarendon, March 1856, Cowley, op. cit., p. 94.
19. Clarendon to Cowley, March, 1856, Cowley, op. cit., 95.
20. Victoria to Louis Napoléon, 3 avril 1856, Victoria, *Letters,* pp. 182–183.
21. *The Times,* Monday, March 31, 1856, quoted Prefect Piétri's bulletin; see also *Moniteur Universel,* lundi, 31 mars 1856.
22. Cowley, op. cit., p. 91; and Viel-Castel, op. cit., vol. III, p. 222, mercredi, avril 2, [1856].
23. Viel-Castel, op. cit., vol. III, p. 222, mercredi, avril 2 [1856].
24. Bernardy, *Walewski,* pp. 211–212.
25. Fisher and Ochsenwald, op. cit., p. 296.
26. Bernardy, op. cit., p. 215.
27. Anceau, op. cit., p. 333–334.
28. Virginie Castiglione, born in Florence in 1835 (or 1837), *DSE,* p. 242; Milza, op. cit., pp. 358–360.
29. Cowley, op. cit., pp. 93–95, 96.
30. Steward, *Eugénie,* pp. 103, 108.
31. Viel-Castel, op. cit., vol. III, p. 221, mardi, 1 avril [1856]; jeudi, 3 avril, and dimanche, 3 mars.
32. Viel-Castel, Ibid., vol. III, p. 221, mardi, 1 avril. The actual expedition launched in 1857 was comprised of 30,000 men, but Napoléon III remained at the Tuileries, not visiting Algeria for the first time until 1860.
33. Claude Martin, *Histoire de l'Algérie française, 1830–1962* (Paris: Editions du 4 Fils Aymon, 1963), pp. 160–161. Martin gives the official number of French troops killed at 1,500. The government figures for wounded or missing invariably tend to underestimate the actual numbers. Total French casualties probably reached 5,000. The number of Berber warriors killed, given at "*bien plus grand*" than those of the French.
34. Viel-Castel, op. cit., vol. III, p. 223, mercredi, 2 avril [1856]. "La France jouit du repos. Elle a conquis la considération. Dieu veuille nous conserver longtemps sous la tutelle de Louis Napoléon."

26. An Italian Opera

1. Orsini to Napoléon III, Aeau, op. cit., pp. 170–171, n. 1.
2. Jerrold, op. cit., vol. IV, p. 165.
3. *The Times,* Friday, Jan. 15, 1858, p. 7, referring to events of Jan. 14.
4. *The Times,* Saturday, Jan. 16, 1858, pp. 7 and 9. All reports here are from their special correspondent, occasionally quoting from the *Moniteur Universel,* of Friday, Jan. 15, 1858.

5. *The Times,* Saturday, Jan. 16, 1858, pp. 7 and 9. "THE ATTEMPTED ASSASSI-NATION OF EMPEROR NAPOLEON."

6. *The Times,* Sat., Jan 16, Ibid.

7. Ibid.

8. Ibid.

9. Ibid.; Cowley [Henry Richard Charles Wellesley], op. cit., p. 152—Cowley to For. Sec. Malmesbury, March 16, 1858; *The Times,* Friday, Jan. 15, 1858, 6 p.m., p. 7.

10. *The Times,* Monday, Jan. 18, 1858, pp. 7, 8 and 9; and *The Times* editorial of Satur-day, Jan. 16, 1858, p. 8. For the Maupas comment, see Emile de Maupas, *Mémoires sur le Second Empire* (Paris: Dentu, 1882), vol. II, p. 81 ff.

11. Marcel Le Clère's article, "Orsini," in the *DSE,* pp. 944–945, and for greater de-tails, "Felice Orsini," in the *Dizionario Biografico Degli Italiani* (Roma: Istituto della Encclopedia Italiana, 2013), vol. 70, pp. 638–642.

12. Bernardy, *Walewski,* op. cit., p. 230; Clarendon to Cowley, Jan. 15, 1858; and Cow-ley to Clarendon, Jan. 18, 1858, Cowley, op. cit., pp. 147, 150.

13. Viel-Castel, op. cit., vol. IV, p. 232.

14. Cowley, op. cit., pp. 150–151, Clarendon to Cowley, Jan. 19, 1858; see Jerrold, op. cit., vol. IV, pp. 184–185.

15. Viel-Castel, op. cit., vol. IV, pp. 234–235. *"Qui le cas échéant."* The new Privy Coun-cil was comprised of Cardinal Nicholas Morlot, Marshal Aimable Pélissier—the new Duke de Malakoff, Minister of State Achille Fould, the newly created Comte de Persigny, Senator Raymond Troplong, and Auguste de Morny.

16. As a result of the passage of the Government of India Act in August 1848, the East India Company ceased to exist, the administration of India now placed under the British Crown. On May 1, 1871, Disraeli was to create Victoria Empress of India.

17. Cowley, op. cit., p. 163. Victoria to Cowley, April 18, 1858; Cowley, Ibid., Malmes-bury to Cowley, April 17, 1858, p. 162; Ibid., Clarendon to Cowley, Jan. 16, 1858, p. 248. My italics.

18. Orsini to Napoléon III, Feb. 1858, Jerrold, op. cit., vol. IV, p. 170, n. 1.

19. Cowley to Clarendon, March 3, 1858, Cowley, op. cit., p. 159.

20. Cowley, op. cit., p. 160, Cowley's farewell to outgoing Clarendon on March 3. Viel-Castel, op. cit., vol. IV, p. 232. According to Blanchard Jerrold, Louis Napoléon was deeply distressed by having to order the execution of Felix Orsini because Orsini's father had fought by Louis Napoléon's side in the Romagna in 1831—he had executed a friend's son. Jerrold, op. cit., vol. IV, p. 169.

21. See the excellent article on "Cavour" in the *Dizionario Biografico Degli Italiani,* vol. 23, pp. 120–128. Camillo Paolo filippo Giulio Benson, Conte di Cavour, was born in Turin on Aug. 10, 1810, dying in that same city on June 6, 1861. His father, Carlo Benso, Conte di Cavour, was a founding leader of the "Risorgimento" (Resurrec-tion) movement leading to a unified Italy.

22. Vittorio Emanuele Mari Alberto Eugenio Ferdinando Tommaso, 1820–1878.

Cavour knew him from the day he was born in Turin on the fourteenth of March [1820]. He served as King of Sardinia, 1849–1861, until Italian independence. His mother, Maria Theresa, was a Habsburg, and he later married Adelaide, a Habsburg cousin, thereby complicating his relations with Vienna over the Italian War of Independence from the Austrians.

23. Jerrold, op. cit., vol. IV, pp. 174–175.

27. Return of a Carbonaro: Italy, 1859

1. Eugénie quote, "our cause," in Jerrold, op. cit., vol. IV, p. 198.
2. Prince Albert, 1858 (?), in Jerrold, Ibid., vol. IV, pp. 194–195.
3. Jerrold, Ibid., vol. IV, p. 198.
4. In March of 1860, Parma, Tuscany, Modena, and the Romagna voted to join the Kingdom of Sardinia. On March 17, 1861, Law No. 4671 was passed, creating the Kingdom of Italy, with Turin as its first capital, until 1865, when it shifted to Florence, 1865–1871, and finally to Rome in 1871.
5. Jerrold, vol. IV, p. 183. Cowley to Malmesbury, Jan. 12, 1859.
6. Jerrold, Ibid., vol. IV, pp. 194–195.
7. *"Ça ne va pas,"* Lajos Kossuth, 1802–1894, quoted in Jerrold, Ibid., vol. IV, p. 192, n. 2, quoting from Kossuth's *Memoirs.*
8. Jerrold, Ibid., vol. IV, pp. 180, 194. Victoria to Louis Napoléon, Dec. 1858.
9. Jerrold, Ibid., vol. IV, p. 181; Milza, op. cit., pp. 417–418; Anceau, op. cit., pp. 302–305.
10. Anceau, op. cit., p. 305.
11. Jerrold's translation of this address, op. cit., vol. IV, pp. 183–186.
12. Milza, op. cit., pp. 418–419; Girard, op. cit., pp. 284 ff.
13. Eventually the French would field an army of 172,000 men. Girard, op. cit., pp. 284–286; Anceau, op. cit., pp. 306–307; Jerrold, op. cit., vol. IV, pp. 194–195, and 198 for Eugénie's declaration.
14. Jerrold, op. cit., vol. IV, pp. 199–200.
15. Anceau, op. cit., p. 309.
16. Girard, op. cit., pp. 286–287. This was just the beginning of a most complex burgeoning crisis, allegedly because of the hostility of England, Prussia, and Austria to the cession of Nice and Savoy to France in 1859. Jerrold, op. cit., vol. IV, pp. 255–271.
17. Anceau, op. cit., pp. 310, 382.
18. Anceau, Ibid., pp. 3882 ff.
19. In order to obtain Venice, Italy joined forces with Prussia on April 8, 1866, and on the twentieth of June [1866] Italy declared war on Austria, resulting in an Italian victory. In the resultant Treaty of Vienna of October 12, 1866, Austrians at long last ceded Venice to the new Italian state. Modern Italy was now complete. In 1871 its capital was transferred permanently from Florence to Rome where the Quirinal Palace became the official residence of the kings of Italy.

28. Four Seasons

1. Metternich on Napoléon III. Pauline de Metternich, *My Years in Paris* (London: Everleigh, Nash & Grayson, 1922), p. 14.
2. Pauline von Metternich, Ibid., pp. 9–10.
3. Metternich, Ibid., p. 127.
4. Metternich, Ibid., pp. 126–127.
5. Metternich, Ibid., pp. 91–92, 96. A very susperstitious Eugénie associated her own existence closely with that of the beheaded Bourbon queen of Louis XVI, always expecting disaster for herself and her son. Napoléon I wore this diamond in the hilt of his coronation sword.
6. I discuss the background to this in my biography of Napoléon I.
7. Metternich, op. cit., p. 128.
8. Prosper Mérimée to the Comtesse de Montijo, Nov. 28, 1861, in Mérimée, *Prosper Mérimée à la Comtsse de Montijo* (Paris: Edition Privée, 1930), vol. II, pp. 197–198.
9. Metternich, op. cit., p. 113.
10. Metternich, Ibid., p. 87.
11. Metternich, Ibid.
12. Metternich, Ibid., pp. 87–90.
13. Auguste de Morny was elevated from count to duke on July 15, 1862.
14. Metternich, Ibid., p. 94
15. Metternich, Ibid., p. 98.
16. Metternich, Ibid., pp. 11–14, 99–102.
17. Mérimée to Comtesse de Montijo, Nov. 18, 1863, Ibid., pp. 242–243.
18. Mérimée to Comtesse de Montijo, June 28, 1864, Ibid., p. 253.
19. Metternich, Ibid., pp. 108–109.
20. Metternich, Ibid., pp. 105–107.
21. Metternich, Ibid., pp. 109–110.
22. Metternich, Ibid., p. 137.
23. Metternich, Ibid., p. 136.
24. Metternich, Ibid., pp. 138–139.

29. Inquisition at Baden: 1860

1. Jerrold, op. cit., vol. IV, pp. 268–270.
2. Jerrold, Ibid., vol. IV, p. 222.
3. Jerrold, vol. IV, p. 237, n. 1. John, Lord Campbell, May 10, 1860. But in France even Louis Napoléon's arch-opponent, Adolphe Thiers, hailed the acquisition of Savoy—"The worst humiliation of 1815 has been wiped out." Jerrold, vol. IV, p. 237; Ibid., vol. IV, p. 255, and Anceau, op. cit., pp. 387–388 regarding the Anglo-French military expedition to Peking in 1860 led by Gen. Sir Hope Grant and Gen. Charles Cousin Montauban, the future Count Palikao. Technically the French and

English were attacking because of the Chinese failure to respect the previous June 1858 Treaty of T'ien Tsin, opening ports to their commerce.

4. See Schom, *Napoléon Bonaparte,* op. cit., pp. 678 ff. Napoléon's staggering defeat at Leipzig in October 1813 effectively shattered his Confederation of the Rhine, France losing 400,000 allied troops in the process.

5. For the text of this secret memorandum dispatched to Albert in England, see Jerrold, op. cit., vol. IV, pp. 268–270, and 220 and 250 for the Prussian army reforms of Jan. 12, 1860.

6. Jerrold, Ibid., vol. IV, p. 270. My italics.

7. Lord John Russell's statement, Feb. 21, 1861, e.g., see Anceau, op. cit., p. 390; and Fisher and Ochsenwald, *The Middle East,* op. cit., p. 297.

8. Jerrold, op. cit., vol. IV, pp. 287–288; Anceau, op. cit., pp. 395–397. Hippolyte Carnot to Mr. Darimon: this decree *"est l'arrêt de l'Empire."*

9. Prosper, Comte de Chasseloup-Laubat, the former minister for Algeria and the Colonies, now served as governor of Algeria, March 1859–Nov. 1860, when he was succeeded by Marshal Aimable Pélissier. See also, Claude Martin, *Histoire de l'Algérie,* op. cit., p. 168. The indigenous peoples of North Africa are Hamites, not Arabs. See René Pillorget's article, published electronically, "Les Deux Voyages de Napoléon III en Algérie (1860 et 1865)," pp. 2 and 3. See also the full coverage, with illustrations, in *Le Monde Illustré,* vol. VII, Juillet-Décembre 1860.

10. Desmond Seward, *Eugénie,* op. cit., pp. 105–106. Eugénie traveled via Edinburgh to Glasgow and to the estate of the Duchess of Hamilton—daughter of Stéphanie de Beauharnais (the late Grand Duchess of Baden). Eugénie continued to act erratically during this period of mourning for a sister and companion she could never replace. She never danced again in public. Eugénie had also been close to Stéphanie, whom she had known since childhood.

30. Offenbachland

1. Jean Claude Yon, *Jacques Offenbach* (Paris: Gallimard, 2000), p. 417. Apocryphal comment attributed to Pius IX.

2. General Boum in the *Grand Duchess of Gerolstein.*

3. Yon, op. cit., p. 405.

4. Despite Zola's subsequent role as librettist to Alfred Bruneau, that novelist literally read nothing beyond literature and newspapers. He had little knowledge of music or any other subject outside contemporary French literature, and a bit about current art trends. Most of these political denunciations were based on his personal moral considerations and class jealousy. I discuss his attitudes throughout my biography, *Emile Zola* (New York: Henry Holt, 1988). See also Yon, op. cit., pp. 405–423.

5. Quote: "Mozart of the Boulevards," by the late conductor Otto Klemperer.

6. Ludovic Halévy to his mother, quoted by Yor, op. cit., pp. 415, 423.

7. Émile Ollivier, *L'Empire Libéral. Etudes, récits, souvenirs* (Paris: Garnier, 1897–1918), vol. V, p. 74; Maxime Du Camp, op. cit., p. 230; and comment to Madame Delessert.

8. For a complete list of Offenbach's works, cf. Yon, Ibid., pp. 759 ff.

9. Anonymous article, "La Belle Hélène et l'Encyclique,"in the reviews of, *La Vie Parisienne,* 7 janvier 1865, Yon, op. cit., p. 307.

10. "Chronique du Gérôme," *L'Univers Illustré,* 24 déc. 1864, also Yon, op. cit., p. 305, Klemperer quote.

11. David Rissin, *Offenbach ou la rire du musique* (Paris: Fayard, 1980), pp. 83, 117, 309; Yon, op. cit., p. 306; "frénésie rythmique."

12. For background on Offenbach's youth, see Yon, op. cit., pp. 9 ff.

13. Carmona, *Morny,* op. cit., pp. 340 ff., explores the major role Morny played in Offenbach's career.

14. Carmona, Ibid., pp. 342–343. Viel Catel, op. cit., vol. III, p. 38.

31. Fields of Empire

1. The London *Times* in the summer of 1850 threatening Viceroy Sa'id Pasha with the invasion of Egypt unless he scuttled Lessp's Suez Canal. Ghislain de Diesbach, *Ferdinand de Lesseps* (Paris: Perrin, 1998), p. 174.

2. Lesseps to Dutch Consul Gen., Cairo, Ruyssenaers, Oct. 24, 1859, Ferdinand de Lesseps, *Lettres, Journal et Documents pour servir à l'histoire du canal de Suez* (Paris: Didier, 1875–1880), vol. III, pp. 235–237; Diesbach, op. cit., p. 179.

3. One is reminded of a similar case resulting from the failure to study history, viz., Eisenhower, Kennedy, and Johnson: Vietnam. As for troops, Louis Napoléon currently had 85,000 men in Algeria, 30,000–50,000 in Mexico, several thousand assisgned to Indochina and Asia, leaving perhaps 150,000 to protect France's frontiers, including Alsace. Prussia alone now had 750,000 men available, including their reserves.

4. Anceau, op. cit., p. 430. Convention of April 10, 1864.

5. Richard Hill and Peter Hogg, *A Black Corps d'Elite; an Egyptian Slave Battalion in the French Army in Mexico, 1863–1867* (Michigan State Press, 1995).

6. Milza, op. cit., p. 646.

7. Milza, Ibid., pp. 645–647.

8. Milza, Ibid., p. 648.

9. Diesbach, op. cit., pp. 112–113.

10. Diesbach, Ibid., Ch. 1–5 for detailed background of his life until 1854; Le Chenaye, op. cit., pp. 114 ff.

11. Diesbach, Ibid., p. 131.

12. Through the *Société d'Etudes du Canal de Suez.*

13. Journalist Amaresh Misra states "millions," but provides no documentation.

14. Diesbach, op. cit., p. 168, cites Enfantin's denunciation of Lesseps.

15. Diesbach, Ibid., p. 174. Threat to deploy the Royal Navy and army units from bases in Malta, Corfu, Bombay, and Aden. The London *Times,* throughout the summer of 1859.

16. Lesseps, *Lettres,* op. cit., vol. I, pp. 132 ff.; Diesbach, op. cit., 143, F. de Lesseps to Barthélemy Saint-Hilaire.

17. Diesbach, op. cit., p. 175, Lesseps to Sa'id Pasha.

18. Diesbach, Ibid., p. 176.

19. Diesbach, Ibid., p. 178, Sa'id to Brit. Consul Waine.

20. Diesbach, Ibid., p. 178.

21. Diesbach, Ibid., pp. 162–164.

22. Lesseps to Dutch Consul Gen. Ruyssenaers, Oct. 24, 1859, Lesseps, *Lettres,* op. cit., vol. III, pp. 235–237; see also Diesbach, op. cit., p. 179.

23. Diesbach, op. cit., p. 181.

32. An Arab Kingdom

1. Claude Martin, *Histoire de l'Algérie Française, 1830–1962* (Paris: Editions des 4 Fils Aymon, 1963), p. 172.

2. Auguste de Morny to Baron Jérôme David, ca. 1863, Martin, Ibid., p. 170.

3. Carmona, *Morny,* p. 446.

4. Anceau, op. cit., p. 408, cites "une crise cardiaque" in Aug. 1964.

5. Martin, op cit, p. 22

6. Cheickh=Shaykh, Si=Sayyid (title, for gentleman, sir, lord). I have kept the French phonetics to keep in line with all the official French citations, terminology, and map references.

7. Martin, op. cit., pp. 176–177.

8. On "The Arab Bureaux," see Pierre Darmon, *Un Siècle de Passions algériens, Une Histoire de l'Algérie Coloniale, 1830–1940* (Paris; Fayard, 1009), pp. 214 ff.

9. Martin, op. cit., pp. 166–167.

10. Martin, Ibid., pp. 176–177. Decree of July 7, 1864.

11. "*Race déchue*," a fallen race, or a people in decline—Louis Napoléon's completely inaccurate description of the Algerians inserted in his June 1865 program sent to Gov. Gen MacMahon—Martin, op. cit., p. 178. Louis Napoléon to Marshal Pélissier, letter published in *Le Moniteur Universel,* 6 février 1863; Martin, op. cit., pp. 172–173; Anceau, op. cit., 415—Nov. 1862.

12. Martin, op. cit., p. 179; Anceau, p. 415; Milza, p. 630: Darmon, pp. 210–211.

13. Martin, pp. 178–180; Anceau, p. 415.

14. Martin, pp. 178–180; Anceau, p. 416; MacMahon's *Mémoires,* p. 305 ff. By 1929 Algeria's commercial imports from France came to 4.5 billion francs, while the colony's exports to France totaled nearly three billion francs. Martin, p. 167, n. 1. This compared with trade figures of 1851—exports from France to Algeria, 86 million, from Algeria to France, 20 million francs, Martin, p. 182.

15. Sénatus-consulte, July 14, 1865, Martin, 180. Pélissier's earlier objections to these new privileges, Martin, Ibid., p. 170.

16. Milza, op. cit., p. 630.

17. Milza, Ibid., pp. 630, 631. According to Martin, by 1872 the Algerian population had fallen to 2,125,000 largely as a result of the terrible drought, natural disasters, and wars. Martin states the Algerian population was 2,750,000 back in 1861. Martin, op. cit., pp. 182–183. If 300,000 deaths could be attributed to "natural causes," this could indicate a genocide of another 325,000 committed by the French army over a ten-year period. In any event, by the time of the 1872 census, the Algerian population had shrunk by 625,000 people, or by nearly 23 percent over the past decade alone.

18. Martin, Ibid., pp. 198 and 174.

19. Martin, Ibid., p. 174; "Black Clouds"—Napoléon's speech delivered at Lille, 27 Aug. 1867, Anceau, op. cit., p. 409.

33. Bismarck: War Watch

1. Jonathan Steinberg, *Bismarck, A Life* (Oxford: Oxford University Press, 2011), pp. 180–181; Lothar Gall, *Bismarck, The White Revolutionary* (London: Unwin Hyman, 1986), vol. I, p. 206, Bismarck, autumn 1862.

2. Steinberg, op. cit., p. 174. Disraeli to Graf Vitzthum von Eckstädt, July 1862. See also "Disraeli" in the *New Oxford Dictionary of National Biography*.

3. Steinberg, Ibid., p. 29. I refer to Steinberg's biography throughout this chapter, as well as Bismarck's memoirs: *Bismarck, the Man & the Statesman: Being the Reflections and Reminiscences of Otto Prince von Bismarck* (London: Harper and Bros. 1899), 2 vols. See also Bismarck's *Bismarck's Briefe, 1836–1873* (Leipzig: Verlag Hagen und Klasing, 1900).

4. Steinberg, Ibid., pp. 28–29.

5. Steinberg, Ibid., pp. 29, 33.

6. Steinberg, Ibid., p. 38.

7. Steinberg, Ibid., pp. 43–44.

8. Albrecht von Stosch, *Denkwürdigkeiten des Generals und Admirals Albrecht von Stosch, Briefe und Tagebücher* (Stuttgart; Deutsche Verlags-Anstalt, 1904), p. 94. This is a very useful source.

9. Steinberg, Ibid., p. 174: *NODNB*, "Disraeli."

10. Bleichröder to James de Rothschild, Sept. 24, 1862, Fritz Stern, *Gold and Iron: Bismarck, Bleichröder and the Building of the German Empire* (London: Allen and Unwin, 1977), p. 28; and Hermann von Petersdorff, *Kleist Retzow: Ein Lebensbild* (Stuttgart: Nachfolger, 1907), p. 338; and Steinberg, op. cit., p. 170, Ludwig von Gerlach to Kleist Retzow, Sept. 20 1862.

11. Sept. 30, 1862, Blood and Iron speech. Otto Planze's excellent *Bismarck and the Development of Germany* (Princeton: Princeton University Press, 1990), pp. 183–185.

12. Steinberg, op. cit., p. 181; Gall, op. cit., p. 206.

13. Steinberg, pp. 179, 181, 183, 257. "C'est un homme!" von Schlozer, Oct. 31, 1862. Steinberg here includes Bavaria's later membership in the Reich; see Planze, op. cit., vol. I, p. 179.

14. Steinberg, op. cit., p. 128; Karina Urbach, *Bismarck's Favorite Englishman: Lord Odo Russell's Mission to Berlin* (London: Tauris, 1999), p. 61.

15. Roon, Waldemar von, *Denkwürdigkeiten aus dem Leben des Generalfeldmarshalls Kriegministers Grafen von Roon* (Breslau: E. Trewendt, 1892), 2 vols—a basic source for Bismarck.

16. Planze, vol. II, p. 35; Storsch to von Prodlitz, July 17, 1866, Stosch, op. cit., p. 102; Steinberg, op. cit., p. 189.

17. Steinberg, op. cit., pp. 345–346, 279; Bismarck to Roon, Aug. 19, 1869, *Bismarcks Briefe,* op. cit., nos. 401, 449.

18. Steinberg, op. cit., p. 301; and Stosch to wife, Dec. 22, 1870, Stosch, op. cit., p. 17.

19. Milza, op. cit., p. 649.

20. "I shall strike at"—cf. endnote 9, Steinberg, op. cit., p. 174; Disraeli's "despot," Steinberg, p. 372, and Odo Russell, "demonic," p. 335; Dierk Walter, *Preussische Heeresreformen, 1807–1870. Militärische Innovation* (Paderborn: Ferdinand Schöningh, 2003), p. 64.

21. By the autumn of 1867, Hannover, Württemberg, Baden, and Bavaria had formed an alliance with Prussia—Steinberg, Ibid., p. 165; and between 1867 and 1870 they adopted a unified currency, unified metric system, and free trade agreements based on Napoléon's previous organization, but now adding freedom of movement as well, Steinberg, Ibid., p. 271. Bavaria's King Ludwig II would be the last to hold out against accepting a German Empire, July–Dec. 1870, and then only after accepting a bribe of 300,000 marks per annum for the next sixteen years—Steinberg, Ibid. p. 304.

34. Ebb Tide

1. Louis Napoléon addressing the opening of the Chambers, Nov. 29, 1869, Jerrold, op. cit., vol. IV, p. 397.

2. Jerrold, vol. IV, p. 397.

3. Lord Clarendon to Lord Cowley, July 31, 1866, Cowley, op. cit., p. 314.

4. Clarendon to Cowley, July 31, 1866, and Cowley to Clarendon, summer of 1866, Cowley, Ibid., pp. 314–315.

5. Eugénie to Prussian Ambassador von der Goltz, and Louis Napoléon to Cowley, Nov. 1866, Louis Napoléon to Cowley, in Cowley, Ibid., pp. 317–318.

6. Cowley, Ibid., p. 316.

7. Cowley, Ibid., pp. 316–318.

8. Clarendon to Cowley, May 1, 1867, Cowley, Ibid., p. 320.

9. Louis Napoléon with Cowley, late Nov. 1866, Cowley, Ibid., p. 319.

10. Cowley to Clarendon, April 7, 1867, Cowley, Ibid., pp. 319–320.

11. Jerrold, op. cit., vol. IV, pp. 370–371.

12. *Le Moniteur Universel,* Jan. 20, 1867; Anceau, op. cit., p. 450.

13. Jerrold, op. cit., vol. IV, p. 396.

14. Quoted by Anceau, op. cit., pp. 473, 476. Louis Napoléon opening a special session of the Corps Législatif, Nov. 29, 1869, *Moniteur,* Nov. 30, 1869.

15. Jerrold, vol. IV, pp. 368–370. In 1860 Louis Napoléon passed a law to prevent further destruction of forests in mountainous regions, reqiring anyone felling timber to replace it with an equal number of trees. By 1867, 645,013 additional hectares had been added to corn production, and the wine yield trebled.

16. 119 acres=48 hectares; 52 acres=21 hectares; 490 meters long, 380 meters wide.

17. Among those countries exhibiting: Austria-Hungary, Belgium, Germany, Denmark, the Ottoman Empire, Persia, Algeria, the United States, etc.

18. Edmond and Jules de Goncourt, *Journal, Mémoires de la Vie Littéraire* (Paris: Robert Laffont, 1956), vol. II (1866–1886), pp. 84–95.

19. The Goncourt quote, Ibid., p. 90.

20. These steam-powered boats were manufactured just south of Lyon in the Quartier Mouche.

21. Goncourt's expression, "il pleuvra des rois," Girard, op. cit., p. 395.

22. Cowley, op. cit., p. 324. Cowley to Clarendon, June 7, 1867, Jerrold, op. cit., vol. IV, p. 355, quotes Mérimée on Bismarck.

23. Louis Napoléon's letter to Maximilian, Aug. 29, 1866, re the "Mexican Question," AN 400 AP 46: on 29 July 1861 Gen. James Watson Webb (U.S. ambassador to Brazil) met with Napoléon at Fountainebleau at the request of President Abraham Lincoln to discuss the French position re the American blockade of the southern ports (U.S. Civil War), and also re Mexico. In 1863 Webb warned Louis Napoléon that the United States would not tolerate a Roman Catholic French-backed empire in Mexico—violating the United States' Monroe Doctrine, and which could lead to a military clash between the U.S. and France. On March 22, 1863 Napoleon III wrote to General Webb that he did not like having to send French troops there in the first place. "In any event it is my intention to withdraw them as soon as the honor and the interests now engaged permit." General Webb, having since resigned his post, nevertheless stopped in Paris to meet with Louis Napoléon yet again on Nov. 10, 1865, regarding the Mexican situation. They drew up an official, if top-secret, agreement to the effect that all French forces would be withdrawn within twenty-four months' time. President Johnson's secretary of state, Seward, kept this agreement secret, even from the American ambassador in Paris. In April 1866 *Le Moniteur* announced the withdrawal of the French army from Mexico, to be completed by February 1867. Maximilian was executed on June 19, 1867. Jerrold, op. cit., vol. IV, pp. 342–346, for letters and details.

24. Cowley quote, "Spanish jealousy," Cowley, op. cit., p. 274. Girard, op. cit., pp. 426–427, Marshal Vaillant notes, Lord Cowley to Clarendon, March 10, 1865, re the death of Auguste de Morny, Cowley, op. cit., pp. 280–281.

25. Edward Shorter and Charles Tilly, *Strikes in France, 1830–1868* (Cambridge University Press, 1974), pp. 110–111. Henri Rochefort's editorial in *Le Rappel, 9 Oct 1869;* see also Milza, op. cit., p. 672.

26. For the itinerary of her voyage and the subsequent events, see Desmond Steward, op. cit., pp. 184 ff.

27. He later killed himself with a pair of scissors. Eugénie did not allow Abdul Aziz to kiss her hand, Seward, op. cit, pp. 186–187.

28. Seward, op. cit., pp. 188–189; Diesbach, op. cit., for general coverage at Suez; and two works by Ferdinand de Lesseps—*Souvenirs de Quarante Ans* (Paris: Nouvelles Revue, 1887), vol. 2, and his *Lettres, Journal et Documents pour servir l'Histoire du Canal de Suez* (Paris: Didier, 1875–1881), vol. 5.

29. See Hugh Chisolm's article, "Ismail," in *The Enclopaedia of Islam, 11th edition,* Cambridge University Press; Celik Zeynep, *Displaying the Orient; Architecture of Islam at the 19th Century World Fairs* (Berkeley: University of California Press, 1992), which, surprisingly, has a decription of the inaugural event of the Suez Canal.

30. Seward, Ibid., p. 189.

31. Louis Napoléon addressing the opening of the Chambers, Nov. 19, 1869.

35. Count Bismarck's War: 1870

1. Steinberg, op. cit., p. 289; Robert Sigmund Lucius von Billhausen, *Bismarck— Erinnerungen des Staatsminsters Freinherrn Lucius von Ballhausen* (Stuttgart: Cotta, 1921), p. 98. Diary entry, Jan. 17, 1877. Reference to For. Min. Gramont and Ems, July 15, 1870.

2. *Journal Officiel,* 2 Juillet 1870, pp. 1147 ff.

3. Milza, op. cit., p. 689. New constitutional reforms, plebiscite of May 8, 1870, Anceau, op. cit., p. 499; *Journal Officiel,* 2 Juillet 1870, pp. 1139 ff.

4. Milza, op. cit., pp. 680–683; Anceau, op. cit., p. 483.

5. Milza, op. cit., pp. 681–684; Anceau, op. cit., pp. 483–485. Like many other Bonapartes, the murderer Prince Pierre remained on Louis Napoléon's Civil List, continuing to receive 100,000 francs a year, courtesy of the French taxpayer.

6. Milza, op. cit., p. 485.

7. Milza, Ibid., p. 490. There were also 1.9 million abstentions.

8. Jules Hansen, *Les Coulisses de la Diplomacie* (Paris: Plon, 1880), p. 208.

9. Anceau, op. cit., p. 501.

10. Anceau, Ibid., p. 501.

11. Anceau, Ibid., p. 464; Gramont and Wilhelm I quote in Steinberg, op. cit., p. 285, 8 July 1870.

12. Jerrold, op. cit., vol. IV, p. 471; Anceau, op. cit., p. 467.

13. Steinberg refers to this meeting, op. cit., p. 287, and the original quote from the *Kriegstagebuch Herbert Bismarck,* quoted by Fritz Stern, op. cit., p. 130.

14. Milza, op. cit., p. 697.

15. Jerrold, op. cit., vol. IV, p. 469; Anceau, op. cit., pp. 502–504.
16. Steinberg, op. cit., p. 288; Johannes Willms, *Bismarck, Dämon der Deutschen* (München: Kinder Verlag, 1997), p. 228.

36. To Berlin!

1. Maxime Du Camp, *Souvenirs*, op. cit., vol. I, p. 297.
2. Milza, op. cit., p. 705. Eugénie to her mother, Aug. 1870, and Mathilde quote.
3. Milza, Ibid., p. 705.
4. Speech to the nation, July 19, 1870, Jerrold, op. cit., vol. IV, pp. 481–482.
5. Anceau, op. cit., pp. 474–476; Jerrold, vol. IV, pp. 484 ff.
6. Jerrold, vol. IV, pp. 483, 488, 490–491; quotes from Louis Napoléon's postwar analysis of the campaign in his *Oeuvres Posthumes de Napoléon III* (Paris: Lachaud, 1873), Deuxième Partie, pp. 89 ff.
7. The French Model 1866, complete with six-foot-two-inch bayonet, fired a single 11-mm *balle* accurately up to 1,300 yards. The Prussians had their own needle gun, single-shot breech-loading rifle—the Dreyse M.41—but with less power and of shorter range. The French Model 1866 replaced the traditional Miniés muzzle-loaders. The French Reffye Mitrailleuse had twenty-five barrels firing 100 13-mm *balles* per minute. It weighed 1,760 pounds and required six horses to transport it. Roger Ford, *The World's Greatest Rifles* (London: Brown Books, 1999), p. 23.
8. Jerrold, vol. IV, p. 477 (Sartpri, Invalides).
9. Jerrold, vol. IV, pp. 477, 491; Napoleon III, *Oeuvres Posthumes,* pp. 89 ff.
10. Other newspapers calling for war included *Le Soir, Le Rappel, La Liberté,* and *L'Opinion Nationale.*
11. Du Camp, op. cit., vol. I, p. 295.
12. Du Camp, Ibid., vol. I, p. 293.
13. Yon, *Offenbach,* op. cit., p. 397. Gen. Boum, a character from *The Grand Duchess of Gerolstein.*
14. Emile Ollivier, *L'Empire Libéral* (Paris: Garnier Frères, 1907), vol. XV, p. 327; Napoléon III, *Oeuvres Posthumes*, p. 214.
15. Milza, op. cit., pp. 706–707; D. Steward, op. cit., p. 223; Louis Girard, op. cit., pp. 476–477; Anceau, op. cit., p. 512; *Oeuvres Posthumes,* pp. 115 ff.; Maurice Paléologue, *Les entretiens l'Impératrice Eugénie* (Paris: Plon, 1928), p. 209. List of battles and skirmishes of the Franco-Prussian War: Saarbrücken, Wissembourg, Forbach-Spicheren, Wörth, Bitche, Borny (Dombey), Mars-la-tour, Toul, St.-Privat-la-Montagne, Metz, Beaumont, Strasbourg, Noiville, Siège de Paris, Bellevue, Château-audun, Dijon, Belfort, Coulmier, Beaune-la-Rolande, Champaigny, Orléans, Loigney, Longeau, Bapaume, Villersexel, Le Mans, Héricourt, Saint-Quentin, and Sedan.
16. Steward, op. cit., p. 225.
17. Palikao—the title received for defeating the Chinese near Peking in 1860; Jerrold, vol. IV, pp. 501–502.

18. Jerrold, vol. IV, pp. 503 and 506; *Oeuvres Posthumes,* op. cit.
19. See Bazaine's *Capitulation de Metz. Rapport Officiel du Maréchal Bazaine* (Lyons: Lapierre-Brille, 1871). Bazaine claimed that by the time of the surrendering of Metz he had 63,000 able-bodied men, and another 20,000 wounded, whereas the official figures state 38,000 casualties and 142,000 POWs.
20. Jerrold, vol. IV, pp. 505–515, quotes Louis Napoléon's personal report of this war. The full original version is found in Louis Napoléon's *Oeuvres Posthumes,* op. cit.
21. For detailed histories of this war see: Quentin Barry, *The Franco-Prussian War, 1870–1871, vol. I, The Conquest of Sedan, Helmuth von Moltke and the Overthrow of the Second Empire; and vol. II. After Sedan* (London: Helion Co., 2007); Jean Delmas, *L'Histoire militaire de la France, vol. II, 1715–1871* (Paris: Presses Universitaires de France, 1995); Michael Howard, *The Franco-Prussian War, The German Invasion of France, 1870* (London: Harte-Davies, 1960); and Geoffrey Wawro, *The Franco-Prussian War, the German Conquest of 1870–1871* (Cambridge University Press, 2003).

37. "Were You at Sedan, Henri?"

1. Steward, op. cit., p. 257. Louis Napoléon to Henri Conneau, Jan. 9, 1873.
2. Steward, Ibid., p. 159. Eugénie to her mother, Doña Maria Manuela, Mar. 1876.
3. Steward, Ibid., pp. 230–231; and Augustin Filon, *Souvenirs de l'Impératrice Eugénie* (Paris: Plon, 1920); see also Jasper Ridley, *Napoléon III and Eugénie* (New York: Columbia University Press, 1983).
4. Steward, op. cit., p. 233
5. Steward, Ibid., p. 235. Eugénie's life was indeed at risk, as the list of the Communards' summary executions in the Champs-Élysées, the Champs de Mars, and behind the Senate in the Luxembourg Gardens, attested.
6. Steward, Ibid., pp. 236–237.
7. Steward, Ibid., pp. 240–241.
8. Steward, Ibid., p. 243.
9. Steward, Ibid., pp. 223, 225.
10. Louis Girard, op. cit., p. 488.
11. Girard, Ibid., p. 489. Eugénie's first letter, Sept. 1870.
12. Milza, op. cit., pp. 715–716; Roger Price's excellent work, *Napoleon III* (Oxford University Press, 2006); Anceau, op. cit., p. 548. E.g., *La Conduite de l'Empereur depuis le Commencement de la Guerre; Les Causes de la Capitulation de Sedan;* and *La France et la Campagne de 1870.*
13. Anceau, op. cit., p. 549; and Girard, op. cit., pp. 492–493.
14. Steinberg, *Bismarck,* op. cit., p. 308.
15. French troops killed, 138,871, wounded 143,000; the Germans, 28,208 killed, 88,488 wounded. Steinberg, p. 293, quotes Moltke's contradictory figures of 50,000 Prussian dead. Steinberg provides no casualty figures. With the defeat of the

Commune, Thiers's government arrested at least 30,000 "Parisians," of whom 10,137 were then convicted—including 23 executions, 251 assigned to forced labor, and 4,586 transported to penal colonies, chiefly to New Caledonia. For theaters burned down by the Communards, see Jean Claude Yon's *Offenbach,* op. cit., p. 434.

16. Jerrold, op. cit., vol. IV, pp. 520–521. Camden Place, May 12, 1872.

17. Jerrold, Ibid., vol. IV, p. 522.

18. Political Testament of 24 avril 1865, advice to his son: AN 4000 AP54; Anceau, op. cit., p. 556.

19. Steward, op. cit., pp. 247 and 248.

20. Quoting Bismarck's famous maiden address before the Landesrat, March 17, 1847, denouncing the French rape of Prussia by Napoléon I, Steinberg, op. cit., p. 77.

21. See Girard, op. cit., p. 496. Arenenberg had been put on the market years before, and his mother's Roman palazzo would bring another 600,000 francs. Literally everything Louis Napoléon owned, down to his family papers, archives, a magnificent library, and galleries of hundreds of works of art now lay smoldering in the ruins of the Tuileries and St. Cloud. It was almost as if he had never existed. Eugénie's cousin, the Duchess of Malakoff (the wife of Marshal Pélissier), had braved the mob before the Tuileries and seized Eugénie's fabled jewelry collection, along with a few paintings, which she then entrusted to Pauline von Metternich, who would dispatch them by "diplomatic pouch" to London. Later Eugénie sold most of her jewels to the Baron de Rothschild for £150,000 ($14.9 million today). In addition, the empress went to Spain at the end of 1871 to sell some real estate that she had inherited. She had also transferred "millions" of her own money just before she fled the country. Her mother was a very wealthy lady in her own right. Cf. Eugénie's biographer, Desmond Steward, op. cit., p. 251.

22. Girard, op. cit., p. 497.

23. Victoria's visit, Nov. 30, 1871. Steward, op. cit., p. 249. Paléologue, op. cit., p. 237. The Prince Imperial was known as Louis, his full first name being Napoléon Eugène Louis Jean Joseph. He was about to put on a big growth spurt, including a severe thinning.

24. Steward, op. cit., pp. 249–252.

25. Steward, Ibid., pp. 251–252.

26. Steward mentions this, Ibid., p. 244.

27. Steward, Ibid., p. 253. Plon-Plon continued his visits because Prince Louis was now the direct heir to the Bonaparte throne, in turn followed by the good Plon-Plon. When he reached his majority, however, Louis got his revenge and had Plon-Plon's name removed from the line of succession.

28. For the proposed January 1873 coup d'état, see Profs. Anceau, op. cit., p. 552 and Girard, op. cit., pp. 500–501. The pro-Bonapartist newspapers at this time included *Le Pays, L'Ordre, La Patrie,* and *L'Expérience Nationale.* See also Steward, op. cit., p. 261, regarding the taking possession of Camden Place.

29. Girard, op. cit., p. 501; Anceau, op. cit., p. 555.
30. Jerrold, op. cit., vol. IV, p. 531. All the conversations quoted above and through-out this book have been taken from eyewitness accounts, letters, or memoirs.

38. Elegy for an Emperor

1. Lady Cowley to Queen Victoria, January, 1873, Ivor Guest, *Napoleon III in England* (London: BT&G Press, 1952), p. 198.
2. The London *Times*, Thursday, January 16, 1873, p. 9, one of the two best accounts of the funeral, and which I shall be referring to throughout this chapter.
3. Special correspondent of Ireland's *Freeman's Journal,* Thursday, January 16, 1873, pp. 2–3.
4. Blanchard Jerrold, *Napoleon III* (London: Longmans, Green, 1982), vol. IV, Appendix XII, p. 575.
5. Pius IX, angered by the withdrawal of French troops protecting Rome, and because of Louis Napoléon's recommendation to abandon the Papal States. This pope [Count Giovanni Mastai-Ferretti], who had recently declared himself "infallible," had for-bidden any senior Roman Catholic ecclesiatic—English or foreign—from perform-ing the rites for the funeral of Napoléon III or from attending those services.
6. According to the custom of the day, only men participated in the funeral cortège, while the women went ahead to the church.
7. *Freemans Journal,* op. cit., p. 3.
8. Ivor Guest, op. cit., p. 198. Alexandra, the Princess of Wales, to Lady Cowley, Sandringham, January 11, 1873, Henry R. C. Wellesley, Earl Cowley, *The Paris Embassy During the Second Empire* (London: Thorton, Butterworth, 1928), p. 330: "I should think France now would feel some remorse for the ingratitude which embittered the last days of one who had devoted the best years of his life to make her great and glorious."
9. Until this date, official French textbooks dispose of Napoléon III and his reign in just a few paragraphs and even then with disdain and ridicule. Fortunately, a new mature generation of historians is now beginning to produce more honest, objec-tive, and professional studies. But even at the exhibit on "The Second Empire " held at the Musée d'Orsay, in 2016, the Exhibit's coordinator denied well-documented historical facts, again presenting Louis Napoléon with derision as a shallow, frivolous, indeed ludicrous man.
10. In 1881 Eugénie built St. Michael's Abbey in Farnborough, Hampshire, as a mau-soleum, where she had the remains of Napoléon III and their son transferred from Chislehurst. (Although it is not generally known, Prince Louis had outstanding natural artistic talents, both in drawing and sculpting.) Upon her death in 1920, Eugénie joined them.

Select Bibliography

D'Alton-Shée, Edmond de Lignères, *Mes Mémoires, 1848–1862* (Paris: Librairie Internationale, 1868).

Anceau, Eric, *Napoléon III* (Paris: Tallandier, 2012).

Antonelli, Guy, *Louis Philippe* (Paris: Fayard, 2002).

Autin, Jean, *Les Frères Péreire* (Paris: Perrin, 1984).

———. *L'Impératrice Eugénie, ou l'empire d'une femme* (Paris: Fayard, 1990).

Bac, Ferdinand, *La Princesse Mathilde, sa vie et ses oeuvres* (Paris: Hachette, 1928).

Barbier, Frédéric, *Finances et Politiques en France à l'Epoque contemporaine. La Dynasties des Fould (XVIIIe-XXe Siècle)* (Paris: A. Colin, 1991).

Barry, Quintin, *The Franco-Prussian War, 1870–1871* (London: Helion, 2007).

Bazaine, Achille, *Capitulation de Metz. Rapport Officiel du Maréchal Bazaine* (Lyons: Lapierre-Brille, 1871).

Bernardy, Françoise, *Son of Talleyrand, Charles Joseph de Flahaut* (London: Collins, 1956).

———. *Alexandre Walewski, 1810–1868* (Paris: Perrin, 1976).

Bertrand, Gille, *Les Banques de France xu XIXe Siècle* (Paris: Droz, 1970).

Bertraut, Jules, *Le Roi Jérôme* (Paris: Flammarion, 1954).

———. *L'Impératrice Eugénie et son temps* (Paris: Amiot-Dumont, 1956).

Bismarck, Otto von, *Bismarcks Briefe, 1836–1877* (Lepizig: Verlag Hager & Klasing, 1900).

———. *Bismarck the Man and Statesman, Being the Reflexions and Reminiscences of Otto, Prince von Bismarck* (New York: Harper & Bros, 1899).

Blanc, Louis, *Révélations Historiques* (Bruxelles: Méline, 1859).

Blanchard, Jerrold, *The Life of Napoleon III* (London: Longmans, Green, 1875–1882).

Blessington, Marguerite, *The Literary Life and Correspondence of the Countess of Blessington* (London: Longmans, 1855).

Bonfadini, Romualdo, *Vitz di Francesco Arese* (Torino: Roux, 1894).

Brabant, Jacques de, *Achille Fould et son temps. L'homme clé du second empire* (Paris: Cairn, 2001).

Bronne, Carlo, *La Comtesse Le Hon et le Première Ambassade de Blegique à Paris* (Bruxelles: Renaissance du Livre, 1952).

Brown, David, *Palmerston, A Biography* (New Haven: Yale University Press, 2010).

Carmona, Michel, *Haussmann* (Paris: Fayard, 2000).

———. *Morny, Le Vice-Empereur* (Paris: Fayard, 2005).

Castries, Duc de, *La Reine Hortense* (Paris: Tallandier, 1984).

Chateaubriand, François Auguste René, *Mémoires d'Outre-Tombe* (Paris: Penau, 1850).

Clément, Pascal, *Persigny: L'Homme qui a inventé Napoléon III* (Paris: Perrin, 2006).

Cochelet, Louise, *Mémoires sur la Reine Hortense* (Paris: Ladvocat, 1836–1838).

Connelly, Owen, *The Gentle Bonaparte, a Biography of Joseph Bonaparte* (New York: MacMillan, 1968).

Cowley, Henry Richard Charles Wellesley, Earl of, *The Paris Embassy of Ambassador Lord Cowley* (London: Butterworth, 1928).

Darmion, Alfred, *Histoire de Douze Ans (1857–1869)* (Paris: Dentu, 1883).

Darmon, Pierre, *Un Siècle de Passions Algériens, Une Histoire de l'Algérie coloniale, 1830–1940* (Paris: Fayard, 2009).

Dansette, Adrien, *L'Attentat d'Orsini* (Paris: Flammarion, 1964).

———. *Les Origines de la Commune de 1871* (Paris: Plon, 1944).

Delmas, Jean, *L'Histoire Militaire de la France* (Paris: Presses Universitaires de France, 1995).

Des Cars, Jean, *La Princesse Mathilde* (Paris: Perrin, 1996).

Diesbac, Ghislain de, *Ferdinand de Lesseps* (Paris: Perrin, 1998).

Du Camp, Maxime, *Souvenirs d'un Demi-Siècle* (Paris: Hachette, 1949).

Dufresne, Claude, *Morny, l'Homme du Second Empire* (Paris: Perrin, 1983).

———. *L'Impératrice Eugénie* (Paris: Perrin, 1986).

———. *La Reine Hortense* (Paris: Pygmalion, 2000).

Eugénie, *Lettres familières de l'Impératrice Eugénie* (Paris: Plon, 1871–1872).

Filon, Pierre Augustin, *Souvenirs de l'Impératrice Eugénie* (Paris: Plon, 1920).

Fisher, Sidney Nettleton, and William Ochswenwald, *The Middle East: A History* (New York: McGraw-Hill, 1990).

Fleury, Emile Félix, *Souvenirs* (Paris: Plon, 1899–1908).

Gall, Lothar, *Bismarck, The White Revolutionary* (London: Unwin, Hyman, 1986).

Garnier-Pagès, Louis Antoine, *Histoires de la Révolution de 1848* (Paris: Pagnerre, 1877).

Girard, Louis, *Napoléon III* (Paris: Fayard, 1987).

Giraudeau, Fernand, *Napoléon III Intime* (Paris: Ollendorff, 1895).

Gorce, Pierre de La, *Histoire du Second Empire* (Paris: Plon, 1902–1903).

Grangier de Cassagnac, Adolphe, *Histoire de la Chute du Roi Louis-Philippe, de la République de 1848, et du Rétablissement de l'Empire* (Paris: Plon, 1857).

Guedalla, Philip, *The Secret of the Coup* (London: Constable, 1924).

Guizot, François, *Mémoires Pour Servir à l'Histoire de Mon Temps, 1807–1858* (Paris: Calman-Levy, 1859).

Halévy, Ludovic, *Carnets* (Paris: Calman-Lévy, 1935).

Hansen, Jules, *Les Coulisses de la Diplomatie* (Paris: Plon, 1880).

Haussmann, Georges, *Mémoires du Baron Haussmann* (Paris: Victor Havard, 1890).

Hill, Richard, and Peter Hogg, *A Black Corps d'Elite, An Egyptian Sudanese Battalion with the French Army in Mexico, 1863–1867* (Michigan State University Press, 1995).

Hortense de Beauharnais, *Mémoires de la Reine Hortense* (Paris: Tallandier, 1927).

Houssaye, Arsène, *Man About Town, Confessions of Arsène Houssaye* (London: Gollancz, 1972).

Howard, Michael, *The Franco-Prussian War, The German Invasion of France, 1870–1871* (London: Harte-Davies, 1960).

Hübner, Alexandre von, *Neuf Ans de Souvenirs d'un Ambassadeur d'Autriche à Paris sous le Second Empire* (Paris: Plon, 1905).

Hugo, Victor, *Oeuvres Complètes* (Paris: Robert Laffont, 1987).

Julien, Charles-André, *Histoire de l'Algérie Contemporaine* (Paris: Presses Universitaires de France, 1964).

Laity, Armand François Rupert, *Relation Historique des Évènements du 30 Octobre 1836* (Paris: private, 1838).

Las Cases, Marie Joseph Emmanuel Dieudoné, *Mémorial de Saint-Hélène* (Paris: private, 1823).

Lesseps, Ferdinand de, *Lettres, Journal et Documents pour servir à l'Histoire du Canal de Suez* (Paris: Didier, 1875–1880).

———. *Souvenirs de Quarante Ans* (Paris: Nouvelle Revue, 1887).

Lofts, Nora, *Rose for Virtue, The Very Private Life of Hortense, Queen of Holland* (London: Hodder and Stoughton, 1973).

Loliée, Frédéric, *Frère d'Empereur, Le Duc de Morny* (Paris: Emile-Paul, 1909).

———. *La Vie d'Une Impératice. Eugénie de Montijo* (Paris: Plon, F. Juven, 1907).

Martin, Claude, *Histoire de l'Algérie Francaise, 1830–1962* (Paris: Edition des 4 Fils Aymon, 1963).

Masson, Frédéric, *Napoléon et sa famille* (Paris: Ollendorff, 1919).

Masuyer, Valérie, *Mémoires de Valérie Masuyer, Dame d'Honneur de la Reine Hortense* (Paris: Plon, 1937).

Mérimée, Prosper, *Correspondance Générale* (Toulouse: private, 1941–1964).

———. *Prosper Mérimée à la Comtesse de Montijo* (Paris: private, 1930).

Metternich, Pauline von, *My Years in Paris* (London: Eveleigh, Nash & Graeper, 1922).

Milza, Pierre, *Napoléon III* (Paris: Perrin, 2006).

Mollien, Jean-Yves, *Louis Hachette* (Paris: Fayard, 1999).

Napoléon III, *Analyse de la question des sucres* (Paris: Government, 1842).

———, *Considérations politiques et militaire sur la Suisse* (Paris: Levavasseur, 1833).

———. *Discours et proclamations* (Paris: Plon, 1860).

———. *Extinction du paupérisme* (Paris: Pagnerre, 1844).

———. *Des Idées Napoléoniennes* (Paris: Plon, 1860).

———. *Histoire de Jules César* (Paris: Plon, 1865–1866).

———. *Notes sur l'organization militaire et la Confédération de l'Allegmagne du Nord* (Wilhelmshöhe, 1871).

———. *Oeuvres de Napoléon III* (Paris: Plon-Amyot, 1854–1869).

———. *Oeuvres posthumes et autographes inédits de Napoléon III en exil* (Paris: Lachaud, 1873).

———. *Histoire du canon dans les armées modernes* (Paris: Martinon, 1848).

———. *Rêveries politiques* (London: private, 1832).

Ollivier, Émile, *L'Empire liberal. Etudes, récits, souvenirs* (Paris: Garnier, 1897–1918).

Pagerie, Stéphanie de Tascher de la, *Mon Séjour au Tuileries, 1852–1871* (Paris: Plon, 1893–1894).

Paléologue, Maurice, *Les Entretriens l'Impératrice Eugénie* (Paris: Plon, 1928).

Pasquier, Etienne Denis, *Histoire de Mon Temps* (Paris: Plon, 1893–94).

Persigny, Jean Gilbert Victor Fialin, Duc de, *Mémoires du Duc de Persigny* Paris: Plon, 1896).

Pflanze, Otto, *Bismarck and the Develoment of Germany* (Princeton University Press, 1990).

Price, Roger, *The French Second Empire. An Anatomy of Political Power* (Cambridge University Press, 2001).

———. *Napoleon III and the French Second Empire* (London: Routledge, 1997).

Rémusat, Charles de, *Mémoires de ma vie* (Paris: Plon, 1860).

Renouvin, Pierre, *La Politique Extérieure du Second Empire* (Paris: Centre de Documentation Universitaire, 1940).

Ridley, Jasper, *Napoléon III and Eugénie* (NY: Columbia University Press, 1983).

Romeo, Rosario, *Cavour e il suo tempo* (Bari: Laterza, 1984).

Schnerb, Robert, *Rouher et le Second Empire* (Paris: Colin, 1949).

[Strauss] Schom, Alan, *Emile Zola, A Bourgeois Rebel* (New York: Henry Holt, 1987).

———. *Napoleon Bonaparte* (New York: HarperCollins, 1997).

Seward, Desmond, *Eugénie, The Empress and Her Empire* (Gloucestershire: Sutton, 2004).

Stern, Fritz, *Gold and Iron: Bismarck, Bleichröder and the Building of the German Empire* (London: Allen and Unwin, 1977).

Stosch, Albrecht von, *Denkwürdigkeiten des Generals und Admirals Albrecht von Stosch, Briefe und Tagebücher* (Stuttgart: Deutsche Verlag-Amhalt, 1904).

Roon, Waldemar von, *Denkwürdigkeiten aus dem Leben des Generalfeldmarshalls Kriegsminister Grafen von Roon* (Breslau: E. Trewendt, 1892).

Thirria, Hippolyte, *Napoléon III avant l'Empire* (Paris: Plon-Nourrit, 1995).

SELECT BIBLIOGRAPHY

479

Tocqueville, Alexis de, *Oeuvres complètes* (Paris: Gallimard, 1991).

Tulard, Jean, ed., *Dictionnaire du Second Empire* (Paris: Fayard, 1995).

Vezzani, François Griscelli, *Mémoires de Griscelli, Baron de Rimini, Agent Secret de Napoléon III (1850–1858), de Cavour (1859–1861)* (Bruxelles, Genève, private, 1867).

Viarengo, Adriano, *Vittorio Emanuelle II* (Roma: Salerno Editrice, 2017).

Victoria, *Leaves from a Journal, 1855* (London: Andre Deutsch, 1961).

———. *The Letters of Queen Victoria, A Selection, 1837–1861* (London: John Murray, 1908).

Viel-Castel, Horace de, *Mémoires sur le règne de Napoléon III* (Paris: Chez Tous les Libraires, 1883).

Wetzel, David, *The Crimean War, A Diplomatic History* (New York: Columbia University Press, 1985).

Willms, Johannes, *Bismarck, Dämon der Deutschen* (München: Kinder Verlage, 1997).

Yon, Jean-Claude, *Jacques Offenbach* (Paris: Gallimard, 2000).

Zeldin, Theodore, *Emile Ollivier and the Liberal Empire of Naploeon III* (Oxford: Clarendon Press, 1963).

Dizionario Biografica Degli Italiani (Roma: Istituto della Enciclopedia, Italiana, 2013), v. 79.

The New Oxford Dictionary of National Biography, 2004.

ARCHIVES NATIONALES

F^{70} 422: Voyages de l'Empereur

Fonds Persigny 44 AP

44 AP 3, 4, 5, 6: Correspondance avec Louis Napoléon Bonaparte

Fonds Rouher 45 AP

45 AP 2, 3, 11

Fonds Morny 116 AP

116 AP 1 (dossier 1), sur le coup d'état, 2 Déc. 1851

116 AP 2 (dossier 9), sur Fanny Le Hon.

116 AP 2 (dossier 11), correspondance avec Nap. III

Fonds Emile Ollivier, 542 AP

542 AP 8, Correspondance avec Nap. III

541 AP 26 and 27, formation of the Government of 2 January 1870

Fonds Canrobert 595 AP

Fonds Fould 154 Mi

OTHER ARCHIVES

Archives de la prefecture de Police

Ministère de la Défense, SHD

Bibliothèque Nationale

Manuscrits Naf 1066–67, Correspondance Hortense Cornu; 1309, lettres de Napoléon III; 12759, 12760, 12765, correspondance Napoléon III; 23064–23066, correspondance Persigny
Fondation Thiers
Musée de l'Armée, the Invalides
Musée Carnavalet
Musée d'Histoire Contemporaine
Musée de la Marine, Archives
The Bodleian Library, Oxford
The British Library, London
The Library, University of California, Berkeley
The Rothschild Archives, London.
Southampton University Library Archives, PP. GC/TE/327-335
Service Historique de la Défense, Algérie, Vincennes Archives
Biblioteca Nazionale Centrale di Firenze
Biblioteca, Scuola Normale Superiore di Pisa

Index

Members of royal families appear under their given name, e.g. Louis Philippe d'Orleans in the 'L's. The subject of this book is Louis Napoléon. Napoléon III is his reign title, used for discussion of the title itself. In subheadings, LN stands for Louis Napoléon.